Handbook of Research on Developments and Future Trends in Transnational Higher Education

Gareth Richard Morris
Perse School Suzhou, China

Li Li
Exeter University, UK

A volume in the Advances in Higher Education and Professional Development (AHEPD) Book Series

IGI Global
PUBLISHER of TIMELY KNOWLEDGE

Published in the United States of America by
IGI Global
Information Science Reference (an imprint of IGI Global)
701 E. Chocolate Avenue
Hershey PA, USA 17033
Tel: 717-533-8845
Fax: 717-533-8661
E-mail: cust@igi-global.com
Web site: http://www.igi-global.com

Library of Congress Cataloging-in-Publication Data

Names: Morris, Gareth Richard, editor. | Li, Li, DATE- editor.
Title: Handbook of research on developments and future trends in transnational higher education / Gareth Morris and Li Li, editors.
Description: Hershey, PA : Information Science Reference, 2023. | Includes bibliographical references and index. | Summary: "With higher education embracing a period of increasingly rapid development prior to the COVID-19 pandemic due to the speed of technological advances, increased global competition, an ever more astute and savvy consumer base and ethical, planetary responsibilities, this book will look ahead at what the future of higher education may look like, what institutions may have to do in order to be successful and provide concrete suggestions to readers in light of this"-- Provided by publisher.
Identifiers: LCCN 2022018634 (print) | LCCN 2022018635 (ebook) | ISBN 9781668452264 (hardcover) | ISBN 9781668452271 (ebook)
Subjects: LCSH: Transnational education. | Education, Higher--Effect of technological innovations on.
Classification: LCC LC1095 .D48 2023 (print) | LCC LC1095 (ebook) | DDC 378.1/75--dc23/eng/20220609
LC record available at https://lccn.loc.gov/2022018634
LC ebook record available at https://lccn.loc.gov/2022018635

This book is published in the IGI Global book series Advances in Higher Education and Professional Development (AHEPD) (ISSN: 2327-6983; eISSN: 2327-6991)

British Cataloguing in Publication Data
A Cataloguing in Publication record for this book is available from the British Library.

For electronic access to this publication, please contact: eresources@igi-global.com.

Advances in Higher Education and Professional Development (AHEPD) Book Series

Jared Keengwe
University of North Dakota, USA

ISSN:2327-6983
EISSN:2327-6991

Mission

As world economies continue to shift and change in response to global financial situations, job markets have begun to demand a more highly-skilled workforce. In many industries a college degree is the minimum requirement and further educational development is expected to advance. With these current trends in mind, the **Advances in Higher Education & Professional Development (AHEPD) Book Series** provides an outlet for researchers and academics to publish their research in these areas and to distribute these works to practitioners and other researchers.

AHEPD encompasses all research dealing with higher education pedagogy, development, and curriculum design, as well as all areas of professional development, regardless of focus.

Coverage

- Adult Education
- Assessment in Higher Education
- Career Training
- Coaching and Mentoring
- Continuing Professional Development
- Governance in Higher Education
- Higher Education Policy
- Pedagogy of Teaching Higher Education
- Vocational Education

IGI Global is currently accepting manuscripts for publication within this series. To submit a proposal for a volume in this series, please contact our Acquisition Editors at Acquisitions@igi-global.com or visit: http://www.igi-global.com/publish/.

The Advances in Higher Education and Professional Development (AHEPD) Book Series (ISSN 2327-6983) is published by IGI Global, 701 E. Chocolate Avenue, Hershey, PA 17033-1240, USA, www.igi-global.com. This series is composed of titles available for purchase individually; each title is edited to be contextually exclusive from any other title within the series. For pricing and ordering information please visit http://www.igi-global.com/book-series/advances-higher-education-professional-development/73681. Postmaster: Send all address changes to above address.

Titles in this Series

For a list of additional titles in this series, please visit: www.igi-global.com/book-series

Formative and Shared Assessment to Promote Global University Learning
José Sánchez-Santamaría (Universidad de Castilla-La Mancha, Spain)
Information Science Reference • © 2023 • 335pp • H/C (ISBN: 9781668435373) • US $215.00

Research, Practice, and Innovations in Teacher Education During a Virtual Age
Aaron Samuel Zimmerman (Texas Tech University, USA)
Information Science Reference • © 2023 • 351pp • H/C (ISBN: 9781668453162) • US $215.00

Best Practices and Programmatic Approaches for Mentoring Educational Leaders
Amanda Wilkerson (University of Central Florida, USA) and Shalander Samuels (Kean University, USA)
Information Science Reference • © 2023 • 320pp • H/C (ISBN: 9781668460498) • US $215.00

Collaborative Models and Frameworks for Inclusive Educator Preparation Programs
Beverly Sande (Prairie View A&M University, USA) and Charles William Kemp (Shawnee State University, USA)
Information Science Reference • © 2022 • 244pp • H/C (ISBN: 9781668434437) • US $215.00

Instilling Diversity and Social Inclusion Practices in Teacher Education and Curriculum Development
Olga María Alegre de la Rosa (University of La Laguna, Spain) and Luis Miguel Villar Angulo (University of Seville, Spain)
Information Science Reference • © 2022 • 252pp • H/C (ISBN: 9781668448120) • US $215.00

Rethinking Perception and Centering the Voices of Unique Individuals Reframing Autism Inclusion in Praxis
Jessica Block Nerren (California State University, San Bernardino, USA)
Information Science Reference • © 2022 • 289pp • H/C (ISBN: 9781668451038) • US $215.00

Handbook of Research on Practices for Advancing Diversity and Inclusion in Higher Education
Eleni Meletiadou (London Metropolitan University, UK)
Information Science Reference • © 2022 • 451pp • H/C (ISBN: 9781799896289) • US $270.00

Self-Care and Stress Management for Academic Well-Being
Karis L. Clarke (Clark Atlanta University, USA)
Information Science Reference • © 2022 • 302pp • H/C (ISBN: 9781668423349) • US $215.00

IGI Global
PUBLISHER of TIMELY KNOWLEDGE

701 East Chocolate Avenue, Hershey, PA 17033, USA
Tel: 717-533-8845 x100 • Fax: 717-533-8661
E-Mail: cust@igi-global.com • www.igi-global.com

Editorial Advisory Board

List of Contributors

Table of Contents

Detailed Table of Contents

Many students experience foreign language speaking anxiety (FLSA). This chapter adopts quantitative and qualitative methods to research the possible causing factors of FLSA and the corresponding solutions. Quantitative data was collected from 41 year one students at XJTLU using questionnaires to test 14 factors' impacts on students' speaking anxiety from three categories: self, peer, and teacher. Qualitative data was collected from the interviews with 11 students which probed into what elements from those three categories could help reduce students' speaking anxiety effectively from their perspectives. The quantitative data analysis showed that most students had a high level FLSA, and the 14 factors influenced their speaking anxiety to different levels. The qualitative data revealed that students generally believed that teacher-related elements could help reduce their speaking anxiety most effectively. With the findings, it is hoped that teachers in transnational higher education can be acquire some inspirations regarding how to effectively reduce their students' FLSA.

This chapter briefly introduces and demonstrates fifteen debate-related analytical and compositional tools that can be implemented in language arts courses such as writing, public speaking, and debate. Based on classical rhetoric and solidly grounded in pedagogical research, these exercises are already in use in both the English language learner (ELL) and native English-speaking environments. Combined with the larger philosophical tenants of ethical communication, which reminds speakers and writers to be mindful of the positive or negative effects their words can have on the societies in which they live and beyond.

The educational value of formative assessment (FA) has been widely acknowledged within higher education. At the same time, there is little consensus on what FA entails, or how it should be defined and understood when looking at the Western education system; this is even more problematic when adapted by TNE institutions. This chapter looks at the definition issues together with key characteristics of quality formative feedback, including the role of the student in co-creating feedback, something that is particularly challenging within the context of this chapter, TNE in China. It looks at the most apparent challenges that are associated with FA implementation within a Chinese higher education context, such as educational heritage and a deep-rooted collectivist approach to learning. It also ventures to propose an alternative conception, formative routines framework FRF), to emphasise the importance of student and teacher training when engaging in formative tasks and using these to support the ongoing development of curricula.

enlighten researchers and policymakers in both developing and developed countries about the role of the family as a micro-agent of socialisation in contributing to the global level politics and power related to the higher education industry. The findings of the chapter reveal that the dreams and desires developed and disseminated by their family young students experienced in Bangladesh are quite neoliberal in character. Thus, it provides the analysis of empirical data for both host and sending countries to ensure transnational higher education in developing countries.

Chinese students have become the largest share of international students in many countries. Meanwhile, the number of transnational higher education (TNHE) programmes has reached a new high in China. This makes it exceptionally important for teachers whose own cultural and educational background are very different from Chinese to understand their learners. The study set out to better understand Chinese students in TNHE by studying a case of a Sino-Anglo cooperation university in China. The foreign teachers' and foreign students' views on Chinese students were collected and juxtaposed with Chinese students' own accounts. The qualitative study finds many commonly cited features of East Asian students evident in this research context. However, this study gains insights of these phenomena and strategies from the very experienced expatriate teachers, who demonstrated a good understanding of their Chinese students. The authors propose a new approach to teach Chinese students. This study is believed to be of reference to teaching in TNHE in vast contexts with students from Confucian heritage cultures (CHC).

Despite the potentials of collaborative work for enhancing the knowledge, skills, and attitudes (KSA) of professionals, the educational field lacks a clear model for co-training. This article aims to develop a conceptual framework for this collaborative professional development (PD) strategy to help novice teacher trainers (TTs) grow professionally. Although a lot has been written in the educational literature about co-teaching, there are merely few self-reported reflections about the use of co-training, and it is not clear how to adopt it as a tool for TTs' PD. In an attempt to fill in this gap, a proposed co-training model is constructed based on the philosophy of co-teaching, novice TTs' needs in terms of KSA, and their role-competency in the training room. These concepts are integrated to design a co-training model that is expected to help in scaffolding novice TTs. The author argues that this model, if properly implemented, can support novice TTs.

education model, HeXie mindset model, and HeXie management model would be addressed followed by an application of these models in XJTLU's management systems. Fourthly, challenges and opportunities would be outlined in terms of student-centered and research-led education, the teaching of research, quality education, future education in the uncertain, ambiguous, complex, and changeable world, and future education, before conclusion is drawn.

Preface

The internationalisation of education, and in particular higher education, is a long-standing development which potentially reached a zenith in the decade 2010-2020. One feature of this movement has been the development of the lucrative cross border, or transnational, market. In the past couple of decades, the scope and scale of programme and qualification offerings have dramatically changed as academic mobility evolved from people to programmes and providers. This has meant that transnational education (TNE) no longer simply involves students and staff, but any discussion now must also consider everything from provisional approaches to institutional structure and development. The pandemic has also heightened the importance of the potential and value of virtual mobility and distance education. The benefits associated with transnational higher education include programme delivery developments, enhanced intercultural understanding, research collaborations, curriculum innovation, alongside institutional growth. On a macro level, there are also sociocultural, economic, and political implications, and often benefits. That said, there are risks, some of which include provision quality, human resource inequalities and disparities and profit at all costs. Given considerations such as these, in a period of unprecedented change ushered in by the pandemic and technological developments now is as important as ever in terms of considering experiences at and reflecting on practice in global transnational higher education providers.

This book considers a diverse range of associated topics. These include curriculum design, information technology, professional development and leadership, alongside educational models, and future directions. Key issues such as the value of transnational education partnerships, environment to nurture TNE opportunities and tackle challenges, and the local impact are also evident throughout the book. On that note, this book begins with a section on teaching and learning, followed be sections of technology, extended provision, broader horizons and practice enhancement, before concluding with future trends. More specifically:

SECTION 1: TEACHING AND LEARNING

Chapter 1: A Module for General Education Curriculum Development in Chinese International Universities: A Practical Example Concerning Law and Morality

Dr. Kai Liu, Xi'an Jiao Tong-Liverpool University, China
Dr. Jie Yang, The University of Adelaide, Australia

This chapter focuses on a discussion of general education curriculum development in international universities, with an emphasis on the reflective pedagogical practice found in China. It defines general education in the context of Chinese academia, and explores its development and future trends influenced by the global impact of the COVID-19 pandemic and contemporary transnational education (TNE). In particular, this chapter examines the curriculum design of the Law and Morality Module (L & M Module) taught at the Chinese Culture Teaching Center (CCTC) at Xi'an Jiaotong-Liverpool University (XJTLU), Suzhou, China, and identifies any practical problems in relation to teaching quality and assessment methods. It also advances corresponding suggestions to enhance students' learning outcomes and efficiency.

Chapter 2: Making Sense of Brainstorming in Transnational Education
Mr. Mattia Miani, The University of Nottingham, Ningbo, China

The chapter investigates the role of brainstorming as an educational tool on the basis of the author's experience in transnational education and a review of the literature. Brainstorming is an ideation technique invented by Alex Osborn in the 40s. Still popular today, it has found numerous applications in education. Despite its diffusion, a large body of literature dismisses brainstorming as less effective in comparison to individuals working alone or other techniques in terms of quantity and quality of idea produced. Advocates of brainstorming claim that when done properly it can be very powerful in generating breakthrough ideas and studies show that factors such as the presence of a facilitator, training, the right time and type of problem assigned can greatly change the outcome of a session. After reviewing this contrasting literature, the author concludes that these studies ignore the cultural origin of brainstorming and attention should be paid to the cultural implications of the technique in transnational contexts outside the US.

Chapter 3: Speaking Anxiety Lower-Level Learners Experienced in Transitional Higher Education in China – The Case Study of Xi'an Jiaotong-Liverpool University
Ms. Shuangxin Zhang, Xi'an Jiao Tong-Liverpool University, China

Many students experience foreign language speaking anxiety (FLSA). This chapter adopts quantitative and qualitative methods to research the possible causing factors of FLSA and the corresponding solutions. Quantitative data was collected from 41 year one students at XJTLU using questionnaires to test 14 factors' impacts on students' speaking anxiety from three categories: self, peer, and teacher. Qualitative data was collected from the interviews with 11 students which probed into what elements from those three categories could help reduce students' speaking anxiety effectively from their perspectives. The quantitative data analysis showed that most students had a high level FLSA, and the 14 factors influenced their speaking anxiety to different levels. The qualitative data revealed that students generally believed that teacher-related elements could help reduce their speaking anxiety most effectively. With the findings, it is hoped that teachers in transnational higher education can be acquire some inspirations regarding how to effectively reduce their students' FLSA.

Chapter 4: Ethical Communication and Argument-Centered Education Can Enhance Transnational Education and Promote a More Ethical and Civil World
Mr. Rahman Kevin Smith, The Chinese University of Hong Kong, China

This chapter briefly introduces and demonstrates fifteen debate-related analytical and compositional tools that can be implemented in language arts courses such as writing, public speaking, and debate. Based on classical rhetoric and solidly grounded in pedagogical research, these exercises are already in use in both the English Language Learner (ELL) and native English-speaking environments. When combined with the larger philosophical tenants of Ethical Communication, which remind speakers and writers to be mindful of the positive or negative effects their words can have on the societies in which they live and beyond.

Chapter 5: A Curious Case of Formative Assessment – A TNE Perspective in EAP and Beyond
Mr. Sebastian Kozbial, University of Nottingham, Ningbo, China

The educational value of formative assessment (FA) has been widely acknowledged within higher education. At the same time, there is little consensus on what FA entails, how it should be defined and understood when looking at the Western education system; this is even more problematic when adapted by TNE institutions. This chapter looks at the definition issues together with key characteristics of quality formative feedback including the role of the student in co-creating feedback, something that is particularly challenging within the context of this chapter, TNE in China. It looks at the most apparent challenges that are associated with FA implementation within a Chinese higher education context, such as educational heritage and a deep-rooted collectivist approach to learning. It also ventures to propose an alternative conception, Formative Routines Framework FRF), to emphasise the importance of student and teacher training when engaging in formative tasks and using these to support the ongoing development of curricula.

SECTION 2: TECHNOLOGY

Chapter 6: The Perils and Potentials Benefits of Machine Translation in Transnational Higher Education
Dr. Michael David High, Xi'an Jiao Tong-Liverpool University, China

Machine translation has recently improved dramatically in accuracy, convenience, and accessibility, and while it has been widely adopted, it remains far from perfect. This chapter considers the perils and potential benefits of machine translation in English-medium of instruction transnational higher education. The perils of machine translation in this context are that it can stunt language learning and cause miscomprehension; it problematizes authorship; it facilitates novel forms of plagiarism; and it can hurt transnational higher education institutions' reputations and devalue their degrees. The potential benefits of machine translation are that it can aid reading comprehension, raise writing level, and help student retention; it provides an opportunity for critically engaging with digital technology and its appropriate use; and it facilitates instruction and research beyond instructor and student language competencies, which can broaden and transnationalize the often Americentric and Eurocentric content of transnational higher education.

SECTION 3: EXTENDED PROVISION

Chapter 7: Joint Delivery and Collaborations in Transnational Higher Education
Dr. Gloria Molinero, Queen Mary University of London, UK

Transnational Higher Education (TNHE) is increasingly experiencing collaborations between Faculty and specialists of English for Academic Purposes (EAP). Issues concerning knowledge transfer, second language practice, and contextual challenges are the main concerns initiating Joint Delivery (JD) programmes. This reports on research exploring the collaborative experiences of thirteen EAP specialists with a reflective standpoint undertaking Interpretative Phenomenological Analysis. The analysis exhibits three main collaborative practices with different levels of engagement and teaching tactics: assisted-delivery, co-teaching, and lecture-seminars delivery. Friend and Cook's (2014) framework evaluates these collaborations providing insights on approaches for optimum and organic collaborations, based on co-designing, openness and adaptation, mutual learning, and a share of outcomes and responsibilities. JD enriches practice, student experience, and the collaborative stands of TNHE.

Chapter 8: The Local Impact of Social Sciences, Humanities, and Educational Dissertations on Transnational Higher Education in Turkey
Professor Ömer Açıkgöz, University of Ankara, Turkey
Dr. Aydın Aslan, Selcuk University, Turkey
Dr. Aslı Günay, University of Ankara, Turkey

Doctoral education, which is a crucial component of transnational higher education, should contribute to the development of national and international science. To get a better insight into the contributions of doctoral education to the literature, 266 dissertations completed in the fields of social sciences, humanities, and education at 12 Turkish state universities between 2014 and 2017 were analyzed with bibliometric analysis. The analysis indicated that the scientific articles generated from the dissertations and the citations to these articles were dominantly published and cited in national indexed journals, which means that the dissertations made more contributions to the national literature than international literature. It can be one of the indicators that display the impact of transnational higher education on these dissertations is quite limited in Turkey. Several suggestions were made for Turkish universities to make more contributions to transnational higher education through doctoral education.

Chapter 9: Teachers' Role in Enhancing Adult Learners' Sense of Autonomy, Competence, and Involvement in Online Higher Education – Learning From an Australian Transnational Higher Education Provider
Dr. Mamun Ala, Australian Institute of Business, Australia
Dr. Sehrish Shahid, Australian Institute of Business, Australia
Dr. Saadia Mahmud, Australian Institute of Business, Australia
Dr. Kuldeep Kaur, Australian Institute of Business, Australia
Dr. Syed Mohyuddin, Australian Institute of Business, Australia

This chapter draws from the learning from an Australian transnational higher education provider in enhancing adult student's sense of belonging, engagement, and interactions. The literature suggests that student engagement and motivation could be enabled by fulfilling certain needs such as autonomy, competence, and relatedness or involvement. The chapter also explores some strategies that could be adopted by teachers to promote behavioural, cognitive, emotional and agentic engagement of online adult learners. It is argued that regular customized communication by online teachers using email and learning management system can promote teaching presence, student engagement and motivation. This approach is in line with the notion of community of enquiry, a social constructivist model of learning process that suggests that educational experience takes place at the intersection of social, cognitive, and teaching presence. Other strategies, namely the effective use of breakout rooms during an online class, the emphasis on reflective learning, and the use of stories in an online classroom.

SECTION 4: BROADENING HORIZONS

Chapter 10: Blended and Transnational Higher Education in Architecture Schools: Examples and Considerations From Two International Joint-Design Studios Between Australia and Japan

Dr. Raffaele Pernice, University of New South Wales, Australia
Dr. Tetsuya Yaguchi, Waseda University, Japan
Dr. Keigo Kobayashi, Waseda University, Japan

In this book chapter, authors will reflect on the challenges, advantages, and pitfalls of the blended teaching in two architectural design studios jointly organized by an Australian and a Japanese university, highlighting key considerations ranging from the variety of learning and teaching on campus and virtual practices, to the design of assessments and related feedback, and the use of various on-line communication and graphic platforms implemented for teaching and learning (Teams, Zoom, Miro, Concept-board). They will also give an account of the experience and direct involvement of both students and faculty during the lock-down, and how flexibility and adaptability to the use of new technologies on their parts has resulted in a valuable experience at least for what concerns international design studios cooperation. As is common practice in architectural schools, the 2 joint design studios focused on different scale of representation and design, exploring issues and characteristics from the territorial to local scales.

Chapter 11: Collaborative Online International Learning to Enhance Employability Skills at TNE Institutions

Dr. Lauren Amber Holly Crabb, Anglia Ruskin University, UK
Dr. Nan Jiang, Coventry University, UK
Dr. Hanna Yakavenka, Coventry University, UK

Employability skills such as intercultural exposure and communication is well established in most business education degree programs. However, there is little knowledge of how these skills are developed in Transnational Education (TNE). Employability will play an increasingly important role in education as working patterns and skills have changed in the wake of Covid-19. This chapter aims to explore the lived experiences of local and non-local students at TNE partners who engaged in international learning experiences and understand how these projects develop employability skills in terms of intercultural communication. Findings suggest students value these international, interactive projects to develop awareness of the home institution and enhance cross-culture exposure.

Chapter 12: Islands and Bridges – Why and How TNE Universities and EMIs Generally Might "Bridge" Into Their Local Communities

Mr. Kevin Ottley, University of Central Asia, Tajikistan

It is recommended that EMIs, including TNE institutions, should formalise 'bridging' between their institutions and the local community, if possible. A definition of 'community' is extended to include non-faculty/local staff within the university. The rationale for this recommendation is that it is predicated upon a win-win-win result: non-local faculty benefit because bridging assists with their integration into the local community; the university benefits because establishing links with the wider community is an invaluable PR initiative; the local community benefits. The authors' own experiences of bridging, formal and informal, official or otherwise, will be offered as examples of what might be achieved. At the same time, a section of this paper notes the challenges which one might experience when bridging, and how an individual and her institution might avoid such difficulties.

Chapter 13: Bangladeshi Students' Family Fertilization for Pursuing Higher Education in Australia

Dr. Md Tariqul Islam, Hiroshima University, Japan

Among the young Bangladeshi people, like many other international students from developing countries, Australian universities created a position as an emerging terminus for higher education. This chapter pursues to explore the family motivations for Bangladeshi higher education students to become physically mobile to chase education in Australian universities. The chapter follows a qualitative methodology and includes the stories of 18 young Bangladeshi students studying at two Australian universities. It aims to enlighten researchers and policymakers in both developing and developed countries about the role of the family as a micro agent of socialisation in contributing to the global level politics and power related to the higher education industry. The findings of the chapter reveal that the dreams and desires developed and disseminated by their family young students experienced in Bangladesh are quite neoliberal in character. Thus it provides the analysis of empirical data for both host and sending countries to ensure transnational higher education in developing countries.

Chapter 14: Understanding Chinese learners in Transnational Higher Education in China

Dr. Yimei Chen, Jiaying University, China

Ms. Yan Wei, Xi'an Jiao Tong-Liverpool University, China

Chinese have become the largest share of international students in many countries. Meanwhile, the number of Transnational Higher Education (TNHE) programmes has reached a new high in China. This makes it exceptionally important for teachers whose own cultural and educational background are very different from Chinese to understand their learners. The study set out to better understand Chinese students in TNHE by studying a case of a Sino-Anglo cooperation university in China. The foreign teachers' and foreign students' views on Chinese students were collected and juxtaposed with Chinese students' own accounts. The qualitative study finds many commonly cited features of East Asian students evident in this research context. However, this study gains insights of these phenomena and strategies from the very experienced expatriate teachers, who demonstrated a good understanding of their Chinese students. We propose a new approach to teach Chinese students. This study is believed to be of reference to teaching in TNHE in vast contexts with students from Confucian Heritage Cultures (CHC).

SECTION 5: ENHANCING PRACTICE

Chapter 15: Scaffolding New Teacher-Trainers Through a Hybrid Co-Training Model From a Transnational Higher Education Perspective

Dr. Saif Said Rashid Al Abri, Ministry of Education, Oman

Despite the potentials of collaborative work for enhancing the knowledge, skills, and attitudes (KSA) of professionals, the educational field lacks a clear model for co-training. This article aims to develop a conceptual framework for this collaborative professional development (PD) strategy to help novice teacher trainers (TTs) grow professionally. Although a lot has been written in the educational literature about co-teaching, there are merely few self-reported reflections about the use of co-training, and it is not clear how to adopt it as a tool for TTs' PD. In an attempt to fill in this gap, a proposed co-training model is constructed based on the philosophy of co-teaching, novice TTs' needs in terms of KSA, and their role-competency in the training room. These concepts are integrated to design a co-training model that is expected to help in scaffolding novice TTs. We argue that this model if properly implemented, can support novice TTs.

Chapter 16: Reflection on Teaching Observation for Computer Science and Engineering to Design Effective Teaching Resources in Transnational Higher Education

Dr. Sukhpal Singh Gill, Queen Mary University of London, UK
Ms. Danielle Thibodeau, Queen Mary University of London, UK
Dr. Rupinder Kaur, Dulwich College, UK
Dr. Usman Naeem, Queen Mary University of London, UK
Dr. Tony Stockman, Queen Mary University of London, UK

Teaching observation plays an important role in the development of educators in higher education institutions, as this practice facilitates an environment where educators can share and be made aware of good pedagogic practices. This also applies to educators who teach on Transnational Higher Education (TNE) programmes. The work in this article presents a theoretical framework for reflection on educator observations that took place on a Semi-Structured Data and Advanced Data Modelling module delivered to the BSc/MSc Computer Science programme at Queen Mary University of London. This article also provides an overview of a research methodology for designing and delivering teaching resources based on educational research and theory, as well as personal evaluations of the teaching teams' previous experience. The article illustrates how the approach adopted for the module can be transferrable to TNE programmes.

Chapter 17: Professional Development and Transnational Education in the Post-COVID-19 Era

Ms. Xitong Dai, Perse School Suzhou, China

This chapter will consider the impact the COVID-19 pandemic has brought on transnational education and focus on the "new normality" following the epidemic. Moreover, it will concentrate on the development of technology-enhanced education after the pandemic along with the crucial role that professional development performs in TNE. On that note, distance education and work-related challenges will be discussed, and solutions and suggestions put forward to TNE educators, with professional development providing the central focal point.

Chapter 18: Enhancing Educational Leadership in Transnational Higher Education

Dr. Gareth Richard Morris, Perse School Suzhou, China
Mr. James Morris, IT Project Management, UK
Ms. Li Lei, SSFLS, China

In every industry and field, and at every institutional level, good leadership is essential. Equally significant Is the remit a leader is tasked with fulfilling, the point in time at which this is expected and the situation one must work within, alongside the context. This all makes defining good leadership and good leaders fraught with difficulty as what may work well in one situation, may not work so well in another. For transnational higher education, the situation is complicated further because providers can vary in terms of location, size, complexity, context, and remit. It is also challenging because of the ongoing COVID pandemic. Consequently, this chapter will briefly introduce transnational higher education, along with the idea of what successful and effective leadership constitutes. It will then go on to consider different leadership styles before examining a specific transnational higher education provider and discussing some of the leadership approaches and features that have been evidenced in a specific academic school at this institution over the past decade.

SECTION 6: FUTURE TRENDS

Chapter 19: Transnational Higher Education Trends in the Internet Era – Case Studies in China

Ms. Wei Xu, SHSID, China

Under the trend of global integration, transnational higher education has become a research upsurge in recent years. In this chapter, the author focuses on the implementations and influences of the modern information technology in transnational higher education. Current researches are mainly based on traditional textual research and data collection analysis. Few research mentioned the influences and changes that modern information technology could bring to the developing of transnational higher education. Furthermore, the global outbreak caused by 2019-nCOVID has also brought a full range of impacts to the whole world and profoundly affected the current situation and future process of transnational higher education. Consequently, the aim of this chapter is to provide an overview of transnational higher education trends in the internet era. The author will analyze it through several cases studies, taking China as an example and conclude those findings to highlight efficient methods using internet technologies to contribute building a better education world.

Chapter 20: Transnational Education in Malaysia – Development, Challenges, and Strategic Alignment

Dr. Joseph Kee-Ming Sia, Curtin University, Malaysia
Dr. Anita Jimmie, Curtin University, Malaysia

Private higher education in Malaysia has undergone radical transformations with the aim of becoming a regional hub for higher education in Southeast Asia, and to transform the country into one that has a fully developed knowledge-based economy. To understand this transformation, the purposes of this chapter are; to identify key prospects and challenges of international branch campuses (IBCs) and propose strategic alignment on the operation and administration of the IBCs in Malaysia. In order to identify and understand the challenges IBCs face when operating in Malaysia, this study adopts a review approach that is supported by findings and from academic and grey literature. The results of this review indicate that IBCs are faced with complex challenges and are on unequal footing with other local universities. This chapter uncovers various demanding issues and discusses strategic alignment of IBCs. Limitations and recommendations for future research are also incorporated in this chapter.

Chapter 21: Envisioning and Exploring Future Transnational Higher Education and Management Models
Professor Youmin Xi, Xi'an Jiao Tong-Liverpool University, China
Ms. Chengcheng Li, Xi'an Jiao Tong-Liverpool University, China

This chapter aims to envision future transnational university educational and management models. In Background, general review of international universities in China would be outlined following by an overview of a specific example international University, Xi'an Jiaotong-Liverpool University. In Literature Review, an evaluation of relevant literature will demonstrate how the examination of key concepts like knowledge, truth, education, enlightenment could contribute to deepened understanding of future transnational higher education. In the third section on Discussion, detailed analysis of HeXie Education Model, HeXie Mindset Model, and HeXie Management Model would be addressed following by an application of these models in XJTLU's management systems. Fourthly, challenges and opportunities would be outlined in terms of student-centered and research-led education, the teaching of research, quality education, future education in the Uncertain, Ambiguous, Complex, and Changeable world, and future education before conclusion is drawn.

The aim of this collection of work is to consider developments and future trends in transnational higher education. To achieve this end global examples, expertise and insights have been drawn upon through bringing together researchers and practitioners from around the world and collating their varied and discerning experiences and work as a coherent and measured review of some of the key features of transnational higher education in 2023 and beyond. This work should be of interest to a wide range of diverse readers, and we invite questions and correspondence on this topic from all interested parties at any point.

We hope that you find the work within this volume as insightful and useful as we do.

Gareth Richard Morris
Perse School Suzhou, China

Li Li
Exeter University, UK

Section 1
Teaching and Learning

Chapter 1
A Module for General Education Curriculum Development in Chinese International Universities:
A Practical Example Concerning Law and Morality

Kai Liu
Xi'an Jiaotong-Liverpool University, China

Jie Yang
The University of Adelaide, Australia

ABSTRACT

This chapter focuses on a discussion of general education curriculum development in international universities, with an emphasis on the reflective pedagogical practice found in China. It defines general education in the context of Chinese academia, and explores its development and future trends influenced by the global impact of the COVID-19 pandemic and contemporary transnational education (TNE). In particular, this chapter examines the curriculum design of the law and morality module (L & M Module) taught at the Chinese Culture Teaching Center (CCTC) at Xi'an Jiaotong-Liverpool University (XJTLU), Suzhou, China, and identifies any practical problems in relation to teaching quality and assessment methods. It also advances corresponding suggestions to enhance students' learning outcomes and efficiency.

DOI: 10.4018/978-1-6684-5226-4.ch001

INTRODUCTION

In its 1945 report, the Harvard Committee defines 'General Education in a Free Society' with an introduction by James Bryant Conant, a former president of Harvard University (The Harvard Committee, 1945). In this definition, general education is regarded as the cornerstone of the Harvard College curriculum, and divided into four categories: aesthetics & culture; ethics & civics; history, society & the individual, and science & technology in society. Since the fall of 2021, Harvard University has offered 40 different courses from these categories. Another example is Temple University, which requires every undergraduate student to complete the general education curriculum before graduating. Its program stresses the development of personal competencies rather than content knowledge (Temple Undergraduate Bulletin, 2022). Students are encouraged to engage in critical thinking, contextualized learning, interdisciplinary thinking, the development of their communication skills, scientific and quantitative reasoning, civic engagement, information literacy and lifelong learning.

In China, the theoretical framework for a general education curriculum has been set up and actively carried out by Peking and Tsinghua Universities. Peking University has introduced 57 courses covering three areas: Human Civilization and Its Traditions; Issues in Modern Society; Studies in the Humanities, Nature, and Methods (Peking University Undergraduate Education, 2022). In 2020, during the pandemic, Tsinghua University launched 18 online courses (Tsinghua SEM, 2022). These courses integrate the concept of general education into a reflection of professional knowledge to improve the ideological thinking and the quality of life of students. The courses aim to help build personality and civic awareness and enable students to further their reading and analytical skills, and their ability to innovate. Communication and presentation skills are also emphasized.

As of August 2022, China had established 10 independent international universities: The University of Nottingham Ningbo China; Beijing Normal University-Hong Kong Baptist University United International College; Xi'an Jiaotong-Liverpool University; New York University Shanghai; Wenzhou-Kean University; Duke Kunshan University; The Chinese University of Hong Kong, Shenzhen; Shenzhen MSU-BIT University; Guangdong Technion-Israel Institute of Technology; and The Hong Kong University of Science and Technology, Guangzhou (Ministry of Education of the People's Republic of China, 2022). Independent departments in these international universities provide students with general education courses. As the largest Sino-foreign cooperative university in China, XJTLU, vigorously explores the new mode of TNE to make up for deficiencies in traditional higher education. It aims to become a Chinese research-led university recognized internationally. CCTC is responsible for providing general education to XJTLU students.

This chapter discusses general education curriculum development within the scope of Chinese international universities, with a particular focus on the L&M Module offered by CCTC at XJTLU. Curriculum development is a fluid process that necessitates ongoing reflection on prior experiences together with design adjustments changing circumstances can be adapted to (Susam et. al., 2020). In this regard, evaluation is of great importance. This chapter examines the L&M Module evaluation model, which plays a decisive role in both measuring the quality of teaching of CCTC staff and XJTLU student learning outcomes for TNE.

The objectives of this chapter are to investigate the curriculum design of the L & M Module so as to pinpoint existing difficulties and potential challenges, and use them to put forward moderate advice for the enhancement of the corresponding teaching and learning performance. Through this investigation, a new model for the general education development used in Chinese international universities in the TNE environment could be established.

As China's stature grows in the world, people outside of its borders would like to understand more about what kind of education system (in this case, its Tertiary education system) that the people of China are receiving. Therefore, the target readers of this chapter include those who teach the L&M Module in Chinese universities, as well as those who teach general education courses in universities outside of China. Qualitative research method is adopted to analyze L&M Module curriculum objectives, content, implementation, assessment and evaluation, and identify any related issues in teaching and learning. This chapter finds that in the post-pandemic era, strengthening the cornerstone and quality of general education for TNE at a tertiary level along with the role of modern network technology is extremely important and of great significance for overall improvement in the sector.

BACKGROUND

General education is acknowledged world-wide as the way to provide students with knowledge and values that can be used among diverse groups in modern society. It was initially outlined by Petrus Paulus Vergerius in his Renaissance treatise 'On Noble Manners and Liberal Studies' in the early 15th century. He recommended that all disciplines in the medieval liberal arts curriculum, (the trivium-grammar, rhetoric, and logic, the quadrivium-arithmetic, geometry, astronomy, and music) and acknowledged, with respect, the advanced professional disciplines of medicine, law, and theology (Woodward, 1906). General education was first linked to university education by Professor Alpheus Spring Packard of Bowdoin College USA, in the early 19th century. At the time, many scholars felt that the academic divisions of modern universities were too specialized and knowledge seriously fragmented. They began to pay attention to the research and development of general education, and designed relevant curricula for universities (Cleaveland & Packard, 1882). Nowadays, general education is considered a defining feature of the humanistic movement, providing students with the tools and thinking to advance their lives and careers. It is now a compulsory subject in many European and American universities.

In the context of modern university education in China, the renowned educator Mr. Mu Qian first proposed the term, General Education, in his article 'On Reforming the University System' in 1940. He proposed that study and life should be integrated; that people should have a wide knowledge and sound scholarship before becoming expert in any area; that university courses should be academic and that university students should have a sound understanding of China's traditional culture (General Education Center of Wuhan University, 2022). Mingyuan Gu (1992), Beijing Normal University Professor and President of China's Education Association, has said that general education should focus on 'nurture' rather than 'teaching', and should be a kind of humanistic education that surpasses utilitarianism and pragmatism. It should provide students with diversified learning options and enable them to expand and develop their thinking and understanding (Liu & Zheng, 2013), with the ultimate goal of tapping the unique potential of all students.

In universities in contemporary China, there is insufficient attention paid to general education (Chen & Xu, 2020). Only a limited number of public universities, e.g., Peking, Zhejiang, Fudan, Wuhan, Guizhou, Hubei Universities, have set up independent general education departments offering relevant courses. These universities are almost all top-tier education providers in China (Huang, 2011). This means that the majority of Chinese public universities do not have independent general education departments. These universities have general education courses offered by either foundation education departments (usually responsible for teaching public courses, such as College Chinese, College English, College Sport, Basic Computer, Advanced Mathematics, Mental Health for undergraduate students, etc.) or lecturers from different departments across the universities (Jiang, 2010).

Because universities can have different understandings and interpretations of general education, many blend general education courses with public foundation courses, or even with ideological and political courses (such as An Introduction to the Basic Principles of Marxism, An Introduction to Mao Zedong Thought, An Outline of Modern and Contemporary Chinese History, Moral and Legal Ideology) which are all compulsory subjects of China's Ministry of Education (MoE). This means that the curriculum and development of general education has many variations in Chinese public universities (Xia, 2021). It is worth mentioning that, in order to meet the requirements of the MoE, the curriculum and development of general education in some Chinese public universities only addresses the role of public foundation and ideological and political courses, while ignoring the importance of the general education component (Ma, 2012). To some extent, this undermines the practical benefits of general education in tertiary education in China.

Although regarding TNE, international universities in China also adopt a hybrid approach for general education, they manage a better balance of the roles and functions of fundamental, ideological and political courses mixed with general education, and so ensure compliance with the requirements of the MoE (Sun, 2014). As a result, their curriculum settings are different from those in public universities (Qian, 2020). CCTC at XJTLU has set up a general education curriculum framework consisting of compulsory courses and free elective courses. The compulsory courses for Year One and Two mainland Chinese undergraduate students, include 'Self-management', 'Comparisons between Chinese and Western Culture', 'The Modernization of China', 'Law and Morality'. 'An Introduction to Chinese Language and Culture' is compulsory for Year One Hong Kong, Macao and Taiwan undergraduate students. Course lecturers are mostly from CCTC, but some have been invited from other universities. More than 100 free elective courses, covering most disciplines including the humanities, the natural sciences, the social sciences, physical education and the arts, are offered to undergraduate, postgraduate and international students at XJTLU. Lecturers for these courses come from different departments (including CCTC) of XJTLU or other universities and institutions.

CURRICULUM DEVELOPMENT FOR THE L&M MODULE AT XJTLU

The L&M Module is one of the compulsory courses offered by CCTC for Year One mainland Chinese undergraduate students at XJTLU. It is designed not only as a general education course, but also as a public foundation course involving the ideology and politics required by the MoE. The lecturers, graduates from the law schools of various prestigious universities, are all from CCTC. They combine student-centered classroom teaching with online teaching, particularly suited to this post-pandemic era, to overcome the weaknesses of traditional lecturer-centered general education in Chinese public universities.

Curriculum Objectives

The module promotes legal awareness and a moral compass amongst students. It aims to improve their independent and critical thinking skills, and further enhance their adaptability, ability to innovate and international competitiveness, so that the needs of industry and society can be better served.

Specifically, this Module is designed to help students:

a. establish appropriate values, morals, life outlook, and legal framework in the context of TNE, to solve any practical problems they may face.
b. gain an understanding of the overall global legal system, while mastering the basic concepts, principles and content of Chinese law.
c. improve their legal awareness, strengthen their legal concepts, and provide an understanding of the basic concepts of the market economy, e.g. efficiency, fairness and honesty for a more effective society.
d. obey the law, and gain the ability to analyze cases, and use the law to protect individual rights and interests.
e. understand the law of different legal systems, study the judgments of similar cases in various countries, and examine the pros and cons of Chinese law.
f. read and understand legal documents, and the basic principles and procedures for court trials.
g. view people and things from the perspective of the law, abide by the law and form appropriate social attitudes based on their legal knowledge, treat social issues rationally and analyze them objectively.
h. go forward in their lives with the spirit of patriotism, and an appreciation of socialist values; adapt to the needs of socialist modernization, and contribute to the Chinese Dream of national rejuvenation.

Curriculum Content

In consideration of TNE, the content of the L&M Module at XJTLU has 13 different topics: Introduction to Law & Morality, Constitutional Law, Criminal Law, Civil Law, Marriage Law, Tort Liability Law, Contract Law, Company Law, Labor Law, Intellectual Property Law, Criminal Procedure Law, Civil Procedure Law, and Contemporary Legal Systems.

The first two topics are designed to meet the requirements of the MoE, with a special focus on ideological and political education undertaken in most Chinese public universities. These topics encourage XJTLU undergraduates to take on the responsibility of national rejuvenation, pursue high ideals, promote the fine traditions of China, and abide by high moral standards. The remaining topics are designed with reference to the core curriculum of most law schools around the world. These topics outline the basic framework of significant laws, and also present basic legal knowledge in different fields in order to better facilitate the study and life of XJTLU undergraduates.

It is worth noting that the last topic in particular (Contemporary Legal Systems), analyzes the differences and similarities between civil law and common law. It is very important for XJTLU undergraduates to understand the application of laws in different legal systems to accommodate their potential life and employment in other countries. Should they choose to complete Years Three and Four at the University of Liverpool (UoL) in the UK, XJTLU provides two learning modes for undergraduates for TNE, i.e., '4+X' & '2+2'. '4+X' means students complete a four-year bachelor degree at XJTLU in China, while

'2+2' means students complete their first two years at XJTLU in China, and the last two years at UoL in the UK.

Curriculum Implementation

Katz (1990) addressed the interaction between student learning styles and teaching methods by saying that the problem-solving ability of students could be enhanced by observing the amount of time needed for learning outside the classroom. The L&M Module is implemented with a combination of student-centered teaching and student-lecturer interactions through technological support such as 'U-talk' (a distinctive online teaching and learning platform established by CCTC in 2010 to promote general education); 'Learning Mall' (a unique online teaching, learning and training platform established by XJTLU in 2020 to promote TNE and lifelong learning in the post-pandemic era); 'Mediasite' and 'BigBlueButton', follow a '2+2+2' model, i.e. two hours for pre-class activities, two hours for in-class activities and two hours for post-class activities.

At the pre-class stage, pre-reading materials in relation to each teaching topic are uploaded onto 'U-talk' a week before the corresponding class begins. These pre-reading materials assist students quickly and accurately accessing the related key points; encourage critical thinking and active learning and stimulate questions that can be used in class for further discussion.

At the in-class stage, courses are delivered in a large-scale multi-media classroom accommodating more than 200 students. Due to time constraints, lecturers usually refer to PPT slides for collective classroom teaching. It is worth mentioning that lecturer-student interactions are primarily based on 'Learning Mall'. Lecturers upload interactive questions through hyperlinks to the pre-class question bank. Students are required to answer these questions via 'Learning Mall' within a set timeframe. Detailed statistics on their answers then appear on the projector screen for grading and discussion in the classroom.

At the post-class stage, online discussions are mainly conducted through 'U-talk'. Each teaching week, five web posts including questions related to the teaching topic are uploaded onto 'U-talk'. Students use these for discussion, and the corresponding comments and grades are then assigned by lecturers.

Auster and Wylie (2006) argued that students should seek out environments where they cannot only obtain knowledge but also learn how to apply that knowledge and exercise judgment. Carr, Palmer and Hagel (2015) say that students must be able to process content themselves in order to learn. Smart, Witt and Scott (2012) point out that students should try to comprehend any new material encountered in terms of concepts they already have. Bain (2004) advocate that students need to continue improving their skills through inquiry-based, case-based, project-based and discovery learnings.

The implementation of the '2+2+2' model of the L&M Module is particularly helpful in facilitating XJTLU students' studies in the following manner: (a) Active Learning, in which students answer questions raised by lecturers, formulate questions of their own, discuss, debate, and brainstorm during class, leading to problem solving. (b) Cooperative Learning, in which students work in teams on specific assignments under conditions assuring both positive interdependence and individual accountability. (c) Inductive Learning, in which students are presented with challenges in advance and then use course materials to address those challenges. Learning, of course, is a continuous process of understanding, mastering, reflecting, redefining, and applying knowledge.

Assessment Methods

Pounder (2000) pointed out that sound assessment methods effectively improve the quality of teaching in universities. Liu, Bridgeman and Adler (2012) added that appropriate assessment methods are the best tools to measure university student learning outcomes. Thus, assessment methods play a vital role in promoting teaching and learning for TNE. Assessment is usually divided into formative and summative assessments. The former aims to supervise student learning by providing timely feedback that can be used by both lecturers and students to improve the quality of teaching and learning. The feedback obtained in this assessment is used for the improvement of both students and trainers. Therefore, formative assessment can be said to be one of the most important elements for reflective learning and teaching (Orakcı, 2020). The latter aims to evaluate student learning outcomes by comparing them with requirements or criteria at the end of a teaching unit. Both formative and summative assessments serve to measure and improve student performance (Wholey, 1996).

The assessment structure for the L&M Module takes the form of an in-class quiz, worth 20%; an online discussion, worth 20%; and a final exam, worth 60%. Both formative and summative assessments are included. As mentioned earlier, the in-class quiz and online discussion are formatively assessed through 'Learning Mall' and 'U-talk' respectively. For the final exam, lecturers prepare two sets of exam papers (one for the actual exam and one for any possible supplementary tests required). This is the summative assessment. After the exam, lecturers mark the papers, and internal moderators spot check the marked papers to avoid any errors. The marks are then submitted to the Registry Office together with the in-class quiz and online discussion grades.

In recent years, due to the COVID-19 pandemic, the CCTC has had to switch its teaching, learning and assessment activities online, as many other organizations and institutions throughout the world have had to. New network platforms such as 'Mediasite' and 'BigBlueButton' were introduced to provide lecturers with flexible options such as teaching videos, to meet the diversified needs of students. This style of teaching maximized the fun and accuracy of teaching, reduced the uncertainty of real-time teaching, and provided students with the best version of the teaching materials. This style of teaching was better able to facilitate large-group teaching and learning, and it also improved work and study efficiency.

Curriculum Evaluation

Evaluation provides teaching staff with a supportive and constructive framework to monitor, reflect and improve teaching quality (Osigweh, 1986). It encourages a culture in which good evaluation practice is accepted and valued (Schmidt, Von Hippel, & Tippelt, 2010). Evaluation also promotes fair and reasonable learning outcome assessments for students to enhance the quality of learning by connecting with their study needs, so that the teaching staff can address those needs (Poole, Harman & Deden, 1998).

A number of curriculum evaluation models have been designed by academics, e.g. Kolb (1984) and Gibbs (1988). The L&M Module adopts the Kirkpatrick's model. Kirkpatrick (2006) proposed a theory of four levels of evaluation: 1) Reaction: assessing what participants thought and felt about the teaching. 2) Learning: assessing the resulting increase in knowledge and skills, and any change in attitude. 3) Behavior: assessing the transfer of knowledge, skills, and attitudes from classroom to job. 4) Result: assessing overall results together with attendance and participation for any particular teaching program. This theory ensures that the evaluation for the L&M Module is sustainable in line with the common interests of XJTLU lecturers and students, to support their self-reflection and self-improvement, and assist in teaching reform and innovation (Masaru & Yuko, 2012).

The evaluation structure for the L&M Module includes Peer-evaluation, External-evaluation, Self-evaluation, a Module Questionnaire Survey, an Internal Periodic Review, a Staff-Student Liaison Committee, and a Professional Development Review for teaching and learning practice.

Peer-evaluation is conducted by colleagues through classroom teaching observation and peer review feedback to identify the strengths, weakness, opportunities and threats of the Module so that improvements can be made (Thomas et. al., 2014). External-evaluation is carried out by experienced external examiners through teaching staff interviews and examination paper evaluation (Menestrel, Walahoski & Mielke, 2014). Self-evaluation is carried out by lecturers themselves through self-reflection and self-criticism to identify any problems and shortcomings that need improvement (Schwarz & Struhkamp, 2007). Self-evaluation is of vital importance as it can help lecturers develop by providing feedback on a variety of topics such as personality, teaching style, assessment techniques, supervisory responsibilities, academic performance, and so on. It has the potential to teach people to be self-critical and take personal responsibility for their work. It can help people both advance professionally and in their overall careers (Orakcı, 2021; Taylor, 2014; Toraman et. al., 2020). The Module Questionnaire is distributed through ‘Learning Mall’ each semester to collect student feedback on the course and any suggestions for improving the teaching and learning of the Module (Spiel, Schober & Reimann, 2006). The Internal Periodic Review is jointly undertaken by the CCTC and the university through module reports (including reports on teaching strategies, assessment approaches, marking schemes, marking descriptors, research supervision, etc.). Peer review reports analyze the deficiencies of the module for improvement. The Staff-Student Liaison Committee encourages dialogue and interaction between staff and students, for improvement of the Module. It collects student suggestions and feedback, measures student satisfaction, and promotes staff self-development. The Professional Development Review works as a supplementary evaluation method to respond to the abovementioned evaluation results and examine individual lecturer performance in the areas of teaching, research and academic supervision.

These evaluation methods comprehensively ensure the teaching quality and learning efficacy of the L&M Module. They form a repeat cycle, through experimentation, experience and reflection, to abstract conceptualization, supporting Kolb’s theory of teaching and learning evaluation (Kolb, Rubin & McIntyre, 1974). This method is the process whereby knowledge is created through the transformation of experience.

FINDINGS AND DISCUSSIONS

Although the XJTLU Online Module Questionnaire showed that many students gave positive feedback to the curriculum development of the L&M Module, problems were also revealed. For example, the online nature of the curriculum setting means that to a great extent, teaching and learning activities are dependent on this technological network environment. So, disturbances in the stability of factors such as mobile devices, network traffic and network disruptions could have a seriously damaging effect on the quality of teaching and learning. Benson and Ward (2013) believed that new technologies could better improve teaching efficiency and evaluate teaching expertise for TNE, but the sophisticated use of electronic technologies does not necessarily enhance student engagement. And a lack of engagement could lead to a loss of student motivation and a weakening of the real interactions between students and lecturers. Some students indicated there was not much point in these interactions since all pre-reading materials, web posts and discussion topics are given and scored by lecturers.

Apart from this, curriculum implementation of the L&M Module also had drawbacks as reflected in the feedback from the Module Questionnaire. Some of these are: (a) The pre-reading activities are completely dependent on student conscientiousness. This means there may be a lack of reasonable internal and external supervision, and the amount and quality of reading may not be guaranteed. (b) Pre-reading materials are usually set by lecturers, and the selection is relatively subjective, and may lack consistency, diversity and flexibility. (c) Teaching activities are very much constrained by the fact that classes are so large. This means that the time for activities such as Q&A and case studies as well as activities such as student presentations and invitational lectures, is greatly reduced. (d) To some extent the very nature of the L&M Module (only worth 3 credits) has an effect on student motivation, and some students with a negative attitude attend only for the purpose of gaining credit. However, there are students with positive attitudes and they expect to learn about the sound professional knowledge of the law in class. Some even suggested that a law school should be established at XJTLU. (e) The English/Chinese bilingual teaching method is questioned by some students who have different career paths planned. Some (usually those who have a stronger interest in, and a higher level of proficiency in English) expect more English to be used in the course, including vocabulary and terminology to facilitate further study abroad. Others (usually those with less interest in, and a lower level of proficiency in English) think that studying the law is difficult enough itself without complicating the study with English. These students want less English used in the teaching.

So, it can be seen that the overall curriculum implementation of the L&M Module needs further improvement to inspire and motivate students, to help build student confidence, supervise the learning process and help guide and facilitate their future career paths.

Brown, Rust and Gibbs (1994) wrote that the choice of an appropriate assessment method to a large extent ensures the effective evaluation of any unit of study. Masaru and Yuko (2012) said that the choice of assessment method by TNE institutions is influential in encouraging a move towards sustainability. The selected assessment methods for the L&M Module break the traditional exam-focused assessment system (i.e. teacher-centered) to ensure the achievement of curriculum objectives and to ensure good feedback from students and peers. This feedback can be used to enhance student access, retention, completion, and satisfaction during their university study (Eckel & King, 2004). Student Feedback can also provide a timely and thorough model for the latest developments within the research field of assessment feedback (Evans, 2013).

Despite the positive comments, deficiencies in the assessment methods for the L&M Module have been found: (a) most web posts for online discussion are based on case analysis, which needs subjective answers from students. But the monotonous answers that students think they are required to give means there is a low degree of differentiation in the overall marking. (b) the subjective questions in the final exam paper have no standard answers, with only reference answers provided to indicate a general approach to answering (i.e. points given for accurate knowledge, minimum word count and neat handwriting). In this case, students wanted the marking descriptors to be more specific and show the points for each section to ensure the fairness and transparency of marking. However, in the field of social science, grading subjective questions is very difficult and the cause of academic debate due to the individuality and diversity of lecturer style and methods. (c) some students said that the in-class quiz and online discussion were not worth much for their overall score, so they just ignored them and relied wholly on their final exam results to pass the module (the weighted pass mark for the L&M Module is 40 out of

100). In view of this, lecturers need to reconsider and redesign the module assessment structure to better balance each assessment component. (d) the existing assessment structure still focuses on memory tasks and set answers. It lacks individual application and practice.

Harvey (1998) expounded on the limited research available on the quality of assessment methods in regard to TNE. He wrote that the related monitoring has become overly bureaucratized with the focus on accountability rather than improvement. Reeves (2000) goes on to say that timeliness, fairness and effectiveness are key measurement criteria for selecting assessment methods for TNE. These criteria can test the quality and function of assessment methods to improve the effectiveness of future teaching and learning.

The problems mentioned above reflect factors found in the L&M Module assessment methods. To solve them, lecturers must, through further discussion and coordination with students and peers, carefully review the overall assessment system, examine and balance each assessment component and streamline the marking scheme and descriptors, to generate a moderate assessment structure for the Module.

Chickering and Gamson (1991) issued the 'Seven Principles for Good Practice in Teaching and Learning', as a guide for the evaluation of higher education. These were meant to help encourage contact between students and faculty; develop reciprocity and cooperation among students; use active learning techniques; give prompt feedback; emphasize the completion of tasks on time; communicate high expectations, and respect the diverse talents and ways of learning of students.

These principles play a significant role in promoting the quality and efficiency of TNE, and are dominant guiding theories for the evaluation and progress of pedagogical instruction techniques. The existing multi-level evaluation structure of the L&M Module follows these principles closely, as they promote effective teaching, learning and research at CCTC, and provide alternative channels for prompt and effective communication among students, lecturers, and even different departments and universities, through the collection and response to, moderate suggestions and feedback.

Evaluation approaches for the L&M Module also revealed flaws in both teaching and learning practice. For example, the Module Questionnaire Survey showed that pre-reading activities did not necessarily achieve the desired outcomes, because, during classroom Q&A, it was found that some students had not read any of the pre-reading materials. So, the solution here would be to include pre-reading activities in the course assessment structure (e.g. testing pre-learning content through the regular in-class quiz and post-class online discussion), to better monitor the efficacy and quality of student learning.

As invigilation is hard to manage in large classrooms, some students also tried to cheat during the in-class quiz. The solution to this would be for 'Learning Mall' to have more technical support during invigilation, to ensure fairness.

Post-class student-lecturer interactions rely entirely on online discussions through uploaded posts on 'U-talk'. These posts are mostly case-based news and articles, inviting analysis and commentary from students. However, they lack flexibility in knowledge and application. To solve this, it is recommended that the number of web posts counted for assessment be reduced, and the types of questions asked from the web posts diversified. It would be beneficial to introduce more ways of interacting (i.e. not just online discussions), to strengthen the active, reflective and cooperative learning of students for the Module.

Staff-Student Liaison Committee Interviews with students further revealed that the in-class quiz emphasized the acquisition of legal theory and class attendance excessively rather than the importance of reflecting on the learning and practical experience. They also showed that quiz questions were not practical or flexible enough. The effect of this on students can be to dampen enthusiasm and possibly lead to plagiarism, collusion and the fabrication of quiz data (Heckler, Forde & Bryan, 2013).

As the L&M Module is a general education course worth limited credits, the online discussions are out of proportion and too time-consuming. Students need to spend more time on English for Academic Purpose (EAP) and other elective studies. To improve learning efficiency and enhance equal-status interactions between students and lecturers, online discussions need to be simplified (Cohen & Lotan, 1995). Subjective questions, e.g. short answer questions and case analysis for the final exam paper of the Module, need to be increased so students have more flexibility in applying their knowledge. This should be accompanied by a more relaxed marking scheme so that students have more autonomy in answering questions on the basis of their own knowledge reflection (Yorke, Bridges & Woolf, 2000).

Peer-evaluation and self-evaluation both showed that research, (and its application) is the way to achieve improvement in teaching and learning. The study of how to improve teaching through integration with research results, has become increasingly significant. There is a growing emphasis by research funding mechanisms on how to enhance and improve student learning activities, for quality assurance (Musthafa & Sajila, 2014).

In view of this, research-led teaching for the Module needs further development to improve and expand both research methods and the teaching skills of lecturers. The link between research and teaching needs to be emphasized clearly and promoted as a productive relationship. Through the coordination of research activities with teaching duties, quality and excellence in all academic endeavors can be assured (Chambers, Parker & Gregory, 2006). The research-led learning for the Module could also be strengthened by combining student research with the existing assessment system. Students could be encouraged to participate in more research seminars and conferences to promote information sharing and the exchange of knowledge.

Overall, the existing pluralistic evaluation structure for the Module is the outcome of continuous curriculum development by the teaching team of the law department. It is structured to consistently assist lecturers in: reflecting on the core values of general education; scrutinizing the pros and cons of the module design, and examining how the teaching, assessment and supervision of students, affects them (Penington, 1998). It is a structure that makes the teaching practice of CCTC unique for TNE and distinct from other public universities in China.

SOLUTIONS AND RECOMMENDATIONS

Biggs (1987) pointed out that higher education learning is affected by the following: personal factors–unique to the particular student; situational factors; process factors and the motive any particular student has, to want to learn, accompanied by the strategies they use to accomplish that learning. This means that a student approach to learning is a composite of motive and appropriate strategy. Skogsberg and Clump (2003) write that there are major differences in student learning styles depending on the particular course studied. Understanding this can be the key to fully utilizing unique learning styles to address the real needs of students. Gopinath (2015) says that teachers need to be constantly reflecting, critiquing and aligning existing assessment methods to guarantee the best teaching quality and learning outcomes for the TNE environment.

In consideration of the issues concerning the teaching and learning process mentioned above, the following recommendations are put forward for potential improvement:

To diversify pre-reading activities, and enhance student participation, materials such as the renowned law lecturers Massive Open Online Course (MOOC) videos; court trial videos, TV programs on legal debates; interesting pictures and screenshots on hot legal issues, could all be uploaded onto 'U-talk' in addition to the regular legal articles and textbook readings. A more reasonable assessment system (e.g. with the addition of more project-based group presentations and assignments, and a reduction in the point value of the final exam) could be designed for the Module to balance formative and summative assessments. In higher education, supervision plays the same role as appraisement and lecturers should not only be concerned with student examination results, but give more assessment weight (i.e. points or marks) to the learning process itself. Only sound learning strategies and habits, guarantee a solid effective learning process. By making formative and summative assessment equal, the comprehensive evaluation of student learning outcomes, can be realized, eliminating any interference factors such as mental stress, physical discomfort, emotional depression etc. This method of evaluation would reflect the real learning status of students.

According to Bryant's (2005 analytical theory), electronic discussions can create a better learning environment and lead to quality student discussions in class. Network platforms could be further diversified for the teaching and learning of the L&M Module. This is particularly important in the current post-pandemic era. As an example, enriching the content of 'U-talk' could be done by adding online tutoring and assignment assessment channels. By making full use of social media, delivering lectures through virtual classrooms, and establishing a bulletin board system and a web forum to share successful experiences of different universities in general education for TNE, the learning environment could be enriched enormously.

For TNE, curriculum evaluation is essential for both accreditation and learning support (Taras, 2008). Lecturer understanding of evaluation terminology and relationships reflects the fragmented theoretical and practical framework available (Wholey, 1996). A good evaluation model will enhance the student experience of both learning and teaching, and also contribute to the monitoring and review of quality and standards. Although the existing evaluation structure of the Module was carefully designed by the law teaching team, critiques from students, peers and external experts reflect a common need for improvement, i.e. that there should be more diversification of evaluation approaches.

The age of information and internationalization are major trends for higher education development (Hawkins, 2008). Online platform evaluation can provide a convenient tool to measure the attainment of higher order educational goals involving a deep understanding and an active use of knowledge in complex contexts (Reeves, 2000). These are an effective method for motivating instructors and students to raise their skills to a global level in comparison with traditional paper-based evaluation environments (Craig, 2001). These new technologies make TNE attractive to both learners and instructors with multiple evaluation approaches available to meet both their needs and the educational goals of universities (Bullock & Ory, 2000).

To facilitate the application of new technologies for a better evaluation model for the L&M Module, it is suggested that a specialized student survey could be conducted. The answers to questions to do with student satisfaction, learning outcomes, evaluation expectations, lecturer performance expectations etc. could be collated from this survey. Interviews could also be carried out with students, instructors and external cooperative professional bodies involved in network interactions, to support the survey. Based on the data collected, a report could then be produced to pinpoint any particular problems to do with the utilization of advanced technologies and platforms for evaluation. The report could also be used to facilitate relevant research in today's information age and to collect moderate feedback from students' peers and external experts, on all aspects of the teaching/learning process to explore more effective and challenging evaluation for innovation in the TNE environment.

Apart from technology, self-evaluation mechanisms could be further enhanced based on the existing curriculum evaluation structure of the L&M Module (Falchikov & Boud, 1989). Self-evaluation is important because it can help lecturers self-reflect by giving them feedback on a variety of areas such as personality, teaching style, assessment methods, supervisory duties, academic performance etc. It can encourage them to be self-critical and take personal responsibility for their practice. It can assist them in developing professionally and in their careers in general (Taylor, 2014).

With regard to the L&M Module, positive self-evaluation could be used through a set of progressive approaches in accordance with Gibbs' Model of Reflection (Gibbs, 1988). These approaches include: reviewing past experience, feelings, agendas and aspirations; examining existing interpersonal teacher-student interactions to address any impact of duty of care or influence of professionalism in group interactions; exploring student perceptions of the importance and meaning of intended learning outcomes and stimulating their self-directed learning; identifying limitations of established concepts, theories and methods to inform and affect teaching and learning practice and determining feasible remedy measures to optimize self-evaluation.

Through self-evaluation lecturers could be encouraged to improve their professional performance and to further consolidate and improve the quality of their teaching. Rogers (1969) says that the most useful learning is gained through an evaluation of any particular learning process; a continued openness to new experience and an ability to embrace the process of change. Positive self-evaluation in particular, needs cooperative and constructive external evaluation support to help lecturers deliver best practice to their students.

FUTURE DIRECTIONS FOR DEVELOPMENT

Sound curriculum development determines the quality for TNE, and should incentivise institutions and encourage them to move towards sustainability (Yarime & Tanaka, 2012). At XJTLU, Critiques from students and feedback from senior colleagues jointly demonstrate that the curriculum design for the L&M Module needs adjusting to offer more reasonable and effective assessment methods which would both improve the overall supervision of the student learning process and give students fairer evaluation. In view of this, to optimize curriculum development for the L&M Module in the future, three actions are proposed: enhancing pre-reading for in-class and post-class assessment; strengthening post-class student-lecturer interactions; and exploring other assessment methods for comprehensive curriculum evaluation.

1. Pre-reading was introduced to better facilitate teaching, learning and assessment for the L&M Module. A wide range of materials in different forms are provided (e.g. related MOOC videos, audios, picture and the work of previous students etc.). These have been carefully selected and uploaded onto 'U-talk' for pre-learning, together with the set article-based pre-reading. It is proposed that in order to better supervise the quality of student learning, these pre-reading activities should also be used in the assessment process. This could be done by testing the pre-learning content through both the regular in-class quiz and the post-class online discussion. By doing this, it is hoped that students would be more likely to read these materials in order to get higher assessment scores. This could also be a way to monitor and ensure lecturer preparation.

2. Post-class student-lecturer interactions should be enhanced to assist teaching, learning and assessment. In particular, the number of web posts should be reduced so that students are not overloaded with written work. Student knowledge, reflection and practice should be encouraged through other kinds of

assignments (e.g. verbal discussion and field work). Questions from web posts could be broadened to present a wider and more diversified experience, which would better serve the testing of both subjective attitudes and objective performance. The introduction of new interactive patterns could include knowledge exchanges through mobile devices; face-to-face communication; practical activities such as legal clinics, mock courts & court hearing, etc. These activities could fundamentally strengthen active, reflective and cooperative learning for the L&M Module, and promote a much fairer assessment system (Herrmann, 2013).

3. Other assessment approaches could also be introduced to optimize curriculum evaluation for the Module. Lecturers could encourage students to conduct self-assessments of their learning process. This might include appraising their pre-reading, classroom learning and post-class interactions for knowledge reflection and appraising their mastery of knowledge in preparation for the final exam. Self-assessment could help students understand and improve their individual learning styles and encourage them to be both more self-aware and self-critical of their own performance in order to take personal responsibility for their learning outcomes (Taylor, 2014).

Peer-assessment could also be used for assessment purposes. This could be done through group tasks to assess learning performance. Students appointed by lecturers, could give feedback on the assignment tasks of peers. Peer group feedback could also be collected through technology-supported software. All of this could help students gain more self-awareness through a comparison of how they see themselves versus how others see them. This form of assessment would also be a tool to motivate students to work harder (e.g. theme presentations, group projects, research papers) as these activities would also be counted towards a certain percentage of the total assessment. This could be an effective way to promote teaching and research innovation with student learning performance directly reflecting the teaching quality and research outcomes.

In addition, lecturers could show students the actual basis (e.g. updated module structure, specific evaluation criteria and detailed marking schemes) on which they are being assessed regardless of who makes the final assessment. Students could also be provided with training and practice on how to satisfy the evaluation criteria for the Module. Students could even be engaged, themselves, in developing assessment methods and criteria, particularly when peer-assessment or self-assessment is involved, to facilitate further study and research.

CONCLUSION

Curriculum development is a dynamic process, which needs both constant reflection from previous experiences and design adjustment to adapt smoothly to the changing TNE environment. To achieve best practice teaching, comprehensive and ongoing curriculum development is essential for the teaching, learning and research quality of the L&M Module. This requires timely and constructive feedback and suggestions from students, lecturers and professional bodies. The motivation of lecturers, the active cooperation of students, pedagogical guidance from experts, and technical and financial support from the university, are also required.

The findings of this chapter show that high-quality curriculum development in general education could not only enable students to be do more active, rather than passive, learning (including more reflective learning), but also comply with the TNE development trend to transform university teaching and assessment from exam-oriented to quality-oriented. In making these changes, student learning, knowledge level and practical ability could all be improved, to ensure a higher quality of education.

This chapter also discusses the diversity of students. Different students have different academic backgrounds and learning experiences, which means that they react to teaching and learning in different ways. To maximize learning outcomes, curriculum development should always take both the diversity and the inclusion of all students, into consideration. With respect to this, curriculum development for the L&M Module at XJTLU could be more individualized to help students interact with, rather than just consume, the knowledge presented to them. More flexible learning options should be provided for students to ensure they have the opportunity to use critical thinking and cooperative learning to achieve the ultimate goals of general education.

ACKNOWLEDGMENT

This research received no specific grant from any funding agency in the public, commercial, or not-for-profit sectors. We would like to take this opportunity to express our sincere gratitude to the colleagues, students and interviewees who assisted us in carrying out this research. We would also like to thank the Chinese Culture Teaching Center of Xi'an Jiaotong-Liverpool University for supporting in the completion of this research. Special thanks to Irma Frieda for proofreading this chapter, and IGI Global for offering us such a good opportunity to share and disseminate our research findings.

REFERENCES

Auster, E., & Wylie, K. (2006). Creating active learning in the classroom: A systematic approach. *Journal of Management Education, USA*, *30*(2), 333–353. doi:10.1177/1052562905283346

Bain, K. (2004). *What the best college teachers do?* Harvard University Press.

Benson, S., & Ward, C. (2013). Teaching with technology: Using TPACK to understand teaching expertise in online higher education. *Journal of Educational Computing Research*, *48*(2), 153–172. doi:10.2190/EC.48.2.c

Biggs, J. (1987). *Learning process questionnaire manual: student approaches to learning and studying*. Australian Council for Educational Research.

Brown, S., Rust, C., & Gibbs, G. (1994). *Strategies for diversifying assessment in higher education*. The Oxford Centre for Staff Development, Oxonion Rewley Press.

Bryant, B. (2005). Electronic discussion sections: a useful tool in teaching large university classes. Teaching of Psychology, 32(4), pp. 271-275.

Bullock, C., & Ory, J. (2000). Evaluating instructional technology implementation in a higher education environment. *American Journal of Evaluation, Illinois, USA*, *21*(3), 315–328. doi:10.1177/109821400002100303

Carr, R., Palmer, S., & Hagel, P. (2015). Active learning: The importance of developing a comprehensive measure. *Active Learning in Higher Education*, *6*(3), 173–186. doi:10.1177/1469787415589529

Chambers, E., Parker, J., & Gregory, M. (2006). Editorial: Research-led teaching/teaching-led research? *Arts and Humanities in Higher Education*, *5*(2), 115–116. doi:10.1177/1474022206063646

Chen, G., & Xu, D. (2020). A review of Chinese general education research [Lexical characteristics of Chinese language]. *Education Review*, *4*, 88–93.

Chickering, W. & Gamson, F. (1991). Appendix A: Seven principles for good practice in undergraduate education. *New Directions for Teaching & Learning*, *1991*(47), pp. 63-69.

Cleaveland, N., & Packard, A. (1882). *History of Bowdoin College: with biographical sketches of its graduates from 1806 to 1879. inclusive*. J.R. Osgood & Co.

Cohen, E., & Lotan, R. (1995). Producing equal-status interaction in the heterogeneous classroom. *American Educational Research Journal, Stanford University, USA*, *32*(1), 99–120. doi:10.3102/00028312032001099

Craig, D. (2001). View from an electronic learning environment: Perceptions and patterns among students in an online graduate education course. *Journal of Educational Technology Systems. Middle Tennessee State University, USA*, *30*(2), 197–219.

Eckel, P. D., & King, J. E. (2004). *An overview of higher education in the United States*. American Council on Education.

Evans, C. (2013). Making sense of assessment feedback in higher education. Review of Educational Research, 83(1), pp. 70-120.

Falchikov, N., & Boud, D. (1989). Student self-assessment in higher education: A meta-analysis. *Review of Educational Research*, *59*(4), 395–430. doi:10.3102/00346543059004395

Gibbs, G. (1988). *Learning by doing: a guide to teaching and learning methods*. Further Educational Unit, Oxford Polytechnic.

Gopinath, D. (2015). Discourses and practices in teaching methods and assessment: Insights from an early career academic. *SAGE Open*, *5*(1), 2158244015573371. doi:10.1177/2158244015573371

Gu, M. (1992). *Dictionary of Education*. Shanghai Educational Publishing House.

Harvey, L. (1998). An assessment of past and current approaches to quality in higher education. *Australian Journal of Education*, *42*(3), 237–255. doi:10.1177/000494419804200303

Hawkins, J. (2008). Higher education transformation: some trends in California and Asia. Policy Futures in Education, 6(5), pp. 532-544.

Heckler, C., Forde, R., & Bryan, C. (2013). Using writing assignment designs to mitigate plagiarism. *Teaching Sociology, USA*, *41*(1), 94–105. doi:10.1177/0092055X12461471

Herrmann, K. (2013). The impact of cooperative learning on student engagement: Results from an intervention. *Active Learning in Higher Education*, *14*(3), 175–187. doi:10.1177/1469787413498035

Huang, S. (2011). An analysis on the general education mode of universities in mainland China [Lexical characteristics of Chinese language] [Social Science Edition]. *Journal of Guangdong University of Technology*, *11*(1), 15.

Jiang, L. (2010). An exploration on the development of general education in China [Lexical characteristics of Chinese language]. *China Education Innovation Heraid*, *29*.

Katz, N. (1990). Problem solving and time: Functions of learning style and teaching methods. *OTJR (Thorofare, N.J.)*, *10*(4), 221–236.

Kirkpatrick, D., & Kirkpatrick, J. (2006). *Evaluating training programs: the four levels* (3rd ed.). Berrett-Koehler Publishers.

Kolb, D. (1984). Expenmental learning experience as a source of learning and development. Englewood Cliffs.

Kolb, D., Rubin, I., & Mclntyre, J. (1974). Organizational psychology: a book of readings. 2nd Edition, Englewood Cliffs.

Liu, J., & Zheng, S. (2013). The enlightenment of Harvard University's core curriculum to China's general education [Lexical characteristics of Chinese language]. *Research and Teaching*, *276*, 17.

Liu, O., Bridgeman, B., & Adler, R. (2012). Measuring learning outcomes in higher education: Motivation matters. *Educational Researcher, Princeton, NJ, USA*, *41*(9), 352–362. doi:10.3102/0013189X12459679

Ma, G. (2012). An analysis of the development situation and predicament of general education in China [Lexical characteristics of Chinese language] [Higher Education Study Edition]. *Journal of Changchun University of Technology*, *33*(2), 46.

Menestrel, S., Walahoski, J., & Mielke, M. (2014). A partnership model for evaluation: Considering an alternate approach to the internal-external evaluation debate. *American Journal of Evaluation, Washington, DC, USA*, *35*(1), 61–72. doi:10.1177/1098214013506600

Musthafa, M., & Sajila, K. (2014). Reconsidering the teaching–research nexus in higher education. Higher Education for the Future, 1(2), pp. 123-138.

Orakcı, Ş. (2020). Teacher candidates' opinions on portfolio implementation. *The Journal of Turkish Educational Sciences*, *18*(1), 266–295.

Osigweh, C. (1986). An evaluation model of training outcomes for higher education. Educational Evaluation and Policy Analysis, 8(2), pp. 167-178.

Penington, D. (1998). Managing quality in higher education institutions of the 21st century: a framework for the future. Australian Journal of Education, 42(3), pp. 256-270.

Poole, M., Harman, E., & Deden, A. (1998). Managing the quality of teaching in higher education institutions in the 21st century. Australian Journal of Education, 42(3), pp. 271-284.

Pounder, J. (2000). Evaluating the relevance of quality to institutional performance assessment in higher education. Evaluation, 6(1), pp. 66-78.

Qian, F. (2020). A preliminary study on the construction of ideological and political curriculum system in Sino-foreign cooperative universities [Lexical characteristics of Chinese language]. *Chinese Character Culture, 4*, pp. 140-141.

Reeves, T. (2000). Alternative assessment approaches for online learning environments in higher education. *Journal of Educational Computing Research. The University of Georgia, USA*, *23*(1), 101–111.

Rogers, C. (1969). Freedom to learn: a view of what education might become. Charles E. Merrill.

Schmidt, B., Von Hippel, A., & Tippelt, R. (2010). Higher education evaluation in Germany. *Research in Comparative and International Education. Ludwig-Maximilians-University of Munich, Germany*, *5*(1), 98–111.

Schwarz, C., & Struhkamp, G. (2007). Does evaluation build or destroy trust?: Insights from case studies on evaluation in higher education reform. *Evaluation, Germany*, *13*(3), 323–339. doi:10.1177/1356389007078625

Skogsberg, K., & Clump, M. (2003). Do Psychology and Biology majors differ in their study processes and learning styles? *College Student Journal*, *37*(1), 27–33.

Smart, K., Witt, C., & Scott, J. (2012). Toward learner-centered teaching: An inductive approach. *Business Communication Quarterly*, *75*(4), 392–403. doi:10.1177/1080569912459752

Spiel, C., Schober, B., & Reimann, R. (2006). Evaluation of curricula in higher education: challenges for evaluators. Evaluation Review, 30(4), pp. 430-450.

Sun, K. (2014). Comprehensive education: an analysis on the path of general education in Sino-foreign cooperative universities [Lexical characteristics of Chinese language]. *Social Science Review, 4*, pp. 154-157.

Susam, T., Durnalı, M., & Orakcı, Ş. (2020). Administering education and training through a web-based system: E-curriculum. In M. Durnalı (Ed.), *Utilizing Technology, Knowledge, and Smart Systems in Educational Administration and Leadership*. IGI Global. doi:10.4018/978-1-7998-1408-5.ch002

Taras, M. (2008). Summative and formative assessment: Perceptions and realities. *Active Learning in Higher Education. University of Sunderland, UK*, *9*(2), 172–192.

Taylor, S. (2014). Student self-assessment and multisource feedback assessment: Exploring benefits, limitations, and remedies. *Journal of Management Education. University of New Mexico, USA*, *38*(3), 359–383.

Thomas, S., Chie, Q. T., Abraham, M., Jalarajan Raj, S., & Beh, L. (2014). A qualitative review of literature on peer review of teaching in high education: An application of the SWOT framework. *Review of Educational Research*, *84*(1), 112–159. doi:10.3102/0034654313499617

Toraman, C., Orakcı, S., & Aktan, O. (2020). Analysis of the relationships between mathematics achievement, reflective thinking of problem solving and metacognitive Awareness. *International Journal of Progressive Education*, *16*(2), 72–90. doi:10.29329/ijpe.2020.241.6

Wholey, J. (1996). Formative and summative evaluation: related issues in performance measurement. American Journal of Evaluation, 17(2), pp. 145-149.

Woodward, W. (1906). *Studies in education during the age of the Renaissance, 1400-1600*. Cambridge University Press.

Xia, W. (2021). The innovative practice of general education system under the background of new liberal arts [Lexical characteristics of Chinese language]. *Chinese Higher Education*, *12*, 20–21.

Yarime, M., & Tanaka, Y. (2012). The issues and methodologies in sustainability assessment tools for higher education institutions: a review of recent trends and future challenges. Journal of Education for Sustainable Development, 6(1), pp. 63-77.

Yorke, M., Bridges, P., & Woolf, H. (2000). Mark distributions and marking practices in UK higher education: Some challenging issues. *Active Learning in Higher Education, UK*, *1*(1), 7–27. doi:10.1177/1469787400001001002

ADDITIONAL READING

Dell, G. (1978). Robert M. Hutchins' philosophy of general education and the college at The University of Chicago. *The Journal of General Education*, *30*(1), 45–58.

General Education Center of Wuhan University. (2022). *General education curriculum of Wuhan University* WHU. http://gec.whu.edu.cn/tskc/jckc.htm

Harvard Committee. (1945). *General education in a free society: report of the Harvard Committee*. Harvard University Press.

Harvard University. (2022). *Harvard college program in general education*. Harvard University Press. https://gened.fas.harvard.edu/

Kostas, G. (2020). *Commitments to make a culture of shared future for humanity* [Paper presentation]. *2nd International Conference on General Education and Contemporary Development*, Wuhan, Hubei Province, China.

Ministry of Education of the People's Republic of China. (2022). *Alliance of Sino-foreign cooperative universities,* https://baike.baidu.com/item/中外合作大学联盟/16183246

Peking University Undergraduate Education. (2022). *General education curriculum of Peking University*. PU.http://www.dean.pku.edu.cn/web/student_info.php?type=1&id=4

Temple Undergraduate Bulletin. (2022). *General education curriculum for Temple undergraduate students.* TU. https://bulletin.temple.edu/undergraduate/general-education/

Tsinghua, S. E. M. (2022). *General education courses of Tsinghua School of Economics and Management.* http://ug.sem.tsinghua.edu.cn/en/undergraduate/cur/general.html

Yin, H. (2020). *How to realize the transformation of university education* [Paper presentation]. Seminar on Innovation and Development of University Education in Post-epidemic Period.

KEY TERMS AND DEFINITIONS

Civil Law System: also known as 'Roman Law System', 'Continental Law System', 'Written Law System', and 'Roman-Germanic Law System'. This is a general term for the laws of continental European countries and other countries and regions established on the basis of Roman law, with the French Napoleonic Code and the German Civil Code as models.

Common Law System: also known as 'Case Law System'. This is a general term for laws developed on the basis of English common law and refers to a legal system that since the 11th century formed gradually over the years in the United Kingdom. It is mainly based on the common law derived from Germanic customary law, and the legal system of some other countries and regions that imitated the United Kingdom.

Curriculum Development: a working process of determining curriculum objectives through demand analysis, then selecting teaching content and related teaching activities of a certain discipline or multiple disciplines for planning, organizing, implementing, evaluating and revising to finally achieve the objectives. Four parts are usually included: curriculum objectives, curriculum content, curriculum implementation and curriculum evaluation.

Foundation Courses: courses of basic theory and skills for the natural sciences, humanities and social sciences offered by higher educational institutions.

General Education: education course that have the objective of providing students with the common knowledge and values of diverse groups of people in modern society.

Ideological and Political Courses: courses in which a society or social group applies certain political viewpoints and moral norms to exert a planned and organized influence on students and make them engage in approved social practice activities that meet the ideological and moral requirements of the society.

Sino-foreign Cooperative Universities: universities jointly run by both Chinese and foreign educational institutions. This is the third type of university found in China along with public and private universities.

Chapter 2
Making Sense of Brainstorming in Transnational Education:
The Challenge of Contextualization

Mattia Miani
The University of Nottingham, Ningbo, China

ABSTRACT

The chapter investigates the role of brainstorming as an educational tool on the basis of the author's experience in transnational education, and a review of the literature. Brainstorming is an ideation technique invented by Alex Osborn in the 40s. Still popular today, it has found numerous applications in education. Despite its diffusion, a large body of literature dismisses brainstorming as less effective in comparison to individuals working alone or other techniques in terms of quantity and quality of idea produced. Advocates of brainstorming claim that when done properly it can be very powerful in generating breakthrough ideas, and studies show that factors such as the presence of a facilitator, training, and the right time and type of problem assigned can greatly change the outcome of a session. After reviewing this contrasting literature, the author concludes that these studies ignore the cultural origin of brainstorming and attention should be paid to the cultural implications of the technique in transnational contexts outside the US.

INTRODUCTION

Picture this: a group of six individuals seating around a table led by a facilitator. The facilitator introduces the discussion topic in the form of a question: "How might we boost the number of visitors to the zoo?". He provides some context on the problem as well (e.g., visitors numbers are declining). The participants start writing down ideas to answer this challenge on post-it notes (one idea, one post-it) and they hand them to the facilitator reading them aloud for everyone to hear. The facilitator puts them on a board and keeps encouraging the group to strive for quantity. By the end of the session there are around 55 ideas on the board and the facilitator announces the next step: looking for themes and clusters among them.

DOI: 10.4018/978-1-6684-5226-4.ch002

This is the description of a mock brainstorming session made publicly available by design firm IDEO (IDEO U, 2019), a strong advocate of this ideation technique (Kelley & Littman, 2001, 2005). Originated in an advertising firm in New York, brainstorming has been around at least since the late 30s of the last century and has found applications in an impressive number of contexts, from business to design, from accounting to our focus, education, just to name a few. In 1961 the term "brainstorming" entered the *Webster's Dictionary* with the meaning of "a conference technique by which a group attempts to find a solution for a specific problem by amassing all the ideas spontaneously contributed by its members" (quoted in Mareis, 2020). Previously, perhaps interestingly, it had indicated a violent state of mind (Mareis, 2020; Rickards, 1999).

The goal of this chapter is twofold. First, the chapter aims at bridging the gap in the educational literature between the studies of brainstorming as an ideation technique and its applications in education. Second, the chapter aims at reflecting on the use of brainstorming outside its context of origin, the US, specifically in transnational settings. The chapter will begin with introducing brainstorming and its current applications in education. Then, it will present a summary of the literature both against the effectiveness of brainstorming as an ideation technique and in favor. The chapter will argue that this knowledge is essential for educators using brainstorming in transnational education and will conclude with some practical recommendations.

The author's experience with brainstorming is grounded in the setting of transnational education in Vietnam (2010-2016) and China (2017-present) working with learners from foundation year to executive level using English as medium of instruction. Transnational education has been defined as the "offering overseas of a 'home university' course and award" and it often involves teaching to students in a language different from their native tongue (Stafford & Taylor, 2016). The context of transnational education often leads to replicate the pedagogical approaches of the 'home institution' in a new setting. Whether and to what degree the curriculum and the pedagogical approaches of a transnational program should adapt to the cultural variables of the local context is a debated issue in the literature (Wallace & Dunn, 2008) with educators on the ground often holding different believes of what work (Magne et al., 2017). While it has been acknowledged that in transnational education "the curriculum is subject to new kinds of pressures for contextual relevance" (Chapman & Pyvis, 2013, p. xi), contextualization often does not go beyond the superficial level of introducing local examples, with pedagogical approaches remaining unquestioned. Brainstorming is a remarkable example of this tendency. A reflection around brainstorming is then interesting as an example of an American thinking tool often a-critically employed in widely new contexts. One might argue that the challenge to contextualize brainstorming reflects at a micro-level the wider challenge of contextualizing transnational education in a host country.

BRAINSTORMING ORIGIN AND EVOLUTION

The originator of brainstorming is undisputed: his name is Alex Osborn, one of the founders of Madison Avenue advertising agency BBDO. According to his account, Osborn began using it in 1939 to tackle clients' problems with his creative teams. Many articles mention his book *Applied Imagination* as the first written description of the process (Diehl & Stroebe, 1991; B. Mullen et al., 1991; Sutton & Hargadon, 1996). However, the idea of brainstorming is first introduced in his 1942 book *How to Think Up* (Chapter 4) and is fully articulated in the precursor of *Applied Imagination*, a 1948 self-help book titled *Your Creative Power*. Here Osborn defined brainstorming as "using the *brain* to *storm* a creative problem – and to do so in *commando* fashion, with each stormer attacking the same objective" (Osborn, 1948, p. 265). The exact same words were used in *Applied Imagination* with just the addition of the adjective "audaciously" in reference to attacking the objective (Osborn, 1953, p. 297).

The rules of brainstorming are clearly laid down in Osborn's books: the group should be formed by "5-10 people, should include both brass and rookies" (Osborn, 1948, p 267) and the problem "should be specific rather than general" (p. 268). Ideas must be written down (p. 270). More importantly, Osborn enunciated the four basic rules of brainstorming (p. 269):

Judicial judgment is ruled out. *Criticism of ideas will be withheld until the next day.*

"Wildness" is welcomed. *The crazier the idea the better...*

Quantity is wanted. *The more ideas we pile up, the more likelihood of winners.*

Combination and improvement are sought. *In addition to contributing ideas of our own, let's suggest how another's idea can be turned into a* better *idea; or how two or more ideas can be joined into still another idea.*

Finally, Osborn introduced the notion that every brainstorming must have a leader that will enforce the rules (what today we call a "facilitator"). It is important to illustrate Osborn's original formulation because every creative thinking article or book providing an account of brainstorming still repeats this original script today. For example, Puccio et al. (2012) list the four rules as "Defer judgment," "Go for quantity," "Make connections," "Seek novelty". The wording has changed, but the underlying substance has not.

Within the perimeter of this classic script there are numerous variations showing that brainstorming is not a unitary concept: brainwriting performed silently by writing down ideas and sharing them within a group (Heslin, 2009; Michinov, 2012; Paulus et al., 2015; VanGundy, 1984), electronic brainstorming through software applications (Maaravi et al., 2021), reverse brainstorming aimed at finding issues rather than solutions (Hagen et al., 2016; Wilson, 2007), structured methods such as the 365 where 6 participants propose 3 ideas every 5-minute run (Tsai et al., 2020) or through the use of checklists (Kobo-Greenhut et al., 2019), not to mention mixed approaches (Korde & Paulus, 2017; Ritter & Mostert, 2018). However, despite this variety, all the approaches share a certain degree of adherence to the four original rules. The four rules and the group setting may be regarded as the essence of the method. When the four rules are not applied, the term brainstorming is inappropriate, even if it is routinely used to describe generic meetings.

BRAINSTORMING IN EDUCATION

While brainstorming originated in business, it soon made inroads into education and it remains popular today. The first testing ground in academia was Buffalo State College where Osborn met Professor Sidney Parnes and the two worked together to develop educational curricula to foster students' creative skills. The effectiveness of these curricula, prominently featuring brainstorming, in boosting creative thinking and overall students' performance was proved through longitudinal experimental studies (Reese et al., 1976).

More recently, Design Thinking with, again, an emphasis on brainstorming, has been widely adopted by educators in two ways. First, design thinking is being used to design or re-design curricula (Boschman et al., 2014). Second, design thinking skills are being embedded into the classroom as a valuable competence for learners at different stages of their educational journey (Goldman & Zielezinski, 2022; Hwee Ling Koh et al., 2015; Melles, 2020; Portnoy, 2020). What is new is that design thinking and tools such as brainstorming are no longer limited to the specialist setting of design education, but have become general skills with the potential to enrich any discipline.

Outside the context of general creative thinking processes, teaching and learning interventions specifically based on brainstorming have been documented with a variety of goals such as encouraging mathematical learning in early childhood (Ryoo et al., 2018), increasing engagement in anatomy classes (Geuna & Giacobini-Robecchi, 2002), fostering curiosity in adolescents (Clark et al., 2019), fueling interest in STEM among high-school students (Fang, 2013), supporting gifted education (Paulus & Paulus, 1997), improving argumentative writing skills in university-level academic English learners (Rashtchi & Porkar, 2020). All of these studies are from American universities. Al-Samarraie and Hurmuzan (2018) reviewed 42 studies on the use of brainstorming in higher education, again mostly from American institutions, showing promising applications in business, psychology, language, industrial design and education studies. Sections about brainstorming can be found in many handbooks and encyclopedias of teaching techniques (see as an example Exley, Dennick and Fisher, 2019, p. 94; Göğüş, 2012). Overall, brainstorming appears to be used either to foster creative thinking skills or to improve engagement (or a mix of the two).

The use of brainstorming in educational contexts outside the North American place of origin is well-documented in the literature, with some studies dating back to the 60s (Lindgren & Lindgren, 1965). For example, in Taiwan, a group of teachers improved engagement and learning outcomes in a K-12 civic class using brainstorming in combination with a flipped-classroom approach (Tsai et al., 2020). Additionally, brainstorming was part of an intervention to improve creative thinking skills in third grade pupils attending science classes in Iran, resulting more effective than traditional teaching methods, but less than another creativity technique, Synectics (Aiamy & Haghani, 2012). Another study from Iran showed higher performance from fifth grade students trained through brainstorming to tackle science problems as opposed to listening to traditional lectures (Rizi et al., 2013). Brainstorming was found effective in improving the English writing performance of university students in Jordan (Hussein Amoush, 2015). In Finland, a major University introduces engineering students to their program with a two-day brainstorming workshop (Matthíasdóttir et al., 2016). In terms of curriculum development, Ali (2020) showed the use of brainstorming to redesign an engineering curriculum in Indonesia as a tool to engage with construction professionals. When reflecting on the author's context, Mainland China, brainstorming is well-known by educational practitioners: called 头脑风暴法 (*Nǎolì jīdàng fǎ*), its first applications date back to the 80s (Xu & Xu, 1997). The current literature about brainstorming is advanced by studies conducted in Chinese Universities, with the classic involvement of undergraduate students (Lu et al., 2019; Rao, 2007). Mullen included China in her longitudinal study of creativity in the curriculum across three countries and made use of brainstorming in her seminars, but it was not her focus (Mullen, 2020). The literature review stage did not reveal any study of brainstorming in transnational settings.

These studies generally show improvements in the learning outcomes after the implementation of brainstorming-based interventions. However, these results should not be overstated, as most interventions can generate some gains from a baseline situation (Hattie, 2008). Also, in some of these studies, it is difficult to disentangle the effect of brainstorming and other aspects of the intervention.

This review is not meant to be exhaustive. Its main goal is illustrating that brainstorming is common outside its context of origin and is routinely employed as an intervention (or part of one) across different educational systems and levels. One interesting aspect of this literature is that the use of brainstorming in a new context is not questioned or problematized. Additionally, educational literature rarely engages with the studies on the productivity of brainstorming as an ideational technique that we are discussing in the next two sections. This situation suggests several gaps. Not only the current literature does not address problems of contextualization in international and transnational settings sufficiently, but it fails to integrate findings from educational and creative thinking interventions. The rest of the chapter will aim at addressing these gaps.

THE CASE AGAINST BRAINSTORMING

The studies on brainstorming in educational settings usually paint a positive picture of the technique focusing on engagement and learning outcomes. However, the effectiveness of brainstorming as an ideation technique is highly debated in the academic literature, to a "surprising" degree, according to some scholars, given its persistence and ubiquity (Puccio et al., 2012, p. 63). Similarly, the professional press is dotted by articles dismissing brainstorming and portraying it as a "myth" (Furnham, 2000; Lehrer, 2012), an outright "waste of time" (Chamorro-Premuzic, 2015) that simply "does not work" (Torres, 2016). By contrast, advocates of brainstorming assert that, if done properly, "it can be innovation magic" (Gobble, 2014, p. 66).

Educators should be aware that there is a long tradition of psychological laboratory experiments that have disproven the effectiveness of brainstorming as an idea generation tool, taking into account quantity and quality of ideas generated. This literature is mostly ignored in educational applications; however, it is important to take this line of research into consideration to better understand brainstorming in educational settings.

The progenitor of this line of research dates back to 1958 and was conducted at Yale University (Taylor et al., 1958). It is worth examining this seminal study as it offered the blueprint for so many to come. The researchers compared the performance of real groups and individuals working on the same set of three problems (how to attract more European tourists to the USA, how to use a sixth thumb, and how to address the issue of an increasing student-teacher ratio in high schools). The researchers evaluated the idea generated in terms of quantity, originality (measured as number of unique ideas across groups), and quality (using three different subjective ratings). To make a comparison between a group and individuals they introduced the notion of the nominal group. The nominal group is a number of individuals working alone equal to the number of participants in a real group used to compare individual and group performance. The results were clear: nominal groups were always outperforming real brainstorming groups. This led the authors to conclude that "group participation when using brainstorming *inhibits* creative thinking" (Taylor et al., 1958, p. 43). The authors speculated that this may have been due to some residual fear of criticism (also known today as evaluation apprehension) experienced by people working in a group or to the group focusing on a specific 'train-of-thought'. The latter hypothesis has been subsequently framed in the literature as a "fixation" issue (Kohn & Smith, 2011).

One might easily criticize this research design. Even if the authors claim that the three problems were selected through extensive pre-testing to be of interest for the participants (all Yale students), clearly these problems could not be felt as urgent by them. Also, only 12 minutes were allocated to discuss each problem, a time that any trained brainstorming professional would judge as insufficient. It may well be that the difference in productivity simply depended by the fact that four individuals working together had to take turns and listen to others, while those working alone could focus all of their attention on the task of generating ideas. This phenomenon has become known as production blocking and is well documented (Diehl & Stroebe, 1991; Nijstad et al., 2003).

These results have been replicated consistently across several decades. Other things being equal, nominal groups almost always beat real brainstorming groups at idea generation leading researchers to coin the expression "productivity loss" to characterize the performance of brainstorming groups (Diehl & Strpebe, 1987; Henningsen & Henningsen, 2013). Mullen et al. (1991), after reviewing the data on productivity loss in 20 previous studies, pointed out that brainstorming groups fared worse also in terms of quality of the ideas generated in comparison to nominal ones. Overall, they found that social-psychological mechanisms played a greater role than procedural mechanisms in determining the productivity loss, while economic mechanisms (i.e., social loafing) did not seem to play any significant role. This led them to conclude that "It appears to be particularly difficult to justify brainstorming techniques in terms of any performance outcomes" (Mullen et al., 1991, p. 18). Since their analysis of socio-psychological mechanisms – their major determinant – is all centered around the presence/absence of the researcher, one may again wonder whether this experimental groups are genuinely representing the construct of brainstorming proposed by Osborn (Mongeau, 1993).

One more interesting line of research has led scholars to question one of the central tenets of brainstorming, the absence of criticism as a way to fuel ideation. A group of researchers compared the performance of three ideation groups in an experimental setting: one group was given the classic brainstorming rules prohibiting criticism, a second group was asked to criticize each other's ideas, and a third was given no specific instructions (Nemeth et al., 2004). They found that the group asked to include criticism in their discussion scored better than the others, while the group given no instructions was the least productive. Researchers at the Center for Applied Imagination at Buffalo State College have noted that the instructions used in the study may have primed participants on producing good ideas, while real brainstorming only strives for quantity (Puccio et al., 2020). A recent study may offer a new explanation: a form of cooperative conflict may benefit brainstorming, while aggressive criticism does not (Curhan et al., 2021).

MAKING BRAINSTORMING WORK

Brainstorming continues to be a key element of many creative thinking processes widely adopted in industry and academia. In its latest iteration, the Creative Problem Solving model comprises of seven steps: brainstorming is central in the step called "Ideation", but it is also used to support other steps (Puccio et al., 2011, 2012). In this framework brainstorming is regarded as a key divergent thinking technique. Divergent thinking is characterized by openness, search for novel connections, and lack of criticism (Puccio et al., 2011). In another popular approach, Design Thinking, brainstorming remains an essential tool. For example, in the model presented by Liedtka and Ogilvie brainstorming is one of the ten tools that are iteratively used along their innovation process (Liedtka & Ogilvie, 2011). Similarly, Stanford D.School includes brainstorming in their arsenal of tools to achieve breakthroughs defining it as "a distinct segment of time when you amp up the generative part of your brain and turn down the evaluative part" (Doorley et al., 2018, card 15).

Advocates of brainstorming employing these processes do not wholly dismiss the results of experimental studies. However, they claim that brainstorming works "if used effectively" (Puccio et al., 2012). There is some consensus on what may make a brainstorming session effective. Once again, these studies generally address brainstorming in abstract laboratory situations (with some exceptions though). While these studies are not framed as pedagogical interventions, they can help educational practitioners in reflecting on the brainstorming variables that can be used to contextualize the technique. The main variables that will be discussed in the rest of this section deal with the role of the facilitator, training, session time, framing questions, group composition, and types of problems.

The literature agrees that a trained facilitator can make a difference (Offner et al., 1996; Oxley et al., 1996). In an exploratory study Isaksen and Gaulin (2005) showed that groups with a trained facilitator greatly outperformed nominal groups: groups with a facilitator created on average 3.5 times as many ideas as those produced by a nominal group. The ratio went up to 4.6 by adding a client being served by the group's ideation effort.

Not only a trained facilitator appears to be important, but also trained team members can greatly improve brainstorming outcomes (Baruah & Paulus, 2008). In a study, even a quick five-minute training on how to avoid putting down others' ideas during the ensuing session was shown as leading to significant increases in the quantity of idea produced, but effects on quality were less clear (Smith, 1993). When one puts together trained team members and facilitators, the brainstorming groups score the best results across multiple productivity measures (Puccio et al., 2020).

From a practitioner's point of view, one of the most unrealistic assumptions of most of the literature based on experiments is the idea that a productive brainstorming session can last just a quarter of hour if not less. It is possible, but it is not the norm. In a professionally facilitated session just the introduction to the brainstorming question can take up to half an hour (Sutton & Hargadon, 1996). Some authors suggest that breakthrough ideas usually come in the later part of a session, after the more accessible and obvious ideas are exhausted (Basadur & Thompson, 1986). Some experts have even suggested to have frequent five-minute breaks (Sawyer, 2017).

The phrasing of the question to be answered in a brainstorming matters and so group composition. There has been some debate in the literature on whether asking participants to focus on quality or creativity, on top or instead of quantity, may support or hinder the process. Overall, the adage advanced by Osborn that quantity breeds quality seems to hold when tested through rigorous experimental research (Paulus et al., 2011). Brainstorming professionals stress that questions to be offered to a brainstorming group should be open using stems such as "how to", "what are all the ways to", and "how might I" (Puccio et al., 2012). Team composition has been studied and there is evidence of a positive effect of culturally diverse teams, generally at odds with the groups of undergraduate students majoring in psychology characterizing most of the experimental literature we reviewed (Proctor, 2020; Tadmor et al., 2012).

The type of problem is another important factor in determining the effectiveness of a brainstorm. Sawyer (2017) after reviewing the literature suggests using group creativity for problems that are complex and require improvisation. Creative groups cannot be expected to be effective for additive tasks that can be performed individually. A brainstorming group should be seen as a jazz ensemble. In a study with the goal to find what problems work best with brainstorming an interesting conclusion was reached: brainstorming works well with problems that require cross-functional teams and are complex, but not overly complex (Kavadias & Sommer, 2009).

As it has been shown earlier, brainstorming is not a unitary concept. Careful variations can help overcoming issues such as production blocking, evaluation apprehension and social loafing. Electronic brainstorming experiments have been particularly promising in overcoming these hurdles (Gallupe et al., 1991; Maaravi et al., 2021).

Some studies suggest that the dichotomy between individual and group brainstorming ideation is a false one. One study adopting the usual experimental design found that combining individual and group ideation through brainstorming led to results superior to individual or group sessions in terms of quantity of ideas generated (Korde & Paulus, 2017). In this study, the experiments attempted to compare tasks conducted entirely in a group, entirely alone, or alternating alone first followed by group interaction or vice versa. The authors argue that an alone phase after the brainstorming can be useful to supplement the initial pool of ideas generated in group as participants may have time to further reflect on the group session. In another study, giving group members some solitary ideation time before joining the brainstorming session was found more effective than giving them alone time afterwards (Baruah & Paulus, 2008).

It is not just about finding ways to make brainstorming effective; the literature also points toward additional benefits of brainstorming beyond those measurable in experiments. This perspective is offered by what is a refreshing departure from the experimental design paradigm: an ethnographic study conducted by two Stanford researchers between March 1995 and February 1996 in the headquarters of famed design firm IDEO (Sutton & Hargadon, 1996). Brainstorming was not their initial focus, but the topic soon emerged as a point of interest as it was and it is a pivotal practice for IDEO staff. The authors challenge studies relying on a "single effectiveness outcome" (i.e., quantity of ideas or their originality) with experimental subjects that do not own the problem, are not going to meet again, and are not going to develop any of the brainstormed solutions. Their ethnographic study sheds light on the way the organizational context can greatly influence the effectiveness of brainstorming and how organizations can benefit from it in subtle ways. According to the authors IDEO engineers can spend between 5% to 10% of their overall work time on brainstorming (including preparation and debriefing) with some of them being involved in tens of sessions over a typical year. It is a substantial commitment. Sutton and Hargadon conclude that brainstorming serves IDEO more than for idea generation. Other benefits evidenced by the authors included helping share design solutions across departments, providing skill variety for the participants, impressing clients, generating income (brainstorming hours can be billed), and, overall, contributing to forming IDEO's unique culture of innovation. Along these lines, at least another study has shown that some aspects of brainstorming can enhance group cohesiveness (Henningsen & Henningsen, 2018).

Sutton and Hargadon's findings resonate with the old concept of illusion of group productivity. This term refers to the observation that participants of brainstorming groups tend to report higher satisfaction and sense of accomplishment than people ideating alone. Some suggest that this may be the case because in a group individuals experience fewer "failures" (i.e., pauses or difficulty to produce a new idea) than in a group where another participant can always step in (Nijstad et al., 2006). It seems clear that brainstorming underlying social dynamics also matter and we cannot discount the individual satisfaction with an experience, as this may contribute to the long-term climate in an organization. Perhaps there is no point of having a few more ideas generated by a nominal group if the result is getting staff or students demotivated.

One might ask whether IDEO is making brainstorming effective or vice versa. Arguably, the causality direction of the relation is impossible to fully disentangle and this is precisely the point: the social dynamics of brainstorming and its context interact in unique ways and this acknowledgement is missing in the experimental studies about brainstorming across the board.

BEYOND THE DEBATE: THE CHALLENGE OF CONTEXTUALIZATION

To move away from the polarizing end of the debate about the effectiveness of brainstorming, it is important to acknowledge that brainstorming is the product of a specific social and cultural context. Mareis wrote an insightful article showing that the "history of brainstorming spawn a specific economically narrowed view of human creativity as productivity (Mareis, 2020, p. 52). In the paper, she explained that the idea of a small group of workers joining forces in a democratic environment finds its roots in early 20th century studies aimed at improving productivity in North American factories. But this is just one conception of human creativity (Miani, 2016). The goal itself to generate ideas to tackle a problem can be seen as culturally situated, as it has been demonstrated that the idea of efficacy as defining an ideal to reach is rooted in Greek-Roman thought and it is not universally shared (Jullien, 2004).

Given this historical backdrop, it is not surprising that brainstorming is sometimes welcomed with skepticism in places outside the US. One fundamental cross-cultural issue with brainstorming is that it is typically framed as a way to tackle problems. It is undeniable that this is an idea that does not resonate equally well across all cultures. At least traditionally, Americans assume that "problems and solutions are basic ingredients of reality" and view themselves as problem solvers, while in other cultures problems may be a taboo or something to live with (Stewart & Bennet, 1991, p. 155). The author witnessed this situation in executive education work in Vietnam, where several times clients expressed reservations about delivering a problem-solving workshop to their managers because it assumed that there were problems to solve (eventually the name of the course was changed into "Breakthrough Thinking" and everyone felt more relaxed). Similarly, when Osborn speaks of "audaciously attacking" a problem in "commando fashion", as seen earlier, he betrays the mindset of a man living in war-time America.

Almost the totality of the literature reviewed in favor and against brainstorming wholly ignores its cultural context of origin and the serious challenges of deploying it in new contexts in what may appear to be a classic ethnocentric approach. One reason is that many authors maintain that thinking processes are universal, but this is not the case. It has been convincingly argued that individuals from different cultures may show striking differences in basic cognition (Nisbett, 2003; Shweder, 1991).

So, what is he use of brainstorming in a transnational educational setting? One benefit of brainstorming is that it brings structure to a very fuzzy task: ideation. If we go back to the two antithetic studies conducted by Puccio and Nemeth, one can argue that both studies point toward the same direction: what makes the difference is the presence of a structure scaffolding group interaction. This was evident in Puccio's study as even untrained groups could boost their productivity following a basic structure of divergent and convergent thinking. Nemeth's studies showed that both debate and traditional brainstorming were superior to a group interacting with no structure.

Arguably, the need for structure is very important for multicultural groups where different cultural assumptions may make the interaction challenging (Ting-Toomey & Oetzel, 2001). This is precisely the case of transnational education that is characterized by a multicultural workforce and some degree of international student population. Within this context, brainstorming can be one of the possible common languages that a group can embrace to strengthen their ties and more research on this point would be needed.

Brainstorming is not the only answer to the need for structure. Another option is to move beyond brainstorming and tap on indigenous knowledge. One example is the KJ method developed by a prominent Japanese ethnographer (Scupin, 1997). Its application to problem solving has been mediated by its use in quality management, making the transition from Japan to North America (Mizuno, 1979). The main difference with problem solving is that group participants explore ideas about a problem and then reach a consensus about possible outcomes. The technique has also worked in conjunction with brainstorming and other approaches (Ohiwa et al., 1997; Park et al., 2018; Widjaja et al., 2013). Mindfulness and meditation techniques appear to offer another avenue worth exploring (Baas et al., 2020; Byrne & Thatchenkery, 2019).

By acknowledging its cultural roots, one can clearly see that brainstorming cannot be regarded as a neutral tool. Brainstorming, as all interventions, can transform and is transformed by its context. In the author's experience in transnational educational in Asia, for example, some adjustments in its delivery came naturally and, retrospectively, can be seen as attempts to mediate with the context. The author improved his sessions using brainwriting and structured methods such as forced connections to stimulate ideation and found many groups benefitting from time dedicated to solitary ideation. This experience can be regarded as consistent with a tendency toward inner dialogue and silent engagement with the topic observed in learners from Confucian-heritage countries (Li & Wegerif, 2014). The added scaffolding is consistent with the thinking preferences of the groups the author worked with – the Foursight assessment to determine trainees' styles was often administered – showing a low preference for ideation. Introducing more structure to support a low preference has been proven effective also in other situations (Puccio et al., 2020).

The author is not the only one who tried to adapt brainstorming in new settings. Ivanov and Zelchenko (2020) working in a Chinese university found that introducing anonymity in an electronic brainstorming raised the satisfaction for group-oriented participants. This adjustment seems directly related to a culturally rooted group orientation. However, even in this relatively homogeneous context, there were also many participants showing more individualist traits that would prefer non-anonymous mechanics. So, if we can learn one lesson is that there are no simple solutions.

At the same time, if the organization – it can be the classroom – is not ready to accept the results of an ideation exercise as the beginning of a transformative journey, brainstorming is doomed from the beginning. The classroom application will just replicate the limits of the experimental designs criticized earlier. From this point of view the experiences of students as partners can offer a good backdrop for a successful use of brainstorming in education (Healey et al., 2016; Matthews et al., 2018).

CONCLUSION AND RECOMMENDATIONS FOR PRACTITIONERS IN TRANSNATIONAL SETTINGS

This chapter has moved along two interwoven lines of inquiry: one has dealt with the contested nature of brainstorming as an ideation technique despite its persistence in business and education; a second line has connected this literature to professional practice in transnational education.

This review has highlighted that there are major gaps in the study of brainstorming in education. The educational literature tends to ignore the findings in the research about the productivity of brainstorming as an idea generation tool. This is a major gap as one might question why educators are using brainstorming if it has been proven to be ineffective according to productivity metrics. Based on our review, the reason for this gap is twofold: on the one hand, when brainstorming is used as an engagement booster in the classroom, metrics of ideation productivity are not the teachers' first concern; on the other hand, when brainstorming is taught as part of a creative process such as Design Thinking or Creative Problem Solving, educators take it as a given. These assumptions are highly problematic. By switching the focus from ideation productivity to classroom engagement, educators often end up divesting brainstorming of its role within a change process. Ironically, this is another way to weaken brainstorming exactly as laboratory studies do by offering abstract and hardly relevant problems to their subjects.

The chapter has shown that both the literature focused on classroom applications and the studies focused on productivity usually overlook the historic and cultural origins of brainstorming and only rarely try to reflect on the complex interactions between the technique and a new context. These gaps suggest that there is space for further research in an area that appears to be over-researched. New research questions could try to see how brainstorming is received and transformed in different contexts and how real groups adopting its logic can be supported or hindered in a real change process.

Identifying these gaps can also be useful to support the development of practitioners interested in creative teaching or teaching creativity. This reflection leads to a number of recommendations that can be taken into account by practitioners in transnational education. These recommendations build on the idea that the tension between offering students the real 'home experience' and providing contextualization to their locality can foster productive dynamics leading to meaningful applications for brainstorming.

First, before using brainstorming, students and teachers should discuss its cultural and historical background to become aware of the specific conception of human creativity that it underpins. Mareis' and Richards' articles could be a good starting point for this conversation (Mareis, 2020; Rickards, 1999). These discussions should highlight assumptions behind the technique and limitations of brainstorming shown in the literature making participants fully aware of the process they are engaging with. These conversations can lead to improve its contextualization in terms of variables such as number of participants or nature of the problem to be addressed. They can also lead to discard it as brainstorming remains a tool, not an end in itself. However, in a transnational setting there might still be reasons to introduce brainstorming even if it runs against students' predispositions when learning it can be beneficial for their future studies abroad (this is the scenario experienced by the author teaching students who would very likely continue their studies in a master's program outside their country of origin).

Second, brainstorming should be used as part of a change process based on a deliberate creative thinking method such as Creative Problem Solving or Design Thinking. Introducing these processes in detail is beyond the scope of this chapter, but introductory literature abounds and some key texts were introduced earlier. What this means is that the ideas generated in a brainstorming session should be further analyzed and developed. Ideally, the brainstorming will be part of a change project affecting students and their environment. To do so, faculty should identify real clients that are willing to engage in the process and are genuinely looking for new ideas to solve a challenge. Even better if the problem owners are the students themselves. As explained earlier, the term problem is culturally loaded, and problems can be reframed as opportunities and challenges. In a management class the author teaches in China, brainstorming is introduced as a tool to support students' group work toward an oral presentation. Students are encouraged to use it as a tool to get everyone participating in group work and generating ideas for their presentation (in particular the section about recommendations).

Third, practitioners should not be afraid of looking for alternatives to brainstorming or integrating different methods to interact with – and not simply adapt to – the context. Earlier some of the adjustments the author made in his classrooms in Vietnam and China were described as an example. The main point is that every context is somewhat unique and educators should make an attempt to understand their learners' reactions to brainstorming to adjust the different variables of the session discussed in the section about studies finding ways to use brainstorming effectively. Every practitioner will find a unique mix that should also take into account indigenous knowledge and approaches. Speaking with students about idea generation methods informally employed or suggested in the local context may help to get a sense of what can be accomplished (or not) through brainstorming. If possible, using a creative thinking style instrument such as Foursight could help improve a practitioner's understanding of his or her students.

Fourth, as transnational education is usually built around the use of the home country dominant language as a medium of instruction (typically English) and most students share a local language, mixing groups of students who have different native languages and can only use the institution's language to communicate may avoid exclusion and promote cohesiveness by curtailing students' tendency to revert to the local language for interactions outside (and sometimes inside) the classroom. This refers to the idea discussed earlier that intercultural teams may benefit from a common interactive script to smooth their social dynamics. This applies to teachers' teams even more as in many transnational institutions the workforce is more diverse than the student population.

Fifth, one should allocate time to train group members and build facilitation skills. The chapter has shown how research is clear on the positive effect of training and this aspect should be embedded in any intervention based on brainstorming. This means, for example, making time for a mock introductory session before getting students or colleagues to tackle the real problems. For these mock sessions, some of the abstract laboratory problems that were criticized earlier are actually very good as they can foster a humorous atmosphere and contribute to flex the creative muscles of the participants (the six thumbs problem is a good one).

Ultimately, the reflection attempted in this chapter on brainstorming could be extended to question the cultural and historic assumptions behind commonly used pedagogical interventions not with the simple aim to support or adverse them, but rather with the aim to get practitioners to become intentional in their deployment in new contexts uncovering their hidden assumptions for both teachers and students.

ACKNOWLEDGMENT

The author wishes to express gratitude for the constructive comments received by Dr. Shih-Ching Picucci-Huang and prof. John Trent on early versions of the paper. The feedback received by two anonymous reviewers was also helpful in improving the chapter.

REFERENCES

Aiamy, M., & Haghani, F. (2012). The effect of Synectics & brainstorming on 3rd grade students' development of creative thinking on science. *Procedia: Social and Behavioral Sciences*, *47*, 610–613. doi:10.1016/j.sbspro.2012.06.704

Al-Samarraie, H., & Hurmuzan, S. (2018). A review of brainstorming techniques in higher education. *Thinking Skills and Creativity*, *27*, 78–91. doi:10.1016/j.tsc.2017.12.002

Ali, M. (2020). Curriculum reconstruction for education and training of electrical engineering for construction employment in Indonesia. *Journal of Physics: Conference Series*, *1625*(1), 012067. doi:10.1088/1742-6596/1625/1/012067

Baas, M., Nevicka, B., & ten Velden, F. S. (2020). When paying attention pays off: The mindfulness skill act with awareness promotes creative idea generation in groups. *European Journal of Work and Organizational Psychology*, *29*(4), 619–632. doi:10.1080/1359432X.2020.1727889

Baruah, J., & Paulus, P. B. (2008). Effects of training on idea generation in groups. *Small Group Research*, *39*(5), 523–541. doi:10.1177/1046496408320049

Basadur, M., & Thompson, R. (1986). Usefulness of the ideation principle of extended effort in real world professional and managerial creative problem solving. *The Journal of Creative Behavior, 20*(1), 23–34. doi:10.1002/j.2162-6057.1986.tb00414.x

Boschman, F., Mckenney, S., & Voogt, J. (2014). Understanding decision making in teachers' curriculum design approaches. *Technology Research and Development, 62*(4), 393–416. doi:10.100711423-014-9341-x

Byrne, E. K., & Thatchenkery, T. (2019). Cultivating creative workplaces through mindfulness. *Journal of Organizational Change Management, 32*(1), 15–31. doi:10.1108/JOCM-10-2017-0387

Chamorro-Premuzic, T. (2015, March 25). Why group brainstorming is a waste of time. *Harvard Business Review.* https://hbr.org/2015/03/why-group-brainstorming-is-a-waste-of-time

Chapman, A., & Pyvis, D. (2013). *Enhancing quality in transnational higher education.* Lexington Books.

Clark, S., Harbaugh, A. G., & Seider, S. (2019). Fostering adolescent curiosity through a question brainstorming intervention. *Journal of Adolescence, 75*(1), 98–112. doi:10.1016/j.adolescence.2019.07.007 PMID:31376781

Curhan, J. R., Labuzova, T., & Mehta, A. (2021). Cooperative criticism: When criticism enhances creativity in brainstorming and negotiation. *Organization Science, 32*(5), 1256–1272. doi:10.1287/orsc.2020.1420

Diehl, M., & Stroebe, W. (1991). Productivity loss in idea-generating groups: Tracking down the blocking effect. *Journal of Personality and Social Psychology, 61*(3), 392–403. doi:10.1037/0022-3514.61.3.392

Diehl, M., & Strpebe, W. (1987). Productivity loss In brainstorming groups: Toward the solution of a riddle. *Journal of Personality and Social Psychology, 53*(3), 497–509. doi:10.1037/0022-3514.53.3.497

Doorley, S., Holcomb, S., Klebahn, P., Segovia, K., & Utley, J. (2018). *Design thinking bootleg.* Stanford University. https://dschool.stanford.edu/resources/design-thinking-bootleg

Exley, K., Dennick, R., & Fisher, A. (2019). *Small group teaching* (2nd ed.). Routledge. doi:10.4324/9780429490897

Fang, N. (2013). Increasing high school students' interest in STEM education through collaborative brainstorming with yo-yos. *Journal of STEM Education: Innovations and Research, 14*(4), 8–13.

Furnham, A. (2000). The brainstorming myth. *Business Strategy Review, 11*(4), 21–28. doi:10.1111/1467-8616.00154

Gallupe, R. B., Bastianutti, L. M., & Cooper, W. H. (1991). Unblocking brainstorms. *The Journal of Applied Psychology, 76*(1), 137–142. doi:10.1037/0021-9010.76.1.137 PMID:2016214

Geuna, S., & Giacobini-Robecchi, M. G. (2002). The use of brainstorming for teaching human anatomy. *The Anatomical Record, 269*(5), 214–216. doi:10.1002/ar.10168 PMID:12379937

Gobble, M. M. (2014). The persistence of brainstorming. *Research Technology Management, 57*(1), 64–66. doi:10.5437/08956308X5701005

Göğüş, A. (2012). Brainstorming and learning. In N. M. Seel (Ed.), *Encyclopedia of the sciences of learning* (pp. 484–488). Springer. doi:10.1007/978-1-4419-1428-6_491

Goldman, S., & Zielezinski, M. B. (2022). *Design thinking for every classroom. A practical guide for educators*. Routledge.

Hagen, M., Bernard, A., & Grube, E. (2016). Do it all wrong! Using reverse-brainstorming to generate ideas, improve discussions, and move students to action. *Management Teaching Review*, *1*(2), 85–90. doi:10.1177/2379298116634738

Hattie, J. (2008). *Visible learning*. Routledge. doi:10.4324/9780203887332

Healey, M., Flint, A., & Harrington, K. (2016). Students as partners: Reflections on a conceptual model. *Teaching & Learning Inquiry*, *4*(2). doi:10.20343/teachlearninqu.4.2.3

Henningsen, D. D., & Henningsen, M. L. M. (2013). Generating ideas about the uses of brainstorming: Reconsidering the losses and gains of brainstorming groups relative to nominal groups. *The Southern Communication Journal*, *78*(1), 42–55. doi:10.1080/1041794X.2012.717684

Henningsen, D. D., & Henningsen, M. L. M. (2018). Does brainstorming promote cohesiveness? How the rules of brainstorming mirror symbolic convergence. *Communication Reports*, *31*(2), 103–114. do i:10.1080/08934215.2017.1394476

Heslin, P. A. (2009). Better than brainstorming? Potential contextual boundary conditions to brainwriting for idea generation in organizations. *Journal of Occupational and Organizational Psychology*, *82*(1), 129–145. doi:10.1348/096317908X285642

Hussein Amoush, K. (2015). The impact of employing brainstorming strategy on improving writing performance of English major students at Balqa Applied University in Jordan. *Journal of Education and Practice*, *6*(35), 88–92.

Hwee Ling Koh, J., Sing Chai, C., Wong, B., & Hong, H.-Y. (2015). *Design thinking for education: Conceptions and applications in teaching and learning*. Springer.

IDEO U. (2019, July 29). *IDEO brainstorming video from IDEO U.* IDEO U. https://www.youtube.com/watch?v=WIVlACbAWio

Isaksen, S. G., & Gaulin, J. P. (2005). A reexamination of brainstorming research: Implications for research and practice. *Gifted Child Quarterly*, *49*(4), 315–329. doi:10.1177/001698620504900405

Ivanov, A., & Zelchenko, P. (2020). Designing an electronic brainstorming environment for engaging East-Asian teams. *International Journal of Human-Computer Interaction*, *36*(5), 414–428. doi:10.1080/10447318.2019.1649970

Jullien, F. (2004). *A treatise on efficacy: Between Western and Chinese thinking*. University of Hawaii Press.

Kavadias, S., & Sommer, S. C. (2009). The effects of problem structure and team diversity on brainstorming effectiveness. *Management Science*, *55*(12), 1899–1913. doi:10.1287/mnsc.1090.1079

Kelley, T., & Littman, J. (2001). *The art of innovation: Lessons in creativity from IDEO, America's leading design firm*. Currency/Doubleday.

Kelley, T., & Littman, J. (2005). *The ten faces of innovation: IDEO's strategies for beating the devil's advocate & driving creativity throughout your organization*. Currency/Doubleday.

Kobo-Greenhut, A., Reuveni, H., Ben Shlomo, I., & Megnezi, R. (2019). Unstructured brainstorming is not enough: Structured brainstorming based on four verification and validation questions yields better hazard identification in healthcare. *International Journal for Quality in Health Care*, *31*(7), G16–G21. doi:10.1093/intqhc/mzy208 PMID:30295820

Kohn, N. W., & Smith, S. M. (2011). Collaborative fixation: Effects of others' ideas on brainstorming. *Applied Cognitive Psychology*, *25*(3), 359–371. doi:10.1002/acp.1699

Korde, R., & Paulus, P. B. (2017). Alternating individual and group idea generation: Finding the elusive synergy. *Journal of Experimental Social Psychology*, *70*, 177–190. doi:10.1016/j.jesp.2016.11.002

Lehrer, J. (2012, January 30). Groupthink. The brainstorming myth. *The New Yorker*, 22–27. https://www.newyorker.com/magazine/2012/01/30/groupthink

Li, L., & Wegerif, R. (2014). What does it mean to teach thinking in China? Challenging and developing notions of "Confucian education.". *Thinking Skills and Creativity*, *11*, 22–32. doi:10.1016/j.tsc.2013.09.003

Liedtka, J., & Ogilvie, T. (2011). *Designing for growth*. Columbia University Press.

Lindgren, H. C., & Lindgren, F. (1965). Creativity, brainstorming, and orneriness: A cross-cultural study. *The Journal of Social Psychology*, *67*(23), 23–30. doi:10.1080/00224545.1965.9922254 PMID:5827919

Lu, K., Qiao, X., & Hao, N. (2019). Praising or keeping silent on partner's ideas: Leading brainstorming in particular ways. *Neuropsychologia*, *124*, 19–30. doi:10.1016/j.neuropsychologia.2019.01.004 PMID:30633875

Maaravi, Y., Heller, B., Shoham, Y., Mohar, S., & Deutsch, B. (2021). Ideation in the digital age: Literature review and integrative model for electronic brainstorming. *Review of Managerial Science*, *15*(6), 1431–1464. doi:10.100711846-020-00400-5

Magne, P., Poverjuc, O., & Heffernan, T. (2017). Pedagogies across borders: Perspectives from teaching staff and students engaged with transnational programmes in Hong Kong. *Practice and Evidence of Scholarship of Teaching and Learning in Higher Education*, *12*(1), 45–62.

Mareis, C. (2020). Brainstorming revisited: On instrumental creativity and human productivity in the mid-twentieth century. *Cultural Politics*, *16*(1), 50–69. doi:10.1215/17432197-8017256

Matthews, K. E., Dwyer, A., Hine, L., & Turner, J. (2018). Conceptions of students as partners. *Higher Education*, *76*(6), 957–971. doi:10.100710734-018-0257-y

Matthíasdóttir, Á., Saemundsdottir, I., Audunsson, H., & Grimsdottir, H. (2016). Focusing on creativity: Faculty motivation in teaching brainstorming and creativity in an introductory course. *Proceedings of the 12th International CDIO Conference*. IEEE.

Melles, G. (Ed.). (2020). *Design thinking in higher education*. Springer. doi:10.1007/978-981-15-5780-4

Miani, M. (2016). Does culture affect creativity? An integrative literature review. In P. D. Reali & C. Burnett (Eds.), *Big questions in creativity 2016* (pp. 127–141). ICSC Press.

Michinov, N. (2012). Is electronic brainstorming or brainwriting the best way to improve creative performance in groups? An overlooked comparison of two idea-generation techniques. *Journal of Applied Social Psychology, 42*(SUPPL. 1), E222–E243. doi:10.1111/j.1559-1816.2012.01024.x

Mizuno, S. (Ed.). (1979). *Management for quality improvement. The seven new QC tools.* Productivity Press.

Mongeau, P. A. (1993). *The brainstorming myth.* https://files.eric.ed.gov/fulltext/ED357399.pdf

Mullen, B., Johnson, C., & Salas, E. (1991). Productivity loss in brainstorming groups: A meta-analytic integration. *Basic and Applied Social Psychology, 12*(1), 3–23. doi:10.120715324834basp1201_1

Mullen, C. A. (2020). *Revealing creativity.* Springer. doi:10.1007/978-3-030-48165-0

Nemeth, C. J., Personnaz, B., Personnaz, M., & Goncalo, J. A. (2004). The liberating role of conflict in group creativity: A study in two countries. *European Journal of Social Psychology, 34*(4), 365–374. doi:10.1002/ejsp.210

Nijstad, B. A., Stroebe, W., & Lodewijkx, H. F. M. (2003). Production blocking and idea generation: Does blocking interfere with cognitive processes? *Journal of Experimental Social Psychology, 39*(6), 531–548. doi:10.1016/S0022-1031(03)00040-4

Nijstad, B. A., Stroebe, W., & Lodewijkx, H. F. M. (2006). The illusion of group productivity: A reduction of failures explanation. *European Journal of Social Psychology, 36*(1), 31–48. doi:10.1002/ejsp.295

Nisbett, R. E. (2003). *The geography of thought: How Asians and Westerners think differently and why.* Free Press.

Offner, A. K., Kramer, T. J., & Winter, J. P. (1996). The effects of facilitation, recording, and pauses on group brainstorming. *Small Group Research, 27*(2), 283–298. doi:10.1177/1046496496272005

Ohiwa, H., Takeda, N., Kawai, K., & Shiomi, A. (1997). KJ editor: A card-handling tool for creative work support. Knowledge-Based Systems, 10, 43–50. doi:10.1016/S0950-7051(97)00015-4

Osborn, A. (1953). *Applied imagination: Principles and procedures of creative problem solving.* Charles Scribner's Sons.

Osborn, A. F. (1948). *Your creative power. How to use imagination.* Charles Scribner's Sons.

Oxley, N. L., Dzindolet, M. T., & Paulus, P. (1996). The effects of facilitators on the performance of brainstorming groups. *Journal of Social Behavior and Personality, 2*(4), 633–646.

Park, S.-Y., Yasue, H., & Nakao, H. (2018). The iSWOT: A web-based SWOT and TOWS analytical tool that promotes new ideas. *Agricultural Information Research (Japanese), 27*(1), 1–13. doi:10.3173/air.27.1

Paulus, P. B., Kohn, N. W., & Arditti, L. E. (2011). Effects of quantity and quality instructions on brainstorming. *The Journal of Creative Behavior, 45*(1), 38–46. doi:10.1002/j.2162-6057.2011.tb01083.x

Paulus, P. B., Korde, R. M., Dickson, J. J., Carmeli, A., & Cohen-Meitar, R. (2015). Asynchronous brainstorming in an industrial setting. *Human Factors, 57*(6), 1076–1094. doi:10.1177/0018720815570374 PMID:25850113

Paulus, P. B., & Paulus, L. E. (1997). Implications of research on group brainstorming for gifted education. *Roeper Review*, *19*(4), 225–229. doi:10.1080/02783199709553834

Portnoy, L. (2020). *Designed to learn: Using design thinking to bring purpose and passion to the classroom*. ASCD.

Proctor, T. (2020). Creative problem-solving techniques, paradigm shift and team performance. *Team Performance Management*, *26*(7–8), 451–466. doi:10.1108/TPM-06-2020-0049

Puccio, G. J., Burnett, C., Acar, S., Yudess, J. A., Holinger, M., & Cabra, J. F. (2020). Creative problem solving in small groups: The effects of creativity training on idea generation, solution creativity, and leadership effectiveness. *The Journal of Creative Behavior*, *54*(2), 453–471. doi:10.1002/jocb.381

Puccio, G. J., Mance, M., & Murdock, M. (2011). *Creative leadership: Skills that drive change* (2nd ed.). Sage.

Puccio, G. J., Mance, M., Switalski, L. B., & Reali, P. (2012). *Creativity rising: Creative thinking and creative problem solving in the 21st century*. ICSC Press, International Center for Studies in Creativity.

Rao, Z. (2007). Training in brainstorming and developing writing skills. *ELT Journal*, *61*(2), 100–106. doi:10.1093/elt/ccm002

Rashtchi, M., & Porkar, R. (2020). Brainstorming revisited: Does technology facilitate argumentative essay writing? *Language Teaching Research Quarterly*, *18*, 1–20. doi:10.32038/ltrq.2020.18.01

Reese, H. W., Treffinger, D. J., Parnes, S. J., & Kaltsounis, G. (1976). Effects of a creative studies program on structure-of-intellect factors. *Journal of Educational Psychology*, *68*(4), 401–410. doi:10.1037/0022-0663.68.4.401 PMID:1002884

Rickards, T. (1999). Brainstorming revisited: A question of context. *International Journal of Management Reviews*, *1*(1), 91–110. doi:10.1111/1468-2370.00006

Ritter, S. M., & Mostert, N. M. (2018). How to facilitate a brainstorming session: The effect of idea generation techniques and of group brainstorm after individual brainstorm. *Creative Industries Journal*, *11*(3), 263–277. doi:10.1080/17510694.2018.1523662

Rizi, C. E., Najafipour, M., haghani, F., & Dehghan, S. (2013). The effect of the using the brainstorming method on the academic achievement of students in grade five in Tehran elementary schools. *Procedia: Social and Behavioral Sciences*, *83*, 230–233. doi:10.1016/j.sbspro.2013.06.045

Ryoo, J. H., Molfese, V. J., & Brown, E. T. (2018). Strategies to encourage mathematics learning in early childhood: Discussions and brainstorming promote stronger performance. *Early Education and Development*, *29*(4), 603–617. doi:10.1080/10409289.2018.1442095

Sawyer, K. R. (2017). Group genius. The creative power of collaboration (Revised). Basic Books.

Scupin, R. (1997). The KJ method: A technique for analyzing data derived from Japanese ethnology. *Human Organization*, *56*(2), 233–237. doi:10.17730/humo.56.2.x335923511444655

Shweder, R. A. (1991). *Thinking through cultures: Expeditions in cultural psychology*. Harvard University Press.

Smith, B. L. (1993). Interpersonal behaviors that damage the productivity of creative problem solving groups. *The Journal of Creative Behavior*, *27*(3), 171–187. doi:10.1002/j.2162-6057.1993.tb00705.x

Stafford, S., & Taylor, J. (2016). Transnational education as an internationalisation strategy: Meeting the institutional management challenges. *Journal of Higher Education Policy and Management*, *38*(6), 625–636. doi:10.1080/1360080X.2016.1202811

Stewart, E. C., & Bennet, M. (1991). *American cultural patterns. A cross-cultural perspective*. Intercultural Press.

Sutton, R. I., & Hargadon, A. (1996). Brainstorming groups in context: Effectiveness in a product design firm. *Administrative Science Quarterly*, *41*(4), 685–718. doi:10.2307/2393872

Tadmor, C. T., Satterstrom, P., Jang, S., & Polzer, J. T. (2012). Beyond individual creativity: The super-additive benefits of multicultural experience for collective creativity in culturally diverse teams. *Journal of Cross-Cultural Psychology*, *43*(3), 384–392. doi:10.1177/0022022111435259

Taylor, D. W., Berry, P. C., & Block, C. H. (1958). Does group participation when using brainstorming facilitate or inhibit creative thinking? *Administrative Science Quarterly*, *3*(1), 23–47. doi:10.2307/2390603

Ting-Toomey, S., & Oetzel, J. G. (2001). Managing intercultural conflict effectively. *Sage (Atlanta, Ga.)*.

Torres, T. (2016, February 4). *Why brainstorming doesn't work (and what to do instead)*. INC. https://www.inc.com/teresa-torres/why-brainstorming-doesnt-work-and-what-to-do-instead.html

Tsai, M. N., Liao, Y. F., Chang, Y. L., & Chen, H. C. (2020). A brainstorming flipped classroom approach for improving students' learning performance, motivation, teacher-student interaction and creativity in a civics education class. *Thinking Skills and Creativity*, *38*, 100747. Advance online publication. doi:10.1016/j.tsc.2020.100747

VanGundy, A. B. (1984). Brainwriting for new product ideas: An alternative to brainstorming. *Journal of Consumer Marketing, 1*(2), 67–74). doi:10.1108/eb008097

Wallace, M., & Dunn, L. (2008). *Teaching in transnational higher education*. Routledge.

Widjaja, W., Yoshii, K., Haga, K., & Takahashi, M. (2013). Discusys: Multiple user real-time digital sticky-note affinity-diagram brainstorming system. *Procedia Computer Science*, *22*, 113–122. doi:10.1016/j.procs.2013.09.087

Wilson, C. E. (2007). Inverse, reverse, and unfocused methods. *Interaction*, *14*(6), 54–55. doi:10.1145/1300655.1300687

Xu, F., & Xu, F. (1997). Letter from China: A survey of creativity research. *Creativity and Innovation Management*, *6*(4), 249–253. doi:10.1111/1467-8691.00075

Chapter 3
Speaking Anxiety Lower-Level Learners Experienced in Transitional Higher Education in China:
The Case Study of Xi'an Jiaotong-Liverpool University

Shuangxin Zhang
Xi'an Jiaotong-Liverpool University, China

ABSTRACT

Many students experience foreign language speaking anxiety (FLSA). This chapter adopts quantitative and qualitative methods to research the possible causing factors of FLSA and the corresponding solutions. Quantitative data was collected from 41 year one students at XJTLU using questionnaires to test 14 factors' impacts on students' speaking anxiety from three categories: self, peer, and teacher. Qualitative data was collected from the interviews with 11 students which probed into what elements from those three categories could help reduce students' speaking anxiety effectively from their perspectives. The quantitative data analysis showed that most students had a high level FLSA, and the 14 factors influenced their speaking anxiety to different levels. The qualitative data revealed that students generally believed that teacher-related elements could help reduce their speaking anxiety most effectively. With the findings, it is hoped that teachers in transnational higher education can be acquire some inspirations regarding how to effectively reduce their students' FLSA.

DOI: 10.4018/978-1-6684-5226-4.ch003

1. INTRODUCTION

There are four skills in learning a language: listening, reading, writing, and speaking. Among the four skills, speaking is a crucial skill in the learning process of the language. According to Nunan (1991), speaking is the most important skill for most students to master, and whether a student can be deemed as a successful language learner depends on their capabilities to conduct oral communication with others. Similarly, Bahrani and Soltani (2012) argue that the principal outcome of teaching speaking to students is to help them achieve the capability to communicate with others using that target language. These arguments are reasonable because when students learn a language, they may have the needs to express their ideas in that target language and get them understood by others. If they only know how to use grammar and the vocabulary to read and write but cannot have even basic communication, which is a common situation for many EFL learners nowadays, they cannot be regarded as having mastered the language genuinely.

Speaking is even more important when today's globalisation context is taken into consideration. In recent years, communication across the world has been made possible due to the development of new technology, and the continuous growth in the integration of people and countries across the world comes along with it (Huang, 2014). Due to this reason, communication with people from different countries are becoming more important, so it will not meet students' needs if they only master the vocabulary and grammar in the target language. Also, because of globalisation, education, especially higher education, has become borderless and transnational. It is easy for students to attend the educational programmes in another country or the transnational educational (TNE) programmes in their motherland, which may need them to use the target language more often. This relates to the term transitional education, a new word that emerged in 1980s, and its definition is the movement of educational programmes from developed English-speaking countries to emerging non-English-speaking countries (Huang, 2014).

Globalisation and the TNE contexts have put English learning and speaking at a more critical status, and therefore have made it more challenging for students under this context to speak English. Globalisation and TNE contexts have promoted English as a medium of instruction (EMI) in higher education in non-native English-speaking countries in recent years (Chou, 2018). In this circumstance, it is more necessary for students to be accustomed to the mode of using English in class to teach academic content and to use English as a tool to communicate with their classmates or teachers. However, Chou (2018) contends that communication using English in the EMI context is a fundamental demand, but it is very challenging for students to achieve, and one reason is that they experience foreign language speaking anxiety (FLSA). Similarly, Suzuki (2017) argues that though EMI in TNE context provides many benefits for students, it also brings forth a problem which is boosting students' anxiety in speaking English. These are not difficult to understand because when students just transit from high school, where English lessons were generally taught in their first language, to an EMI university under TNE context, and suddenly start to attend the English lectures and seminars in their disciplines, discuss with classmates and teachers in English, and use complete English teaching materials and workbook, quite many of them may not be accustomed to this rapid transformation which can lead to the increase of their FLSA dramatically. This is in line with Arunasalam and Burton's (2018) research that some of their participants were discouraged to continue their learning with the EMI teaching mode under TNE context, not because of the different western and eastern educational cultures but due to the deficiencies of their English language skills and levels. Therefore, teachers in the TNE context are suggested to examine what factors may cause the anxiety and help students deal with them positively. Also, methods that college teachers can adopt in this context to help students overcome anxiety are worth exploring and researching.

2. LITERATURE

2.1. Foreign Language Speaking Anxiety

It is not difficult for teachers to find that their students generally have foreign language speaking anxiety (FLSA) in class to certain degrees. According to He (2018, p. 4), a commonly accepted definition of FLSA has not been reached after several decades-of research, and he claims that it can be defined as "an individual's fear or nervousness associated with either real or anticipated oral communication in foreign language with another person or persons." Horwitz et al. (1986, p. 128) assert that foreign language speaking anxiety is "a distinct complex of self-perceptions, beliefs, feelings, and behaviors related to classroom language learning arising from the uniqueness of the language learning process." Though FLSA can be detrimental to students' language learning or their performance, not all degrees of FLSA are adverse to students. According to Erdiana et al. (2020), FLSA can be categorised into three levels: mild, moderate, and high. If students have low anxiety level, they may show indifferent attitudes towards speaking activities or even tests; if their anxiety level is moderate, this can lead to a bit of worry about the speaking activities or tests, which may motivate these students to concentrate on preparing for the speaking activities or tests. Therefore, only when students' anxiety levels are high or extreme, their performance in speaking will be influenced, like the loss of concentration or the incapability to finish the tasks. The FLSA discussed in the following sections refers to the level which influences on students' performance, namely high or extreme levels. According to Horwitz et al. (1986), students always find anxiety a significant hindrance when they learn to speak a foreign language. It is found that, when learning a foreign language, students reported most often that they are anxious about their speaking, and they need to seek relevant help. Horwitz et al. (1986) have classified three types of anxiety concerning foreign language learning: communication apprehension, test anxiety, and fear of negative evaluation. Communication apprehension refers to the anxiety caused by the worries or shyness when communicating with others; test anxiety represents the one resulting from the worries about the failure of the test; fear of negative evaluation stands for the one stems from other people's negative evaluations which lead to the pessimistic evaluation towards oneself. All of these three aspects can be responsible for FLSA as Horwitz et al. (1986) contend that speaking anxiety can be caused by the communication with others and oral tests, and it is also reasonable that negative evaluation from teachers can cause anxiety to students who are speaking a foreign language in class. When students have anxiety while speaking a foreign language, they may have physical or psychological signs. He (2018) conducted the empirical research on 302 university students in mainland China from four disciplines, Science, Arts, Business, and Engineering. During the interviews, they recalled the following reactions when they feel anxiety while speaking a foreign language: "Failing to recall familiar words, stammer, vacant mind, faster heartbeats, trembling voice (or body), red or pale face, unconscious behaviours (e.g., touch hair), feeling embarrassed, not knowing where to put hands, panic, being afraid of looking at the interlocutor(s), having an impulse to escape and being annoyed." Rajitha and Alamelu (2020) argue that speaking anxiety has an adverse influence on students' oral performance, and it can lead to different levels of physical and psychological fears, which are shown through different symptoms including "handing shaking, sweating fear, forgetfulness, blankness, butterflies in the stomach, dry mouth and throat, fast heartbeat and squeaky voice." These signs are not unfamiliar to college students when they answer questions or have discussions with their partners in class. It can be seen that FLSA is a topic worth attention, but it is a new trend in foreign language learning anxiety, and little research has been conducted on this aspect (He, 2018). Exploring the anxiety students feel in speaking a foreign language in different dimensions and the signals that students show when they feel anxious to speak a foreign language are worth researching.

2.2. Factors Leading to Foreign Language Speaking Anxiety & Relevant Empirical Research

A quantity of research has been done on the factors resulting in foreign language speaking anxiety. They can be grouped into different categories: self-related, peer-related, and teacher-related reasons (Saputra, 2018). *2.1 Self-Related Reasons* The first category of self-related reasons may be relevant to students' psychological conditions. Based on the finding of Chen and Lee's (2011) research, if a student's personality is easy to be anxious in daily life, it will lead to FLSA. Similarly, Saputra (2018) claims that some students are shy in social interaction, so they have anxiety when communicating with people. They normally prefer to stay silent and are unwilling to express their own opinions, though some may have constructed the answers already in their minds. Also, if students lack confidence in speaking a foreign language, it can lead to anxiety in speaking (He, 2018). FLSA can also arise from students' low language competence. Hewitt and Stephenson (2012) also posit that students' poor language competence or achievement, like poor accent, can lead to their FLSA. This agrees with the finding of He's (2018) research conducted on 302 university students that, most prominently, mastering insufficient vocabulary of the foreign language accounts for FLSA. Apart from vocabulary, students' poor grammar, pronunciation, intonation, and fluency in speaking a foreign language can also lead to FLSA. Similarly, students may experience anxiety in speaking due to their poor listening, like when they cannot comprehend teacher's instructions or questions (Erdiana et al., 2020). These are frequent worries for EFL students. When these students have difficulty recalling appropriate vocabulary to express certain ideas or when they believe their oral English sounds unnatural and has a strong accent, they unconsciously and uncontrollably start to be anxious. *2.2 Peer-Related Elements* For the category of peer-related elements, one cause of FLSA is that some students are worried about making pronunciation and grammar mistakes and will be looked down on or laughed at by others. This usually happens when students believe their partners' competencies are superior to them in speaking foreign languages, and they will therefore prefer to stay silent during the speaking activities in the foreign language classroom (Saputra, 2018; Djahimo et al., 2018; Erdiana et al., 2020; He, 2018). The possible reason that leads to students' this wrong belief is that they do not have the correct understanding of making mistakes, which is a necessary part of mastering a foreign language, and all learners may have encountered it more or less (He, 2018). Another peer-related influential factor is students' mother tongue use in class. Students from the same country who do not enjoy talking in a foreign language tend to use their mother tongue during the discussion in class because it is more convenient for them to share ideas in their first language (Djahimo et al., 2018; Erdiana et al., 2020). This can be a problem that leads to students' speaking anxiety when they have to use the target foreign language during the speaking activities in class, as their chances of practicing this language have been decreased, and they have not been fluent in translating their ideas from their mother tongue to the target language.

2.3 Teacher-Related Factors

When it moves to teacher-related factors, the first subcategory is the materials used by teachers. Teachers' materials can cause students' anxiety in speaking if they do not suit students' levels or the context is not familiar to them, which cannot be related to real-world situations (Suadiyatno et al., 2020). Djahimo et al. (2018) also point out that if students do not know the topic or anything relevant to the context of the discussion, they cannot share their ideas confidently. These arguments are in line with He's (2018) findings. He conducts the research on 302 students and finds one element causing students' FLSA is the unfamiliar topic. Students with low language proficiency have already been stressed when they talk in a foreign language, and the situation can be worse if they are required to talk about the topics they have no idea about, like the ones they even do not know how to respond to in their mother tongue. Similarly, Chen and Lee (2011) conduct the research researching 10 volunteers' speaking anxiety and found all of them are calm when speaking on familiar topics, like family, and they are anxious when talking about less familiar topics, such as examinations and the future. One more research mentioned this factor is by Leong and Ahmadi (2017). They argue that students may not say anything if the topic chosen by teachers is inappropriate for them or if they do not know much about it.

Suadiyatno et al. (2020) also argue that teachers' teaching method can cause students' anxiety in speaking if it is used inappropriately. This is because if students are required to work alone during the speaking activities, without the help of cooperative learning environment provided by learning groups, students' speaking anxiety will be increased and they will be unable to solve complex problems individually. Similarly, if dividing students into groups that are too large, it may result in students' speaking anxiety too (Erdiana et al., 2020). Therefore, to reduce students' FLSA, controlling the scale of groups to within a reasonable range is necessary. Another factor influencing FLSA is time for preparation. When letting students complete speaking activities in class, if teachers do not allocate enough time or if they dominate the talk, students cannot gain enough speaking practice during the activity, which may lead to the rise of their anxiety levels (Djahimo et al., 2018; Erdiana et al., 2020).

Teachers' feedback and corrections can also cause students' anxiety in speaking (Djahimo et al., 2018; Erdiana et al., 2020). According to Molloy, et al. (2019), if teachers only provide negative feedback to students, it may destroy students' self-esteem and make them anxious and even feel ashamed about their own performance. The effect sometimes can last for a long time. Djahimo et al. (2018) assert that giving feedback to students can cause their FLSA because if teachers interrupt students and give them corrective feedback during the speaking activities, it may demotivate them and make it hard for students to concentrate on and continue their speaking. However, this problem is intricate as if teachers choose to give the feedback when students finish talking, the mistakes students have made in their speaking may have slipped from their memories already.

3. Approaches To Help Students Deal with Anxiety In Speaking And Achieve Speaking Competence & Relevant Empirical Research

3.1 Self-Related Reasons

For self-related reasons, one reason students may lack self-confidence in speaking is caused by their personality. To help these students, He (2018) suggests that teachers can apply some techniques to strengthen their confidence, including practise being themselves and stopping imitating others, trying to be positive, hindering themselves from worrying about failures, and being nice to themselves.

When moving to students' language competence, if students' FLSA is caused by their low foreign language competence, like lack of vocabulary and poor pronunciation, intonation, and fluency, teachers should encourage students to cultivate a good learning habit (He, 2018). For example, if students concern about their vocabulary, teachers can boost them by creating a learning system to accumulate new words and expressions and create chances to practice them consciously on a daily basis, no matter in and out of class. It works the same for fluency as students can also make more preparation and practice more in or after class to improve it. Another approach He (2018) recommends for dealing with the problem of competency is that teachers should let students be aware that language skills are interweaved with each other, so if they want to cut their anxiety in speaking down, they should make progress in other skills too, like vocabulary, grammar, and listening.

3.2 Peer-Related Elements

Next, approaches dealing with peer-related elements will be provided. Peer pressure can lead to FLSA because students may worry about losing face resulting from making mistakes in front of peers and then getting negative evaluations accordingly. In order to cope with this problem, teachers should first establish the correct values among students that making mistakes is a necessary step for all language learners to reduce students' relevant concerns (He, 2018). Also, to avoid peer pressure from language classrooms and create a supportive speaking environment, it needs to be declared to students that they should not push other students with anxiety or pressure. At the same time, making fun of students' mistakes should be forbidden in class.

With respect to the use of mother tongue, contrary to what has been listed above about the detrimental use of mother tongue in a language class, Mahboob and Lin (2016) claim that taking advantage of students' mother tongue or local language under the EFL context as the communicative resources can bring ideal learning outcomes. For example, teachers can appeal to shared local cultures or draw on students' life experiences to elicit their expressions in a foreign language by switching between their mother tongue and the foreign language in teaching. As no agreement has been achieved, the further exploration needs to be conducted in this research.

3.3 Teacher-Related Factors

In the following paragraphs, numerous approaches to how to deal with teacher-related factors will be discussed. First, when conducting speaking activities in class, a favourable method is dividing students into groups allowing students to beat FLSA with the help of collaborative learning among group members in a less threatening environment (Menggo et al., 2019; Goh, 2016). Bailey and Nunan (2005) suggest that, for low-level students, grouping them in pairs or smaller groups can build up their confidence and reduce the FLSA during speaking activities. Similarly, He (2018) also suggests that dividing students into pairs or smaller groups can lower students' FLSA because students may feel safe and be willing to speak then. It is also worth teachers' attention that a sense of small community is desired within the group members to evade the unnecessary competitiveness or peer pressure, and groups are better to be divided randomly with mixed students completing academically equal tasks to avoid the situation that students feel they are treated unfairly.

Also, teachers should prepare enough language input and explain the tasks clearly before letting students complete the speaking tasks. Saputra (2018) suggests that teachers should explain the speaking task clearly and prepare some language input or illustrative examples that students may need to carry on their speaking activities. Step-by-step guidance is even needed when necessary, especially in those speaking activities where students need to work individually (Suadiyatno et al., 2020). Likewise, Burns (2019) argues that it is necessary for teachers to implement support to help students defeat the FLSA, which includes introducing new language, activating their existing language reserve, and easing the procedures of the tasks. Likewise, Goh (2016) believes that teachers supplying students with the strategies that they will use later in the speaking activities can help them prepare well and make the speaking less challenging.

To deal with the problems brought by unfamiliar topics, teachers can lead in with simpler and familiar topics and elicit more knowledge from students before moving to more complex and unfamiliar topics. He (2018) argues that teachers can consider starting with some simple and everyday topics before moving on to hard and unfamiliar topics. This is because if students have a lot to say in their first language, it will be smoother for them to acquire and use relevant words in a foreign language which can establish their confidence. For the topics students even do not have much to say in their native language will be more difficult for them to express in a foreign language. In addition, after conducting the speaking task, to better help students master the skills, teachers are suggested to repeat this task to build students' fluency and confidence and thereby reduce their FLSA (Burns, 2019; Goh, 2016; Bailey & Nunan, 2005). During this process, students can better apply and practice the language they have learned, which can reduce the FLSA effectively.

Next, regarding the learning environment, Saputra (2018) believes that teachers should create a friendly and encouraging learning environment where they do not blame students for the mistakes they make, as making mistakes is a necessary step leading to improvement. This is in line with the viewpoint of Erdiana et al. (2020) that it is crucial for teachers to create a friendly and supportive teaching atmosphere that can help to lessen students' anxiety about speaking English. Teachers are never suggested to laugh at students' wrong answers, and a tolerance of such answers to certain degrees should be established in class. Similarly, He (2018) believes that teachers should be patient, humorous, friendly, and tolerate students' negligible errors, which do not impede the understanding during the communication. Even when students are unexpectedly silent, teachers should wait patiently and not push or force them to say which can make students anxious to speak.

In addition, communicative language teaching (CLT) method can also reduce students' FLSA. Saputra (2018) claims that adopting the CLT approach is necessary to deal with students' speaking problems as it provides students with more chances to communicate and interact with others. To apply CLT in class productively, teachers are expected to adopt the real settings where the communications are unpredictable and lead students to have down-to-earth reactions (Farooq, 2015). If students are only able to speak based on their preparation based on the questions or after they have rehearsed for times, it is not the real communication that students are supposed to master in language class.

Lastly, to help students defeat the FLSA caused by feedback in class, instead of giving negative evaluations for students' speaking performance, teachers should provide more positive feedback (He, 2018). However, an important metric that teachers should bear in mind is that if students only have achieved a small achievement which is just around the average level, teacher's compliment may let those students feel that the teacher is indicating lack of confidence in their speaking capabilities and the belief they cannot achieve a further improvement shortly (He, 2018). It is suggested that a smiling face or a positive gesture is more suitable on this occasion. He (2018) also suggests that teachers should not interrupt students and give them direct corrections because it may change their focus from fluency to accuracy, which will lead them to pay more attention to their mistakes and may let them be under more pressure. Instead, an indirect correction and self-correction or peer-correction may be better to embrace. As to the kinds of problems that teachers should point out, Wong (2016) asserts that if learners have the persist errors or errors caused by their first language, teachers should get students' awareness of them as, otherwise, students will overlook and keep making these mistakes. When giving feedback, honest and critical feedback is more desired, and it may not necessarily lead to students' negative emotions (Jaidev & Blackstone, 2016; Molloy et al., 2019). Therefore, their FLSA will not increase because of the true and honest corrective feedback.

As stated above, it can be seen that there are plenty of studies in the current literature have been conducted to research the factors leading to students' anxiety in speaking English and the corresponding consequences. At the same time, plenty of methods that college teachers can adopt to help students deal with anxiety have been explored. However, not many of them have researched the possible factors causing speaking anxiety to lower-level students in the EMI teaching mode under TNE context in China, nor have they provided enough approaches for teachers to utilise in helping this group of students to overcome their anxiety. For these reasons, this chapter aims to fill the gap by providing an understanding of what factors lead to lower-level students' speaking anxiety of the foreign language in the EMI context and what are the effective ways college teachers can use to help them conquer such feelings through doing a case study at Xi'an Jiaotong-Liverpool University (XJTLU) in China. In this context, the foreign language refers to English. This research is guided by the following two research questions:

1. Do lower-level students in year one (Y1) at XJTLU experience anxiety when speaking English, and what factors may cause their anxiety? (RQ1)
2. What elements embedded in teaching or language class can reduce Y1 lower-level students' anxiety in speaking English at XJTLU? (RQ2)

4. METHODOLOGY

4.1 Context, Background, And Participants of The Study

Xi'an Jiaotong-Liverpool University (XJTLU), located in Suzhou, China, is a university that conforms to the context of transnational higher education as it is an international joint venture university founded by Xi'an Jiaotong University in China and the University of Liverpool in the United Kingdom. XJTLU uses English as the medium of instruction (EMI), and apart from some general and basic courses, more than one hundred degree programmes are taught in English. It aims to create an internationalised environment and develop students into global citizens.

At the beginning of the academic year 2021-2022, the English Language Support (ELS) programme was founded in the Continuous Support (CS) Division. It was committed to providing pastoral language support and care to around 600 lower-level students in Y1. There were two kinds of language courses provided by ELS, which were optional for students, and most students attended only one lesson from the ELS programme.

The questionnaire was sent out to around 100 students who had attended the same teacher's lessons in the ELS programme and received 41 responses, with 25 males and 16 females. Among them, 11 students, 7 females and 4 males decided to attend the follow-up interviews. Considering they were lower-level students, all questions in the questionnaire were in English but accompanied by a Chinese translation, and the interviewees were also informed that they could choose to attend the interview either in English or Chinese in accordance with their will.

5. DATA COLLECTION AND ANALYSIS

5.1 Mixed Data Collection Methods

According to Creswell and Creswell (2017), mixed data collection methods combine both qualitative and quantitative data in a study. Responses of qualitative data are usually open-ended and do not tend to be determined beforehand, whereas responses of quantitative data are usually close-ended with pre-determined answers, like those found on questionnaires. They believe both methods have their specific bias and shortcomings, and the mixed method of collecting data can neutralise the weaknesses of both forms of data. Therefore, the mixed method of collecting data will be used in this study.

5.2 Questionnaire And Analysis

For RQ1 of this case study, the quantitative data was collected through questionnaires. The values of the options of the questions from the questionnaire were granted and analysed through SPSS Ver. 21.

The questionnaire consisted of two parts which were designed to determine whether lower-level students in Y1 at XJTLU experience anxiety when speaking anxiety and what factors may cause their anxiety in speaking, respectively. The first part of the questionnaire was designed by adapting 5 questions from the 33 questions of FLCAS (Horwitz et al., 1986), such as "I'm more nervous and anxious when doing speaking activities in language class than doing other activities in that class, like reading or listening" and "Even if I'm well prepared for the questions raised by teachers, I still feel anxious about speaking in class." The 17 questions in the second part of the questionnaire were designed by referring to the possible reasons which may lead to students' anxiety in speaking a foreign language from the literature mentioned above, such as "If I work in a larger group, I will be more anxious in speaking English than in a smaller group" and "Making mistakes will make me feel more anxious when speaking English as I'm afraid of being laughed or judged by others." Among them, 14 are closed questions, which list the possible causes of students' FLSA, while the other 3 are open questions which are adopted to get students' in-depth ideas about individual, peer, and teacher's influence on their FLSA.

For the closed questions in both parts of the questionnaire, a 4-graded Likert scale, including options of Strongly Disagree (SD), Disagree (D), Agree (A), and Strongly Agree (SA), was adopted to collect data from students instead of the 5-graded one from the study of Horwitz et al. (1986), as the option of "neutral" was eliminated. There are two reasons that account for this adjustment, with the first one referring to the non-differentiating characteristic of "neutral," which shows students' indifferent attitudes towards the questions in the questionnaire (Edwards, 1946). This kind of ambiguous attitude can lead to problems in interpreting the choices of neutrality and difficulties in deciphering the reasons behind such choices. Another reason is that when there are the neutral options listed on the questionnaire, some students who do not like making a decision tend to choose this one (Brown, 2000). Accordingly, a probable solution to this is that an even number of Likert-scale, say 4-graded one, can be adopted to push students to make their choices. In the context of this study, as one previous research had been done on the same group of students before this study, and most of them had chosen neutral options, it also helped the adjustment from the 5-graded Likert scale to the 4-graded one.

5.3 Interview And Analysis

For the RQ2 of this case study, the qualitative data was collected through the interviews. The interpretation of the qualitative data of this research was using MAXQDA Ver. 20. The interviews were semi-structured to get students' thorough and detailed ideas about what elements embedded in teaching or language class can reduce their anxiety in speaking English. The 7 questions determined before the interview were solutions referring to those three categories which can affect students' anxiety in speaking English mentioned in the previous literature, such as "How can teachers or the teaching content influence your anxiety in speaking English in class?" and "How can your peers, namely your group members or classmates, affect your anxiety in speaking English in class?" If students' answers had not been thorough or detailed, further guiding questions were asked. For example, if students' answers were just simply "yes" or "no" to the first question mentioned above about teachers' and teaching content's influence, further questions like "What kind of teachers can reduce your anxiety?" or "How do you want your teachers to design the activity/teaching content?"

6. FINDINGS & DISCUSSION

Findings and discussion of RQ1 will be demonstrated in the first four sections below and the fifth section illustrates the findings and discussion of RQ2.

6.1. The Levels Of Y1 Lower-Level Students' Speaking Anxiety At XJTLU

To get the possible answers to the RQ1, the quantitative data from the questionnaire will be analysed, and relevant results will be shown from findings 1 to 5.

The first part of the questionnaire consists of 5 questions adapted from FLCAS, which tests whether lower-level students in Y1 at XJTLU experience anxiety in speaking English. These questions have four options, namely SD, D, A, and SA, and the values for these options range from 1 to 4, respectively. The way of interpreting the data is learned from Debreli and Demirkan' (2015) study. Based on their article, for the FLCAS with a total score of 165, a score of 99-132 indicates students' moderate-anxiety level, a score higher than 132 means the high-anxiety level, and a score lower than 99 represents the low-anxiety level. If calculating the percentage of these scores, 99 accounts for 60.00% of 165, and 132 accounts for 80.00% of 165. These two percentages (60% and 80%) will be utilised in deciding students' different anxiety levels of foreign language speaking at XJTLU when interpreting the data of the first part of the questionnaire of this study, which means students' scores higher than 80% (16 out of 20) have high FLSA, lower than 60% (12 out of 20) have low FLSA, and those in between (12-16) have moderate FLSA.

Table 1. Y1 lower-level students' speaking anxiety levels at XJTLU

Student No.	Gender	Students' total scores	Proportion of total scores (20)	Levels of FLSA
1	Female	9	45.00%	low
2	Female	20	100.00%	high
3	Male	5	25.00%	low
4	Female	18	90.00%	high
5	Female	16	80.00%	high
6	Male	17	85.00%	high
7	Male	16	80.00%	high
8	Female	20	100.00%	high
9	Male	12	60.00%	Moderate
10	Female	13	65.00%	Moderate
11	Male	20	100.00%	high
12	Female	18	90.00%	high
13	Male	5	25.00%	low
14	Male	20	100.00%	high
15	Male	5	25.00%	low
16	Female	17	85.00%	high
17	Male	5	25.00%	low
18	Male	17	85.00%	high
19	Male	5	25.00%	low
20	Female	20	100.00%	high
21	Male	20	100.00%	high
22	Male	5	25.00%	low
23	Female	5	25.00%	low
24	Male	18	90.00%	high
25	Male	5	25.00%	low
26	Female	20	100.00%	high
27	Male	16	80.00%	high
28	Female	17	85.00%	high
29	Male	20	100.00%	high
30	Male	10	50.00%	low
31	Female	20	100.00%	high
32	Male	10	50.00%	low
33	Female	17	85.00%	high
34	Male	8	40.00%	low
35	Male	5	25.00%	low
36	Male	20	100.00%	high
37	Male	20	100.00%	high

continues on following page

Table 1. Contineud

Student No.	Gender	Students' total scores	Proportion of total scores (20)	Levels of FLSA
38	Female	20	100.00%	high
39	Male	20	100.00%	high
40	Female	5	25.00%	low
41	Male	20	100.00%	high

Based on this interpreting method, as shown in table 1, it can be drawn that most of the participants, 25 students out of 41, had a high anxiety level when they spoke English in a language class, 14 of them experienced low anxiety, and 2 of them had moderate anxiety. It is worth mentioning that 14 students chose SA for all these five questions, which means their anxiety level is super high, and they are more easily feeling anxious than others when speaking English in language class. Therefore, a conclusion can be made based on the data that around two-thirds of participants experienced a high anxiety level, and more than half of these students' levels were extremely high. Another one-third of students revealed a low anxiety level, and only a few of them showed a moderate anxiety level.

Table 2. Each item's total scores and average score per student

Items in the questionnaire	Total scores (all scores added up)	Mean scores (total scores/ students' numbers)
I'm more nervous and anxious when doing speaking activities in language class than doing other activities in that class, like reading or listening.	115	2.80
I'm not confident in sharing my ideas in class and tend to worry about making mistakes when speaking.	127	3.10
I will panic if I'm not prepared to answer questions but have to speak in class.	121	2.95
Even if I'm well prepared for the questions raised by teachers, I still feel anxious about speaking in class.	98	2.39
If I'm allocated more chances to speak in language class than others, I will feel more anxious.	118	2.88

According to table 2, it can reveal that among these 5 five questions testing students' anxiety levels in speaking English in class, the second question gets the highest scores while the fourth question has the lowest scores. This suggests that students tend to feel more anxious about speaking English in class because they worry about making mistakes, which may cause them to be laughed at by classmates or judged by teachers, which is in line with several studies in the literature (Saputra, 2018; Djahimo et al., 2018; Erdiana et al., 2020; He, 2018). It also suggests that if students are well-prepared for their speaking activities, their anxiety levels are likely to be reduced, which also demonstrates the importance of providing students with support, language input, illustrative examples, strategies, and enough time, which can help them prepare better and reduce their anxiety mentioned in some of the studies in the literature (Erdiana et al., 2020; Saputra, 2018; Goh, 2016).

6.2. Gender's Influence on Y1 Lower-Level Students' Speaking Anxiety At XJTLU

Based on figure 1, the mean score of female students' speaking anxiety levels is 2.56 (out of 4), while the value for male students is 2.08, which means female students generally have a higher anxiety level in speaking English than male students. As the sig is 0.006 on the second column, less than 0.05, the sig of the fifth column depends on the value of the second row. Therefore, it means the sig for the t-test of genders' influence on FLSA is 0.099, higher than the benchmark of 0.05, which means there is no statistically significant difference in the levels of FLSA between female and male students, and it indicates that the difference between female and male students' levels of FLSA is only moderate.

Figure 1. Independent sample t-test for genders' influence on FLSA

Group statistics

	gender	N	Mean	Std. Deviation	Std. Error Mean
anxietylevel	female	16	2.5625	.81394	.20349
	male	25	2.0800	.99666	.19933

Independent Samples Test

		Levene's Test for Equality of Variances		t-test for Equality of Means						
		F	Sig.	t	df	Sig. (2-tailed)	Mean Difference	Std. Error Difference	95% Confidence Interval of the Difference	
									Lower	Upper
anxiety level	Equal variances assumed	8.592	.006	1.619	39	.113	.48250	.29795	-.12016	1.08516
	Equal variances not assumed			1.694	36.560	.099	.48250	.28485	-.09490	1.05990

6.3. Attitudes Of Students with Different Levels Of FLSA Towards The 14 Factors

The ANOVA test has been conducted to test whether students with different levels of FLSA (low, moderate, and high) have different opinions about the factors resulting in their FLSA. In table 3, 14 factors referring to the literature are listed in the first column. According to the test results, the values of sig shown in the last column for all of the 14 factors in each row are higher than the benchmark of 0.05, which reveals that no apparent differences are found among the attitudes of student groups with different anxiety levels towards the 14 factors leading to their FLSA. Therefore, the conclusion can be drawn that no matter what students' levels of FLSA are, they have similar opinions about these factors, which can give rise to their FLSA.

Table 3. ANOVA test for the influence of students' different levels of FLSA on their choices of factors leading to their FLSA

		Sum of Squares	df	Mean Square	F	Sig.
@9 My poor pronunciation and accent make me anxious to speak English in class.	Between Groups	1.452	2	.726	1.147	.328
	Within Groups	24.060	38	.633		
@10 Not knowing enough vocabulary makes me anxious to speak English in class.	Between Groups	.371	2	.185	.499	.611
	Within Groups	14.117	38	.372		
@11 My poor grammar knowledge makes me anxious to speak English in class.	Between Groups	.583	2	.291	.518	.600
	Within Groups	21.369	38	.562		
@12 Not understanding others (teachers or classmates) makes me anxious to speak English in class.	Between Groups	.324	2	.162	.320	.728
	Within Groups	19.189	38	.505		
@14 Making mistakes makes me anxious as I'm afraid of being laughed at or judged	Between Groups	.132	2	.066	.114	.892
	Within Groups	21.917	38	.577		
@15 My partners who speak better than me make me anxious about speaking English in class.	Between Groups	1.568	2	.784	1.166	.323
	Within Groups	25.554	38	.672		
@16 If I work individually, I will get more nervous during the speaking activities.	Between Groups	.455	2	.228	.398	.675
	Within Groups	21.740	38	.572		
@17 If I do the group discussion in a larger group, I will be more anxious than in smaller groups.	Between Groups	.316	2	.158	.389	.680
	Within Groups	15.440	38	.406		
@18 If using my mother tongue (Chinese) in the group discussion, I will be more anxious to share my answers in English later in class.	Between Groups	2.778	2	1.389	1.382	.263
	Within Groups	38.197	38	1.005		
@20 Not receiving positive feedback from the teacher makes me anxious to speak English in class.	Between Groups	.004	2	.002	.005	.995
	Within Groups	14.240	38	.375		
@21 If the teacher keeps correcting my mistakes, I will be more anxious to speak English in class.	Between Groups	.038	2	.019	.037	.964
	Within Groups	19.474	38	.512		
@22 If the teacher does not provide enough language input or illustrative examples, I will be more anxious to speak English in class.	Between Groups	.009	2	.004	.009	.991
	Within Groups	18.089	38	.476		
@23 If the teacher does not provide enough time for me to prepare, I will be more anxious to share my ideas in English later.	Between Groups	1.239	2	.619	1.147	.328
	Within Groups	20.517	38	.540		
@24 If I am not familiar with the topics, I will be more anxious to speak English in class.	Between Groups	2.426	2	1.213	1.268	.293
	Within Groups	36.354	38	.957		

6.4. Students' Attitudes Towards The 14 Factors' Influence On Their Flsa

Table 4 shows the scores (second column) and the mean scores (third column) from students' answers to the questionnaire for the14 factors drawn from the literature, which can cause students' anxiety in speaking a foreign language in class. It is listed in the order of the mean scores for each question, from the lowest to the highest. The questions based on the 14 factors are listed in the first column. As mentioned above, the foreign language in this context refers to English, so the questions are all about students' anxiety about speaking English in class. As the data was collected from 41 students and the answers to these 14 questions are 4-graded Likert-scale, the total score for each question is 164. Students' scores in the second column mean the sum of 41 students' scores for each question, and the mean scores (third column) represent each student's average score for each question. The last column refers to the proportion that students' mean scores for each question account for the total score of 4.

Table 4. Mean scores of the 14 factors affecting students' FLSA

14 items influencing students' FLSA	Students' cores	Mean scores	Proportion of total scores (4)
@24 If I am not familiar with the topics, I will be more anxious to speak English in class.	120	2.93	73.17%
@18 If using my mother tongue (Chinese) in the group discussion, I will be more anxious to share my answers in English later in class.	124	3.02	75.61%
@15 My partners who speak better than me make me anxious about speaking English in class	129	3.15	78.66%
@14 Making mistakes makes me anxious as I'm afraid of being laughed at or judged	134	3.27	81.71%
@9 My poor pronunciation and accent make me anxious to speak English in class.	138	3.36	84.15%
@12 Not understanding others (teachers or classmates) makes me anxious to speak English in class.	138	3.37	84.15%
@21 If the teacher keeps correcting my mistakes, I will be more anxious to speak English in class.	138	3.37	84.15%
@17 If I do the group discussion in a larger group, I will be more anxious than in smaller groups.	139	3.39	84.76%
@23 If the teacher does not provide enough time for me to prepare, I will be more anxious to share my ideas in English later.	139	3.39	84.76%
@11 My poor grammar knowledge makes me anxious to speak English in class.	140	3.41	85.37%
@22 If the teacher does not provide enough language input or illustrative examples, I will be more anxious to speak English in class.	141	3.44	85.98%
@20 Not receiving positive feedback from the teacher makes me anxious to speak English in class.	144	3.51	87.80%
@16 If I work individually, I will get more nervous during the speaking activities.	145	3.54	88.41%
@10 Not knowing enough vocabulary makes me anxious to speak English in class.	152	3.71	92.68%

According to this table, mean scores of these 14 influential factors analysed from students' answers range from 2.93 to 3.71, and the average of these two scores is 3.32 (orange line in Figure 2). Based on this average, the 14 factors can be divided into two groups: strong influence, if the score is higher than

3.32, and weak influence, if the score is lower than 3.32, on students' anxiety toward speaking English in class. Therefore, the first four factors in Figure 2. have a weaker influence, and the rest 10 have a stronger influence. However, this classification may be too simple and can only help create two groups. If the median is also adopted, the analysis can be more accurate. The median of the 14 mean scores is 3.38 (grey line in Figure 2). The rule of classifying these impact factors into different levels can be set as if the factor's mean scores are below both the average and median, they can be seen as factors of weak impact (first four in Figure 2), and vice versa (last seven in Figure 2). Then the factors left can be deemed as a moderate impact on students' anxiety in speaking English in class (5th to 7th factors in Figure 2).

Figure 2. Mean scores of the 14 factors affecting students' FLSA

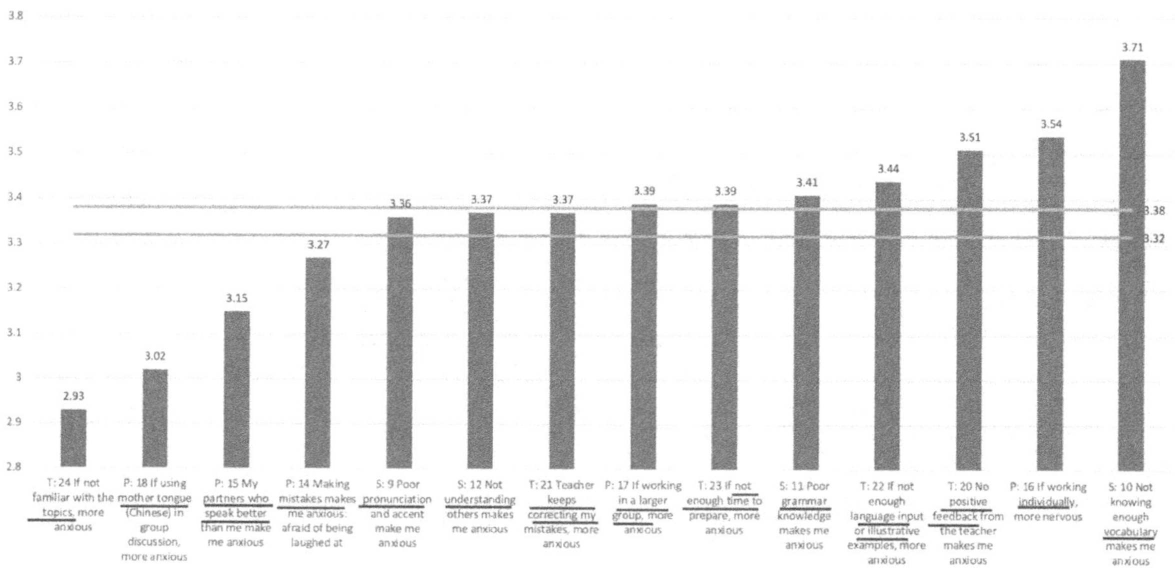

Next, the analysis of these factors' impact levels based on the three categories of self-related, peer-related, and teacher-related reasons mentioned in the literature will be provided.

6.4.1 Self-Related Reasons

For the classification of self-related reasons, the relevant questions are 9, 10, 11, and 12, which refer to "poor pronunciation/accent," "comprehension problems with others (teachers of classmates)," "poor grammar," and "poor vocabulary" respectively. Among them, the "poor pronunciation and accent" and "comprehension problems with others" have a moderate influence on students' FLSA, while "poor grammar" and "poor vocabulary" can greatly affect students' FLSA. Moreover, these results reveal that XJTLU Y1 lower-level students' anxiety levels are relatively influenced more by factors of poor grammar and vocabulary. What is worth mentioning is that not having enough vocabulary is the top 1 impact factor on students' FLSA, with a score of 3.71 out of 4. A possible solution for teachers is to use the time not only in but also out of class to help students cultivate the habit of gaining and practicing more vocabulary and grammar, which can help them lower the level of FLSA. To conclude, these results conform to He's (2018) finding that the most prominent factor influencing students' FLSA is the insufficient vocabulary of the target language, and students' poor pronunciation, accent, and grammar can also lead to the FLSA.

6.4.2 Peer-Related Elements

Next, for the type of peer-related elements, the related questions are 14, 15, 16, 17, and 18. They include the following factors: "more competent partner," "making mistakes and laughed at by others," "working individually," "larger group," and "using mother tongue (Chinese)." Based on their scores, the "more competent partner," "making mistakes and laughed by others," and "using mother tongue (Chinese)" have a weak impact, whereas "working individually" and "larger group" tend to have a stronger influence on students' FLSA. It can be inferred from these results that for the peer-related factors, lower-level Y1 students in XJTLU do not care much about partners' performance or judgement, but they value more the way of preparing for the speaking activities. If they can prepare with others in a smaller group instead of working alone or in a larger group, it can reduce their anxiety about speaking English effectively. Furthermore, among the results, "working individually" has a notable impact on students' FLSA with a score of 3.54 out of 4, and the suggestion can be drawn from it for teachers is that it is better not to let students work alone for the speaking activities unless they have to. In addition, students are inclined to believe "Using mother tongue (Chinese)" only has a small influence on their FLSA, with a score of 3.02 out of 4. However, whether they believe it is useful or not to use Chinese during the preparation or discussion cannot be clearly drawn from the data, and further analysis needs to be done through the interviews.

6.4.3 Teacher-Related Factors

As to the teacher-related factors, the correlated questions are 20, 21, 22, 23, and 24, including the factors of "not receiving positive feedback," "teachers keep correcting the mistakes," "not providing language input or examples," "not providing enough preparation time," and "unfamiliar topics." From the results, "unfamiliar topics" enjoys a weak influence, "teachers keep correcting mistakes" has a moderate influence while "not providing language input or examples," "not providing enough preparation time," and "not receiving positive feedback" possess a strong influence on students' FLSA. It is deserved to be mentioned that "unfamiliar topics" provided by teachers enjoys the lowest score, which is 2.93 out of 4. This does not mean the finding contradicts the research in the literature review (He, 2018; Chen and Lee, 2011) because 2.93 is still a relatively high score compared with 4, which means students generally chose "Agree" (a score of Agree is 3.00) to this question. It can be interpreted that students do not think that unfamiliar topics can strongly increase their anxiety in speaking English in class, so teachers may not need to care too much about the unfamiliar topics when preparing for the language class. Apart from this point, the participants seem to do not mind if teachers keep correcting their mistakes in speaking, but they still hope to get some positive feedback from teachers, which can cut down their FLSA. In addition, greater importance is also attached to enough language input, illustrative examples, and time for preparation by these participants. If these factors are not guaranteed, their FLSA will increase.

After comparing the scores of each factor within the three categories listed above and conducting the analysis accordingly, a holistic analysis of the impact level of each category will be provided. Based on the mean scores of each question of the three categories, the mean scores for them are 3.46 for self-related reasons, 3.27 for peer-related factors, and 3.33 for teacher's influence. Therefore, it reveals that self-related factors tend to have the biggest influence on students' FLSA among all the three types, while peer-related reasons are inclined to have the comparatively weakest influence.

7. STUDENTS' VIEWPOINTS ON WHAT ELEMENTS CAN REDUCE THEIR FLSA

To analyse and get the results of the second research question, qualitative data from the interviews with students was analysed through the software QDA, version 20. The 11 interviewees, 7 females and 4 males, covered all three levels of FLSA, including eight students with high-level of FLSA (No.5, 6, 8, 12, 18, 20, 21, and 31), 2 students with low-level of FLSA (No. 3 and 23) and 1 student with moderate-level of FLSA (No. 12). The participants were selected randomly. However, most voluntary participants were classified as having high-level of FLSA, only a few had low-level anxiety, and no moderate-level student was voluntary because there were only 2 out of 41 students were deemed as moderate-level. Therefore, the interview of that moderate-level student was conducted successfully after three rounds of contact to make sure that the data of the interviews covered ideas from all three types of students. In the end, 55 codes and sub-codes were compiled from the interview transcripts of 11 students, which were mentioned 203 times altogether and the codes belonging to those three categories showed up for 182 times. The most frequent codes are listed in the form of a code cloud below (Figure 3). The darker the colour is and the larger the text is, the more frequent it was mentioned in the interviews by students.

In Figure 4, the left column lists the 55 codes and sub-codes compiled from the students' interview transcripts. The codes are classified into four types, including three types of influential factors from literature (self, peer, and teacher) and one category of FLSA (self-evaluation and importance). The symbols of + and – represent increasing and decreasing anxiety, respectively. Though the interviews were conducted to understand students' attitudes towards how the elements in teaching or language class can decrease their anxiety levels in speaking English, students would mention some ideas or examples from a different angle that can increase their anxiety, such as using some conditional sentences like "if the teacher is too strict on my language, I will be nervous." The first row in this figure shows students' anxiety levels and numbers. For instance, M10 means the No.10 student to submit the questionnaire, and their anxiety level is moderate, which is analysed from their answers to the questions in the questionnaire. On the right side of this figure, the numerous numbers show the frequency of these codes appearing in each student's interview transcript.

7.1 Findings on the Codes About FLSA

The first category of codes, in yellow, is about students' self-evaluation of FLSA and their understanding of the importance of reducing it. At the beginning of the interview, all the interviewees were asked to give a self-evaluation of their levels of FLSA. The results were that 7 students' self-evaluation levels were in accordance with the results analysed from the questionnaire, including 6 high and 1 low anxiety level, while the other 4 students' self-evaluations contradicted the results from the questionnaire. In these four samples, 3 students thought their anxiety levels were low but were moderate or high actually, and one student believed their anxiety level was high but turned out to be low. This can suggest that not all the students have a clear and correct acknowledgement of their anxiety levels. For those who tend to underestimate their anxiety levels, they may neglect the hazards of having speaking anxiety and do not prepare well to deal with their potential anxiety in speaking a foreign language; for those inclined to overestimate their anxiety levels, they may get overstressed when speaking English while they do not need to. Therefore, teachers should let students realise their actual levels of FLSA and then prepare them for their problems accordingly.

Another finding here is about the importance of reducing FLSA. All students agreed on the importance of reducing FLSA, but when talking about the reasons, only 3 mentioned it is for a better future or better themselves. 6 students alluded to the objective reason that they were studying in XJTLU, where all lessons are taught in English which makes it necessary for them to reduce FLSA as they need to communicate with their classmates and teachers in English. This finding suggests that if students study in transnational higher education where EMI is adopted, students tend to have a clearer understanding of the necessity of reducing FLSA and will be more motivated to achieve this goal. This finding is in line with Chou's (2018) argument that it is more necessary for students to be used to communicating with others in English in transnational higher education because of the EMI mode of teaching. In teaching, when students in transnational higher education ignore the importance of lowering their FLSA, teachers can adopt this theory to guide students and arouse their inner motivation and determination to reduce their FLSA.

Figure 3. Most frequent codes compiled from students' interview transcripts

Figure 4. Codes compiled from 11 students' interview transcripts

	H5	H6	H8	H12	H18	H20	H21	H31	M10	L3	L23
FLSA											
Self evaluation of FLSA											
Low-Low(Q)										1	
High-Low(Q)											1
Low-Moderate or High(Q)	1			1					1		
High-High(Q)		1	1		1	1	1	1			
Importance of reducing FLSA											
Motivation/future self -		1							1		1
Studying in XJTLU -	1			1		1		1	1		1
EMI environment						1					
Teacher-related factors											
Better to have native speaker teachers -											1
Teachers design class											
More/diverse topics	1		1	1					1		1
Step by step activities			1								
Design more speaking lessons than other skills		1			2						
accent		1									
phonetic symbols		1									
Teachers design more vocabulary lessons -									1		
Familiar topics -							2				
Input/illustrative examples from T -	1		1	1	1	1	2		1		1
Teacher lists and reviews common mistakes -											1
Teach based on ss' interests -		1					3			1	
Keep up with trends -							1				
Teach more about spk exam -			1	1	1					1	
Teachers design more pronunciation lessons -		1				2	1		1		
More interaction in class -		1	1		1		1		2		
Teachers monitor groups			1								
Teacher's feedback + -											
Teacher corrects mistakes with humour -									1		
Teacher corrects mistakes (frequently) -		2		1	1	1	1	1	2		1
Correcting mistakes in front of others +							1				
Teachers blame/punish for mistakes +	1		1		1			1			1
Teacher's positive feedback -	1			1	1			1			1
Encouraging teacher -	1		2		1	1	2	1			1
Teacher ignores/interrupt ss +								1			
Teachers high requirement +	1			1							
Friendly teacher -	1		2	1	1	1	2	1	1		2
Peer-related factors											
Use Chinese in discussion -			1			1					
Discussing with partners in English -	2	1			1			1			
Learn from others' answers				1	1		1				
Work individually +							1				
No partners but more teachers -										1	1
Being looked down upon due to mistakes +		1				1	1		2		
Groups, especially active groups -			2	1		1		1	1		1
low competence partner - (vice versa +)			1	1	1		1		1		
Self-related factors											
Solutions											
Learn grammar -			1	1							
Teachers supervise after class	1		1			1		1			
Practice with native speakers -										1	1
Shouldn't be afraid of making mistakes											1
Talk more during practice -	1	1			1		1	1		1	1
Speak more after class -	1	1		2	1		1	1		2	1
Teachers can give advice -	1	1		1							
Clear pronunciation -	1										
Building vocabulary -	1	1	1			1	1	1			
Practice listening -		1						1			
Language competence											
poor vocabulary +			2	1			2	1	2		
Poor pronunciation +		1				1			1		
poor grammar +			1	1	1	1	1		1		
comprehend problems due to poor listening +					2			1			
Being shy +	1										

7.2 Findings on Codes About Self-Related Factors

Codes about self-related factors are marked in red from Figure 4. Students were asked two questions in this section which were "what self-related factors can influence your FLSA?" and "how can you reduce FLSA?" Most of the self-related factors emphasised by students were about language competency. Among them, influential factors of vocabulary and grammar were mentioned the most frequently, with the frequency of 8 and 6 times, which conforms to the quantitative analysis mentioned above. As to students' viewpoints about the solutions to reduce their FLSA, speaking more after class enjoyed the highest frequency (10 times), and three students mentioned the point that teachers could provide some suggestions about how to effectively practice and improve their speaking capabilities. Student 12 stated that:

"Sometimes we know the importance of practicing more and more on our speaking, but we don't know how to achieve the goal. So, teachers should tell us how to do it."

A similar solution alluded to 7 times was talking more during practice in class instead of being silent. Apart from these two, building more vocabulary (6 times) and grammar (2 times), practicing listening to improve comprehension when speaking (2 times), and improving pronunciation (1 time) after class were also mentioned. A relevant unexpected finding was that the necessity of teachers' supervision after class (4 times) was pointed out by four students with high-anxiety levels. This can imply that students with a higher level of anxiety in speaking may hope to practice more after class but tend to worry more about whether they can persist. This is coherent with He's (2018) claim that to cut down students' FLSA, teachers may encourage students to foster the great learning habit like doing more self-study to gain the improvement after class, and if necessary, teachers can create chances for students to practice daily on what they have learned in and out of class. If teachers notice some students have similar needs, they can provide similar help and support to them to reduce their FLSA. The last finding is that two students mentioned practicing speaking with native speakers can deal with their FLSA. Similarly, one student said having a native speaker as their teacher could also help. These statements were all from students belonging to the low-level anxiety group. Thus, it can be inferred that if students have less FLSA, namely higher speaking confidence, they may have the needs to talk to some native speakers, including students or teachers. Teachers can guide students to achieve this aim when their certain needs are noticed.

7.3 Findings on Codes About Peer-Related Reasons

Peer-related reasons are shown as purple codes in Figure 4, which appeared to be the least frequently (30 times) in students' interview transcripts compared with self-related (59 times) and teacher-related factors (93 times). Therefore, it can be concluded that peer-related reasons tend to have the least influence on students' FLSA. Based on students' responses, most students (8 times) believed working in groups instead of working individually can reduce their anxiety in speaking English, which is consistent with He's (2018) and Bailey and Nunan's (2015) assertions that students, especially lower-level ones, are more willing to work in pairs or smaller groups which can lessen their FLSA and increase their confidence. A related prominent finding in this area is 6 students happened to mention that active groups can reduce their FLSA. This point was novel as it had not been referred to in the literature nor in the questionnaire sent to students, but they coincidentally came to an agreement on this point. Student 8 claimed that:

"If all the, or most partners can talk, then I can talk. If they don't, I will be uncomfortable to speak. But teachers will ask us to give answers soon, so I will start to be anxious."

For another improvised question went much further about how to encourage active groups, this student asserted that it not only needed teachers' encouragement and supervision towards the groups during the activities but also needed students' efforts as they need to foster a friendly atmosphere with their partners to reduce the awkwardness when talking to each other. If both can be done, student 8 believes he can talk in English freely without anxiety in class. A similar argument mentioned by students was that if they were looked upon during the group discussion, their FLSA would boost (5 times). These viewpoints are in line with He's (2018) that teachers can create a sense of small community among group members to produce a more friendly and supportive learning environment and stop students from putting pressure on each other. Another inspiration for teachers is that it is quite necessary for them to supervise the groups during the speaking activities and make sure they are active, just in case they will be silent and stop talking, which may bring pressure on those who would like to talk more about the topic.

Another finding here is about the use of Chinese in group discussions. Based on students' questionnaires, the result was concluded that speaking Chinese has a weaker influence on students' increased FLSA, but students' attitudes towards speaking Chinese in discussion in English class were not clearly drawn. From the analysis of the codes, 2 students (2 times) referred to the point that using Chinese to aid their discussion can help to mitigate their FLSA. On the contrary, 4 students (5 times) put forward that speaking in English during the preparation could better help them deal with the speaking activities and diminish their FLSA. One shared benefit among them was that 3 out of 4 of these students argued that they could learn from each other's answers which can be combined with their ideas to produce a better answer if they were nominated by the teacher to answer the question later. In addition, all the 6 students were grouped as having high-level speaking anxiety. One conclusion can be reached that if students have high-level FLSA, they may have different opinions about the use of their mother tongue in their group discussion, but most of them tend to believe that using the target language can lead to a better practice effect which is beneficial to lower their FLSA. This may differ from arguments mentioned in the literature (Saputra, 2018; Djahimo et al., 2018; Erdiana et al., 2020; He, 2018; Mahboob & Lin, 2016) to some extent as it cannot be concluded easily whether using mother tongue will decrease or increase students' FLSA. Therefore, teachers may not need to introduce the use of students' mother tongue in the discussion on purpose or ban students from using it entirely. If some students' needs of using their mother tongue are noticed, teachers can collect all the students' opinions and then make the decision flexibly based on different results.

7.4 Findings on Codes About Teacher-Related Reasons

As illustrated in table 6, teacher-related reasons, codes in green, were probed in by students the most frequently. Altogether, they were mentioned 93 times by students during the interviews. The code that occurred the most times was "friendly teacher" (12 times). This can suggest that among the factors linked with teachers, students value the most about the teacher's characteristics. If teachers can be friendly and kind to students, their FLSA can be cut down effectively. Student 5 asserted that:

"If teachers are patient, kind, and willing to be close with us in class, I will be more relaxed when speaking English with them. However, if they have higher requirements and are strict, I will not be able to think and say any English."

A connected factor mentioned is "teachers having high requirements," which was mentioned by 2 students during the interviews. Both of them believed their anxiety about speaking English would be higher if they had a stricter teacher.

One key finding in the section on teachers' influence is about teachers' design of the lesson. First, though student 21 mentioned twice that familiar topics would reduce his FLSA, 5 other students from all three levels of anxiety contended that they hoped to have more topics that could meet their needs of practicing speaking in diverse contexts. In this way, they believed that their FLSA could drop when they meet a similar context next time. A similar argument was that 3 students put forth the importance of designing lessons based on students' interests, and one of them required teachers to keep up with trends. Student 21 raised a claim:

"If teachers can design lessons based on our interests, I mean young people's interests, I will feel more willing and relaxed to join the lesson. For example, a recent trend among us is the game Glory of King. If teachers can teach us speaking in the context of this game, more students will benefit from the class."

These arguments reveal students' needs to have diverse contexts and topics and updated teaching materials in class. From their opinions, these can help them stay focused, engage more in class and reduce their FLSA efficiently at the same time. Especially when they meet a similar topic next time, their FLSA can go down obviously, even though this time the topic is unfamiliar for them and may bring a certain degree of anxiety. This contradicts He's (2018), Chen and Lee's (2011), and Leong and Ahmadi's (2017) arguments partially that students' FLSA will rise if they meet unfamiliar topics. The results suggest that teachers do not need to care too much about unfamiliar topics as most students may have the needs to practice speaking on diverse topics to reduce their FLSA next time in the long run. Also, combined with another code, "input/illustrative examples from teachers," showed up 9 times from 8 students, which represents students' needs to have enough input or examples for different activities to reduce their FLSA, it can be concluded if teachers provide enough input and illustrative examples for students' unfamiliar topics and activities, students' FLSA will not be increased extremely even it is their first time dealing with these topics or activities.

Some other noticeable findings of teacher's design of lessons are that students want more speaking classes (2 students, 3 times), especially for the skill of pronunciation (4 students, 5 times) and preparation for speaking exams (4 times), which they believe are useful in diminishing their FLSA. Based on students' responses during the interviews, this can be understood as although students feel poor vocabulary and grammar can aggravate their FLSA more severely, they believed these were what they should do on their own after class, as mentioned in 5.2. In class, they showed their point of views that they would like to learn more about the pronunciation from teachers as they could not notice the pronunciation errors and make improvements accordingly easily by themselves.

Another key finding of teacher's influence falls into the area of feedback. Students like teachers giving encouraging (9 times) and positive (5 times) feedback as they believe such feedback can make them less nervous in class. Similarly, teachers ignoring or interrupting students (1 time) or even blaming students for their mistakes (5 times) can stimulate students' FLSA easily. Student 31 argued that:

"No one of us likes teachers who always blame us in class. Even if they want to help us, if they interrupt me and correct my mistakes, they just make me cannot speak. It's not because I'm not willing to, but because I am too anxious to speak then."

Teachers can learn from the results that it is more suitable to give students positive and encouraging feedback based on their performance and do not ignore, interrupt, or blame students if they cannot perform well in the activities. These can help decrease students' FLSA in class.

However, it does not mean that teachers could never correct students' mistakes. Based on Figure 4, students' attitudes towards teachers' correcting their mistakes (10 times) are positive as they believe this could improve their language competency and their confidence in speaking accordingly. The opinion of student 20 was as follows:

"I don't think teachers correcting our mistakes is making us lose face. They are helping us to improve. I always want my teachers to give me some suggestions or corrections in class."

This may disprove the statements in the literature that teachers' corrective feedback can build up students' FLSA (Djahimo et al., 2018; Erdiana et al., 2020), as most students from this research prefer their teachers to give them corrective feedback in class, which conforms to Jaidev and Blackstone's (2016) and Molloy et al. (2019) arguments that honest corrective feedback are more desired and they would not surely lead to negative feelings and increase of FLSA. At the same time, the result also proves the claim of Djahimo et al. (2018) claim that it is better to let students finish their speaking and give feedback then; otherwise, it may make students not easy to continue their speaking. Teachers can bear these suggestions in mind during their teaching.

8. CONCLUSION

This case study examines students' anxiety about speaking English in class at XJTLU, analysed the influence on students' FLSA of 14 impact factors from three categories, and the correspondent elements that can help deal with students' speaking anxiety. Data from the first two parts were collected through questionnaires from 41 students, while the third one was acquired from interviews with 11 students.

The results of RQ1 showed that only a tiny fraction of students' anxiety in speaking English was moderate. Most of the participants experienced high levels of anxiety in speaking English, and around one-third of them had low levels of anxiety. As to the analysis of the 14 impact factors from self-related, peer-related, and teacher-related aspects, this research demonstrates that all of the 14 factors from the literature led to students' FLSA to certain degrees, but the influential power of each factor was different based on students' opinions, and there was no obvious difference noticed between female and male groups' attitudes. Among these 14 factors, seven of them had a greater influence on students' FLSA because their scores were higher than both the median and average, which were "poor grammar," "poor vocabulary," "working individually," "larger group," "not providing language input or examples," "not providing enough preparation time," and "not receiving positive feedback." When analysed the impact levels of three categories' factors holistically, the mean score of self-related reasons was 3.46, which ranked the first among the three types, while peer-related factors' mean score was 3.27, which was the lowest one. This finding revealed that students' FLSA was most likely caused by self-related reasons and was least likely resulted from peer-related factors.

Concerning the analysis of RQ2 based on the interview scripts of 11 students, 55 codes and subcodes that showed up 182 times were compiled under those three categories. A general result was that students from transnational higher education tended to have a clearer understanding of the necessity of the importance of reducing FLSA in such context and may have a stronger inner motivation to achieve this goal. Another general finding was that it could be concluded that students regarded teacher-related factors as the most effective tools to reduce their FLSA, as the codes of this type appeared most frequently (93 times) in students' interviews, far higher than self-related (59 times) and peer-related factors (30 times). Detailed results from analysing codes of three categories are listed below.

After analysing the codes falling into the category of self-related reasons, the result showed that many students actually needed guidance and supervision from teachers after class to aid them in improving their competencies to deal with FLSA because they may lack the professional knowledge of how to improve their speaking effectively and may not persist in achieving the goals. When moving to peer-related elements, the main finding was that apart from preferring to work in groups than individually, students also cared about whether the group was active. This gives teachers an implication that it is important to monitor all the groups to make sure they are active throughout the whole activity to reduce students' FLSA. Another finding of peer-related elements was that different students had different attitudes towards the use of their mother tongue, but based on the analysis, most students were inclined to speak the target foreign language during the group discussion. Hence, teachers can be flexible based on students' different needs. Lastly, for the codes of teacher-related factors, a noticeable finding was that students cared the most about teachers' characteristics. "Friendly teacher" was mentioned 12 times by students, and they believed their FLSA would decrease strikingly if teachers were friendly, encouraging, helpful, and not harsh. Another finding was that many students preferred the teaching which was based on their interests or the current trends, as such lessons could make them relaxed and lower their FLSA. What is more, the opinions of students towards the unfamiliar topics were different from those listed in the literature. Students believed that if the language input and illustrative examples of unfamiliar topics were provided, they would not be afraid of such topics, and some of them even preferred unfamiliar topics to expand their horizons. The last finding of teacher-related factors was about teacher's feedback. Generally speaking, different students preferred different styles of feedback, but many students wanted teachers' positive feedback. However, it did not mean they did not welcome the corrective feedback from teachers because some of them reported that true and honest feedback is more preferred as it could help them improve. Teachers can be inspired accordingly to provide true and honest feedback together with some positive and encouraging ones.

As mentioned before, transnational higher education has developed and become popular recently. Under this context, students are expected to use English as a fundamental tool to have effective communication with their classmates and teachers. Therefore, it is necessary for them to cope with FLSA. Based on the findings of this study listed above, hopefully, teachers working in transnational higher education can get some inspiration regarding how to reduce their students' FLSA. Also, the causes of lower-level students' speaking anxiety in transnational higher education and the corresponding solutions can be a topic that is going to be further investigated in future research.

REFERENCES

Arunasalam, N. D., & Burton, R. (2018). Investigating Malaysian Nurses' perspectives of intercultural teaching in transnational higher education learning environments. *Nurse Education Today*, *69*, 165–171. doi:10.1016/j.nedt.2018.07.011 PMID:30092544

Bahrani, T., & Soltani, R. (2012). How to teach speaking skill. *Journal of Education and Practice*, *3*(2), 25–29.

Bailey, K. M., & Nunan, D. (2005). Practical English Language Teaching: Speaking. *Scientific Research.*

Brown, J. D. (2000). What issues affect Likert-scale questionnaire formats. *Shiken: JALT Testing & Evaluation SIG Newsletter, 4*(1).

Burns, A. (2019). Concepts for teaching speaking in the English language classroom. *LEARN Journal: Language Education and Acquisition Research Network*, *12*(1), 1–11.

Chen, C. M., & Lee, T. H. (2011). Emotion recognition and communication for reducing second-language speaking anxiety in a web-based one-to-one synchronous learning environment. *British Journal of Educational Technology*, *42*(3), 417–440. doi:10.1111/j.1467-8535.2009.01035.x

Chou, M. H. (2018). Speaking anxiety and strategy use for learning English as a foreign language in full and partial English-medium instruction contexts. *TESOL Quarterly*, *52*(3), 611–633. doi:10.1002/tesq.455

Creswell, J. W., & Creswell, J. D. (2017). *Research design: Qualitative, quantitative, and mixed methods approaches*. Sage publications.

Debreli, E., & Demirkan, S. (2015). Sources and levels of foreign language speaking anxiety of English as a foreign language university students with regard to language proficiency and gender. *International Journal of English Language Education*, *4*(1), 49–62. doi:10.5296/ijele.v4i1.8715

Djahimo, S., Bili Bora, D., & Huan, E. (2018). Student anxiety and their speaking performance: Teaching EFL to Indonesian student. *International Journal of Social Science and Humanity*, *2*(3), 187–195.

Edwards, A. L. (1946). A critique of 'neutral' items in attitude scales constructed by the method of equal appearing intervals. *Psychological Review*, *53*(3), 159–169. doi:10.1037/h0054184

Erdiana, N., Daud, B., Sari, D. F., & Dwitami, S. K. (2020). A study of anxiety experienced by EFL students in speaking performance. *Studies in English Language and Education*, *7*(2), 334–346. doi:10.24815iele.v7i2.16768

Farooq, M. U. (2015). Creating a Communicative Language Teaching Environment for Improving Students' Communicative Competence at EFL/EAP University Level. *International Education Studies*, *8*(4), 179–191. doi:10.5539/ies.v8n4p179

Goh, C. (2016). *Teaching speaking. English Language Teaching Today, 143-159.* Springer.

He, D. (2018). *Foreign Language Learning Anxiety in China: Theories and Applications in English Language Teaching*. Springer. doi:10.1007/978-981-10-7662-6

Hewitt, E., & Stephenson, J. (2012). Foreign language anxiety and oral exam performance: A replication of Phillips's MLJ study. *Modern Language Journal*, *96*(2), 170–189. doi:10.1111/j.1540-4781.2011.01174.x

Horwitz, E. K., Horwitz, M. B., & Cope, J. (1986). Foreign language classroom anxiety. *Modern Language Journal*, *70*(2), 125–132. doi:10.1111/j.1540-4781.1986.tb05256.x

Huang, F. (2014). *The internationalisation of the academic profession. The internationalization of the academy, 1-21.* Springer. doi:10.1007/978-94-007-7278-6

Jaidev, R., & Blackstone, B. (2016). *Facilitating Workplace Communicative Competence. English Language Teaching Today, 293-307.* Springer.

Leong, L. M., & Ahmadi, S. M. (2017). FLUENCING LEARNERS'ENGLISH SPEAKING SKILL. *International Journal of English Education.*

Mahboob, A., & Lin, A. M. (2016). *Using local languages in English language classrooms. English language teaching today, 25-40.* Springer.

Menggo, S., Suastra, I., Budiarsa, M., & Padmadewi, N. N. (2019). Needs Analysis of Academic-English Speaking Material in Promoting 21st Century Skills. *International Journal of Instruction, 12*(2), 739–754. doi:10.29333/iji.2019.12247a

Molloy, E., Noble, C., & Ajjawi, R. (2019). *Attending to emotion in feedback. The impact of feedback in higher education, 83-105.* Palgrave Macmillan.

Nunan, D. (1991). *Language teaching methodology: A textbook for teachers.* Prentice hall.

Poggensee, A. (2016). *The effects of globalization on English language learning: Perspectives from Senegal and the United States.* WMU.

Rajitha, K., & Alamelu, C. (2020). A study of factors affecting and causing speaking anxiety. *Procedia Computer Science, 172*, 1053–1058. doi:10.1016/j.procs.2020.05.154

Saputra, J. B. (2018). An analysis of students' speaking anxiety toward their speaking skill. *Premise: Journal of English Education, 7*(1), 111–123. doi:10.24127/pj.v7i1.1334

Suadiyatno, T., Firman, E., Hanan, A., & Sumarsono, D. (2020). Examining the effect of contextual teaching-learning and anxiety towards students' speaking skills. *Journal of Languages and Language Teaching, 8*(1), 100–107. doi:10.33394/jollt.v8i1.2266

Suzuki, N. (2017). Foreign language speaking anxiety in the English-medium instruction (EMI) program in a Japanese university. *Casele Research Bulletin, 47*, 11–21.

Wong, C. S. (2016). *Teaching pronunciation to learners of English as a lingua franca. English language teaching today, 241-255.* Springer.

Chapter 4

Ethical Communication and Argument-Centered Education Can Enhance Transnational Education and Promote a More Ethical and Civil World

Rahman Kevin Smith
https://orcid.org/0000-0001-6586-4641
The Chinese University of Hong Kong, Shenzhen, China

ABSTRACT

This chapter briefly introduces and demonstrates fifteen debate-related analytical and compositional tools that can be implemented in language arts courses such as writing, public speaking, and debate. Based on classical rhetoric and solidly grounded in pedagogical research, these exercises are already in use in both the English language learner (ELL) and native English-speaking environments. Combined with the larger philosophical tenants of ethical communication, which reminds speakers and writers to be mindful of the positive or negative effects their words can have on the societies in which they live and beyond.

INTRODUCTION

This chapter presents a suite of interconnected concepts extracted from the conventions of competitive debate that can be of significant benefit to teachers and learners within the Transnational Education (TNE) community. A philosophy of Ethical argument, a detailed pedagogical framework, a review of the most excellent literature available, and a brief demonstration of 15 classroom activities are provided. The information in this document is sufficient for institutions and individual educators to begin a deliberate shift to a more argument-focused approach to teaching. Data will be presented showing that such a shift can be a helpful method of improving educational outcomes. Furthermore, these concepts can be imple-

DOI: 10.4018/978-1-6684-5226-4.ch004

mented with minimal investment in cost and resources. Therefore, adopting some or all of the pedagogical principles provided here could reasonably become a part of any TNE institution's educational strategy.

BACKGROUND

In 2008, the author of this chapter started his teaching career in China with little experience and, therefore, not much confidence. Additionally, the international context brought significant cultural barriers, which meant that prospects for success in this chosen field were sometimes in doubt. However, during the second teaching year, an unexpected turning point came from an assignment to take over as the coach of the university's competitive debate team. This required attending a week-long training session in Beijing provided by a well-known national publishing company.

The annual event brought together hundreds of coaches, students, and adjudicators from every corner of China and nearly every continent. Additionally, well-known argument scholars and national-championship-winning instructors from Singapore, the United States, Great Britain, and Australia were also present.

Each year, a full day was set aside for teacher-to-teacher interaction. During these sessions, best teaching practices were shared and exchanged. Since each lecturer was also a debate coach, the presentations revolved around how debate-related techniques could be fused into day-to-day teaching practices. With these lessons learned and applied, the author of this chapter quickly began to see improved interaction and enthusiasm in his classes. With these argument-centered methods, students were learning more and displaying greater competence and confidence, especially regarding writing and public speaking. Thanks to this "debatification" process, success as university-level writing and public speaking teacher was no longer in doubt.

In 2015, the author moved to a newly founded university almost exclusively focused on sending its graduates to further studies in western countries. This meant the responsibility to prepare students to write, speak, and communicate confidently was a significant part of the teaching responsibilities. However, there was a more significant problem developing that would affect future teaching styles.

The world was beginning to change during those years. Words like "deglobalization" and "decoupling" were starting to be heard regularly. Previous international trends that helped bring people together were starting to be reversed. In accordance with the university's mission statement, which is in part "to bring together East and West," the school's leaders wanted to produce young people who might one day be part of the solution. With this purpose in mind, the author began a formal academic inquiry into ways in which the argument and debate-centered approach could be effective in the classroom and valuable to society and the world beyond.

Ethical Communication is the result of this multi-year inquiry. It is a mixture of formal debate techniques combined with principles that guide educators and students in directions conducive to a more peaceful world. It is designed to equip students with communication and listening tools that will help prepare them for global citizenship.

UTILITY TO THE TNE COMMUNITY

The concepts presented in this chapter can fit the mission of any TNE institution. For example, a well-known TNE university in China (Xi'an Jiaotong Liverpool University - XJTLU) has a mission statement that includes: "to educate [students] with international perspectives." Additionally, as part of its 5-year education enhancement strategy it lays out the following goals:

- Enhance student-centered education models and provide a transformative, enriching learning experience in an international education environment.
- Support students to develop lifelong and global citizenship with knowledge and capabilities for contributing to the well-being of human society.

As will be demonstrated later in this document, argument and debate-centered teaching is very much student-centered as it reduces the time teachers spend lecturing. The rapidity in which students can tangibly improve their communication skills can indeed have a transformative effect on their confidence. This learning system is designed to help students place themselves in the context of "the greater good." In other words, they learn to be cognizant of how quality communication can promote global citizenship and the well-being of people worldwide. The XJTLU 5-year planning document also includes the following objectives:

- Increase international and domestic brand awareness.
- Support student recruitment in international and domestic markets both in quality and quantity.

At the author's university, every student, regardless of major, will spend some time debating in class. Furthermore, every English major must take a full-credit course (Ethical Public Speaking and Debate) in order to graduate. Thus, the formal study of argument and debate is now a part of the school's brand. Prospective students understand that they will receive extensive training in the subject. Therefore, they are likely to graduate with considerable English writing and speaking skills. This can only help the school recruit excellent students.

It is for all of these reasons that Ethical Communication, with its argument-centered and debate-related tools can benefit the managers, educators, and students of the TNE community. With this chapter, the process of "debatification" can begin. Specifically, this chapter introduces 15 tools that anyone within the TNE community can utilize to begin the debatifying process of thinking and composition. These extant pedagogical moves have already proved to bring forth the types of critically thinking, communicationally competent, authentically confident, and problem-solving young people that the world now needs more than ever.

THEORETICAL FOUNDATION

Throughout the centuries, philosophers, speakers, and thinkers from both China and the United States have unequivocally declared that any excellent speaker cannot, by definition, be exceptional without operating from a high moral character adhering to an enduring, ethical code of conduct. (Trapp, 2016, p. 17)

Table 1. Definitions

Terms	Definitions
Argument	A sophisticated grouping of rhetorical elements, words, and sentences, artfully arranged into configurations that maximize their persuasive effect.
ACE	A set of tools that allow teachers and learners to act as partners in an active process of intellectual inquiry that seeks the generation of ethical ideas while pursuing enhanced critical thinking and improved written and oral expression. ACE can be thought of as the engine of an ethical-communication-based curriculum which can encompass writing, public speaking, and informal debate exercises and assessments.
Debatify	A colloquial term meaning to utilize tools from competitive debate in a language arts curriculum.
Generative debate	A style of intellectual inquiry that does not pursue victory as in a competitive or tournament debate. Instead, this style of inquiry sets up scaffolds that lead participants toward generating new and valuable ideas through the course of analysis of issues and composition of texts. Generative debate is suitable for practical teaching and learning in ways in which competitive debate is not.
Ethical communication	An approach to rhetorical compositions of all types that emphasize a sense of responsibility on the sender's part to avoid messaging that will purposely create negative outcomes in society. Specifically, ethical communication adheres to the following principles: · Speakers and writers commit to encouraging unity instead of disunity. · Speakers and writers commit to helping generate nonviolent solutions to human being's inevitable differences of opinion.
Rhetoric	Rhetoric is a set of tools that provide frameworks for improved composition, persuasion, analysis, and critical thinking. Rhetoric can be metaphorically understood as the foundation of argument and the glue which connects writing, public speaking, and debate together into a cohesive whole.
Scaffolding	Scaffolding consists of the activities provided by the educator, more competent peer or rhetorical/ argumentative tool to support the student as they are led through the zone of proximal development (ZPD). This support decreases as it becomes unnecessary, much as a scaffold is removed from a building during construction. The result is an autonomous learner able to use presently mastered skills to take on increasingly challenging tasks.
ZPD	The ZPD describes the difference between a learner's limited achievements without help and what a learner can achieve with guidance and encouragement from a skilled partner. Thus, the term "proximal" refers to those skills that the learner is "close" to mastering. While in this "zone," learners are being challenged and making gains. Thus, getting students into the ZPD should be the goal of every academic activity.

Societies flourish or decline based on the collective decisions their people make (Trapp, 2016). Therefore, it is logical to consider that the most persuasive individuals, those who can convince others of what future paths need to be taken to advance society and solve its problems, are those who can also have an extraordinarily disproportionate effect on the quality of societal outcomes.

With this in mind, Trapp places the importance of quality persuasion as central to the greater societal good. He writes about the important roles persuasive writers and speakers have played in both ancient Chinese and ancient western (Greek/Roman) contexts. This fits his role as a transnational educator who taught debate in China and the United States. Many of these students have gone on to teaching careers, thus carrying forth his message about the importance of good writing, clear speaking, and principled debate (Trapp, 2016).

Ethical communication is derived from these principles. Trapp frames human conflict to be inevitable. This means that any study of human society will show that humans will always disagree with each other. Different interests, different ideas of how to solve problems, and different outlooks on life will always have the potential to create angry clashes over these differences. Thus, responsible members of society must ask themselves: Must these differences always lead to negative outcomes in society, or is there a better way?

Ethical communication is that better way. Since humans will always disagree, why not exercise restraints on the negative outcomes of these inevitable disagreements? This is done by placing guardrails on persuasive communication efforts. Instead of using words to attack others, exacerbate tensions or encourage strife within society, humans would instead limit themselves to debating and critiquing ideas, not criticizing those who hold those ideas. Hence, the author may summarize an ethical communicator as one who:

- Communicates with the intent to increase, not decrease, unity within societies and the larger world.
- Communicates with a problem-solving mentality that aims to help humans find nonviolent solutions to individuals' inevitable differences.

Whether it entails writing an essay for class or an article for a newspaper or a social media blog, whether it is preparing a persuasive speech or a debate on an important topic, the responsible communicator maintains a sense of responsibility to the greater good. The composer is always conscious not to make the divisions in society and the world worse with their words. Before hitting send, before making that speech, and before turning in that essay, the ethical communicator asks: "Am I contributing to the greater good by putting these words into the world?"

As Trapp (2016) teaches, there will never be a day when humans will not disagree with each other. These disagreements can lead to devastating outcomes such as deglobalization, decoupling, and even war. Therefore, people of goodwill must always face this question: "What can an individual do to help make a better tomorrow?"

Training to be an ethical communicator is a good answer. However, it must be admitted that formal debates, whether they are on cable news, Youtube or primetime television during an election year, are rarely ethical. When speakers are trying to defeat an opponent, the tenets of competitive debate can hinder quality discussion. In the thirsty pursuit of a victory, the journalist or presidential candidate is likely to choose a position and stick to it regardless of what contradictory evidence might be presented. This is not what is taught in the TNE community. Instead, TNE can rise above unethical communication styles and begin to apply generative debate across the curriculum.

According to Trapp (2016), generative debate is largely an ideological construct, as it does not occur between competitors. As the term implies, the goal of generative debate is to generate reasoned arguments grounded in effective evidence toward a goal of peacefully managing or resolving problems created by disagreeing ideas. Importantly, the disagreement is characterized as existing between ideas, rather than persons (Trapp, 2016). Therefore, in a classroom setting, generative debaters, even when they are advancing opposing ideas, can be considered teammates. They are teammates because together they are exercising critical thinking, improving communication skills, and engage in cooperative efforts to discover truths often hidden below the surface of common narratives.

Whenever individuals use argument as the primary teaching and learning tool, while pursuing answers to issues or solutions to problems, they practice generative debate. This can take the form of classroom discussion, friendly debates, argument writing assignments or any related assessment based on language arts.

The key difference is quality. For example, name-calling or questioning an ideological opponent's ulterior motives can hardly be considered quality conversation. Such inarticulate communication could best be labeled quarreling. The argumentative approach introduces the requirement that quality argument rests on claims based on evidence, logic, and reasoning. Such standards move readers to recognize new problems and consider new solutions

Hence, people's understanding of argument is that is it ethical and generative, and its quality rises with the amount of carefully considered logic and evidence it includes. These are the guardrails that composers of written and spoken texts are to keep in mind as they decide to engage in persuasive effort that lead to positive outcomes in society. Based on these parameters, the following section provides a demonstration of how ACE works.

THE ARGUMENT-CENTERED EDUCATION TOOLBOX

"Most of the things about which we make decisions, and into which therefore we inquire, present us with alternative possibilities" (Aristotle et al., 1954).

What follows is a series of exercises that take place at the start of a debate called "motion analysis." These tools allow debaters to unpack, analyze, and prepare an intelligent response to any issue, question or problem. In competitive debates, participants are trained to go through these basic steps to understand a given issue from multiple sides and prepare a speech or essay to argue for or against the given topic.

Along this demonstration, the following points have to be kept in mind:

- The tools are flexible. They can be used for writing, public speaking or formal debate purposes. They may be used only to spark intelligent conversations. They may also be modified to suit individual preferences.
- These are the most basic tools. The field of argument is vast enough that there are always new discoveries. However, the tools demonstrated here are more than sufficient for any teacher or learner to get started. Once autonomous learner status is achieved, the study of argument can last a lifetime.
- Each tool can be used as a standalone exercise, discussion or assignment. It is not necessary to try to use them all at once.
- These tools can be used in generative debate, meaning no winners or losers need to be declared (unless teachers and learners want to engage in actual competition). Instead, the purpose is to generate ideas, spark conversations, and further one's understanding of issues and problems.
- At the end of the demo, the following question may test the quality of the content of this chapter: Can these tools generate enough questions, information, arguments, and material to spark a fruitful conversation, get started writing an essay, begin a research project on the topic discussed, prepare a formal speech or participate in a debate? If the answer is yes, then an understanding of the power of ACE has been achieved.

Tool 1: Motion/Resolution Analysis

The "debatification" process starts by taking a systematic look at an issue or a problem. These are commonly known as motions or resolutions. They are prompts for thinking, speaking, writing or generative discussion. They are usually, but not always, based on a real-world problem. The objective of this first step is to decide which tools can be applied to resolve the motion in the form of new arguments in support or refutation of the topic. Below are several typical motions/resolutions.

This House Would Use Artificial Intelligence to Replace the Current Criminal Justice System

The word "house" represents a theoretical house of parliament or congress. This wording sets the stage for simulating the types of problem-solving activities that would take place in actual decision-making bodies. Here, the verb "would" prompts debaters to create arguments that include specific actions or policies to be implemented. Hence, arguments supporting the truth of this motion might focus on how this could be implemented using modern technology that exists to reduce bias in judicial rulings or sentencings.

This House Supports the Implementation of Universal Basic Income

The word "support" identifies this as another value motion, meaning writers or speakers should argue from the perspective of what is right and wrong, in addition to considering concrete policy arrangements. Arguments in favor of this motion might aim to convince an audience that a universal basic income (UBI) would benefit nearly everyone in society, because it would reduce crime despite the cost to taxpayers. This could then be looked at as an investment in safety for citizens. As protecting the lives and safety of citizens is a central role of government, supporting this motion could be argued as the morally sound thing to do.

This House Believes That Batman Should Be Arrested!

"This House Believes That" is similar to "This House Supports" in that debaters are expected to focus on the proposal's morality or the greater good the proposal might have in society. For example, arguments in favor of this motion would look for reasons to take a popular hero off the streets. But why? Arguments could be made about the harms of vigilante justice. Perhaps Batman's actions, although popular, undermine the authority of legitimate police forces. Alternatively, maybe Batman has unintentionally inspired copycats who try to fight crime like him, but get themselves hurt because they have neither the resources nor training Batman has.

Resolved: Globalization Has Done More Good Than Harm

The author will unpack this resolution to see how much can be done to generate conversation about a given topic. Here, globalization will be defended against arguments that it should be curtailed because of the harm it creates for individuals and entities worldwide.

Tool 2: Choose Stock Issues

"When discussing the invention of arguments, rhetorical scholars from Aristotle to Perelman have cataloged starting points for the creation of arguments in an attempt to assist arguers with this generative process" (Johnson, 2009, p. 21). These starting points are called stock issues Table 2).

Table 2. Stock issues

Stock Issues (Johnson, (2009)	Subject of Arguments
Cultural	Arguments about the collective identity shared by people in a particular group.
Economic	Arguments concerning financial matters.
Educational	Arguments relevant to the effort to instruct citizens.
Environmental	Arguments about the natural world.
Legal	Arguments related to what is required or prohibited by a society's rules.
Moral	Arguments concerning ethical consequences of a proposition.
Political	Arguments relevant to the acquisition and exercise of power.
Rights	Arguments about freedoms or privileges.
Security	Arguments that address the subject of a nation's safety.
Social	Arguments regarding relationships between people.
Symbolic	Arguments concerning the interpreted meaning of phenomena.
Welfare	Arguments about public health and well-being.

In this context, stock issues mean common issues. They are used as the first step to unpacking the problem and breaking it into smaller and more digestible pieces for analytical purposes. Each subcomponent is a prompt that can be used to create quality arguments during future steps of the analytical process. This tool has another key function. By identifying stock issues, the writer is forced not just to identify two sides of a given problem, but all possible sides. This is an important point because it may often be too simplistic to divide every issue up into two directly opposing sides. This risks making the resultant conversation a dualistic competition. In generative debate, we try to find truth from several perspectives. To find stock issues, simply consider which categories might have something to do with the given topic.

Not all students will choose the same stock issues. Each debater can choose the categories they think fit best. Hence, freedom of thought and choice are already built into upcoming compositions. As Table 3 shows, a debater might choose the economic, educational, and political stock issues for the resolution. Continuing with "Globalization has done more good than harm,"

Table 3. Stock issues – Scaffold

Stock Issue	Scaffold (Language Students Can Use to Get Their Writing Started)
Economic	"Globalization brings up economic issues because it concerns financial transactions between multinational corporations."
Educational	"Globalization brings up important matters of education because TNE schools operate across borders."
Political	"Globalization makes us consider political matters because governments from different regions are forced to interact and maintain peace."

Tool 3: Stasis Theory

"Yet, another way of categorizing arguments is to consider their status or stasis, that is, the specific kinds of issues they address" (Fletcher, 2015). Stasis theory is a series of interconnected questions that help writers and speakers identify points where they should focus their persuasive efforts. In use by speakers since the days of ancient Greece, this tool helps unpack the resolution from different aspects. Combined with stock issues, this tool helps guarantee that multiple sides of any given issue are explored.

Table 4. Stasis questions and student -generated answers

Stasis Question	Student-Generated Answers
What happened?	In the past few years, globalization has been on the retreat.
What are the key terms/definitions (or what is the nature of the issue?)	Governments are decoupling. Supply chains have broken down. Some jobs are being lost.
What is its cause?	The role governments play in economic policies differs in different countries. Nationalism is on the rise based on populism in the media.
What actions should be taken?	Diplomats and journalists should adopt the principles of ethical communication. This will help control nationalist and populist urges because countries will no longer insult each other. This might also provide diplomats with space to have more positive conversations with each other. Over time, this could reverse the deglobalization process.

Tool 4: Stakeholder Analysis

This tool allows to figure out who benefits and who is harmed by globalization. Stakeholder analysis comes from the world of competitive debate and consists of a simple test: "Identify at least three individuals or entities that are somehow affected by the topic. Then, classify each stakeholder as being harmed or benefitting."

Table 5. Stakeholders

Stakeholder	Benefit/Harm
Import-export business owners	These stakeholders benefit from globalization because they can sell their products to potential customers worldwide.
TNE schools	Educators and students in the TNE community benefit from globalization. They get to work and study with colleagues and classmates from multiple continents. This helps them get an excellent education.
Governments	Globalization can actually harm some governments or political leaders because, when citizens from different countries can get along harmoniously, populist and unethical messages are less effective. Hence, the bombastic and communicationally-incompetent leader may even lose the next election. Therfore, it is necessary to consider the counterintuitive idea that, even for self-interested and nationalistic politicians, promoting deglobalization and decoupling might turn out to be a bad idea for them.

Stakeholder analysis tells that two of the three identified stakeholders benefit from globalization. This is evidence allows to argue that globalization brings the world more good than harm.

Tool 5: Assertion, Reasoning, Example/Evidence, and Impact

Assertion, reasoning, example/evidence, and impact (AIRE) make a practical tool for building a complex argument. AREI also functions as an excellent structure for a single paragraph or even part of a longer essay.

Table 6. Elements

Elements	Explanation
A stands for assertion.	The raw idea being put forward in an effort to persuade. The A is what the speaker wants to prove.
R stands for reasoning	The logical support added to the assertion to build argumentative power.
E stands for either specific evidence or a specific example.	A concrete piece of information to prove the assertion true.
I stands for impact.	Perhaps the most important element of AREI. The impact is why the assertion matters. The I answers the question that every speaker should ask themselves as they build an argument: "Why does this matter to my audience, why should they care?" When properly constructed, an AREI argument can be a formidable piece of persuasion.

Considering Tool 2, each of the three stock issues could be developed into three AREIs. Alternatively, each stakeholder could be turned into an AREI. All of the tools can be used interchangeably. Hence, building arguments will begin to resemble a creative activity. Choosing to expand on the economic stock issue, an AREI structure might look like the following:

Table 7. AREI

AREI	Scaffold and Possible Verbiage
Assertion (employing the economic stock issue)	"We believe that widespread economic benefits of globalization are among the most compelling reasons to believe it does more good than harm."
Reasoning	"That is positive because globalization has allowed each country to maximize its comparative advantage. This results in highly efficient supply chains and lower prices."
Example/evidence	"For example, since most Apple products are made in China, they are more affordable for consumers all over the world."
Impact	"This matters because when people feel richer, they usually feel more satisfied with their lives. Furthermore, when everyone can afford premium products such as the latest iPhones, a feeling of equality can spread. This results in more stable societies around the world."

Tool 6: "Yes, and..."

It is crucial to remember that there is no such thing as a perfect argument. All arguments can be refuted. Every argument contains some type of fallacy that a skilled debater can uncover.

This fact reflects the conditions of the real world. As Stanford economist Thomas Sowell (2014) said of efforts to solve problems or resolve major societal debates, "there are no solutions, there are only trade-offs". Therefore, when working with argument, teachers and learners should suspend the human instinct to find fault with or immediately declare any argument "right" or "wrong."

Instead, in a "debatified" educational environment, teachers and learners elicit further elaboration and strengthening of arguments by employing the "yes, and..." phrase. This validates the student's response while also inviting them to provide more evidence, better logic or more reasoning to add persuasive power to the arguments they are building step by step.

For example, when confronted with the challenge of arguing in favor of the economic benefits of globalization, upon hearing the first answer, "...because it results in lower prices." An ACE-trained teacher will not immediately judge or look for faults. Instead, the conversation should go something like this:

"Yes, lower prices, and?"

"Well, lower prices lead to higher consumption."

"Yes, and?"

"Higher consumption means better profits for most businesses."

"Yes, and?"

"Better profits means more jobs, more prosperity."

Obviously, these points can all be rebutted. For example, an opposing argument might take exception to the idea that better profits will mean increased hiring. Moreover, some businesses might use those extra profits not to provide more jobs, but to pay dividends to wealthy shareholders.

In a reflection of how the real world works, there is often truth to the arguments of both sides. Therefore, in the ACE system, remaining flexible is more important than finding immediate rights or wrongs. What matters more quickly than judging whether to agree or disagree with someone's argument is the elevated quality of the conversation, the critical thinking sparked, and the continuous search for truth in a civil environment where no one is insulting each other. Adding the guardrails of unity and nonviolence allows to see how argument-centered and ethical and highly intellectual conversations can work. The author argues that such conversations can better human relations one dialog at a time.

Tool 7: Rhetorical Structures - The Classical Oration

Making powerful arguments and communicating with eloquence can be achieved by anyone who pays careful attention to structure. A good structure can create logic just by its form.

The tools of classical rhetoric provide good structures. Using such tools, which have been proven effective since ancient Greece and Rome, ensure the ability to communicate with clarity. The classical oration is an excellent choice for building an argument. "This structure is powerful because it covers all the bases: Readers or listeners want to know what your topic is, how you intend to cover it, and what evidence you have to offer" (Lunsford & Ruszkiewicz, 2015).

Table 8. The classical oration

Section and Function*	Scaffold and Possible Verbiage
Exordium: Gain the attention and goodwill of the audience by urging them forward to support the argument.	"Resolved: Globalization has created more good outcomes for the world than harm. Therefore, we urge our fellow citizens to support proglobalization candidates."
Narratio: Provide the background and context of the issue at hand.	"In 2022, globalization is under attack from multiple directions. Populism and nationalism are spreading. Economic dislocation and inequality have led some to believe that decoupling economies should happen. However, careful analysis has led others to believe that globalization should continue."
Partitio: Provide the audience a logical and easy-to-follow division of the topic.	This speech will contain three arguments. Two arguments will be built according to the economic and educational stock issues. They will be structured using AREI. The third argument will be based on stakeholder analysis. Counterarguments will then be addressed. This essay/speech/ article will conclude with a summary.
Confirmatio: Confirm the case by providing the specific arguments.	1. "There are significant economic benefits to the continuation of globalization to include..." 2. "TNE is another excellent reason to support globalization..." 3. "Stakeholder analysis reveals that internationally minded entrepreneurs and international students benefit from globalization..."
Refutatio: Engage and respond to opposing arguments or evidence.	"It must be admitted that globalization harms some. However, their disadvantages can best be turned into advantages with more, not less, internationalization."
Peroratio: Summarize the case and move the audience forward to accepting towards acceptance.	"Globalization is not perfect. However, it is the best way to improve the lives of most stakeholders. With the evidence and reasoning provided, it is clear that humanity should continue this process as it delivers more good than harm."

Note: *these are Latin terms with Latin spelling.

Tool 8: Rhetorical Structures - Concept Sets

Coming up with an idea and turning it into a structured argument is an excellent skill for teachers and learners to possess. This can be thought of as push-thinking.

However, it can also work the other way around. For example, starting with a structure in the form of the concept sets depicted below (Table 9) can help pull an argument into being. For example, by choosing the "past-present-future" concept set, a debater may be compelled to build a composition starting with the history of globalization. Next, the present state of globalization will be discussed to include arguments related to whether it delivers more good than harm. Finally, the structured essay or speech would conclude with a discussion of what the future of globalization may hold for the world (Johnson, 2009).

Table 9. Concept sets (Johnson, 2009)

Concept Sets
Past-Present-Future
Idealism-Realism
Moral-Pragmatic
General Principle-Specific Instance
Social-Political-Economic
Diplomatic Influence-Economic Influence-Military Influence
Domestic-Foreign
National-Regional-Global
Problem-Cause-Solution
Cause-Effect
Behaviors-Motivation
Individual-Community
Empirical-Logical
Scientific-Spiritual

Tool 9: Rogerian Rhetoric

The sophisticated and high-quality conversations that ethical communication and ACE encourage require more than just one person making good points. True dialogue requires sincere listening. In other words, it is just as important to learn how to listen as it is to learn how to speak.

Table 10. Section and function

Section and Function	Possible Responses
Introduction: Describe an issue or a problem in detail to show respect for the opposing side.	The other side supports deglobalization and decoupling for several good reasons, such as the loss of jobs in certain parts of the developed world and a disagreement over important values.
Contexts: Describe a situation in which the opposing side's opinions would be valid.	In certain contexts, they are right. The fact is countries and their cultures can be very different. Also, many jobs have been lost and different countries indeed hold values that are not the same.
Writer's position: Provide arguments and explain how it is correct in the present circumstance.	However, due to robotics, artificial intelligence technology, and social changes in developed worlds, no amount of deglobalization and decoupling will bring those factory jobs back. Additionally, just as individuals in Western countries are taught to get along with people of different religions and ethnicities, nation-states can do the same. Cultural diversity is good for individuals so surely it can be good for the countries in which they live.
Benefits to opponents: Explain how the opposing side would benefit.	Since factory jobs will not be coming back, young people in a globalized world can be encouraged to choose education over attempts to find factories in which to toil away. TNE can help them grow into an internationally-oriented person who can travel to countries that offer the best employment prospects. Moreover, surely these people-to-people contacts could eventually lead to better relations among countries, even those with different cultures or styles of government.

Listening is a skill that can be practiced and improved. A well-known 20th Century psychologist named Carl Rogers used his vast experience counseling couples to come up with a style of argument that accomplishes these goals. The key idea of the Rogerian structure is to listen and strive for a full understanding of opposing opinions before responding (Lunsford & Ruszkiewicz, 2015).

Tool 10: The Toulmin Model

Invented by a British philosopher in the 1950s, Toulmin rhetoric is designed so that ordinary people, students, teachers, lawyers, and businesspersons could make skillful arguments. Powerful and practical, "Toulmin's system acknowledges the complications of life situations when we qualify our thoughts with words such as sometimes, often, presumable, unless, and almost" (Hillocks, 2011, p. 6).

Table 11. Component

Component	Scaffold
Claim	Globalization should be supported because it creates the conditions for a better world for our children and children's children.
Support	For example, TNE is a product of a globalized world. TNE puts educators and young people of various nationalities in the same classrooms. Through cross-cultural contact, they gain understanding and empathy. Furthermore, it can help people figure out how to travel to different countries to maximize their comparative advantages, leading to better employment opportunities.
Warrant	We should support systems that can help young people reach self-actualization and lead to humans with more empathy and, possibly, more money.
Backing	For example, schools like NYU-Shanghai, Xi'an Jiaotong Liverpool University all provide students the opportunities to study in their home country and spend time in at least one other country. This improves their language ability, helps them understand different business cultures, and ultimately gives them more employment choices than non-TNE schools.
Qualification	This does not mean we ignore the job losses and other negative aspects of globalization. We understand that not everyone wins when the world changes rapidly.
Refutation	However, it is clear that opportunities related to education and cultural exchange can bring prosperity and peace to most people in the world. For these reasons, it should be supported.

Tool 11: Logical Fallacies

These help identify and label flawed or poorly constructed arguments. For example, some might argue that since politicians benefit from the breakdown of globalization, the supporters of those leaders' political parties should favor deglobalization and decoupling.

However, this is a fallacy called "hasty generalization." This means the argument does not fully consider the ways the politician may be harmed. For example, tariffs are a tool of deglobalization, but they are known to bring inflation. Such inflation is likely to make consumers angry. It might even harm the antiglobalization politician. The end result could be that the leader loses the next election. Therefore, the argument that deglobalization can be good for certain politicians failed to consider the possible consequences. The argument was too hastily put together. The ACE-thinker must always be on a quest for deeper analysis.

Table 12. Fallacy

Fallacy	Verbiage
Ad hominem: Attacks the individual instead of the argument.	"Some say globalism is bad, but that is only because they are too lazy to work hard and compete in the globally connected world."
Ad populum: Appeal to patriotism, not logic.	"We should support globalism because with our advantages in trade and hard power, we will surely dominate all the other small countries in the world. That is why we should support globalism."
Card stacking: Selecting only the evidence that supports a friendly argument while ignoring existing evidence to the contrary.	"Globalism is perfect because it leads to the creation of much wealth for each and every person on earth. Since all people benefit globalization is a perfect system."

Tool 12: Refutation

Although many rhetorical structures for rebuttal and refutation are available, many are highly complex. Nevertheless, for the purposes of this toolbox, the ICE protocol is sufficient. The I stands for identify the argument to be refuted; the C stands for critique the argument, and the E means elaborate on why the rebuttal matters (Johnson, 2009). Table 13 provides an example.

Table 13. ICE protocol

ICE Protocol	Verbiage
Identify the counterargument	"Some say that globalization leads to an unacceptable loss of sovereignty."
Critique the counterargument	"However, we believe that such an argument commits the card-stacking fallacy because it focuses only on the negative aspects of a rules and respect-based international order."
Elaborate on why it matters.	"This matters because, when we respect the affairs and customs of other countries, even if they are different from ours, we are repaid for that respect with economic gains that benefit our own people. Additionally, if we are willing to respect the international community's rules, it can help us maintain positive diplomatic relations with most countries in the world. These are positive outcomes of globalization that our opponents fail to discuss."

Tool 13: Graham's Hierarchy of Refutation

This tool constantly reminds that individuals should focus their refutational efforts on staying near or at the top of this pyramid. Name-calling and *ad hominin* attacks are unethical. However, by critiquing the idea and not the arguer, the quality of all conversations is improved, despite the possibility of sharp differences of opinion.

Tool 14: Moral Philosophy – Maslow's Hierarchy of Needs

Models such as Maslow's hierarchy can help build robust arguments that can stand up to vigorous challenges. Employing such moral philosophies can add context, credibility, and eloquence to any essay, speech or generative conversation.

Figure 1. Graham's hierarchy of refutation (Meyer, 2022)

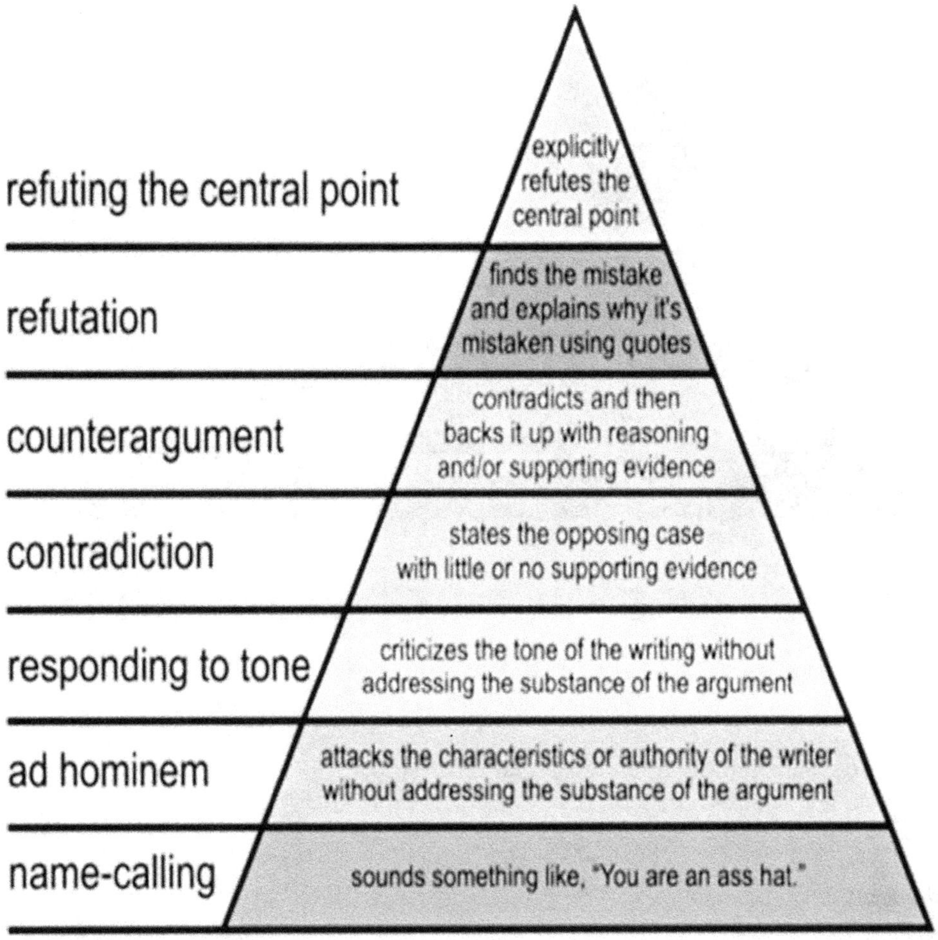

For example, one might credibly argue that Batman should not be arrested. This argument is based on the fact that a responsible government should provide the opportunity for citizens to rise to the top of Maslow's pyramid. However, citizens cannot reach the good life or self-actualization, if they must worry about their safety every day. Since the government has failed to keep citizens safe in recent years, vigilantes such as Batman are justified in their actions.

Tool 15: Moral Philosophy - Justice

Harvard's Michael J. Sandel (2010) defines justice as members of society getting what they deserve and need from a given policy. He provides an analytical tool to determine the good and the bad of certain motions or resolutions:

- **Welfare:** Does the policy or value support the general well-being of the people?
- **Virtue:** Does the policy or value encourage virtuous behavior among citizens?
- **Freedom:** Does the policy or value support freedom within the society?

Figure 2. Maslow's hierarchy of needs (Mcleod, 2020).

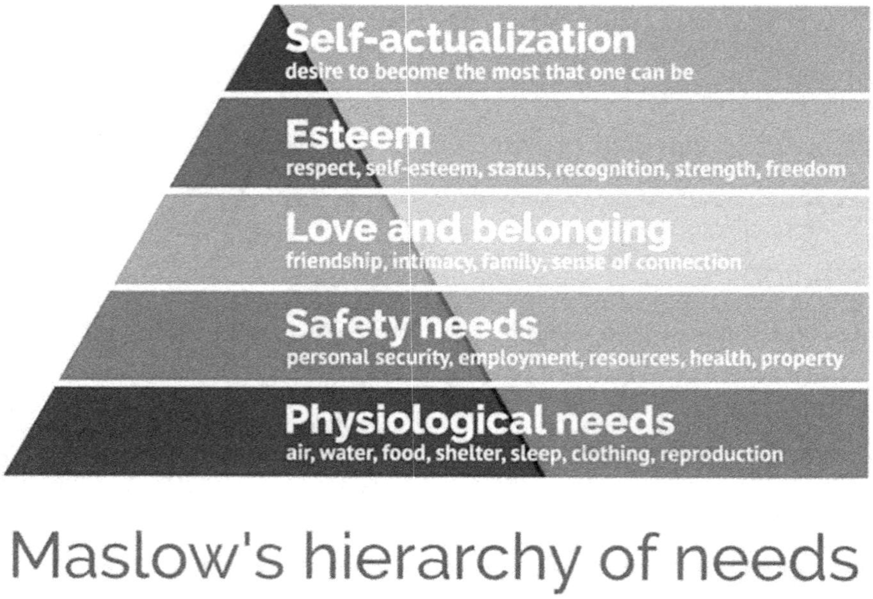

Table 14 provides an example referring to the UBI topic.

Table 14. Elements

Elements	Verbiage
Welfare	"As UBI supports the public's welfare as it would effectively eliminate severe poverty.
Virtue	"A UBI might support the virtue of society, because the general public is freed from the burden of jobs they do not like, are able to follow their dreams, and contribute more art and enjoyment to the society, thus reaching the top of Maslow's hierarchy. However, a UBI might decrease virtue as it would encourage some not to work at all."
Freedom	"A UBI would place a big tax burden on most successful people. They are likely to interpret that as a loss of freedom. This would create widespread resentment within the society as some citizens would subsidize the possibly non-working lifestyles of others."
Conclusion	"Since the justice test does not show a clear consensus on what should be done about UBI, perhaps it would be better not to force it on society, at this time. Such a course of action would be divisive and possibly lead to violence. This goes against the principles of ethical communication. Therefore, our class will not publicly argue for the implementation of a UBI because jeopardizing the peace and stability of the society is a negative outcome that we do not want to encourage."

BENEFITS OF THE ARGUMENT-CENTERED APPROACH

Benefit 1: Rhetoric on New Teaching Expertise

ACE gives teachers new expertise. ACE can be understood as an umbrella with argument-writing, public speaking, and debate underneath. The common thread linking those three disciplines together is rhetoric. Thus, by learning to understand and wield one craft, namely rhetoric, teachers can teach three crafts, namely argument writing, public speaking, and debate.

"Rhetoric targets the conventions and processes of high academic literacy, including the sophisticated responsiveness to the context that characterizes college and workplace writing," according to Fletcher (2015). She uses the word "writing" here, but rhetoric is flexible, so it is useful in teaching and learning debate and public speaking, too.

Rhetoric—in addition to being versatile—has always been both eminently rigorous and practical. Throughout the centuries, rhetoric has been a remarkably adaptive means to prepare critical thinkers and effective communicators for real-world decisions. Rhetoric develops what literacy researchers Richard Beach, Amanda Haertling Thein, and Daryl Parks identify as an equalizing competency for working-class teens: The ability to negotiate the competing demands of diverse social worlds. (Fletcher, 2015)

Benefit 2: Social Learning, With Society in Mind

An influential researcher in the field of education was Russian psychologist Lev Vygotsky. According to Gibbons (2014), Vygotsky offered sociocultural theory as an explanation of how students learn. This theory "sees human development as social rather than individualistic...In a very real sense, what and how we learn depends very much on the company we keep". Moreover, what kind of company does ACE-learning group together? Students focused on exchanging arguments verbally or *engaging* deeply with the ideas of others in their writing. The word *engagement* comes from competitive debate and means fully understanding and responding to those who hold opposed ideas. This is different and deeper than simple persuasion.

In Hillocks's (2011) view, "The most advanced secondary textbooks for English do not teach students to think critically or to write argument. Rather, they opt for vague discussion of *persuasive writing*". This raises a crucial point: Persuasion is not exactly the same as *argument.* To persuade means one simply picks the most favorable evidence, dresses it up, and tries to convince someone else. This is a crucial human activity and good teachers teach students how to do it. However, *argument* is much more sophisticated.

Disinformation is designed to *persuade.* Fake news is designed to *persuade.* Neither of these tend to do society much good in the long run. However, *argument* is, Hillocks continues, "about logical appeals and involves claims, evidence, warrants, backing and rebuttals...argument is at the heart of critical thinking and academic discourse; it is the kind of writing students need to know for success in college and in life".

Thus, the educator who can wield *argument* as a teaching tool is immediately distinguished because they will be seen as one who is presenting something related, but also totally different from the norm. The ACE teacher is not teaching students to form their own narrow opinions and repeat them over and over to the world with the expectation that someone's mind will be changed. Instead, the ACE teacher cultivates students who think more *communally.* For composing an argument is not fully an act of individuality. According to Fletcher, *when we analyze and develop arguments, we have to consider more than just the printed word on the page. We have to consider the full social world in which the argument does its work. Arguments try to accomplish something; they seek a specific outcome, a change in people's actions or beliefs. To change people's minds, we must first understand them.*

Understanding others. Looking into important issues more carefully. Deciding to contribute to ingoing societal conversations, but remaining determined not to make the situation worse with careless words. In this chapter, the author argues that these worthy goals can be accomplished through the "debatification" or TNE curriculums.

Benefit 3: The Process vs. Product Dichotomy Is Overturned

Many teachers struggle with getting students to think through the process without rushing to finish the assignment. Students may finish the task, but did they fully absorb the teaching objectives?

It is easy to preach that process matters. It is another thing to get students to buy-in. However, ACE argument is both a process and a product

According to the University of Michigan ("*Teaching argumentation*," n.d.),

people who write about argument (and teaching argument) imagine argument as two things:

1. a process of (the *act of*) of inquiry, discovery, and truth-seeking, and
2. a product (an *end result)*—one that includes mature reasoning, understanding, persuasion, and/or Communication.

Neither the process nor the product exists in a vacuum but instead responds to a specific rhetorical situation.

Thus, the ACE teacher does not often lecture. The ACE teacher, instead, asks students questions, presents them with problems to solve, and guides them through the process of creating excellent essays and speeches.

Benefit 4: Lecture-Dependent Teaching Becomes Less Necessary

"Tell me and I forget. Teach me and remember. Involve me and I learn." Ben Franklin

According to Robert Litan (2020) of the Brookings Institute, "students are more likely to remember what they researched and debated than some or even much of the material that is delivered to them in lecture format and then regurgitated on an exam". In the ACE system, the teacher is weaned off of lectures. Once students learn how to argue on paper or debate in class, the teachers' job is simply to feed them challenging problems to solve. Academic arguments, whether meant for writing or speaking, start with prompts, known as motions or resolutions.

These prompts represent real-world topics, questions, problems or issues. Some recent topics engaged by middle school students in China include: Does crypto currency do more good than harm? Does foreign aid help or hinder improved quality of life in developing nations?

After learning to *argue*, students then spend time researching, writing, rewriting, discussing, and debating. They are forced to confront opposing ideas. They often change their minds. They must compose essays and speeches for both sides of the issue. They are no longer the lectured-to; instead, they are now apprentices in their own learning, the teacher taking the role of a facilitator and partner in the experience.

It is often said that the best way to learn something is to teach. Debate-centered education takes this adage up a notch, requiring students not only to teach but also to be persuasive on both sides, requiring anticipation of questions and counterarguments, activities that teacher delivered lectures do not promote. (Litan, 2020)

Benefit 5: Students Learn

"Other students have found that in a high-challenge/high-support curriculum equity gaps diminish and all learners, regardless of background, achieve at higher levels" (Gibbons, 2014).

Lev Vygotsky gifted the teaching community the term ZPD. Students learn when teachers push them out of their comfort zone into their ZPD. However, students will grow frustrated if they are pushed too far or not given sufficient support. To strike the delicate balance between challenge and frustration, educators use *scaffolding*. According to Gibbons, scaffolding can be thought of as "a special kind of help that assists learners in moving towards new skills, concepts or levels of understanding. It is future-oriented and aimed at increasing a learner's autonomy".

Metaphorically, scaffolding is the same as the structures of an unfinished building. Scaffolding is what allows teachers to push students beyond the comfort zone of only being able to write or speak to persuade. Scaffolding is what gives students the ability to advance to the point in which they can compose arguments and have the courage to have them tested in the real world against someone with the opposite opinion. The essence of ACE is scaffolding. ACE itself can be thought of as a set of structures based mostly on classical rhetoric that gives the arguer the ability to read with insight, write with precision, speak with power, and debate with confidence.

With the scaffolding provided by ACE, students are consistently in a high challenge, high support classroom environment.

In such an environment, students become apprentices in their own education. The ACE techniques teach them to be autonomous learners, that is critical thinkers with the skills to understand and engage with society's most complex problems.

RESEARCH BASIS

There is a growing wave of educators and education leaders making the case that argument and debate, as key learning tools, should become much more central than they are in the K-12 curriculum. They maintain that classroom instruction organized around argument and debate across all the academic subjects and grades would engage and educate students far better than the existing curriculum does. (Graff & Birkenstein, 2021)

First, a quick review. ACE focuses on rhetoric and academic argument. Learning this system can give educators the skills to teach argument-writing, public speaking, and debate. The concept of ethical communication orients the words written and spoken toward the good-for-society and healing principles of promoting unity and nonviolence in this historical moment of decoupling, racial conflict, and war. In this chapter, the author further argues that ACE enhances the quality of teaching and learning. However, what is the evidence for such claims?

The acronym comes from the ACE organization, which is a nonprofit that works with school districts to help them implement argument across the curriculum. Amazingly, this includes not just language arts, but also math and science.

The ACE's Web site https://argumentcentered education.com/impact/research-basis/ reports the following findings:

- In a 2004 study that appeared in *The Journal of Adult and Adolescent Literacy*, Mark Felton and Suzanne Herko observed that high school students who engage in structured arguments and debates in the classroom have substantially higher scores on argumentative writing assessments.
- Deanna Kuhn has studied argument-centered instruction for more than a decade. She writes that the biggest academic impact of a curriculum rich in structured argument is how dramatically it can increase the percentage of students who demonstrate college-level writing proficiency, including students who begin in a low-ability grouping.
- In a 2013 study published in *Cognition and Instruction*, Professor Kuhn showed that high school students enrolled in a Columbia University debate-based curriculum for two years outperformed a control group by 41% on a standardized college-level writing assessment.
- In the *Research Appendix* to the *Common Core State Standards*, the authors quote Gerald Graff: college is an "argument culture," and "argument literacy" is the key to college readiness, though currently only 20% of High School graduates are argument literate.
- Deborah Meier (2002), in *The Power of Their Ideas*, summarizes her own research in NYC high schools: a curriculum that places debate and discussion at the core can improve college matriculation and retention by as much as 80% among Title I and at-risk students.
- Mike Schmoker (2007), in *Educational Leadership*, reported that low-income students in Phoenix who were taught core subject areas using a method rooted in "argument literacy" had scores on the Arizona Instrument to Measure Standards exams that were more than twice as high as students in classes that were not argument-centered.
- In three peer-reviewed, carefully controlled studies–published in *The Journal of Negro Education* (2009), *Educational Research and Reviews* (2011), and *The Journal of Adolescence* (2012)–researchers from Virginia University found that Chicago students who participate in academic debate programs are twice as likely to attain the (ACT) college-readiness benchmark in English and 70% more likely to attain the ACT college-readiness benchmark in reading as comparable peers who did participate in academic debate in high school.

https://argumentcentereducation.com/impact/research-basis/

- According to Robert Litan (2020), publishing for the Brookings Institute,

One study published in 2011 by Professor Briana Mezuk, an epidemiologist at the University of Michigan compared the educational performance of debaters and nondebaters in the Chicago Public School district. They find that, even after accounting for the influence of self-selection, debaters were "more likely to graduate from high school, performed better on the ACT, and showed greater gains in cumulative GPA relative to similar comparison students."

Figure 3. Teaching learning zones

LITERATURE REVIEW

The following are the best available publications that inform this style of teaching. With these books on the shelf, any educator can become an expert at the argumentative approach. With the exception of AREI, which is a concept from the Chinese university debate circuit, most of what is set forth in this chapter can be found in the following texts:

- **Fine, G. (2001).** ***Gifted Tongues: High School Debate and Adolescent Culture*****. Princeton University Press.** To understand how high-school students learn to debate and what they get from the activity, Northwestern University Sociologist,, Gary Fine embedded himself in two high schools and followed the teams around for several months. His research concluded that students gained improved writing and speaking skills when compared to nondebaters. Additionally, students felt more confident when the time came for them to apply to university.
- **Gibbons, P. (2014).** ***Scaffolding Language, Scaffolding Learning, Second Edition: Teaching English Language Learners in the Mainstream Classroom*** **(2nd ed.). Heinemann.** Pauline Gibbons teaches as the University of New South Wales and consults with educators from more than a dozen countries. An expert at teaching English to non-native speakers, she stresses the importance of a social learning in which educators aim to get students into their ZPD and using stretched language.
- **Graff, G., & Birkenstein, C. (2018).** ***They Say / I Say: The Moves That Matter in Academic Writing*** **(Fourth ed.). W. W. Norton & Company.** Gerald Graff is a former president of the Modern Languages Association and Cathy Birkenstein is co-director of the Writing in the Disciplines program at the University of Illinois, Chicago. They are both members of the ACE

nonprofit organization. Their text provides easy-to-use templates that students can use to quickly produce well-organized written and spoken arguments.

- **Fletcher, J. (2015).** ***Teaching Arguments: Rhetorical Comprehension, Critique, and Response.*** **Stenhouse Publishers.** Before joining California State University, Monterey Bay as an associate professor of English, Jennifer Fletcher taught high school for a decade. This has given provided insight into the learning styles and processes of a wide age range of students. Her text expounds on the argument-centered teaching process as well as provides practical lesson plans.
- **Hillocks, G. (2011).** ***Teaching Grades 6–12 Argument Writing.*** **Heinemann.** George Hillocks of the University of Chicago has been training some of America's best writing students for more than three decades. His text provides step-by-step instructions any teacher can use to get students as young as eleven years old analyzing and producing their own academic arguments.
- **Johnson, S. (2009).** ***Winning Debates: A Guide to Debating in the Style of the World Universities Debating Championships.*** **International Debate Education Association.** Steven Johnson has coached the University of Alaska debate team to a national championship. Along with Robert Trapp, Johnson was one of the original scholars to introduce debate to China in the early 2000s. The more advanced argumentative techniques can be found in this text.
- **Litan, R. (2020).** ***Resolved: Debate Can Revolutionize Education and Help Save Our Democracy.*** **Brookings Institution Press.** With the world famous thinktank known as the Brookings Institute, Robert Litan has emerged as a major advocate for infusing teaching pedagogy with debate tools. As the title of his book makes clear, he believes that by educating students and future citizens in the tools of argumentation, a better future can be result.
- **Lunsford, A. A., & Ruszkiewicz, J. J. (2015).** ***Everything's an Argument*** **(Seventh ed.). Bedford/St. Martin's.** This text published by professors at Stanford and the University of Texas, Austin has become perhaps the most well-known and most-used text on how to understand and teach academic argument. According to the authors, most of the material has been tested in class with actual students at the Ohio State University, Stanford, and Portland State University. Many of the tools can be found in this book.
- **Sandel, M. J. (2010).** ***Justice: What's the Right Thing to Do?*** **(Reprint ed.). Farrar, Straus and Giroux.** Harvard's Michael Sandel pioneered international education with his wildly popular Justice videos which gave millions of students, especially in China, a peek into his argument-centered moral philosophy course. The book will help educators learn to think like a debater.
- **Trapp, R. (2016).** ***Building global relations through debate.*** **The Foreign Language and Research Press.** One of the original scholars involved in launching China's robust university debate culture, Willamette University's Robert Trapp epitomizes TNE. Prior to retirement, he split his time between teaching in Shanghai and America while also hosting and training a number of Chinese rhetorical scholars. This text provides the history and background of argument and debate and forms the definition of ethical communication.

CONCLUSION

I do not claim that the sources of division in our (world)—economic, cultural, religious, or racial—would be any less intense. Rather, my claim is that many, perhaps even most of us, would react differently to these underlying differences and be more tolerant of them, perhaps even celebrate them or recognize that the diversity of backgrounds and experiences is a strength and not a weakness. (Litan, 2021)

As social media continue to proliferate, it will be increasingly difficult to shield young people from controversies regarding race, gender, gender identity, inequality, deglobalization, decoupling, and demagoguery. Additionally, fake news abounds.

This chapter proposes a response: ACE as a system that empowers teachers and learners to turn any problem into an opportunity for a generative debate. This type of discussion and dialogue can spark critical thinking and new ideas among a group of people. Mutual respect and civility reign.

Furthermore, the author argues that successful countries, especially those from the ancient Greek, Roman, and Chinese philosophical traditions, made the training of citizens to write and speak in ways that promoted the common good a national priority (Trapp, 2016).

Ethical communication picks up and reframes these traditions for the transnational classroom.

The argument-centered approach the author modeled in this chapter is the engine that makes ethical communication work. Trapp defines ethical communicators as those who use their persuasive and argumentative talents to urge their societies to make decisions that lead to flourishing rather than decaying societies. Specifically, ethical communicators shape their words and sentences with two outcomes in mind: unity and nonviolent solutions to problems. Finally, rhetoric is the glue that binds them together into a cohesive whole. Educators and learners that understand these concepts can develop the skills to each writing, public speaking, and debate at a high level of proficiency.

The author of this chapter offers ethical communication as a mission for which anyone can sign up. When educators and learners teach the ACE way, they build confidence. They make arguments. They promote unity and nonviolence. They take responsibility for their words. By doing so, they make a positive difference in the world.

ABOUT THE AUTHOR

The writer of this chapter has taught writing, public speaking, and debate, formerly at Shenzhen University and presently at the Chinese University of Hong Kong, Shenzhen (CUHK,SZ) for a total of fifteen years. He founded and coached the debate teams at both universities. Presently, he trains both the Shenzhen University and CUHK,SZ competitive writing teams which compete in Beijing each year. He coached a Shenzhen-based middle school debate team to a national championship victory in 2020. Along with teaching a course called *Ethical Public Speaking and Debate,* he also tutors and conducts weekly workshops in the CUHK,SZ writing center. He credits the argumentative tools presented in this chapter (along with many others) with most of the success he has attained in his various teaching roles. Rahman K. Smith is from the United States and holds a BA in Political Science from The Ohio State University, an MS in International Relations from Troy University, and an MA in Teaching Writing from Johns Hopkins University.

REFERENCES

Argument-Centered Education. (n.d.). *Home*. Argument Centered Education. https://argumentcenterededucation.com

Aristotle, Roberts, W. R., Bywater, I., & Solmsen, F. (1954). *Rhetoric*. Modern Library.

Fletcher, J. (2015). *Teaching arguments: Rhetorical comprehension, critique, and response*. Stenhouse Publishers.

Gibbons, P. (2014). *Scaffolding language, scaffolding learning: Teaching English language learners in the mainstream classroom* (2nd ed.). Heinemann.

Graff, G., & Birkenstein, C. (2018). *They Say, I Say*. W. W. Norton, Incorporated.

Hillocks, G. (2011). *Teaching grades 6–12 argument writing*. Heinemann.

Huang, C. W., & Archer, A. (2017). "Academic literacies" as moving beyond writing: Investigating multimodal approaches to academic argument. *London Review of Education*, *15*(1), 63–72. doi:10.18546/LRE.15.1.06

Johnson, S. L. (2009). *Winning debates: A guide to debating in the style of the world universities debating championships*. International Debate Education Association.

Lieva, J., Tsiligkiris, V., Killingley, P., & Brandenburg, U. (2021). *Local impact of transnational education: A pilot study in selected European countries*. British Council. https://www.britishcouncil.org/education/he-science/knowledge-centre/transnational-education/local-impact-TNE-Europe

Litan, R. (2020). *Resolved: Debate can revolutionize education and help save our democracy*. Brookings Institution Press.

Lunsford, A. A., & Ruszkiewicz, J. J. (2015). *Everything's an Argument* (7th ed.). Bedford/St. Martin's.

Mcleod, S. (2019, March 24). The zone of proximal development and scaffolding. *Simply Psychology*. https://www.simplypsychology.org/Zone-of-Proximal-Development.html

Mcleod, S. (2020, December 29). Maslow's hierarchy of needs. *Simply Psychology*. https://www.simplypsychology.org/maslow.html

Meyer, C. (2022, June 3). *Graham's hierarchy of disagreement: How to argue like an expert*. The Mind Collection. https://themindcollection.com/revisiting-grahams-hierarchy-of-disagreement/

Norman, A. (2021, May 18). The cause of America's post-truth predicament. *Scientific American*. https://www.scientificamerican.com/article/the-cause-of-americas-post-truth-predicament/

Sandel, M. J. (2010). Justice: What's the Right Thing to Do? (Reprint ed.). Farrar, Straus, and Giroux.

Schädler, T. (2020, May 4). *The role of international schools amid the new anti-globalization sentiment*. Linden Education. https://www.linden-education.com/post/the-role-of-international-schools-amid-the-new-anti-globalization-sentiment

Sowell, T. (2014). *Basic Economics* (5th ed.). Basic Books.

Stafford, S., & Taylor, J. (2016). Transnational education as an internationalisation strategy: Meeting the institutional management challenges. *Journal of Higher Education Policy and Management*, *38*(6), 625–636. doi:10.1080/1360080X.2016.1202811

Trapp, R. (2016). *Building global relations through debate*. The Foreign Language and Research Press.

WMU. (n.d.). *Teaching argumentation*. The University of Michigan Writing Center. https://lsa.umich.edu/sweetland/instructors/teaching-resources/teaching-argumentation.html

Chapter 5
A Curious Case of Formative Assessment: A TNE Perspective in EAP and Beyond

Sebastian Kozbial
University of Nottingham, Ningbo, China

ABSTRACT

The educational value of formative assessment (FA) has been widely acknowledged within higher education. At the same time, there is little consensus on what FA entails, or how it should be defined and understood when looking at the Western education system; this is even more problematic when adapted by TNE institutions. This chapter looks at the definition issues together with key characteristics of quality formative feedback, including the role of the student in co-creating feedback, something that is particularly challenging within the context of this chapter, TNE in China. It looks at the most apparent challenges that are associated with FA implementation within a Chinese higher education context, such as educational heritage and a deep-rooted collectivist approach to learning. It also ventures to propose an alternative conception, formative routines framework FRF), to emphasise the importance of student and teacher training when engaging in formative tasks and using these to support the ongoing development of curricula.

1. INTRODUCTION

An intercultural interaction is neither a question of maintaining one's own cultural frame nor of assimilating to one's interactant's cultural frame. It is rather a question of finding an intermediary place between these two positions – of adopting a third place. In so doing the participant in the interaction is an experiencer, not an observer of difference (Crozet, Liddicoat and Lo Bianco, 1999, p 5).

DOI: 10.4018/978-1-6684-5226-4.ch005

It has been suggested that the demand for higher education programmes around the world will continue to grow and will quadruple its current numbers to 414 million students by 2030 (European Parliamentary Research Service, 2013). This presents an opportunity to countries with well-established and emerging international education industries, including China, to 'export' their 'educational products' to international students (Education at Glance, 2013). This business opportunity comes with inherent pedagogical challenges that are often the result of the characteristics of the target culture, and the business model that frames how educational institutions operate. For instance, a stronger emphasis on profit or revenue generation rather than contributions to society and educational gains is surprisingly proven to be more effective in the long term within the application of Transnational Education (TNE) business sustainability (Dyllick and Muff, 2015). Something that may have a negative effect on the quality of the pedagogical gains for the target students.

TNE in China can be divided into three sector settings:

1. Chinese-foreign cooperation universities (e.g. University of Nottingham Ningbo China, Xi'an Jiaotong-Liverpool University and New York University Shanghai)
2. Chinese-foreign cooperation second-tier colleges (affiliated to Chinese universities; e.g. Sydney Institute of Languages and Commerce at Shanghai University)
3. Chinese-foreign cooperation programmes (Joint Undergraduate Program in Accounting between

Wenzhou University, China and Kean University, the United States) (Hu, Eisenchlas and Trevaskes (2019, p. 308)

With 9 Chinese-foreign cooperation universities, 79 second-tier colleges and a further 1024 cooperation programmes, it is not difficult to tudentr both the scale and impact of such collaborations (Centre of Research on CFCRS, 2018). However, a number of joint ventures have been stopped by China's education ministry. For instance, 30% of 149 Australian and 25% of the 245 UK cooperation programmes opened since 1994 have now been terminated for a number of reasons including a mismatch between foreign staff, students and local authorities' expectations (Sharma, 2018). This suggests that establishing and maintaining a successful TNE initiative can be challenging and does not always lead to successful outcomes.

Several authors (Briguglio, 2000, Heffernan et al., 2010, Mok and Han, 2016, Hu, Eisenchlas and Trevaskes, 2019) have suggested that TNE has evolved into a phenomenon across the global borders of tudentraliza tudentralizationn; however, TNE often falls short of its vision. This might be due to the various stakeholders' differing understanding of 'educational success' and the best way of achieving it. In other words, the differences between host and partner-country in governance, management of staff (Stafford and Taylor, p. 2016), student support (Bhuian, 2016) or implementing foreign clerical support systems by professional services (Henderson, Barnett and Barnett, 2017) could be seen as problematic. Echoing the opening quote, Hu, Eisenchlas and Trevaskes (2019, p. 307) stated that the key challenge to address, mainly by host countries, is 'how to assure the quality of transnational higher education on the one hand and how to maintain a national identity and character on the other'. This can be further tudentraliz when students within a TNE context have minimal exposure and opportunity to interact with other cultures, something that has been increasingly visible throughout the Covid-19 pandemic. These aspects can visibly influence how certain pedagogical initiatives and tools are both understood and implemented by teachers and students.

Using as its focus the example of a British Branch Campus in China (UNNC), this chapter identifies one particular focus for universities, namely, approaches to implementing formative assessment (FA). The importance of this FA assessment related issue is associated with misconceptions of what FA represents, and how it should be used with Chinese students who often perceive FA as an invaluable form of pedagogy. Such key characteristics of FA and formative feedback (Ffe) as dialogical discussions, co-creating learning, peer and self-assessment, reflective thinking and learning directed feedback are all crucial elements of current active learning. At the same time, the majority of students educated in China often struggle with adjusting to the above after joining international universities, as they have different expectations of what constitutes a 'good learner' (Yu and Moskal, 2019, Pham and Hoang Pham, 2021). This is not to suggest that these students are reluctant to adapt or are not willing to take responsibility for their own learning. Rather, it means that TNE professionals tudend carefully consider how to engage their students within such educational experiences and support the adaptation to different expectations these students may face (Kozbial, 2022). The objective of this chapter is not to convince readers of the importance of FA as a valid pedagogical tool, as this is assumed as true and is indicated throughout with reference to research. The key objective is to suggest a workable framework within which FA takes a central role when planning, designing and delivering programmes of studies. In other words to emphasise that FA is not a tool but something far more reaching, which needs a more established and structured approaches in implementation.

This chapter is divided into five sections. The background briefly introduces the theoretical perspective on educational assessment. The second section focuses on the definition of FA, stressing the problematic label (formative assessment) and its implication for teaching-staff and students within a TNE environment, It also identifies the key elements of FA and Ffe. Next, several characteristics of a 'Chinese student' that may be overlooked or misunderstood by international staff are discussed, particularly when considering FA. The penultimate section introduces Formative Routines Framework (FRF), which builds on constructive alignment theory (Biggs, 1999). FRF has been devised to ensure that FA is considered at the curriculum planning and design stage and used with a TNE perspective in mind. Finally, this chapter closes by signalling potential applications of FRF onto one of the predominant assessment theories within HE – learning outcomes assessment. This section also ventures into the importance of reflective learning as necessary to take full advantage of FRF.

2. BACKGROUND

Before focusing on the characteristics of FA, which are further distorted when transferred into TNE in China, a few words to set the context and outline the theoretical perception of the key concepts related to assessment are needed. Language assessments have been used for decades but 1961 when Robert Lado published his work *Language Testing,* is arguably the starting point for institutional assessments as they are known today. The suggestion that testing can be based on 'a systematic linguistic comparison of the two language structures' (Lado, 1967:24) may not now be the most popular, but the principle underlying theory can still be perceived as extremely influential:

Language must be tested in the way in which it is taught; and in the early 1960s teaching orthodoxy was in favour of language components (Davies, 1990:132).

This is particularly important when considering the implementation of varied, and often very different, educational approaches and systems within TNE.

Although approaches to teaching have changed, Lado explicitly states that the assessment should also adapt to what is being done in the classroom. This could also be labelled 'timeless' as 50 years later a similar conclusion is drawn by Bachman and Palmer, who stated that all assessment tasks should be designed and developed in accordance with the teaching plan by both teaching staff and assessment experts (2010, p. 9). This, one may argue, is well implemented within the Chinese educational system where summative approaches to assessment inform and sometimes hijack teaching and influence learning (Chen, Zhang and Li, 2021).

Although terms such as testing, assessment, evaluation, appraisal, estimation or judgement often refer to the same act of looking into a student's performance or work and using this to inform various decisions, there is little consensus about the precise meaning or differences between them amongst practitioners who often use such labels interchangeably. Bachman (2004) suggests that language assessment is an act of gathering information about a learner's language ability. He further expounds that assessment differs from others forms of gathering information as a result of two main factors; *systematicity* and *substantive grounding*.

The first refers to the idea of clear and established procedures that every assessment should adhere to. These are normally prescriptive, replicable and open to scrutiny. This also means that the same piece of assessment can be implemented in different contexts or institutions by different people.

The second quality refers to the idea of 'verifiable area of content' (Bachman and Palmer, 2010, p.20). Examples include a defined chapter in a course book, a course syllabus or widely accepted teaching practices such as observations. It should be mentioned that the notion of labelling or allocating value to something that is used as an assessment event (e.g. essay, poster presentation) usually using a mathematical approach, for instance percentages, is more closely connected with 'evaluation' rather than assessment. In other words, assessment is the process of collecting evidence about a student's knowledge and/or ability, and 'evaluation' refers to the actual process of making judgements based on this evidence, which makes it the main purpose for using assessment (Davies, 1990). One important point relating to the above is the overwhelming notion that summative assessment is generally associated with strict procedures that include both systematicity and substantive grounding whereas FA is not.

Nonetheless, this chapter will use the word 'assessment' as an umbrella term that refers to measurement, evaluation and testing as synonyms and will not focus on distinguishing between these terms.

3. FORMATIVE ASSESSMENT (FA) – THE DEFINITION ISSUE AND…THE IMPORTANCE OF FEEDBACK

It is important to commence this section by highlighting FA as a phenomenon that may seem easy to understand in principle, but which is far more complex on closer inspection. This is particularly important for TNE teaching professionals from differing contexts and who often hold different beliefs regarding FA. Therefore, it is crucial to consider various perspectives and highlight key characteristics, as a lack of clarity when discussing innovation, prevents meaningful discussion and evaluation of its effectiveness.

If we can't clearly define an innovation, we can't meaningfully summarise results across studies because we won't know which instances to include in our summary. Last, we won't be able to transport it to our own context, for how will we know the characteristics on which to focus in doing the transport? (Bennett, 2011:8)

When defining FA, Bennett (ibid., p.1) concludes that 'the term *formative assessment* does not yet represent a well-defined set of artefacts or practices'. This was, of course, over a decade ago but it remains the most recent extensive review paper of the tudentralizatio of FA. Enabling 'administrators to decide whether the entire finished curriculum, refined by use of the evaluation process in its first role, represents a sufficiently significant advance on the available alternatives to justify the expense of adoption by a school system' and 'having 'a role in the on-going improvement of the curriculum' were two main aspects of evaluation identified by Scrivener (1967, pp. 41-42). Scrivener was also one of the first scholars to propose a distinction between 'summative' and 'formative' evaluation in accordance to the two aspects above. For Bloom (1984, p.6), the purpose of formative evaluation was '[…] to provide feedback and correctives at each stage in the teaching-learning process'. Bloom however does not venture his own definition of FA. This could also be paired with Bloom's (1969) general differentiation between formative and summative types of assessments. A summative approach was suggested to evaluate programmes of study, rather than students, at the end of a programme while FA was used to informally gather feedback during the running of this programme (Bennett, 2011).

Another exemplification of FA states that it '[…] is concerned with how judgments about the quality of student responses [output] can be used to shape and improve the stud'nt's competence by short-circuiting the randomness and inefficiency of trial-and-error learning' (Sadler, 1989, p. 119). Here, the author focuses on a continuous aspect of FA, the link with an ongoing use of formative feedback (FFe) and, evidently, its importance tudentraing a learner's inefficient 'trial and error' learning. This could mean, however, that learners in general learn English using the above approach and that this process is random and ineffective. This understanding is a step towards 'formativeness' and 'continuity' but it does not mention who is responsible for feedback creation or how exactly this evidence can or should be used. This was acknowledged by Wiliam and Thompson (2007, p. 9) who stated that:

Practice in a classroom is formative to the extent that evidence about a student achievement is elicited, interpreted, and used by teachers, learners, or their peers, to make decisions about the next steps in instruction that are likely to be better, or better founded, than the decisions they would have taken in the absence of the evidence that was elicited.

This is perhaps a more appropriate and relevant definition in terms of TNE and contexts similar to UNNC. The definition stresses the importance of feedback providers (teachers and students/peers), the context within which the evidence is collected (classroom and not only formal exams) and, finally, the decisions informed by this evidence. However, the reference to 'practice' might be interpreted as any form of teaching that includes elements of FA but which may not be structured or designed based on concrete and established learning objectives – an argument why FA (created by teachers) was often treated as less important than summative assessment (created by assessment experts). Here FA was often described as a product of individual teacher's idiosyncrasy (Bennett, 2011, Clarke, 2014).

Another perspective on understanding FA presented by publishers and test developers describes it as 'an instrument, as in a diagnostic test, an interim assessment' (Bennett, 2010, p. 6). This is a rather dangerous assumption and could lead to the conclusion that allocating a score on its own could be considered developmental, something that has been widely discredited (Black and William, 2009; Bachman and Palmer, 2010, Bennett, 2010, Bennett, 2011, Clarke, 2014 or Green, 2014). There is, of course, certain value in using summative tests as FA tasks but, as it is suggested throughout this chapter, FA is far more than a series of practice exam papers.

It might be safe to assume, therefore, that FA can include tests of various design to elicit evidence of students' performance but it could also be suggested that '[…] formative assessment is not a test but a process' (Popham 2008, p. 6). McManus (2008, p. 3) adds that 'Formative assessment is a process used by teachers and students during instruction that provides feedback to adjust ongoing teaching and learning to improve students' achievement of intended instructional outcomes'. This explanation includes such characteristics as: the involvement of both teachers and students, the context (during the instruction), the use of feedback to guide both teaching and learning and, something that had not been included previously, the link to the learning aims ('intended instructional outcomes'). The final characteristic is particularly important to challenge the notion that FA is often created by non-assessment experts and lacks connection to the final intended learning outcomes (judged by summative assessment). However, as suggested by Bennett (2011), Clarke (2014) and Jones and Saville (2016), a popular misunderstanding atudentralizationion is that any task can be used formatively regardless of its original purpose as long as it results in altering the instruction (e.g. class content, teaching methods), therefore making the argument of well-designed and thoughtfully crafted FA tasks redundant.

FA then might be best conceived as neither a test nor a process, but a thoughtful integration of process and purposefully designed methodology or instrumentation. In addition, calling formative assessment by another name may only exacerbate, rather than resolve, the issue of definition (Bennett, 2011, p. 7).

The above could be treated as a signpost when establishing what FA is and what characteristics are necessary to be included when considering designing FA tasks. The proposal that FA is neither actually a process nor a tool can be treated as insightful because it suggests that FA needs to be skilfully integrated within the syllabus (course design). It requires a clearly defined structure and purpose (who does what when and why), and it should not include tasks that would have been designed with another purpose in mind, as this can skew the overall plan. Using a tool that was designed for another task might only frustrate the users, tutors atudentdents. Moreover, a purposeful and strategic use of FFe could play a crucial role in ensuring that FA is perceived as, at least, equal to summative assessment in terms of importance when discussing curriculum development. The last statement can be extremely powerful in the TNE context of domestic Chinese students, whose learning is often directed towards passing exams as the most crucial outcome of learning (Chen, Zhang, & Li, 2021). Shifting some of the focus from the product (summative assessment) to the process (learning) would be the most important impact of FA within TNE in China.

This can lead to a general conclusion that in order to ensure validity, reliability and, something extremely difficult to maintain with summative exams and tests, to optimise the *positive* washback effects when discussing the application of FA, the following aspects need to be met. FA:

1. is a part of effective planning
2. focuses on how students learn
3. is central to classroom practice
4. is a key professional skill
5. is sensitive and constructive
6. fosters motivation
7. promotes understanding of goals and criteria

8. helps leaners know how to improve
9. develops capacity for self-assessment
10. recognises all educational achievements

To summarise what has been discussed in relation to various definitions, FA can be understood as a skilful integration of meaningful tasks that are designed to 1) support learners development using quality formative feedback, 2) diagnose attainment of intended learning outcomes by gathering quality information, and 3) be used by teachers, learners and their peers as evidence of progress and thus signpost directions for further development.

The term 'assessment', however, can often direct HE professionals, particularly those less familiar with testing and assessment jargon, towards the notion of evaluation or strict judgement. This, in turn, can detract from teaching and development and unintentionally focus on summative understanding of evaluation, for instance using backward looking feedback only. Here one further piece of information should be highlighted: FA also entails focusing on formative feedback (FFe) without using marks. Research shows that when FFe is supplemented by marks, this often diverts students' attention from the usefulness of the comments created by tutors (Nicol & Macfarlane-Dick, 2006, Fluckiger et al., 2010). Although the author understands Bennet's stance (2011, p. 7) that changing the label can add to the confusion, and the term 'assessment' entails an ongoing engagement with evaluating students' output, this only refers to a small part of what the bigger conception of FA, in the author's view point, represents. Therefore, although the term FA has been used throughout this part of the chapter, perhaps a new overarching label should be proposed. This is to illustrate the hypothesis that FA could be better understood as a *theoretical perspective* on how to approach designing curricula and that it could include formative assessment tasks within a given programme. This will be further exemplified in the final section of this chapter. Before this, however, there is an immediate need to focus on the necessity of understanding the key aspects of formative feedback (FFe).

As suggested previously, feedback can be treated as the most powerful tool at any teacher's disposal (Guskey, 2007; Hattie & Timperley, 2007; Sadler, 2010), but under what circumstances can feedback be considered quality or effective in terms of its formative function? The first challenge here, relates to the idea of perception and understanding, as with any written or spoken text. An intention of the feedback creator, either faculty staff or peer (Atmaca, 2016), could be misconstrued by the feedback receiver for a number of reasons including the difficulty or inaccuracy of the language used (Crook et al., 2012) or the usefulness of the feedback, namely a lack of necessary detail and/or personalisation (Carless, 2006; Kim and Bowless, 2019). This is increasingly apparent when considering students for whom English is not a mother language or when the education beliefs of the involved (creator/receiver) are at odds. Another crucial issue mentioned in literature links to timing. Feedback should be provided soon after the event that it refers to, so it is still fresh in the student's mind. Simultaneously, students should have sufficient time to apply this feedback before the following submission that is directly linked to the feedback process. Focusing on mark justification (summative feedback) rather than being created for developmental purposes (formative, feeding forward feedback) should also be taken into consideration when training teachers and students in FFe (Nicol & Macfarlane-Dick, 2006; Hattie & Timperley, 2007; Carless & Boud, 2018). Another aspect of feedback is slightly more contentious, particularly in the TNE context, and it is based on the assumption that learners are not as interested in feedback as they are in their marks (Carless, 2006). Therefore, the way in which feedback is delivered should also be considered as crucial, as the one directional approach where comments of one's work are delivered without a possibility of discussion or further queries is no longer acceptable as effective for the majority of HE learning (Hounsell, McCune, Hounsell & Litjens, 2008; cited in Planar & Moya, 2016, p. 197). It needs to be emphasised that providing even high quality feedback by itself is not enough to see appropriate outcomes (Guskey, 2007), especially if we are considering students who are not familiar with how to engage and respond to feedback. In order to ensure that FFe aims at supporting students' development beyond one particular task, it is crucial to have a bigger picture in mind that focuses on enhancing learners' knowledge on how to improve and how to learn. In the context of TNE in China, this can be particularly problematic as many university programmes exclude activities such as 'working with feedback', 'understanding feedback' or relating feedback to a holistic improvement that a student makes throughout one particular module or better still, an academic year. This lack of non-graded and qualitative evidence of a student's progress should be addressed together with idea of the feedback users, the students, being more reflective. This could be labelled as increasing feedback users' proficiency in applying and working with qualitative comments to support learner independence in thinking about learning (Nicol & Macfarlane-Dick, 2006; Ritchhart, Church and Morrison, 2011).

Summarising the above, Hattie and Timperley (2007) suggested four different levels of feedback that include:

- Focus on task (provides comments on the answer's correctness or offers guidance on obtaining more information)
- Focus on the process (information about the strategies used to approach and complete the task as well as suggesting alternative approaches)
- About self-regulation (might comment on self-confidence or encourage appropriate help-seeking behaviour)
- About the person (use of praise or criticism)

Nicol and Macfarlane-Dick (2006) proposed an FFe model established on the above, suggesting seven principles of effective formative feedback related to self-regulation within learning. They suggest that FFe needs to provide high quality and actionable information to students about their learning; be easy to understand and encourage students to improve their work; and include both strengths and areas to improve. These characteristics, of course, are broad and could be interpreted differently in different contexts. Providing feedback in a timely fashion for instance, could mean something different within a year-long programme and for learners doing high-stakes intensive courses for eight weeks (see Fluckiger et al., 2010; Fisher, Cavanagh, & Bowles, 2011 or Evans, 2013). However, it is important to note at this point that there are key guiding principles that should be used when designing courses of study and preparing teaching staff for delivery. It has also been suggested that:

... the assessment system needs to be structured around a series of learning activities which enable students to master the contents and to form an adequate representation of the objectives and evaluation criteria whilst at the same time familiarizing themselves with the regulation and control tasks (Planar & Moya, 2016, p. 198).

This means that HE professionals should pay attention to the design and use of assessments and feedback (FFe in particular) in order for students to develop self-regulation. Therefore, FFe should be approached with more care and attention to ensure maximum effectiveness. It is also important to train

EAP learners and tutors how to give and receive FFe. This has also been acknowledged within the wider scope of HE (Nicol & Macfarlane-Dick, 2006; Carless, 2006).

4. THE TRANSITION ISSUE FOR A 'CHINESE LEARNER'

Biggs and Tang (2011) discuss 'academic' versus 'non-academic' students, noting the importance of sparking and supporting engagement with active teaching approaches that need to be far more engaging for the latter group. Therefore, a key difference could be the intrinsic 'interest' exhibited by these two groups. However, the idea of social/educational standards and norms, which may predetermine how learners perceive their own roles and responsibilities within a classroom, might be equally important when considering the context for domestically educated Chinese students in the context of a UK university in China, with predominately domestically educated students. Acknowledging the above when teaching and supporting the learning of Chinese students could be the difference between success and failure when it comes to educational aims and more specific Intended Learning Outcomes (ILOs). This is particularly important when targeting a perceived lack of self-monitoring and independence amongst this group of students (Chan, 1999) – two essential characteristics of a successful application of FA (Bennett, 2011), this chapter's primary interest.

Although the overall value of FA is generally supported by research (Bennett, 2011, Black, 2015 or Wanner & Palmer, 2018), several challenges in establishing a clear definition of FA, and hence its implementation, may be magnified when using and applying FA within the TNE context. Here, a compatibility issue might arise that may be based on different politics, policies and cultures in the situated contexts, namely China (Black & Wiliam, 2005).

Hamid (1995) suggests that Western societies' individualism favours personal objectives over group goals, which can be contrasted with the collectivist culture of Chinese society. He further suggests that within the principles of collectivism 'one creates opportunities in life by learning and obeying the rules of conduct, and the major means of social progress is the establishment of harmonious and predictable conditions' (ibid., p. 354). When applying this to the context of higher education, there might be an apparent clash involving the Western teaching methodologies stressing independence and critical thinking and Chinese students' understanding of their role and responsibilities. One example could be related to understanding of the usefulness and application of FA and FFe that rely on learner differentiation, as well as dialogical and student-centred activities (Clarke, 2014).

Most Chinese students complete National College Entrance Examination (Gaokao) before entering university, including UNNC. They often anticipate a similar approach to teaching that heavily relies on teacher-centred approaches, where learners are explicitly told what to do (Zhou, Knoke, & Sakamoto, 2005). Gaokao represents the Chinese education system and its mechanisms, which are rooted in the country's history. Kéjǔ (科举), a nationwide examination system that can be traced back to the Han Dynasty (206 BC–220 AD), was used to appoint civil officials for administration purposes (Spolsky, 1995). This approach to education has had a profound effect on how examination in Chinese education is perceived, and how it is incorporated within the current system as a typically high-stakes, summative exam (Han and Yang, 2001 p. 5), which 'over time has developed an intensely testing-dominated assessment culture' (Chen, Zhang, & Li, 2021, p. 652).

Although it needs to be emphasised that the label 'Chinese learner' is rather artificial and does not refer to all learners from China, Chan (1999) suggests several general aspects that influence how Chinese students learn and perceive their role within a classroom. These include: the strong influence of an authority figure that should not be questioned; strong reliance on memorisation; emphasis on concrete rather than universals; harmony and balance within a learning environment; and the notion of 'face' that could be divided into 'lien' (each person has a 'moral character') and 'mien tsu' ('prestige arising from one's social status') (ibid., p. 297-299). FFe, an example of a developmental tool that is of key importance within Western teaching approaches, has less significance in the above conception of classroom teaching. Teachers who ask open questions, rely on student-initiated content to co-create a lesson and ask students to take a central stage within a learning activity may struggle with the Chinese students who are used to teacher-centred delivery, which can be further related to following the authority figure. This is perhaps why Chinese students are often successful at subjects related to finance, accounting or law where independent and reflective thinking are not as essential (Chen, 2020). Another observable issue is a lack of engagement with FFe as a potential consequence of deep-rooted approaches to a student role within the classroom. Chinese students often receive instructions on what needs to be done rather than how this could be done (Poole, 2016), which may lead to the false conclusion that they lack the motivation to seek answers independently and are only interested in summative assessments when they join a Western higher education institution. In fact, 'the Chinese addition of a measurement function to formative assessment illustrates the ongoing historical and cultural influence of the summative orientation to assessment in China' (Chen et al., 2013, p. 843). In many cases, two-way communication is discouraged or restricted for Chinese students; however, this does not translate directly to students' lack of motivation, or being shy or quiet, but only illustrates their compliance with the deep-rooted expectations. Therefore, as suggested by Tan (2015), it is paramount to understand these generic characteristics and how they influence the achievement of effective TNE education without falling in misleading bias and false assumptions.

Although FA has been widely acknowledged as key when supporting learning and has been adopted around the globe, 'the gaps between policy intention, interpretation and implementation remain a problem to be solved' (Chen, Zhang, & Liang, 2021, p. 649). Adding to the issues of clear definition, and the challenges that Chinese students face in TNE, the implementation of FA in such contexts could be even more challenging due to the assumption that what works in one culture or context will work in another (ARG, 2009, p.7).

5. BEYOND ASSESSMENT IN FORMATIVE ASSESSMENT (FA) – FORMATIVE ROUTINES FRAMEWORK (FRF)

Discussion in section 3 ended with a suggestion that FA as a label needs to be rethought. In order to maximise the effectiveness of FA tasks within any context, and particularly within TNE, the importance of learner training and adaptation needs to be acknowledged. The challenges of dialogic and independent learning using FFe, should be at the heart of curriculum design. Returning to the matter of definition, the active participation of relevant stakeholders can lead to a general conclusion that FA is neither a tool, nor a process (as suggested previously), nor is it a methodology (how certain tools are used). It might be a much larger entity that can be used to guide the approach to course and material design, teacher and learner training (for instance how to create quality formative feedback by teachers and students; how to work with this feedback) and the implementation of different approaches to teaching and learning (the incorporation of FA tasks to maximise learning and motivation).

If this is the case, it might be more appropriate to perceive and approach FA as a theoretical perspective on course design, within which certain aspects of delivery/input would need to take place. For instance, the active use of marking criteria when creating feedback, and students' evidenced understanding of these marking criteria in order to deconstruct FFe and be able to create feedback for peers. If this was assumed plausible, FA would no longer be an example of the idiosyncrasies of individual teachers, rather it could be presented as a more complex phenomenon requiring far more attention from qualified staff to ensure the validity and reliability of its design. This would still leave room for personalisation and tailored changes within individual classes or a given programme; for example, personalised FFe, correctives (tasks to target misconceptions support underachievers), enrichments tasks (to push overachievers). These, in turn, could lead to tailored changes to teaching based on students' mastery of input as judged by evidence gathered through formative tasks, but this would be within the scope of more rigid instructions of what can and cannot change, which would also bring FA more in line with summative assessment tasks. In other words, the idea of constructive alignment (Biggs and Tang, 2010) would explicitly need to include the use of FA.

With the above in mind, an alternative label could be used to emphasise the notion of a bigger picture and wider applicability of FA. The label that the author offers is Formative Routines Framework (henceforth FRF).

In the background section, the understanding of the word 'assessment' was outlined. Based on these explanations, and being aware of the suggested issues that 'assessment' entails examination, high-stakes processes with conclusive marks, it is suggested that the term 'assessment' be removed from the new label. However, The process of evaluation, or the use of previously mentioned evidence is not discarded, but advocated as part of a larger whole. The word 'formative', on the other hand, has not been mentioned nor labelled problematic in a sense that it could be misleading or that it implies something that is difficult to decode. Dictionary definitions of 'formative' include:

Table 1. Definitions of the word 'formative'

Source	Definition
Oxford Dictionary	· *having an important and lasting influence on the development of something or of somebody's character*
Cambridge Dictionary	· *relating to the time when someone or something is starting to develop in character*
Longman Dictionary	· *having an important influence on the way someone or something develops*
Meriam-Webster Dictionary	· *capable of alteration by growth and development* · *of, relating to, or characterized by formative effects or formation*

The various definitions in Figure 2 primarily concern development, important influence, growth and formation. Owing to the above, the word 'formative' has been incorporated into the new label. One final word, however, that needs to be justified is 'routines'. As suggested by Ritchhart, Church and Morrison (2011), this implies the notion of cyclical and developmental behaviour used to enhance effective thinking and teaching; the author also suggests adding 'assessment' to these two areas (although some may argue that assessment is a part of teaching). Moreover, as the idea of FRF is based on a broader notion of collaborative practice between teachers, students and their peers, the 'formative routines' within the

FRF should also be understood as ''shared scripts' [that the students] are able to use with increasing independence' (ibid:48) to enhance their ability to self-monitor and improve their learning. FRF, therefore, could be defined as a theoretical framework consisting of a list of pedagogically developmental tools, approaches and clearly defined methodologies of how to use these tools to aid HE professionals in designing curricula, developing teacher training and planning learning tasks. How these learning tasks are delivered in terms of teaching methodology is a separate matter. After all, teaching methodology changes with time and is highly dependent on context and resources.

Moving towards further explanation of FRF, there is an apparent need to show that the concept of constructive alignment (Biggs & Tang, 2011), extremely influential within higher education, can still be used.

Figure 1. Constructive Alignment (based on Biggs and Tang, 2011:97-100)

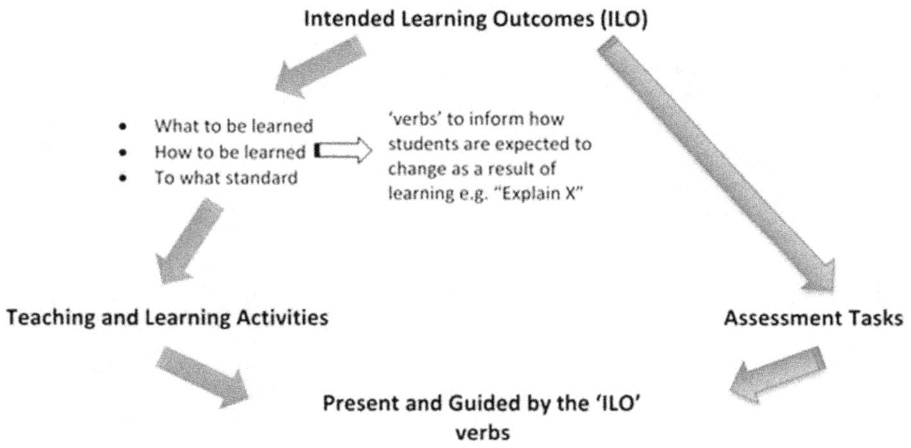

The above figure can be explained in relation to four distinct stages:

1) describe the intended learning outcome in the form of a verb (learning activity), its object (the content) and specify the context and a standard the students are to attain;
2) create a learning environment using teaching/learning activities that address that verb and therefore are likely to bring about the intended outcome;
3) use assessment tasks that also contain that verb, thus enabling you to judge with the help of rubrics if and how well students' performances meet the criteria; and
4) *transform these judgements into standard grading criteria* (ibid.: 101)

When discussing FRF, *Teaching and Learning Activities* together with *Assessment Tasks*, requires specified tools and clearly defined implementation. Three groups of stakeholders would need to be involved: curriculum designers (relevant staff), curriculum implementers (teaching staff) and curriculum receivers (students). As can be seen in Appendix 1, FRF could be integrated in four stages to both ensure that formative tasks are planned and designed together at the curriculum design stage), and to ensure the curriculum designers are guided by the key principles of FRF outlined below. This integration is not unorthodox, and several authors (Bachman & Palmer, 2010; Biggs & Tang, 2011 or Hattie, 2012) include the idea of FA within curriculum design and emphasise the role it plays in both teaching and assessing learners. Experience of EAP and training in TNE would suggest that the current conception of FA is often confined to the role of a backup class-assessment or the 'extra' practice of summative tests. This is exactly why there should be a systemic approach to designing, implementing and training staff how to use formative tasks and FFe within any given programme of studies is vital / necessary. The following is the author's further exemplification of the new framework.

Table 2. Formative Routines Framework

		Guidance	Explanation
Stakeholders	Curricula designers	**How each learning unit uses formative opportunities for practice, consolidation, recycling and extending the target input**	Each learning outcome includes a set of formative tasks designed in accordance to teaching and assessment methods/approaches (how ss learn/ how ss are assessed) Each set is designed with a threshold pass (minimal ILO attainment) in mind but also having in mind higher ILO Formative tasks should include corrective and enriching tasks to aid learners differentiation and ILO attainment
		How each ILO attainment is being tracked and how this information is used to improve the programme and teaching	Each set of formative tasks includes a concluding task that focuses on a particular ILO or part of this ILO to provide meaningful information in respect to this ILO's attainment The concluding task is directly based on or related to summative grading criteria
	Curricula implementers	**What pedagogically developmental tools are needed to support the mastery of target input and track the attainment of ILO**	Explicit and sustained use of grading criteria in teaching (teaching tasks, homework, self-access materials designed with active use of grading criteria by students in mind) Formative tasks are designed to include sufficient target skills practice and recycle (e.g. re-submissions of the same task after applying FFe); formative tasks focus on development and providing meaningful sources for FFe
		What FFe standardisation approaches are used with teaching staff	Sustained teacher support in relation to a set approach to providing FFe and use of formative tasks Setting standards, exemplifying ILO and linking these to particular sets of formative tasks Highlighting opportunities for personalisation of formative tasks; exemplifying channels to provide feedback to curriculum designers on what is (not) needed to change
	Curricula Reviews	**What routines are needed to be developed and established to foster and sustain motivation and track the attainment of ILO**	Sustained learner training in using marking criteria and using and creating FFe to support learning Reflective practice established as a meaningful teaching and learning tool to optimise learners' self-regulation and independence (e.g. use of FFe to direct self-study) Creating opportunities for learners to evaluate own learning and ILO attainment

The above table ventures further exemplification of the FRF concept, suggesting key steps that stakeholders needs to perform in order to maximise the effects of formative practice on teaching and learning. Again, the actual theories behind designing and incorporating formative tasks within teaching materials would depend on a selected theory of types of curriculum design and an associated understanding of the ways students learn (e.g. constructivism and student-centred teaching; Doyle & Doyle, 2020). FRF, therefore, could be used as a guiding framework when designing curricula (see Appendix 1, and figure 4)

Table 3. Formative Routines Framework – ILO level planning – guidance for curriculum designers

Intended Learning Outcome (ILO)			
Individual class ILO (sub-skills involved)	**Assumed baseline knowledge**	**Approximated no. of hours to achieve ILO**	**Links to summative assessment**
Teaching materials necessary to attain individual ILO (develop selected sub-skills)	Formative tools to evaluate knowledge at selected points of reference parallel to teaching materials (e.g. start – middle – finish)	Breakdown of hours for input, practice, consolidation, recycling and extending the target input over the duration of the programme	Assessment design mapped to teaching material and formative tools
Individual teaching tasks (class and self-study including learning how to use and create FFe)	Individual formative tasks (e.g. working with marking criteria and FFe, corrective and enrichment tasks)	Specific breakdown of time for input, learner production and formative tasks	Individual assessment tasks mapped to individual teaching and formative tasks

The table above, ventures slightly deeper into the design of teaching and learning activities using FRF whilst looking at individual ILOs. Key areas include the process of conscious design and mapping of specific formative tasks with both teaching and summative assessment tasks.

6. LEARNING OUTCOMES ASSESSMENT AND FORMATIVE ROUTINES FRAMEWORK

The ultimate goal of any learning theory and accompanying framework is to optimise students learning. An indispensable element of Constructive Alignment (Biggs & Tang, 2011) is the role of assessment in the process of teaching and learning, and the approaches to 'checking' the extent of the learning that has taken place. The Learning Outcomes Assessment (LOA) is an example of a predominant assessment theory that focuses on the importance of broader curriculum that would ensure graduates develop 'core skills' that can be transferred across various contexts (Martin, 2014). Based on the creation of meaningful, intended learning outcomes, it emphasises the need for clearer mechanisms that are 'manifestations of the global standards movement' (Ewell, 2010 in Martin, 2014, p. 51). In other words, quality assurance entities that can be adapted by HE around the world, for instance the European Bologna process or Graduate Attributes Framework. This could potentially allow for better comparison between HE institutions, however as Ewell (2010 in Martin, 2014, p. 51) suggests, there are several possible pitfalls that include:

1. *Conceptual and operational difficulties in defining the outcomes*;
2. Potential to lose important distinctions between the programmes offered by different institutions;
3. *The problem of not being able to specify all important outcomes in advance.*

Furthermore, sets of identified and meaningfully constructed learning outcomes can include skills, knowledge and personal attributes that are not directly impacted by teaching but are shaped and influenced by experiences outside of the HE environment. Here, FRF could prove useful as a way to minimise the pitfalls and optimise the impact of extracurricular activities on teaching. LOA could be generally illustrated as a series of steps: 1) identification and specifications of the intended learning outcomes, 2) assessment and evaluation of individual achievement, 3) aggregation and comparison of assessment results (students achievement representation), and 4) formulation of performance indicators capable of differentiation between institutions' capacity in helping students obtain learning outcomes (i.e. gain knowledge, skills and other attributes) (Martin, 2014, p. 52). Each of these steps is based on formal and established methods of assessments that are described as 'testing regimes' able to measure achievement of a given outcome. Although the need for summative approaches is unquestionable, the author's recommendation for more structured and standardised approaches to implementing formative tasks capable of supporting the above process could be further strengthened in conjunction with addressing the key pitfalls identified earlier.

Firstly, FRF allows for a broader application and 'analysis' of intended learning outcomes (ILOs), as it is not limited to summative tasks (often a small number of assessment events) nor formative assessments but, in comparison, it is a more comprehensive framework focusing on development. The second pitfall could be addressed by FRF based on the approaches to creating standardised but personalised feedback, which could also take into account pitfall number 3, as with FRF, both teaching staff and students would be presented with qualitative evidence to inform the next step in learning. In other words, depending on progress and attainment, supplementary ILOs could be constructed and presented at an appropriate time during the programme of study ensuring tree-like growth rather than linear progress; perhaps lacking when considering the implementation of LOA in China (Xia & Zhong, 2014).

Returning to the Curriculum Receiver/Co-creator level, arguably, the most important goal for FA and FFe is to support a learner's development in terms of their self-regulation and independence (Bennet, 2011), extremely challenging for learners moving from the Chinese education system into TNE. In an ideal scenario, a learner would be able to use feedback from a tutor/mentor and his/her peers to become better at doing something. Going one step further, this learner, over time, would be able to self-assess and provide continuously improved quality feedback to other peers, thus optimising their own development, and at the same time noticing and comparing their own strengths and areas for improvement with others. Both these scenarios include the ability to understand and meaningfully use feedback, and thus create constructive feedback for others and oneself through critically engaging with formative tasks and being able to reflect on one's performance. Being able to skilfully create and engage with feedback should also be based on knowledge of what quality feedback is and how it should be delivered (e.g. the importance of empathy). Although focusing on the idea of learning in HE, the above should also be understood as the 'core skill' that could be transferred to other contexts, namely employment. However, this may be particularly problematic in the 'Chinese context' with the 'Chinese learners' described in previous sections. Obvious challenges are related to at least three aspects not in order of importance: 1) teaching context, 2) quality of formative tasks and FFe and 3) learners' characteristics that directly affect number 1. Number 1 and number 2 are both very much dependent on curriculum design and teacher training, and both are more related to course designers and tutors approaches to teaching. This could potentially be supported by the implementation of FRF. Number 3, on the other hand, is linked to learners' ability to engage with input, reflect on their own learning, identify their strengths and areas for improvement and use available tools to develop both. As mentioned previously, the ability or inability to do this could be deep-rooted and based on learners' educational experiences. At this point, it might be useful to return to the idea of learner training and the need for adaptation or change from a teacher-centred system, towards another more student-centred one. Here, the importance of developing the ability to be reflective comes into play (Bassot, 2016) as a possible way to aid Chinese home-students transition within TNE (Kozbial, 2022). Being reflective and able to engage might be the difference between successful and unsuccessful, or appropriate and inappropriate application of FFe. This, of course, could be optimised by creating an engaging environment and tasks to work with FFe; one side of the argument that emphasises the need for active learning. This is even more visible with EAP learners, who often treat English preparatory courses as an interim, box-ticking necessity.

If one approach to providing feedback (without additional, pre-planned tasks that asks students to engage with this feedback) works with a few students, and it can evidence their progress, other less successful students are often blamed for not engaging with feedback or with the content of the session. Here there are several challenges that could directly affect students' engagement and with learning more broadly. Possible reasons of a lack of engagement from/progression of other students are often related to the conception that feedback from teachers in essence will improve their performance. It is unreasonable to expect a learner to engage with something that is unclear or focuses on areas too broad or too detailed, that may be presented without sufficient time to process or is of general poor quality (for characteristics of quality FFe see Hattie & Timperley, 2007, Evans, 2013, Clarke, 2014, Carless & Boud, 2018). On the other hand, assuming that FFe is of appropriate quality, it is still unreasonable to expect a learner to apply it without prior practice and ongoing focus on developing the skill of using and giving FFe. As argued by Biggs and Tang (2011), a growing number of students may require additional active support to spark the engagement with learning, and the author also argues that the same goes for engaging with feedback and, by extension, becoming a more reflective learner. Therefore, returning to Appendix 1 and using the Revised Bloom's Taxonomy (Anderson & Krathwohl, 2001), all stakeholders (curriculum designers, curriculum implementers and curriculum receivers/co-creators) should consider explicit focus on skills and abilities that are directly involved in gradual development of:

- ***understanding*** of the importance of formative tasks and FFe;
- ***application*** of FFe;
- ***analysing*** and ***evaluating*** FFe and its impact on overall curricular and professional development;
- ***creating*** FFe for peers and for self-assessment.

7. CONCLUSION

In spite of its value within HE, Formative Assessment (FA), as discussed throughout this chapter, still does not represent a clearly established set of rules, policies or definitions that can be easily applied within the TNE context. This chapter has suggested that there is still a need for further research and suggestions on how to better support curriculum designers, teachers and students, so the developmental value of formative feedback (FFe) and FA are enhanced and effectively exercised.

The first section argued that summative assessment has received more attention from exam experts who adhere to strict procedures when developing examinations. The second section examined the definition of FA and concluded that there are several conceptions of FA that do not fully acknowledge the status and potential that formative tasks can offer when designing a programme of studies. This section also included a brief overview of the essential features of developmental feedback, suggesting that both the feedback levels and characteristics should be explicitly incorporated in teaching and learning, as these are not only a teacher's domain. The chapter then continued by outlining several challenges for Chinese students in an international education institution, primarily focusing on their education bakcground and deep-rooted expectations that can impact on attainment of learning and on the teachers' perception of their students' engagement and independence. In the final section, an alternative framework and a definition explaining FA as a larger entity was introduced. It was suggested that formative tasks could meaningfully influence the way curriculum is perceived and how all stakeholders (curriculum designers, teachers and students) cooperate to constructively align learning that is authentic, meaningful and targeted to students' needs. This conception, Formative Routines Framework (FRF), was aligned with several influential theories including Constructive Alignment, Revised Bloom's Taxonomy and Learning Outcome Assessment. Further research into the application of this framework is needed to test its applicability within various HE contexts and to suggest potential advantages and improvements, namely specific designs of curricula that observe FRF and the impact of these on students' independence .

REFERENCES

Anderson, L. W., & Krathwohl, D. (2001). *A Taxonomy for Learning, Teaching and Assessing: a Revision of Bloom's Taxonomy of Educational Objectives*. Longman.

ARG. (2002) *Assessment for Learning: 10 Principles.* ARG. www.hkeaa.edu.hk/DocLibrary/SBA/HKDSE/Eng_DVD/doc/Afl_principles.pdf

ARG. (2009). *Changing assessment practice: Process, principles and standards.* ARG. http:// www.assessment-reform-group.org/ARIA%20English.pdf

Atmaca, Ç. (2016). Contrasting perceptions of students and teachers: Written corrective feedback. *Journal of Language and Linguistic Studies*, *12*(2), 166–182. https://files.eric.ed.gov/fulltext/EJ1117969.pdf

Bachman, L. (2004). Linking observations to interpretations and uses in TESOL research. *TESOL Quarterly*, *38*(4), 723–728. doi:10.2307/3588290

Bachman, L., & Palmer, A. (2010). Language Assessment in Practice. Oxford: Oxford University Press.

Bassot, B. (2016). *The Reflective Journal* (2nd ed.). Palgrave.

Bennett, R. E. (2010). 'Cognitively based assessment of, for, and as learning: A preliminary theory of action for summative and formative assessment'. *Measurement: Interdisciplinary Research and Perspectives*, *8*(3), 70–91. doi:10.1080/15366367.2010.508686

Bennett, R. E. (2011). Formative assessment: A critical review. *Assessment in Education: Principles, Policy & Practice*, *18*(1), 5–25. doi:10.1080/0969594X.2010.513678

Bhuian, S. N. (2016). 'Sustainability of Western branch campuses in the Gulf Region: Students' perspectives of service quality'. *International Journal of Educational Development*, *49*, 314–323. doi:10.1016/j.ijedudev.2016.05.001

Biggs, J. (1999). *Teaching for Quality Learning at University Buckingham.* The Society for Research in Higher Education and Open University Press.

Biggs, J., & Tang, C. (2011). *Teaching for Quality Learning at University*. McGraw-Hill Education.

Black, P. (2015). Formative assessment – An optimistic but incomplete vision. *Assessment in Education: Principles, Policy & Practice*, *22*(1), 161–177. doi:10.1080/0969594X.2014.999643

Black, P., & Wiliam, D. (2005). Lessons from around the world: How policies, politics and cultures constrain and afford assessment practices. *Curriculum Journal, 16*(2), 249–261. doi:10.1080/09585170500136218

Bloom, B. (1969) 'Some theoretical issues relating to educational evaluation', In Tyler, R.W. (ed.), Educational evaluation: new roles, new means: the 63rd yearbook of the National Society for the Study of Education (part II), 69(2), pp. 26-50. doi:10.1177/016146816907001003

Bloom, B. S. (1984). The search for methods of instruction as effective as one-to-one tutoring. *Educational Leadership*, *41*(8), 4–17.

Briguglio, C. (2000) 'Language and cultural issues for English-as-a-second/foreign language students in transnational educational settings', *Higher education in Europe. Enseignement supérieur en Europe. Vysshee obrazovanie v Evrope*, *25*(3), pp. 425–434.

Carless, D. (2006). Differing perceptions in the feedback process. *Studies in Higher Education*, *31*(2), 219–233. doi:10.1080/03075070600572132

Carless, D., & Boud, D. (2018). The development of student feedback literacy: Enabling uptake of feedback. *Assessment & Evaluation in Higher Education*, *43*(8), 1315–1325. doi:10.1080/02602938.2018.1463354

Centre of Research on CFCRS. (2018) Grand opening of the 9th National Conference on CFCRS in Yantai City (in Chinese). CFCRS. https://cfcrs.xmu.edu.cn/2018/0920/c4034a352953/page.htm

Chan, S. (1999). The Chinese learners – a question of style. *Education + Training*, *41*(6), 294–304. doi:10.1108/00400919910285345

Chen, L. (2020). 'Problematising the English-Only Policy in EAP: A Mixed-Methods Investigation of Chinese International Students' Perspectives of Academic Language Policy'. *Journal of Multilingual and Multicultural Development*, *41*(8), 718–735. doi:10.1080/01434632.2019.1643355

Chen, Q., Kettle, M., Klenowski, V., & May, L. (2013). Interpretations of formative assessment in the teaching of English at two Chinese universities: A sociocultural perspective. *Assessment & Evaluation in Higher Education*, *38*(7), 831–846. doi:10.1080/02602938.2012.726963

Chen, Q., Zhang, J., & Li, L. (2021). Problematising formative assessment in an undeveloped region of China: Voices from practitioners. *Educational Assessment, Evaluation and Accountability*, *33*(2), 649–673. doi:10.100711092-021-09369-5 PMID:34394769

Clarke, S. (2014). *Outstanding formative assessment: culture and practice*. Hodder Education.

Crook, A., Mauchline, A., Maw, S., Lawson, C., Drinkwater, R., Lundqvist, K., & Park, J. (2012). The use of video technology for providing feedback to students: Can it enhance the feedback experience for staff and students? *Computers & Education*, *58*(1), 386–396. doi:10.1016/j.compedu.2011.08.025

Crozet, C., Liddicoat, A. J., & Lo Bianco, J. (1999). Intercultural Competence: From language policy to language education. In J. Lo Bianco, A. J. Liddicoat, & C. Crozet (Eds.), *Striving for the Third Place: Intercultural Competence through Language Education*. Language Australia.

Davies, A. (1990). *Principles of language testing*. Blackwell.

Doyle, T., & Doyle, B. (2020). Learning and Teaching in harmony with the Brain. Insight from neuroscience, biology, cognitive science and psychology. In S. Hoidn & M. Klemenicic (Eds.), *The Routledge International Handbook of Student-Centered Learning and Teaching in Higher Education*. Routledge. doi:10.4324/9780429259371-6

Dyllick, T., & Muff, K. (2015). Clarifying the meaning of sustainable business: Introducing a typology from business-as-usual to true business sustainability. *Organization & Environment*, *29*(2), 1–19.

European Parliamentary Research Service. (2013)'Internationalisation of higher education', *European Parliament*. https://epthinktank.eu/2013/09/29/internationalisation-of-higher-education/

Evans, C. (2013). Making Sense of Assessment Feedback in Higher Education. *Review of Educational Research*, *83*(1), 70–120. doi:10.3102/0034654312474350

Fisher, R., Cavanagh, J., & Bowles, A. (2011). Assisting transition to university: Using assessment as a formative learning tool. *Assessment & Evaluation in Higher Education*, *36*(2), 225–237. doi:10.1080/02602930903308241

Fluckiger, J., Vigil, Y., Tixier, Y., Pasco, R., & Danielson, K. (2010). Formative feedback: Involving students as partners in assessment to enhance learning. *College Teaching*, *58*(4), 136–140. doi:10.1080/87567555.2010.484031

Green, A. (2014). *Exploring Language Assessment and Testing*. Routledge.

Guskey, T. R. (2007). Closing Achievement Gaps: Revisiting Benjamin S. Bloom's "Learning for Mastery". *Journal of Advanced Academics*, *19*(1), 8–31. doi:10.4219/jaa-2007-704

Hamid, P. N. (1995). Self-monitoring, locus of control, and social encounters of Chinese and New Zealand students. *Journal of Cross-Cultural Psychology*, *25*(3), 353–268. doi:10.1177/0022022194253004

Han, M., & Yang, X. (2001). Educational Assessment in China: Lessons from history and future prospects. *Assessment in Education: Principles, Policy & Practice*, *8*(1), 5–10. doi:10.1080/09695940120033216

Hattie, J. (2012). *Visible learning for teachers: maximizing impact on learning*. Taylor and Francis. doi:10.4324/9780203181522

Hattie, J., & Timperley, H. (2007). The Power of Feedback. *Review of Educational Research*, *77*(1), 81–112. doi:10.3102/003465430298487

Heffernan, T., Morrison, M., Basu, P., & Sweeney, A. (2010). Cultural differences, learning styles and transnational education. *Journal of Higher Education Policy and Management*, *32*(1), 27–39. doi:10.1080/13600800903440535

Henderson, M., Barnett, R., & Barnett, H. (2017) 'New development in transnational education and the challenges for higher education professional staff.' *Perspectives: Policy and Practice in Higher Education*, *21*(1), pp. 11–19.

Hu, M., Eisenchlas, S. A., & Trevaskes, S. (2019). Factors affecting the quality of transnational higher education in China: A qualitative content analysis on Chinese host universities' self-appraisal reports. *Journal of Higher Education Policy and Management*, *41*(3), 306–321. doi:10.1080/1360080X.2019.1591679

Jones, N., & Saville, N. (2016). *Learning Oriented Assessment: A Systemic Approach, Studies in Language Testing* (Vol. 45). Cambridge University Press.

Kim, H. R., & Bowless, M. (2019). How Deeply Do Second Language Learners Process Written Corrective Feedback? Insights Gained From Think-Alouds. *TESOL Quarterly, 53*(4), 913–938. doi:10.1002/tesq.522

Kozbial, S. (2022). Towards Student-Centred Learning: Using Exploratory Practice with Undergraduate Students in an International Branch Campus in China. *Inform (Silver Spring, Md.), 21*, 12–15. https://www.reading.ac.uk/web/files/inform/B28079_InForm_Issue_21_FINAL.pdf

Lado, R. (1967). *Language Testing: A Teacher's Book*. Longmans.

Martin, L. (2014). Assessing student learning outcomes: Research trajectories. In H. Coates (Ed.), *Higher education learning outcomes assessment: international perspectives* (pp. 49–65). Peter Lang GmbH.

McManus, S. (2008). *Attributes of effective formative assessment*. Council for Chief State School Officers. http://www.ccsso.org/publications/details.cfm?PublicationID=362.

Mok, K. H., & Han, X. (2016). From 'brain drain' to 'brain bridging': Transnational higher education development and graduate employment in China. *Journal of Higher Education Policy and Management, 38*(3), 369–389. doi:10.1080/1360080X.2016.1174409

Nicol, D. J., & Macfarlane-Dick, D. (2006). Formative assessment and self-regulated learning: A model and seven principles of good feedback practice. *Studies in Higher Education, 31*(2), 199–218. doi:10.1080/03075070600572090

OECD. (2013) Education at a Glance: 'OECD indicators', *OECD*. https://www.oecd.org/edu/eag2013%20(eng)--FINAL%2020%20June%202013.pdf

Pham, T., & Hoang Pham, L. (2021). 'Enhancing Asian students' engagement by incorporating Asian intellectual and pedagogical resources in teaching and learning. In S. Hoidn & M. Klemenčič (Eds.), *The Routledge international handbook of student-centred learning and teaching in higher education* (pp. 171–185). Routledge.

Planar, D., & Moya, S. (2016) 'The Effectiveness of Instructor Personalized and Formative Feedback Provided by Instructor in an Online Setting: Some Unresolved Issues', *The Electronic Journal of e-Learning, 14*(3), pp. 196-203. https://files.eric.ed.gov/fulltext/EJ1107130.pdf

Poole, A. (2016) 'Complex teaching realities' and 'deep rooted cultural traditions': Barriers to the implementation and internalisation of formative assessment in China. *Cogent Education, 3*(1), pp. 1-14.

Popham, W. J. (2006). Phony formative assessments: Buyer beware! *Educational Leadership, 64*(3), 86–87.

Ritchhart, R., Church, M., & Morrison, K. (2011). *Making thinking visible: how to promote engagement, understanding, and independence for all learners*. Jossey-Bass.

Sadler, D. (1989). Formative assessment and the design of instructional systems. *Instructional Science, 18*(1), 119–144. doi:10.1007/BF00117714

Sadler, D. (2010). Beyond feedback: Developing student capability in complex appraisal. *Assessment & Evaluation in Higher Education, 35*(5), 535–550. doi:10.1080/02602930903541015

Scriven, M. (1967). The Methodology of Evaluation. In R. W. Tyler (Ed.), *Perspectives of Curriculum Evaluation* (pp. 39–83). Rand McNally.

Sharma, Y. (2018) Ministry ends hundreds of Sino-foreign HE partnerships. *University World News.* https://www.universityworldnews.com/post.php?story=20180706154106269#:~:text=According%20to%20official%20figures%2C%20as,Some%2070%20are%20joint%20institutes

Spolsky, B. (1995). *Measured words: the development of objective testing.* Oxford University Press.

Stafford, S., & Taylor, J. (2016). Transnational education as an internationalization strategy: Meeting the institutional management challenges. *Journal of Higher Education Policy and Management, 38*(6), 625–636.

Tan, C. (2015). 'Education Policy Borrowing and Cultural Scripts for Teaching in China'. *Comparative Education, 51*(2), 196–211. doi:10.1080/03050068.2014.966485

Wanner, T., & Palmer, E. (2018). Formative self-and peer assessment for improved student learning: The crucial factors of design, teacher participation and feedback. *Assessment & Evaluation in Higher Education, 43*(7), 1032–1047. doi:10.1080/02602938.2018.1427698

Wiliam, D., & Thompson, M. (2007). Integrating assessment with instruction: What will it take to make it work? In C. A. Dwyer (Ed.), *The future of assessment: Shaping teaching and learning* (pp. 53–82). Erlbaum.

Xia, H., & Zhong, B. (2014). Learning outcomes assessment in China: Primitive foundations. In H. Coates (Ed.), *Higher education learning outcomes assessment: international perspectives* (pp. 113–134). Peter Lang GmbH.

Yu, Y., & Moskal, M. (2019). Missing intercultural engagements in the university experiences of Chinese international students in the UK. *Compare: A Journal of Comparative Education, 49*(4), 654–671.

Zhou, R. Y., Knoke, D., & Sakamoto, I. (2005). 'Rethinking silence in the classroom: Chinese students' experiences of sharing indigenous knowledge'. *International Journal of Inclusive Education, 9*(3), 287–311. doi:10.1080/13603110500075180

APPENDIX 1

Table 4.

	Intended Learning Outcomes (ILO)	Teaching methods/ approaches	Formative Routines Framework	Summative Assessment
Curriculum Designers (Senior staff)	How appropriate ILOs* tailored to the specific needs of a given cohort are constructed *ILO – educational aims, learning objectives and learning outcomes	How syllabi and teaching materials are created within a selected theoretical approach	How each learning unit uses formative opportunities for practice, consolidation, recycling and extending the target input How each ILO attainment is being tracked and how this information is used to improve the programme and teaching	How summative tasks are created to evaluate the extent to which ILO have been attained How standard grading criteria are created
Curriculum Implementers (All staff with teaching duties)	What knowledge, skills and abilities are needed to successfully implement ILO	What teaching methods and approaches are most appropriate to achieve ILO	What pedagogically developmental tools are needed to support the mastery of target input and track the attainment of ILO What FFe standardisation approaches are used with teaching staff	What methods of delivering summative assessments are used What standardisation approaches are used with teaching staff
Curriculum Receiver/ Co-creators (Students)	What skills and abilities are needed to access the programme	What skills and behaviours are needed to successfully master the target input	What routines are needed to be developed and established to foster and sustain motivation and track the attainment of ILO	What skills and abilities are needed to successfully complete the programme and achieve ILO

è Student ®needs analysis, particularly skills or level of knowledge that ss must have to access a newly created programme®what ss do on a regular basis within the programme (e.g. each class ® week by week or unit by unit) ®how to foster and sustain motivation throughout the programme (and beyond).
è FRF, therefore, could be defined as a theoretical framework consisting a list of pedagogically developmental tools, approaches and clearly defined methodologies of how to use these tools to aid HE professionals in designing curricula, developing teacher training and planning learning tasks. How these learning tasks are delivered in terms of teaching methodology could be a separate aspect, after all

Section 2
Technology

Chapter 6
The Perils and Potential Benefits of Machine Translation in Transnational Higher Education

Michael David High
https://orcid.org/0000-0002-7898-1078
Xi'an Jiaotong-Liverpool University, China

ABSTRACT

Machine translation has recently improved dramatically in accuracy, convenience, and accessibility, and while it has been widely adopted, it remains far from perfect. This chapter considers the perils and potential benefits of machine translation in English-medium of instruction transnational higher education. The perils of machine translation in this context are that it can stunt language learning and cause miscomprehension; it problematizes authorship; it facilitates novel forms of plagiarism; and it can hurt transnational higher education institutions' reputations and devalue their degrees. The potential benefits of machine translation are that it can aid reading comprehension, raise writing level, and help student retention; it provides an opportunity for critically engaging with digital technology and its appropriate use; and it facilitates instruction and research beyond instructor and student language competencies, which can broaden and transnationalize the often Americentric and Eurocentric content of transnational higher education.

1. INTRODUCTION

Machine translation (MT) has recently improved dramatically in accuracy, convenience, and accessibility. What was once an inaccurate and limited technology is now a standard feature in computer and smartphone operating systems and software applications. Nevertheless, there has been little discussion of this technology in higher education outside the disciplines of translation and language learning. This chapter considers the use of MT in the context of transnational higher education (TNHE), as TNHE brings together instructors and students from different linguistic backgrounds and requires students to study in the language of the provider institution. Foreign and second language instruction contexts like

DOI: 10.4018/978-1-6684-5226-4.ch006

TNHE naturally invite the use of MT, and MT has the potential to radically transform TNHE "since students may be, in the future, able to use technology to circumvent traditional language learning processes" (Mundt & Groves, 2016, p. 387).

While research on MT usage in TNHE is still in its infancy, studies in language classes portend that use in other educational contexts is likely widespread. These studies show that students are using MT to understand course materials, lectures, and university communications and to draft written assessments. Yet despite these findings, language instructors have been slow to account for and adapt to this technology (Lacore-Martin, 2019). With this likely usage and hesitance in mind, this chapter brings together research from various disciplines to ponder MT's benefits and drawbacks for English-medium instruction (EMI) at TNHE institutions. While TNHE encompasses a broad range of modes, this chapter focuses primarily on transnational in-country providers of EMI, though the claims and perspectives put forward will also apply to distance learning, international education, and medium of instruction education in languages other than English.

The following section details the history, benefits, and issues with MT and TNHE and the relationship between language learning and educational context. The chapter then discusses the perils of MT, namely that, if used as a replacement for reading and writing in the language of instruction, MT can stunt language learning and cause miscomprehension, problematize notions of authorship, facilitate novel forms of plagiarism, and hurt TNHE institutions' reputations and devalue their degrees. The discussion of the perils is followed by a consideration of the potential benefits of MT, namely that it can aid reading comprehension, raise writing levels in the language of instruction, and contribute to student retention; it provides an opportunity for critically engaging with digital technology and its appropriate use; and it facilitates instruction and research beyond the instructors and students' language competencies, which can broaden and transnationalize TNHE content provision. The chapter then ends with a discussion of future research possibilities and the recommendation that TNHE institutions maximize the potential benefits of MT by rapidly developing MT policy and training students and instructors in its responsible and appropriate use.

2. BACKGROUND

2.1 Machine Translation

"Machine translation" is the "name for computerised systems responsible for the production of translations from one natural language into another" (Hutchins & Somers, 1992, p. 3). Practical research into computer translation began in earnest in the 1950s (Hutchins & Somers, 1992), but it was only in 2016 that MT systems became able to consider the meaning of entire sentences rather than separate words and phrases. Due to the development of MT neural networks incorporating machine learning, these new MT systems decreased translation errors by over 60% from their predecessors (Wu et al., 2016). Trained on ever-growing data sets, improved by volunteer suggestions, and optimized constantly, these systems continue to improve (Caswell & Liang, 2020; Poibeau, 2017). MT is now available through standalone websites, designated applications, and as a feature of software applications, operating systems, social networking sites, digital personal assistants, and cloud and web servers. MT can now translate text in images and audio and video files and simultaneously translate live, multilingual conversations (Poibeau, 2017). With the adoption and proliferation of smartphones, MT is mobile and can be used anywhere. By

2021, Google Translate had been installed over 1 billion times on Android smartphones and supported 109 languages (Pitman, 2021). These increases in accuracy, accessibility, and convenience have made this technology a routine aspect of contemporary life.

At the same time, though, neural MT systems still "lag significantly behind human performance in all but the most specific translation tasks" (Caswell & Liang, 2020, para. 1). They fail to translate all words in original texts, have trouble with proper names and rare terms, and do not consider the context of a sentence in a paragraph, section, or entire text (Le & Schuster, 2016). Like all MT systems, they are limited by their training material, and low-resource languages (i.e., languages with smaller amounts of training material) are less likely to be accurately translated. More generally, "Part of the reason why translation is difficult for computers is that translation is just difficult: difficult even for humans" (Arnold, 2003, p. 119). Just how aware MT users are of the technology's limitations remains an open question, but if the histories of other digital technologies are any indication, critical understanding, critical use, and ethical consideration of MT will significantly lag behind adoption.

2.2 Transnational Higher Education

There has been a significant increase in the amount and importance of mobility in higher education since the 1990s, a trend closely related to economic and technological globalization (Scott, 2011). This increase in educational mobility has led to a wide variety of international, transnational, and global education practices. While there is some confusion and overlap between the terms, "international education" has increasingly been used to describe students studying abroad. In contrast, "transnational education" is used to describe the mobility of institutions across borders, and "global education" is used to describe a pedagogical focus on the global (Francois, 2016). TNHE may include international education if students move between host and provider campuses and may include global education if TNHE curriculum focuses on it, but neither is fundamental to the TNHE enterprise. TNHE comes in a variety of modes: some are collaborative, as when foreign providers and a local partner work together on the delivery and design of education (e.g., twinning programs, cofounded institutions, and joint/double/multiple degree programs); and some are independent, as when foreign providers without local partners deliver education or when local partners deliver education but do not design curricula (e.g., international branch campuses, franchises, and distance education) (Knight, 2016).

With the inclusion of educational services in the General Agreement on Trade in Services in 1995, transnational education as a tradable commodity became part of the World Trade Organization's trade liberalization aims. Since then, the number of transnational programs and students has increased rapidly (Paniagua et al., 2022; Wilkins, 2020). The emergence and expansion of transnational higher education has resulted from trends and developments within both developed and developing countries. From the perspective of developed countries, declining funding for universities and the increasing privatization of higher education have led universities to adopt a more entrepreneurial focus. Decreasing amounts of domestic students are also leading institutions to search out new populations. Meanwhile, globalization has increased the need for cultural understandings across national boundaries. Universities are eager to internationalize and produce more competitive graduates, attract foreign talent, and contribute to local and regional cultural and economic development. From the perspective of developing countries, demographic shifts have produced increasing numbers of students. Many countries in the developing world lack the higher education capacity to satisfy their populations. With the respect that Western education commands globally, many students in the developing world desire to study abroad but cannot do so due to economic, political, or family reasons. TNHE programs allow students to study a foreign curriculum and receive a foreign degree without leaving their country, often paying less than they would if they studied abroad. Foreign faculty and instruction in developing countries can also lead to knowledge transfer (Francois, 2016, pp. 13–18; Wilkins & Huisman, 2012).

The benefits of TNHE for those in both developed and developing countries are apparent. It gives educational institutions in the developed world access to new markets and increased revenue (from student tuition and host country government support) during a time of defunding (Kim & Zhu, 2010), and it provides them the opportunity to internationalize and develop their institutional brand. Students in developing countries gain access to education that may not be available domestically but without the governmental hurdles, tuition, living costs, and cultural difficulties of studying abroad. Developing countries that cannot meet the demand (in terms of both amount and quality) for higher education can provide in-country alternatives to support long-term domestic economic and cultural development. Through transnational contact, those in developed and developing countries engage in cultural exchange and technology transfer. Because TNHE crosses and bridges national boundaries, it can express "a way of seeing the world" that has the "potential to foster transcultural understandings over time" (Francois, 2016, p. 6). TNHE can enable symbiosis between the local and the global and provide glocal understanding (Francois, 2015). It can prepare graduates to comprehend and work on local, regional, national, international, and transnational issues (Francois, 2016, p. 6). TNHE branch campuses and programs also create and maintain soft power and influence in foreign countries, something on which governments are increasingly keen (Wilkins, 2020). However, TNHE is far from an unalloyed good.

As a tradable commodity, TNHE provision results from neoliberal policies that favor commercial competition over public service and international development (Knight, 2016; Marginson, 2004). Such "global academic capitalism" is predicated on the inequality of educational opportunity between developing and developed countries (Gill & Kirkpatrick, 2013, para. 10; Marginson, 2004). When universities operate overseas, they are more likely to act as business firms than at home where they are still (somewhat) beholden to public service obligations (Kim & Zhu, 2010). "Western HEIs [Higher Education Institutions] have many different motives for establishing international branch campuses," Wilkins and Huisman relate, "but the most important seem to involve money, influence and status" (2012, p. 640). While institutions in developing countries have recently begun to export more educational services (Wilkins & Urbanovič, 2014), and there is a large amount of TNHE provision (particularly branch campuses) between developed countries (Garrett et al., 2016), TNHE generally continues the colonial dynamic of developed countries extracting wealth from developing ones (Caillods & Varghese, 2011, p. 10). In 2018, the UK had £650 million in repatriated TNHE revenue, an increase of 85% since 2010 (*UK Revenue from Education Related Exports and Transnational Education Activity 2018*, 2022, p. 5). In that same year, the United Kingdom, followed by the USA, Australia, and then France, provide the most transnational education services, while China, followed by the United Arab Emirates, Malaysia, Singapore, and Qatar, had the most students enrolled in international branch campuses and transnational education programs (*Transnational Education (TNE) Data Report*, 2018). Though joint and dual degree programs often allow for mutual mobility between institutions, a study by the American Council on Education found that such programs mainly enroll non-U.S. students and "may be serving primarily as a mechanism **for U.S. institutions to recruit international students**" (Helms, 2014, p. 18; bold in original).

Relatedly, there has been a proliferation of EMI programs throughout the globe. EMI describes the "use of the English language to teach academic subjects (other than English itself) in countries or jurisdictions where the first language of the majority of the population is not English" (Macaro et al.,

2018, p. 37). As the leading providers of TNHE are from Anglophone countries, "EMI is enabled by TNHE, and the latter is often mediated through EMI" (Costa et al., 2021, p. 117), which is to say most transnational education provision is in English (Wilkins & Urbanovič, 2014). In 2021, there were 27,874 English taught bachelor's and master's programs outside of the U.S., the U.K., Canada, and Australia, up 77% since 2017 (*The Changing Landscape of English-Taught Programmes*, 2021).

Several critics have argued that the spread of EMI mirrors the domination of European colonialism and American imperialism: "By spreading English language and Americanised practises, global education markets colonise non-English cultures and identities.... Along with global hegemony comes global insularity, a blindness to other languages and the cultures embedded in them, regardless of the immense richness these entail" (Marginson, 2004, p. 24). Tellingly, a colonial relationship is the most significant cultural determinant for a host country having a branch campus from another country (more significant than shared religion or language) (Paniagua et al., 2022). Though English language education can provide economic advantages and social mobility to students, this advantage is not available to all, and it can displace instruction in local languages that would have a more beneficial impact on students' lives (Ricento, 2015). A simple view of post-colonial relations fails, though, to account for the complex dynamics and neo-colonial state-building occurring through TNHE agreements, as many developing countries are glad to Westernize and repeat colonial patterns of discrimination and domination within their borders (Le-Ha, 2017; Waters & Leung, 2022). As such, providers and hosts must weigh "the potential benefits of transnational education programs against the risks of educational imperialism" (Bannier, 2016, p. 83).

Due to the distance between the host institution and the provider institution, quality assurance in TNHE remains an continuous challenge (Kosmützky & Putty, 2016). National organizations like the British Quality Assurance Agency, the Australian Universities Quality Agency, and the UAE's Knowledge and Human Development Authority and national regulatory bodies like the Chinese Ministry of Education aim to ensure the quality and parity of TNHE provision. However, provider and host institutions can often differ significantly in provision. Even if they share curriculum and staff frequently interact, "the physical distance, staff and student demographics, and teaching and learning preferences across multi-campus structures suggest variability in expectations, decision-making, and academic performance itself" (Coleman, 2003, p. 359). Such differences may not be pedagogically harmful, as variation may lead to more student-centered pedagogy, but they nonetheless have the potential to undermine quality assurance (Coleman, 2003). Due to issues with quality, which are also related to the rapid commercialization of the market, TNHE has been criticized as "mediocre" and inferior to international education (Le-Ha, 2017, p. 143; Waters & Leung, 2013). It is also important to note that quality is not just a pedagogical issue; quality control ensures elite universities maintain their reputations after establishing transnational programs (Kim & Zhu, 2010).

2.3 Language Learning and Educational Context

International education research shows that non-native speakers face considerable linguistic challenges, such as difficulty understanding spoken lectures and course content and taking notes in class. These challenges can undermine academic success, lead to hesitance to participate, and cause loss of confidence. International students also often have trouble understanding their institution's national and regional academic conventions (Khanal & Gaulee, 2019; Peters & Anderson, 2021). Research has found that EMI students encounter similar linguistic challenges as those in international education (Kagwesage,

2012) and that there may be little language support for EMI students after pre-sessional and English for academic purposes (EAP) courses because EMI content instructors do not feel it is their responsibility to teach language (Kir & Akyüz, 2020; Trent, 2017).

Importantly, there is still considerable debate as to whether EMI leads to increased English language proficiency (Macaro et al., 2018), as simply "teaching in English and requiring students to submit their work in English will not automatically lead to improved proficiency in English" (Galloway et al., 2017, p. 6). Studies on EMI in and beyond higher education have stressed the need to allow students to use their native language for comprehending concepts (i.e., to code-switch), a need that problematizes the underlying idea that English immersion will increase proficiency (Paxton, 2009). EMI can also hinder the reception of content material, as Le Han (2017, p. 23) stresses: "many [TNHE] students stop acquiring content knowledge in their stronger language(s) while struggling to comprehend knowledge through their rather limited English in their English medium education." Regardless, students find international education and EMI valuable and report that both educational contexts improve their English language skills (Kagwesage, 2012; Kir & Akyüz, 2020). This improvement is especially pronounced in the case of international education, as the environment of foreign campuses can encourage even non-native English speakers to speak English with each other if they are from different language groups (Andrade, 2009, p. 23).

The use of MT will undoubtedly further complicate debates over the effectiveness of EMI, and there has yet to be a large-scale study of MT usage by TNHE students. However, studies in language classes, international education, and TNHE pre-sessional English courses indicate that usage is very high. A study of English majors in Saudi Arabia found that 96.2% reported using Google Translate (Alhaisoni & Alhaysony, 2017, p. 77), and a study of Korean undergraduate students in elective English courses found that 85% of students used MT inside and outside the classroom (Briggs, 2018, p. 10). 56% of international students at the University of Nottingham Trent University reported using MT most days, quite often, or sometimes, with only 22% reporting never using it. MT usage was higher amongst those that needed to take pre-sessional English courses before beginning their studies (compared to international students that entered directly), which is to say that students with lower language ability are more likely to use MT (Nowlan, 2019). At Xi'an Jiaotong-Liverpool University, a joint venture TNHE institution in mainland China, over 75% of pre-sessional master's students reported using MT daily to look up words and phrases, 50% reported using it daily to look up entire paragraphs, and 50% reported using it daily to look up longer chunks of text. When those same students were asked about the importance of MT to their academic studies, 38% replied "very important," 48% replied "important," and 14% replied "slightly important." No students replied "unimportant" (Son et al., 2021). These studies strongly indicate that most students studying another language or in another language regularly use MT systems.

3. THE PERILS

3.1 Language Learning and Miscomprehension

The most significant peril that MT poses for TNHE is that students will use MT to replace learning the language of instruction. Students, when surveyed and interviewed on the different ways they use MT, claim to very infrequently or never use it to translate entire texts while reading and writing (Chompurach, 2021; Organ, 2019; Son et al., 2021). Yet it is wise to be skeptical about this self-reported behavior. Nowlan (2019), in his study of international students at Nottingham Trent University, reported that students claimed to rarely translate entire texts while reading and never while writing. Tellingly though, these same students feared that using MT would negatively affect their language learning, even though they were supposedly only using it to look up words, phrases, and translate single sentences (see also Ryu et al. [2022]). Niño, in a small study (N=16) pre-dating the development of neural MT, found that 75% of surveyed Spanish language students used MT to produce a starting draft (2009, p. 249). Alhaisoni and Alhaysony, in their study of English students in Saudi Arabia, note that some students "rely heavily on GT [Google Translate], do not read the English text and cannot retrieve or guess the meaning of unknown words. Furthermore, they do not write English based on their own efforts and they rely on GT to help them" (2017, p. 78).

MT usage can also lead to miscomprehension, especially when the user's language ability in the target language is low, the amount of translated text is long, or when the original text has errors. While research shows that students are aware that MT is not perfect (Lee, 2021; Son et al., 2021), students with a lower ability in the target language (tested and self-reported) are less able to recognize errors in MT output (Briggs, 2018; Ducar & Schocket, 2018; Fredholm, 2019; Lee, 2020; Ryu et al., 2022). The use of MT in TNHE is also problematic because the technology remains imperfect and TNHE is culturally complex, making cultural misunderstandings more likely to occur than in domestic higher education. Such misunderstandings can be especially serious when foreign instructors teach politically, culturally, and religiously sensitive topics in authoritarian countries (see, for example, Hessler [2022] on the increasing ideological policing of foreign instructors in China and Rostrong [2016] on the precarious position of foreign instructors in Qatar). Adding to the problem, many offshore and branch campus instructors do not receive training for transnational education (Wilkins & Annabi, 2021). Therefore, MT errors can exacerbate deficiencies and cultural differences already present in TNHE.

3.2 Authorship

EAP and English for specific purposes (ESP) instructors have been debating the re-use of language by non-native English students for decades (e.g., see Deckert [1993] and the responses to his text), and they generally hold that notions of authorship are historical and cultural and should not be held up as universal ideals (Pennycook, 1994). As such, EAP and ESP instructors tend to take a more expansive view of textual authorship, noting that language learning involves memorizing and using formulaic expressions. From within this tradition, Groves and Mundt (2015) advocate for a technological acceptance view of MT authorship. Though they acknowledge that "one could argue that a translated text is no longer the student's own work," they ultimately "concede that the text (translated or not) is still produced and owned by the student, and is, thus, their achievement" (p. 119). In another article (Mundt & Groves, 2016), they question whether a student using MT to translate their text into English is problematic at all, comparing it to reading texts in translation and "asking a friend (or paying a stranger) to proofread work before submission" (p. 395).

This view of MT and authorship can be challenged though. While it is correct that academics accept the reading of texts in translation, this is discipline specific: scholars in area studies, anthropology, literature, and other culturally focused disciplines are expected to be fluent in the languages related to their specialty. Flowerdew and Li (2007) cautiously note that "the primary concern of the scientific community in evaluating an article is the 'originality' of its 'science', rather than its language" (p. 461), but such concern would not extend to the Humanities were the relationship between an idea and its expression is considered much more critical. Moreover, there is debate as to whether students and academics hiring proofreading, editing, and translation services constitute academic integrity violations and co-authorship, respectively (Lozano, 2014; Luo & Hyland, 2019; Turner, 2011). If there are disciplinary differences the view of the idea/expression relationship, and there is contention about the ethical and professional use of writing and editing services, instructor tolerance for MT usage is likely to vary widely.

Further complicating the matter, academic organizations have yet to grapple with the questions MT poses for authorship. None of the most recent versions of the Chicago Manual of Style (17th edition; 2017), the Publication Manual of the American Psychological Association

(7th edition; 2019), nor the Modern Language Association Handbook (9th edition; 2021) mention MT. Instead, these handbooks assume that translations come from published sources or that writers translate texts themselves. Yet a machine translation is not a published source nor a writer's translation. While citing the software company or app developer is a logical workaround (and is like current provisions for citing databases as containers of texts), it is not Google (for example) that ultimately authors a Google Translate translation. Instead, the author of a machine translation is a complex mixture of the engineers who program and optimize MT algorithms, the writers and translators of the texts in the data set, the volunteers who suggest translation improvements, and the instantiating user that enters text into the system. "Authorship, in the algorithmic context, is both pluriform and problematic" (Uricchio, 2017, p. 134), which makes determining and documenting such authorship extremely difficult.

3.3 Academic Integrity

There is a lack of clarity on whether and to what extent student use of MT is an academic integrity violation (Case, 2015; Ducar & Schocket, 2018; Lacore-Martin, 2019). If machine translating a word or phrase is acceptable (akin to using a dictionary) and machine translating an entire essay is not, where would use cease to be acceptable on the continuum between the two? Would the same continuum hold for both reading and writing? In 2019, York St John University included MT in its forms of academic misconduct: "inappropriate use of online translation tools to conceal the source of text, or otherwise present work that it [*sic*] not a student's own" (York St John University, 2021). As well, students in language classes suspected of extensive MT use at York St John must reproduce their work unassisted (Organ, 2019). However, this institution is an outlier, as most institutions lack MT policy. Studies of academic integrity have shown the need for clear institutional policy and training to guide student behavior (Kim & LaBianca, 2018; Palmer et al., 2019), and researchers have called for developing clear MT guidelines and policies for some time (Groves & Mundt, 2021; Mundt & Groves, 2016). Without clear MT policy students and instructors are likely to act in discordant and inconsistent ways, especially considering that there are discrepancies between these groups' attitudes towards appropriate MT use (e.g., students naturally have a more expansive view of the kinds of practices that should be allowed than instructors) (Lee, 2021).

International students are accused more often of cheating and plagiarism than domestic students. While some have claimed these accusations are a form of cultural stereotyping (Le-Ha, 2006; Liu, 2005), there are contextual reasons why international students may violate academic integrity more: difficulty studying in non-native languages, cultural differences regarding knowledge production, lack of instruction on referencing guidelines and plagiarism, and other situational factors like family pressure may prompt such behavior at higher rates (Hill, 2017). There is less study of plagiarism at TNHE institutions, but there is reason to believe the situation is similar if not more extreme due to the greater percentage of non-native speakers, the at times limited support services provided to them, and the more entrepreneurial nature of TNHE education, which encourages institutions to see students as paying customers and accommodate their demands and lower academic and linguistic levels (Palmer et al., 2019).

MT facilitates novel ways for students to plagiarize without being detected, adding another dimension to this context. Non-native English speakers can now easily machine translate a text from their native language into English and present it as their own, a practice known as cross-language plagiarism (Barrón-Cedeño et al., 2013). Students can also take an English language text and translate it into another language and back so it will not be flagged by similarity detection software, a practice known as back translation plagiarism (Jones & Sheridan, 2015). Though computer scientists have developed approaches to address these kinds of plagiarism (Barrón-Cedeño et al., 2013; Al-Bayed & Abu-Naser, 2018; Jones & Sheridan, 2015), the approaches have not been widely deployed. For example, though Turnitin has begun machine translating non-English submitted texts into English and checking them against the service's archives, it cannot translate English texts into other languages and detect similarity, as its archive of student texts, internet web pages, and academic texts are primarily in English. Instructors suspecting cross-language plagiarism must translate a potentially plagiarized text into the suspected original language and then search the internet and accessible academic databases for the original text. If the instructor is not competent in the suspected original language, they must use MT to translate the suspected text, the search engine responses, and any potential source texts, which creates layers of MT errors and makes finding (and understanding) the originally plagiarized source difficult and time consuming.

3.4 Institutional Reputation and TNHE Value

MT as a substitute for language learning can hurt TNHE institutions' reputations and lower the value of their degrees. Students who graduate from TNHE programs but cannot speak, read, and write well in the language of instruction will undermine the reputations of both the provider and host institutions. Research in international education indicates that professors adjust their mode of delivery and possibly the content, deadlines, and rigor of their courses to accommodate non-native English speakers (Andrade, 2009; Peters & Anderson, 2021). If this occurs in majority English speaker institutions, then such adjustments are even more likely in TNHE situations where the student population is overwhelmingly or exclusively non-native English speakers. Moreover, differences in provision and outcomes between provider and host institutions are already an issue in TNHE education. As Waters and Leung report, TNHE students in British programs in Hong Kong "are quite simply unable, through a static TNE [transnational education] programme, to acquire the specific kinds of skills that employers and colleagues would expect from an international degree employment" (Waters & Leung, 2013, p. 614). Instructors in international education have expressed concern over students' use of MT and its adverse effects on institutional reputation (Mundt & Groves, 2016). It is only a matter of time before MT prompts similar concerns in TNHE and, as TNHE already has a reputation for lower quality than international education (Le-Ha, 2017), MT has the potential to exacerbate this perception and affect the entire TNHE market.

Finally, MT usage can undermine the value of TNHE degrees. Language is always cultural: it conveys semantic and pragmatic information about the history and culture of the people who use it (Risager 2007). Students who substitute MT for language learning will not engage with the cultural aspects of a language, impoverishing the experience and value of TNHE. This also has a professional component: students who replace language engagement with MT will not be able to read and write well in the language of instruction, a skill that a degree from a TNHE institution should provide and on which employers likely count.

Underdeveloped language skills can also affect future educational opportunities, as master's and Ph.D. programs are increasingly asking reference writers to verify students' language ability (not their ability to use MT). A TNHE degree promises employers and graduate schools a level of cultural knowledge and language ability that may not develop if MT use replaces engagement with the language of instruction.

4. THE POTENTIAL BENEFITS

4.1 Language Learning, Writing, and Retention

Though the perils of MT use are frightening, the potential benefits are also significant. MT can enable study, instruction, and research beyond students' *and* instructors' language competencies, broadening their experience and knowledge if used as an aid to reading and writing in the language of instruction (rather than as a replacement for it). Overall, research on MT in foreign language learning demonstrates a positive impact (Lee, 2021, p. 16) and it has repeatedly been shown that language learners perceive MT as beneficial (Alhaisoni & Alhaysony, 2017; Chompurach, 2021; Niño, 2009; Nowlan, 2019; Organ, 2019; Ryu et al., 2022). As previously mentioned, research shows that allowing students to use their native language can increase EMI content understanding (Paxton, 2009). Thus, MT can become a means for integrating native language support without code-switching aloud in the classroom.

Research on MT and foreign and second language composition indicates that it can be a valuable tool for increasing the quality of student writing. Lee (2020), in a study of unassisted and MT-assisted writing in English by South Korean students, found "that MT functioned similar to peer-editing: neither is perfect, but both are helpful to student writing" (p. 168). Lee also found that MT "greatly improved the quality of student English writing in terms of vocabulary, grammar, and expression, but it could not help the students beyond that" (p. 169). Studying the writing output of Taiwanese students, Tsai (2020) found that MT generally improved the richness, grammatical accuracy, and vocabulary of writing in English, and MT was even more beneficial for students with lower English proficiency. While both English and non-English majors in the study benefitted from MT, non-English majors benefited the most.

The benefits of MT will be more pronounced when students are instructed on its use, and when asked, students report that they want such instruction (Bowker, 2020; Son et al., 2021). In one study, Ryu et al. (2022) instructed Korean foreign language students on MT usage, had them complete five composition assessments over a semester, and provided them with feedback on and strategies for MT use after each composition. The students "perceived the GUMT [Guided Use of Machine Translation] model as an effective automated feedback tool for clarifying meanings, correcting grammatical errors, and finding better expressions while also being aware of possible multiple meanings depending on the context of writing" (Ryu et al., 2022, p. 146). Considering that EMI content instructors do not view language instruction as part of their teaching remit, student use of MT as a feedback tool can help supplement a lack of language support.

MT has the potential to help TNHE students comprehend the onslaught of academic and disciplinary terms they encounter. Academic and disciplinary norms and terms are difficult for students entering TNHE programs and studying in another language. MT may especially benefit first and second-year TNHE students as they struggle to understand assessment instructions, university policies, and academic culture (Evans & Morrison, 2011), all of which can contribute to in-country culture shock (Pyvis & Chapman, 2005). Relatedly, MT has been found to help students struggling with instruction in foreign languages remain engaged (Briggs, 2018), and it may be able to do so beyond the language classroom, thereby encouraging student retention. Students that can maintain their studies and understand course and university material with the aid of MT will be more satisfied with their experience. Increased retention and student satisfaction are particularly significant for new TNHE institutions as they must quickly begin producing revenue or are likely to be shuttered (Helms, 2014; Wilkins, 2020). More generally, maintaining student satisfaction is a key to the success of higher education institutions, and it can lead to a competitive advantage in the TNHE market (Wilkins & Balakrishnan, 2013).

4.2 MT Literacy and Appropriate Use

As students are likely already using MT, it is vital to train them in MT literacy to encourage appropriate, efficient, and critical use (Bowker, 2020). Educating students on how to use MT and on the technology's limitations will make usage more beneficial in that "whether an existing MT system is useful or not depends not only on how well it can translate but also largely on how it is utilized" (Kit & Wong, 2008, p. 321). Unsurprisingly, many researchers recommend such training (Bowker, 2020; Chompurach, 2021; Ducar & Schocket, 2018; Knowles, 2022; Lee, 2020; Ryu et al., 2022; Son et al., 2021; Urlaub & Dessein, 2022). However, only educating students is insufficient; instructors must be trained as well. Though language instructors have increasingly come to accept MT usage as inevitable, the belief that it is detrimental to language learning persists (Case, 2015). This belief is likely shared by academics in other disciplines (for example, see Groves and Mundt [2021]). Training students and instructors on MT and its limitations will help address such concerns and create the mutual understanding necessary for instruction and guidance.

MT literacy workshops can be added to digital literacy modules, offered as standalone events, or integrated into language, EAP, and introductory content courses. Bowker (2020) has already developed MT literacy training focused on six topics: privacy/confidentiality, academic integrity, algorithmic bias, MT tool variety, task awareness, and the relationship between MT input and output. This training can be adapted to the TNHE context and the needs of diverse students and instructors. MT literacy instruction by itself is not enough to ensure ethical behavior though; a holistic response is needed. MT-assisted plagiarism can be discouraged through intelligent assessment design (Jones & Sheridan, 2015; Velliaris & Pierce, 2019), and instructors can adjust assessment weights to de-emphasize those that allow for MT usage (Lacore-Martin, 2019). Admittedly, some MT-resistant assessments (such as closed book exams and unscripted discussions) are challenging to deliver online and can increase workload, making them less likely to be adopted. However, if institutions formulate clear policies, students and instructors will be more likely to adopt new behavoirs and practices (Pan et al., 2019).

MT Literacy can also introduce students to post-editing, which is editing, modifying, or correcting a text translated by a MT system (Allen, 2003). Post-editing has emerged as a professional translation practice that is likely to be widely adopted in many industries due to its efficiency and low cost. Being aware of MT systems' common errors and the "levels" of post-editing will be an asset to those who work for transnational companies or live in multilingual environments (Hu & Cadwell, 2016, p. 346). Instructing students in MT literacy and introducing them to post-editing aligns with calls to move away from prohibitory and punitive approaches to academic integrity towards those aimed at "fostering a learning-oriented environment, improving instruction, enhancing institutional support for teaching and learning, and reducing institutional constraints to teaching and learning" (Bertram Gallant, 2008, p. 89).

4.3 Transnationalizing TNHE

For TNHE to be truly transnational and "foster transcultural understandings" (Francois, 2016, p. 6), it must facilitate "two-way interactions and exchanges of ideas and information" (Lowery, 2016, p. 63). However, because of the need for institutional equivalence in TNHE provision, the curriculum of host institutions is often developed far away from the location of instruction. Even when the curriculum is developed locally, it is heavily tilted toward material from the provider institution's national tradition, as the need to assign reading materials in the language of instruction limits the range of potential texts and perspectives. Governments in host countries can somewhat offset this tendency (e.g., China mandates first-year courses focused on Chinese culture and politics), but the devaluing of local culture can easily accompany EMI, resulting in "internationalization without a multicultural perspective" (Tsuneyoshi, 2018, p. 50).

To combat the devaluing of local culture, staff at TNHE host institutions can bring local examples and knowledge into their courses, thereby modeling respect for indigenous culture and enabling cross-cultural knowledge production (Malete, 2016). TNHE instructors' autonomy varies depending on the type of provision (with twinning programs providing the most autonomy and franchises and online education providing the least). Within these parameters, though, there is the freedom to introduce culturally relevant content. However, doing so relies not only on staff willingness but also on their linguistic ability. Non-local faculty (i.e., flying faculty or immigrants) often do not speak the local language and must rely on professionally translated texts or secondary sources, which can limit access to local texts and preclude engagement with domestic current events. Through MT, non-locals can bring in topical and obscure local language texts. Instructors using machine-translated local texts can also productively shift the authority of the classroom, as local students will be the experts on the local content. Such a shift of authority encourages student-centered learning and co-construction of knowledge and including local texts can decrease cultural imperialism.

Students can also use MT to research in languages other than their own and their language of instruction, allowing for the study of material that has not yet been professionally translated but is still academically valuable. This can enable transcultural student research and encourage students to see themselves as members of a diverse global society. While the amount of machine-translated content able to be integrated into TNHE provision is admittedly limited, and the inaccuracies of MT need to be accounted for, it can nonetheless enable students and instructors to cross linguistic and national boundaries beyond those crossed by the provider entering the host country.

5. FUTURE RESEARCH DIRECTIONS

Research on MT usage in TNHE needs to begin in all areas. It is currently unknown with what frequency and to what extent TNHE students use MT. Empirical studies of the scope and scale of MT usage must consider the diversity of TNHE students and institutions, researching in different countries, contexts, and TNHE modes. Studies of TNHE student and staff perceptions and beliefs about MT must be undertaken and considered against similar research in language learning and international education. Longitudinal studies of the effect of MT on language learning and performance in content courses are also essential. As Mundt and Groves (2016) recommend, researching how different stakeholders (students, universities, and employers) value language learning is indispensable. Such research can inform MT policy and guide curriculum and assessment revision. Finally, research on MT policy and literacy is also needed to gauge the efficacy of interventions to encourage appropriate and beneficial MT use.

6. CONCLUSION

Engagement with MT and discussion of its benefits and drawbacks should become part of entry-level courses in EMI TNHE institutions so that students use MT efficiently, critically, and ethically. Integrating MT literacy into digital and information literacy curricula, whether in language courses, research courses, or library instruction, should be undertaken as soon as possible. Instructors should likewise undergo MT training to encourage their use of the technology and make them better able to instruct and guide student use. Instructors must make students "realize that even when words seem to map directly from one language to the next, the cultural concepts, products, practices, beliefs, and values that are conveyed are not necessarily the same" (Ducar & Schocket, 2018, p. 789). Language teachers and EAP instructors are already implementing assessment strategies that preclude or render unhelpful the use of MT and are revising course learning objectives (Groves & Mundt, 2015, 2021; Lacore-Martin, 2019; Urlaub & Dessein, 2022). TNHE instructors should do the same.

Ultimately, such changes must happen at the institutional level, and university management must be made aware of the perils and potential benefits of MT. Not only should institutions rapidly develop MT usage policies and student and instructor training, but they must also ensure that student language levels are high enough upon enrollment so that students can use MT as a tool, not as a crutch. Quality assurance organizations and local governments should press TNHE institutions to address MT usage before it undermines the value of EMI and the market for TNHE. Plagiarism checking services also need to develop the capability to flag characteristic MT errors and cross-language and back translation plagiarism, providing instructors with the tools to investigate academic integrity cases.

Extrapolating from the rapid improvements of MT systems, the TNHE market's historical growth, and the current use of MT in language learning, MT will undoubtedly have a profound and lasting impact on EMI TNHE. While it is impossible to predict the exact contours of this impact, it is possible to help shape it. Now is the time to begin developing policy and best practices and preparing instructors and students for a future in which the potential benefits of MT are realized, and its perils are avoided.

REFERENCES

Al-Bayed, M. H., & Abu-Naser, S. S. (2018). Intelligent multi-language plagiarism detection system. *International Journal of Academic Information Systems Research, 2*(3), 19–34. http://dstore.alazhar.edu.ps/xmlui/handle/123456789/125

Alhaisoni, E., & Alhaysony, M. (2017). An investigation of Saudi EFL university students' attitudes towards the use of Google Translate. *International Journal of English Language Education, 5*(1), 72–82. doi:10.5296/ijele.v5i1.10696

Allen, J. (2003). Post-editing. In H. Somers (Ed.), *Computers and translation: A translator's guide* (pp. 297–318). John Benjamins Publishing. doi:10.1075/btl.35.19all

Andrade, M. S. (2009). The effects of English language proficiency on adjustment to university life. *International Multilingual Research Journal*, *3*(1), 16–34. doi:10.1080/19313150802668249

Arnold, D. (2003). Why translation is difficult for computers. In H. Somers (Ed.), *Computers and translation: A translator's guide* (pp. 119–142). John Benjamins Publishing Company. doi:10.1075/btl.35.11arn

Bannier, B. (2016). Global trends in transnational education. *International Journal of Information and Education Technology (IJIET)*, *6*(1), 80–84. doi:10.7763/IJIET.2016.V6.663

Barrón-Cedeño, A., Gupta, P., & Rosso, P. (2013). Methods for cross-language plagiarism detection. *Knowledge-Based Systems*, *50*, 211–217. doi:10.1016/j.knosys.2013.06.018

Bertram Gallant, T. (2008). *Academic integrity in the Twenty-First Century: A teaching and learning imperative*. Jossey-Bass.

Bowker, L. (2020). Machine translation literacy instruction for international business students and business English instructors. *Journal of Business & Finance Librarianship*, *25*(1–2), 25–43. doi:10.1080/08963568.2020.1794739

Briggs, N. (2018). Neural machine translation tools in the language learning classroom: Students' use, perceptions, and analyses. *The JALT CALL Journal*, *14*(1), 2–24. doi:10.29140/jaltcall.v14n1.221

Caillods, F., & Varghese, N. V. (2011). Preface. In J. B. G. Tilak, *Trade in higher education: The role of the General Agreement on Trade in Services (GATS)—UNESCO Digital Library* (pp. 9-10). UNESCO: International Institute for Educational Planning. https://www.iiep.unesco.org/en/trade-higher-education-role-general-agreement-trade-services-gats-9582

Case, M. (2015). Machine translation and the disruption of foreign language learning activities. *eLearning Papers, 45*, 4–16.

Caswell, I., & Liang, B. (2020, June 8). Recent advances in google translate. *Google AI Blog*. https://ai.googleblog.com/2020/06/recent-advances-in-google-translate.html

Chompurach, W. (2021). "Please let me use Google Translate": Thai EFL students' behavior and attitudes toward Google Translate use in English writing. *English Language Teaching*, *14*(12), 23–35. doi:10.5539/elt.v14n12p23

Coleman, D. (2003). Quality assurance in transnational education. *Journal of Studies in International Education*, *7*(4), 354–378. doi:10.1177/1028315303255597

Costa, P. I. D., Green-Eneix, C., & Li, W. (2021). Problematizing language policy and practice in EMI and transnational higher education: Challenges and possibilities. *Australian Review of Applied Linguistics*, *44*(2), 115–128. doi:10.1075/aral.00036.edi

Deckert, G. D. (1993). Perspectives on plagiarism from ESL students in Hong Kong. *Journal of Second Language Writing*, *2*(2), 131–148. doi:10.1016/1060-3743(93)90014-T

Department of Education. *activity 2018*. (2022). *UK revenue from education related exports and transnational education.* Department of Education. https://www.gov.uk/government/statistics/uk-revenue-from-education-related-exports-and-transnational-education-activity-2018

Ducar, C., & Schocket, D. H. (2018). Machine translation and the L2 classroom: Pedagogical solutions for making peace with Google Translate. *Foreign Language Annals, 51*(4), 779–795. doi:10.1111/flan.12366

Evans, S., & Morrison, B. (2011). Meeting the challenges of English-medium higher education: The first-year experience in Hong Kong. *English for Specific Purposes, 30*(3), 198–208. doi:10.1016/j.esp.2011.01.001

Flowerdew, J., & Li, Y. (2007). Language re-use among Chinese apprentice scientists writing for publication. *Applied Linguistics, 28*(3), 440–465. doi:10.1093/applin/amm031

Francois, E. J. (2015). *Building global education with a local perspective: An introduction to glocal higher education*. Palgrave Macmillan. doi:10.1057/9781137386779

Francois, E. J. (2016). What is transnational education? In E. J. Francois, M. B. Avoseh, & W. Griswold (Eds.), Perspectives in transnational higher education (pp. 3–23). Sense Publishers. doi:10.1007/978-94-6300-420-6_1

Fredholm, K. (2019). Effects of Google Translate on lexical diversity: Vocabulary development among learners of Spanish as a foreign language. *Revista Nebrija, 13*(26), 98–117. doi:10.26378/rnlael1326300

Galloway, N., Kriukow, J., & Numajiri, T. (2017). *Internationalisation, higher education and the growing demand for English: An investigation into the EMI movement in China and Japan* (ELT Research Papers 17.02). British Council. https://www.teachingenglish.org.uk/article/internationalisation-higher-education-and-growing-demand-english-investigation-emi-movement

Garrett, R., Kinser, K., Lane, J. E., & Merola, R. (2016). *International branch campuses: Trends and developments*. The Observatory of Borderless Higher Education and C-BERT. https://www.obhe.org/resources/international-branch-campuses-trends-and-developments-2016

Gill, S. K., & Kirkpatrick, A. (2013). English in Asian and European higher education. In C. Chapelle (Ed.), *The encyclopedia of applied linguistics*. Wiley-Blackwell., doi:10.1002/9781405198431.wbeal0383.pub2

Groves, M., & Mundt, K. (2015). Friend or foe? Google Translate in language for academic purposes. *English for Specific Purposes, 37*, 112–121. doi:10.1016/j.esp.2014.09.001

Groves, M., & Mundt, K. (2021). A ghostwriter in the machine? Attitudes of academic staff towards machine translation use in internationalised Higher Education. *Journal of English for Academic Purposes, 50*, 100957. Advance online publication. doi:10.1016/j.jeap.2021.100957

Helms, R. M. (2014). *Mapping international joint and dual degrees: US program profiles and perspectives*. American Council on Education and Center for Internationalization and Global Engagement. https://www.acenet.edu/Documents/Mapping-International-Joint-and-Dual-Degrees.pdf

Hessler, P. (2022, May 9). A teacher in China learns the limits of free expression. *The New Yorker*.

Hill, C. (2017). *Knowledge creators or knowledge hijackers? Plagiarism in international education*. The Observatory on Borderless Higher Education. https://www.obhe.org/resources/knowledge-creators-or-knowledge-hijackers-plagiarism-in-international-education

Hu, K., & Cadwell, P. (2016). A comparative study of post-editing guidelines. *Baltic Journal of Modern Computing*, *4*(2), 346–353. doi:10.13140/RG.2.1.2253.1446

Hutchins, W. J., & Somers, H. L. (1992). *An introduction to machine translation*. Academic Press.

JISC and Internet2. (2018). *Transnational education (TNE) data report*. [Data set]. JISC and Internet2. https://wiki.geant.org/download/attachments/103713412/TNE%20data%20by%20country_v12_final.pdf?version=1&modificationDate=1525804573391&api=v2

Jones, M., & Sheridan, L. (2015). Back translation: An emerging sophisticated cyber strategy to subvert advances in 'digital age' plagiarism detection and prevention. *Assessment & Evaluation in Higher Education*, *40*(5), 712–724. doi:10.1080/02602938.2014.950553

Kagwesage, A. M. (2012). Higher education students' reflections on learning in times of academic language shift. *International Journal for the Scholarship of Teaching and Learning*, *6*(2), 1–14. doi:10.20429/ijsotl.2012.060218

Khanal, J., & Gaulee, U. (2019). Challenges of international students from pre-departure to post-study: A literature review. *Journal of International Students*, *9*(2), 560–581. doi:10.32674/jis.v9i2.673

Kim, E. H., & Zhu, M. (2010). Universities as firms: The case of US overseas programs. In C. T. Clotfelter (Ed.), *American universities in a global market* (pp. 163–201). University of Chicago Press. doi:10.7208/chicago/9780226110455.003.0006

Kim, E. Y. J., & LaBianca, A. S. (2018). Ethics in academic writing help for international students in higher education: Perceptions of faculty and students. *Journal of Academic Ethics*, *16*(1), 39–59. doi:10.100710805-017-9299-5

Kir, E., & Akyüz, A. (2020). An exploration of perceptions of faculty members and students: The effects of English-medium instruction on language ability. In M. L. Carrió-Pastor (Ed.), *Internationalising learning in higher education: The challenges of English as a medium of instruction* (pp. 155–177). Springer. doi:10.1007/978-3-030-21587-3_8

Kit, C., & Wong, T. M. (2008). Comparative evaluation of online machine translation systems with legal texts. *Law Library Journal*, *100*(2), 299–31.

Knight, J. (2016). Transnational education remodeled: Toward a common TNE framework and definitions. *Journal of Studies in International Education*, *20*(1), 34–47. doi:10.1177/1028315315602927

Knowles, C. L. (2022). Using an ADAPT approach to integrate Google Translate into the second language classroom. *Journal of Linguistics and Language Teaching*, *14*(1), 195–236. doi:10.5070/L214151690

Kosmützky, A., & Putty, R. (2016). Transcending borders and traversing boundaries: A systematic review of the literature on transnational, offshore, cross-border, and borderless higher education. *Journal of Studies in International Education*, *20*(1), 8–33. doi:10.1177/1028315315604719

Lacore-Martin, E. (2019, July 5). *The elephant in the room: Rethinking language assessment in the times of Google Translate* [Symposium]. Translation Technology in Education – Facilitator or Risk? Nottingham Trent University.

Le, Q. V., & Schuster, M. (2016, September 27). A neural network for machine translation, at production scale. *Google AI Blog*. https://ai.googleblog.com/2016/09/a-neural-network-for-machine.html

Le-Ha, P. (2006). Plagiarism and overseas students: Stereotypes again? *ELT Journal*, *60*(1), 76–78. doi:10.1093/elt/cci085

Le-Ha, P. (2017). *Transnational education crossing 'Asia' and 'the West': Adjusted desire, transformative mediocrity and neo-colonial disguise*. Routledge.

Lee, S. M. (2020). The impact of using machine translation on EFL students' writing. *Computer Assisted Language Learning*, *33*(3), 157–175. doi:10.1080/09588221.2018.1553186

Lee, S. M. (2021). The effectiveness of machine translation in foreign language education: A systematic review and meta-analysis. *Computer Assisted Language Learning*, 1–23. doi:10.1080/09588221.2021.1901746

Liu, D. (2005). Plagiarism in ESOL students: Is cultural conditioning truly the major culprit? *ELT Journal*, *59*(3), 234–241. doi:10.1093/elt/cci043

Lowery, C. L. (2016). Critical transnational pedagogy: Toward a critical theory of transnational education and learning. In E. J. Francois, M. B. Avoseh, & W. Griswold (Eds.), Perspectives in transnational higher education (pp. 55–73). Sense Publishers.

Lozano, G. A. (2014). Ethics of using language editing services in an era of digital communication and heavily multi-authored papers. *Science and Engineering Ethics*, *20*(2), 363–377. doi:10.100711948-013-9451-6 PMID:23690133

Luo, N., & Hyland, K. (2019). "I won't publish in Chinese now": Publishing, translation, and the non-English speaking academic. *Journal of English for Academic Purposes*, *39*, 37–47. doi:10.1016/j.jeap.2019.03.003

Macaro, E., Curle, S., Pun, J., An, J., & Dearden, J. (2018). A systematic review of English medium instruction in higher education. *Language Teaching*, *51*(1), 36–76. doi:10.1017/S0261444817000350

Malete, L. (2016). Transnational education and internationalization of education as tools for higher education: Transformation and economic development in emerging economies. In E. J. Francois, M. B. Avoseh, & W. Griswold (Eds.), Perspectives in transnational higher education (pp. 39–54). Sense Publishers.

Marginson, S. (2004). National and global competition in higher education. *Australian Educational Researcher*, *31*(2), 1–28. doi:10.1007/BF03249517

Mundt, K., & Groves, M. (2016). A double-edged sword: The merits and the policy implications of Google Translate in higher education. *European Journal of Higher Education*, *6*(4), 387–401. doi:10.1080/21568235.2016.1172248

Niño, A. (2009). Machine translation in foreign language learning: Language learners' and tutors' perceptions of its advantages and disadvantages. *ReCALL*, *21*(2), 241–258. doi:10.1017/S0958344009000172

Nowlan, W. (2019, July 5). *Translation software: An insight into student use and non-EAP lecturer attitudes to translation software in university learning and assessments* [Symposium]. Translation Technology in Education – Facilitator or Risk? Nottingham Trent University.

Organ, A. (2019, December 10). *Blissful ignorance? Or turning a blind eye? Language departments' attitudes to student use of Google Translate* [Symposium]. Language Teaching Forum, University of York.

Palmer, A., Pegrum, M., & Oakley, G. (2019). A wake-up call? Issues with plagiarism in transnational higher education. *Ethics & Behavior*, *29*(1), 23–50. doi:10.1080/10508422.2018.1466301

Pan, M., Stiles, B. L., Tempelmeyer, T. C., & Wong, N. (2019). A cross-cultural exploration of academic dishonesty: Current challenges, preventive measures, and future directions. In D. M. Velliaris (Ed.), *Prevention and detection of academic misconduct in higher education* (pp. 63–82). IGI Global. doi:10.4018/978-1-5225-7531-3.ch003

Paniagua, J., Villó, C., & Escrivà-Beltran, M. (2022). Cross-border higher education: The expansion of international branch campuses. *Research in Higher Education*, *63*(6), 1–21. doi:10.100711162-022-09674-y PMID:35068659

Paxton, M. I. J. (2009). 'It's easy to learn when you using your home language but with English you need to start learning language before you get to the concept': Bilingual concept development in an English medium university in South Africa. *Journal of Multilingual and Multicultural Development*, *30*(4), 345–359. doi:10.1080/01434630902780731

Pennycook, A. (1994). The complex contexts of plagiarism: A reply to Deckert. *Journal of Second Language Writing*, *3*(3), 277–284. doi:10.1016/1060-3743(94)90020-5

Peters, B. D., & Anderson, M. E. (2021). Supporting nonnative English speakers at the university: A survey of faculty and staff. *Journal of International Students*, *11*(1), 103–121. doi:10.32674/jis.v11i1.1200

Pitman, J. (2021, April 28). *Google Translate: One billion installs, one billion stories*. Google. https://blog.google/products/translate/one-billion-installs/

Poibeau, T. (2017). *Machine translation*. MIT Press. doi:10.7551/mitpress/11043.001.0001

Pyvis, D., & Chapman, A. (2005). Culture shock and the international student 'offshore.'. *Journal of Research in International Education*, *4*(1), 23–42. doi:10.1177/1475240905050289

Ricento, T. (2015). Political economy and English as a "global" language. In T. Ricento (Ed.), *Language policy and political economy: English in a global context* (pp. 27–47). Oxford University Press. doi:10.1093/acprof:oso/9780199363391.003.0002

Risager, K. (2007). *Language and culture pedagogy: From a national to a transnational paradigm*. Multilingual Matters LTD. doi:10.21832/9781853599613

Rostrong, M. (2016). A cultural other in transnational education: Impact of globalization on student and teacher identities. In L. Seawright & A. Hodges (Eds.), *Learning across borders: Perspectives on international and transnational higher education* (pp. 193–215). Cambridge Scholars Publishing.

Ryu, J., Kim, Y., Park, S., Eum, S., Chun, S., & Yang, S. (2022). Exploring foreign language students' perceptions of the Guided Use of Machine Translation (GUMT) model for Korean writing. *Journal of Linguistics and Language Teaching*, *14*(1), 136–165. doi:10.5070/L214151759

Scott, P. (2011, June 7). Universities are all "internationalising" now. *The Guardian*. https://www.theguardian.com/education/2011/jun/07/universities-global-ambitions-internationalising

Son, B., Liang, X., & McIntosh, A. (2021). *An exploration of attitudes towards machine translation and a consideration of good practice* [Symposium]. School of Languages Symposium, Xi'an Jiaotong-Liverpool University.

Study Portals. (2021). *The changing landscape of English-taught programmes*. British Council and Study Portals. https://studyportals.com/intelligence/19347-2/

Trent, J. (2017). "Being a professor and doing EMI properly isn't easy": An identity-theoretic investigation of content teachers' attitudes towards EMI at a university in Hong Kong. In B. Fenton-Smith (Ed.), *English medium instruction in higher education in Asia-Pacific* (pp. 219–239). Springer. doi:10.1007/978-3-319-51976-0_12

Tsai, S. C. (2020). Chinese students' perceptions of using Google Translate as a translingual CALL tool in EFL writing. *Computer Assisted Language Learning*, 1–23. doi:10.1080/09588221.2020.1799412

Tsuneyoshi, R. (2018). The internationalization of Japanese education: "International" without the "multicultural.". *Educational Studies in Japan*, *12*(0), 49–59. doi:10.7571/esjkyoiku.12.49

Turner, J. (2011). Rewriting writing in higher education: The contested spaces of proofreading. *Studies in Higher Education*, *36*(4), 427–440. doi:10.1080/03075071003671786

Uricchio, W. (2017). Data, culture and the ambivalence of algorithms. In K. Van Es & M. T. Schäfer (Eds.), *The datafied society: Studying culture through data* (pp. 125–137). Amsterdam University Press. doi:10.1515/9789048531011-011

Urlaub, P., & Dessein, E. (2022). From disrupted classrooms to human-machine collaboration? The pocket calculator, Google Translate, and the future of language education. *Journal of Linguistics and Language Teaching*, *14*(1), 45–59. doi:10.5070/L214151790

Velliaris, D. M., & Pierce, J. M. (2019). Cheaters beware: (Re)designing assessment practices to reduce academic misconduct. In D. M. Velliaris (Ed.), *Prevention and detection of academic misconduct in higher education* (pp. 1–38). IGI Global. doi:10.4018/978-1-5225-7531-3.ch001

Wake, D., Ryan, G., & Ramos, E. (2020). *The scale of UK higher education transnational education 2018-19* (No. 4). Universities UK International. https://www.universitiesuk.ac.uk/universities-uk-international/insights-and-publications/uuki-publications/scale-uk-higher-education-transnational-1

Waters, J., & Leung, M. (2013). Immobile transnationalisms? Young people and their *in situ* experiences of 'international' education in Hong Kong. *Urban Studies (Edinburgh, Scotland)*, *50*(3), 606–620. doi:10.1177/0042098012468902

Waters, J., & Leung, M. W. H. (2022). Transnational higher education. In B. S. A. Yeoh & F. L. Collins (Eds.), *Handbook on transnationalism* (pp. 230–245). Edward Elgar Publishing.

Wilkins, S. (2020). Two decades of international branch campus development, 2000–2020: A review. *International Journal of Educational Management, 35*(1), 311–326. doi:10.1108/IJEM-08-2020-0409

Wilkins, S., & Annabi, C. A. (2021). Academic careers in transnational higher education: The rewards and challenges of teaching at international branch campuses. *Journal of Studies in International Education*. doi:10.1177/10283153211052782

Wilkins, S., & Balakrishnan, M. S. (2013). Assessing student satisfaction in transnational higher education. *International Journal of Educational Management, 27*(2), 143–156. doi:10.1108/09513541311297568

Wilkins, S., & Huisman, J. (2012). The international branch campus as transnational strategy in higher education. *Higher Education, 64*(5), 627–645. doi:10.100710734-012-9516-5

Wilkins, S., & Urbanovič, J. (2014). English as the lingua franca in transnational higher education: Motives and prospects of institutions that teach in languages other than English. *Journal of Studies in International Education, 18*(5), 405–425. doi:10.1177/1028315313517267

Wu, Y., Schuster, M., Chen, Z., Le, Q. V., Norouzi, M., Macherey, W., Krikun, M., Cao, Y., Gao, Q., Macherey, K., Klingner, J., Shah, A., Johnson, M., Liu, X., Kaiser, Ł., Gouws, S., Kato, Y., Kudo, T., Kazawa, H., & Dean, J. (2016). *Google's neural machine translation system: Bridging the gap between human and machine translation. ArXiv*. https://arxiv.org/abs/1609.08144

York St John University. (2021). *Code of Practice for Assessment and Academic-related Matters 2021-22 (Section 23)*. York St John University. https://www.yorksj.ac.uk/media/content-assets/registry/policies/code-of-practice-for-assessment/23.Academic_Misconduct_Policy_2021-22.pdf

ADDITIONAL READING

Bowker, L., & Buitrago Ciro, J. (2019). *Machine translation and global research: Towards improved machine translation literacy in the scholarly community*. Emerald Group Publishing.

Chapman, A., & Pyvis, D. (2012). *Enhancing quality in transnational higher education: Experiences of teaching and learning in Australian offshore programs*. Lexington Books.

Chowdhury, R., & Le Ha, P. (2014). *Desiring TESOL and international education: Market abuse and exploitation*. Multilingual Matters. doi:10.21832/9781783091492

Dafouz, E., & Smit, U. (2021). English-medium education revisited: Arguing for a comprehensive conceptualisation in the age of internationalised universities. *European Journal of Language Policy, 13*(2), 141–159. doi:10.3828/ejlp.2021.9

Dunn, L., & Wallace, M. (Eds.). (2008). *Teaching in transnational higher education*. Routledge.

Jolley, J. R., & Maimone, L. (2022). Thirty years of machine translation in language teaching and learning: A review of the literature. *Journal of Linguistics and Language Teaching, 14*(1), 26–44. doi:10.5070/L214151760

Klekovkina, V., & Denié-Higney, L. (2022). Machine Translation: Friend or Foe in the Language Classroom? *Journal of Linguistics and Language Teaching*, *14*(1), 105–135. doi:10.5070/L214151723

Somers, H. (Ed.). (2003). *Computers and translation: A translator's guide*. John Benjamins Publishing. doi:10.1075/btl.35

KEY TERMS AND DEFINITIONS

Academic Integrity: the appropriate values, practices, and behavior within academia.

English Medium-Instruction: the teaching in English of subjects other than English in countries where English is not the primary language.

Language Learning: the process whereby a person acquires competence in speaking, reading, and writing in a language.

Machine Translation: a computer's automated translation of one language into another.

Plagiarism: taking information without citation from other sources to deceptively present it as one's own.

Post-Editing: the editing, modifying, or correcting of a text translated by an MT system.

Transnational Higher Education: the provision of higher education across national boundaries.

Section 3
Extended Provision

Chapter 7
Joint Delivery and Collaboration in Transnational Higher Education:
A Phenomenological Analysis

Gloria Molinero
Queen Mary University of London, UK

ABSTRACT

Transnational higher education (TNHE) is increasingly experiencing collaborations between faculty and specialists of English for academic purposes (EAP). Issues concerning knowledge transfer, second language practice, and contextual challenges are the main concerns initiating joint delivery (JD) programmes. This reports on research exploring the collaborative experiences of thirteen EAP specialists with a reflective standpoint undertaking interpretative phenomenological analysis. The analysis exhibits three main collaborative practices with different levels of engagement and teaching tactics: assisted-delivery, co-teaching, and lecture-seminars delivery. Friend and Cook's (2014) framework evaluates these collaborations, providing insights on approaches for optimum and organic collaborations based on co-designing, openness and adaptation, mutual learning, and a share of outcomes and responsibilities. JD enriches practice, student experience, and the collaborative stands of TNHE.

INTRODUCTION

Within transnational higher education (TNHE) in the Chinese context, this paper reports on a research study based on collaborations between Faculty and English for Academic Purposes (EAP) specialists. These integrate disciplinary content with academic skills and language provision—a programme we name here Joint Delivery (JD).

Two main factors helped establish JD. One was to facilitate students with a contextualised EAP (Jordan, 1997; Jacobs, 2005, 2007), embedding with this the rationale and importance of learning the skills EAP offers in its modules since its courses are often shelved as general English. A second factor

DOI: 10.4018/978-1-6684-5226-4.ch007

aimed at bridging EAP with disciplinary course requirements encourage departmental collaboration and lecture partnerships in an expanding university that aspires for a cohesive setting where students can enrich their learning experience in a transnational environment.

The interest of this piece is in looking at the transformations TNHE is experiencing to accommodate world changes. From an increase in sophisticated technological advances aiding learning and the form in which information is acquired today to the overall geopolitical and environmental changes affecting students' futures, these are contained in classrooms whose purposes may need to be reconsidered.

This paper explores forms of collaboration and their dynamisms binding EAP specialists and Faculty in the JD programme. It provides insights into how EAP lecturers in TNHE understand their experiences and the implications of collaboration in practice and rethinking the role of Transnational Education (TNE) at large.

This study explores the reflective accounts of EAP specialists collaborating in Joint Delivery by analysing their narratives of their experiences and studying their construct of the JD phenomenon through Smith, Flowers and Larkin's (2009) interpretative cycle and hermeneutic approach.

BACKGROUND

Education has transformed quickly in approach and nature (Stensaker et al., 2012). The constant and rapid flow of students and faculty (Altbach, 2007; Ho, 2010; González-Ardeo, 2012) and technological improvements in information access have redesigned the dynamics, logistics and purpose of our classrooms with initiatives such as *blended learning* (Ehlers, 2013; Hew & Cheung, 2014), *flipped-classrooms* (Reidsema et al., 2017), and *Content Language Integrated Learning* (CLIL) (Mehisto, 2012; Evans et al., 2009). Thus shaping the overall palette of teaching practices. A palette that in TNE mixes standards and values in learning and teaching (LnT) traditions with differences in expectations between learners and teachers.

These mixed educational values were observed with the first TNHE in China in 2004 (Ennew & Fujia, 2009). Changes, adaptations and innovations are continuously taking place to meet students' learning needs. Within the TNHE context, some of these issues are denoted, for instance, in the ability to utilise and transfer skills from one course to another, others are in using English as the medium of instruction (EMI) in non-language related courses, and in general, the expectation that knowledge is centralised in textbooks and the teacher. These can affect acquiring micro-skills such as group work, peer-review, participation or taking the initiative to offer answers in the classroom without previous instruction. Experiences in pre-tertiary education, background and exposure to English can differentiate local and international students (Zha, 2013), while at the same time, both cohorts require similar academic competencies (Wang & Curdt-Christiansen, 2016).

In this EMI context, our Language Center (LC) is the pillar for students' continuation of their degrees, providing support throughout courses and levels. The LC provision focuses on the first two years where, until recently, half of the cohort continued their studies at the partner university in the UK. In recognizing some of these mixed values and issues, collaborative initiatives emerged to aid observed changes in students' learning needs developing thus; a programme that can synergise departmental teaching input and give cohesion to their learning. With this, JD evolved from an initial trial module in the first year, providing a taste of departmental literacy followed by LC-led seminars to multidisciplinary content with LC support at 3rd-4th year levels. The research finds a menu of combinations in interdepartmental collaborations, cohort size, classroom settings, teaching approaches, and use of virtual learning environments (VLE).

This TNHE context offers a variety of specialisms and backgrounds that can enrich teaching collaborations and multidisciplinary provision for learning (Bryant et al., 2014). Experiences in these collaborations can shed light on the underpinnings of collaborative practices and future teaching settings in similar contexts.

With globalisation, knowledge exchange, cultural diversity and collaborations at all levels have progressed global intellectual capital (Altbach & Knight, 2007). In this context, however, there are noticeable imbalances between on-the-ground practices today and the initial motivations that facilitated licensing approvals for TNE in China, aiming at attaining first-class education. TNE and geopolitical structures are becoming more complex (Hou, Montgomery & McDowell, 2014), while progressively, drivers are changing direction (Kirby & van der Wende, 2019). Yet, transnational collaborations can shape the future of LnT and research through interdisciplinary programs that can further combine eastern and western educational values that could mitigate future world challenges and generate not only intellectuals but also global citizens.

Theoretical Approach and Rationale

Contextualising Learning Values

To understand the fabric of today's educational system in China, we briefly examine Confucianism and Taoism as the two main core philosophies. These intertwine in their foundation (De Bary & Bloom, 1999; Lin, Ho & Lin, 2013) and complement each other in teachings such as the Yin-Yang School (Kirkland, 2004). Confucianism concerns the norms and hierarchical social structures; the "*order, duty, ceremony… respect of family and authority*" (Lin et al., 2013 p. 91), while Taoism's interest is in the forces of life and the process and cycle of nature. Their endurance today is in the complementary harmony they provide, satisfying rulers' character and people's beliefs. These ideas resonate in the classroom, balancing the forces of Yin-Yang (Chan, 1999) and dual '*paradoxical strength of passivity and the power of compliance*' (Lin et al., 2013 p. 91) central in Taoism. While Taoists avoid conflict through passivity, Confucians observe rules and procedures. For instance, the loss of face in order to prevent a superior's humiliation (Chan, 1999), or the Confucian collectivist attitude (Shi, 2006) that cares for the self in the view of others as a social magnetic force like cosmic movements as depicted below (Lu & Jover, 2019, Fig. 2, p. 429). These philosophies can be subtle moments in the LnT community. In a diverse TNHE, an awareness of this subtleness can be important in bringing the 'self' (*Figure 1*) closer to the wider community.

The learning values in Confucianism rest on the perfection of character (Hayhoe, 2008; Yao, 2000). Crafted exams allowed young males to reach the status of scholar-officials, the emperor's intelligentsia, the '*sidafu*' of the Confucian society, standing above the craftsman and merchant (Hayhoe, 2008; Xiong, 2011). This is reflected in today's preferred career paths with less vocational professions (Xiong, 2011; Frankel, Leshner & Yang, 2016). These exams tested morality and the memorisation of the classics (Xiong, 2011; Jin & Cortazzi, 2020). Rigorous and competitive exams saw candidates recite their ancient texts tirelessly as life value rather than enjoyment (Yao, 2000 p. 211), similar to the countless students this author has met since 1997 reciting aloud at dawn English sentences. Thus, the importance of exams transcends today's educational ethos with its strict processes and set of learning styles ingrained in Chinese education (Cortazzi & Jin, 2013 p. 6). Analogous to the '*sidafu*' exams, the university entrance exams or *Gaokao* curbs students' teen years on exams, determining their social status and future equally. Yet, although "*education today still focuses on the acquisition of a vast store of knowledge through rote memorisation, at the expense of creativity*" (Chan, 1999 p. 228), these rote-learning stereotypes and traditions are fading whilst the Chinese education transforms and synergises (Jin & Cortazzi, 2020).

Figure 1. The Anthropocentric Confucian Philosophy

"The broadening process of the self. Reprinted from Confucian Thought: Selfhood as Creative Transformation" (Adapted from Tu, 1985, as cited in Lu and Jover, 2019, Fig. 2, p. 429)

Within this synergy of philosophies, including religion and Western thought (excluded but considered here), programmes such as JD can provide blended LnT approaches that best cater to students with different learning needs. In TNHE, JD's interdepartmental collaborations in planning, delivery and assessment can offer exchanges in an educational ethos that facilitates best educational practices.

Collaborations in Education

The collaborative culture embedded in TNHE comprises an elaborate embroiled network of collective work and LnT teamwork (Grangeat & Gray, 2008; Snyder, 2009). The explicit definition of *collaboration* seems blurry in the everyday discourse, which "*created problems when the concept and phenomenon became the objects of investigation*" (Croker, 2016 p.56). Yet, an explicit definition can aid the description of the practice, initiatives and approaches, establishing potential collaborative interactions (Friend & Cook, 2014 p.7). This specificity includes the requisites for working together with peers comprised in Friend and Cook's (2014 p.8) definition, placing *collaboration* as a 'unique professional concept':

"Interpersonal collaboration is a style for direct interaction between at least two coequal parties voluntarily engaged in shared decision making as they work towards a common goal"

(Friend & Cook, 2014 p. 8)

Although set in pre-tertiary education, its collaborative insights on integrated and inclusive learning give basis to our context. This definition allows us to recognise the importance of personalities in the '*interpersonal style(s)*' of each peer, who is in '*direct interaction'*, actively '*sharing decisions*', and with fundamentally '*one common goal*', which Friend and Cook (2014) identify as essential in collaborations. In Healthcare collaborations, this is also identified with a distinction between the notion of the concept and the experience (Croker, Trede & Higgs, 2014), which interests us since the experience of *collaborating* is the phenomenon studied here as a human endeavour.

The components of this endeavour are best analysed in Friend and Cook (2014), offering a scaffold framework of the collaboration mechanisms, including personal commitments, skills required, process, facilities, and the oval context as represented below (*Figure 2*). Paradoxically, this representation echoes similarities to the depiction of Confucian Philosophy (*Figure 1*), symbolising both human nature and social construct. Attributed to the 'self/personal' can be the personal and professional learning gains of collaborating, while the 'communication/interaction processes' relate to the commitments to peers and students as the family and the community.

Figure 2. Components of collaboration

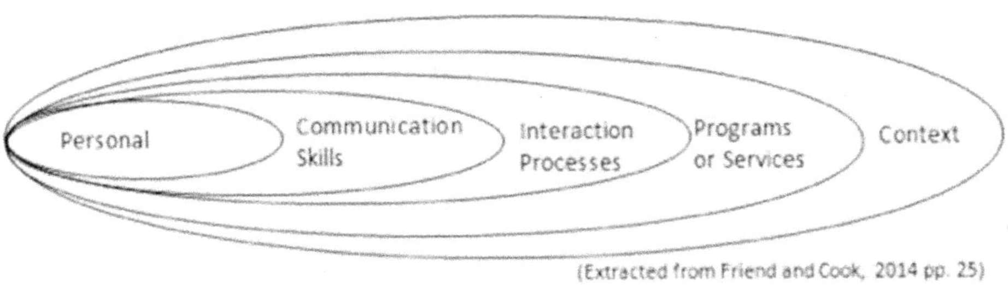

Collaborations in Education and Healthcare concur that they can only exist with a 'common goal' and in 'different interactive forms' (Friend & Cook, 2014; Croker et al., 2014). The evaluation of an *optimum collaboration* involves *voluntary* disposition, *parity* in decision-making, at least one *mutual goal*, a share of *duties, responsibilities and resources,* and *accountability for the outcomes* (Friend & Cook, 2014 p. 8). With these, the collaborative success can be assessed, determined, and modified as needed. With time and equilibrium between strengths and weaknesses, trust strengthens building community (Friend & Cook, 2014) while providing work ownership, commitment and professional development. Collaborative motivators may intensify as sharing and trust build, while students may emulate the lecturers' collaborations in teamwork, which is essential in this diverse and transnational setting.

Collaborations can present challenges, complexities and imbalances. In Healthcare, Croker et al. (2014; Croker, Higgs, & Trede, 2016) classify two collaborative modes: one *ordered* with discipline, planning, structure, and purpose; and another more *organic* with synergy awareness and focus on plasticity spawning *creativity, trust, respect, taking the initiative, willingness and responsibility.*

Although of different degrees, these collaborative modes align in four dimensions: *people, place, purpose* and *process* (Croker et al., 2014, 2016). In Education, these dimensions should include *resources, time, space* and *proximity* as they can affect other dimensions and learning outcomes. As Croker (2016) finds, the context may determine particular dimensions, accentuating the complexity of this phenomenon. For instance, in Massey's (2016) collaboration of a healthcare practitioner and a schoolteacher, the *space* dimension experienced identified "*the interactive space*", "*collaborative space*", and "*the collaborative space*" (p. 205), suggesting further analysis in this dimension within the collaborative mode. As Fisher, Squires and Woodley (2016) find, overwhelming *ordered* modes with regulations constrain collaborations, while *organic* collaborations outside the working context can generate rewards "*fostering connections, using imagination, being resourceful, and ensuring vigilance*" (Fisher et al., 2016 p.211). Thus, reflecting an inclination towards *organic* collaborations, where rules may be embedded, ensuring quality and community engagement.

Nonetheless, *organic collaborations* evolve naturally with time. As Littlefield, Taddei and Radosh's (2015) observe in Education, four building blocks can identify the *common goal* in shared attitude and motivations; *group dynamics* in support and commitment; *peer-to-peer support* in a community of practice; and *intentional relational learning* in sharing. Hence, to reach the *organic collaboration* layer (*Figure 3)*, previous blocks need to take place, reproducing together Friend and Cook's (2014) collaboration components.

Figure 3. Nested Venn diagram of Organic Collaboration

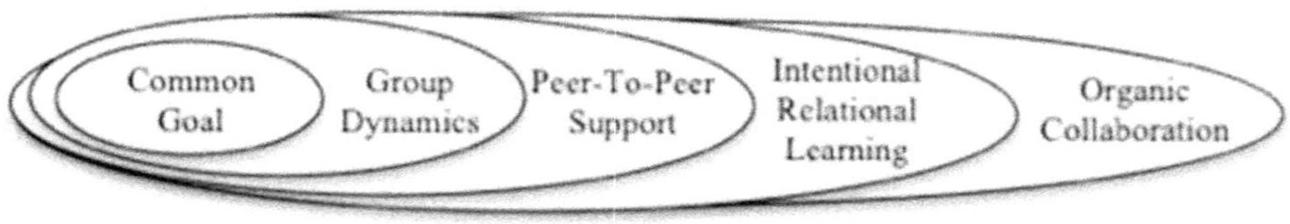

(Adapted from Littlefield, Taddei and Radosh, 2015 p.138)

Littlefield et al. (2015 p.131) define *organic collaborations* as "*a naturally formed dynamic peer-to-peer support group, built on individual strengths and differences, while focused on a common goal*". These *organic collaborations* require informal or open spaces for interaction without the academic setting constraints where learning may not be implied but may occur unintentionally and naturally, encouraging and sustaining the collaboration (Weiler, 2004; Littlefield et al., 2015; Massey, 2016; Fisher et al., 2016; MacLeod, Yang & Xiang, 2017).

Collaborative Teaching Approaches

Collaborative teaching adds value to learning and students' social development, particularly in a technologically individualised era. Lecturers' collaboration can motivate students in collaborative tasks, benefiting learning, developing teamwork soft-skills, and "*improv[ing] understanding and performance*" (Vangrieken et al., 2015 p.27), seldom explained in instruction. However, conflicting views exist between lecturers' beliefs on collaborative learning practices and traditional teaching (De Hei et al., 2015; Vangrieken et al., 2017), which can affect the collaboration even when LnT benefits are clear. For instance, "*according to the majority of co-teachers, inclusion facilitated the social development of students*" (Austin, 2001 p.254), while informal settings effectively aid and 'sustain collaborations' (Rice & Pinnergar, 2010). Thus, combining formal/informal interactions can aid all views and help students learn.

Collaborations in/out of the classroom form part of a constant *workflow* of *collective processes.* A teacher is under continuous observation mode, absorbing from all environments and transforming material into functional and active classroom tasks. Grangeat and Gray (2008) organise these *collective processes* into a *vertical* delegation of work and a *horizontal* agent of equals where tasks, goals, support and space are shared in cooperation towards a greater purpose, while management and administration, they argue, should take an active role in facilitating this *collective processes* that ultimately benefit the overall educational setting. For instance, a community of practice formed organically in Chinese universities (Fang, 2010), facilitating collaborations in formal/informal settings, thereby assisting with the paradoxes of co-teaching and *teaming* (Vangrieken et al., 2017) and indirectly providing a better learning experience for students. It is therefore vital to recognise in these collaborations that although an *order mode* may prove more operational, they would constrain organic modes that sustain collaborations. In this way, with time, richer outcomes at the professional and personal levels are obtained, while co-teaching and *teaming* can contribute as a model to students' teamwork and social skills.

In teaching collaborations, a 'life-cycle' is observed, including *team forming, storming, norming*, and *performing* (Tuckman, 1967 as cited in Friend & Cook, 2014). This process can be associated with most forms of long-term collaborations; complex for TNHE's high turnover and limited time to build rapport. In English for Specific Purposes (ESP), where specialists collaborate with Faculty in providing content-language support, Dudley-Evans and St John (1998) identify three primary collaborative levels denoting gradual collaborative closeness towards greater classroom cohesion: *cooperation,* enquiring about the subject; *collaboration*, sharing learning outcomes; and, *team-teaching* with full LnT involvement. These cooperative stages are progressive from an early demarcation of roles to a holistic contribution that can include students collaborating and enhancing the learning experience (Almagro & Vallejo, 2002).

The Collaborative Classroom Dynamics

The collaborative classroom dynamics can be divided into six '*co-teaching approaches*' (Friend & Cook, 2014 p.113) (*Figure 4*). A demarcation of roles is significant in *observation* and *teacher/assist* models, while 2-4 models alternate content and assistance, and *teaming* denotes classroom cohesion and *organic collaboration* potential. Teachers may complement each other and bring different perspectives in assisting second language (L2) acquisition (Baeten & Simons, 2014). This coordination may vary depending on planning, status and responsibilities in/out of the classroom, while maintaining inclusion at all levels of the experience. These models are pivotal in TNHE working with L2 mixed-abilities and/or large groups and essential in teacher training.

Figure 4. Co-teaching approaches

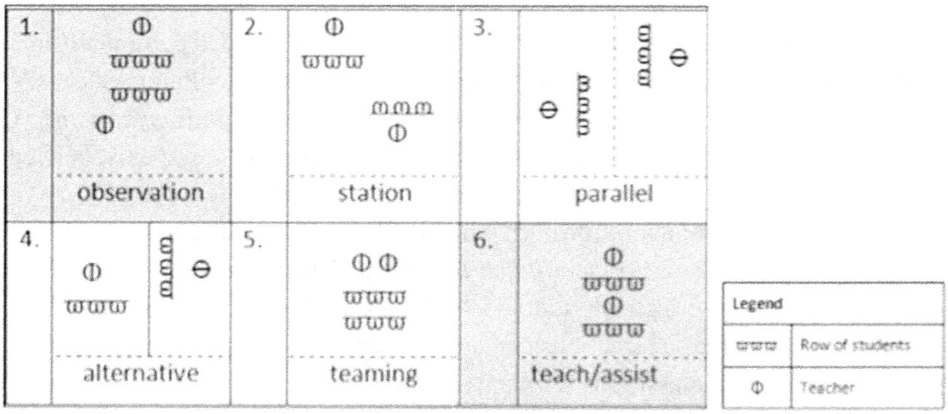

(Adapted from Friend and Cook, 2014 Figure 1. p.133)

Within the ideological context fostering techniques to acquire the 'unique right' answer to pass exams and the teacher as "*the omniscient authority who transmits knowledge to passive recipients*" (Hanusch, Obijiofor, & Volcic, 2009 p.66), co-teaching can "*help students learn how to learn… develop flexibility, analytic awareness, and a self-critical value system*" (Wenger & Hornyak, 1999 p.312). Effective co-teaching should consider the balance between the nature of the student, the curriculum and the learning outcomes, with the practitioners' practices and layered cooperation added, providing "*creative strategies that bring out the best in students and teachers*" (Friend & Cook, 2014 p.132). Therefore, in TNHE, with its diverse specialists' viewpoints and backgrounds (Hanusch et al., 2009) and students' collaborative inclusion (Almagro & Vallejo, 2002), team-teaching can enhance the learning experience and aid the social construct that the logistics of TNE needs (Altbach, 2007).

In recent decades, HE has seen significant change due to international mobility (Altbach, 2007; HESA, 2018), with greater demand for general English (TESOL), EAP and ESP provisions. Separated by a thin line, these are often intertwined and misinterpreted by non-specialists. EAP's study skills specialisms are crucial to all national and international students (Jordan, 1997). Conversely, EAP provision is not always recognised for its academic literacy skills outside the LC (Sloan & Porter, 2010), which detaches EAP from other programmes. This connection is necessary for TNHE settings since broader access to digital information adds complexity to LnT, such as in the confrontational perception of academic argumentation (Frankel et al., 2016) and confusion in adhering to academic integrity conventions, evaluation of sources or critical reading.

While ESP is particular to content and genre (Hutchinson & Waters, 1987), both ESP and EAP can contribute to team-teaching bringing authenticity and credibility to the course where "*the students see that their subject tutors take the EAP/ESAP classes seriously*" (Jordan, 1997 p. 121). Dudley-Evans and St. John (1998) classify team-teaching as a gradual increase of engagement: *collaboration, cooperation and team-teaching*, in which success requires willingness, demarcation of responsibilities and practice complementing each other's delivery. Still, both EAP/ESP practitioners are "*supposed to have not only functional academic literacy but also content knowledge of the field*" (González-Ardeo, 2012 p.233). Although ESP has that disciplinary dimension, EAP can contribute to all aspects of academic learning and research (Dudley-Evans & St. John, 1998), adding more widely to multiple programmes and multidisciplinary courses.

Integrated Learning

There has been a gradual increase in team-teaching initiatives denoting integration and contextualisation of literacies (Jacobs, 2005; Gustafsson & Jacobs, 2013; Dafouz, 2014; Leonardi, 2015). Content Language Integrated Learning (CLIL), seen in European bilingual schools, compiles recent literature on collaborations and team-teaching. At the tertiary level, these initiatives have various complexities, contexts, interpretations (Coyle, 2018) and terminology ICLHE (Wilkinson, 2018). Holistically, '*Joint Delivery*' offers a greater spectrum of flexibility to the language-content integration phenomenon where the two entities went out of their way to collaborate in meeting shared learning outcomes providing a more significant learning spectrum within the TNHE context.

Although sharing similarities, ESP is less content driven, while CLIL is more scaffolded content-based (Leonardi, 2015 p.18-25). In this contrast, Arno-Macia and Mancho-Bares (2014) find that while students are concerned with the lack of language in CLIL, their teachers support their 'learning by doing' ethos. This is consistent with Brown's (2017) findings in Japanese HE and Leonardi's (2015) conclusions stating that more cross-disciplinary development and interdisciplinary approaches with more specialists in team-teaching would help bridge the content-language gap experienced in ESP and CLIL.

EMI settings prepare students to articulate and interact within their fields of study. This goal in language support and literacies (Jacobs, 2005; Schmidt-Unterberger, 2018) places EAP/ESP in the first row. Although often unrecognised, EAP lecturers provide a range of linguistic support in genre and authenticity, as well as tackle learning issues and the overall academic ethos that would otherwise be disconcerting to subject specialists (Schmidt-Unterberger, 2018). Thus, to complement their expertise, departments and EAP/ESP specialists should be encouraged to generate collaborative planning and teaching initiatives even when it is administratively challenging.

Disciplines do not act in isolation; they coordinate in research and industries (Newell & Bain, 2018). Transdisciplinary collaborations in a rapidly advancing era need greater recognition in Education, as questions become more complex and challenging (Becher & Trowler, 2001; Bryant et al., 2014). Students should become specialists in different fields, exposed to structures of collaboration that allow them to transfer, interrelate and connect transdisciplinary concepts into new knowledge, creating processes that meet the challenges of the future. In *relational learning* programmes, for instance, students learn about new fields and their connections through interdisciplinary approaches (Holloway & Alexandre, 2012), thus, enhancing criticality, initiative, interactivity, and cooperative skills. As Becher and Trowler (2001 p.20) recognise, "*traditional forms of knowledge generation are being phased out in favour of collective, applied transdisciplinary developments*". Indeed there is more interweaving of fields in research (Cagle & Tillery, 2015) which should reflect in learning, such as in a cohesive JD course interrelating business concepts with environmental science, providing students with an awareness of their world.

Choi and Pak (2006) classify *transdisciplinary* collaborations as more holistic, while *interdisciplinary* concerns the synthesis of disciplines and *multidisciplinary* relates to the discipline's value added to a programme. This taxonomy can be evaluated through Friend and Cook's (2014 p.106) framework and Croker et al.'s (2014, 2016) areas of interaction, responsibility, and trust (*Figure 5*). Learning in 'transdisciplinary collectives' (Jacobs, 2005, 2007), trust amongst practitioners is built through "*cur-*

riculum, pedagogy, and student well-being" (Zappa-Hollman, 2018 p. 603), indicating thus the amplitude of benefits in the 'process of engagement', 'sense of belonging', 'applications of learning', and professional development.

Figure 5. Team interaction models

	Multidisciplinary	**Interdisciplinary**	**Transdisciplinary**
Sharing	participants might **not belong to a team** within different environments	share goals and **responsibilities related to each discipline**	common **goals**, and **responsibility**
Committing	disciplines collaborate while **remaining independent**	Committing to shared services primarily specific to their disciplines	working **across disciplines** integrating **planning and services**
Planning	**independently** develop plans in their discipline	Planning section related to disciplinary	**develop** plans together
Learning	brief encounters and **independent learning** in separate environments	regular **meetings** to share and learning on assessment **results** from each discipline	**regular** meetings to learn from each other's disciplines
Trust	unrelated - plans are implemented **separately** and **by discipline**	some **coordination** - members trust each part of the plan is implemented	shared responsibility - **trust building** - collaborative assessments, observations and **team building**,

(Adapted from Friend and Cook, 2014 p. 106, bold my emphasis)

In sustaining language-content collaborations, Zappa-Hollman (2018) observes an alignment in aims, engagement, parity and recognition of EAP practitioners' pedagogical authority, but an imbalance in the lack of the EAP instructors' perspective. Thus, a trial is needed to reach positive organic collaborations, where goals are maintained and moved forward. For this reason, several longitudinal studies accomplish collaborative maturity with elements of process and reflection (Jacobs, 2005; Zappa-Hollman, 2018; Lock et al., 2016; Jameau & Le Henaff, 2018). Reflective accounts are valuable elements of good practice in co-teaching (Lock et al., 2016), which Jameau and Le Henaff (2018) coin 'reflective investigation' as stages of development and advancement shaping the collaboration. Hence, this study utilises these insights by collecting reflective accounts focused on the EAP practitioner in JD contexts.

Reflective accounts allow participants to conceptualise and reflect on the efficacy of their co-teaching practices. Through these Lock et al. (2016) find continuity, understanding of peers' teaching styles and views of the classroom to be the basis of the rhythm, fluidity and organic approach of the collaborative practice, strengthened by an open and reciprocal learning relationship grounded on constructive feedback. There are, however, areas of conflict, as Perry and Stewart (2005) observe in interdisciplinary team-teaching in Japan: 1) co-teaching initial fears, classroom-spontaneity, clashes in experience and general power struggle; 2) mismatched working styles and personalities; and, 3) beliefs about learning. Zappa-Hollman (2018) classifies these observations into two paradigms, *organisational* and *interpersonal*. Her study on EAP-language-content programmes in Canada identifies additional elements concerning lack of commitment, patience and territorialism. Hence, it seems apparent that a better "*understanding of roles and expectations… helping, observing and talking with each other*" (Perry & Stewart, 2005 p. 572-573) as well as reflecting actively with colleagues on collaborative practices and pedagogical philosophies can energise engagement in team-teaching and joint initiatives such as JD.

Joint Delivery in the Transnational Context

The JD initiative allows students to practice, connect, and intrinsically associate language with subject-specific content in a tangible and reachable manner. It provides students with multidisciplinary perspectives and support that aids critical thinking and collaborative skills as students witness a collaborative Faculty. Closer linguistic and academic skills support subject-specific work, enhancing problem-solving and contextualising language and academic skills while making connections and enriching language learning, curriculum, and materials more meaningful and interestingly. There are, however, challenges demanding EAP specialists to identify the genre and language specificity of lecture content, a crafting talent to incorporate that language into digestible active tasks, rationalising the integration of language/skills in the subject classroom (e.g. to science learners), and an ability to recognise logic in language patterns applicable to scientific minds. Even though the learning opportunities are significant with JD collaborations, the content-language specialists' liaison presents challenges. Thus, these collaborations require further analysis to maximise the potential of the JD programme within the synergy nature of TNHE.

Consequently, with the recent and significant increase in collaborative initiatives (Mehisto, 2012; Leonardi, 2015; Lasagabaster, 2017; Coyle, 2018), particularly following CLIL approaches, the literature concerning Special Education and Healthcare offers matured and transferrable insights to HE collaborations; from Friend and Cook's (2014) framework for evaluating collaborations to Littlefield et al.'s (2015) depictions of organic collaborations. While the former guides us in classroom dynamics and co-teaching practices, the latter advises us about territorialism issues and shows us the potential of transdisciplinary and organic collaboration. Yet, Jacobs' (2005) encouragement of contextualising academic literacies in multilingual South Africa, and authors depicting similar contexts in Canada, Europe, and Japan, prove an increasing need to observe in detail what JD programmes have to offer with collaborative structures where content and language specialists synchronise in collaboration and how these move TNHE forward.

RESEARCH AND METHODS

The research analyses the reflective accounts of thirteen EAP specialists and their collaborative experiences in the JD programme. Participants were experts with a good number of years of experience in the field. Some were in management and all were interviewed at the end of the programme, providing a reflective angle to the study.

The study's paradigm adheres to Smith et al.'s (2009) applications to Interpretative Phenomenological Analysis (IPA), which focuses on the ideography of participants and their sense-making of their lived experiences (Creswell, 2013; Smith et al., 2009). This analytical platform allows the understanding of how participants make sense of their experiences, the researcher's interpretations as an insider and participant in the JD programme, and insights into the context. This paradigm is chosen for its flexibility and the organic form in which JD emerges in tackling issues concerning students' learning needs, mainly transferring skills and utilising a second language.

The study utilises *conversational interviews* as a two-level reflective approach where the professional background is shared. The researcher and participant engage in reflection and interpretation (Normann, 2017), while presuppositions and extrapolations refrain through distancing and bracketing (Smith et al., 2009). From a continuous reflexive and emic perspective, the interpretation is constantly active during the research process (Postholm & Skrøvset, 2013). The interview questions were based on openings such as perceptions, experience, changes and suggestions for improvement and possible future scenarios for JD. Follow-up questions adhered to the phenomenological ethos '*what was it like?*' and ideographic thrust '*how did you feel about that?*' (Smith et al., 2009) offering a wide range of tangled themes and items to a cluster.

Patterns of meaning were identified and thematically mapped, establishing relationships. In recollecting detail, particular interest focused on interviewees' intonation and use of pauses in the interviews aiding the interpretation of interactive language features. IPA uses hermeneutic cycling and recycling processes in iterative and inductive approaches (Smith et al., 2009).

Analysis of Findings

The analysis provides an umbrella of JD modes with various degrees of collaboration and teaching approaches integrating content, skills and language. Three main forms of delivery are identified:

- Assisted delivery – departmental courses with light EAP support;
- Co-delivery – language and content specialists co-teaching courses that combine both lectures and seminars within a session.
- Full lecture-seminar delivery or Joint Delivery – content-focused lectures followed by EAP-specialists-led seminars co-teaching in some cases, or multidisciplinary with various visiting lecturers delivering content synthesised in seminars.

Figure 6. Joint delivery's collaborative scenarios

Structural	Lecture - LC Supported	Co-Delivery Dep.-LC	Joint Delivery Lecture & Seminar
Voluntary	Semi-voluntary for LC-tutors & generally assigned for lecturers according to subject	Semi-voluntary for LC-tutors & generally assigned for lecturers according to subject	Semi-voluntary for LC-tutors & generally assigned for lecturers accordingto subject
Parity	Content – Dep. led Structure and assessments – LC led	Content, structure & assessments – Dep. led	Content – Dep. led Structure and assessments – LC led
Mutual goals	Students' Learning subject and related language. Promoting & introducing Dep.'s topic Language & Skills improvement	Students' Learning subject and related language. Promoting & introducing Dep.'s topic Language & Skills improvement	Students' Learning subject and related language. Promoting & introducing Dep.'s topic Language & Skills improvement
Shared responsibilities & decision-making	Demarcation of tasks Some common decision making	Shared participation	Demarcation of tasks Shared participation for LC-tutors in seminars
Share of resources	Share of lecture's PPTs Generally	Share of lecture's PPTs	Share of lecture's PPTs
Share of accountability of outcomes	May share grading assessments, often speaking assessments. Module's outcomes shared to a degree. Responsible the departmental module coordinator	May share grading assessments, often speaking and writing for large cohorts. Module's outcomes shared to a degree. Shared responsibility, but mostly on module coordinator	Usually LC designs and grades assessments. Module's outcomes shared to a degree. Responsibility - LC's module coordinator

Applying JD Features to Friend and Cook's (2014 pp. 8-11) Characteristics of Collaboration

These collaborative scenarios share common goals, responsibilities and resources of various degrees, which place them as '*collaborative*' in Friend and Cook's (2014 p.8) framework for optimum collaborations (*Figure 6*). *Assisted delivery*, as faculty-led courses, has the least parity in shared responsibilities, accountability and outcomes than *co-delivery* or the *lecture-seminar delivery* modes. While the latter have clearer demarcation of duties, in *co-delivery* content and language specialists coordinate and share all aspects of a course, including planning, sources and assessments. With this, *co-delivery* can be identified as the most *optimum collaboration* mode as both specialists cooperate in all aspects of a course.

Although with imminent obstacles, JD was mainly seen as a positive and valuable experience for LnT armoured with clear tactics and avenues for improvements and optimistic solutions, participants had a clear understanding of their practice and a desire to continue developing the JD programme, as observed in attitudes and perceptions of all accounts (*Figure 7*).

Figure 7. Joint Delivery – The Phenomenon

Lectures		
Positive experiences	Less positive experiences	Needs and improvements
- Having the student experience in lectures - Learning or re-learning subject matter - Lecture teaching observations	- No interaction with lecturers in semi-detached courses - Some assisting in lectures - Lack of peer observation - Too many people in the course, some visiting lecturers	- Feedback on teaching for/from lecturers - More communication in exchanging expertise - More continuation to build rapport
Seminars		
Positive experiences	Less positive experiences	Needs and improvements
- JD bridges between EAP and Content - Contextualising EAP	- Overlaps between skills taught in EAP and those in JD	- Remedial and supplementary work on skills and language
The co-teaching experience		
Positive experiences	Less positive experiences	Needs and improvements
- Satisfaction - Interesting - Good to have a co-teacher - Support - Fantastic - Being assisted - Professionalism - A 'fortune' when working with people that corresponds to one's personality - Greater use of technology	- Adaptation - New dynamics - A Gradual process - Reservation - Observation - Learning process - Judging - Co-reaction - Acting accordingly	- Early expressions of teaching preferences - Preferences as part of the plan (course plan) - Clear understanding of each other's teaching approaches - Open dialogue - Respect and professionalism

Participants' expectations and perceptions of JD gravitated towards greater specificity and content focus than EAP provision. Although optimistic about JD, they experienced an initial sense of apprehension and anxiety concerning unfamiliarity with the subject matter and preparation time. They "*envisioned more content specific*", the "precise" reason for "*want[ing] to do it*", though greater preparation time "*going back to study and refresh my memory" and being "a kind of learner too... if I have to teach about something, I have to learn about it... regardless of whether I am an expert or not, it was a bit intimidating"*. These require thorough organisation and coordination between lectures and seminars, "*sometimes 24 hours before... I was a bit anxious"*.

At the same time, participants expressed thrilling enthusiasm to start JD, looking forward to breaking from EAP's prescriptive mechanisms. One reason was to contextualise EAP since *"students may have a well-constructed paragraph, but had nothing to say about the subject... with content, we have something to deal with being EAP limited in a way"*. Another was the input to professional development and practice; "*a lot of the support in assisted delivery takes place outside the classroom [i.e. VLE]... [and] I wanted to see how big room teaching worked in practice"*.

The JD programme experience within each of the three main modes offers different language and skills support levels, depending on the course's particulars and students' needs analysis. Course 'ownership' can also affect the level of engagement and contribution.

In *Assisted delivery*, participants felt distant in designing courses led by content specialists, while *Co-delivery* offered closer contact between specialists in course planning. The dynamics for the *lecture-seminar delivery* settings are more detached, yet the course ownership and assessment rest on the language specialists, providing more room for change and course development.

In co-teaching, participants expressed reservations at the start of the programme, finding it '*strange*', '*disconcerting*', or feeling '*nervous*' concerning the number of people involved. At the same time, they had '*a fantastic experience*', '*a co-teacher to work together*' with, and '*learning different styles and approaches*'. For established teachers, co-teaching can be disconcerting in having to adapt to colleagues' teaching approaches, to share the control of the classroom and classroom management; *'it's like an orchestra conductor, directing where you want to, but suddenly there is more dynamics involved... it's very different'*. This suggests gradual adaptation, coordination, and an understanding of what co-teaching entails.

The adaptation process articulated by responders suggests an initial reservation, followed by observation, and then a learning process through an evaluative time of judgement that responds to a colleague's feedback to one's teaching, where practitioners observe each other's reaction to respond and cooperate accordingly.

"Yes, it feels as though I learned something because I only taught on my own so, I was a little bit nervous at the beginning because you never know when you're sitting in someone lecture; 'should I speak? Can I speak? Would he mind if I say something? ... I was quiet at the beginning but... I delivered my session and he was quite active in my session so, I thought 'oh great, he doesn't mind... so I would just jump-in if he was talking and say 'we should clarify that point' and he was more than happy to let me do it"

An initial open dialogue determining co-teachers preferences and expectations can avoid this long process. This open communication should be part of the shared goals (Friend & Cook, 2014), highlighting respect and engagement in the collaboration (Croker et al., 2016) and leading to an organic collaboration (Littlefield et al., 2015). These can, therefore, energise new approaches and improvements to JD practice as we anticipate in EAP's future. Other participants found having a demarcation of duties "*deciding who will lead which part*" more functional. While one teaches, the peer is in 'supporting capacity' volunteering elements to the collaboration (Friend & Cook, 2014) while building rapport and trust.

Participants conceptualised JD as courses offering students a '*transfer learning from and to other classes'* adding value to EAP academic skills and language, '*an extension of the lecture format*' providing authenticity and context to EAP's academic work, '*lecturers' echo chambers'* to transition smoothly to the subject matter, and '*specificity'* to the '*embedded language support'*. Regarding staffing, managers perceive JD as a way to '*reach across different modules*', which for some '*requires less people for the number of students involved'*. Other practitioners questioned the student-centred pedagogical value in managing large rooms and the complexity of dealing with different subjects.

The value of JD is seen unanimously as a way to '*prepare students for content'*, '*provide greeter communication*' and '*bridge between EAP and academic input'*, though these objectives need to be more explicit for students as JD settings may seem unusual and confusing. Still, participants call for more co-teaching communication since they could '*have a better idea of the pitfalls and language straggles'* and can predict and '*solve problems before coming to the classroom'*. Thus, the consensus is that the JD programme '*is the future of EAP...[for] talking about ideas, teaching ideas, [and] sharing ideas*' in TNHE contexts.

The Lecture Experience_

For *lecture-seminar* experiences, attending lectures is part of the LC-tutor's schedule; '*you have to go*', with some flexibility. Attending lectures can '*help you to see what students experience is*' and add value to students' skills learning such as note taking with a '*model they can refer to... students like it*'. They can assist in monitoring group and lab work, sketching, and language practice depending on the nature of the course. Though detachment affects the collaboration, '*we just sit there, listen... there is not much social interaction... because there is no structural requirement for us to collaborate, ...we're quite semi-detached'*.

There are pedagogical learning moments in lecture observation. From mechanical approaches, '*I felt as if he was going to get through the material regardless of what was actually happening in the class... there wouldn't be a moment to... stop and go back and review*'. To inspiring and meaningful moments, '*...the way he delivered this was more digestible, and he was so slow in doing this, ...with the little notes everyone was just expecting... the language was simple with examples of our everyday life... It was amazing. So that's when I thought, a lecture can make a huge difference'*.

As trained teachers, participants identify and complement lecture practices in using learning spaces and student-centred approaches, while at the same time they determine students' learning needs in content, skills and language to prepare seminars and further formative assessment. Peers' constant observations, however, can be intimidating since teaching experience and English proficiency may defer in TNHE settings.

For LC-led *lecture-seminar* modules, lecturers provide the course content with sporadic LC-consultation suggesting readings sometimes '*without specifics on activities'*. For departmental *assisted-delivery* modules, the learning outcomes, content, curriculum and assessment are designed without LC involvement, thus leading to frustration; "*I felt like a spare part, almost like a secretary ... [without] any meaningful contribution... I wasn't utilised*". For all delivery forms, therefore, the curriculum design should incorporate voice and accountability to all involved, avoiding alienation and demotivation to add value to the LnT experience.

The Seminar Experience

Seminars follow the lecture after a day or two, tailored to provide the space and time to digest and discuss lecture content while reinforcing EAP elements. This allows students to reflect on the subject and build on academic literacies. For cohorts ranging from 60 to 200+ students, two co-teaching LC-specialists swiftly turn the lecture content into manageable learning chunks and activities that ease content learning, which can be demanding:

"In a sense we're repeating the content; I give little mini-lectures, ...repeating aspects of the lecture from the day before and explaining things in greater detail, ...there would be a series of questions of what we've done, discussion questions, ...at the end we'd have feedback.... It would not be just student-centred..., we'd also give some kind of perspective of our own, so therefore is a little like in the lecture again"

Seminars are spaces for students to identify and discuss the lecture's key ideas in more detail. For some complex content, pre- and post-lecture seminars facilitate lecture preparation and review, allowing a deeper understanding of the lecture. LC-specialists summarise the lecture content in seminars, evaluating students' learning needs and covering any missing information and further explanations while connecting all the different subjects concurrently. Likewise, in multidisciplinary courses: '*I can help with content, it takes time, but it helps students to think*'. This complexity leads to participants' common concern about the lack of time to transfer content and course material into a meaningful formative practice with EAP features. Thus, adding a layer to the JD experience outside the seminars and on VLE, utilising blended learning and flipped-classroom approaches (Ehlers, 2013; Hew & Cheung, 2014; Reidsema et al., 2017).

Lecture-seminar modules demand greater responsibility, empowering participants as they bring their ingredients to subject learning. Some respondents dread *'when the lecturer had to go away, and I was to lead the seminar discussion on the content-based topic'*, while others see an opportunity for change. This suggests a range of intellectual backgrounds and attitudes towards content delivery in JD. This dependency also adds to TNHE's high turnover bringing concerns about collaborations and absenteeism. Although *"when the lecturer change(s), the content tends to evolve... up-to-date or new [content] or new examples"*, continuity can bring progression to course design and content while maintaining collaborative rapport. Therefore, when co-teachers maintain co-working, the success is tangible, providing examples of 'true collaboration' through a share of responsibilities, better performance and experience, amending and reflecting on provision and benefiting the overall learning experience.

True collaborations can also determine the flexibility in which co-teachers spontaneously interrupt each other during class. Spontaneous interjections can reflect the dynamics of the collaboration marked by personalities, culture, roles, and teaching styles. While some preferred a demarcation of roles without a peer's clarifications or adds-on, others were *'very flexible [and] willing to try new ideas... it felt like team-teaching'*, reflecting a sense of belonging and inclusion in co-delivery.

Observing the language dynamics between L1/L2, it is distinctive in the JD classroom how students respond readily in L2 to the lecturer sharing L1 but feel compelled to use L2 with the international practitioner. During teamwork, students code-switch as the practitioner, monitoring the groups, approaches but continue discussing in L1 when the co-lecturer observes their work. Hence, students associate L1 with the discipline's content where teamwork is primarily done in L1, limiting L2 acquisition.

Teaching Experience

Although participants recognise the challenges and complexities that JD collaborations bring to their practice, they also identify the benefits offered to students' cognitive experience in subject-language integration (Evans et al., 2009; Mehisto, 2012; Arno-Macia, & Mancho-Bares, 2014), which helps them transferring the necessary skills across disciplines in EMI transnational contexts (Brown, 2017). Participants agreed when reporting success in incorporating content into their language teaching and exploring new subjects and ways to teach EAP.

Participants recognised all JD collaboration to help students transfer skills and literacies, contextualise their studies and make connections between concepts (Jacobs, 2005, 2007). For TNHE settings, this is important where EAP is seen as an additional course or exam cultures demarcate the ending of courses (Becher & Trowler, 2001; Cortazzi & Jin, 2013). These collaborations align subject courses and the assessments with the core purpose of EAP, often misjudged by students with higher English levels in this context. JD in this setting also helps to contextualise both practical skills such as note taking and more abstract skills; for instance, taking the initiative, working in teams, or suggesting an answer to the classroom without instruction. Such collaborations also address rooted learning and pragmatic traditions such as expecting the teacher, not peers, to provide the right and unique answer. Therefore, JD equips students with a collaborative learning environment and a palette of learning styles that can help them explore new learning approaches and identify their preferences.

Although administrative and logistics aspects of course ownership may influence the functionality of JD collaborations, its participants' encouraging attitudes added significant value to the program. As in Jacobs (2005), participants' objectives are to conceptualise EAP further through support, authenticity and specificity. While also aspire to new teaching experiences to further professional development. These prompt positive and innovative approaches to JD collaborations, offering constructive feedback and solutions to the encountered issues in participants' experiences, suggesting forward thinking towards the programme and strengthening attitudes towards further initiatives.

Implications for Practice

Three main areas strive for the meaning and significance of JD practices in participants' experiences: collaboration, pedagogy and professional development. These elements intertwine in the analysis, with *collaboration* as JD's main essence.

The participants' discourse on collaboration gravitated towards three main questions: 'how the collaboration worked', 'what was their role' and, 'what would they gain from the experience'. Within the notion that all collaborations share at least one common goal (Friend & Cook, 2014), this study infers three main essential practices for successful collaborations that can apply to comparable centres and universities: 1) co-design a clear and thorough initial plan; 2) maintain and adapt shared responsibilities; and, 3) grow at both personal and professional levels. These can be defined and elaborated as follows:

1. **To plan and design together** a clear and thorough course outline before the course starts, including discussions about roles and expectations. This shared task would help build trust, accountability and direction. Practical options include:
    1. Co-planning (Li et al., 2019) and co-designing the course and assessments, including the course's learning outcomes, each other's roles and expectations.
    2. Guidelines form, helping co-teachers establish their expectations and preferences in teaching (e.g. task-based approaches, classroom interjections, lesson adaptations).
    3. Establishing and adapting the degree of fluidity in co-teaching, from an initial demarcation of roles to a subsequent organic collaborative teaching.
    4. Including students in the planning and collaboration, for instance, by recording a presentation with the co-lecturers, the curriculum, students' roles, and how the JD course would benefit them.
2. **To adapt and share course responsibilities** through an open, adaptive and supportive share of sources sustaining and developing the collaboration. A sustainable co-teaching delivery, including an open attitude towards adaptation to change, coordination, and reciprocal inclusivity. Practical options include:
    1. Sharing spaces, teaching resources, instructional responsibilities and assessment (Hedin & Conderman, 2019)
    2. Creating a mixture of formal and informal spaces (Massey, 2016; Fisher et al., 2016; Austin, 2001; Rice & Pinnergar, 2010), aiding rapport building and engagement in a dynamic and inclusive classroom environment toward organic collaborations (Croker, 2016).
    3. Set courses based on practical and hands-on tasks where small and large cohorts can work in open and flexible spaces, shifting teacher-centred approaches to online delivery and hybrid classroom methods, blended learning, flipped classrooms, HyFlex and other more recent online approaches (Ehlers, 2013; *Hew & Cheung, 2014; Reidsema et al., 2017;* Leijon & Lundgren, 2019; Scull et al., 2020).
3. **To grow at personal and professional levels** by learning from the JD experience, the departmental subject matter, and the various teaching practices. In turn, this should motivate and maintain an interest in the collaboration. Practical options include:
    1. Cultural and pedagogical exchanges within TNHE, activating a co-teaching community of practice, welcoming fluid reflective discussions about JD co-practices.
    2. Taking the time to exchange expertise and skills in subject-content and pedagogical skills.
    3. Keeping a JD diary recording significant (or not) components learned weekly, reflecting on practice and collaboration and exchanging viewpoints for positive change and practical adaptations.
    4. Developing JD training in co-teaching and teaching strategies from observations and reflective practices.
    5. Sharing the JD experience university-wide and beyond of practices and potential research in consortiums, conferences, journals and similar.

These essential and practical options suggest a cyclical evolving process throughout the semester (*Figures 8* and *9* below). This basic approach can implement JD provision in similar TNHE and EMI contexts, adding improved elements from the analysis, such as regulating the number of visiting lectur-

Figure 8. Collaborative Process

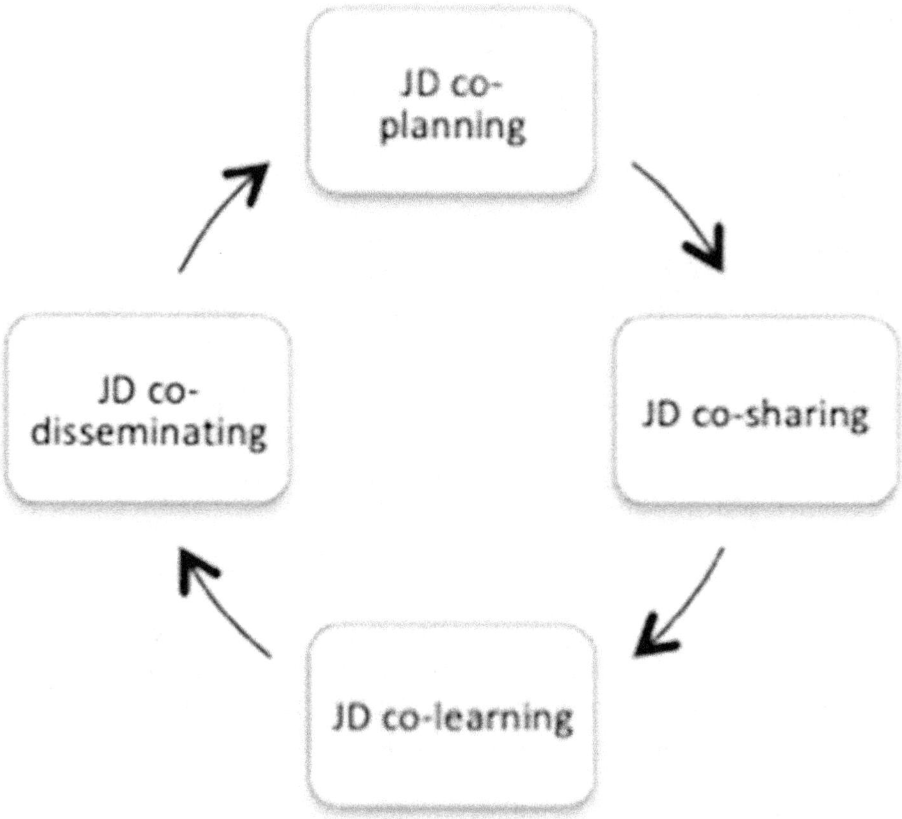

ers, empowering co-teachers with course development and providing departmental shared ownership of the JD courses.

Localised course ownership for multidisciplinary and JD syllabi forces one department to regulate and take full responsibility for the course, isolating the participation of others. This can generate tensions and damage the collaboration, as seen in the assessment and course materials analysis. Likewise, fewer lecturers rather than course-visiting lectures would minimise fluctuations in engagement and provide accountability, empowering teachers in their craft.

To alleviate conflict and ensure a truly effective collaborative practice, guaranteeing extensive applications of JD, course ownership and participation need sharing amongst departments. Courses could be owned centrally at the university level or as a new entity for all JD and multidisciplinary related courses. A university hub comprising a collaborative network of practice for teaching and research is the way forward.

Indeed, not all practices can be undertaken efficiently, as protocols, regulations, and life often tend to interfere. *Figure 9* summarises some fundamental areas and optional approaches to implement greater collaborations in institutions with JD programme implementation potentials.

Figure 9. Essential and optional areas for successful collaborations

JD Collaboration essentials	- To co-plan and design the course establishing teaching styles and co-teaching preferences - To adapt and share course responsibilities including all involved - To engage in mutual learning at personally and professionally levels
JD collaboration optional	- To limit the number of lectures involved - To focus classroom work on practical and interactive tasks that teams can perform in large and flexible spaces, placing lectures to asynchronous online platforms - To share course ownership pushing for cross-departmental multidisciplinary work in both teaching and research generating equality between departments and centres. - To implement a co-teaching community of practice sharing experiences and developments in learning and teaching. - To disseminate through co-research and presentations the impact of collaborative curricula and learning outcomes.

Some of these potentials can encourage collaborations at departmental levels by offering language and academic skills input to already established subject-based courses. Initiated as testers and moving toward planning and delivery sharing could include exchanging peer-observations of subject-based and EAP sessions, acquiring a taste of different pedagogies, a learning experience, and avoiding fossilising presuppositions.

Management may enable interdepartmental communication to understand each other's teaching content and practice as in a university-wide community of practice. At the same time, policy changes could include course ownership and transdisciplinary curricula, which can contribute to TNHE cohesion. The stature of JD collaborations needs dissemination, circulation and influence in groups such as BALEAP, where EAP specialists with similar backgrounds can influence their contexts, bringing value to their practices, adding to the development of skills in teacher training, and disseminating through research and journals circulation.

CONCLUSION

This chapter reported on research contributing to the literature on Joint Delivery integrating disciplinary content and academic language and skills provision, analysing collaborations between EAP practitioners and Faculty. Through IPA, the study discloses the essence of JD through the analysis of EAP specialists' experiences in JD, answering the research questions concerning JD's impact on LnT, professional development and the future of education in TNHE settings. Although many elements were consistent with those found in the literature, JD's contributions could significantly enhance pedagogical practices and professional development. Effective collaborations were found in initial solid co-planning and designing courses, maintaining a share of responsibilities and having continuous motivational learning, either in teaching practices or subject matter. These would enhance and lead to more organic collaborations in multidisciplinary settings. More practical approaches for JD collaborations across departments can be a community of practice that can aid the exchange and sharing of experiences and advance future collaboration in TNHE.

REFERENCES

Almagro, A. E., & Vallejo, M. C. M. (2002). A case study of collaboration among the ESP practitioner, the content teacher, and the students. *Revista Alicantina de Estudios Ingleses*, *15*(15), 7–21. doi:10.14198/raei.2002.15.01

Altbach, P. G. (2007). Globalization and the University: Realities in an unequal world. In J. J. F. Forest & P. G. Altbach (Eds.), *International handbook of higher education* (pp. 121–139). Springer.

Altbach, P. G., & Knight, J. (2007). The Internationalization of Higher Education: Motivations and Realities. *Journal of Studies in International Education*, *11*(3–4), 290–305. doi:10.1177/1028315307303542

Arno-Macia, E., & Mancho-Bares, G. (2014). The role of content and language in content and language integrated learning (CLIL) at university: Challenges and implications for ESP. *English for Specific Purposes*, *37*, 63–73. doi:10.1016/j.esp.2014.06.007

Austin, V. L. (2001). Teachers' beliefs about co-teaching. *Remedial and Special Education*, *22*(4), 245–255. doi:10.1177/074193250102200408

Baeten, M., & Simons, M. (2014). Student teachers' team teaching: Models, effects, and conditions for implementation. *Teaching and Teacher Education*, *41*, 92–110. doi:10.1016/j.tate.2014.03.010

Becher, T., & Trowler, P. (2001). *Academic tribes and territories: Intellectual enquiry and the culture of disciplines* (2nd ed.). SHRE & Open University Press.

Brown, H. (2017). Cooperation and collaboration in undergraduate EMI: Adapting EAP to the emergence of blended academic norms and practices in a Japanese University. In J. Valcke & R. Wilkinson (Eds.), *Integrating content and language in Higher Education: Perspectives on professional practice* (pp. 151–167). Peter Lang GmbH.

Bryant, L. H., Niewolny, K., Clark, S., & Watson, C. E. (2014). Complicated spaces: Negotiating collaborative teaching and interdisciplinarity in higher education. *The Journal of Effective Teaching*, *14*(2), 83–101.

Cagle, L. E., & Tillery, D. (2015). Climate change research across disciplines: The value and uses of multidisciplinary research reviews for technical communication. *Technical Communication Quarterly*, *24*(2), 147–163. doi:10.1080/10572252.2015.1001296

Chan, S. (1999). The Chinese learner - A question of style. *Education + Training*, *41*(6/7), 294–305. doi:10.1108/00400919910285345

Cortazzi, M., & Jin, L. (2013). *Researching cultures of learning: International perspectives on language learning and education* [electronic version]. Palgrave Macmillan. doi:10.1057/9781137296344

Coyle, D. (2018). The place of CLIL in (bilingual) education. *Theory into Practice*, *57*(3), 166–176. doi:10.1080/00405841.2018.1459096

Creswell, J. W. (2013). *Qualitative inquiry & research design: Choosing among five approaches* (3rd ed.). Sage Publications, Inc.

Croker, A. (2016). Valuing ordered and organic collaboration: People, place, process and purpose. In A. Croker, J. Higgs, & F. Trede (Eds.), *Collaborating in healthcare: Reinterpreting therapeutic relationships* (pp. 55–81). Sense Publishers. doi:10.1007/978-94-6300-806-8_5

Croker, A., Higgs, J., & Trede, F. (Eds.). (2016). *Collaborating in healthcare: Reinterpreting therapeutic relationships* Sense Publishers. doi:10.1007/978-94-6300-806-8

Croker, A., Trede, F., & Higgs, J. (2014). Collaboration and collaborating. In J. Higgs, A. Croker, D. Tasker, J. Hummell, & N. Patton (Eds.), *Health practice relationships* (pp. 75–85). Sense Publishers. doi:10.1007/978-94-6209-788-9_9

De Bary, W. T., & Bloom, I. (1999). *Sources of Chinese tradition from earliest times to 1600* (2nd ed., Vol. 1). Columbia University Press.

De Hei, M. S. A., Strijbos, J. W., Sjoer, E., & Admiraal, W. (2015). Collaborative learning in higher education: Lecturers' practices and beliefs. *Research Papers in Education*, *30*(2), 232–247. doi:10.1080/02671522.2014.908407

Dudley-Evans, T., & St. John, M. J. (1998). *Developments in ESP: A multi-disciplinary approach.* Cambridge University Press.

Ehlers, U. D. (2013). *Open learning cultures: A guide to quality, evaluation and assessment for future learning*. Springer. doi:10.1007/978-3-642-38174-4

Ennew, C. T., & Fujia, Y. (2009). Foreign universities in China: A case study. *European Journal of Education*, *44*(1), 21–36. doi:10.1111/j.1465-3435.2008.01368.x

Evans, E., Tindale, J., Cable, D., & Hamil-Mead, S. (2009). Collaborative Teaching in a Linguistically and Culturally Diverse Higher Education Setting: A Case Study of a Postgraduate Accounting Program. *Higher Education Research & Development*, *28*(6), 597–613. doi:10.1080/07294360903226403

Fang, Y. (2010). The cultural pedagogy of errors: Teacher Wang's homework practice in teaching geometric proofs. *Journal of Curriculum Studies*, *42*(5), 597–619. doi:10.1080/00220271003773901

Fisher, K., Squires, K., & Woodley, I. (2016). Community collaboration beyond the red tape: Complying without being constrained. In A. Croker, J. Higgs, & F. Trede (Eds.), *Health practice relationships.* (pp. 203–211).

Frankel, M. S., Leshner, A. I., & Yang, W. (2016). Research integrity: Perspectives from China and the United States. In T. Bretag (Ed.), *Handbook of Academic Integrity* (pp. 848–864). Springer. doi:10.1007/978-981-287-098-8_65

Friend, M., & Cook, L. (2014). *Interactions: Collaboration Skills for School Professionals, Enhanced.* Pearson Education Limited.

González-Ardeo, J. M. (2012). Overlapping of ESP/EAP and Content Courses Revisited. *Revista de Lenguas para Fines Específicos, 18*, 213–236.

Grangeat, M., & Gray, P. (2008). Teaching as a collective work: Analysis, current research and implications for teacher education. *Journal of Education for Teaching, 34*(3), 177–189. doi:10.1080/02607470802212306

Gustafsson, M., & Jacobs, C. (2013). Student Learning and ICLHE - Frameworks and Contexts. *Journal of Academic Writing, 3*(1), ii–xii. doi:10.18552/joaw.v3i1.141

Hanusch, F., Obijiofor, L., & Volcic, Z. (2009). Theoretical and practical issues in team-teaching a large undergraduate class. *International Journal on Teaching and Learning in Higher Education, 21*(1), 66–74.

Hayhoe, R. (2008). Philosophy and Comparative Education: What can we learn from East Asia? In K. Mundy, K. Bickmore, R. Hayhoe, M. Madden, & K. Madjidi (Eds.), *Comparative and International Education: Issues for Teachers*. Canadian Scholars' Press Inc.

Hedin, L., & Conderman, G. (2019). Pairing Teachers for Effective Co-Teaching Teams. *Kappa Delta Pi Record, 55*(4), 169–173. doi:10.1080/00228958.2019.1659063

Hew, K. F., & Cheung, W. S. (2014). *Using blended learning: Evidence-based practices*. Springer Ltd. doi:10.1007/978-981-287-089-6

Higher Education Student Statistics [HESA] (2018). *Higher Education Student Statistics: UK, 2016/17 - Where students come from and go to study*. HESA. https://www.hesa.ac.uk/data-and-analysis/students/where-from

Ho, R. (2010). Assessment of Chinese students' experience with foreign faculty: A case study from a Chinese University. *Journal of Teaching in International Business, 21*(3), 156–177. doi:10.1080/08975930.2010.504461

Holloway, E. L., & Alexandre, L. (2012). Crossing boundaries in doctoral education: Relational learning, cohort communities, and dissertation committees. *New Directions for Teaching & Learning, 2012*(131), 85-97.

Hou, J., Montgomery, C., & McDowell, L. (2014). Exploring the diverse motivations of transnational higher education in China: Complexities and contradictions. *Journal of Education for Teaching: International research and pedagogy, 40*(3), 300-318.

Hutchinson, T., & Waters, A. (1987). *English for Specific Purposes*. Cambridge UP. doi:10.1017/CBO9780511733031

Jacobs, C. (2005). On being an insider on the outside: New spaces for integrating academic literacies. *Teaching in Higher Education, 10*(4), 475–487. doi:10.1080/13562510500239091

Jacobs, C. (2007). Towards a critical understanding of the teaching of discipline-specific academic literacies: Making the tacit explicit. *Journal of Education, 41*(1), 59–81.

Jameau, A., & Le Henaff, C. (2018). "Content and Language Integrated Learning" teaching in science: A didactic analysis of a case study. *Review of Science Mathematics & ICT Education, 12*(2), 21.

Jin, L., & Cortazzi, M. (2020). Reaching for the gold standard: Metaphors and good university teachers. [De Gruyter]. *Canadian Journal of Applied Linguistics*, *43*(2), 131–149.

Jordan, R. R. (1997). *English for academic purposes: A guide and resource book for teachers* (11th ed.). Cambridge University Press. doi:10.1017/CBO9780511733062

Kirby, W., & van der Wende, M. (2019). New Silk Road: Implications for higher education in China and the West? *Cambridge Journal of Regions, Economy and Society*, *12*(1), 127–144. doi:10.1093/cjres/rsy034

Kirkland, R. (2004). *Taoism: The enduring tradition*. Routledge. doi:10.4324/9780203646717

Lasagabaster, D. (2017). "I always speak English in my classes": Reflections on the use of the L1/L2 in English-medium instruction. In A. Llinares & T. Morton (Eds.), *Applied linguistics perspectives on CLIL* (pp. 251–267). John Benjamins Publishing Company. doi:10.1075/lllt.47.15las

Leijon, M., & Lundgren, B. (2019). Connecting physical and virtual spaces in a HyFlex pedagogic model with a focus on teacher interaction. *Journal of Learning Spaces*, *8*(1), 1–9. http://libjournal.uncg.edu/jls/article/view/1640

Leonardi, V. (2015). Bridging the gap between ESP and CliL in the university context. *Testi Letterature Linguaggi*, *5*, 18-26. https://www.iperstoria.it/joomla/images/PDF/Numero%205%20giusto/saggi_monografica/Leonardi_ESPCLIL.pdf

Li, Y., Cargill, M., Gao, X., Wang, X., & O'Connor, P. (2019). A scientist in interdisciplinary team-teaching in an English for Research Publication Purposes classroom: Beyond a "cameo role". *Journal of English for Academic Purposes*, *40*, 129–140. doi:10.1016/j.jeap.2019.06.005

Lin, L. H., Ho, Y. L., & Lin, W. H. (2013). Confucian and Taoist Work Values: An Exploratory Study of the Chinese Transformational Leadership Behavior. *Journal of Business Ethics*, *113*(1), 91–103. doi:10.100710551-012-1284-8

Littlefield, C. M., Taddei, L. M., & Radosh, M. E. (2015). Organic collaborative teams: The role of collaboration and peer to peer support for part-time doctoral completion. *International Journal of Doctoral Studies*, *10*, 129–142. http://ijds.org/Volume10/IJDSv10p129-142Littlefield0790.pdf. doi:10.28945/2113

Lock, J., Clancy, T., Lisella, R., Rosenau, P., Ferreira, C., & Rainsbury, J. (2016). The Lived Experiences of Instructors Co-Teaching in Higher Education. *Brock Journal of Education*, *26*(1), 22–35.

Lu, Y., & Jover, G. (2019). An anthropocosmic view: What Confucian traditions can teach us about the past and future of Chinese Higher Education. *Higher Education: The International Journal of Higher Education Research*, *77*(3), 423–436. doi:10.100710734-018-0280-z

MacLeod, J., Yang, H. H., & Xiang, Z. (2017). Understanding College Students' Intrinsic Motivation and Social Interdependence in Intercultural Computer-Supported Collaborative Learning between USA and China. *The Asia-Pacific Education Researcher*, *26*(3), 205–217. doi:10.100740299-017-0341-6

Massey, S. (2016). Working across health and education sectors. In A. Croker, J. Higgs, & F. Trede (Eds.), *Health practice relationships*.

Mehisto, P. (2012). Criteria for producing CLIL learning material. *Encuentro: Revista de investigación e innovación en la clase de idiomas, 21,* 15-33. http://www.encuentrojournal.org/textos/3.%20Mehisto_rev.pdf

Newell, C., & Bain, A. (2018). *Team-based collaboration in higher education learning and teaching: A review of the literature*. Springer. doi:10.1007/978-981-13-1855-9

Normann, A. (2017). Becoming a phenomenologically skilled researcher - An account of a journey started. *Reflective Practice*, *18*(5), 613–626. doi:10.1080/14623943.2017.1307720

Perry, B., & Stewart, T. (2005). Insights into effective partnership in interdisciplinary team teaching. *System*, *33*(4), 563–573. doi:10.1016/j.system.2005.01.006

Postholm, B. M., & Skrøvset, S. (2013). The researcher reflecting on her own role during action research. *Educational Action Research*, *21*(4), 506–518. doi:10.1080/09650792.2013.833798

Reidsema, C., Kavanagh, L., Hadgraft, R., & Smith, N. (Eds.). (2017). The Flipped Classroom: Practice and Practices in Higher Education. Springer Science and Business Media. doi:10.1007/978-981-10-3413-8

Rice, M., & Pinnegar, S. (2010). Organic collaboration: Sustaining teachers and teacher educators in the cottage industry of curriculum making. *Teachers and Teaching*, *16*(3), 373–387. doi:10.1080/13540601003634537

Schmidt-Unterberger, B. (2018). The English-medium paradigm: A conceptualisation of English-medium teaching in higher education. *International Journal of Bilingual Education and Bilingualism*, *21*(5), 527–539. doi:10.1080/13670050.2018.1491949

Scull, J., Phillips, M., Sharma, U., & Garnier, K. (2020). Innovations in teacher education at the time of COVID19: An Australian perspective. *Journal of Education for Teaching*, *46*(4), 497–506. doi:10.1080/02607476.2020.1802701

Shi, L. (2006). The Successors to Confucianism or a New Generation? A Questionnaire Study on Chinese Students' Culture of Learning English. *Language, Culture and Curriculum*, *19*(1), 122–147. doi:10.1080/07908310608668758

Sloan, D., & Porter, E. (2010). Changing international student and business staff perceptions of in-sessional EAP: Using the CEM model. *Journal of English for Academic Purposes*, *9*(3), 198–210. doi:10.1016/j.jeap.2010.03.001

Smith, J. A., Flowers, P., & Larkin, M. (2009). *Interpretative Phenomenological Analysis: Theory, Method and Research*. Sage Publications, Inc.

Snyder, L. G. (2009). Teaching Teams about Teamwork: Preparation, Practice, and Performance Review. *Business Communication Quarterly*, *72*(1), 74–79. doi:10.1177/1080569908330372

Stensaker, B., Henkel, M., Välimaa, J., & Sarrico, C. S. (2012). Introduction: How is change in Higher Education managed? In B. Stensaker, J. Välimaa, & C. S. Sarrico (Eds.), *Managing Reform in Universities: The Dynamics of Culture, Identity and Organizational Change*. Palgrave Macmillan. doi:10.1057/9781137284297_1

Vangrieken, K., Dochy, F., Raes, E., & Kyndt, E. (2015). Teacher collaboration: A systematic review. *Educational Research Review*, *15*, 17–40. doi:10.1016/j.edurev.2015.04.002

Vangrieken, K., Grosemans, I., Dochy, F., & Kyndt, E. (2017). Teacher autonomy and collaboration: A paradox? Conceptualising and measuring teachers' autonomy and collaborative attitude. *Teaching and Teacher Education*, *67*, 302–315. doi:10.1016/j.tate.2017.06.021

Wang, W., & Curdt-Christiansen, X. L. (2016). Teaching Chinese to international students in China: Political rhetoric and ground realities. *The Asia-Pacific Education Researcher*, *25*(5-6), 723–734. doi:10.100740299-016-0316-z

Weiler, A. (2004). Information-seeking behavior in generation Y students: Motivation, critical thinking, and learning theory. *Journal of Academic Librarianship*, *31*(1), 46–53. doi:10.1016/j.acalib.2004.09.009

Wenger, M. S., & Hornyak, M. J. (1999). Team Teaching for Higher Level Learning: A Framework of Professional Collaboration. *Journal of Management Education*, *23*(3), 311–327. doi:10.1177/105256299902300308

Wilkinson, R. (2018). Content and language integration at universities? Collaborative reflections. *International Journal of Bilingual Education and Bilingualism*, *21*(59), 607–615. doi:10.1080/13670050.2018.1491948

Xiong, J. (2011). Understanding higher vocational education in China: Vocationalism vs Confucianism. *Frontiers of Education in China*, *6*(4), 495–520. doi:10.100711516-011-0143-1

Yao, X. (2000). *An introduction to Confucianism*. Cambridge University Press. [electronic version] doi:10.1017/CBO9780511800887

Zappa-Hollman, S. (2018). Collaborations between language and content university instructors: Factors and indicators of positive partnerships. *International Journal of Bilingual Education and Bilingualism*, *21*(5), 591–606. doi:10.1080/13670050.2018.1491946

Zha, Q. (Ed.). (2013). *Education in China*. Berk Publishing Group LLC.

Chapter 8
The Local Impact of Social Sciences, Humanities, and Educational Dissertations on Transnational Higher Education in Turkey

Ömer Açıkgöz
Social Sciences University of Ankara, Turkey

Aydın Aslan
Selcuk University, Turkey

Aslı Günay
Social Sciences University of Ankara, Turkey

ABSTRACT

Doctoral education, which is a crucial component of transnational higher education, should contribute to the development of national and international science. To get a better insight into the contributions of doctoral education to the literature, 266 dissertations completed in the fields of social sciences, humanities, and education at 12 Turkish state universities between 2014 and 2017 were analyzed with bibliometric analysis. The analysis indicated that the scientific articles generated from the dissertations and the citations to these articles were dominantly published and cited in national indexed journals, which means that the dissertations made more contributions to the national literature than international literature. It can be one of the indicators that display the impact of transnational higher education on these dissertations are quite limited in Turkey. Several suggestions were made for Turkish universities to make more contributions to transnational higher education through doctoral education.

DOI: 10.4018/978-1-6684-5226-4.ch008

INTRODUCTION

In the modern world, one of the most significant roles of universities is to contribute to the generation of a knowledge-based economy and a welfare economy by looking for and developing answers to society's issues at the national and international levels. These answers should first deal with and come up with solutions and suggestions for society's issues at the national level. Academic systems and organizations as well as individuals can use the solutions and suggestions developed at the national level to cope with the global academic environment at the international level. Commercial gain, knowledge and language acquisition, curriculum enhancement with international materials, and many other reasons are the main motivations of universities for internationalization (Altbach & Knight, 2007).

At the international level, universities can find solutions and suggestions for the global challenges through transnational higher education. In transnational higher education, learners are awarded by the awarding institutions, which are based in different countries other than the learners' locations (UNESCO/Council of Europe, 2001). In the literature, there are several terms such as cross-border, offshore, and borderless higher education to describe transnational higher education (Knight, 2016). Transnational higher education involves providers and programs crossing national borders. Providers take a variety of forms, with different ownership structures, objectives, strategies, disciplines, and types of students (Wilkins, 2018). Moreover, it can promote the intellectual enrichment of the universities of countries and provide a stimulus to their programs and research (Stella & Woodhouse, 2011). In this regard, it can play a significant role in knowledge transfer among higher education institutions around the world. Transnational higher education will be used throughout this paper (Huang, 2007) because it is an important part of internationalization.

Today, doctoral education must be a key element in the planning of science and technology and social policies for countries. Doctoral graduates, with their knowledge and skills, should help the economic growth and social well-being of their country at the national level and the global academic environment at the international level. Doctoral education is precisely the place to go beyond national boundaries and outside the academic world to explore how particular techniques help or hurt people outside national spheres. This means that research can no longer be thought of as being done only locally or at universities (Nerad, 2010). In this regard, doctoral education can be considered a crucial component of transnational higher education, which has evolved as a prominent type of internationalization at universities over the past two decades.

Doctoral dissertations constitute the most important product of doctoral education. They should identify and account for the challenges that people face in terms of social, cultural, and economic factors. They demonstrate their holders' knowledge, skills, and competency they have acquired in their doctoral training. Therefore, they are regarded as an "academic genre ladder" (Swales & Feak, 2000). Researchers should reflect on how they have developed their knowledge, skills, and competency in their study area, as well as solve problems in working and learning environments on their own or provide the most innovative ideas in these environments (European Qualification Framework [EQF], 2020; Turkish Qualification Framework [TQF], 2015) in their dissertations. Every country expects its researchers to introduce innovation to science in their dissertations. EQF is a common European reference framework whose purpose is to make qualifications more readable and understandable across different countries and systems. So, this might be seen as an important part of transnational higher education in recent years since the credits and qualifications of higher education students can be carried out among countries by this framework (EQF, 2020). This process seems likely to have a profound effect on the development of transnational doctorate education globally since the beginning (Miller, Selvanathan, & Meredith, 2012).

Hasgall et al. (2019) and Granovsky et al. (1992) suggest that the number of scientific publications from dissertations and the number of times other researchers cite them could be used to measure the quality of doctoral education. This is because the number of scientific publications and the number of times other researchers cite an author's scientific publications are usually used to measure their scientific impact on their field or discipline (Aslan et al., 2021). Besides, one of today's questionable issues in higher education is how transnational education might improve the quality of doctoral dissertations. It is thought that this study will contribute to these discussions.

In this context, the organization of the paper is as follows: The next section indicates the objective of this study. While the third section displays the literature review about the topic of this study, the fourth one addresses background about the study. The following ones give the methodology and findings of this study, respectively. Then the discussion part is given, and the next one is about future research directions. Finally, the study is concluded.

OBJECTIVES OF THE STUDY

There are two objectives of this study. The first objective is to assess the quality of Turkish social sciences and humanities, as well as educational dissertations, based on scientific impact variables such as the number of scientific publications extracted from them and citation counts. The second one is to examine how transnational higher education can affect dissertation quality. Because they show how well students can do research on their own, dissertations are meant to have a big impact on the development of policies and applications in the social sciences, humanities, and education, even outside of the country where they were done. In accordance with these objectives, the answers to the following questions will be sought:

Q1: What is the quality of Turkish social sciences and humanities, as well as educational dissertations, based on scientific impact variables such as the number of scientific publications extracted from them and citation counts?

Q2: How can transnational higher education affect the quality of Turkish social sciences and humanities, as well as educational dissertations?

LITERATURE REVIEW

Knowledge mobility lies at the heart of transnational higher education across countries and cultures with academic mobility and information and communication technologies (Waters & Leung, 2017). That is, knowledge transfer is an inevitable part of transnational higher education. To get a comprehensive insight into the nature of transnational higher education, the knowledge transfer issue (e.g., Sutrisno & Pillay, 2015; Truong, Hasanen & Laihonen, 2020) is frequently studied in the literature. Sutrisno & Pillay (2015) investigated this issue between Indonesian and Australian universities through an undergraduate transnational program partnership. Truong, Hasanen, & Laihonen (2020) examined knowledge transfer in the context with transnational education according to a Finnish-Vietnamese transnational education program. It is understood that knowledge mobility or transfer is an inevitable component of transnational higher education.

Today, the academic 'marketplace' is becoming increasingly transnational under the influence of economic globalization due to the global knowledge economy (Kim, 2009). Since the 1990s, new recruitment policies and strategies have greatly increased the size and speed of cross-border academic mobility, especially among highly skilled mobile knowledge workers and academics, especially in science and technology (Kim, 2009; Kuptsch & Pang, 2006; Tremblay, 2005).

The literature is quite limited to studies on the basis of transnational doctoral education. For example, Miller, Selvanathan, & Meredith (2012) informed those involved or interested in doctoral education in the business and management genre about transnational doctoral education in the Asian region. Moreover, Bendrups, Candelaria, & Hogan (2021) described the experiences of doctoral candidates involved in the first year of a transnational research training partnership between Australia and the Philippines. They aimed to ascertain how the partnership model of the program had been perceived by doctoral candidates and to understand its associated benefits and challenges.

BACKGROUND

In Turkey, there are 207 higher education institutions with 8 296 959 students and 184 702 academics as of the 2021–2022 academic term (Council of Higher Education [CoHE], 2022). Besides, in state and foundation universities, 109 540 students continue their studies in 11 193 doctoral programs. In Turkey, Ph.D. programs typically run four years, and students must complete coursework, pass doctoral qualification examinations, write a dissertation, and defend it orally (Aslan et al., 2021). Dissertations certify their holders' knowledge, skills, and competency. To what extent they contribute to the development of knowledge and policies in knowledge-based economies can be regarded as an indicator in the evaluation of doctoral programs.

The dissertations in this study were undertaken in the fields of social sciences, humanities, and education. Dissertations in the social sciences and humanities were chosen because they can help people understand the conditions to which they are exposed through digitalization, globalization, and population (Organisation for Economic Co-operation and Development [OECD], 2019) and come up with solutions to the problems they encounter, such as climate change, interdependent financial systems, immigration, conflict, and social inequality (OECD, 2018). Furthermore, educational dissertations were chosen since global trends like technological advancement, competitiveness, knowledge-based economies, and shifting workforce demands have resulted in changes in the qualifications that students should have to participate in today's society (Levy & Murnane, 2005; Stewart, 2010; Wilmarth, 2010). So, people with a doctorate degree in these fields are expected to improve the quality and competitiveness of human capital, get involved in social and organizational life, and come up with creative and innovative solutions to social and economic problems.

Aslan et al. (2021) and Aslan & Açıkgöz (2022) investigated the impact of the Turkish social sciences, humanities, and educational dissertations through the scientific impact criterion dealing with the scientific publications extracted from the dissertations in peer-reviewed indexed journals and their citation counts. This study might be considered a combination of both studies in terms of internationalization and transnational higher education. From the studies conducted at the national level, it can be deduced that the local impact of the dissertations in the fields of social sciences, humanities, and education in terms of internationalization and transnational higher education aspects has not been evaluated yet. Hence, this study can be considered to be filling this gap in this area.

METHODOLOGY

Between 2014 and 2017, the output quality of doctoral dissertations completed in several disciplines in the fields of social sciences, humanities, and education was assessed through bibliometric analysis, which is usually used to identify the distribution of scientific publications by nation, institution, publication type, and research topics (Kaya & Erbay, 2020). So, this method was used to measure the contributions of dissertations to knowledge in the social sciences, humanities, and educational fields by looking at the number of scientific publications that came from dissertations and the number of times they were cited.

The universities included in this study were chosen based on a set of criteria (Suri, 2011). Only one university is chosen in each of Turkey's regions based on the following criteria: the number of students enrolled in doctoral programs, the number of doctoral program graduates; the number of academics employed by higher education institutions; and the number of publications per academic in national and international indexed journals (CoHE, 2018). The universities in each region with the greatest values for these criteria were selected by considering the 12 Nomenclature of Territorial Units for Statistics-1 (NUTS-1) regions in Turkey developed by the European Office for Statistics (EUROSTAT) (European Commission, 2020). To maintain homogeneity among the universities, it was decided that they should be state universities founded in or before 1992, and their language of teaching should be Turkish. So, 12 universities were included in this study, and their names are listed in Table 1.

This study was made up of 266 dissertations, 124 of which were in the field of education and 142 of which were in the fields of social sciences and humanities.

Table 1. Number of dissertations by universities

Universities	Educational Dissertations	Social Science and Humanities Dissertations	Total
Ankara University	12	12	24
Ataturk University	12	12	24
Canakkale Onsekiz Mart University	12	12	24
Cukurova University	12	12	24
Dokuz Eylul University	12	12	24
Erciyes University	2	12	14
Gaziantep University	11	10	21
Inonu University	12	12	24
Istanbul University	7	12	19
Karadeniz Technical University	12	12	24
Ondokuz Mayis University	12	12	24
Uludag University	8	12	20
Total	**124**	**142**	**266**

First, the doctoral dissertations were retrieved from the Turkish Council of Higher Education (CoHE) National Thesis Center. Second, the publications collected from these dissertations and their citation counts were searched in the following databases: CoHE Academic, ERIC, Google Scholar, ResearchGate, ScienceDirect, SCOPUS, and Web of Science (WoS). All of the data was recorded in the Microsoft Excel Office Program.

In the determination of the scientific impact of the value of the indexed journals, the indexed criteria for associate professorship applications in the field of education by the Turkish Interuniversity Council (IUC) were considered (IUC, 2018). According to the criteria, the publications indexed in the Social Sciences Citation Index (SSCI), Science Citation Index (SCI), Science Citation Index Expanded (SCI-Expanded), Arts and Humanities Citation Index (ACHI), and Emerging Sources Citation Index (ESCI) are regarded the most prestigious in the international scientific community owing to their impact factor values. Universities can be judged by how well they do in the international arena based on how many publications they have in these indexes. The international publications indexed in Education Resources Information Center (ERIC), EBSCO Information Services (EBSCO), Directory of Open Access Journals (DOAJ), and Index Copernicus have lower impact factor values compared with the former indexed publications. The national articles indexed in the Turkish Academic Network and Information Center (ULAKBIM), the SOBIAD, and the Turkish Education Index are locally indexed journals, which have lower impact factor values compared to others.

FINDINGS

Quality of the Dissertations

The scientific impact of the Turkish doctorate dissertations in the fields of social sciences, humanities, and education was first determined by considering the scientific publications extracted from 266 dissertations in national and international indexed journals. The publications generated from these dissertations are indicated in Table 2. According to the data in Table 2, almost one in two dissertations has not been made available in a scientific publication. What is more, 11 publications extracted from dissertations were discovered in the international SSCI, SCI, SCI-Expanded, ACHI, and ESCI indexed journals. There were 41 publications in international indexed journals such as ERIC, EBSCO, DOAJ, and Index Copernicus. There were also 80 publications in the national indexed journals like ULAKBIM, SOBIAD, and Turkish Education. According to the data, the bulk of the scientific articles generated from the dissertations was published in journals with a lower impact factor. When compared to social science and humanities dissertations, educational dissertations performed better since the number of publications in the international indexed journals was higher. The quality of the dissertation is generally quite low taking into account the number of publications extracted from the dissertation and the indexed publications.

The citation counts for these scientific publications extracted from the dissertations in the fields of social sciences, humanities, and education according to the indexed journals are listed in Table 3. The total number of citations given to the scientific publication was 354. However, it is also observed that the dissertations were mostly cited in low-impact factor indexed journals. The number of citations received by the scientific publications extracted from the dissertations in the SSCI, SCI, SCI-Expanded, ACHI, and ESCI indexed journals was 21. There were 142 citations received from publications in the ERIC, EBSCO, DOAJ, and Index Copernicus international indexed journals and 191 citations received from publications in the local national indexed journals. As a result, this finding implies that the scientific impact of dissertations in the social sciences, humanities, and education is very low in Turkey. However, scientific publications extracted from the education field have more citations in the SSCI, SCI, SCI-Expanded, ACHI, and ESCI indexed journals compared to publications extracted from the social science and humanities field. Based on these figures, it can be deduced that the citations are mostly clustered in the local indexed journals, which means that the Turkish researchers have largely reached and cited these publications.

Table 2. Number of the publications generated from the dissertations

Indexes	Number of Publications Generated from Educational Dissertations	Number of Publications Generated from Social Sciences and Humanities Dissertations	Total
SSCI, SCI-Expanded, ACHI, ESCI	6	5	11
ERIC, EBSCO, DOAJ, INDEX COPERNICUS	27	14	41
Turkish ULAKBIM, SOBIAD, Turkish Education Index	29	51	80
Total	**62**	**70**	**132**

Table 3. Citation counts of the publications generated from the dissertations

Indexes	Citation Counts of Publications Generated from Educational Dissertations	Citation Counts of Publications Generated from Social Sciences and Humanities Dissertations	Total
SSCI, SCI-Expanded, ACHI, ESCI	13	8	21
ERIC, EBSCO, DOAJ, INDEX COPERNICUS	62	80	142
Turkish ULAKBIM, SOBIAD, Turkish Education Index	40	151	191
Total	**115**	**139**	**354**

The Impact of Transnational Higher Education on the Quality of Dissertations

The scientific publications generated from the dissertations and their citation counts indicate that their scientific impact is significantly restricted within the borders of Turkish academia. So, Turkish researchers generally have difficulty in transferring the knowledge generated from the research conducted in their dissertations to other researchers across the world. It can be argued that the effect of transnational higher education on these dissertations is quite limited. It is so obvious that Turkish doctorate education should more focus on publications done with international cooperation.

DISCUSSION

In this study, 266 dissertations completed at 12 state universities in the fields of social sciences, humanities, and education were analyzed using bibliometric analysis to gain a better understanding of their local impact on transnational education. When the published scientific studies retrieved from the dissertations are regarded, 132 studies were made available in the national indexed journals (nearly 60%), ERIC, EBSCO, DOAJ, and Index Copernicus international indexed journals (nearly 31%), and SSCI, SCI, SCI-Expanded, ACHI, and ESCI indexed journals (8%). Besides, the publications that received the most citations from the studies indexed in the national indexed journals (about 54%), ERIC, EBSCO, DOAJ, and Index Copernicus indexed journals (about 40%), and SSCI, SCI, SCI-Expanded, ACHI, and ESCI indexed journals (about 5%). This finding is in parallel with the study conducted by Baloğlu & Bilgiç (2021). The researchers investigated the international scientific performance of the Turkish academics' in the WoS database and concluded that their scientific impact is national rather than international. It is obvious that the scientific impact factor and implicit quality of Turkish scientific publications are very low. Thus, the Turkish universities should increase the quality of their research outputs to become world-class universities, as the quality of research outputs has an important role in the performance measurement of the universities.

Today, the global performance of universities is measured by world university rankings like The Times Higher Education (THE) World University Ranking and Academic Ranking of World Universities (ARWU). As part of their framework, they use "research productivity (or scientific publications)" and "citations" as a performance indicator to measure research influence. For example, the weight of research productivity is 6% in THE World University Rankings and 40% in the ARWU (THE, 2022; ARWU, 2022). Besides, the weight of citations is 30% in THE and the weight of highly cited researchers is 20% in ARWU (THE, 2022; ARWU, 2022). However, the Turkish universities included in the study are not represented in the 500 top universities in the world except Istanbul University (QS, 2021; THE, 2021; ARWU, 2021). This result might explain why the scientific impact of the scientific products generated from social science, humanities, and education dissertations has a low impact value in Turkey. Besides, the Turkish number of scientific publications was 67.150 and Turkey ranked 17th, but the number of citations per document was 0.94, with a rank of 135 in the world in 2021 (Scimago Journal Rankings [SJR], 2021). This shows that the scientific impact factor and implicit quality of Turkish scientific publications are very low. On the other hand, the share of international students at the top of the universities in the international rankings system is almost at least 20% (THE, 2021). But this ratio is a maximum of 10% at the examined universities in this study (CoHE, 2022). Hence, these results indicate the transnational higher education impact is low in Turkish higher education. This also affects the collaboration within the international scientific community of Turkish universities.

In order to improve the quality and performance of doctorate education, the doctoral programs offered by Turkish universities might have transnational awards. Candidates for these programs come from across the globe. Turkish universities have evolved their organizational structures, systems, and processes to meet the demand for their doctoral programs and to provide quality delivery mechanisms. This involves entering into collaborative educational partnerships with overseas universities to allow the doctoral programs to be offered at overseas locations. For example, Turkish universities might establish a "pod" supervision model whereby a group of candidates at particular overseas locations were assigned to a particular Turkish university full-time staff supervisor (the principal supervisor) to work together with the local in-country supervisor to create a formal link between the local supervisors and the universities' qualified and experienced staff and to ensure supervision standards, quality, and procedures are matched at the overseas locations (Meredith & Miller, 2012). Therefore, this transnational structure might facilitate knowledge sharing between countries.

On the other hand, Bendrups, Candelaria, & Hogan (2021) stated that interpersonal relationships with and between supervisors and program administrators provided a trusted reference point that became part of the candidates' sense of belonging for doctoral candidates involved in the first year of transnational research training. Hence, improving transnational doctorate education might be crucial to doctorate candidates' well-being and educational process. In addition, the number of projects implemented with others abroad by these state universities has increased in Turkey since only 342 projects were conducted with their counterparts abroad (CoHE, 2021). Also, they should offer more joint doctoral degrees and scholarships with their international partner universities.

Nevertheless, the COVID-19 pandemic has also had a severe impact on higher education, and globally, the number of online courses has risen steeply during the pandemic. Currently, most universities around the world are preparing for a safe and effective digital learning environment by altering their normal schedules and organization at the institutional and national levels (Aristovnik et al., 2020). Therefore, transnational doctoral education might take place in an online learning environment with partner universities in other countries.

From this perspective, internationalization and transnational education are two of the core features of CoHE in Turkey. For this purpose, CoHE tries to develop and enhance joint education and training programs between universities from all over the world. Joint education and training programs can be established at all levels (associate, undergraduate, and graduate) by signing a protocol between the parties. A new "Regulation on Joint Education and Training Programs among Higher Education Institutions and International Higher Education Institutions" was enacted on October 6, 2016, after the first one was enacted in 2006. As a result, institutions can now receive their authorized protocols from the CoHE more speedily and practically. The main enhancements made with this regulation include transfer between current programs, varied teaching languages, and various diploma samples. Furthermore, the Erasmus+ Program, the Mevlana Exchange Program, and the Project-Based International Exchange Program are some of the most powerful initiatives taken by CoHE in the direction of internationalization and transnational higher education. The Council of Higher Education also set up the "Research Scholarship for Doctoral Studies Abroad for Research Assistants" (YOK-YUDAB) to encourage academic staff working as research assistants at state universities and writing doctoral theses in CoHE-designated priority fields to do research abroad for at least six months and up to a year (CoHE, 2019).

The Council of Higher Education (CoHE) provides researchers who are in the phase of completing their doctoral dissertations at the state universities with the scholarship to study abroad for at least six months or one year in the context of the Abroad Research Scholarship Programme. Besides, the Turkish universities send their students to study abroad through the Erasmus bilateral agreements they sign with the other universities abroad. Actually, the scholarship programs and bilateral agreements enable students and researchers to study abroad and exchange ideas with their peers and colleagues. This contributes to expanding the borders of national education to include transnational education.

FUTURE RESEARCH DIRECTIONS

This study is limited to the bibliometric analysis of the dissertations conducted in the fields of social sciences, humanities, and education at 12 state universities in Turkey. The researchers could examine the local impact of the dissertations completed in the other programs, such as basic science programs, including mathematics, physics, chemistry, and biology, through bibliometric analysis of the transnational doctoral education. Besides, since the instruction language of doctoral programs of the universities examined in this paper is Turkish, other universities whose medium of instruction is English might be taken into account in terms of transnational higher education. Although these 12 state universities have exchange programs even for doctorate level, there is no information available for PhD holders experiences with regard to transnational education in their doctoral training program. Also, the local effects of the dissertations looked at in this paper could be compared to those of universities in other countries to get a better idea of how transnational higher education works.

CONCLUSION

It seems a necessity for the Turkish universities, and more specifically, the 12 state universities, to adopt new approaches in their policies to increase the quality of their doctoral education and their scientific outputs on an international platform. In this context, the mass movement of academics and students across borders at the same time increases knowledge production and strengthens the corporation of the university on a global scale. In other words, more international academic career development has been made possible by the growth of transnational doctorate education.

In more recent years, doctoral programs have universally become diverse in terms of their aims, curriculum, and structure. Therefore, transnational doctorate education in terms of collaborative educational partnerships with overseas universities is one of the new models to increase the quality and performance of doctoral education. In the context of knowledge transfer or mobility, doctoral dissertations that have been done in collaborative educational partnerships with universities abroad might contribute a lot to the invention of new information and the expansion of existing knowledge through doctoral education in Turkey. Hence, the low scientific impact of outputs of doctoral dissertations might also improve, and Turkey's higher education and scientific performance around the world might also rise.

REFERENCES

Academic Ranking of World Universities. (2021). *2021 Academic ranking of world universities.* ARWUhttps://www.shanghairanking.com/rankings/arwu/2021

Academic Ranking of World Universities. (2022). *Academic ranking of world universities: Methodology.* ARWU. https://www.shanghairanking.com/methodology/arwu/2021

Altbach, P. G., & Knight, J. (2007). The internationalization of higher Education: Motivations and realities. *Journal of Studies in International Education*, *11*(3-4), 290–305. doi:10.1177/1028315307303542

Aristovnik, A., Keržič, D., Ravšelj, D., Tomaževič, N., & Umek, L. (2020). Impacts of the Covid-19 pandemic on life of higher education students: A global perspective. *Sustainability*, *12*(20), 8438. doi:10.3390u12208438

Aslan, A., & Açıkgöz, Ö. (2022). Bibliometric Analysis of the Turkish Doctoral Dissertations: A Case Study of Economy, Law, Psychology, Political Science, and International Relations Disciplines. *Yükseköğretim Dergisi*, *12*(2), 363–372. doi:10.2399/yod.21.820951

Aslan, A., Açıkgöz, Ö., & Günay, A. (2021). Scientific impact of the Turkish educational dissertations. *Turkish Journal of Education*, *10*(3), 237–250. doi:10.19128/turje.850728

Baloğlu, M., & Bilgiç, Ş. (2021). *Türkiye'de akademisyenlerin WoS yayın performansları*. Nobel Yayıncılık.

Bendrups, D., Candelaria, A. L. K., & Hogan, T. (2021). Collaborative transnational doctoral education: Insights from a Philippines-Australia partnership. *Innovations in Education and Teaching International*, *58*(6), 682–692. doi:10.1080/14703297.2021.1991833

CoHE. (2018). *The regulation for thesis submission to the National Thesis Center database of the CoHE*. CoHE. https://www.mevzuat.gov.tr/MevzuatMetin/1.5.2547.pdf

CoHE. (2019). *Higher education system in Turkey*. CoHE. https://www.yok.gov.tr/Documents/Yayinlar/Yayinlarimiz/2019/Higher_Education_in_Turkey_2019_en.pdf

CoHE. (2021). *University monitoring and evaluation general report 2021*. CoHE. https://www.yok.gov.tr/Documents/Yayinlar/Yayinlarimiz/2022/universite-izleme-ve-degerlendirme-genel-raporu-2021.pdf

CoHE. (2022). *Statistics for Turkish higher education*. CoHE. https://istatistik.yok.gov.tr/

D'Annunzio-Green, N., & Barron, P. (2019). Learning whilst working: Perceptions on barriers and enablers to transfer of learning amongst part-time students on a professional MSc programme. *Education + Training*, *61*(2), 187–200. doi:10.1108/ET-04-2018-0098

European Commission. (2020). *Eurostat*. EC.https://ec.europa.eu/eurostat/web/nuts/background

European Qualifications Framework. (2020). *European qualifications framework*. European Qualifications. https://ec.europa.eu/ploteus/content/descriptors-page

Granovsky, Y. V., Luibimova, T. N., Murashova, T. I., & Myatlev, V. D. (1992). Information-based evaluation of the quality of doctoral theses. *Scientometrics*, *23*(3), 361–376. doi:10.1007/BF02029804

Hasgall, A., Saenen, B., & Borrell-Damian, L. (2019). *Doctoral education in Europe today: Approaches and institutional structures*. European University Association.

Huang, F. (2007). Internalization of higher education in the developing and emerging countries: A focus on transnational higher education in Asia. *Journal of Studies in International Education*, *11*(3-4), 421–432. doi:10.1177/1028315307303919

InterUniversity Council. (2018). *The criteria for the promotion and appointment for the associate professorship*. UAK. https://www.uak.gov.tr/Documents/docentlik/2021-eylul-donemi/basvuru-sartlari/TA_Tablo11_2021E_15092021.pdf

Kaya, M., & Erbay, E. (2020). Global trends of the researches on COVID-19: A bibliometric analysis via VOSviewer. *Ankara Sağlık Bilimleri Dergisi,* 201-216. https://www.doi.org/10.46971/ausbid.817925

Kim, T. (2009). Transnational academic mobility, internationalization and interculturality in higher education. *Intercultural Education, 20*(5), 395–405. doi:10.1080/14675980903371241

Knight, J. (2016). Transnational education remodeled: Toward a common TNE framework and definitions. *Journal of Studies in International Education, 20*(1), 34–47. doi:10.1177/1028315315602927

Kuptsch, C., & Pang, E. F. (Eds.). (2006). *Competing for global talent*. International Labour Organization.

Levy, F., & Murnane, R. J. (2005). *The new division of labor how computers are creating the next job market*. Princeton University Press.

Meredith, G., & Miller, P. (2012). Transnational doctoral education and research: A case study. In P. Miller, A. Selvanathan, & G. Meredith (Eds.), *Transnational doctoral education and research: An Asian focus* (pp. 11–32). Southern Cross University Press.

Miller, P., Selvanathan, A., & Meredith, G. (Eds.). (2012). *Transnational doctoral education and research: An Asian focus*. Southern Cross University Press.

Nerad, M. (2010). Globalization and the internationalization of graduate education: A macro and micro view. *Canadian Journal of Higher Education, 40*(1), 1–12. doi:10.47678/cjhe.v40i1.1566

OECD. (2018). *The future of education and skills. Education 2030 the future we want*. OECD Publishing.

OECD. (2019). *OECD employment outlook 2019: The future of work*. OECD Publishing.

Quacquarelli Symonds World University Ranking. (2021). QS world university rankings 2021. *Top Universities*. https://www.topuniversities.com/university-rankings/world-university-rankings/2021

Scimago Journal Rank. (2021). *Country Rank*. Scimago. https://www.scimagojr.com/countryrank.php

Stella, A., & Woodhouse, D. (2011). Evolving dimensions of transnational education. In A. Stella & S. Bhushan (Eds.), *Quality assurance of transnational higher education the experiences of Australia and India* (pp. 3–18). Australian Universities Quality Agency and National University of Educational Planning and Administration.

Stewart, V. (2010). A classroom as wide as the world. In H. Hayes Jacobs (Ed.), *Curriculum 21: Essential education for a changing world* (pp. 97–114). Association for Supervision and Curriculum Development.

Suri, H. (2011). Purposeful sampling in qualitative research synthesis. *Qualitative Research Journal, 11*(2), 63–75. doi:10.3316/QRJ1102063

Sutrisno, A., & Pillay, H. (2015). Knowledge transfer through a transnational program partnership between Indonesian and Australian universities. *Asia Pacific Education Review, 16*(3), 379–388. doi:10.100712564-015-9384-7

Swales, J., & Feak, C. (2000). *English in today's research world: A writing guide*. University of Michigan Press. doi:10.3998/mpub.9059

The Times Higher Education World University Ranking. (2021). THE world university rankings 2021. *Times*. https://www.timeshighereducation.com/world-university-rankings/2021/world-ranking#!/page/0/length/25/sort_by/rank/sort_order/asc/cols/stats

The Times Higher Education World University Ranking. (2022). World university rankings 2022 methodology. *Times*. https://www.timeshighereducation.com/sites/default/files/breaking_news_files/the_2022_world_university_rankings_methodology_31082021_final.pdf

Tremblay, K. (2005). Academic mobility and immigration. *Journal of Studies in International Education*, *9*(3), 196–228. doi:10.1177/1028315305277618

Truong, Van T., Hasansen, K., & Laihonen, H. (2020). Students as knowledge mediators in transnational higher education. *Multidisciplinary Perspectives in Higher Education*, *5*(2), 48–65.

Turkish Qualifications Framework. (2015). *Turkish qualifications framework*. MYK. https://www.myk.gov.tr//TRR/File6.pdf

UNESCO/Council of Europe. (2001). *Code of good practice in the provision of transnational education*. UNESCO. https://www.coe.int/en/web/higher-education-and-research/lisbon-recognition-convention

Waters, J., & Leung, M. (2017). Trans-knowledge? Geography, mobility,and knowledge in transnational education. In H. Jöns, P. Meusburger, & M. Heffernan (Eds.), *Mobilities of knowledge. Knowledge and space* (pp. 269–285). Springer. doi:10.1007/978-3-319-44654-7_14

Wilkins, S. (2018). Definitions of transnational higher education. *Industry and Higher Education*, *95*(95), 5–7. doi:10.6017/ihe.2018.95.10717

Wilmarth, S. (2010). Five socio-technology trends that change everything in learning and teaching. In H. Hayes Jacobs (Ed.), *In Curriculum 21: Essential education for a changing world* (pp. 80–96). Association for Supervision and Curriculum Development.

ADDITIONAL READINGS

Bendrups, D., Diaz-Gasca, S., Martinez Ortiz, G. C., Guarneros Sanchez, P., & Mena-Maldonado, E. (2020). Australia as a destination for Latin American doctoral candidates: Four personal reflections. *Transitions: Journal of Transient Migration*, *4*(1), 69–85. doi:10.1386/tjtm_00013_1

Gao, Y. (2021). How transnational experiences and political, economic policies inform transnational intellectuals' identities and mobility: An autoethnographic study. *Higher Education Policy*, *34*(4), 992–1009. doi:10.105741307-020-00187-w

Hill, C., Lamie, J., & Gore, T. (2022). *The evolution of transnational education pathways, globalization and emerging trends*. Routledge.

Justice, K. M., & Aslan, A. ve Zhu, C. (2020). Educational innovation in higher education. In R. Papa (Ed.), Oxford research encyclopedia of education (pp. 1-16). Oxford University Press.

Naidoo, V. (2009). Transnational higher education. A stock take of current activity. *Journal of Studies in International Higher Education*, *13*(3), 310–330.

KEY TERMS AND DEFINITIONS

Bibliometric Analysis: It involves the use of statistical methods to analyze the bibliometric publications such as peer-reviewed journal articles.

Dissertation: An essay or thesis written on a particular subject by a candidate to earn the doctorate degree.

Doctoral Education: It refers to the highest educational level in higher education.

Educational Sciences: It is any branch of academic study to describe, understand and prescribe the policies and practices to be developed in education.

Humanity: It is any branch of academic study or science that deals with literature, philosophy, art etc.

Internationalization in Higher Education: It refers to the policies and methods implemented by academic systems and organizations, as well as individuals, in order to cope with the global academic environment.

Social Sciences: It is any branch of academic study or science that deals with human behavior in its social and cultural aspects.

Transnational Higher Education: It refers to study programs or educational services in which the learners are located in a country different from the one where the awarding institution is based.

Chapter 9
Teachers' Role in Enhancing Adult Learners' Sense of Autonomy, Competence, and Involvement in Online Higher Education:
Learning From an Australian Transnational Higher Education Provider

Mamun Ala
Australian Institute of Business, Australia

Saadia Mahmud
Australian Institute of Business, Australia

Sehrish Shahid
https://orcid.org/0000-0001-7021-5152
Australian Institute of Business, Australia

Kuldeep Kaur
Australian Institute of Business, Australia

Syed Mohyuddin
Australian Institute of Business, Australia

ABSTRACT

This chapter draws from the learning from an Australian transnational higher education provider in enhancing adult students' sense of belonging, engagement, and interactions. The literature suggests that student engagement and motivation could be enabled by fulfilling certain needs such as autonomy, competence, and relatedness or involvement. The chapter also explores some strategies that could be adopted by teachers to promote behavioural, cognitive, emotional, and agentic engagement in online adult learners. It is argued that regular customized communication by online teachers using email and learning management systems can promote teaching presence, as well as student engagement and motivation. This approach is in line with the notion of community of enquiry, a social constructivist model of learning process that suggests that educational experience takes place at the intersection of social, cognitive, and teaching presences. Other strategies, namely the effective use of breakout rooms during an online class, the emphasis on reflective learning, and the use of stories in an online classroom, are also discussed.

DOI: 10.4018/978-1-6684-5226-4.ch009

INTRODUCTION

Student engagement is generally understood as a process that involves the active involvement of students in effective educational practices that are linked to desired outcomes such as acquiring knowledge, academic achievement (e.g., competition of a course, achieving higher grades, etc.), and cognitive development (Koh, 2009; Christenson et al., 2012; Meyer, 2014; Stone et al., 2014; Banna et al., 2015; Britt, 2015). The literature suggests that student engagement is a multidimensional concept consisting of four dimensions: 1) behavioural 2) cognitive 3) emotional and 4) agentic. Behavioural engagement refers to students' involvement through activities such as attention, participation, effort, intensity, or persistence (Reeve, 2013; Reeve & Tseng, 2011). Cognitive engagement involves using mental effort to complete educational and learning tasks. Emotional engagement refers to a sense of belonging and attachment with teachers, peers, school experience, and learning activities, while agentic engagement entails taking initiative that contributes to learning and teaching (Reeve, 2013; Reeve & Tseng, 2011).

Since student engagement is mostly seen as a motivational process, nurturing different aspects of motivation is useful for students to be involved and absorbed in learning activities (Reeve, 2013). Therefore, it makes sense to explain student engagement through the lens of self-determination theory (Ryan & Deci, 2017, 2020). The theory defines sources of motivation as intrinsic and extrinsic and focuses on how external factors such as social and cultural could be conducive to an individual's well-being and performance. It is a theory of human emotion, growth, motivation and development where internal and external factors play a huge role in facilitating the growth of people. This theory is of much use in the area of education and possibly educators can tap on the student's natural inclination to learn.

The theory suggests four types of motivation namely 1) external regulation 2) introjected regulation (outside of personal control) 3) identified regulation and 4) integrated regulation (which are autonomous). It could be argued that students' engagement or motivational orientation to move through these motivation types could be enabled by fulfilling certain needs such as *autonomy* (the need for being in control of goals), *competence* (being competent and challenged), and *involvement or relatedness*, in other words, the feeling of being connected and involves interaction and care for others (Ryan & Deci, 2017, 2020).

When the educational pedagogy addresses the psychological needs of students, they are more engaged in the learning activities (Hsu et al., 2019). The class sessions that address the psychological needs of students, they are more engaged in the learning (Reeve, 2013). Hence this theory can help us understand the influence of the fulfilment of needs on students' engagement, motivation and learning. Accordingly, this study draws from the learning from the Australian Institute of Business (AIB), a leading Australian transnational online higher education provider, to examine the teachers' role in enhancing adult learners' sense of autonomy, competence, and relatedness (involvement).

The rest of the paper is organized as follows. Section 2 discusses the context of the study (the higher education provider) which highlights the key teaching and learning principles of the institute. Section 3 discusses the dimensions of effective teaching practices in online higher education. Section 4 presents different examples of strategies to enhance online learners' sense of autonomy, competence and involvement, namely the use of customized communication using email and learning management system, the effective use of breakout rooms during an online class, the emphasis on reflective learning, the importance of inclusion, and the use of stories in an online classroom. Section 5 concludes this paper.

AUSTRALIAN INSTITUTE OF BUSINESS (AIB): GLOBAL LEADER IN ONLINE HIGHER EDUCATION

AIB is one of the leading online business schools worldwide. In addition to its flagship Master of Business Administration (MBA) program, AIB also offers the Doctor of Philosophy (PhD), the Doctor of Business Administration (DBA), the Master of Management (MMgt), and the Graduate Certificate in Research Methodologies (GCRM) (AIB, n.d.). These accredited programs are widely recognised globally. The programs are delivered online with a specific focus on industry engagement and flexible learning at the student's own pace. AIB's mission statement is "to provide distinctive business and management education in national and international environments based on AIB's orientation towards work-applied learning" (AIB Constitution, 2017). Work-applied learning is the central premise in course design and delivery. The work-applied learning model focuses on 1) knowledge, 2) project and 3) questioning. Further, there is a feedback look between academic knowledge and industry experience that generates excellent performance outcomes.

Experiential learning is at the heart of AIB's learning and teaching philosophy (Zuber-Skerritt & Abraham, 2017). This involves stimulating the critical thinking process to learn from reflecting on experience. To incorporate reflective critical thinking within the subjects offered at AIB, an authentic range of corporate, industry-based assessments have been made a vital component of the curriculum. These assessments require students to link theory to practice, stimulating critical reflection. In addition, the academics refresh the assessments each term to ensure that they are contemporary and relevant to the current corporate environment and issues (AIB 2022).

The majority of the AIB student cohort are full-time working adults spread across various continents in different time zones; critically, most of these students are time-poor. Therefore, the AIB academic team ensures its teaching presence is optimised by offering a wide range of time options for students to attend online webinars/tutorials. Further, all online lectures are recorded and made available to students later, especially those who are unable to attend them live. One of AIB's key philosophies is to offer "life changing experiences" to its students. The institution achieves this by facilitating AIB students furthering their professional careers by completing a world-class, practical and work-applied MBA degree (AIB, n.d.).

DIMENSIONS OF EFFECTIVE TEACHING PRACTICES IN ONLINE HIGHER EDUCATION

Enhancing adult students' sense of belonging, engagement, and interactions in online higher education requires a set of unique strategies (Coates, 2007; Harbour et al., 2015; Abayadeera et al., 2019). In light of the self-determination theory, teaching practices could be grouped into the following *autonomy support* (autonomy), *structure* (competence), and *involvement* (relatedness) (Lietaert et al., 2015; Ryan & Deci, 2017, 2020; Sierens et al., 2009; Vansteenkiste et al., 2009; Vollet et al., 2017):

- **Autonomy Support** – It refers to encouraging and helping students to achieve their personal goals and supporting their learning. In an online context, it involves having an open approach to learning, allowing for choices, and reducing stressors and demands on students. Examples include giving access to learning sources, personalized learning opportunities based on individual needs and interests, options to choose different learning materials, and flexibility in responding to learning activities (Alamri et al., 2020; Bedenlier et al., 2020; Hartnett, 2015; Lee et al., 2015; Trenshaw et al., 2016).

As a result, students have the freedom to make decisions that align with their goals and self-efficacy and hence feel more empowered in their learning process. In addition, autonomy support can nurture student engagement as well as support concentration and time management. Improved concentration and time management help fulfil the behavioural engagement. Furthermore, autonomy enables students to enjoy the lessons and activities which helps achieve emotional engagement (Skinner et al., 2008). Attaining emotional engagement promotes the student's communication with the educator in achieving the learning outcomes. This helps improve agentic engagement (Reeve, 2013). Autonomy helps students to choose their learning outcomes which enhances cognitive engagement (Bedenlier et al., 2020).

- **Competence Support** – It refers to being clear and transparent in expectations with students (Sierens et al., 2009). In an online context, it involves having well-structured class discussion forums, user-friendly instructions, peer moderation, facilitating and guiding during online webinars/ lectures, establishing boundaries of learning activities, giving formative and summative feedback, and expressing a sense of confidence in student's abilities (Chiu et al., 2020; Chiu & Lim, 2020; Chiu & Mok, 2017; Ng & Chiu, 2017; Xie & Ke, 2011).

Structure or competence support enables to enhance student engagement. The clarity in the learning structure would enable students to feel capable, effective and challenged in learning outcomes which are considered to be a key motivating factor for enhancing cognitive student engagement (Skinner et al., 2008). When this motivation need is met, it enables students to have some command over the topics covered and they feel encouraged to participate. It enhances the behavioural and emotional engagement element (Reeve, 2013).

- **Relatedness (Involvement) Support** – It involves the behaviour exhibited by teachers such as affection, support, encouragement, and developing a teacher-student bond (Skinner et al., 2008). In an online context, it implies providing emotional and motivational support, pedagogical caring, and development of trust in a collaborative learning space and in a small discussion group setting (Alamri et al., 2020; Xie & Ke, 2011; Vonderwell et al., 2007). These initiatives would make students feel more included, safe, welcome, and autonomous; they would also exhibit greater engagement with the content (Reeve, 2013; Ryan & Deci, 2017, 2020).

Relatedness influence the three dimensions of student engagement such as behavioural, emotional and agentic engagement because a good relationship between teacher and student helps students to participate in the different activities of the course (behavioural engagement), and enhances their positive feeling toward the course and its activities (emotional engagement), enhances student's efficacy to complete challenging activities (cognitive engagement) and enable students to express their concern regarding learning needs (agentic engagement) (Vollet et al., 2017)

Essentially, each of the teaching support dimensions explained above involves the effective use of educational technology, which is quite different from support provided in a traditional face-to-face setting. The focus is to ensure that students are engaged behaviourally, cognitively, emotionally, and agentically.

EXAMPLES OF STRATEGIES TO ENHANCE ONLINE LEARNERS' SENSE OF AUTONOMY, COMPETENCE AND INVOLVEMENT

The Use of Customized Communication Using Email and Learning Management System (LMS)

Online learning environments are often characterised by the lack of personal touch and emotional connection and the lack of sense of community (Anderson, 2008; Ashworth et al., 2014). To address students' feeling of isolation that comes with studying online and to minimise the instructor-student power distance and to improve student autonomy, regular customized communication using emails and learning management system (e.g., Moodle) could be an effective way. This approach is in line with the notion of community of enquiry (COI) - a social constructivist model of learning processes that suggests that educational experience that takes place at the intersection of social, cognitive and teaching presence (Garrison, Anderson & Archer, 2003; Lambert & Fisher, 2013; Swan, Garrison & Richardson, 2009). As part of the customized communication approach, the following types of emails could be sent to students enrolled in an online course:

- **Touch Base Communication** - general inquiry about academic progress, assignments, etc.
- **Encouragement Communication** - regarding accessing the subject Moodle on a regular basis, timely submission of assignments, encouraging to seek support when needed, advising to attend weekly webinars or contributing to online discussion forums, sharing non-confidential workplace insights/experiences with peers, making the best use of course resources including turnitin, etc.
- **Recognition Communication** - sending 'thank you' or appreciation emails/messages for early/timely submission of assignments, creating high quality assignments, regular webinar attendance, proactive participation in group discussion, valuable contribution in discussion boards, great group/team performance, sharing resources with peers, etc.
- **Supportive Communication** - providing additional information about assignments, sharing online materials that could be useful for individual students, reminder about the submission deadline, unsought information regarding grade release date, etc.
- **Follow Up Communication** - regarding non-confidential/non-sensitive personal information that individual students have shared with the instructor (such as about health, travel, work, family, pet, hobby, etc).

The Effective Use of Breakout Rooms During an Online Class

Breakout Rooms are a feature in the Zoom platform that allows instructors to create online spaces for small group activities (Li et al., 2021). They are an effective online tool to promote student engagement (Ahshan, 2021). Students can be allocated to a specified number of rooms automatically or assigned manually. The duration is flexible, and the instructor can broadcast a message to all the breakout rooms before closing them. This gives participants a minute to join the main class. Students can interact with a smaller group of peers and their instructor in each breakout room. Studies indicate the flexibility and interaction with fellow students as the key positive features (Oraif & Elyas, 2021) and these sentiments are echoed in the positive feedback from students about the use of breakout rooms by the authors of this paper.

Using the lens of self-determination theory, it can be argued that the primary impact of breakout rooms is to create 'involvement' through students working in small groups. nevertheless, it can further be argued that they also provide 'autonomy support' and 'structure' as learners find them useful and easy to use (Oraif & Elyas, 2021). The smaller groups allow students a safe space to interact more freely and build rapport with their peers while building on their learning. Along with autonomy, it would increase their involvement and provides a structure for students to share their ideas.

An overview of the limited research on the use of breakout room to create student engagement in online learning indicate that breakout rooms can be used to create all four dimensions of student engagement i.e., behavioural, cognitive, emotional, and agentic. A recent study found that students rated breakout rooms the highest (mean value of 6.3 on a scale of 7) for "perceived usefulness—work more quickly, increases productivity, effectiveness, makes job easier, and useful" and (6.26 on a scale of 7) for "perceived ease of use: easy to learn, controllable, clear and easy to understand, flexible, easy to become skillful, and easy to use" (Oraif & Elyas, 2021). Cognitive engagement can be considered as a proxy for learning (Pickering, 2017). According to earlier research on cognitive engagement, the elements are authenticity, inquiry, collaboration and teamwork, and technology (Blumenfeld, Kempler & Krajcik, 2005). Studies have found advantages of using breakout rooms for interactive group activity (Read et al., 2022) and brainstorming (Mirzoeva, 2021). These advantages reflect the capability of using breakout rooms to create behavioural and cognitive engagement through inquiry, collaboration, and teamwork. The synchronous teaching pedagogy of breakout rooms provides social presence and promotes emotional engagement with student-student and student-teacher interaction (Ahshan, 2021). The 'involvement' of students in breakout rooms contributes to enhanced student engagement.

Breakout rooms can also be used to create 'psychological safety' in online meetings (Edmondson & Daley, 2020). In larger online classes, participants may choose to turn their camera off. Research has found that the main reason for students not turning their camera on is concern for their appearance (Castelli & Sarvary, 2021) in a large group. However, in a smaller group such as in a breakout room, a more inclusive environment can be created which can encourage participants to have their camera on. This also provides an opportunity to build trust in communication and a 'safe space' to discuss issues in more depth. This is supported by Pollom et al. (2021) who found that while participants found break out rooms easy to use, they preferred a smaller group size and a duration longer than 10-15 minutes. However, the duration in the breakout room depends on the number of participants and task undertaken. In a recent article sharing best practices in the use of breakout rooms across disciplines (Reina, 2021), virtual group activities to engage students included digital gaming, peer learning and brainstorming. Students tended to hold each other accountable in smaller groups and introverted students were able to participate more effectively. Another study on the individual comfort level of students in breakout rooms (Zhouri & Running, 2021) supports the use of small groups (i.e. 2-3 students) in each room. In larger groups (more than 5 students) participants reported feeling bored and unable to contribute (Smith & Kaya, 2021). These studies provide useful insights for practitioners seeking to build student engagement using break out rooms. The important role played by the facilitator is underscored in studies with the creation of small group breakout rooms, assignment of specific tasks, and visits to each room (Zhouri & Running, 2021, Smith & Kaya, 2021). Providing links to resources in the chat and broadcasting messages to the group during the breakout sessions build collaborative activity and student interest.

Additionally, teachers can effectively use chat options in an online classroom to engage the non-active students, especially those are reluctant to join the breakout room discussion for various reasons such as language difficulty, shyness, disabilities, etc. Creating inclusivity and equity using breakout rooms

(Garza, 2021) teachers can engage all students in collaborative activity. By having learners engage in critical thinking and reflection, breakout rooms offer and opportunity to use Freire's notion of critical pedagogy (Freire, 1998 cited in Garza, 2021).

Importantly, the effective use of breakout rooms needs to be part of the teaching and learning framework (Ahshan, 2021). Studies suggest that using breakout rooms as part of a combination of tools/technologies is more effective (Ahshan, 2021). Additional research is needed for the optimum mix to promote active learning. At AIB, the Moodle Learning Management System supports student engagement through the forums and formative activities. Facilitated open discussion has been found to lead to positive learner outcomes (Oraif & Elyas, 2021). The skill of the facilitator in the guidance of the small group discussion using breakout rooms is reflected in the approach of linking it to topics in the course materials and activities. Some facilitators pose a single question for the groups to discuss with one member reporting back on behalf of the group. Such an approach builds 'autonomy support' for learners. He et al. (2020) found that in virtual medical teaching clinics, facilitation was improved by the use of 'co-hosts' where learners had greater autonomy to assign themselves to different breakout rooms. The use of structure in breakout rooms is an area for development.

While there are many benefits of using breakout rooms, there are barriers that impact effective use of this tool. Chandler (2016) found the skill and confidence of teaching staff to be a significant barrier which prevented tutors from using breakout rooms in online tutorials. Training alone was not found to be sufficient to build confidence as experience in using breakout rooms develops over time. Collaboration and sharing of ideas among the teaching team can support staff in using breakout rooms creatively. Support is needed for teaching staff to overcome technical issues and build student confidence while using the tool. The call to share expertise in online education (Barnes, Cole & Nix 2018), has now become imperative with the advent of Covid 19. The move to online delivery in higher education as a response to the pandemic had accelerated the need to develop teaching and learning skills in the use of technologies such as breakout rooms (Agustina & Suharya, 2021, Strawbridge et al., 2022).

THE EMPHASIS ON REFLECTIVE LEARNING

According to the World Economic Forum (2020), there are considerable talent disparities across the globe as our education system is still based on the industrial revolution model. Our education system's current skills are based on memorization, which may in the near future be taken over by automation and artificial intelligence. A teacher needs to understand that the traditional book-based lecture method is no longer effective in stimulating critical thinking mainly because it underestimates the value of student engagement and creativity (Schmidt et al., 2015). Using the traditional methods of teaching and learning, engaging online learners sitting across the globe is even more challenging (O'Mahony, 2014).

The success of online higher education largely depends on the extent to which teachers can engage their students. Providing a deeper understanding of the concept and its application in the real world helps increase learners' confidence (Knowles, Holton & Swanson, 2015). As indicated by Kolb and Kolb (2009) and Kolb (2014), adults are moulded by their experiences and interactions with the environment, and they interact differently based on whom they are interacting. In transnational education, providing a safe, open-ended learning environment helps build students' self-image (Gunawardena, Wilson & Nolla, 2003). Students can learn more about other countries and cultures since they can openly share their own experiences (Shackelford & Maxwell, 2012). These interactions produce stable and permanent patterns of human learning as they try to make sense of theories and successfully apply them in their environment. Therefore, getting students out of their textbooks and encouraging them to learn from each other's experiences is an excellent method to increase student engagement and enhance meaningful learning that meets the industry's needs (Ferreira, MacLean & Center, 2018; McGuire, 2006).

Some practical ways to promote experiential or reflective learning in the online environment include the use of scenarios (e.g., real-world business problems), role-playing exercises, case studies, discussion on current events, videos, and industry expert discussion (Britt, Goon & Timmerman, 2015; Lombardi & Oblinger, 2007; Miettinen, 2000). Adopting these initiatives in transnational teaching practices offers many benefits. In addition to improving students' engagement with the learning content (Cornell et al., 2013), the focus on reflective learning is likely to 1) make the learner more confident in their abilities and could be transferrable to their jobs; 2) enhance their involvement in the learning process by specifically asking their input; and 3) allow them to discuss their ideas with their peers.

The learner's engagement in professional activities using real-world scenarios is particularly crucial for professional courses, including business management and engineering (Pittaway & Moss, 2014). In line with self-determination theory (Ryan & Deci, 2017, 2020), the approach also satisfies students' need for autonomy, competence and relatedness. Nevertheless, it is important to recognise individual learner differences, especially in transnational education (in terms of communication style, cultural issues, experience etc.), and examples should be chosen to create purposeful engagement opportunities for all learners.

When exposed to real-world settings, adult learners may quickly observe how the concept works in practice and gain a thorough understanding of it (Keller, 2010). Adult learners are more likely to retain newly acquired knowledge (Chrestensen, 2007) and are more likely to identify the transferability of these skills to their workplace (Roberts, 2017).

THE IMPORTANCE OF INCLUSION

According to Conrad and Donaldson (2012), the relationship between a teacher and a student can be best understood using the example of the relationship between a gardener and seeds. They believe that a teacher should be compared to a gardener and students should be viewed as seeds. When a teacher gives adequate attention and support to their students (similar to how a gardener gives the seeds the proper conditions and nourishment), in due time, all of them will blossom and be able to enjoy their achievements. This indicates that teachers play a significant impact in determining the futures of their students.

To provide this transformative learning, the teachers in transnational education should create courses that are inclusive to all learner groups. In simple terms, inclusive teaching means recognising the value of student diversity in all manifestations, including but not limited to colour, experience, ethnicity, gender, disability, socioeconomic background, ideology and personality. It involves developing a curriculum and delivering lessons in a way that encourages talent development in all students (Sathy & Hogan, 2019). Students should be allowed to take the control of their learning and freely express their thoughts in the classroom as well as outside the classroom using using various educational meadia. Further, to promote an inclusive learning environment in higher education, teachers must also reflect on their own experiences, thoughts, opinions, beliefs, and language use and be aware of their unconscious biases (Fussell, Bianco & Polkina, 2021).

Importantly, students' dedication and interest in the subject matter being covered in the class might vary widely. Therefore, it is important that teachers grasp the attributes, needs and motivation of individual learners enrolled in an online classroom (Merriam, Caffarella & Baumgartner, 2007). Furthermore, teachers should recognise individual students' learning learning behabiour and styles (for example, while some students are comfortable sharing their experiences, others are hesitant to do so). The literature suggests that technology plays a crucial role in creating an inclusive culture. Using appropriate and adequate technology in an online environment (while keeping the learner's needs and challenges in mind) helps in better understanding the digital structure of the course (Tainsh, 2016).

In addition, an inclusive course design reinforces successful self-directed learning and facilitates interaction among students (Blondy, 2007). A welcoming learning environment helps build better bonding and promotes engagement and participation throughout the course delivery (Conrad and Donaldson, 2012). When it comes to transnational education, providing the right opportunities to diverse adult learners can reap many benefits. Some of these benefits include understanding the application of concepts across multiple industries, providing opportunities for learning to both teachers and peers, and preparing students for a knowledge-based society while also meeting the demands of industry (Appana, 2008).

THE USE OF STORIES IN AN ONLINE CLASSROOM

In their seminal study, Connelly and Clandinin (1990) suggest that human-beings are storytelling organisms; stories significantly impact their individual and social lives. Stories represent the lived experience of people. Human brains process information in the form cause and effect, which is very much like how stories are structured (Mohan & Nair, 2018). According to Ketelle (2017), stories are not only cognitive, but they also contain ideas and emotions. Scholars suggest that the use of anecdotes and storytelling can facilitate the learning process of adult learners by making them more involved and engaged (Mohan & Nair, 2018). Storytelling can also cultivate empathy among learners (Ketelle, 2017). Storytelling is one of the common methods used by academics to emotionally connect to the students and to establish connection and relatability for them to the course content, however academics need to have clarity and understanding that invoking stories in the classrooms is only to add educational value, not just to entertain students (Greene et.al., 2015).

Although remote learning and virtual classrooms was not a new scenario for higher education, COVID-19 pandemic lockdowns and closure of educational institutions promoted a rapid transformation to virtual and digital learning, using many innovative educational technologies including Digital Storytelling (DST. According to Yang and Wu (2012), DST is about utilising the new technological advancements to improve critical thinking and enhancing learning among the students. DST requires instructors to use computers and multimedia effectively to generate student interest into complex learning concepts. Another, aspect of rise in the use of digital storytelling in the form of educational videos now a days is due to easy and economically viable options to create such content e.g., low-cost cameras and downloadable editing online software (González-Tennant, 2017).

When it comes to online classroom learning the spread of diverse students can be across the globe, therefore academics also need to take cultural differences in to account when using anecdotes and storytelling in their virtual classrooms, as students from different cultural backgrounds can have different motivating factors (Yong, 2021).

Teachers who are also good storytellers can trigger the imagination of adult learners that can help them gain personal insights into their own experiences. Importantly, teachers need to present themselves as co-learners and encourage students to share their own stories. However, to demonstrate the link between theory to practice, it is important to ensure that anecdotes and stories are relevant to the context of the subject. In line with self-determination theory (Ryan & Deci 2017, 2020), stories would enhance students' involvement in the class.

CONCLUSION

Thanks to COVID-19 pandemic, online education has become more important than ever before. Nevertheless, effective online teaching and learning warrants a careful utilization of digital educational technologies that would enhance adult learners' sense of autonomy, competence and involvement. These dimensions of effective teaching practices are crucial for higher levels of student performance, satisfaction, and retention. As discussed in the preceding sections, some effective teaching practices including customized communication using email and learning management system (LMS), the effective use of breakout rooms during an online class, the emphasis on reflective learning, and the use of stories in an online classroom would lead to adult learners' sense of autonomy, competence and involvement, and therefore, help educators achieve superior learning outcomes.

REFERENCES

Abayadeera, N., Mihret, D. G., & Dulige, J. H. (2019). Acculturation of non-native English-speaking teachers in accounting: An ethnographic study. *Accounting Research Journal*, *33*(1), 1–15. doi:10.1108/ARJ-01-2017-0005

Agustina, E., & Suharya, T. (2021). Zoom breakout room for students' collaborative skill enhancement in history learning during Covid-19 outbreak. *International Journal of Research in Counseling and Education*, *5*(1), 33–38. doi:10.24036/00430za0002

Ahshan, R. (2021). A framework of implementing strategies for active student engagement in remote/online teaching and learning during the COVID-19 pandemic. *Education in Science*, *11*(9), 483. doi:10.3390/educsci11090483

AIB. (2017). *Constitution of Australian Institute of Business Pty Ltd*. AIB. https://www.aib.edu.au/wp-content/uploads/2019/03/aib-constitution.pdf

AIB. (2022). *AIB Academic Quality Assurance Framework*. AIB. https://www.aib.edu.au/wp-content/uploads/2019/05/Academic-Quality-Assurance-Framework.pdf

AIB. (n.d.). Why Study With Us. AIB. .https://www.aib.edu.au/study-with-us/why-study-with-us/

Alamri, H., Lowell, V., Watson, W., & Watson, S. L. (2020). Using personalized learning as an instructional approach to motivate learners in online higher education: Learner self-determination and intrinsic motivation. *Journal of Research on Technology in Education*, *52*(3), 322–352. doi:10.1080/15391523.2020.1728449

Anderson, T. (Ed.). (2008). *The theory and practice of online learning*. Athabasca University Press.

Appana, S. (2008). A Review of Benefits and Limitations of Online Learning in the Context of the Student, the Instructor and the Tenured Faculty. *International Journal on E-Learning*, *7*(1), 5–22.

Ashworth, F, Brennan, G, Egan, K, Hamilton, R & Sáenz, O, 2004. Learning theories and higher education. *Level 3, 2*(1), p.4.

Banna, J., Lin, M. F. G., Stewart, M., & Fialkowski, M. K. (2015). Interaction matters: Strategies to promote engaged learning in an online introductory nutrition course. *Journal of online learning and teaching/MERLOT, 11*(2), 249.

Barnes, F., Cole, S., & Nix, I. (2018). Supporting and enabling scholarship: Developing and sharing expertise in online learning and teaching. *Journal of Perspectives in Applied Academic Practice*, *6*(1), 66–74. doi:10.14297/jpaap.v6i1.323

Bedenlier, S., Bond, M., Buntins, K., Zawacki-Richter, O., & Kerres, M. (2020). Facilitating student engagement through educational technology in higher education: A systematic review in the field of arts and humanities. *Australasian Journal of Educational Technology*, *36*(4), 126–150. doi:10.14742/ajet.5477

Blondy, L. C. (2007). Evaluation and application of andragogical assumptions to the adult online learning environment. *Journal of Interactive Online Learning*, *6*(2), 116–130.

Blumenfeld, P., Kempler, T., & Krajcik, J. (2005). Motivation and Cognitive Engagement in Learning Environments. In R. Sawyer (Ed.), *The Cambridge Handbook of the Learning Sciences (Cambridge Handbooks in Psychology* (pp. 475–488). Cambridge University Press. doi:10.1017/CBO9780511816833.029

Britt, M., Goon, D., & Timmerman, M. (2015). How to better engage online students with online strategies. *College Student Journal*, *49*(3), 399–404.

Castelli, F. R., & Sarvary, M. A. (2021). Why students do not turn on their video cameras during online classes and an equitable and inclusive plan to encourage them to do so. *Ecology and Evolution*, *11*(8), 3565–3576. doi:10.1002/ece3.7123 PMID:33898009

Chandler, K. (2016). Using breakout rooms in synchronous online tutorials. *Journal of Perspectives in Applied Academic Practice*, *4*(3), 16–23. doi:10.14297/jpaap.v4i3.216

Chiu, T. K., & Lim, C. P. (2020). Strategic use of technology for inclusive education in Hong Kong: A content-level perspective. *ECNU Review of Education*, *3*(4), 715–734. doi:10.1177/2096531120930861

Chiu, T. K., & Mok, I. A. (2017). Learner expertise and mathematics different order thinking skills in multimedia learning. *Computers & Education*, *107*, 147–164. doi:10.1016/j.compedu.2017.01.008

Chrestensen, A. (2007). Real-world context, interest, understanding, and retention.[Thesis, Michigan Technological University, USA]. https://digitalcommons.mtu.edu/etds/536/

Christenson, S., Reschly, A. L., & Wylie, C. (2012). *Handbook of research on student engagement* (Vol. 840). Springer. doi:10.1007/978-1-4614-2018-7

Coates, H. (2007). A model of online and general campus-based student engagement. *Assessment & Evaluation in Higher Education*, *32*(2), 121–141. doi:10.1080/02602930600801878

Connelly, F. M., & Clandinin, D. J. (1990). Stories of experience and narrative inquiry. *Educational Researcher*, *19*(5), 2–14. doi:10.3102/0013189X019005002

Conrad, R. M., & Donaldson, J. A. (2012). *Continuing to engage the online learner: More activities and resources for creative instruction*. John Wiley & Sons.

Cornell, R. M., Johnson, C. B., & Schwartz, W. C. Jr. (2013). Enhancing student experiential learning with structured interviews. *Journal of Education for Business*, *88*(3), 136–146. doi:10.1080/08832323.2012.659296

Edmondson, A. C., & Daley, G. (2020). How to foster psychological safety in virtual meetings. HBR. https://hbr.org/2020/08/how-to-foster-psychological-safety-in-virtual-meetings

Ferreira, D., MacLean, G., & Center, G. E. (2018). Andragogy in the 21st century: Applying the assumptions of adult learning online. *Language Research Bulletin*, *32*(11), 10–19.

Fussell, G., Bianco, M., & Polkina, G. (2021). Fostering Diversity, Equity, and Inclusion in Online Classes. In E. Langran, & D. Rutledge (Eds.), *Proceedings of SITE Interactive Conference* (pp. 15-19). Association for the Advancement of Computing in Education (AACE).

Garrison, D. R., Anderson, T., & Archer, W. (2003). A theory of critical inquiry in online distance education. Handbook of distance education, 1(4), 113-127.

Garrison, D. R., Cleveland-Innes, M., & Fung, T. S. (2010). Exploring causal relationships among teaching, cognitive and social presence: Student perceptions of the community of inquiry framework. *The internet and higher education*, *13*(1-2), 31–36. doi:10.1016/j.iheduc.2009.10.002

Garza, T. J. (2021). Raise Your Hand: Online Language and Culture Instruction, Inclusivity, and Critical Pedagogy. *Russian Language Journal*, *71*(2), 15.

González-Tennant, E. (2017). Digital Storytelling in the Classroom: New Media Techniques for an Engaged Anthropological Pedagogy. In M. Nuñez-Janes, A. Thornburg, A. Booker, I. Penier, S. Pack, & A. Leverton (Eds.), *Practicing, Teaching, and Learning Anthropology with Digital Storytelling* (pp. 152–169). De Gruyter. doi:10.1515/9783110539356-012

Greene, H., Koh, K., Bonnici, J., & Chase, J. (2015). The value of storytelling in the marketing curriculum. *Journal of the Academy of Business Education*, *16*, 111–128.

Gunawardena, C. N., Wilson, P. L., & Nolla, A. C. (2003). Culture and online education. In M. G. Moore & W. G. Anderson (Eds.), *Handbook of distance education* (pp. 753–775). Routledge.

Harbour, K. E., Evanovich, L. L., Sweigart, C. A., & Hughes, L. E. (2015). A brief review of effective teaching practices that maximize student engagement. *Preventing School Failure*, *59*(1), 5–13. doi:10.1080/1045988X.2014.919136

Hartnett, M. K. (2015). Influences that undermine learners' perceptions of autonomy, competence and relatedness in an online context. *Australasian Journal of Educational Technology*, *31*(1). doi:10.14742/ajet.1526

He, X., Shelden, D., Kraftson, A., Else, T., & Auchus, R. J. (2020). A virtual teaching clinic for virtual care during the COVID-19 pandemic. *Clinical Diabetes and Endocrinology*, *6*(1), 1–3. doi:10.118640842-020-00108-1 PMID:33251027

Hsu, H. C. K., Wang, C. V., & Levesque-Bristol, C. (2019). Reexamining the impact of self-determination theory on learning outcomes in the online learning environment. *Education and Information Technologies*, *24*(3), 2159–2174. doi:10.100710639-019-09863-w

Keller, J. M. (2010). Motivational design research and development. In *Motivational design for learning and performance* (pp. 297–323). Springer. doi:10.1007/978-1-4419-1250-3_12

Ketelle, D. (2017). Introduction to the Special Issue: What Is Storytelling in the Higher Education Classroom? *Storytelling, Self, Society*, *13*(2), 143–150. doi:10.13110torselfsoci.13.2.0143

Knowles, M. S., Holton, E. F. III, & Swanson, R. A. (2014). *The adult learner: The definitive classic in adult education and human resource development*. Routledge. doi:10.4324/9781315816951

Kolb, A. Y., & Kolb, D. A. (2009). Experiential learning theory: A dynamic, holistic approach to management learning, education and development. The SAGE handbook of management learning, education and development, 42, 68.

Kolb, D. A. (2014). *Experiential learning: Experience as the source of learning and development*. FT press.

Krause, K. L., & Coates, H. (2008). Students' engagement in first-year university. *Assessment & Evaluation in Higher Education*, *33*(5), 493–505. doi:10.1080/02602930701698892

Kuh, G. D. (2009). What student affairs professionals need to know about student engagement. *Journal of College Student Development*, *50*(6), 683–706. doi:10.1353/csd.0.0099

Lambert, J. L., & Fisher, J. L. (2013). Community of inquiry framework: Establishing community in an online course. *Journal of Interactive Online Learning*, *12*(1), 1–16.

Lee, E., Pate, J. A., & Cozart, D. (2015). Autonomy support for online students. *TechTrends*, *59*(4), 54–61. doi:10.100711528-015-0871-9

Li, L., Xu, L. D., He, Y., He, W., Pribesh, S., Watson, S. M., & Major, D. A. (2021). Facilitating online learning via zoom breakout room technology: A case of pair programming involving students with learning disabilities. *Communications of the Association for Information Systems*, *48*(1), 12. doi:10.17705/1CAIS.04812

Lietaert, S., Roorda, D., Laevers, F., Verschueren, K., & De Fraine, B. (2015). The gender gap in student engagement: The role of teachers' autonomy support, structure, and involvement. *The British Journal of Educational Psychology*, *85*(4), 498–518. doi:10.1111/bjep.12095 PMID:26446905

Lombardi, M. M., & Oblinger, D. G. (2007). Authentic learning for the 21st century: An overview. *Educause learning initiative, 1*(2007), 1-12.

McGuire, S. Y. (2006). The impact of supplemental instruction on teaching students how to learn. *New Directions for Teaching and Learning*, *2006*(106), 3–10. doi:10.1002/tl.228

Merriam, S. B., Caffarella, R. S., & Baumgartner, L. (2007). Self-directed learning. In S. B. Merriam, R. S. Caffarella, & L. Baumgartner (Eds.), *Learning in adulthood: a comprehensive guide* (pp. 105–129). Jossey-Bass.

Meyer, K. A. (2014). Student engagement in online learning: What works and why. *ASHE Higher Education Report*, *40*(6), 1–114. doi:10.1002/aehe.20018

Miettinen, R. (2000). The concept of experiential learning and John Dewey's theory of reflective thought and action. *International Journal of Lifelong Education*, *19*(1), 54–72. doi:10.1080/026013700293458

Mirzoeva, L. Y. (2021). Using breakout rooms in online language teaching: Advantages and disadvantages. *International Journal of Innovative Research in Education*, *8*(2), 94–101. doi:10.18844/ijire.v8i2.6807

Mohan, B., & Nair, L. R. (2018). Story tellingan effective pedagogy for multicultural education. *SCMS Journal of Indian Management*, *15*(3), 81–90.

Ng, K. H., & Chiu, T. K. (2017). Emotional multimedia design for developing mathematical problem-solving skills. In *New ecology for education—Communication x learning* (pp. 131–141). Springer. doi:10.1007/978-981-10-4346-8_11

O'Mahony, J. (2014). *Enhancing student learning and teacher development in transnational education.* Higher Education Academy.

Oraif, I., & Elyas, T. (2021). Applicability of collaborative work in the COVID-19 Era: Use of breakout groups in teaching L2 translation. *Electronics (Basel)*, *10*(22), 2846. doi:10.3390/electronics10222846

Pickering, J. D. (2017). Cognitive engagement: A more reliable proxy for learning? *Medical Science Educator*, *27*(4), 821–823. doi:10.100740670-017-0447-8

Pittaway, S. M., & Moss, T. (2014). 'Initially, we were just names on a computer screen': Designing engagement in online teacher education. *The Australian Journal of Teacher Education*, *39*(7), 140–156. doi:10.14221/ajte.2014v39n7.10

Pollom, E. L., Sandhu, N., Deig, C. R., Obeid, J. P., Miller, J. A., & Kahn, J. M. (2021). Networking and applying to radiation oncology during a pandemic: Cross-sectional survey of medical student concerns. *Advances in Radiation Oncology*, *6*(3), 100643. doi:10.1016/j.adro.2021.100643 PMID:33748546

Read, D., Barnes, S. M., Hughes, O., Ivanova, I. T., Sessions, A., & Wilson, P. J. (2022). Supporting student collaboration in online breakout rooms through interactive group activities. *New Directions in the Teaching of Physical Sciences, 17*(1).

Reeve, J. (2013). How students create motivationally supportive learning environments for themselves: The concept of agentic engagement. *Journal of Educational Psychology*, *105*(3), 579–595. doi:10.1037/a0032690

Reeve, J., & Tseng, C. M. (2011). Agency as a fourth aspect of students' engagement during learning activities. *Contemporary Educational Psychology*, *36*(4), 257–267. doi:10.1016/j.cedpsych.2011.05.002

Reina, S. (2021). Get Creative with Your Use of Breakout Rooms. Harvard Business Publishing Education. https://hbsp.harvard.edu/inspiring-minds/get-creative-with-your-use-of-breakout-rooms?msclkid=fe01b671c50011ec9be359fd9d509506

Roberts, L. (2017). Research in the real world: Improving adult learners web search and evaluation skills through motivational design and problem-based learning. *College & Research Libraries*, *78*(4), 527. doi:10.5860/crl.78.4.527

Ryan, R. M., & Deci, E. L. (2017). *Self-determination theory: Basic psychological needs in motivation, development, and wellness*. Guilford Publications. doi:10.1521/978.14625/28806

Ryan, R. M., & Deci, E. L. (2020). Intrinsic and extrinsic motivation from a self-determination theory perspective: Definitions, theory, practices, and future directions. *Contemporary Educational Psychology*, *61*, 101860. doi:10.1016/j.cedpsych.2020.101860

Sathy, V., & Hogan, K. A. (2019). How to make your teaching more inclusive. The Chronicle of Higher Education.

Schmidt, H. G., Wagener, S. L., Smeets, G. A. C. M., Keemink, L. M., & van der Molen, H. T. (2015). Guus ACM Smeets, Lianne M. Keemink, and Henk T. van Der Molen. "On the use and misuse of lectures in higher education. *Health Profession Education*, *1*(1), 12–18. doi:10.1016/j.hpe.2015.11.010

Shackelford, J. L., & Maxwell, M. (2012). Sense of community in graduate online education: Contribution of learner to learner interaction. *International Review of Research in Open and Distributed Learning*, *13*(4), 228–249. doi:10.19173/irrodl.v13i4.1339

Sierens, E., Vansteenkiste, M., Goossens, L., Soenens, B., & Dochy, F. (2009). The synergistic relationship of perceived autonomy support and structure in the prediction of self-regulated learning. *The British Journal of Educational Psychology*, *79*(1), 57–68. doi:10.1348/000709908X304398 PMID:18466671

Skinner, E. A., Kindermann, T. A., & Furrer, C. J. (2009). A motivational perspective on engagement and disaffection: Conceptualization and assessment of children's behavioral and emotional participation in academic activities in the classroom. *Educational and Psychological Measurement*, *69*(3), 493–525. doi:10.1177/0013164408323233

Smith, E. K., & Kaya, E. (2021). Online university teaching at the time of COVID-19 (2020): An Australian perspective. *IAFOR Journal of Education*, *9*(2), 183–200. doi:10.22492/ije.9.2.11

Stone, G., Fiedler, B. A., & Kandunias, C. (2014). Harnessing Facebook for student engagement in accounting education: Guiding principles for accounting students and educators. *Accounting Education*, *23*(4), 295–321. doi:10.1080/09639284.2014.908730

Strawbridge, J., Hayden, J. C., Robson, T., Flood, M., Cullinan, S., Lynch, M., Morgan, A. T., O'Brien, F., Reynolds, R., Kerrigan, S. W., Cavalleri, G., Kirby, B. P., Tighe, O., Maher, A., & Barlow, J. W. (2022). Educating pharmacy students through a pandemic: Reflecting on our COVID-19 experience. *Research in Social & Administrative Pharmacy*, *18*(7), 3204–3209. doi:10.1016/j.sapharm.2021.08.007 PMID:34483082

Swan, K., Garrison, D. R., & Richardson, J. C. (2009). A constructivist approach to online learning: The community of inquiry framework. In *Information technology and constructivism in higher education: Progressive learning frameworks* (pp. 43–57). IGI global. doi:10.4018/978-1-60566-654-9.ch004

Tainsh, R. (2016). Thoughtfully designed online courses as effective adult learning tools. *Journal of Adult Education*, *45*(1), 7–9.

Trenshaw, K. F., Revelo, R. A., Earl, K. A., & Herman, G. L. (2016). Using self-determination theory principles to promote engineering students' intrinsic motivation to learn. *International Journal of Engineering Education*, *32*(3), 1194–1207.

Vansteenkiste, M., Sierens, E., Soenens, B., Luyckx, K., & Lens, W. (2009). Motivational profiles from a self-determination perspective: The quality of motivation matters. *Journal of Educational Psychology*, *101*(3), 671–688. doi:10.1037/a0015083

Vollet, J. W., Kindermann, T. A., & Skinner, E. A. (2017). In peer matters, teachers matter: Peer group influences on students' engagement depend on teacher involvement. *Journal of Educational Psychology*, *109*(5), 635–652. doi:10.1037/edu0000172

Vonderwell, S., Liang, X., & Alderman, K. (2007). Asynchronous discussions and assessment in online learning. *Journal of Research on Technology in Education*, *39*(3), 309–328. doi:10.1080/15391523.2007.10782485

Wilkinson, A., Gollan, P. J., Marchington, M., & Lewin, D. (2010). Conceptualizing employee participation in organizations. In A. Wilkinson, P. Gollan, M. Marchington, & D. Lewin (Eds.), *The Oxford handbook of participation in organizations* (pp. 1–125). Oxford University Press.

World Economic Forum. 2020. *The future of jobs report 2020.* World Economic Forum, Geneva, Switzerland.

Xie, K., & Ke, F. (2011). The role of students' motivation in peer-moderated asynchronous online discussions. *British Journal of Educational Technology*, *42*(6), 916–930. doi:10.1111/j.1467-8535.2010.01140.x

Yang, Y. T. C., & Wu, W. C. I. (2012). Digital storytelling for enhancing student academic achievement, critical thinking, and learning motivation: A year-long experimental study. *Computers & Education*, *59*(2), 339–352. doi:10.1016/j.compedu.2011.12.012

Yong, S. (2021). A reflective commentary about teaching international non-accounting postgraduates amid COVID-19. *Pacific Accounting Review*, *33*(5), 616–624. doi:10.1108/PAR-09-2020-0156

Zouhri, K., & Running, C. L. (2021, July). Different Zoom Breakout Room Methods and Techniques' Effects on Engineering Students' Learning Outcomes for Engineering Courses. In *2021 ASEE Virtual Annual Conference Content Access.*

Zuber-Skerritt, O., & Abraham, S. (2017). A conceptual framework for work-applied learning for developing managers as practitioner researchers. *Higher Education. Skills and Work-Based Learning*, *7*(1), 35–50. doi:10.1108/HESWBL-05-2016-0037

Section 4

Broadening Horizons

Chapter 10
Blended and Transnational Higher Education in Architecture Schools:
Examples and Considerations From Two International Joint-Design Studios Between Australia and Japan

Raffaele Pernice
University of New South Wales, Australia

Tetsuya Yaguchi
Waseda University, Japan

Keigo Kobayashi
Waseda University, Japan

ABSTRACT

In this book chapter, authors will reflect on the challenges, advantages, and pitfalls of the blended teaching in 2 architectural design studios jointly organized by an Australian and a Japanese university, highlighting key considerations ranging from the variety of learning and teaching on campus and virtual practices, to the design of assessments and related feedback, and the use of various on-line communication and graphic platforms implemented for teaching and learning (Teams, Zoom, Miro, Concept-board). They will also give an account of the experience and direct involvement of both students and faculty during the lock-down, and how flexibility and adaptability to the use of new technologies on their parts has resulted in a valuable experience at least for what concerns international design studios cooperation. As is common practice in architectural schools, the 2 joint design studios focused on different scale of representation and design, exploring issues and characteristics from the territorial to local scales.

DOI: 10.4018/978-1-6684-5226-4.ch010

INTRODUCTION

The COVID-19 pandemic which hit and transformed the world in the last 2 years has been a fundamental reason behind an extended and far-reaching revolution in the methods and practice on teaching in higher education globally. Extended lockdowns and the consequent transition from face-to-face interaction towards the rapidly worldwide implementation of remote learning and teaching has completely reshaped the education methods and techniques in the academic world.

Among the main consequence of this revolution has the development of a so-called "hybrid" and "blended" teaching practice which blends in-class on campus practices with on-line activities. This has resulted in challenges for both students and teaching staff/faculty given the rapidity of the change and the lack of experience related to this new condition.

Based on first-hand experience of the authors, this book chapter discusses and critically outlines the activities planned and executed during 2 joint design studios organized by the School of Built Environment at the University of New South Wales (UNSW Sydney) and the Department of Architecture at Waseda University in Tokyo in the period 2020-2021. It intends to give a qualitative and reflective account of this experience (within its limits) and to assess and evaluate the efficacy of blended delivery (on-line and offline learning) while sharing some examples of good practice on the hybrid teaching and remote learning approaches which have been implemented during 2 international joint-design studios which involved students and faculty of the architecture program of these 2 universities in Australia and Japan.

As is common practice in architectural schools, the 2 joint design studios focused on different scale of representation and design, exploring issues and characteristics from the territorial to local scales.

The final work resulted in strategic architectural and urban design projects built on the knowledge and data collected, analysed, and elaborated during the various phases of studios and through a combination of seminars, virtual fieldwork, on-line tutorials and design charrette and interim and final reviews with faculty and student groups of the two institutions.

In both cases, through a series of blended teaching and learning methods, Australian and Japanese students were invited to develop urban design proposals and architectural responses through mapping, the review and analysis of relevant information, leading to conclusive detailed projects relaying on shared materials and coordinated (remote) joint activities.

METHODOLOGY

The content of the present chapter is grounded on the personal experience of the authors and other direct empirical observations which have been integrated with substantial literature review and ad hoc internal/external feedbacks from both students and invited staff during the interim and final reviews of the students' works. The reflections presented are mainly based on and matured through several years of teaching design studios in local context (namely Australia and Japan) which also offered several opportunities of conducting joint activities with foreign partners during the pre-covid years.

The collaboration for the joint design studios illustrated in this chapter were the follow up of personal contacts among the co-authors, who after initial discussion eventually decided to experiment with a communal teaching project at the beginning of the covid pandemic in 2020.

While both studios in Australia and Japan worked on the same site and the same theme and had mostly the same kind of deliverables and assessments, still there was flexibility in deciding the focus of the design project (more architectural or urban) and the temporal frame, in order to satisfy the academic requirements of the respective university.

Feedback was formally and informally collected during the different stages of the teaching activities and after the exam period to assess the effectiveness of the teaching and the experience of the students, especially in terms of overall satisfaction and suggestions for further improvement of the proposed courses.

LEARNING AND TEACHING IN THE 21ST CENTURY AND THE RATIONALE FOR THE JOINT DESIGN STUDIOS

"Tell me and I forget.
Teach me and I remember.
Involve me and I learn."
Benjamin Franklin (1706-1790)

Modern pedagogy tends to privilege an approach that see the students as embedded in a 'knowledge society' in perpetual evolution, and as such foster their training to prepare them for many new and unforeseen challenges derived by the constant advance of science (Tilak, 2002). In a context where everyone is urged to acquire knowledge in a perpetual status of "continuous learning" to cope with an extremely complex world (Barnett, 2000) the acquisition of systematic skills to obtain not only information but to learn how to obtain information is a paramount importance. Recent decades have highlighted the importance of a progressive shift from passive to active learning (Baxter Magolda, 2008), a context where the student is no more a passive recipient of information but assume a more active role in various learning activities.

Some methodologies are particularly important and largely implemented in the teaching in the field of architectural studies and in design studios in particular, like for instance: reflective practice, the research by design and the comparative studies. Each of these exert relevant impact on the acquisition of knowledge and the professional formation students and their formation as future professionals.

The reflective practice envisions learning structured as a continuous conversation, criticism and "restructuring" of the professional practice in the society (Schon, 1983). Research by design and research-based teaching and learning for students are very valuable pedagogical approaches which build a process which focuses on the formulation of a conceptual framework which describes the research process itself and is focused essentially on a system relating the proposition of research questions, the investigation of literature review and the use of case studies (Healey, Flint, and Harrington, 2014). The conclusion transcribes the phases of the research process which results in an alteration or the conceptual framework. The importance of comparative studies has been largely recognized in different field of research and subject (Werner and Zimmermann, 2004) and it is particularly valuable in the field of architecture and urban design as this allows a direct comparison of different techniques and strategies which can inform the process of learning through the critical analysis and testing of different solutions in the transformation of the built environment.

The nature of the professional practice for architects and urban designers indeed requires very broad skillsets, great curiosity and a vast culture, spanning from aesthetics to art, from general graphic skills to sound understanding of mathematics and physics and design principles, which are usually transferred via face-to-face interaction and collegial activities. Observation, full immersion in local and foreign contexts, the analysis and the comparison of similarities and differences of the cultural, social and urban environment which they are called to investigate and understand are among factors determinant for the smooth development of skills and practical management abilities in order to enrich the fundamental knowledge which informs the professional activity after the conclusion of the formal academic training.

JOINT DESIGN STUDIOS IN ARCHITECTURE BETWEEN UNSW SYDNEY AND WASEDA UNIVERSITY 2020-2022

A multiplicity of theoretical and practical activities, spanning from literature and case studies reviews to model making, sketching and drafting, is typical in the curricula of the design studios, which are the backbones of the preparation of the student of architecture in a knowledgeable professional with necessary competence and skills able to operate at various level of the architectural and urban project. Various tasks in the different stages of the research and design studio practice consist in literature and case studies review, attendance to guest lectures, general research-oriented presentations, research and making skill training (e.g., model making).

2 joint design studios have been selected as model of transnational teaching cooperation which has been proposed between UNSW Sydney and Waseda University between 2020 and 2022. Some communalities are that these joint courses were proposed, developed and delivered during the acute phase of the pandemic when remote learning and online classes were mandatory in both the institutions, being all lessons being moved on Microsoft Teams.

In general, the studios were organized as a series of lectures, tutorial tasks and collective/individual reviews focused on studio discussion which takes place in general once per week and divided into 2 parts, with lectures and seminars in the morning (usually 1-2 hours) followed by 5-6 hours of tutorial practice.

In principle continuous attendance is a firm pre-requisite in architecture schools, and all students were encouraged to attend the weekly sessions. During various activities and despite the presence on campus, students were generally expected to work proactively and share the progress of their works on Miro or Concept Board (2 of the most popular digital visual communication platforms) in order to foster a studio culture from which all participants can profit, and which keeps in high regard the *peer-to-peer learning* (where everyone learn directly from their classmates by observing their work and talking with them, or during the various tutorials with tutors, guest lectures and other students) and *learning-by-doing* approach (which is an active learning tool where students engage different tasks to learn from their own experience, and direct involvement and efforts, for instance in the preparation of posters and construction of and testing of physical scale models).

Like other design studios around the world, the pedagogy for both studios were also inspired by a *Design-By-Research* approach which values both the final design project (as a finished product and conclusive objective) and the entire process of design development guided by research, which is an important tool of inquiry and fundamental occasion for individual and collegial research activity.

In all stages of the design studios, students were encouraged to participate in the planned seminars and hands-on weekly tutorials (on-line or face-to-face). Lectures, workshops, and series of brain-storming sessions helped expanding the understanding of theoretical concepts and their application to the project's resolution.

Activities and Topics of the Courses ARCH7112 2020 and BEIL 6013 (2021-2022)

The course ARCH7112 – Integrated Studio Urban Conditions ran from early September to late November 2020 with an attendance of 30 students at UNSW Sydney and 12 at Waseda University. A second course BEIL6013 – Nomad Japan Studio was structured as a 2-week intensive summer course which was split into 2 parts running in December 2021 and in January 2022. For this course due to the coincidence of the holiday summer period in Australia only a limited number of students attended with a total of 11 participants, despite a significant financial support for its promotion and organization came from a competitive grant awarded by the Australian Department of Foreign Affairs and Trade (DFAT) and the Australian Japan Foundation (AJF) in 2021(Grant Ref. AJF2021113).

With some obvious differences, both courses were structured in a similar way and consisted in 3 main phases with the involvement of both the faculty and students of the 2 universities. Initially, students conducted a literature review as group and then individually to engage them with the teaching subject, followed by a critical analysis of others relevant selected case studies for the initial stage of the design task. All classes were in a hybrid mode consisting in in-presence and remote contacts, with students from home or gathering on campus but using Microsoft Teams as virtual platform to interact with colleagues and peers overseas. Joint tutorials were then organized together with guest lectures and structured lectures which related to the studio theme were delivered by both faculty and guest scholars to enable students' research inquiry into the interest topics. During the interim and the final reviews, students conducted group and individual presentations on their studio project to gain feedback from instructors and learn from peer discussions.

THE EXPERIENCE WITH ARCH7112 (2020)

Inspired by a real project initiative, the topic for the ARCH7112 - Integrated design studio was the development and design of an alternative masterplan on the same blocks of the proposed space for the design of the new UNSW Canberra campus. All students were divided into teams started first with the design of the masterplan, then individually developed an education building architecturally. As is typical for architectural school for design studios, feedback was continuous and mainly provided during the daily tutorials and seminars, and the presentation and discussion of graphic materials and/or other required outputs.

The design studio was organized every Monday from 10am-4pm, Sydney local time, with 1 hour lunch break. The students initially undertook a site appraisal and SWOT analysis (which consists in a framework indicating a critical assessment of the site in terms of its strength, weakness, opportunities and threads, presented as a matrix of various data and other relevant information), which was integrated with the review and analysis of selected precedents as exemplary case studies. The activity then concentrated on the development of a comprehensive spatial strategy, culminating in the development of a general masterplan, followed by the preliminary architectural design of a building by the end of the trimester.

The results of the site and precedent studies were shared by the whole studio both at UNSW and Waseda University. This resource acted as a springboard for students to collectively and individually develop their architectural project brief based on the studio premise alongside their own ideas and strategies, whether these were contextual, environmental, social, political, economic, philosophical, technological, or cultural.

The Beginning

Many schools of architecture these days established international bi-lateral academic exchange programs. In the fall of 2019, just before the pandemic, the University of New South Wales in Sydney (UNSW) and Waseda University in Tokyo initiated a discussion to establish an agreement between two institutions. Our goal was to create the platform for mutual coordination and cooperation in joint research and global educational, academic, and cultural exchanges.

Soon after the initial discussion, the covid-19 pandemic hit in full scale. Both institutions were forced to revisit the teaching methodologies and techniques without compromising the academic principles that support students to grow and become creative professionals with global perspectives.

The Challenges in the Remote Design Education

Like many other academic institutions, UNSW and Waseda shifted from in-person instruction to online education. Luckily enough, Waseda University had a plan to introduce a robust and newly customized online education platform, Moodle[1] from April 2020, and all faculty members had been trained for the initial launch. Therefore, the transition was relatively smooth but revealed the new online education system's challenges and limitations both for educators/ students, specific to architectural/ urban design education.

From our experience during the transitional period, we observed that mobility, interactive communication, and a peer-reviewed working environment were something we lost in our studio milieu.

The mobility restriction was an apparent challenge. Due to strict quarantine orders under the state of emergency, all students cannot conduct site visits and grasp the "neighbourhood feel". This limitation tended to result in the design without sensibility to the local context, such as existing land uses, scale, natural resources, cultural assets, etc. Uses of widely available online data could mitigate these challenges, like google earth, open street maps[2], and GIS data from municipal governments and GIS benders. However, these alternatives could not fill the gap between first-hand and virtual site visit experiences.

Second, communication through a 2-Dimensional screen could not completely substitute the use of physical models during the design development stage. The advancement of 3-Dimensional CAD software made it possible to create sophisticated professional-level renderings even by undergraduate students. On the other hand, 3-D software has not developed enough as a communicative tool for searching for better design alternatives and solutions. The 3-D cad model allows for exploration of the forms that may be difficult to build by the traditional physical study model but could not become the tool to share the narrative of the design concept because of its inflexible interface. Additionally, informal communication between instructors and students in the studio, which sounds relatively minor but was an essential part of the creative learning environment as the extension and supplement of the desk critique, was completely missing in the online platform.

Lastly, in the physical studio environment, students could learn by seeing their friends' and seniors' drawing/ model making techniques, exchanging ideas, and conducting peer-reviewed studio projects. Nevertheless, the pandemic completely disassembled this studio culture and hit very hard on lower-division students with limited experience and skillset.

The Pilot Virtual Joint Studio with UNSW and Waseda University

Although there are obvious challenges and limitations mentioned earlier, UNSW and Waseda University started the experimental virtual joint studio in September 2020 to seek a new and improved pedagogy in the age of the pandemic. Through the remote instruction experience from April to July of 2020, we believe we could turn these disadvantages into advantages of architectural design education on the online platform.

First, we all suffer from limitations in mobility, and the situation will not be alleviated for several years. In the traditional design studio, students are expected to visit the site for the comprehensive assessment of the characteristics of the area (SWOT analysis) before the initial development of the design project. This norm is not the case any longer after the pandemic. Since mobility limitations impacted equally all students, the project site could be located anywhere in the world as long as they have access to sufficient datasets.

As for communicative design tools in lieu of traditional ones, online whiteboards application, such as Miro and Concept board, became powerful tools. These applications allowed us to store numerous idea sketches and images. Unlike a physical studio setting, there is no limitation for the pin-up spaces. In addition, studio instructors could chronologically see the progress of students' design ideas and concept development during the weekly tutorials in person or online. This process involved the display and discussion of students works (with online tutorials freely accessible via Miro or Concept board), resulting in a continuous flow of coherent and effective critiques from the instructors.

In September 2020, there was no substitute for a peer-review environment in the physical studio setting, so Waseda University employed an in-person/ online blended approach. Students were allowed access to the school for the group work, while all classroom lectures and joint presentations with UNSW and Waseda University went online.

Knowing the constraints and opportunities, we designed the pilot virtual studio for the master level students using the existing courses at both institutions, namely "ARCH7112 Urban Conditions" at UNSW and "Regenerative Design of Built Environment Exercise B" at Waseda University. This virtual studio aimed to widen students' eyes to the urban conditions and encourage them to develop strategic solutions through urban and architectural design, contributing to the city's liveability and global competitiveness. The eight-week virtual joint studio is organized in weekly lectures, individual and group tutorials, and periodic individual/collective reviews developed from the in-person curriculum before 2019 (see table 1).

Table 1. Schedule of 2020 pilot joint studio UNSW/Waseda University (author: Yaguchi T.)

Schedule
Sep.14, 2020: Orientation and Introduction (lecture by Suzanna Holmes, program manager of UNSW campus development)
Sep.21, 2020: Lecture by Morgan Lumen (General Information on Campus Design)
Sep.28, 2020: Lecture by Raffaele Pernice (Site appraisal and SWOT analysis)
Oct.05, 2022*: Mid-presentation (site analysis, case studies and SWOT analysis)
Oct.12, 2022: Lecture by Tetsuya Yaguchi (Campus Planning 101)
Oct.26, 2020*: Virtual critique
Nov.02, 2020*: Virtual critique (general masterplan and design strategies)
Nov.30, 2020*: Final presentation (masterplan and conceptual architectural design)
* Students from both institutions meet and present the projects on the Microsoft Teams videoconferencing platform

The project site for the studio was near the city centre of Canberra city, the federal capital of Australia, where UNSW is planning the development of a new campus. Since all students, including those in Australia, could not access the site due to the lockdown under the covid-19 pandemic restrictions, instructors invited several guests from Canberra to assist students in filling the gap of readily available data and first-hand site visit experience. A draft master plan of the campus is currently being prepared, and the project should be completed within ten years. Students were expected to work as a small group and develop the conceptual master plan for the new Canberra campus. The online group work was intended to re-create a peer-review studio environment even in the virtual format.

Then UNSW students would develop a schematic architectural design of the education building (approx. 8000-9000m2). The final result of the virtual pilot studio from both institutions has been edited in booklet format and uploaded to the ISSUU platform for our record and public review[34].

Lesson Learned for the Future Improvement

Our pilot virtual joint studio was a blessing in disguise. Both institutions planned to host the in-person workshop in 2019. We observed many educational benefits of the joint virtual studio over the in-person workshop. First, students can develop the design idea over several weeks (in this case, students spent an entire semester developing urban design ideas) rather than be forced to make a final presentation in a short time. Second, international travel is not necessarily required, resulting in time and cost savings. Cost-saving-benefit is also applicable to the jury system. Juries can be invited from every corner of the world if the time difference works nicely. For this specific pilot studio, eight jury members joined from Australia (Sydney and Canberra), China, Japan, and Italy. We are lucky enough that Sydney and Tokyo have a one-hour time difference only, so coordination was relatively easy for all.

The use of new technology as a communication tool was another blessing in disguise. Many people, including myself, still prefer communicating design ideas through traditional media, such as physical study models and 2-D illustrations. At the same time, we found that the use of online whiteboard applications showed enormous potential when recording the progress of design development (figures 1,2,3,4).

THE EXPERIENCE WITH BEIL6013 (2021/22)

The 2 weeks intensive summer course BEIL 6013 Nomad 2022 Japan Studio at UNSW Sydney was open to undergraduate and post graduate students and focussed on the theme of waterfront regeneration in Tokyo Bay, focussing on the selected sites of Odaiba artificial and land and Harumi pier, whereby all main activities were carried out in strong cooperation with students of Waseda University in Tokyo.

Through mapping, the review and analysis of case studies and other relevant information, students developed initial visions of selected sites which informed their individual design response. For this course students were invited to propose, develop and present innovative concepts and practical ideas leading to sustainable and eco-friendly architectural solutions, effective city planning strategies and urban design proposals to cope with the specific problems existing in the local built environment in order to deliver healthy and liveable spaces, and high-quality urban places.

Figure 1. Virtual Presentation at Waseda University. Student group built a physical model (source: Yaguchi T.)

Figure 2. Presentation by campus planer from UNSW Canberra for initial project briefing (source: Yaguchi T.)

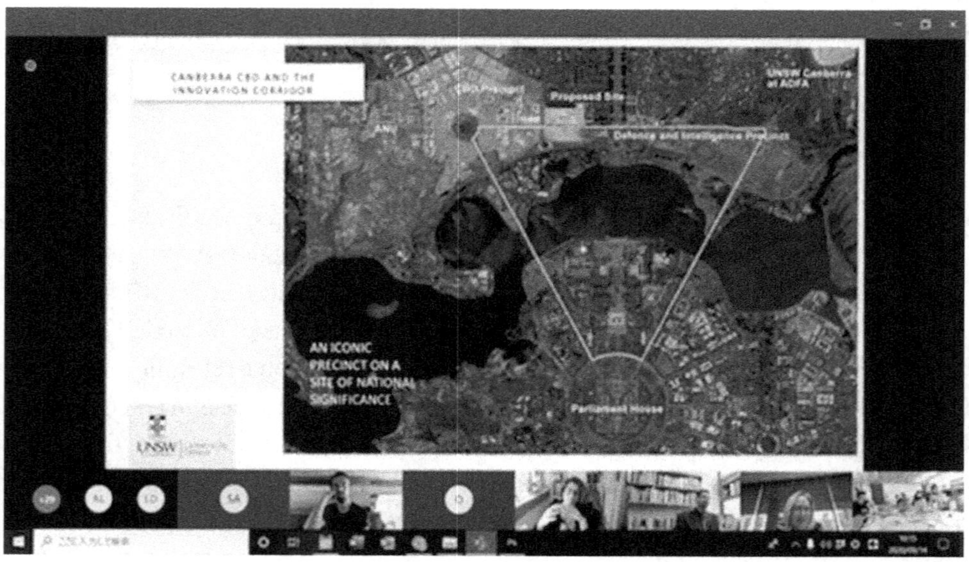

Figure 3. Final presentation materials were professionally binded and published for the record (source: Yaguchi T.)

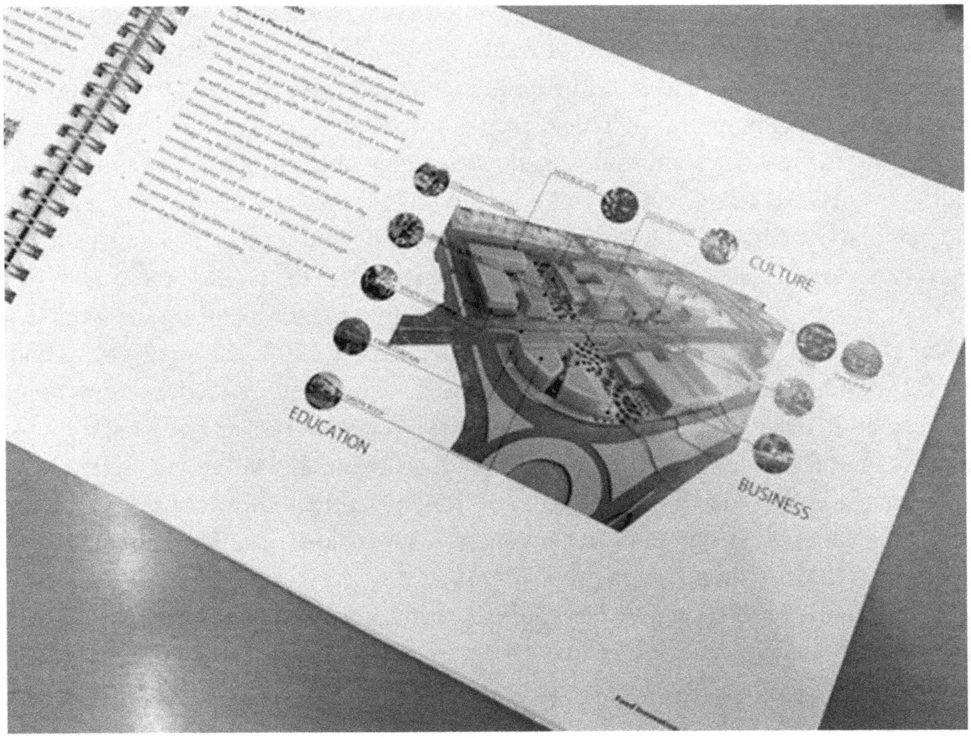

Figure 4. Final presentation of the student's masterplan and architectural projects via Microsoft Teams, November 2020 (source: Pernice R.)

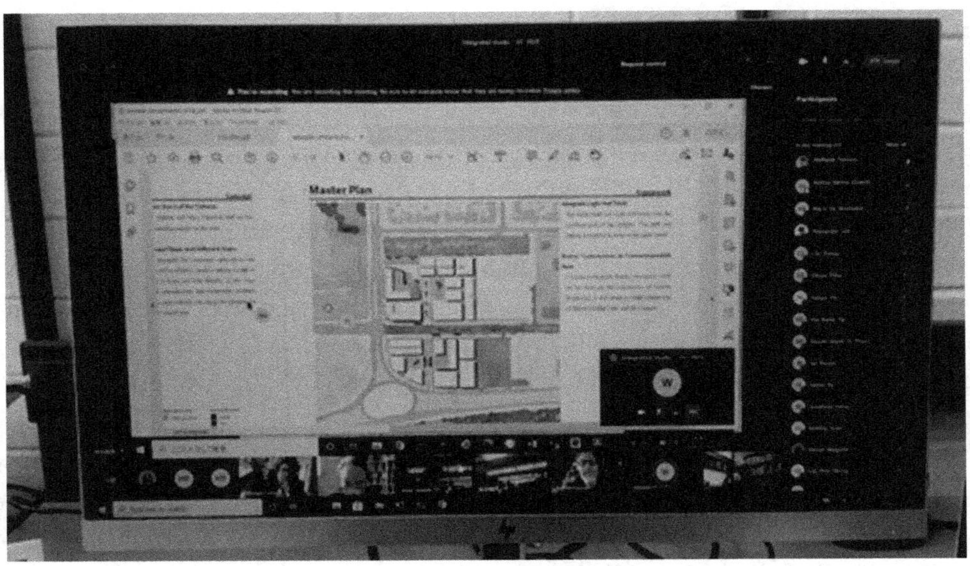

This course was taught in intensive blended/online mode of delivery, including lectures, tutorials, online learning activities and international, and students were fostered to collaborate with their partner international university colleagues. Because of the intensive nature of the summer course, the structure for this studio (teaching and learning) was designed to expand their knowledge on how integrate and elaborate information to trigger and develop architectural and urban design strategies of intervention, while refining their critical thinking, analytical and teamwork and communications skills. In the process one intention was to make Australian students knowledgeable about urban Japan and world city Tokyo.

The studio was divided into 2 blocks and consisted in a combination of virtual site visits, on-line lectures and seminars, critical discussions, intensive charrette and tutorials sessions (face-to-face and online). It was expected that each student being fully engaged with the tasks of the studio. Students were expected to research, draw, diagram and/or model on a continuing basis during the workshop.

The typical studio day started at 9am to 5pm, Sydney local time. While the lectures and the tutorials were shared continuously, it was agreed to have 1 hour daily open for students' communication and sharing of information during the first week which concentrated on the analysis and initial study of the site before the actual initial design of the project. Students from UNSW Sydney relied heavily on different information from Waseda University peers to fill gaps in their knowledge of the site and retrieve precious data and a variety of documents, images and statistics (mostly available only in Japanese) which eventually informed directly their design propositions.

Although it was a brief course, and in the same way as the precedent course ARCH7112m, it provided both schools with a chance to experiment a new form of collaboration through use of remote technologies and methodologies that can further expand the possibilities and deepen understanding of the values of transnational educations.

Reflection Of the Instructors on The Joint Design Experience For Beil6013: New Opportunities Through Remote Lectures

BEIL6013 summer studio started off with several lectures given by professors and an architect, explaining about the Japanese context from historical, cultural, and architectural point of views, using remote video conferencing applications. Since the theme of the studio was about the waterfront regeneration in Tokyo Bay, one of the lectures covered the topic of urban design and waterfront developments, explaining several references as well as in depth information on the site and its surroundings. Another lecture given by a guest architect, Toyo Ito, a renown practitioner who covered the topic of general history of Tokyo and Tokyo Bay area, followed by explanation about his own projects and their concepts. The third lecture further elaborated the history of modern architecture in Japan and how it's reflected in some of the buildings at the site area. It also covered the critical issues which is faced by Japan today, such as the issue of rapid population decline, ageing and increase of singles households, using statistical information. All the lectures were provided in English and while the topics were more aimed towards the students of UNSW who had limited knowledge about the context of the project site, the Japanese students also seemed to be benefited from the lectures as they too lacked in-depth knowledge about their own history and environments. This process of providing lectures at the beginning of the transnational workshops and studios, is often shared with other cases of similar workshops and studios, which has been proven to be effective in accelerating the process of teaching about the contexts and setting a minimum common ground amongst the students before engaging in the same assignment.

Through personal experience and empirical evidence, based on informal discussion and official students' feedback during and after the workshops, these lectures were very helpful for them to understand the contexts as well as understanding the general directions to which they need to focus for the development of their design.

One of the great benefits of using remote technologies which became apparent with lectures for BEIL6013 is the possibility of inviting guest lecturer such as Toyo Ito, who is one of the established and renowned architects worldwide, into the studio. Although the realization of such an event was only possible due to close relationship between a faculty and Ito himself, the flexibility and facilitation of joining the studio through use of remote technologies must've played an important role in accomplishing such a prestigious event. While this benefit is not only limited to educational occasions, but it can also be further utilized in this kind of international studios where the special speakers from anywhere in the world can be invited to speak and motivate the students engaging into studio works without the hustle of travelling nor using too much of their precious time.

On the other hand, there are some disadvantages as well. Since the lecturer is not physically present, there are very limited chance of interactions with the students and the instructors, and this is particularly evident for highly visual subjects like architecture and urban design, where the main medium of communication is drawing and graphic representation. Furthermore, in pre-COVID times, in addition to the lecture, sometimes the lecturer can provide on-site guide of his or her built projects in the area and explain the physical and more intangible qualities of the built environment. With remote interactions, this kind of possibilities are extremely difficult to achieve.

Re-Discovery of Own Environment

Pre-COVID transnational collaborations often took place in the context of one of the participating institutions. Whether through looking at the site of the project or researching about various references, these opportunities of visiting new environment and welcoming outsiders, provide great benefits for the students of both sides. Visiting any new place with the help of local guides is a great way to experience and understand the unfamiliar context, and the students can be exposed to innumerable discoveries and inspirations. Simultaneously, it's equally important for the welcoming students to guide and explain about the places where they are familiar with, which forces them to be experts about their own context. Furthermore, by guiding the students from abroad, they are exposed to fresh views on something which they thought was very ordinary, providing chances of discoveries and re-evaluation on their own environment. Throughout several transnational workshops in the past that were held in Tokyo, this re-discovery aspect always left a large impact for the Japanese students, where they are often fascinated by the way visiting students found interests in what seemed like normal things and turning them into sources of inspirations and innovations.

Unfortunately, post-COVID situation with remote tools greatly hinders the students from receiving these blessings. As it was the case of BEIL6013, without the actual visit, the students are unable to experience the context of the projects outside of the designated site area, and the time spent for the students of both sides to collectively engage into projects and explore the city are greatly reduced. While digital tools such as Google Earth and street view function can allow foreign students to visit the site virtually, the experience is still very much limited with static scenes without human actions. In BEIL6013, the Japanese students tried to cope with this situation by documenting the site area with additional photographs and video clips to supplement the Google information, which provided extra help for the UNSW students. Also, the studio was organized so that the students were able to ask any questions using video calls (which were kept connected during studio hours as much as possible) and SNS's between each other, where some of the UNSW students were asking the Waseda students direct questions about the site and about Tokyo. Taking these experiences into consideration, in the future sessions, one can perhaps imagine a virtual site visits where hosting students can walk through the city using live video chat with 360 degrees camera, while exchanging information and questions between students from abroad. Unlike the Google's street views, this may supplement some of the lacking experiences and discoveries for both parties.

With Covid Communication as New Potential

Communication, or rather the intense need of communication, between the students from different contexts, is essential part of the transnational education. The students engaged in these exercises are often forced out of their usual comfort zone, supported by same language, same value, same moral, same knowledge, etc. In order to collaborate, the students are inevitably required to explain not only about what they think, but also about why, which often requires explaining about the background of certain context as well as use of various references. Particularly for the Japanese students who in general hesitate to speak out their opinions, these opportunities where they are forced to communicate was in-itself a great educational value.

In addition, the use of English as secondary language seemed to play an important role, where the lack of vocabulary often forces them to be more direct in communicating their opinions and ideas.

For example, Japanese students using their native language of Japanese could explain about their ideas with lots of words and articulations but failed to communicate the main point or specific intensions. On the other hand, the use of English and the concomitant lack of enough vocabulary to over articulate one's ideas, often resulted in a more clear and direct explanations about their design ideas and concepts when speaking to their Australian peers.

If there is one thing from which we had greatly benefited by the COVID, it's the global distribution and advancement of the remote communication tools. As in the case of transnational education, these communication tools allowed easier remote critique sessions and reviews. During BEIL6013, the students of both sides were able to receive comments from professors at both universities using the video meeting functions, showing the progress by sharing screens as well as capturing the pin-up contents on the walls and physical models with cameras. Final review was also held using the same technique with several additional guest critiques, the session was successfully carried out without any difficulty (fig.5). As the visit to another country for transnational collaborations often have very limited time of stay, and most of the workshops and studios choses the timing of the physical visit at the beginning of the studio rather than at the end, these remote communication tools can allow the smooth continuation of the studio beyond the time of the shared physical visit, as held in the BEIL6013.

Sharing Skills and Methods

Another positive aspect of transnational education can be said about the sharing opportunity of visual techniques and design methodologies. Today, while magazines and digital information can provide students with professional examples, it's not easy for the students to know about how the other students in different contexts are formalizing and representing their works. More and more, the digital tools have been shared amongst all the students globally, but each institutions tends to have different techniques and tendencies which can be inspiring for students of other institutions. In the case of recent BEIL6013 studio, UNSW students have shown their great strength in sorting researched materials into beautiful graphic representations in very short time. As for the Waseda students, besides their interesting approaches to the site, they had shown great strength in physical model representations, which was very contrasting to the use of digital 3D modeling and collage representations by UNSW students. The students of both sides, by being exposed to such differences, can learn about their strengths and weaknesses as well as representational skills and visuals. Although in BEIL6013 the students of both school were working separately in terms of proposing schemes, in the near future, this may also be improved by utilizing digital tools, where the students of both sides can work together on a single scheme constructed and studied within a 3D modeling software (such as Rhinoceros) and digitally shared working board (such as Miro). Rapid prototyping tools such as 3D printers and milling machines can also support the process by providing opportunity to evaluate the schemes in physical models at both schools.

Encouraging Differences Through Further Connection

Whether it's the communication skills or the representational skills, the transnational education can provide the students with many positive influences which are not easily acquired from purely domestic experiences. However, as the technological advancement further helps to overcome the physical distances, communication difficulties, and even financial burdens such as the travel expenses and the costs for the purchase of study related materials (e.g. in architectural school it is typical for students to print posters and produce physical models), each educational institutions will be forced to further strengthen its own identities, required to be more conscious of their emphasis and differences in research and educations towards shared global goals. As in the case of BEIL6013 for example, the issue of ageing and increasing singles households were introduced by the Japanese students during the course of their research, reflecting the extreme demographical transformation Japan and city of Tokyo is facing today. As for the UNSW students, emphasis on landscape and the ecological approach were presented as a key strategy in transforming the artificial land of Tokyo Bay area into sustainable living environment. Both of these ideas were shared between the students of two institutions and provided vital backgrounds and inspiration for their final design proposals.

Today, as more students are exposed to opportunities of working internationally, the importance of being conscious about their own ability, specialty and identity are further encouraged. The exchanging views and information through transnational education can provide both students and institutions a crucial chance to identify their own environment and strengths as well as weaknesses, necessary for developing identities crucial within rapidly connecting world.

CONCLUSION

The 2 joint designs studios organized between UNSW Sydney and Waseda University Tokyo which have been outlined in the chapter provided a significant opportunity to re-visit the importance of transnational education.

Figure 5. Final presentation for BEIL6013 studio project (via Microsoft Teams) with all staff and students from Australia and Japan, December 2021 (source: Pernice R.)

Through experiences in teaching at higher education, transnational workshops and design studios has been proven to be vital part of an architectural education as well as an essential experience for the students. Whether as a short charrette or as a proper design studio for extended periods of time, it's safe to say that the values these international collaborations can provide has been widely recognized and implemented at many universities today. With COVID or without, one of the most important aspects of transnational education is that it's trans-cultural, where groups of students from very different contexts and cultures can encounter each other, discovering differences and similarities at numerous levels, ranging from thoughts and ideas to skills, methodologies, visual representations, and presentations. Today, with the COVID situation still prevailing, these benefits of transnational collaborations which used to be almost unconsciously shared are now under a great challenge, but simultaneously provides us with great opportunity to revisit its meanings and values.

During the various phases of the joint design studios, a few (albeit surmountable) challenges were set because factors like different age of participants and their different level of education and experience (UG and PG students recruited for BEIL6013), together with different level of (English) language fluency, which had some limited repercussion for a more active participation of all the cohort. Another obvious problem, which also didn't interfere much with the studio experience, were sporadic technological glitches/malfunctioning of the wifi and unstable connection during tutorials. Besides, despite the enormous advantages of Information and Communication Technologies (ICT) for the blended model of teaching and learning (Alexander, 2010), empirical evidence and feedback from architecture students suggested for design studio tutorials with face-to-face in-person inquiry work much better that virtual interaction. But overall, all the above issues were manageable and didn't impact on the final outcomes and whole teaching and learning experience.

There are still challenges ahead to be addressed in the virtual studio format. The foremost issue is the site visit. Many students used "google map street view" as a virtual visit. However, the still photos of the street did not provide sufficient information, such as traffic volume, micro-climate, land use compatibilities, local vegetation, etc. There is no perfect solution replacing the first-hand experience today, but civic tech will gradually fill the missing information near future.

The combination of the remote conference and whiteboard application worked best for quality communication and a peer-review milieu of the physical studio. It will be an alternative to the physical design studio if necessary. However, as pointed out earlier in this text, there is no room for informal communication on online platforms. Therefore, studio instructors should carefully select strategies that facilitate informality through a blended/ hybrid approach, virtual group work environment, etc.

Lastly, it might be challenging when two institutions run completely different academic calendars, like the quoter system, tri-semester system, semester system, September enrolment, April enrolment, and such, from an administrative viewpoint.

Among the most valuable aspect of this transnational albeit virtual teaching and learning experience was eventually the human experience in terms of direct contacts and participation, and the gain of a better reciprocal knowledge for the respective foreign partners (for both faculty and students), as well as the possibility to expand all participants social and professional network. Also, very relevant was the possibility to have access to documents and other relevant information in foreign language, while simultaneously fostering ideas and plans for future international cooperation and research activity towards concrete communal endeavours, such as new joint symposium, publications, and research projects.

REFERENCES

Alexander, S. (2010). Flexible Learning in Higher Education. In P. Peterson, E. Baker, & B. McGaws (Eds.), *International Encyclopedia of Education* (3rd ed., pp. 441–447). Elsevier. doi:10.1016/B978-0-08-044894-7.00868-X

Altbach, P. G., & Knight, J. (2007). The internationalization of higher education: Motivations and realities. *Journal of Studies in International Education, 11*(3-4), 290–305. doi:10.1177/1028315307303542

Barnett, R. (2000). *University Knowledge in an Age of Supercomplexity; Higher Education N. 40*. Kluwer Academic Publishers.

Baxter Magolda, M. (2008, July/August). Three Elements of Self-Authorship. *Journal of College Student Development, 49*(4), 269–284. doi:10.1353/csd.0.0016

Chapman, A., & Pyvis, D. (2006). Quality, identity and practice in offshore university programmes: Issues in the internationalization of Australian higher education. *Teaching in Higher Education, 11*(2), 233–245. doi:10.1080/13562510500527818

Dunn, L., & Wallace, M. (2006). Australian academics and transnational teaching: An exploratory study of their preparedness and experiences. *Higher Education Research & Development, 25*(4), 357–369. doi:10.1080/07294360600947343

Gray, C. M. (2013, December 1). Informal peer critique and the negotiation of habitus in a design studio. *Art, Design & Communication in Higher Education, 12*(2), 195–209. doi:10.1386/adch.12.2.195_1

Harman, G. (2005). Internationalization of Australian higher education: A critical review of literature and research. In P. Ninnes & M. Hellstén (Eds.), *Internationalizing Higher Education* (Vol. 16, pp. 119–140). Springer-Verlag. doi:10.1007/1-4020-3784-8_7

Healey, M., & Bordogna, C. (2014). From transnational to multinational education: Emerging trends in international higher education. In E. Beerkens, M. Magna, M. Söderqvist, & H.-G. van Liempd (Eds.), *Internationalisation of higher education*. Raabe Academic Publishers.

Healey, M., Flint, A., & Harrington, K. (2014). *Engagement through partnership: Students as partners in learning and teaching in higher education*. HE Academy.

Kawaguchi, Y. (2005). 7010 Possibility of International Exchange Student Workshop: Case Study of Japan-Korea Architectural Design Workshop (Urban Planning). *Proceeding of the architectural research meetings: architectural planning and design, urban planning, rural planning, building economics, history and theory of architecture,* (75), 253-256.

Kosmützky, A., & Putty, R. (2016). Transcending Borders and Traversing Boundaries: A Systematic Review of the Literature on Transnational, Offshore, Cross-Border, and Borderless Higher Education. *Journal of Studies in International Education, 20*(1), 8–33. doi:10.1177/1028315315604719

Kuriyama, N., & Miwa, K. (2010). Report on WAT Kobe 2009, the international workshop on urban landscape and the environment in Kobe UNESCO City of Design. *Journal of the City Planning Institute of Japan, 45*(3), 295–300. doi:10.11361/journalcpij.45.3.295

Matsumoto, H. (2013). Return of Scientific Knowledge to the Researched Society: Fieldwork in Other Countries. E-journal. *Geo: Geography and Environment, 8*(1), 3–14.

Matsushita, K. (2017). 2F18 Education System of International Architectural Design Workshop, Method to Encourage Continuous Collaboration among Students. *Proceedings of Annual Conference of Japanese Society for Engineering Education*, pp. 346-347. JEE.

Robertson, R. (1992). *Globalization: Social theory and global culture*. Sage.

Schon, D. (1983). *The Reflective Practitioner*. Temple Smith.

Tilak, J. B. (2002). Knowledge Society, Education and Aid. *Compare: A Journal of Comparative Education, 3*(32), 297–310. doi:10.1080/0305792022000007463

Togashi, R., Goto, H., Morita, R., Yamachika, Y., & Yamazaki, Y. (2019). Transformation of Activity and Consciousness of AA School and Residents through the Past 22 years in Koshirakura village, Niigata Prefecture. *Journal of the City Planning Institute of Japan, 54*(3), 1460–1467. doi:10.11361/journalcpij.54.1460

Werner, M., & Zimmermann, B. (2006, February). Histoire Croisée and the Challenge of Reflexivity. *History and Theory, 45*(1), 30–50. doi:10.1111/j.1468-2303.2006.00347.x

Yamamoto, R., Konno, T., Kishi, M., & Kubota, K. (2012). A Study of Learning Factors on International Fieldwork: Focus on Interaction with Partners in the Program. *Japan Journal of Educational Technology, 36*(Suppl.), 213–216.

ENDNOTES

1. A free and open-source learning management system that is used all over the world. Waseda University developed a customized platform for its specific curricula
2. A user-initiated open-source map creation project https://www.openstreetmap.org/
3. https://issuu.com/raffaelepernice/docs/unswsydney-arch7112_-urban_condtions_2020-comp
4. https://issuu.com/yagchi_lab./docs/20210115_unsw_canberra_campus_small3

Chapter 11
Collaborative Online International Learning to Enhance Employability Skills at TNE Institutions:
A Case From a London-Based University

Lauren Amber Holly Crabb
Anglia Ruskin University, UK

Nan (Johanna) Jiang
Coventry University London, UK

Hanna Yakavenka
Coventry University London, UK

ABSTRACT

Employability skills such as intercultural exposure and communication are well established in most business education degree programs. However, there is little knowledge of how these skills are developed in transnational education (TNE). Employability will play an increasingly important role in education as working patterns and skills have changed in the wake of Covid-19. This chapter aims to explore the lived experiences of local and non-local students at TNE partners who engaged in international learning experiences and understand how these projects develop employability skills in terms of intercultural communication. Findings suggest students value these international, interactive projects to develop awareness of the home institution and enhance cross-culture exposure.

DOI: 10.4018/978-1-6684-5226-4.ch011

INTRODUCTION

International education continues to be lucrative for Western, and more recently, non-Western Higher Education Institutions (HEI) despite Covid-19 preventing student mobility and severely affecting how curriculums are taught (Galloway et al., 2020). For example, in 2019 international education was Australia's third largest export category (Chowdhury, 2022), and in the UK the volume of higher education exports is expected to reach £35billion per year by 2023 (Department for Education and Department for International Trade, 2021). Aside from the short-term impacts of Covid-19, rapid technology enhancements and increasing strategic importance of Transnational Education (TNE) had led to distinctive changes in how HEIs provide the service to their customers. Widely implemented solutions such as flexibility in mode and place of study, cross-border curricula sharing, and flying faculty (Wylie, 2021) have been complemented by newer innovations such as distance and multi-site learning, dual degrees and individually tailored programs and routes to qualifications. These innovations have created new opportunities for both home and host institutions. With internationalisation becoming an integral part of the business and management curriculum, current student expectations go beyond an internationally recognised degree, with virtual and collaborative international experiences taking priority irrespective whether studies are taken at home or host education providers (Gorgodze et al., 2020). This book chapter aims to shed light on the impact of these changes using a case of TNE relationships of a London based University.

Predominantly, TNE relationships have been transactional with programs taught at host institutions mirroring the home institution curriculum. Common TNE models included articulation agreements, flying faculty, validation, franchise, and foreign campus arrangements (for full definitions please see Henderson et al., 2017). The emergence of new TNE models and innovations created more opportunities for HEIs, but required significant investment to ensure the governance of quality assurance maintained a positive student experience whilst enhancing financial sustainability. Additional benefits to institutions derive from the opportunities around nurturing deep institutional connections, facilitating meaningful staff and student exchanges, instilling high academic quality, and enhancing student experience (Henderson et al., 2017) and international reputation.

Alongside these developments in TNE the perception of student experience has also evolved, meaning that obtaining an internationally recognised degree alone was not sufficient to make students competitive on the global labor market. Students at host institutions have been expecting more from their education providers, especially in terms of transferrable skills and international exposure to enter global graduate careers (Whitsed & Green, 2015). The ban on international travel during Covid-19 meant traditional internationalisation activities such as field trips and exchanges became impossible. However, in a way despite the added complexity to the TNE operation, it offered HEIs ample opportunities for innovation and enabled participation of those students who would not normally be able to access international opportunities.

Collaborative Online International Learning (COIL) has been one of the innovations which have spearheaded HEIs response to student demands for internationalisation during the pandemic. Although COIL projects have been utilised for internationalisation by home institutions before the pandemic, they gained strategic prominence after the ban on international travel. The premise of COIL is virtual mobility, enriching student international experiences and improving cross-cultural literacy through experiential design in the virtual setting (Orsini-Jones et al., 2017). When the content of these projects is co-created among the participants, COIL projects also offer a way for students to form an international peer network while having legitimate cross-cultural experiences (Ryabova, 2020)

This chapter aims to understand the lived experiences of local and non-local students, studying a business degree through a TNE agreement at two host providers located in South-East Asia, who participated in a COIL project with home institution students. Responding to Wilkins and Jussola's (2018) call for more research into students' perspective on their experiences in TNE, this book chapter explores whether international exposure through COIL projects creates an additional element to the internationalisation of the curriculum in Business Schools. In doing so the authors seek to understand (i) how the COIL project was perceived by participants at host institutions, (ii) whether it contributed to enhancing their transferrable employability skills, and most importantly, (iii) whether internationalisation of the curriculum did take place in the eyes of students studying at international partner institutions through TNE agreements given the impact of current challenges, such as the increasing level of travel restrictions and costs.

BACKGROUND

The globalisation of higher education has impacted how, when and where students study. The global scope of education is a lucrative business for Western HEIs who have experienced domestic recruitment fall due to the emergence of other qualification routes, including apprenticeships, and the increased tuition fee cost. With a globally growing middle class, the possibility of entering Higher Education is opening to many, with an estimated 5 million students moving country to pursue their studies (Jing et al., 2020).

Innovations in TNE has also diversified the ways of obtaining an internationally recognised degree. According to Knight (2018), there are three generations of international education. Student mobility, in terms of international students on campus, exchange programs and field trips, was the first generation. The second was when provider and program mobility took place through traditional TNE models including flying faculty and franchise arrangements. The third generation said to be the emergence of educational hubs, at country or city level where various local and international institutions, students, and research organisations collaborate. In South-East Asia, Malaysia, Singapore, and Hong Kong have been the most successful examples of education hubs (Knight, 2011 & Knight and Morshidi, 2011) driven by government policies around access to education, upskilling the workforce, or striving for knowledge development and innovations. In the case of Singapore, knowledge and innovation underpinned the development strategy adopted by the Singaporean government to develop and retain top talent (Sidhu et al., 2011). Malaysia focused more on international collaboration, using education to increase the cross-border flow of talent and knowledge (Aziz and Abdullah, 2004). In Manila, the focus has been on widening access to students unable to access prestigious universities. The industries training providers focused on were those in which Philippine labor is internationally recognised (Ortiga, 2018). The students choose to study in one of the educational hubs as they wish to experience some level of mobility by leaving their home country, however, do not wish to travel as far as Western Europe where majority of the awarding institutions are. Motivations of these students vary but findings show they have perceived different education levels in their home country compared to internationally recognised degrees. Factors influence decision include the lower cost of living in the education hubs compared to the institutions located in Europe and finally, and perceived relative safety of country for studying or familiarity with customs or religion (Ahmad & Buchanan, 2016).

Although there are clear benefits for students studying in host countries, challenges remain in respect to vital parts of their student experience. Pieper & Beall (2014) found that students studying at host institutions have experienced some development of intercultural awareness, flexibility and improved career prospects. However, traditional experiences of home institutions such as societies, sports teams and an 'on campus' community were missing. Increasingly, students want to feel part of the university community, have extra- activities and social experiences regardless of their mode of study (Hamdullahpur, 2020). Leask (2004) argued that host country institutions could help internationalise students at the home institution, however this research avenue has not been developed further in the literature.

The growth of TNE has coincided with changes to the global labour market where having an internationally recognised degree is not enough to equip students with a competitive edge in the regional labour market (Wilkins & Juusola, 2018). Curricula across the world have re-focused on developing skills vital for careers. Common additions to the curriculum include internships, focus on case studies, presentations, and analytical assignments rather than exams (The Economist Intelligence Unit, 2014). This shift has also been followed by debate within the academic literature and recently two main arguments in the employability literature have prevailed - the international aspect of employability and the impact of Covid-19 on employability.

In a special issue introduction, Fakunle and Higson (2021) argue the Covid-19 pandemic has not only changed the way students learn, but also how they would work in the future. Employability skills will need to be reconceptualised to include the need to respond to future potential disruptions and uncertainty. For example, graduates are now expected to live and work with technology, calling for technology use in the university curriculum to go beyond normal uses as being a complementary pedagogic tool. In addition to this there is a growing literature looking at understanding global employability patterns. There has been a recent call for 'employability in context' (Thi Tran et al., 2021) which appreciates employability complexities and relation to cultural contexts. Employability in a Western HE context usually is defined by skills such as leadership, enterprise and decision making. Whereas in South-East Asia, different attributes such as hardworking, conformity and adaptation are expected (Gribble, 2014). Understanding individual career pathways and identifying skills needed for diverse cultural contexts might therefore be an important part of employability of the future.

Navigating diverse cultural contexts is agreed to be integral to any skill set of future graduates. As the global workforce expands and technology enables more collaborative working across national borders, students expect to have similar experiences as part of their learning. However, the Covid-19 pandemic has impacted the skills required from the global labour force and how those skills are developed and enhanced throughout students' learning journey. Traditional methods of socialising students into the global economy, such as field trips, exchanges, and sandwich years with international partners (Beerkens & Derwende, 2007) are becoming rarer. Students from diverse backgrounds or with limited resources are demanding socialisation into the global economy without the additional financial burden (Heffernan et al., 2019). The restrictions on international travel throughout the Covid-19 pandemic also forced HEIs to rethink the internationalisation of curricula placing stronger emphasis on learning with remote design and digital platforms whilst enabling intercultural exchange (Liu & Gao, 2022).

There are competing ways to view and test the effects of intercultural exchanges on developing the skills required to be culturally sensitive and culture-literate. The most popular framework used is intercultural competence, also known as global competence (Cao & Meng, 2020). The definition and understanding of intercultural competence - originally known as intercultural contact theory - has evolved since its inception into academic literature in the 1950s. It was developed in the wake of World War II and aimed to understand and reduce intergroup prejudice (Allport, 1954: cited in Peng and Wu, 2016). Since then, intercultural competence as a theory and a framework has been advanced by many. Although a succinct definition is yet to be agreed, scholars have said intercultural competence is "a set of abilities to interact effectively and appropriately across cultures in the various contexts" (Peng & Wu, 2016 p. 17). Additionally, for intercultural competence to develop successfully, critical learning components must be included (Ari & Mula, 2017).

The ubiquitous demand of intercultural competence in all curriculums has led different disciplines, regions and schools of thought to have applied and measured intercultural competence in differing ways. Most literature agrees there are cognitive, affective, and behavioural dimensions to intercultural competence development (Arasaratnam-Smith, 2017) but the labels used, and measurements applied differ. Within the business and management literature, one of the most developed models of intercultural competence comes from Deardorff (2006). She suggests successful cross-cultural communication requires distinct characteristics within individuals. These characteristics of empathy, flexibility in choosing appropriate communication style, ethnorelativity and tolerance for ambiguity can be trained and enhanced. In order to obtain these characteristics an individual needs to first have certain knowledge. This includes knowledge of cultural self-awareness, sociolingistic awareness, and knowledge of cultural viewpoints. Although Higher Education can include this learning into curriculums, Deardorff (2006) suggests this knowledge will not be personalised and engrained without a set of attitudes. Attitudes such as curiosity, openness and respect are seen as the foundation for knowledge retention and are prerequisites for the intercultural competence. The task of the HEI is to provide students with the time and space to develop their own intercultural competence (Ryabova, 2020). Intercultural competence has been measured during cross-cultural projects by numerous researchers in different contexts, including the Netherlands (de Hei et al., 2020), China (Wu et al., 2013) and Israel (Ari & Mual, 2017). Whilst these quantitative studies test the development of intercultural competences, they neglect the exploration of the lived experiences of the students as these skills are being developed and try to understand the nuance of various motivations and challenges for the skill development and perceptions of its value to their career development.

Developing intercultural competency can be accomplished in many ways; immersive simulations (Johnson, 2010) e-learning from English as Foreign Language students (Liaw, 2006) and email exchange (Schenker, 2012) have all been used. However, experiential and collaborative learning activities have been seen as the most effective method (Barrett, 2018). As well as adding value to learning experience, collaborative learning also has additional benefits of developing transferrable skills such as comparison, analysis, reflection, co-operation (Barrett et al., 2014; Croucher et al., 2020). However, these activities have been found less significant compared to the individual students' agency (Kudo et al., 2020). Institutions should facilitate opportunities for intercultural exchange, but the learning should be driven by the students' needs, building further on their life experiences. This supports the operationalisation of virtual experiential design over other more costly activities (Neuwirth, 2021).

There lies an additional challenge for HEIs as alternatives for conventional international learning need to be seen to have the same level of significance for students. Adapting to the new pedagogies and ways of learning during Covid-19 saw satisfaction rates drop with students perceiving online experiences as poor value for their investment in Higher Education (Neves and Hewitt, 2021). Perceived value for money in the post-pandemic environment is critical as student expectations change and pedagogy continues to evolve. Whilst many institutions are returning to face-to-face teaching, some elements of the curriculum are likely to stay virtual (Tsiligkiris & Ilieva, 2022). COIL projects, with their inherent virtual opportunities for intercultural communication could be a platform for genuine intercultural exchanges, replacing physical international fieldtrips.

COIL projects have the potential to create added value to business curriculums and offer students studying at host institutions the opportunity to create international peer networks and access genuine international collaboration experience. They also offer a practical replacement for costly international travel. The gap remains in understanding the TNE students' experience of COIL projects and specifically whether the international learning within this disruptive environment could result in quality learning experiences for the students studying on franchised programs at South-East Asian education hubs. Gaining deeper insights into the lived experiences of students on COIL projects as an international learning experience will fill this gap. The aim is to bring students' voice into the discussion of benefits and challenges of TNE; in particular, their experience of improving intercultural competence through collaborative online learning.

Main Focus of The Chapter

In the wake of Covid-19, technological advancements and changing working and learning practices within the University setting, COIL projects are increasing in popularity on all curriculums. COIL projects offer internationalisation at home and international exposure to students who may not have been able to participate in previous intercultural exchanges. A COIL project between host and home institutions has been used to explore the perceived use of these projects in enhancing international communication and learning of students at South-East Asian educational hubs studying under franchise TNE agreements. The home institution, a London based campus of a large university, has a majority international student population and is the home institution to the TNE partnerships in the case. The two host institutions include a private education academy in Singapore and a private college in Malaysia, both have a mixture of part-time local students who are in full-time employment and full-time non-local students from the region. As previously discussed, both Singapore and Malaysia can be considered international educational hubs (Richards, 2019).

Figure 1. Expectations of a COIL project from institutional guidelines

Institutional COIL minimum requirements guidelines

1) students interact with an HE institution/company abroad, either with peers (if HE institution) or with professionals (if from the private sector/work sector) and among themselves. For the second option, the project leader needs to be sure that the guests are interacting with the students; please be aware that a standalone guest speaker lecture with presentation and limited Q&As is not enough to satisfy the first criterion.
2) the interaction is online (synchronous, asynchronous or both)
3) the project leader planned and designed some international learning outcomes - see attached file for examples
4) the project leader manages the reflection element of the project (the medium and characteristics of the reflective elements are to be decided by the project leader). In this reflective final product/project or submission, the learning is evidenced and critically reflected upon by the students – the project leader can contact the COIL team for further details.

The COIL project used in this case has been one of 12 international learning projects aligned to a range of UG and PG business related degrees, undertaken between 2020 and 2022 with students based in UK, EU, Canada, South and South-East Asia. All COIL projects have support from a central administration unit, although the projects themselves are designed and facilitated by an academic team (See box 1 for institutional guidelines). The COIL project in this case has been around a business idea pitch competition between MSc Enterprise and Innovation (E&I) students at the home campus, and MBA Global Business (GB), and International Marketing (IM) students at host institution. All course teams worked together to organise, create and advertise the event which was held online using the Zoom conference call platform. All students study the same Entrepreneurship module as part of their courses which offers a set of key academic principles to develop a business opportunity feasibility study. Students who successfully complete the module are expected to have enhanced pitching, evaluation, and networking skills, skills entrepreneurs are expected to have. The COIL project aimed to offer an additional space to enhance these key skills and gain extra peer feedback. In previous years students from all institutions pitched within their own cohort and location, then selected students from each location pitched again in the COIL project. In the studied iteration of the project, due to the module delivery patterns and timing within the academic year, the decision was for the home institution students who had studied the module ahead of the TNE partners to pitch to host students who would perform in the role of the evaluation panel.

COIL projects are said to be more successful when tied to an assessment as it gives students involved more focus (Wimpenny & Orsini-Jones, 2020). The pitch was based on proposed new ventures, which were underpinned by a critical evaluation of the viability of an untapped or under-served market in the industry they aimed to target. Students competed for the 'Best Pitch' and 'Best Business Idea' awards. The partner institution participants had an active role in the project and gave an opportunity to play different roles in assessing ideas whilst enhancing their networking skills. Participating students from the TNE partners formed the selection panel who undertook some background research on the proposed markets and designed and posed questions to the presenters on their pitches with support from the academic staff as advised by Key and Duening (2020). A criteria (Box 2) was developed by the academic team for the pitch competition in this COIL to assist the students to prepare and comment according to the learning outcomes of entrepreneurship module.

In terms of developing intercultural skills, all participants had to adjust one's pitch style and feedback style including use of vocabulary and concepts required in intercultural situations. This experience would allow them gain knowledge of international audience and improve their abilities to shift between cultural environments dealing with audience from different cultural background or with less experience of intercultural networks. Therefore, the COIL design was for students at home and host institutions to play different roles of pitching and assessing ideas whilst enhancing their networking skills.

Table 1. Feedback sheet given to students to peer assess based on module learning outcomes

	Criteria	Rate from 1-5	Comments/ notes/ follow up questions
1	Business Idea (Clear justification of value proposition, exact customer, consumer pain point, overall entrepreneurial marketing approach)		
2	Micro Factors (Ability to communicate the critical success factors of the business ideas; competitor analysis; entrepreneurial team; finances and any other industry relevant points)		
3	Macro Factors (Ability to discuss how the wider environmental, market and cultural trends shape the business idea as well as the sustainability and innovativeness of product offering)		
4	Pitch Presentation/Articulation and effectiveness of Slide Deck		

Primary data was collected by the authors and formed an additional, reflective part of the project for the participants. It enabled students to demonstrate their understanding of personal development through this experience. The qualitative interviews aimed to explore if the COIL project was able to enhance the internationalisation of the curriculum and develop intercultural communication to facilitate student learning. In total 10 interviews were conducted of 25-55 minutes each, 4 based at the Malaysian partner and 6 from the Singapore partner. Of these, 1 participant in Malaysia was an international student from Morocco, 3 international students based in Singapore were from Indonesia, China, and Malaysia. The students from Malaysia and Singapore were all part-time students in full-time employment. The interviews were recorded on Microsoft Teams and used the automatic transcription software. All transcripts were cleaned by the authors before analysis.

Semi-structured interview format was adopted as key concepts had already been identified in the literature and used as guiding principles when designing the interview questions. The core interview themes were around enhanced intercultural competence (Deardoff, 2006) and learning community at TNE home and host institutions (Pieper & Beall, 2014 and Hamdullahour, 2020). Semi-structured format enabled space for additional topics to be explored within the interview raised by individual participants. For many of the participants it was the first time they had undertook an academic interview. It took time to develop a level of trust and break the teacher/student relationship, particularly in on-line setting. This was primarily helped by the lead interviewer not being part of the delivery of the COIL project and therefore not having an initial power relation with the participant.

The sampling strategy was initially self-selecting as student participants who expressed an interest in the research project were approached to participate. In the later stages to complete the substantive theory development, snowball sampling approach was implemented where previous participants encouraged peers to participate (Bell et al., 2022). Data analysis took a constructionist approach based on a process of interpreting various views of different parties involved in the COIL project and constant data comparison. This enabled the researchers to create and continuously develop codes and categories until substantive theory was created (Santos et al., 2018). Substantive theory means the theories developed from this research can only apply to the context that was researched. For formal theory to be developed, a wider, more holistic approach would be more relevant (Heath & Cowley, 2004). This is outside the confines of this research project. The constructionist theory approach to data analysis allowed the researchers to add the supplementary theme - added value - into the later interviews. This theme was not identified in the preliminary literature review and is a significant finding of current research. The value and future of TNE is constructed through better understanding arrived from the interviews by students and staff reflections in the COIL project. Ethics clearance for data collection was sought through the relevant channels and secured by the University Ethics Committee. Microsoft Teams were used to record the semi-structured interviews and focused on reflective experience of students engaging in COIL after securing participants' consent.

ISSUES, CONTROVERSIES, CHALLENGES

Internationalisation is a key feature of any curriculum and is an expectation of many students. Those studying at a TNE host institution tend to have family responsibilities or financial constraints which mean travelling to the home institution is not be possible. The students on franchised programs, due to their nature, wish to experience the similar to home institution education and student experience as students studying at a home institution. The following sections present the findings categorised into the themes around community, intercultural skills, and added value.

1. The Use of COIL to Enhance Learner Characteristics, Knowledge and Attitudes for Intercultural Competence

COIL projects are said to increase intercultural competence which is seen as a key skill for creating career ready graduates (Deardorff, 2006). Whilst the COIL project for this research was not long enough to establish if these skills were developed, it was possible to explore how students felt about their experience during the project and its influence on their intercultural exposure. An agreement was that majority of students felt the need of being able to work more in cross-cultural teams and wanted more opportunities to practice this skill. For example, one student explained:

I need to be exposed to an international environment or have an idea of what to expect from people from a different cultural environment. To prepare yourself that will be different from what you are used to. To reduce stereotypes and not getting shocked by the unfamiliar environment. This project has been helpful for understanding the perspectives of different people. I think I learned a lot. (Interview M4)

The student's appreciation of 'not being shocked' by the unfamiliar, speaks to the Deardorff's (2006) characteristic of tolerance for ambiguity. Being exposed to a wider range of cultural differences among the participants, communication and learning styles would mean students have an opportunity to experience and navigate their way through. The tolerance for ambiguity was further supported by students' attitude of curiosity and given as a key motivation for initially agreeing to participate in the project, as the outcomes or participation was not assessed as part of either of the programs.

I wanted to do the project because I was interested to see what the students from London were like. How they learn and how they presented their work.(Interview S4).

I did the project to see the London students, I wanted to know who studied there and how they learn. I thought this was interesting for me (Interview M3)

Post-project students did reflect on differences between the learners, tutors, and learning at the home and host institution. As well as satisfying their curiosity such reflections enabled them to appreciate the different type of knowledge and skills demonstrated by others, such as choosing appropriate communication style, as explained below.

After the COIL project I feel like as a student that is studying in Singapore, it is more relevant for me to study in Singapore. Like the students in [home institution] seemed way older than me and I think our local lecturers, the way they teach us is deeper. I felt, when they presented, they were doing more data analytics. But it was good to see what the students were learning is similar. (Interview S1)

Particularly I took notes on how they presented. Especially when they answered the questions. This is always the bit of the presentation I hate, one guy always said 'thank you for the question', I thought this sounded professional, I took notes on this (Interview M3).

It is important to note that the development of intercultural competence is a long-term endeavour, but these small-scale projects can contribute to the development of the initial willingness and attitudes required to develop the intercultural competence. Whilst students found it worthwhile to engage with peers internationally, the extent to which this has been influential depended on the previous international exposure of the participants. More mature part-time students, who had significant work experience did not seem to value the experience as much as those students with less international exposure. That was also noticeable in the depth of reflection demonstrated. Nevertheless, with the participation in the COIL project being voluntary the evidence of curiosity from all students who participated was evident and often rewarding.

I have worked for over 15 years internationally. The skills needed to do this take time. I do not think this project helped me to develop international skills and I do not feel any different after this project. It is nice however to put on my CV and social media. (Interview S1)

Unlike other classmates, they are working adults. I did not have much time to work as I had to finish my degree whilst doing the first lockdown. After that there was not much chance to work or do internships. So, my first goal is to have a stable job and try to grow from there. These projects help me to understand international business better. (Interview M2)

There was evidence the project helped students enhance already existing attitudes, knowledge and skills needed to be interculturally competent. While not being able to measure any quantitative gain in these skills, student reflections were clear that many were already aware of the skills required to be culturally literate and that those with little exposure to the international workplace valued these experiences more than mature part-time students who already have significant exposure.

2. COIL as a Way to Improve Learning Communities Across Home And Host Institutions

International students at host institutions need to be inducted into the host institution, local community, and the home institution. These multiple communities and sets of belonging could feel complex and overwhelming. As students become more invested in their education, they want to feel part of the home institution as this is where they are getting their award from. The COIL project was found to be a helpful way to induct host students into the home learning community.

I only get the feedback from my local lecturer. I do not know who the lecturers are in [home institution] and I never met any students. Now I feel like a part of the community as you invited me to participate in this project and I met some students. (Interview M1)

Cultivating deeper engagement through this community was not successful through the project. The COIL project was seen as too short to continue the relationship between the participants beyond the learning interaction. Students felt this was the responsibility of the institutions to facilitate further collaboration opportunities, rather than the responsibility of the individual participants.

After the COIL project that day, I felt for the students to keep in contact there could be a mini game or Q&A session, so it was like more informal for us to get to know each other. So after the project, another session would make it easier to then keep in touch. (Interview S1)

The need for encouraging and facilitation of networking also became apparent when students fed back, as they did not network with other students:

The project for me was too short to make friendships or close relations. I mean, I found a lecturer on LinkedIn, but no students. (Interview M3)

Community forming is a vital part of the student experience as it sets foundations for effective communication skills and building future professional networks. The COIL project seemed to develop a sense of community for students at home institution, as they worked on something beyond their course and felt they had to 'impress' the peers they did not know. Shorter COIL projects such as these should require significant individual preparation by the participants to ensure their commitment to the project and have exposure to the culture/organisation before direct communication commences. This will also allow participants to develop a degree of confidence in the unfamiliar environment before the project commences. Overall, further tailored activities beyond the project were needed for longer-lasting relationships to be formed.

3. COIL as Added Value for TNE Students

COIL can also be a way to increase the added value of degree programs. Some COIL projects are linked to assessment on the program and require compulsory participation. The COIL project researched here was voluntary and therefore in addition to the curriculum learning. As TNE students' expectations change in accordance with the international labor market, programs are expected to deliver additional experiences or skill enhancement opportunities.

The findings indicate that earning an internationally recognised degree was still the key motivation for most international students studying at the host institutions. It was seen as added value for their investment. For example, the following excerpt highlights the added value of a UK degree.

Getting a UK degree is good if I wanted to work internationally. Because I only have a local degree from Morocco, it is from a private University. It does not hold the same value as having one from a state University and also as it is Global Business, this looks good for my CV. (Interview M2)

However, additional extra-curricular activities, such as COIL were also valued in terms of building experiences and developing skills.

I want to settle down in Singapore and coming from a different country I need to stand out compared to local applicants. So, by having this opportunity to study a foreign degree in a different foreign country, it will make my CV stand out. Also, by having extra experience with international students will be helpful for me. So, for me the project is important, I already have it on my CV. (Interview S2)

These findings were largely expected as international students sought out extra international exposure. However, an unexpected finding was how students valued exposure to diversity as something they did not achieve in their program:

There is international exposure in my MBA. We get to look at different opinions through the course and at different writers, different theories and apply different ideas. But it is just theory. I was amazed at the different countries represented in the presentations, India, Nigeria and so on. I would not have met these people in my program otherwise. (Interview M2)

The added value of COIL to the curriculum is multi-dimensional. The opportunity to develop concrete experiences which can build to a portfolio of international exposure to enhance student employability is one feature. COIL also offers exposure to diversity which some TNE students do not yet experience in their own classrooms.

Another aspect of added value, was that COIL project was perceived as enhancing the students experience at the home institution with lesser impact on the host students:

For me, the COIL project was to help the [home] students to achieve something in their career. To add value to their studies. The projects were really interesting and if they were implemented, they would really revolutionise their industry. For example, the electrical vehicle presentation was great... I think it not only to adds value to their course but also helps them to build their own brand. (Interview S1)

This further emphasised the need for clearly set goals for all participants involved. To ensure all students have a substantial role, and understand the purpose and expected outcomes of the project. This feedback also speaks to using the experience of mature learners into the project to encourage their commitment and participation in the project. This learning has facilitated the development of the COIL toolkit presented later in the chapter offering the considerations on how to implement a COIL project at TNE institutions.

The COIL project was facilitated over Microsoft Teams. Findings indicate that students did not feel the online nature of the projects affected the success or the experience. Although students said meeting face to face would be helpful, they suggested that responsibilities and financial constraints meant the online projects were a suitable alternative and allowed for internationalisation at home.

RECOMMENDATIONS AND PRACTICE IMPLICATIONS

This chapter set out to explore the lived experiences of students at host institutions during COIL projects.

Kudo et al., (2020) suggested that student's agency in developing cross-cultural relationships and networking is more important than the institution. This contrasts with the findings in this case where students sought more support from the University in developing peer relationships. Students were unable to find each other on LinkedIn or did not make contact again after the project. This was despite the project dedicated group created on Microsoft Teams. Future COIL projects between TNE partners would therefore need to have more emphasis on the students doing individual networking or a clearer space for students to network after the organised event.

However, the students' motivation to initially participate in the research was borne of curiosity of the home institution itself or the students studying there on similar programs. This aligns with Kudo's et al. (2020) research in the student has most agency. It also aligns to the attitudes required to develop intercultural competence (Deardorff, 2006). COIL projects can provide valuable opportunities for these already existing attitudes to develop into skills. In shorter COIL projects in particular, ensuring the participants have some exposure to the community/ culture before the project also helps enhance intercultural skills and ensures commitment before interaction with peers.

The qualitative approach enabled the evaluation of the lived experiences of students on TNE programs, unlike most of the literature on intercultural competence. Barrett et al., (2014) in their study found that experiential learning situations were said to develop skills of comparison, analysis, reflection, and co-operative action. Similar behaviours were observed among the MBA students who were on the panel of the Entrepreneurship presentations. Students felt they benefitted from comparing business ideas, presentation styles, and communication skills with their colleagues. Some students also reflected on the ability of the business ideas to work in their home countries. Even this surface-type reflection and comparisons demonstrate the importance of international learning projects for students. However, it would not be possible to suggest these projects developed deeper characteristics for intercultural competence as suggested by Deardorff (2006). The shorter length projects and limited time for reflection, meant developing the deeper characteristics was not possible.

Internationalisation of the curriculum is often overlooked by TNE host institutions who have historically seen the internationally recognised degree as a sufficient competitive advantage for studying TNE programs (Wilkins & Juusola, 2018). As the global labour market becomes more accessible and working patterns change, students expect more from their university experience. The COIL projects also enabled a further element of added value where students were able to use this experience as evidence on their CVs. Although not orientated to provide 'employability in context' (Thi Tran et al., 2021) COIL projects can expose students to intercultural exchanges which appears to be a global employability skill (Gribble, 2014) leading to networking skills in professional setting.

Although there are more international students studying at host institutions, it is still common for there to be little diversity within the classroom. This was highlighted by respondents who commented on being exposed to different students at the host institution and the diversity of those students. COIL projects can therefore be advocated as a way to facilitate internationalisation at home activities for non-local students at host institutions.

Internationalisation was seen as an important part of the learning journey for students and being exposed to their host learning environment, as well as the home institution. COIL projects with TNE partners in the future could expand this to include cultural activities for non-local institution or would have the opportunity to do so during the length of the programme. Therefore, exposing them to the home institution is a valuable internationalisation at home feature.

Creating a community of students between the home and host institutions have unlimited benefits for learners, institutions, and the reputation of the partnerships (Hamdullahpur, 2020). The participants in current case commented on not knowing the lecturers at the home institution and felt the COIL project gave them the opportunity to interact with them. This is something which is often overlooked in the literature, non-local students in particular are keen to know that the standard and the approach adopted on similar programs at home institution is comparable to that at the host institution.

Toolkit for Delivering Successful COIL Projects

There were issues and challenges for the course teaching and service teams to work together and coordinate in the setup of this COIL, such as time difference, student and staff timetable arrangement and the IT system comparability. These issues and challenges were dealt quickly due to the strong partnership was already built to develop a positive attitude and mutual strategic understanding. The link tutor of this partnership has acted as the mediation is critical for creating new COIL based intercultural teams to manage and overcome intercultural conflict. The partnership has been strengthened through this regular exercise of intercultural relationship building COIL project.

Observations and lessons learnt from current research, supported by past experiences as practitioners of COIL, enabled the design of the toolkit which can be used to guide future COIL projects.

1) Have clear goals and intended learning outcomes for all participants involved in the project
2) Engage with the tutors at partner institutions to gouge out the students' characteristics and expectations
3) Set pre-learning for all involved
4) Highlight the benefits in clear terms.
5) Ensure students understand the skills they are enhancing and added value (e.g., to their CVs).
6) Market the project. Students need to be aware of the opportunity and how it can develop their knowledge. Use social media or Virtual Learning Environments for advertising the project.
7) Consider time difference. Including normal delivery times and schedules, this is vital for part-time students whose contact hours may be evening and weekends
8) Consider the running order of modules at a partner. If the COIL project is linked to a particular module, the students need to have some understanding of the content.
9) Consider the term delivery structure. If students are studying the same module at the same time, the weeks in the term might be different and students would have diverse levels of knowledge and/or perceived value of proposed activities
10) Use institutional support or infrastructure to facilitate certification of the experience.
11) Ensure there is structured and unstructured time for students to network.
12) Enable time for reflection for students.
13) Use photos to circulate the event on social media. This is a straightforward way for students to tag themselves and find other participants on the project.
14) Ensure you and the wider team are invested in the COIL project.
15) Utilise the current knowledge of participants, including mature students with work experience.

FUTURE RESEARCH DIRECTIONS

With current sparse research into internationalisation of curriculums under the TNE arrangements, future investigations could include studying the experiences of students across different models, for example validation, distant learning, or articulation agreements.

CONCLUSION

This chapter sought to explore the lived experiences of students studying under franchised provision through a COIL project at TNE hosting institutions. COIL projects have been used to enhance intercultural exposure through 'internationalisation at home' agendas by HEIs. This agenda became more prominent during the Covid-19 pandemic and set to remain an integral of internationalisation strategies at universities.

At the same time, there is an increase in international students who see studying at host institutions cheaper, more practical, and safer than travelling all the way to a home institution. These students similarly to those at home seek international experiences with COIL projects offering them the opportunities to develop their international skills sought after by global employers.

This research found that these students who sought such international experiences often had less international exposure compared to part-time home students who often worked internationally. Clear benefits were identified by the participants highlighting the increased engagement in learning of the subject, familiarity with the standards and experience of students at home institutions, and most importantly the valuable foundations for the development of transferrable skills. At the same time, future COIL projects should make space and time for students to network, encouraging further contact through LinkedIn or social media relationships to generate professional networks. Although most COIL projects are short-term in nature, longer projects would develop more behaviours seen in Deardoff's (2006) model. Finally, future COIL projects should encourage reflections on the individual students and staff experiences and how that fits into the shared knowledge and TNE practice created because of the project.

We could draw few insights from one limited case study of COIL project in a London-based university to show that how different expectations shall be taken into consideration, when utilising the collaborative partnership for enhancing student experience and values perceived. There are clear benefits to include COIL projects as a feature of the TNE curricula as it enhances international exposure of students studying under franchise agreements. Further benefits of COIL projects include the creation of wider multi-site student community and growing awareness of home institution. The collaborations enhance the partnership by celebrating dynamics rather than merely focus on compliance. They can also generate opportunities for wider networking and smoother progression into other degrees. We recommend future research could further explore on why local and non-local students could have different experience of a TNE programme and its implication on practice in other TNE partner institutions.

REFERENCES

Ahmad, S. Z., & Buchanan, F. R. (2016). Choices of destination for transnational higher education: "pull" factors in an Asia Pacific market. *Educational Studies*, *42*(2), 163–180. doi:10.1080/03055698.2016.1152171

Ahmad, S. Z., & Buchanan, F. R. (2017). Motivation factors in students' decision to study at international branch campuses in Malaysia. *Studies in Higher Education*, *42*(4), 651–668.

Altbach, P. G. (2013). Is there a future for branch campuses? In *The international imperative in higher education* (pp. 101–106). SensePublishers. doi:10.1007/978-94-6209-338-6_22

Arasaratnam-Smith, L. A. (2017). Intercultural competence: An overview. *Intercultural competence in higher education*, 7-18.

Ari, L. L., & Mula, W. (2017). "Us and them": Towards intercultural competence among Jewish and Arab graduate students at Israeli colleges of education. *Higher Education*, *74*(6), 979–996. doi:10.100710734-016-0088-7

Aziz, M. I. A., & Abdullah, D. (2014). Malaysia: Becoming an education hub to serve national development. In *International education hubs* (pp. 101–119). Springer. doi:10.1007/978-94-007-7025-6_7

Barrett, M. (2018). How schools can promote the intercultural competence of young people. *European Psychologist*, *23*(1), 93–104. doi:10.1027/1016-9040/a000308

Barrett, M. D., Huber, J., & Reynolds, C. (2014). *Developing intercultural competence through education*. Council of Europe Publishing.

Beerkens, E., & Derwende, M. (2007). The paradox in international cooperation: Institutionally embedded universities in a global environment. *Higher Education*, *53*(1), 61–79. doi:10.100710734-007-9061-9

Bell, E., Harley, B., & Bryman, A. (2022). *Business research methods*. Oxford university press.

Bennell, P., & Pearce, T. (2003). The internationalisation of higher education: Exporting education to developing and transitional economies. *International Journal of Educational Development*, *23*(2), 215–232. doi:10.1016/S0738-0593(02)00024-X

Cao, C., & Meng, Q. (2020). Effects of online and direct contact on Chinese international students' social capital in intercultural networks: Testing moderation of direct contact and mediation of global competence. *Higher Education*, *80*(4), 1–19. doi:10.100710734-020-00501-w

Chowdhury, M. B. (2022). Internationalisation of education and its effect on economic growth and development. *World Economy*, *45*(1), 200–219. doi:10.1111/twec.13174

Croucher, G., Elliott, K., Locke, W., & Yencken, E. (2020). *Australia's higher education delivery offshore and online–trends, barriers and opportunities*. Melbourne Centre for the Study of Higher Education.

de Hei, M., Tabacaru, C., Sjoer, E., Rippe, R., & Walenkamp, J. (2020). Developing intercultural competence through collaborative learning in international higher education. *Journal of Studies in International Education*, *24*(2), 190–211. doi:10.1177/1028315319826226

Deardorff, D. K. (2006). Identification and assessment of intercultural competence as a student outcome of internationalization. *Journal of Studies in International Education*, *10*(3), 241–266. doi:10.1177/1028315306287002

Department for Education and Department for International Trade. (2021). International Education Strategy: 2021 update. Supporting recovery, driving growth. DIT. https://assets.publishing.service.gov.uk/government/uploads/system/uploads/attachment_data/file/958990/International-Education-Strategy-_2021-Update.pdf. Accessed on: 16/05/2022

Fakunle, O., & Higson, H. (2021). Interrogating theoretical and empirical approaches to employability in different global regions. *Higher Education Quarterly*, *75*(4), 525–534. doi:10.1111/hequ.12345

Galloway, N., Numajiri, T., & Rees, N. (2020). The 'internationalisation', or 'Englishisation', of higher education in East Asia. *Higher Education, 80*(3), 395–414. doi:10.100710734-019-00486-1

Gorgodze, S., Macharashvili, L., & Kamladze, A. (2020). Learning for Earning: Student Expectations and Perceptions of University. *International Education Studies, 13*(1), 42–53. doi:10.5539/ies.v13n1p42

Gribble, C. (2014). Exploring 'employability' in different cultural contexts. *Final Report: Scoping Study. Society for Research into higher Education (SRHE).* Deakin University, Australia.

Hamdullahpur, F. (2020). Global citizens for the twenty-first century: the role of international partnerships in university education. In *Successful Global Collaborations in Higher Education Institutions* (pp. 23–30). Springer. doi:10.1007/978-3-030-25525-1_3

Heath, H., & Cowley, S. (2004). Developing a grounded theory approach: A comparison of Glaser and Strauss. *International Journal of Nursing Studies, 41*(2), 141–150. doi:10.1016/S0020-7489(03)00113-5 PMID:14725778

Heffernan, T., Morrison, D., Magne, P., Payne, S., & Cotton, D. (2019). Internalising internationalisation: Views of internationalisation of the curriculum among non-mobile home students. *Studies in Higher Education, 44*(12), 2359–2373. doi:10.1080/03075079.2018.1499716

Henderson, M., Barnett, R., & Barrett, H. (2017). New developments in transnational education and the challenges for higher education professional staff. *Perspectives: Policy and Practice in Higher Education, 21*(1), 11–19.

Jing, X., Ghosh, R., Sun, Z., & Liu, Q. (2020). Mapping global research related to international students: A scientometric review. *Higher Education, 80*(3), 1–19. doi:10.100710734-019-00489-y

Johnson, W. L. (2010). Using immersive simulations to develop intercultural competence. In *Culture and computing* (pp. 1–15). Springer. doi:10.1007/978-3-642-17184-0_1

Key, T., & Duening, T. (2020). Strategic Entrepreneurial Storytelling: An Applied Framework for Better Pitches. *Contemporary Management Research, 16*(4), 279–300. doi:10.7903/cmr.19684

Knight, J. (2011). Education hubs: A fad, a brand, an innovation? *Journal of Studies in International Education, 15*(3), 221–240. doi:10.1177/1028315311398046

Knight, J. (2018). International education hubs. *Geographies of the university*, 637-655.

Knight, J., & Morshidi, S. (2011). The complexities and challenges of regional education hubs: Focus on Malaysia. *Higher Education, 62*(5), 593–606. doi:10.100710734-011-9467-2

Kudo, K., Volet, S., & Whitsed, C. (2020). Intercultural relationship development and higher education internationalisation: A qualitative investigation based on a three-stage ecological and person-in-context conceptual framework. *Higher Education, 80*(5), 913–932. doi:10.100710734-020-00523-4

Leask, B. (2004). Transnational education and intercultural learning: Reconstructing the offshore teaching team to enhance internationalisation. Australia: *Australian Universities Quality Forum.*

Liaw, M. L. (2006). E-learning and the development of intercultural competence. *Language Learning & Technology, 10*(3), 49–64.

Liu, J., & Gao, Y. (2022). Higher education internationalisation at the crossroads: Effects of the coronavirus pandemic. *Tertiary Education and Management*, *28*(1), 1–15. doi:10.100711233-021-09082-4

Neuwirth, L. S., Jović, S., & Mukherji, B. R. (2021). Reimagining higher education during and post-COVID-19: Challenges and opportunities. *Journal of Adult and Continuing Education*, *27*(2), 141–156. doi:10.1177/1477971420947738

Neves, J., & Hewitt, R. (2021) *Students highlight the challenges of their 2021 academic experience.* Advance HE. https://www.advance-he.ac.uk/news-and-views/students-highlight-challenges-their-2021-academic-experience.

Orsini-Jones, M. E., Lloyd, E., Cribb, M., Lee, F., Bescond, G., Ennagadi, A., & García, B. I. (2017). The trouble with cyberpragmatics: Embedding an online intercultural learning project into the curriculum. [IJCALLT]. *International Journal of Computer-Assisted Language Learning and Teaching*, *7*(1), 50–65. doi:10.4018/IJCALLT.2017010104

Ortiga, Y. Y. (2018). Constructing a global education hub: The unlikely case of Manila. *Discourse (Abingdon)*, *39*(5), 767–781. doi:10.1080/01596306.2018.1448703

Payne, B., Cigularova, D., Costanzo, J., Das, S., Mann, M., & Perez, K. (2021). Impact of articulation agreements on student transfer between higher education institutions: A case study of a cybersecurity program. *Community College Journal of Research and Practice*, 1–16.

Peng, R. Z., & Wu, W. P. (2016). Measuring intercultural contact and its effects on intercultural competence: A structural equation modelling approach. *International Journal of Intercultural Relations*, *53*, 16–27. doi:10.1016/j.ijintrel.2016.05.003

Pieper, A., & Beall, J. (2014). *Impacts of transnational education on host countries: Academic, cultural, economic and skills impacts and implications of program and provider mobility*. British Council/ DAAD.

Richards, C. (2019). Higher education privatisation, internationalisation and marketisation: Singaporean versus Malaysian models of Asian education hub policy. *Compare: A Journal of Comparative Education*, *49*(3), 375–392. doi:10.1080/03057925.2017.1413638

Ryabova, A. (2020). Collaborative online international learning projects in the context of contemporary pedagogical challenges. *Pedagogical Journal*, *10*(3A), 238–246.

Santos, J. L. G. D., Cunha, K. S. D., Adamy, E. K., Backes, M. T. S., Leite, J. L., & Sousa, F. G. M. D. (2018). Data analysis: Comparison between the different methodological perspectives of the Grounded Theory. *Revista da Escola de Enfermagem da U S P.*, 52. PMID:29668789

Schenker, T. (2012). Intercultural competence and cultural learning through telecollaboration. *CALICO Journal*, *29*(3), 449–470. doi:10.11139/cj.29.3.449-470

Sidhu, R., Ho, K. C., & Yeoh, B. (2011). Emerging education hubs: The case of Singapore. *Higher Education*, *61*(1), 23–40. doi:10.100710734-010-9323-9

Skipp, A., & Hopwood, V. (2017). *Alternative providers of higher education: Views of the validation and franchise process and innovation in the sector.* London Department for Education.

The Economist Intelligence Unit. (2014), High university enrolment, low graduate employment: Analysing the paradox in Afghanistan, Bangladesh, India, Nepal, Pakistan and Sri Lanka. *The Economist.*

Thi Tran, L., Thi Quy Do, T., & Bui, H. (2021). 'Employability in context': The importance of considering contextual factors in reimagining employability through Australian student mobility to the Indo-Pacific region. *Higher Education Quarterly*, *75*(4), 591–607. doi:10.1111/hequ.12303

Tsiligkiris, V., & Ilieva, J. (2022). Global engagement in the post-pandemic world: Challenges and responses. Perspective from the UK. *Higher Education Quarterly*, *76*(2), 343–366. doi:10.1111/hequ.12390

Westerlaken, M., Christiaans-Dingelhoff, I., Filius, R. M., De Vries, B., De Bruijne, M., & Van Dam, M. (2019). Blended learning for postgraduates; an interactive experience. *BMC Medical Education*, *19*(1), 1–7. doi:10.118612909-019-1717-5 PMID:31362735

Whitsed, C., & Green, W. (2015). Internationalising the Curriculum in Education: An Overview. *Critical perspectives on internationalising the curriculum in disciplines*, 83-90.

Wilkins, S., & Juusola, K. (2018). The benefits & drawbacks of transnational higher education: Myths and realities. *Australian Universities Review*, *6*, 68–76.

Wimpenny, K., & Orsini-Jones, M. (2020). Innovation in collaborative online international learning: A holistic blend. In *Radical solutions and eLearning* (pp. 1–25). Springer. doi:10.1007/978-981-15-4952-6_1

Wu, W. P., Fan, W. W., & Peng, R. Z. (2013). An analysis of the assessment tools for Chinese college students' intercultural competence. *Foreign Language Teaching and Research*, *4*, 581–592.

Wylie, I. (2021) Business schools aim for an international experience at home. *Financial Times*. https://www.ft.com/content/f3e0931b-0ab3-48c1-87a5-151303327f59.

Chapter 12

Islands and Bridges:
Why and How TNE Universities and EMIs Generally Might "Bridge" Into Their Local Communities

Kevin Ottley
University Central Asia, Khorog, Tajikistan

ABSTRACT

It is recommended that EMIs, including TNE institutions, should formalise 'bridging' between their institutions and the local community, if possible. A definition of 'community' is extended to include non-faculty/local staff within the university. The rationale for this recommendation is that it is predicated upon a win-win-win result: non-local faculty benefit because bridging assists with their integration into the local community; the university benefits because establishing links with the wider community is an invaluable PR initiative; the local community benefits. The authors' own experiences of bridging, formal and informal, official or otherwise, will be offered as examples of what might be achieved. At the same time, a section of this paper notes the challenges which one might experience when bridging, and how an individual and her institution might avoid such difficulties.

INTRODUCTION

Transnational Education (TNE) Universities and English Medium Institutions (EMI): The Same Model for Bridging

Strictly speaking, transnational education (TNE) is when learning takes place where "learners are located in a country different from the one where the awarding institution is based." (Council of Europe, 2000). According to this definition, TNE is not limited to higher education (HE) institutions: the document in question goes on to note that TNE includes not only "all types of higher education study programmes", but also "sets of courses of study, or educational services." (Bannier, 2016; Mc Burnie & Ziguras, 2006). However, this chapter restricts TNE to a narrow definition, that is, where it operates in HE institutions.

DOI: 10.4018/978-1-6684-5226-4.ch012

This is for the reason that the content of the current chapter is based completely on the author's experiences, and the greater percentage of these experiences have been gained while he was employed at HE institutions.

Where a formal definition of TNE might also be narrow is in the proviso that learners are in another country from the 'awarding' institution. Regarding HE, this would rule out the large number of HE English medium institutions (EMI) which operate courses of study in English in a country where English is not the first or official language but which have their own degree programmes; institutions, that is, which are regulated by the HE system of the host country. However, the current study includes such places of study, subsuming them, for convenience's sake, within TNE. This is because many overlaps exist, especially with regards to English teaching, between TNEs and EMIs. The first of these is obvious: English is the medium of instruction at such institutions. Second, the majority of learners are based in their home environment (with the exception of a sprinkling of international students). Third, the university and many of its faculty are operating in a foreign environment. Points one and two should be clear. Point three, however, requires some clarification.

A TNE/EMI university operating in a country other than a native English-speaking country would normally include English language support classes, perhaps an English foundation or Preparatory programme (but not always), for which many, probably the majority of instructors, are native English speakers. Second, such a university would normally employ subject teachers, lecturers and professors, who are either native English speakers or who would be using English as a second language, both in the classroom and, as a language of convenience, outside, too. Third, English would normally be the language of academic management in such an institution. Fourth, although such institutions would employ local staff to facilitate HR, administration, security duties, and so on, many of these would nevertheless be expected to have a good working knowledge of English, if only because they work for, and alongside, faculty who might not be confident with local languages. It might even be the case that such staff are encouraged to use English as a usual medium for operations. Taking all the above together, TNE/EMIs would usually operate and function in a language other than that of the country in which they are located. Or to put it another way, they are, linguistically speaking, small alien territories, or islands, within a foreign ocean.

It might be the case that many of the above-mentioned foreign teachers, lecturers and professors, living and working in a foreign country, do not fully avail themselves of the manifold cultural opportunities which day-to-day living in an alien environment might afford. Maybe they don't want to (Bodycot & Walker, 2000; Garson, 2005). That's their choice. However, what about their place of work, the university itself? What formal measures, if any, do TNE universities have in place to 'bridge' between themselves and local communities? Actually, it might be argued that such institutions operating in a foreign country should have a duty to bridge locally, this being in their own PR interests; they might also have a duty of care to staff who require assistance to reach out, explore and integrate. And to turn this round: what of the local communities themselves? Would not local people, adults, schoolchildren, academics and other professionals want in some way to be a part of the operations of a university, to benefit, that is, from its location within their community?

The current paper is based on the author's experiences of bridging between three English medium institutions where he has taught and the local communities. It is focussed on English language teaching, the author's profession. Of the three institutions that are written about, all offered different and varying degrees of opportunity to bridge. First, an English language in Kazakhstan had a contractual clause that required its English foundation English programme teachers to undertake two hours of so-called 'community service' per week. However, it was not specified what form this should take. Moreover, there was no requirement that the service be based in the wider, local community. As it was, most foundation teachers ended up performing extra-curricular activities within the university, these usually centred on the learning experiences of the foundation students themselves. Meanwhile, another English language university where the author worked, this located in China, had no insistence that its English teachers provide community service. However, under the auspices of its postgraduate (PG) English division there operated an 'outreach' programme, the aim of this being to link up with compulsory training programmes which the university ran for its Chinese-speaking staff; an 'internal outreach', in other words. In short, Chinese-speaking staff in the university were required to participate in regular training sessions, and English courses offered by the outreach programme were one of several options they might choose in order to fulfil this obligation. This Staff English programme, as it was called, was managed by the author of this paper, a .2 allocation of his normal teaching schedule facilitating this. Finally, the author's current employer in Tajikistan insists on community service. Indeed, one third of his contracted employment hours are required to be spent in this way. Despite such a formal requirement, however, the author has been free to set up his own initiatives, these being internal, within the university, and external, in the community outside his place of work. At the same time, his university has assisted with, for example, the setting up of meetings with educational institutions in the wider community.

The current study gives an account of the author's successes and challenges regarding bridging from places of work and into communities, internally and externally, of the institutions themselves. It is not limited to a discussion of practices within TNE universities for the clear reason that the models of outreach or local-based community service that are proposed (this being the main purpose of the current study) are viable for any EMI. I would add, too, that a rationale of the current study is to encourage universities to invest in reaching out (again, internally and externally), and for the following reasons: on account of the wellbeing of foreign faculty; and as a responsibility to the community, one which, we might bear in mind, affords the university and its faculty the ability to function fully and effectively.

In short, the content of the current paper is as follows. It is recommended that TNE institutions which operate in a foreign country should formalise 'bridging' between their institutions and the local community, if possible. A definition of 'community' is extended to include non-faculty/local staff within the university. The rationale for this recommendation is that it is predicated upon a win-win-win result: non-local faculty benefit because bridging assists with their integration into the local community; the university benefits because establishing links with the wider community is an invaluable PR initiative; the local community benefits because, well, why wouldn't they? The authors' own experiences of bridging, formal and informal, official or otherwise, will be offered as examples of what might be achieved. At the same time, a section of this paper notes the challenges which one might experience when bridging, and how an individual and her institution might avoid such difficulties.

Why An Institution Should Tread Carefully When Supporting Bridging

A main difference between TNE institutions specifically and EMIs generally is that the former function as offshore campuses for institutions based in other countries (Bannier, 2016; McBurnie & Ziguras, 2006; Mellors-Bourne et al, 2014), whereas non-TNE universities are a part of the educational framework of the country in which they are located. Such differences are technical and legal and, often, problematic (Knight, 2015; McBurnie & Ziguras, 2006); for example, to whom is the university legally responsible? Moreover, some nations and their educational/legal frameworks are stricter (or more controlling) than others. To put this in a nutshell: any substantial changes that one wished to make to a foundation EAP syllabus at a TNE the author worked for in China needed only to be approved by the institution's awarding body in the UK. In contrast, at a non-TNE EMI in Kazakhstan, such modifications required approvement at state level. Furthermore, another EMI (non-TNE) in central Asia insisted changes could not be made to the teaching syllabus because it was certain these would not be approved by the country's education ministry. These are important and necessary considerations to bear in mind if, for example, one wishes to introduce into the teaching syllabus (as I have; see below) more locally-biased materials.

However, such influences (if we might call them that) are usually transparent and overt. If state documentation is not already available, it can be obtained. Furthermore, large institutions are normally aware, because they need to be, of where local customs and laws are likely to impact on the teaching experience. It might be the case, however, that when teaching outside the classroom, either within or outside her normal place of work, a teacher believes that she is less constrained by normal practice, especially if the work is non-contractual. This would be a mistake, however; and it is for this reason, and others (see below), that an HE institution operating in a foreign country needs to be careful when setting up bridging opportunities.

There are also less overt issues to contend with, these being what might be termed socio-cultural rather than technical-legal. For example, at a HE institution in the Kurdistan region of Iraq, the author was required to sign a paper which prohibited him from being critical towards Kurdish customs and culture. Likewise, anyone who has taught in China knows in that country an educator's role is given due seriousness, one being presented with a document which outlines the expected role of a teacher (Si, 2019; Zhu & Li, 2018). Finally, the author once inadvertently criticised an aspect of 'official' Kazakh *history during a history lecture there, to which some local people in the audience objected. These* examples are, however, broad. What is Kurdish culture? The Chinese document in question is couched in very general terms. And when Kazakh scholars objected to the author, was it because his facts were wrong or because he was trespassing? Again, however, an institution needs to tread carefully.

How 'Bridging' Might Occur Inside the Classroom: Materials and Materials Development

Culture always creeps into language teaching: to argue it does not would be to claim, absurdly, that language is not a part of culture. This might manifest itself in several ways. First, a foreign teacher will always be regarded by members of the host country (like it or not) as a representative of her own culture, her speech, her behaviour, her styles of communication and interaction being judged thus. This works the other way round, too: a teacher will make generalisations about the host country's culture, these often based on the educational performances of her students. Third, teaching materials promote culture, obviously, and often (at least regarding a general English syllabus), these favour the teacher's own culture, being what we might term west-centric. Finally, if a teacher wishes to be imaginative, creative and more student-centred, she might adapt teaching materials to suit a local perspective, thus introducing the learners' culture into the classroom (this is addressed in the author's 2016 publication: Ottley, 2016).

Some countries and their educational institutions already offer teaching materials that contain a local flavour. The teaching of history in English-medium secondary schools in Kazakhstan, for example, has been revolutionised recently by the arrival of new textbooks produced by the country's education ministry (Mun, 2014). Not only do these offer different narratives and perspectives regarding local and world events (different, that is, from either West-centric narratives or Soviet-produced materials), but their details are significant, too: individual characters might be presented with dark skin tones, they often wear traditional costume, and the rural and urban backgrounds of the narratives have a local flavour. The same narrative – one might term it thus – has been underway in China for some years, where today school history textbooks normally present a Sino-centric view of history. (Qiang, 2002; Si, 2019). In Kurdistan, meanwhile, there was (at least when the author worked there) a law that foreigners were simply not allowed to teach Kurdish history. The author has observed examples of how English learning school textbooks are following the same pattern. In China, for example, characters in these publications and their stories have changed: rather than featuring, say, a Chinese visitor to the UK learning English while at the same time grappling with issues of local culture, the protagonist in more-modern publications is equally likely to get their English from a visitor to China, and to assist him with cultural complexities and differences. Moreover, these are only formal, published examples; they do not include the numerous instances when an instructor (the current author included) has adapted texts or other sources of local interest into teaching materials.

It is at this interface, namely that of materials development (whole syllabuses as well as individual lessons), and specifically by adapting local-themed texts into teaching materials, that 'bridging' with a local community might begin to be practiced. This can be approached on a consultative basis. To illustrate this: the author is employed by a university in central Asia which is run by a charitable foundation, and he is expected to commit to community service. He was put in touch with a local state university, one which, compared to his own place of work, has fewer resources generally, especially regarding teaching aids, including materials. This is not an unusual experience or discovery for an international teacher working abroad (Keay et al., 2014). The university's English school, for example, which offers English for Academic Purpose (EAP) courses to students within an arts and social sciences department, possesses only GE textbooks; moreover, these are recycled year-on-year, are tatty and are full of scribbled notes. During the author's first meeting with a dozen EAP lecturers from the university, the latter were asked what role he should be fulfilling. Although the responses of the lecturers were wide and varied, a majority expressed a desire for assistance with the creation of new teaching materials. Moreover, and as the discussion developed, the lecturers welcomed the idea that such materials be developed based on or around local-interest subjects. Over the next weeks, several sessions were devoted to sourcing materials, adapting these, and collating them into a bank. At its close, after ten weeks, all the participants expressed satisfaction with what was achieved.

If the above was a successful initiative, it was because the participants believed they had developed a useful skill. Furthermore, they now possess a rich resource of extra teaching and learning materials. Moreover, the materials are relevant to the culture of their own cultural environment and, of course, that of their students'. Finally, the participants have expressed confidence in continuing to develop their own materials. What the author of this article gained from the experience, meanwhile, was invaluable. First, he acquired friends in the local community: the sessions were relaxed, friendly and informal; furthermore, they led to numerous social engagements. Second, he gained precious and helpful insights into the character of the local culture, both from the individual participants and, more widely, from the materials which were sourced. This stood him in good stead when integrating with the wider community. He also feels that he has become a more confident teacher at his own university, being, that is, more tolerant to and understanding and appreciate of the behaviours and culture of his own students. These are not merely casual results. Rather, the author believes this particular bridging initiative guaranteed these personal and professional dividends.

Reflecting the above point about professionalism, the exercise was a success for the author's place of work, too. As a result of its formal encouragement that faculty provide community service, as well as assisting with the setting-up of initial meetings with the local state university, the author's university got back a twofold dividend. First, an international teacher they had invested in had begun to integrate successfully with the wider community, becoming as a result more grounded; moreover, the teacher indicated that he subsequently felt more assured in delivering his own teaching. Second, the institution itself will have increased its recognition and prestige in the wider community, as well as deepening an already-existing relationship with the state university in question. In short, a bridge was built out from the author's employer: this, the author traversed, and he returned more confident. At the same time, those at the bridge's further pole expressed professional satisfaction as a result of the initiative.

Bridging and the Wider Cultural Context

As already noted, culture always creeps into language teaching. This may be one reason why some countries, or their educational establishments, are rephrasing English language teaching in a modified and more-local context. However, this is, according to Bannier (2016, p. 82), a "culturally complex" subject, one that forms part of a post-colonial debate regarding education generally and English language teaching specifically. According to Martin Cornoy, international education in English is an aspect of cultural imperialism, it being "implanted" in order to "support the imperial powers' continued political and economic interests." (Ziguras, 2008). To be sure, this argument might be outdated and no longer relevant in the post-Cold War world. It could even be the case that many English learners, young and aspirant by nature, expect English language to be bundled, as it were, with Western cultural norms, especially if they are university students majoring in subjects such as finance, economics, urban planning, fashion, and so on. In this sense, there is a valid argument that international education in its widest sense might actually be demand-led. At the same time, and especially for countries that are emerging from under a foreign yoke, which formerly had foreign-influenced education systems imposed upon them, and which might still function with languages that were once to all intents and purpose imported (Kurdistan/Iraq, Africa, the Middle East and the Far East/European colonial powers, Central Asia/the Soviet Union), the full use of English as a *lingua franca* within home-based universities might sometimes be a little controversial (Mun, 2014; Ziguras, 2008).

The example of China is an illustration of this. Chinese history presents the period between the First Opium War (1839-1842) and the close of The Second Sino-Japanese War (1937–1945) as a century of national humiliation. Although the British were not the only instigators of this humiliation, it is they (and the Japanese) who are generally regarded as its main perpetrator. Therefore, there exists a (possibly uncomfortable) situation whereby the language, and even the culture, of a former oppressor is at the same time the *modus operandi* of many he institutions in the country today. The same argument might also be made for post-colonial Africa, the Middle East, and other Far East nations.

There is another side to this, however. To repeat, with language goes culture, and it might be that an English teacher's cultural subskills are as much in demand as her teaching experiences, especially when she is requested to provide language support to homegrown staff, such as HR and admin. Within an EMI and outside of it, HR and admin need to routinely communicate in English, a large part of this communication being by phone and email. Indeed, it might be the case that although the English language competence levels of such staff are already high, they express less confidence when dealing with phone enquiries or when writing professional emails, for example. There is – one might argue – an entire etiquette surrounding these and similar professional skills, one whose origin, it might be added, is as much a product of the teacher's culture as is her language. Here, then, is another example of how an EMI might usefully bridge with its community.

The author developed and taught a professional email writing course while employed at a TNE university in China under the auspices of a Staff English programme he managed. This was adapted for later use at an EMI in central Asia. Although the course's focus was primarily on the composition of emails (following the completion of eight hours of tuition, the participants were required to submit a portfolio of emails), it was positioned within a cross-cultural communication framework. Moreover, many subskills were introduced, analysed and taught, including planning, time management, formal and informal language, and politeness and informality; as well as more specific skills such as salutations, subject headings, 'polite but firm' strategies, sharing bad news, and customer satisfaction. When the pandemic hit, in the summer of 2020, the programme was recorded and put online.

That the professional email writing programme was successful at the Chinese university was measured by positive feedback, from participants and their managers. That it was a successful bridging initiative, meanwhile, can be judged by the fact that in attracting participants from HR, admin, marketing, finance and student affairs officers, as well as faculty from a diversity of departments, it effectively promoted the author's own place of work, the university's language centre, and more specifically the PG division where the Staff English programme was located, to the whole university. Moreover, once a bridge is built it can continue to be used, even for different purposes. For example, when the PG division required assistance with the production of a promotional booklet, or when the individual who organised and taught the course (the author) needed help with a tricky visa-related issue, names could be checked from the original list of course participants and contacts conveniently re-established. Many bridges, then, rather than just one.

The success of another email writing course at a Central Asia university followed a similar but slightly different pattern. Here, the outreach was personal and professional. This is a small institution with no more than a dozen full-time faculty; as a result, its HR and admin support team is small, too. The author arrived at the institution at the commencement of his contract at the start of autumn, just before a half-term break from teaching, and, having time on his hands while at the same time wishing to connect with the wider university community, he offered the professional email writing course to HR and admin staff after only two weeks of employment. Thus, he was able to promote himself as a new member of staff. At the same time, and because of the small size of the HR and admin team, it was offered that the bridge that had been built would remain open; that is, staff were invited to come forward with language-related enquiries which they might continue to have after the email-writing course was completed.

The author has been involved with similar bridging opportunities, or initiatives, at other institutions. For example, it is not unusual for staff and faculty at EMI universities overseas to study IELTS; indeed, IELTS and other courses are often encouraged and supported by an employer, financially and otherwise; staff might even be required to obtain formal English qualifications. It is often the case that the high levels of English competence that local workers in EMIs possess have been acquired through a process of osmosis, largely because they work in an English-speaking environment. However, they might lack formal English qualifications. (A lot of the literature on THEs and EMIs devotes itself to international staff and the challenges they face (Keayet al., 2014; Leask, 2004; McBurnie & Ziguras, 2006; O'Mahony, 2014); however, there appears to be little content, reports or surveys that focus on homegrown staff). As Alexander, Argent and Spencer (2008) have demonstrated, the usual rites of passage for a teacher of EAP is from GE and, detouring through IELTS teaching, to arrive at a full-time EAP career. Although the statistics are not available, the author would guess that a majority of EAP teachers at TNEs and EMIs have experience of teaching IELTS. This being the case, another bridge suggests itself.

The current author, a qualified IELTS examiner, had two experiences of teaching IELTS while working at an EMI in Kazakhstan. Both offered great bridging opportunities. First, he was asked by his English Foundation programme to devise an IELTS course for HR and admin staff, this running over several weeks. Because of teaching and office hour commitments, the course took place one evening per week or on Saturday mornings. It was well attended. Later, when the author's family visited the country, admin staff willingly assisted with local transport arrangements, including airport pick-ups. A similar course was organised for managers of the university's accommodation department. Again, it took place one evening per week. Both courses helped to bridge between the English language faculty and HR, academic and non-academic staff within the university community generally.

POSSIBLE CHALLENGES OF BRIDGING FOR THE TEACHER

It may be the case that a reading of the above examples leads to the conclusion that goodwill was being sought from local staff, and that a renumeration in kind was then accepted. If that is so, the author would like to make two points. First, a concept of favours given and returned operates across many cultures. In the UK, for example, this would be the time-honoured practice of 'you scratch my back and I'll scratch yours.' In some eastern cultures, a similar concept is often more deeply-embedded culturally as well as practiced more openly. In China, this is known as *guanxi*, a practice which, when conducting business, is not to be taken lightly or dismissed as a kind of low-level corruption. On the contrary, learning to navigate *guanxi* successfully, understanding, for example, that a favour will always be returned and that a refusal is likely to cause offence, is, arguably, a lesson in cross-cultural communication. This being so, would this not then be an instance of bridging, too: that of an individual learning through experience how to navigate the cultural subtleties of his new home? Second (and as the teaching-times above would hint at), the two IELTS courses in question were organised privately; that is, as something extra to the institution's requirement for community service. The author was asked, and he agreed. However, if an institution were sensitive to such arrangements (and it might be the case that the laws of the country or the regulations of the university, or both, do not allow international staff to perform work outside of their existing contract, paid or unpaid), then it would need to safeguard against this by making clear stipulations in the work contract, or it might specify that community service can only be undertaken within the local, university community. Such contractual clauses are not unusual after all in the teachers' home countries (for example, institutions might require that permission be sought if an employee wishes to take on additional external work).

Legal restrictions regarding one's ability to work are a factor that would obviously mitigate against bridging, or at least make it more challenging. There are others, too, these being cultural, academic and legal, or a combination of these. Although such challenges would apply primarily within the educational establishment where one works (it is within this context that most of the commentators referenced below position their narratives), they would be relevant to external community initiatives also. Indeed, this might be more the case given that in the wider community one is more likely to be operating in different cultural and educational environments. Less in one comfort's zone, in other words.

A lot of the existing literature on TNEs operating in foreign countries discusses these issues. For example, Michael Fonkem writes about how a foreign teacher working in HE is needing to transition between cultures, a skill which may be more difficult to achieve given the fact (Fonkem's point) that "many foreign-born or immigrant professors arrive in the host country in their middle adulthood," at a time in their lives, that is, when they have "become used to certain patterns of work…consonant with their home county…" He likens this to navigating "two cultural universes." (Fonkem, p. 99; in Francois et al., 2016). Betsy Bannier, meanwhile, discusses both cultural and quality concerns that EMIs and their faculty need to be aware of (2016). Keay, May and O'Mahony (2014) write about the challenges of different learning styles, as well as communication and cultural differences. Betty Leask (2002) warns that for foreign staff working overseas, there is "an imperative to work towards intercultural understanding." McBurnie and Ziguras (2006) widen the net, meanwhile, writing as they do about the challenges posed by TNE universities for governments, educators and HE managers, the financial challenges surrounding "foreign investment", as well as outlining what they term the "pedagogical and cultural controversies" experienced by some TNE institutions.

The current author has experienced several challenges relating to bridging initiatives. Perhaps the most difficult experience he undertook was while employed in Kazakhstan. This involved multiple connections or bridges, both within the community of the university and into the wider community, too. It occurred through a chance encounter. Following a conversation with a colleague from his university's School of Education, the author learned that a local secondary school was embarking on an ambitious pilot programme to become the first school of its kind in the country to offer inclusive education: children with physical disabilities, in particular cerebral palsy, would have classes within the same school as able-bodied children. Actually, teaching had already commenced, and the author was asked if he would like to participate in the English language classes because, simply, the school did not have enough English teachers. Arriving from a separate school, the children with physical disabilities had had no English to date, whereas their able-bodied peers had already enjoyed a few years of English. Thus, they would not have English classes together.

The author had no previous experience of special needs education, this being the main reason why the experience proved difficult. Second, and again echoing an earlier point (Keay et al., 2014), the school in question had limited resources: blackboards and chalk rather than whiteboards, and no IT and projector facilities; even, several chairs and table were broken, as was a classroom window. Furthermore, the school's limited resources extended to staffing: for children who were more physically-challenged than others (the author's class), parents or helpers needed to be in attendance (rather than professional educators); moreover, some children, arriving early or late, were actually left unattended in cold corridors, seemingly as a result of poor or miscommunication between the school and parents.

The purpose of the university's involvement in the initiative under discussion was for its School of Education faculty to observe the inclusive classes, obtain feedback from teachers, and to collate the information for publication. This was done. However, the author's own classes with the special needs children were unobserved, and neither was he interviewed; probably because the classes were not, strictly speaking, inclusive. Notwithstanding the latter point, the author did feel rather like a spare part in the programme; moreover, when he expressed the opinion that the classes he was teaching were challenging, he was promised a teaching assistant, but this never materialised. Finally, and following a situation when a pair of students were again left in the school corridor unattended (unbeknown to the teacher who was busy within the classroom), and their parents, upon discovering the children an hour later, complained to the teacher (the author), it was decided that his involvement in the initiative would end.

The above example is included in the current study as a warning. As the literature makes clear (Allan & Omarova, 2020), special needs education is indeed special; it requires professionals who are trained and experienced. The author was invited to participate in what was, basically, a formal programme of research, and yet his role was peripheral. Moreover, he had, or was given, no training for the role and no formal support. He was largely unsupervised. Better, then, to stick to one's own area of professional expertise.

QUALITY ASSURANCE AND LEGAL ISSUES

To be sure, there will always be question marks about the quality of education offered by TNEs (Bannier, 2016; Ziguras, 2013), as indeed there ought to be, and it may be the case that there should exist, as indeed there often is, a double- or even multi-scrutiny of a foreign institution's academic quality, as well as the admin and technical aspects of its operations (an offshore campus, for example, would normally be responsible to the educational authorities of its host country and its parent university, as well as other partner institutions). At the same time, there may exist confusion over roles of quality assurance (McBurnie & Ziguras 2006). However, what about outreach and community service initiatives, especially if these are undertaken in the wider community outside of the institution? Can these be fully and professionally scrutinised? What might be the quality assurance models at play here, if any? Indeed, if a serious problem were to ensue, who would be responsible or likely to be held to account? Would this be the teacher's normal employer, i.e., the institution which has encouraged (or at least not objected to) an employee's bridging initiative? Would it be the community institution, such as a local university or a school? Or would it be the individual herself?

Levels of regulation vary between countries. For example, in the UK, schools and universities are pretty much open-access. In other countries, meanwhile, an educational institution might have private or even police security at its gates; others might deny entry to visitors who have not had their credentials previously checked and confirmed. There might even be variations within countries. In China, for example, the author was permitted entry to a primary school with no checks (although he was accompanied by a local teacher), whereas on another occasion he was denied entry even to the gardens of a HE establishment. In a central Asian country, moreover, he might routinely enter a further education (FE) college to meet up with local friends with no checks whatsoever, but when entering his own place of work, he needs to show ID.

This plethora of complexity and confusion might well be reflected at a formal level, too. Potentially, these are legal issues rather than educational ones, matters for government rather than individual institutions. Therefore, given the fact that very different legal codes and regulations might exist between a teacher's own country and that of her foreign, host institution (and they probably do), and given also the reality that a foreign teacher is probably operating behind a language and cultural barrier, one can understand why an EMI might be unwilling to allow its staff to work in the community outside of the university. Indeed, it may be that on account of legal reasons that a university cannot allow such work, this being a policy of government rather than the institution. While employed in China, for example, the author had many requests to work in the wider community turned down by his employer.

ACADEMIC DIFFERENCES

Academic differences, principally between what a teacher is used to and what she experiences in a new educational context, might result in challenges for bridging initiatives. As Bannier (2016), Keay, May and O'Mahony (2014) and Leask (2004) all observe, teaching and learning styles are grounded in culture and can be very different between different countries. Thus, when one bridges outside of one's place of work and into a local educational establishment where both teachers and learners might have less experience of 'international' teaching styles and methodologies, this could prove challenging.

At its most general, this can be observed in class sizes. In the UK, for example, the author's experiences of class sizes for the teaching of English in HE is that they are small and manageable, seldom reaching beyond twenty students, often fewer. Small class sizes conveniently allow for communicative language teaching (CLT). In countries with emerging economies, where the majority of TNEs and EMIs tend to be located, class sizes at all levels of education and especially in public institutions are usually larger, this being the result of clear socio-economic factors (teachers needs to be paid and larger class sizes means fewer teachers; moreover, many countries are still transitioning to English teaching and fewer qualified teachers are thus available; finally, the demographic trends in many countries with emerging economies tend to a large youth population). Furthermore, the author's experiences of teaching English at universities in China and central Asia is that student attendance is often strictly compulsory, it forming part of assessment (via 'engagement' or 'contribution'); another reason, then, why class sizes would be larger.

Arguably, CLT is the bread-and-butter methodology of ELT for the majority of English language teachers. However, because the fundamental aim of CLT is that of communication in the target language (from instructor to learner as well as between learners), it is less convenient and less manageable when teaching larger class sizes. Therefore, when working with learners and teachers (especially the latter) whose language acquisition skills and learning and teaching experience (including of their first language) have been based on different models (for example, grammatical competence), one is likely to encounter a radically different experience in the classroom; more so, and for reasons already stated, when one is bridging into a wider community.

The author has one such challenging experience to share. He was conducting a teacher-training session in a high school in Kazakhstan. He wished to demonstrate how local subject matter might be successfully incorporated into an English lesson; the subject was national Olympic athletes. The lesson ran through several cycles, including a section when learners needed to do some online research on their phones, discussing in small groups what they had found out before sharing this with the whole class. This invitation to student autonomy was met with resistance from several of the teachers observing the class, as was the free and open discussion that followed, and especially the instruction that students should use their mobile phones. For example, the author was asked in a post-teaching feedback session why he didn't correct student output; furthermore, he was told that normally there was a zero-tolerance policy towards the use of mobile devices in class. Moreover, the pilot group comprised eight students, and the author was asked by a teacher after the session if the class would also work for larger groups of students. When he asked how large her class of students normally was, he was shocked to hear the reply, 'eighty'.

Without stretching the point, it might be stated that CLT is more about trust than control. Because CLT positions the teacher as a facilitator rather than an instructor, it is, arguably, a more 'democratic' method of classroom engagement than other 'top-down' styles of teaching (Richards, 2005; Spada, 2007). Within a CLT environment, learners are often paired together or work in small groups and are trusted to communicate in the target language. While it could be argued that this aspect of CLT makes it better-suited to large class sizes, the current author has observed local teachers in central Asia struggle with this fundamental feature of CLT, it being alien to their own notions of classroom management, as well as their own experiences of how they were taught. Moreover, the assumption that CLT is somehow the default method of ELT has been challenged on the grounds that this point of view might be a neo-liberal conceit (Hu, 2005).

Finally, there is the fact that learners in China and other east Asian countries often appear less willing to engage in their learning (from a communicative point of view) than students of other societies and nations. Again, this is probably because they have been less exposed to CLT practices. There are other, deeper-seated reasons, too. As Hu (2005), Marginson (2011), and Zhu and Li (2018) demonstrate, education in such countries is normally based on a Confucian model, whereby students are less likely to define themselves as independent learners and more as a collective body, one in which, moreover, an individual learner would be less likely to speak up or speak out, and would be averse, furthermore, to challenging the authority of the teacher. In bridging into the wider educational community in countries where such educational norms prevail, attitudes such as these might prove challenging to a foreign teacher.

THE PANDEMIC

As the 'Introduction' for the Call for Chapters for the current publication states, "the global pandemic has made TNE a timely topic because traditional international education, which relies on the mobility of staff and students, experienced unprecedent challenges…" (ICI Global, 2021). In countries that pursue a zero-tolerance policy towards containment of the pandemic, this has been and still is profound. The example given above, where the author was allowed access to a school on account of merely accompanying a member of the institution's teaching staff, would no longer be valid. On the contrary, the author himself would now only be able to access the buildings of his own university campus after showing an active QR code identifying who he is, an active QR code issued by the local province confirming his health status, and an active health code that confirms his travel status within a previous fourteen-day time period. Those wishing to visit the university, meanwhile, would now need to have their visit confirmed in advance, which would include evidence of a negative PCR-test. Applicants for courses, moreover, now have their interviews online. Other countries have different pandemic-related rules and regulations, of course, and these might be more relaxed than the above examples. What is consistent, though, is the fact that locally and globally nothing is fixed or certain, and that successive waves of the Covid-19 virus will mean a continuation of restrictions, these often imposed at short notice.

Limitations on movement and on access within and between countries, a continuation, that is, of a so-called 'new normal' into the foreseeable future, imply corresponding restrictions on bridging. In societies which operate zero tolerance policies regarding the pandemic, it may be the case that external bridging opportunities shrink to nothing. Even in countries with less restrictive policies, there will undoubtably be fewer opportunities to bridge than existed before the pandemic, at least for the next year or so.

CONCLUSION

Bridging initiatives might be challenging, even to the point of proving prohibitively difficult. Even where opportunities for bridging initiatives remain, it is recommended that an individual and the employing

TNE institution be aware of several factors. First, when bridging, either inside one's institution or into the wider community, parties need to be aware of the legal situation regarding employment, paid and unpaid. Often, such laws will be different for foreign workers from those of the local population. Because this is a legal issue, the onus is on the employer to provide guidance. Second, a teacher needs to be aware of, and sensitive to, the different cultural practices of her new country of work. Here, she might avail herself: who wouldn't, after all, desire to read up on and acquire knowledge of the culture of the country one is planning to live and work in for a lengthy period of time? At the same time, an institution might consider formalising such guidance: a short series of lectures, language classes, and brochures, would suffice. Third, the author would recommend that an institution stipulate that its foreign faculty undertake bridging initiatives and, this being the case, embed such requirements into the work contract. It is recommended, moreover, that institutions actively assist with the setting up of such initiatives. This needn't be difficult or time-consuming: a well-run university will already have well-established contacts within the local community, especially with educational establishments, as well as contacts with alumni who are employed locally. Furthermore, the formal involvement of an employer might help safeguard against well-meaning but ad-hoc initiatives that ultimately prove difficult and disappointing, or are not legitimate. Finally, a teacher working in a foreign university and bridging into educational establishments in the host country needs to bear in mind that the styles and methodologies of teaching she routinely practices in the classroom might prove alien in outreach teaching environments, for learners and for teachers.

Arriving in a country and looking ahead to months or even years of employment at a foreign university, one cannot fail to be excited. One is a stranger in a strange land. Venturing into the wider community for the first time, one is assailed by new sights, smells and experiences. Essentially, this is a part of that well-documented period of culture shock known as 'the honeymoon period' (Irwin, 2007). We have all been there (have we not?). Although a subjective state, this manifests itself in the following ways: because you are foreign, local inhabitants seem attracted to you: they will make conversation, practice their English, ask for photographs; local workers, meanwhile, will offer you a good table in their restaurants, shopkeepers will be patient as you struggle to convert prices into your own currency. Later, you will return to a comfortable and clean university-subsidised apartment (as is usually the case when employed in a HE institution abroad). Sure, the accommodation might seem like an island in the local community, but, really, this is what is needed during these first, strange weeks.

When the sun shines, islands can be lovely places.

Familiarity, it is said, can breed contempt. Living and working in the same well-defined and exclusive environment can easily lead to feelings of over-dependence and insularity, a mild sense of deprivation, even of cheating. Islands can readily become irksome places.

A bridge, meanwhile, is defined as a construction that serves the purpose of providing passage over an obstacle, this being otherwise difficult to cross. In the context of this current paper, the bridge is outreach, from one's place of work in a foreign country and into the wider community: utilising one's skills, that is, in order to integrate. The obstacle, moreover, is the same: because integration is never straightforward or easy. Of course, integration does not guarantee there will not be problems and challenges in the future. However, the more one integrates, the fewer of these one is likely to encounter. That, surely, is a definition of successful integration.

REFERENCES

Alexander, O., Argent, S., & Spencer, J. (2008). *EAP essentials: A teacher's guide to principles and practice*. Garnet Education.

Allan, J., & Omarova, T. (2020). Disability and inclusion in Kazakhstan. *Disability & Society*, 1–18. https://www.tandfonline.com/doi/full/10.1080/09687599.2020.1867073?scroll=top&needAccess=true

Bannier, B. J. (2016). Global trends in transnational education. *International Journal of Information and Education Technology (IJIET)*, *6*(1), 80–84. https://www.researchgate.net/profile/Betsy-Bannier/publication/280758526_Global_Trends_in_Transnational_Education/links/57c8252b08ae28c01d51ac83/Global-Trends-in-Transnational-Education.pdf. doi:10.7763/IJIET.2016.V6.663

Bodycott, P., & Walker, A. (2000). Teaching abroad: Lessons learned about inter-cultural understanding for teachers in higher education. [Code of Good Practice in the Provision of Transnational Education. UNESCO-CEPES Bucharest.]. *Teaching in Higher Education*, *5*(1), 79–94. https://www.tandfonline.com/doi/pdf/10.1080/135625100114975?needAccess=true Council of Europe/UNESCO. doi:10.1080/135625100114975

Francois, E. J., Avoseh Mejia, B. M., & Griswold, W. (2016). What is Transnational Education? In *Perspectives in transnational higher education* (pp. 1–22). Brill Sense. https://brill.com/view/book/edcoll/9789463004206/BP000002.xml doi:10.1007/978-94-6300-420-6_1

Garson, B. (2005). Teaching abroad: A cross-cultural journey. *Journal of Education for Business*, *80*(6), 322–326. https://www.tandfonline.com/doi/pdf/10.3200/joeb.80.6.322-326?casa_token=7cR5erGR0nUAAAAA:LrE7Bk5dBSB_qpIpY-mVBdsWjfACX1HGHnjEtIfOqyVgS4kKqwdiOWVPg3S_XJZYt-FZLHHCL4Vlz. doi:10.3200/JOEB.80.6.322-326

Hu, G. (2005, January). 'CLT is best for China'— An untenable absolutist claim. *ELT Journal*, *59*(1), 65–68. doi:10.1093/elt/cci009

IGI Global. (2021). Call for Chapters: Developments and Future Trends. In *Transnational Higher Education*. IGI Global. https://www.igi-global.com/publish/call-for-papers/call-details/5725

Irwin, R. (2007). Culture shock: negotiating feelings in the field. *Anthropology Matters*, *9*(1). https://anthropologymatters.com/index.php/anth_matters/article/view/64/124

Keay, J., May, H., & O'Mahony, J. (2014). Improving learning and teaching in transnational education: Can communities of practice help? *Journal of Education for Teaching*, *40*(3), 251–266. https://www.tandfonline.com/doi/full/10.1080/02607476.2014.903025?scroll=top&needAccess=true. doi:10.1080/02607476.2014.903025

Knight, J. (2015). International universities: Misunderstandings and emerging models? *Journal of Studies in International Education*, *19*(2), 107–121. https://journals.sagepub.com/doi/abs/10.1177/1028315315572899. doi:10.1177/1028315315572899

Leask, B. (2004). Transnational education and intercultural learning: Reconstructing the offshore teaching team to enhance internationalisation. *Australian Universities Quality Forum.* https://www.researchgate.net/profile/Betty-Leask/publication/266277495_Transnational_Education_and_Intercultural_Learning_Reconstructing_the_Offshore_Teaching_Team_to_Enhance_Internationalisation/links/565dfe2608ae4988a7bd294e/Transnational-Education-and-Intercultural-Learning-Reconstructing-the-Offshore-Teaching-Team-to-Enhance-Internationalisation.pdf

Marginson, S. (2011). The Confucian model of higher education in East Asia and Singapore. In *Higher education in the Asia-Pacific* (pp. 53–75). Springer. https://link.springer.com/chapter/10.1007/978-94-007-1500-4_3 doi:10.1007/978-94-007-1500-4_3

McBurnie, G., & Ziguras, C. (2006). *Transnational education: Issues and trends in offshore higher education.* Routledge. doi:10.4324/9780203968352

Mellors-Bourne, R., Fielden, J., Kemp, N., Middlehurst, R., & Woodfield, S. (2014). *The value of transnational education to the UK.* Higher Education Academy. https://assets.publishing.service.gov.uk/government/uploads/system/uploads/attachment_data/file/387910/bis-14-1202-the-value-of-transnational-education-to-the-uk.pdf

Mun, O. (2014). Re-imagining national identity through early literacy textbooks in Kazakhstan. [Master's thesis. Lehigh University, England]. https://core.ac.uk/download/pdf/228638588.pdf

O'Mahony, J. (2014). *Enhancing student learning and teacher development in transnational education.* Higher Education Academy.

Ottley, K. (2016). Why One-Size-Fits-All Is Not Fit for Purpose: The Problem With Mass-Produced Teaching Materials, and How One Might Creatively and Sensitively Confront this Problem. In *SLA research and materials development for language learning* (pp. 284–295). Routledge.

Qiang, W. (2002). Primary school English teaching in China: New developments. *English Language Teacher Education and Development, 7,* 99-108. http://www.elted.net/uploads/7/3/1/6/7316005/v7qiang.pdf

Richards, J. C. (2005). *Communicative language teaching today.* SEAMEO Regional Language Centre. https://d1wqtxts1xzle7.cloudfront.net/55716819/Communicative_Language_Teaching_Today-with-cover-page-v2.pdf?Expires=1660584453&Signature=BTWrAwfHZaMKhPLa4kF~u261bnmwFYudpjiHb-14GK4xwNJkaOluuRmzqIj~7qP7zZfHJmVcF6iOPcnoqFQSPayF6WW4rM7mQ7Y07XQAw6z249O9MxcGgzun33eZzmTLa5mPV0T2hDjwMwbjl5w6yIjhbwEtn8Fs3Jo5B36g1gjt6EcBEC-QgLt4Eao5K~yPPrvSKr9PgZXc-l7q2r~NPAPmYAL7bNwLkK-QenxqSc0TL4RRu36RAngNzOz5QA-1z51xY3Zly~3LsbCDkwDmGBqhFfJ4JYOvpYy1EkH4RgaBnXS3f~2dhfCPqFagt~kfWP7EDS1QcUN6lP-yQWX9E9g__&Key-Pair-Id=APKAJLOHF5GGSLRBV4ZA

Si, J. (2019). English as a lingua franca: A new approach for English language teaching in China? *Canadian Journal of Applied Linguistics, 42*(1), 113–135. doi:10.1515/CJAL-2019-0007

Spada, N. (2007). Communicative language teaching. In *International handbook of English language teaching* (pp. 271–288). Springer. doi:10.1007/978-0-387-46301-8_20

Wilkins, S., & Huisman, J. (2012). The international branch campus as transnational strategy in higher education. *Higher Education*, *64*(5), 627–645. doi:10.100710734-012-9516-5

Zhu, X., & Li, J. (2018). Conceptualizing the ontology of higher education with Chinese characteristics. *Educational Philosophy and Theory*, *50*(12), 1144–1156. https://www.tandfonline.com/doi/full/10.1080/00131857.2018.1504707?scroll=top&needAccess=true. doi:10.1080/00131857.2018.1504707

Ziguras, C. (2013). The Cultural Politics of Transnational Education: Ideological and Pedagogical Issues for Teaching Staff. In *Teaching in transnational higher education* (pp. 68–78). Routledge.

Chapter 13
Bangladeshi Students' Family Fertilization for Pursuing Higher Education in Australia

Md Tariqul Islam
https://orcid.org/0000-0002-4165-5594
Hiroshima University, Japan

ABSTRACT

Among the young Bangladeshi people, like many other international students from developing countries, Australian universities created a position as an emerging terminus for higher education. This chapter pursues to explore the family motivations for Bangladeshi higher education students in becoming physically mobile to chase education in Australian universities. The chapter follows a qualitative methodology and includes the stories of 18 young Bangladeshi students studying at two Australian universities. It aims to enlighten researchers and policymakers in both developing and developed countries about the role of the family as a micro-agent of socialisation in contributing to the global level politics and power related to the higher education industry. The findings of the chapter reveal that the dreams and desires developed and disseminated by their family young students experienced in Bangladesh are quite neo-liberal in character. Thus, it provides the analysis of empirical data for both host and sending countries to ensure transnational higher education in developing countries.

INTRODUCTION

A dominant characteristic of capable young students or consumers of higher education in the globalised world appears to be their willingness to be mobile through education (Brooks & Abrahams, 2018; Cuzzocrea & Mandich, 2015). The international mobility of students pursuing higher education is the focus of a growing body of education policies and academic practices in almost all the countries in the globalised world (Bhandari & Blumenthal, 2011). Acknowledging the limitation of a research paper, this chapter explores only the family culture (not the educational culture) that influenced or motivated (not the support of the family during international studies) young Bangladeshi students to become internationally

DOI: 10.4018/978-1-6684-5226-4.ch013

mobile in pursuing higher education. The research question that the author explores through this chapter is: what family factors have motivated young Bangladeshi students to seek a qualification from Australian universities? This chapter aims to address the unexplored relationship of young Bangladeshi students' international mobility for higher education with family as a social institution in the globalised world.

The author has grounded this chapter in the context of globalisation where young higher education students are considered as the micro aspect of the globalised world. Here, he finds how some macro globalising forces through family motivate young Bangladeshi students to pursue higher education in Australian universities. These mobility factors create neoliberal imaginations among young Bangladeshi students in a way that has led them to become neoliberal actors. Finally, young students express their dreams and desires in developing themselves as global citizens through foreign higher education. Thus, the chapter presents a critical analysis of current practices of globalised cultures and associated politics and power visible in the actions of young students' families related to mobilities in the name of global citizenship. The findings of the chapter will help the universities and policymakers of both host and sending countries to take decisions and make policies in terms of transnational education. In other words, the findings will provide them with the analysis of empirical data to ensure transnational higher education in Bangladesh addresses the issues of international benchmark and affordable international higher education opportunities in-country.

NATIONAL, INTERNATIONAL, TRANSNATIONAL EDUCATION AND FAMILY

In Bangladesh, 52 public universities, 108 private universities and 3 international universities are listed under the University Grants Commission (UGC, 2022). According to the UGC Annual Report of 2019, the total number of students in Bangladeshi higher education institutions is 44,34,451 (UGC, 2020). Moreover, 70,000-90,000 Bangladeshi students move abroad for higher education every year (Siddiqui & Jasim, 2022). In addition to national and overseas higher education, Transnational Education (TNE) is seen as significant for the higher education sector in Bangladesh. TNE ensures the mobility of higher education i.e., education programmes and providers between countries (Knight, 2016). Transnational Education (TNE) is being discussed as a burning issue in the higher education sector in Bangladesh for several reasons. For example, local students will get the chance to get a global education in the country and local teachers will be able to receive international standard training (Haque, 2021). In addition to the quality of higher education, TNE in Bangladesh might bring positive changes to the economy of Bangladesh by producing skilled graduates and reducing the cost of overseas higher education. In this situation, it is important to understand the reasons for students' international mobility in pursuing higher education. The identified reasons will provide the logic and factors that need to be considered for promoting and ensuring quality TNE in Bangladesh.

M. T. Islam (2019) identifies 3Cs – i.e. culture, course and career through analysing the literature on international students' mobility. According to him 3Cs emerge as the three broad categories and cover most of the identified motivations behind mobility in international higher education. In terms of culture, M. T. Islam (2021) claims that the consumerist culture of neoliberalism in both home and the host country motivates students from developing or underdeveloped countries to go to developed countries to pursue higher education. To be specific, mobility motivators for young students from developing countries comprise the influence of local mobility and network capitals (Hannam et al., 2006; M. T. Islam, 2022a, 2022c; Sheller, 2014), i.e. local cultural practices in the job market, their family and global media, and their imaginations for the future. In other words, these motivators are the outcomes of the neoliberal market mechanism of the globalisation process. Cultural factors include the educational and family culture of students' home country and the cultural offerings of the host city and country. Giralt and Bailey (2010) focus on the lived experiences of young people to examine 'spatial imaginaries,' drawing on Bauman's thesis on 'liquid life paths' in liquid modernity. In understanding the impact of migration stories on personal identity formation, they found the process of young migrants' development through negotiation with family heritage, host cultures, and cultural reproduction.

The role of the family in higher studies affecting students studying abroad is well known and documented in the literature. For example, Bailey (2021) highlights the influence of objective social structure that families have on young people through direct and indirect values and cultural rules for decision-making about higher education. Further, researchers find family background (Larose et al., 2019) or family characteristics (Y. Liu, 2019) as important factors for young people's transition to higher education. Bahna (2018) identifies the 'family background or characteristics' as cultural capital that influence higher education students' international mobility as well as mobility to the more admired host countries. Specifically, higher levels of family education and higher family income are associated with the enrolment in higher education institutions abroad and completion of the most prestigious educational path (Cao et al., 2016; Dias Lopes, 2020; Vergolini & Vlach, 2017; Weiss & Steininger, 2013). Likewise, Pimpa (2005) recognises family motivation on Thai students for international mobility pursuing higher education into five categories i.e., finance, information, expectation, persuasion, and competition. All the reviewed literature concerns the backing and support of the family for one to become an international student. In other words, all of these perspectives matter, and so matters the social, cultural and economic capital of families because they can predict the likelihood that a student effectively has the idea of studying abroad.

THEORETICAL UNDERPINNINGS OF GLOBALISED MOBILITY FOR HIGHER EDUCATION

At present, we can consider globalised mobility as an essential issue regarding the individual, local and global context. Physical and virtual global movements of people, capital and products are drastically changing social conditions and personal lived experiences. Zygmunt Bauman (1998a, 1998b, 1999, 2003, 2005, 2009, 2013a, 2013b, 2014), in his works, regards globalisation as the core context as well as one of the key influencing factors for understanding modern individual and social life. Bauman also considers both types of mobility as significant and observes mobility as an element differentiating instead of unifying the human condition.

Bauman presents his thoughts about the life of mobile people in the aftermath of globalisation and liquid modernity (Bauman & Donskis, 2013; M. T. Islam, 2022b). According to him, "globalization is geared to the tourists' dreams and desires" (Bauman, 1998b, p. 47), and for that reason, we are all on the move (Bauman, 1999). In liquid modern time, in line with Bauman's theory, young students are physically mobile when they travel to another country to pursue higher education. They do this to address their dreams and desires, which are generated by and in response to the forces of globalisation.

In the globalised world, for Bauman, the mobility of young students pursuing higher education from an overseas university is a matter of choice or fate. We can consider the young students from developing countries who decide to undertake a degree from a university in a developed country to achieve a higher status in their society as tourists in the globalised society. On the contrary, some young students are also mobile because of their intention to improve their economic condition (fate) after achieving an overseas degree and after that a better job. Considering young Bangladeshi students' mobility to Australia from Bauman's critical theoretical point of view, it can be argued that because of some underlying globalising forces they move from their past locality (Bangladesh) to the new locality (Australia).

METHODOLOGY

To explore the family factors behind the physical mobility of the young Bangladeshi students to Australian universities in pursuing higher education the author follows a qualitative methodology in this chapter. For Australian universities, Bangladeshi students are representative of many other students from developing countries who have different socio-cultural and economic backgrounds. However, the author's intention is not to generalise the findings but to understand individuals' perspectives from their stories.

The Research Participants and Sites

For this study, 18 young Bangladeshi students studying in two Australian universities are the key participants, whose stories and views provide important insights regarding the research question. Through snowball sampling (Creswell, 2013) the mentioned number of research participants were recruited "who are accessible, willing to provide information, and distinctive for their accomplishments and ordinariness or who shed light on a specific phenomenon or issue being explored". Further, the author was conscious of the need to collect credible data from the participants of the research. In the snowball sampling procedure, there is an "inherent risk of disclosure of personal information to others" (Sadler et al., 2010, p. 371), and the "samples tend to be biased towards more cooperative individuals or those who have a large personal network" (Baltar & Brunet, 2012, p. 60). However, keeping these limitations into consideration, the author first identified two participants from two research sites. To be specific, a Bangladeshi acquaintance in Melbourne suggested the name of one participant from Eastern University and the author found another participant by searching 'Bangladeshi student at Southern University, Melbourne' through social media. Firstly, he approached them to participate in my study and secondly, he requested them to suggest more participants for the study if they knew any. In total, he identified 24 young Bangladeshi students from two research sites through snowball sampling, with 18 (9 from each research site) of them participating in the study. One out of twenty-four identified participants was not interested in sharing his data for research purposes. Similarly, the other five participants who showed interest in participating were not able to find the time to do so, as most of them were involved in part-time jobs during the semester or trimester break and some of them went to visit their family members in Bangladesh. Likewise, the author was not able to maintain the anticipated age range (18 to 24) of the participants according to the UN's youth definition (UNDESA, 2013). However, UNDESA (2013) accepts that the definition of young people varies in several UN entities and different societies to keep pace with global socio-cultural, economic and demographic changes. For example, the Commonwealth (2016) defines young people as those between 15 to 29 years of age. The author was not able to include an equal number of male and female participants in the study, either. To ensure the collection of quality data up to a significant level of data saturation and increase the number of female participants in this research, he moved the maximum age level of the participants from 24 to 25 years, which allowed him to include two more female participants (total of four females out of eighteen participants) in the study.

He selected two universities in Melbourne, considering the availability of Bangladeshi students. In the selected universities, there is a large intake of international students, including Bangladeshi students, compared with other Australian universities.

To ensure the anonymity of the nominated Australian universities, he refers to them as Eastern University (EU) and Southern University (SU).

The Individual Interviews

The recruited research participants were involved in individual interviews to gather qualitative data about the family factors that motivated them to seek a qualification from Australian universities on their own words. In other way, participants' story provides the actual data on the factors that need to be considered for promoting and ensuring quality TNE in Bangladesh. The author's intention for using the interview method was to counter invisibility through the in-depth articulation of the hidden discourses from the life stories of mobile young students in a global context (Brinkmann, 2013). Before conducting the interviews, he considered the settings in which he would conduct the interviews. A private, neutral and distraction-free environment was ensured to guarantee the comfort of the young participants and to obtain high-quality information from them. Although all of the participant's mother tongue is Bangla, he interviewed them in English for two reasons: firstly, all of them are attending Australian universities where the medium of instruction is English, and secondly, he used the English language in all aspects of this study. Semi-structured interviews allow the interviewees to offer their narrative accounts of their lived experiences, providing knowledge through dialogue in line with the essential aspects of the research (Elliott & Urry, 2010). As a researcher, to bring out their experiences, the author concentrated on creating a space where young students could talk safely and freely (Gaskell, 2013). Moreover, on the one hand, such an interview structure provides him with the opportunity to focus on the conversations whether they are progressing according to the research goal or not. It also allows the author the flexibility to elucidate the questions of the semi-structured interviews at the time of the interview for gathering more appropriate information regarding the phenomena under study (Ary et al., 2013). Moreover, the author applied the same semi-structured interview guide for all interviews as a key technique for increasing the reliability of qualitative research with young students, which enables him to follow the line of inquiry in an unbiased manner (Yin, 2003) and analyse the data from a comparative aspect (Flick, 2008) in this chapter. Besides, using the same interview guide strengthens the reliability of the collected data because any change in wording, context and emphasis would undermine the reliability of the interview method (Louis et al., 2007).

Data Analysis

To gather the stories from the research participants the author asked them only one question i.e., what made you decide to undertake a degree in an Australian university? Through this question, a wide range of stories came from the participants. However, for this chapter, he analysed the data collected through interviews in response to the research question (Schmidt, 2004) only. Bauman's suggestion guides the author in analysing data, allowing an experimental plurality of perspectives in the globalised world and offering interpretations without claiming conclusiveness (Junge, 2008; R. L. M. Lee, 2005). In the data analysis process, he examined and re-examined the research questions to be answered by the available data collected through individual interviews as the critical hermeneutical phenomenology focuses on understanding the meaning of the text (Annells, 2006). As a qualitative researcher, the author believes that "there is no one single or correct way to analyse and present qualitative data; how one does it should abide by the issue of fitness for purpose" (Louis et al., 2007, p. 461). In this chapter, a thematic analysis approach was followed where the author examined each new piece of data in light of the followed theoretical underpinnings and research question to find out the answer to the question.

Table 1. Data coding and categorising

<table>
<tr><th>Data</th><th>Child code</th><th>Parent code</th><th>Category</th></tr>
<tr><td>My parents always wanted me to be the best at school, the best in the class, and everything. I was ended up getting good grades, and so, yea that's why I never looked down all I want to grow up that is why I wanted to study in the best university. (Farhan)</td><td>Motivation to be the best</td><td rowspan="2">Implicit motivation</td><td rowspan="4">Family fertilisation</td></tr>
<tr><td>I think the reason they [my parents] chose Canadian school [in Bangladesh] because … they wanted me just to have an idea of outside, if I do want to go abroad what it would be like, so, just like a glimpse. (Pikachu)</td><td>School selection</td></tr>
<tr><td>He [my father] always said that Bangladesh is not a place where you can live or pursue your higher education or do a job because it is already corrupted. So, it is better to go … abroad but not in Bangladesh. (Fariha)</td><td>Develop consciousness</td><td rowspan="2">Explicit motivation</td></tr>
<tr><td>My father came to Australia many times, and he thought it is a good country to study my higher education. (Fahmid)</td><td>Set destination</td></tr>
</table>

Following the inductive process, the interview data was organised from the 'bottom-up' and developed their codes and categories (Table 1). In doing so, the author followed several steps. Firstly, for example, he developed a child code, namely 'Motivation to be the best', based on the story between lines 104 and 106 of Farhan's transcript. Similarly, 'School selection' is a child code developed based on Pikachu's transcript (lines 102-106). Secondly, he analysed the developed child codes to find out their patterns and relationships, therefore found parent codes. For example, 'Implicit motivation' is a parent code developed on the basis of three child codes: 'Motivation to be the best', 'School selection' and 'Familial norms'. Likewise, 'Explicit motivation' is another parent code that is developed based on two child codes, i.e., 'Develop consciousness' and 'Set destination'. Parent codes were analysed in the third step to categorise them, and he found categories from all interview data. In line with the example mentioned above, 'Family fertilisation' is a category that he found from analysing 'Implicit motivation' and 'Explicit motivation' parent codes. In all of the steps mentioned above, he employed the qualitative data analysis software 'NVivo' to manage, retrieve, and connect data, but not to analyse them (Forman & Damschroder, 2007).

RESULTS AND DISCUSSION: FAMILY FERTILIZATION

The category of 'family fertilisation' emerged from the interview data. The author claims this category as the motivation coming from family and friends for a better life for the students. The role of family on young students for their international mobility is visible at different stages of their life, i.e., early childhood to young age. In other words, young students feel the need to develop their desires and dreams of future mobility within the educational, social and psychological interventions of their families. For many of the young Bangladeshi students whom the author interviewed, family motivation for overseas higher education may be associated with neoliberal consumerist dreams and desires. For this reason, he refers to the construction process of dreams and desires by family members for international mobility as 'family fertilisation'. For the participants' international mobility, family fertilisation works both implicitly and explicitly. Brooks and Waters (2011) term these implicit and explicit interventions as 'family project', as parents want to secure the future of the child through an overseas degree. These family interventions will be discussed in this section by analysing and discussing some of the interview data.

Briefly, implicit interventions include admitting children to a school that implements an overseas curriculum and developing their consciousness regarding place, culture and career. Implicit intervention is a long-term process that takes time to motivate young people for international mobility. On the other hand, explicit interventions comprise rationalising the area of study through the lens of economic gain, presenting the future career prospects of an overseas degree, and deciding young students' destination country for higher education by family members. Explicit family interventions bring immediate results regarding young students' international mobility in pursuing higher education.

Implicit Motivation

Brooks and Waters (2015) in their study observed that parents are increasingly concerned regarding the acquisition of valued multicultural 'global capital' by their children and help them to be competitive in both local and global labour markets. For this purpose, families engage with the children's school life (Larose et al., 2019) and try to prepare their children psychologically and culturally for future mobility by enrolling them in 'elite international' (M. Lee & Wright, 2016) or 'English medium' schools in their home country. In Bangladesh, English medium schools are registered with the relevant authorities in compliance with set rules (MoE, 2010), follow a foreign curriculum and provide TNE. Al-Quaderi and Al Mahmud (2010, pp. 213–214) observe that "the English medium caters most to the needs of the very rich to moderately rich sections of society, and has the strongest connection with the former colonial power and present Anglo-US/US-European hegemony". The author finds the implicit family intervention for international mobility by enrolling their child in an English medium school in the story of Pikachu, who studied in a school in Bangladesh that follows an overseas curriculum taught by foreign teaching staff. To her,

I think the reason they [my parents] chose Canadian school [in Bangladesh] because ... they wanted me just to have an idea of outside, if I do want to go abroad what it would be like, so, just like a glimpse. (Pikachu)

Kim (2011) explains the above-mentioned type of parents' involvement in children's education from the school level as a strong influencing factor for the development of their aspirations for an overseas degree. From this schooling process, children achieve the ability to assimilate into the society and culture of the host country (Chung et al., 2009). This is because these international schools reproduce and reinforce dominant values and beliefs driven by a dynamic global culture (Baker & LeTendre, 2005). This kind of parents' involvement in children's education may relate to the British colonial policy and practice in Bangladesh to develop English-speaking auxiliary administrators from local people. During the period of the British administration (1757-1947), most of the students from English medium schools saw themselves in Bangladesh for a while but with an ultimate desire to migrate to an English-speaking country. At present, in Bangladesh, many people consider studying in English medium schools as a tool for economic and social advancement. Education from English medium schools provides individuals with the opportunity to access elite social positions within the country, and the possibility to gain more freedom, high-profile jobs and a life of luxury abroad (Imam, 2005). To ensure this secure and higher standard of living for their children (Waters, 2005, 2006), parents are practising their right as consumers of education and investing money in English-medium education, which provides a foreign environment and the necessary resources to prepare young people for overseas higher education.

Regarding parental support in the decision-making process for overseas higher education, Waters (2006) finds the family's aspiration for 'social class status' to be instrumental in the exercise of 'parental choice' in children's mobility. Similarly, by analysing the socially distributed benefits available to internationally mobile students, researchers identify overseas higher education as an upgraded social class-maker (M. Singh et al., 2007) and a victory for the family (Choi & Nieminen, 2013). For this reason, families and ultimately the children are under pressure to succeed (Waters, 2005): firstly in the local education system, and eventually in the top-ranked overseas universities. From early childhood, many Bangladeshi parents convey the notion that most overseas universities are providing a better education than local universities. This implicit family intervention for achieving a certain social class status emerges from Farhan's account. Now studying at one of the best Australian universities, he expresses his story of entering one of the globally higher-ranked universities in Australia:

My parents always wanted me to be the best at school, the best in the class, and everything. I was ended up getting good grades, and so, yea that's why I never looked down all I want to grow up that is why I wanted to study in the best university. (Farhan)

In this context, it can be suggested that to see their desires for social status in reality, many Bangladeshi parents give importance to 'position and ranking' and provide psychological and educational interventions to their children from the early years. In other words, the family develops the desire among the children to be the best in the school or community. Family interventions also develop young students' dreams and desire to study at one of the best overseas universities. From the above analysis, it can be said that the availability of quality transnational higher education in Bangladesh might create implicit family motivation for that.

Explicit Motivation

Besides selecting and doing well in school, familial norms play a substantial explicit role in educational decision-making at the tertiary level, especially across different Asian countries, which has been evident in literature (Brooks & Waters, 2010; Choi & Nieminen, 2013; W. Liu, 2016). Moreover, young people from families with direct experience of international higher education are most likely to be internationally mobile than students from the family without direct experience (Pimpa, 2005). Like many of the participants, Fazi says that one of his family members who studied and started living abroad motivated him to become physically mobile pursuing higher education. According to him,

I have always had this thing for abroad studies. Because my elder brother also studied from the UK, he just finished his graduation. So, being he is my elder brother I took him as an idol, so I thought since he is studying abroad is something to attract obviously. (Fazi)

In the stories of the participants, it is evident that family members play an explicitly influential role to develop the spatial consciousness that motivates young students to be internationally mobile in undertaking higher education. As an example, Fariha's father took one of the problems in Bangladesh, namely corruption, and linked it with higher education, job prospects and future life to motivate her to pursue international mobility:

He [my father] always said that Bangladesh is not a place where you can live, pursue your higher education, or do a job because it is already corrupted. So, it is better to go … abroad but not in Bangladesh. (Fariha)

Similarly, Chung et al. (2009) in their study found the appeal of New Zealand society as a higher education destination to Chinese students comes from its high level of fairness and honesty and low corruption. In the list of most corrupted countries, according to Transparency International's corruption perceptions index, the position of Bangladesh is 143rd out of 180 in ascending order (R. Islam, 2018). The position in the corruption index reveals that everyone in this country is more or less affected directly or indirectly by this negative practice. In Bangladesh, the projected number of tertiary enrolments in 2026 is 4.6 million (Monitor, 2017) while some 31,737 people, i.e. 0.7%, will be globally mobile for higher education in 2025 (Banks et al., 2007). As economically and socially privileged groups of people are most likely to grab the opportunities available in the globalised higher education market (Altbach et al., 2010; Lörz et al., 2016), this big difference between total enrolments and international mobility for higher education in Bangladesh indicates that a very few financially capable parents will be sending their children overseas for higher education.

In this situation, it can be argued that this international mobility is not happening because of the Bangladeshi cultural and spatial 'push' factors but, rather, that it is a 'push-pull' factor between neoliberal global imaginaries and individual (family members and young students) desires. To attain a higher standard of living by participating in overseas higher education, provoked by family members, some young Bangladeshi students use their family funds and prove themselves as successful choosers in the global free market of education.

Like developing spatial consciousness, family members play an explicit role to increase awareness among the young Bangladeshi students regarding the present and future demands of the job market in Bangladesh and the valuation of overseas degrees in the globalised world. Privileged families are in a situation to position themselves as the choosers in the education market who can reject the domestic education system and chase global alternatives. This investment brings international credentials (Waters, 2012) for their children and its associated rewards (Jung, 2013) (e.g. social status and future income) at home. Anisul, one of the research participants, describes how his parents motivated him for an overseas degree explaining its importance in the job market:

They [my parents] said that job sector in Bangladesh is not good enough … and they want me to be highly qualified, even if I have to go back to Bangladesh so that I can get a job in a higher position, so that is the main thing. They also believe that if I have a degree from abroad, I might be able to get a job in Bangladesh easily. (Anisul)

Conversely, none of the participants mentioned family motivation for their education, which Bauman (2003) refers to as education for critical consciousness as global citizens. Several studies also reveal that a family's explicit interventions in the global mobility of their young student/s are driven by the perceived possibility of the student/s' economic gain, which outweighs educational achievements (e.g., Bodycott, 2009; Hong Nguyen, 2013; Pimpa, 2003). Family intentions include an overseas academic degree, improved employment options in the host or home country, immigration prospects in the host country, developed life experience and social security.

The explicit role of the family in young students' international mobility for higher education is not only limited to developing spatial and career consciousness but also concerns the choice of destination. Studies on higher education destinations suggest that friendship networks, social relationships, familiarity with other countries and family travel are implicitly influencing educational mobility (Brooks & Waters, 2010; M. Singh et al., 2007). Similarly, expectations from family members have a great explicit impact on young students' decision in choosing a country, academic programme and institution. The collected data also suggest that family members of the participants played a strong explicit role in selecting the country, university and discipline of study. For example, Fahmid's father travels to different countries and suggested Australia as his higher education destination:

My father came to Australia many times, and he thought it is a good country to study my higher education. (Fahmid)

In the context of selecting a better destination, Cubillo, Sánchez, and Cerviño (2006) and Perez-Encinas and Rodriguez-Pomeda (2018) find that prospective education consumers consider various aspects related to present and future living in the host country. In a similar study, J. K. N. Singh, Schapper, and Jack (2014) suggest Malaysia as a potential destination for many Asian young students for higher education because of its safe environment, multicultural practices, low tuition and living cost and geographical proximity. However, one of the research participants' father rejected Malaysia because of its image as a workforce importer country in Bangladesh. According to my participant Tamal,

He [my father] told me like if you go somewhere overseas why not are you going to Canada, Australia, New Zealand or the USA. Okay, so he told me like if someone goes for Malaysia, he goes for work or something like that, he does not go for study there. (Tamal)

Here, Tamal's father expressed his desire for a higher status through his son's overseas education, while every year a significant number of young Bangladeshi students go for higher education in Malaysia. Similarly, family members present the positive image of an educational institution to young students to motivate them to be part of a world-renowned university for a better future. Family members' explicit intervention in university selection is evident in the story of Dina:

When I got the [admission offer] letter from Eastern University I mention it to my mom because she was [the] first person who said just give it a shot and she said, as far as I know, Eastern University is a really good reputed university. (Dina)

The narratives of the participants suggest that their parents consider overseas degrees as able to bring future career security for the young generation. For this reason, in choosing an academic discipline for their children they show consciousness in analysing the future market prospect of that discipline. For example, Beatrix, who is studying Literature at Southern University, expresses her father's unhappiness regarding her discipline selection:

My family was not happy with the degree I choose. He [my father] wanted me to study medicine, which did not happen, and … as a father, he is like ok fine you can study what you want to study, but I am not going to be super happy about the degree. So he was a little unhappy about the degree I choose. (Beatrix)

Family members calculate their future economic gain from the mobility of their children, where country, university and area of study are the most important. This is because, in the globalised world, these three elements of the global free market of education determine the value of the degree that a student may achieve after completion of a programme. For this reason, in some cases, the role of the family regarding young students' international mobility moves from being just a motivating factor to develop desires among children, and to becoming an imposition, whereby young students do not enjoy the freedom of choice. As mentioned by my participant Imti:

As we all know, the Australian education system is very developing itself, and my family insisted me to come here and take this course [Information Technology and Cloud Computing]. (Imti)

For the author's PhD degree in Australia, his father's intervention was explicit. His father did not enrol him in an English medium school because of his limited investment capacity in children's education, but he always encouraged him to do the best in class and exams. Similarly, his father was not ready to invest money for his overseas PhD degree, but his father drew examples of some people in front of me who were doing overseas degrees with scholarships and tried to encourage me to take that challenge. All of his father's explicit interventions contributed to his development as a potential consumer of global education; however, because of his limited investment capacity, he was not readily a 'chooser' but was dependent on receiving a scholarship. The reason for his father's continuous interventions for his higher education in an abroad country was not to see him as a moral global citizen but to create a greater opportunity for improved status in his society for himself, and to see him as a successful actor in the labour market of the globalised world. In contrast to his experience, Vergolini and Vlach (2017) find that high-performing students from less wealthy families show a lower probability of becoming mobile and pursuing higher education abroad considering it a risky field of investment. Besides, Lörz et al. (2016) mention that most students from lower economic backgrounds are showing a lower intention to go abroad for higher education as a result of their low performance in previous educational tests and events. However, in Bangladesh, the number of high-performing students from lower economic backgrounds is very less in number and many of them show less interest to go abroad to pursue higher education but a secured government job in the home country.

In Bangladesh, parents tend to feel proud of their child's overseas education as most of them consider it a status symbol. In other words, in Bangladesh, participation in international higher education by children brings families status in their community. At present, the iPhone has become a revolutionary status symbol in many Asian countries (Lasco, 2015; Marginson, 2006; Roy, 2014; Toptal et al., 2015). The author argues that the status that comes from a person's overseas higher education is similar to having an iPhone in Asian society. To achieve this status through the next generation, parents plan, save and invest money in their children's schooling, and at the end of this race, they invest in higher education at an overseas university. To fulfil the purpose of bringing social status and fulfilling their economic desire through their children's international mobility pursuing higher education, a family makes interventions on the next generation through school selection, contributing towards the development of consciousness about comparative cultural practice, future career aspects and determining mobility destinations. To some extent, family members make strategic decisions about their child's overseas education in a way that might secure an economic and social advantage for the whole family.

In this context, it can be argued that the family members of 'enlightened classes' make interventions about young generations' international mobility that are likely to bring wealth faster than ever before. In other words, family interventions are the result of a social imagination about a wider set of possible lives for young students in other parts of the world that they did not enjoy before. Thus, in the global society of consumers, consumerist family interventions are affecting young Bangladeshi students' international mobility in pursuit of higher education in Australia. The visible neoliberal consumerist desires among young Bangladeshi students and their family members are the by-product of global media representations of the poor economic condition, political practices and standard of life in Bangladesh on the one hand, and the alluring aspiration for unlimited possibilities of a better life in the developed countries on the other. In this situation, TNE can be an alternative of overseas higher education for Bangladeshi students ensuring linkage with globally renowned universities and providing degrees in market demanding disciplines.

CONCLUSION

In this chapter, the author analysed the stories of some young Bangladeshi students on their physical mobility pursuing higher education in Australian universities and discussed the family factors behind this mobility. Family members consider the international mobility of their children pursuing higher education in the developed country as a powerful and stratifying factor for them in their community and society. Within the framework of neoliberal imaginaries, family members develop these imaginations, and they transfer these to the young students through implicit and explicit mechanisms. The author argues that young students' desire for mobility is a constructed desire, where their families are the first ones to stoke it. Moreover, this understanding of young students' dreams and desires for international mobility gives an essential base for further study to investigate Bangladeshi students' present life in the Australian community and future aspirations after graduating from an Australian university. Finally, transnational higher education can be seen as an alternative to international mobility for higher education. Transnational higher education, on one hand, can meet the family expectations of the young people related to higher education. On the other hand, it will address the quality and cost issues for the host country. Moreover, transnational higher education will create new opportunities for the host countries to expand quality higher education in developing countries like Bangladesh.

REFERENCES

Al-Quaderi, G. G., & Al Mahmud, A. (2010). English literature at English-medium schools of Bangladesh: The question of culture. *Pedagogy, Culture & Society*, *18*(2), 211–226. doi:10.1080/14681366.2010.488046

Altbach, P. G., Reisberg, L., & Rumbley, L. E. (2010). Tracking a global academic revolution. *Change: The Magazine of Higher Learning*, *42*(2), 30–39. doi:10.1080/00091381003590845

Annells, M. (2006). Triangulation of qualitative approaches: Hermeneutical phenomenology and grounded theory. *Journal of Advanced Nursing*, *56*(1), 55–61. doi:10.1111/j.1365-2648.2006.03979.x PMID:16972918

Ary, D., Jacobs, L. C., Sorensen, C. K., & Walker, D. (2013). *Introduction to research in education*. Cengage Learning.

Bahna, M. (2018). Study choices and returns of international students: On the role of cultural and economic capital of the family. *Population Space and Place*, *24*(2), e2082. doi:10.1002/psp.2082

Bailey, W. (2021). Parental influence and HE decision making: The continuing power of local culture. *Journal of Further and Higher Education*, *45*(2), 149–161. doi:10.1080/0309877X.2020.1744540

Baker, D., & LeTendre, G. K. (2005). *National differences, global similarities: World culture and the future of schooling*. Stanford University Press. doi:10.1515/9781503624870

Baltar, F., & Brunet, I. (2012). Social research 2.0: Virtual snowball sampling method using Facebook. *Internet Research*, *22*(1), 57–74. doi:10.1108/10662241211199960

Banks, M., Olsen, A., & Pearce, D. (2007). *Global student mobility: An Australian perspective five years on*. IDP Education Pty Ltd.

Bauman, Z. (1998a). *Globalization: The human consequences*. Columbia University Press.

Bauman, Z. (1998b). On glocalization: Or globalization for some, localization for some others. *Thesis Eleven*, *54*(1), 37–49.

Bauman, Z. (1999). The self in a consumer society. *The Hedgehog Review*, *1*(1), 35–40.

Bauman, Z. (2003). Educational challenges of the liquid-modern era. *Diogenes*, *50*(197), 15–26. doi:10.1177/039219210305000103

Bauman, Z. (2005). Work, consumerism and the new poor. In T. May (Ed.), *Issues in society*. Open University Press.

Bauman, Z. (2009). *Does ethics have a chance in a world of consumers?* Harvard University Press.

Bauman, Z. (2013a). Liquid modernity. In *Polity*. Polity.

Bauman, Z. (2013b). *Postmodernity and its discontents*. New York University Press.

Bauman, Z. (2014). *Wasted lives: Modernity and its outcasts*. John Wiley & Sons.

Bauman, Z., & Donskis, L. (2013). Moral blindness: The loss of sensitivity in liquid modernity. *Polity.*

Bhandari, R., & Blumenthal, P. (2011). *International students and global mobility in higher education: National trends and new directions*. Palgrave Macmillan. doi:10.1057/9780230117143

Bodycott, P. (2009). Choosing a higher education study abroad destination: What mainland Chinese parents and students rate as important. *Journal of Research in International Education*, *8*(3), 349–373. doi:10.1177/1475240909345818

Brinkmann, S. (2013). *Qualitative interviewing*. Oxford University Press. doi:10.1093/acprof:oso bl/9780199861392.001.0001

Brooks, R., & Abrahams, J. (2018). Higher education students as consumers? Evidence from England. In N. Ingram & A. Tarabini (Eds.), *Educational choices, aspirations and transitions in Europe : systemic, institutional and subjective challenges*. Routledge. doi:10.4324/9781315102368-11

Brooks, R., & Waters, J. (2010). Social networks and educational mobility: The experiences of UK students. *Globalisation, Societies and Education*, *8*(1), 143–157. doi:10.1080/14767720903574132

Brooks, R., & Waters, J. (2011). *Student mobilities, migration and the internationalization of higher education*. Palgrave Macmillan. doi:10.1057/9780230305588

Brooks, R., & Waters, J. (2015). The hidden internationalism of elite English schools. *Sociology*, *49*(2), 212–228. doi:10.1177/0038038514525517

Cao, C., Zhu, C., & Meng, Q. (2016). A Survey of the Influencing Factors for International Academic Mobility of Chinese University Students. *Higher Education Quarterly*, *70*(2), 200–220. doi:10.1111/hequ.12084

Choi, S. H.-J., & Nieminen, T. A. (2013). Factors influencing the higher education of international students from Confucian East Asia. *Higher Education Research & Development*, *32*(2), 161–173. doi:10.1080/07294360.2012.673165

Chung, K.-C., Holdsworth, D. K., Li, Y., & Fam, K.-S. (2009). Chinese "Little Emperor", cultural values and preferred communication sources for university choice. *Young Consumers*, *10*(2), 120–132. doi:10.1108/17473610910964705

Commonwealth. (2016). Youth. *The Commonwealth.* https://thecommonwealth.org/youth

Creswell, J. W. (2013). *Qualitative inquiry and research design: Choosing among five approaches*. Sage Publications.

Cubillo, J. M., Sánchez, J., & Cerviño, J. (2006). International students' decision-making process. *International Journal of Educational Management*, *20*(2), 101–115. doi:10.1108/09513540610646091

Cuzzocrea, V., & Mandich, G. (2015). Students' narratives of the future: Imagined mobilities as forms of youth agency? *Journal of Youth Studies*, *19*(4), 552–567. doi:10.1080/13676261.2015.1098773

Dias Lopes, A. (2020). International mobility and education inequality among Brazilian undergraduate students. *Higher Education*, *80*(4), 779–796. doi:10.100710734-020-00514-5

Elliott, A., & Urry, J. (2010). *Mobile lives*. Routledge. doi:10.4324/9780203887042

Flick, U. (2008). *Designing qualitative research*. Sage Publications.

Forman, J., & Damschroder, L. (2007). Qualitative content analysis. In L. A. S. Liva Jacoby (Ed.), *Empirical methods for bioethics: A primer* (Vol. 11, pp. 39–62). Emerald Group Publishing Limited. doi:10.1016/S1479-3709(07)11003-7

Gaskell, C. (2013). 'Isolation and distress'?(Re) thinking the place of emotions in youth research. In L. van Blerk & M. Kesby (Eds.), *Doing Children's Geographies: Methodological Issues in Research with Young People* (pp. 404–439). Routledge.

Giralt, R. M., & Bailey, A. J. (2010). Transnational familyhood and the liquid life paths of South Americans in the UK. *Global Networks*, *10*(3), 383–400. doi:10.1111/j.1471-0374.2010.00294.x

Hannam, K., Sheller, M., & Urry, J. (2006). Mobilities, immobilities and moorings. *Mobilities*, *1*(1), 1–22. doi:10.1080/17450100500489189

Haque, S. (2021). In-country international higher education: The right step forward. *The Daily Star*. https://www.thedailystar.net/opinion/news/country-international-higher-education-the-right-step-forward-2107257

Hong Nguyen, C. (2013). Vietnamese international student mobility: Past and current trends. *Asian Education and Development Studies*, *2*(2), 127–148. doi:10.1108/20463161311321411

Imam, S. R. (2005). English as a global language and the question of nation-building education in Bangladesh. *Comparative Education*, *41*(4), 471–486. doi:10.1080/03050060500317588

Islam, M. T. (2019). (Re)searching for the development of a conceptual model of education for citizenship in the context of young people's globalised mobility in higher education. *Globalisation, Societies and Education*, *17*(2), 194–207. doi:10.1080/14767724.2019.1583093

Islam, M. T. (2021). Cultural cultivation for the mobility of Bangladeshi higher education students in Australia. *Higher Education Research & Development*, *41*(5), 1572–1585. doi:10.1080/07294360.2021.1902950

Islam, M. T. (2022a). (Un)employability and (un)employment issues towards international mobility for higher education. In P. O. de Pablos, X. Zhang, & M. N. Almunawar (Eds.), *Education Institutions, Skills, and Jobs in the Digital Era: Toward a More Inclusive and Resilient Society*. IGI Global. doi:10.4018/978-1-6684-5914-0.ch008

Islam, M. T. (2022b). Bauman or Appadurai? In theorising mobilities of the Southern higher education students in the North. In K. Jermsittiparsert, P. Suanpang, A. Nuemaihom, & P. Siriattaku (Eds.), *Handbook of Research on Current Trends in Asian Education, Psychology, and Sociology*. IGI Global.

Islam, M. T. (2022c). Media mediation on academic advancement for youths' international mobility pursuing higher education. In S. Bansal, V. Ahuja, V. Chaturvedi, & V. Jain (Eds.), *Multidisciplinary Perspectives Towards Building a Digitally Competent Society*. IGI Global. doi:10.4018/978-1-6684-5274-5.ch012

Islam, R. (2018). Bangladesh ranks 143rd in corruption index. *Dhaka Tribune*. https://www.dhakatribune.com/bangladesh/2018/02/22/tib-bangladesh-progresses-two-positions-corruption-perceptions-index/

Jung, J. Y. (2013). Adolescent Decision-Making Processes Regarding University Entry: A model incorporating cultural orientation, motivation and occupational variables. *Tertiary Education and Management, 19*(2), 97–111. doi:10.1080/13583883.2012.747107

Junge, M. (2008). Bauman on ambivalence: Fully acknowledging the ambiguity of ambivalence. In M. H. Jacobsen (Ed.), *The sociology of Zygmaunt Bauman: Challenges and critique* (pp. 41–56). Routledge.

Kim, J. (2011). Aspiration for global cultural capital in the stratified realm of global higher education: Why do Korean students go to US graduate schools? *British Journal of Sociology of Education, 32*(1), 109–126. doi:10.1080/01425692.2011.527725

Knight, J. (2016). Transnational Education Remodeled: Toward a Common TNE Framework and Definitions. *Journal of Studies in International Education, 20*(1), 34–47. doi:10.1177/1028315315602927

Larose, S., Duchesne, S., Litalien, D., Denault, A.-S., & Boivin, M. (2019). Adjustment Trajectories During the College Transition: Types, Personal and Family Antecedents, and Academic Outcomes. *Research in Higher Education, 60*(5), 684–710. doi:10.100711162-018-9538-7

Lasco, G. (2015). The smartphone as status symbol. *Philippine Daily Inquirer*. https://opinion.inquirer.net/89605/the-smartphone-as-status-symbol

Lee, M., & Wright, E. (2016). Moving from elite international schools to the world's elite universities: A critical perspective. *International Journal of Comparative Education and Development, 18*(2), 120–136. doi:10.1108/IJCED-01-2016-0002

Lee, R. L. M. (2005). Bauman, liquid modernity and dilemmas of development. *Thesis Eleven, 83*(1), 61–77.

Liu, W. (2016). The international mobility of chinese students: A cultural perspective. *Canadian Journal of Higher Education, 46*(4), 41–59. doi:10.47678/cjhe.v46i4.186143

Liu, Y. (2019). Choices, risks and rational conformity: Extending Boudon's positional theory to understand higher education choices in contemporary China. *Higher Education, 77*(3), 525–540. doi:10.100710734-018-0285-7

Lörz, M., Netz, N., & Quast, H. (2016). Why do students from underprivileged families less often intend to study abroad? *Higher Education, 72*(2), 153–174. doi:10.100710734-015-9943-1

Louis, C., Lawrence, M., & Keith, M. (2007). *Research methods in education*. Routledge.

Marginson, S. (2006). Dynamics of national and global competition in higher education. *Higher Education, 52*(1), 1–39. doi:10.100710734-004-7649-x

MoE. (2010). National Education Policy-2010 (M. of Education (ed.)). Government of People's Republic of Bangladesh.

Monitor. (2017). Bangladesh: Middle class growth helping to drive demand for study abroad. *Monitor.* https://monitor.icef.com/2017/02/bangladesh-middle-class-growth-helping-to-drive-demand-for-study-abroad/

Perez-Encinas, A., & Rodriguez-Pomeda, J. (2018). International students' perceptions of their needs when going abroad: Services on demand. *Journal of Studies in International Education, 22*(1), 20–36. doi:10.1177/1028315317724556

Pimpa, N. (2003). The influence of family on Thai students' choices of international education. *International Journal of Educational Management, 17*(5), 211–219. doi:10.1108/09513540310484931

Pimpa, N. (2005). A family affair: The effect of family on Thai students' choices of international education. *Higher Education, 49*(4), 431–448. doi:10.100710734-004-2825-6

Roy, S. (2014). Status insanity: Why the iPhone is the perfect status symbol. In *Huffington Post* https://www.huffingtonpost.com/sandip-roy/status-insanity-why-the-i_b_5801748.html

Sadler, G. R., Lee, H., Lim, R. S., & Fullerton, J. (2010). Recruitment of hard-to-reach population subgroups via adaptations of the snowball sampling strategy. *Nursing & Health Sciences, 12*(3), 369–374. doi:10.1111/j.1442-2018.2010.00541.x PMID:20727089

Schmidt, C. (2004). The analysis of semi-structured interviews. In U. Flick, E. von Kardoff, & I. Steinke (Eds.), *A companion to qualitative research* (pp. 253–258). Sage Publications.

Sheller, M. (2014). Sociology after the mobilities turn. In P. Adey, D. Bissell, K. Hannam, P. Merriman, & M. Sheller (Eds.), *The Routledge handbook of mobilities* (pp. 65–74). Routledge.

Siddiqui, K., & Jasim, M. M. (2022). Why brain drain is set to rise. *The Business Standard.* https://www.tbsnews.net/bangladesh/migration/why-brain-drain-set-rise-403834

Singh, J. K. N., Schapper, J., & Jack, G. (2014). The importance of place for international students' choice of university: A case study at a Malaysian university. *Journal of Studies in International Education, 18*(5), 463–474. doi:10.1177/1028315314523990

Singh, M., Rizvi, F., & Shrestha, M. (2007). Student mobility and the spatial production of cosmopolitan identities. In K. N. Gulson & C. Symes (Eds.), *Spatial theories of education: Policy and geography matters* (pp. 195–214). Routledge.

Toptal, V. M., Toptal, & Vogel, M. (2015). *Does owning an iPhone elevate a persons social standing in society?* Quora. https://www.quora.com/Does-owning-an-iPhone-elevate-a-persons-social-standing-in-society

UGC. (2020). *46th Annual Report 2019.*[Data set]. UGC.

UGC. (2022). *List of Universities.* UGC. http://www.ugc-universities.gov.bd/public-universities

UNDESA. (2013). *Definition of youth* (Issue 10/08/2016). United Nations Department of Economic and Social Affairs. https://www.un.org/esa/socdev/documents/youth/fact-sheets/youth-definition.pdf

Vergolini, L., & Vlach, E. (2017). Family background and educational path of Italian graduates. *Higher Education, 73*(2), 245–259. doi:10.100710734-016-0011-2

Waters, J. L. (2005). Transnational family strategies and education in the contemporary Chinese diaspora. *Global Networks*, *5*(4), 359–377. doi:10.1111/j.1471-0374.2005.00124.x

Waters, J. L. (2006). Geographies of cultural capital: Education, international migration and family strategies between Hong Kong and Canada. *Transactions of the Institute of British Geographers*, *31*(2), 179–192. doi:10.1111/j.1475-5661.2006.00202.x

Waters, J. L. (2012). Geographies of international education: Mobilities and the reproduction of social (dis)advantage. *Geography Compass*, *6*(3), 123–136. doi:10.1111/j.1749-8198.2011.00473.x

Weiss, F., & Steininger, H.-M. (2013). Educational family background and the realisation of educational career intentions: Participation of German upper secondary graduates in higher education over time. *Higher Education*, *66*(2), 189–202. doi:10.100710734-012-9598-0

Yin, R. K. (2003). *Case study research: Design and methods*. Sage publications.

Chapter 14
Understanding Chinese Learners in Transnational Higher Education in China

Yi-Mei Chen
Jiaying University, China

Yan Wei
https://orcid.org/0000-0002-7187-9433
Xi'an Jiaotong-Liverpool University, China

ABSTRACT

Chinese students have become the largest share of international students in many countries. Meanwhile, the number of transnational higher education (TNHE) programmes has reached a new high in China. This makes it exceptionally important for teachers whose own cultural and educational background are very different from Chinese to understand their learners. The study set out to better understand Chinese students in TNHE by studying a case of a Sino-Anglo cooperation university in China. The foreign teachers' and foreign students' views on Chinese students were collected and juxtaposed with Chinese students' own accounts. The qualitative study finds many commonly cited features of East Asian students evident in this research context. However, this study gains insights of these phenomena and strategies from the very experienced expatriate teachers, who demonstrated a good understanding of their Chinese students. The authors propose a new approach to teach Chinese students. This study is believed to be of reference to teaching in TNHE in vast contexts with students from Confucian heritage cultures (CHC).

INTRODUCTION

Transnational education (TNE) "refers to study programs or educational services in which the learners are located in a country different from the one where the awarding institution is based" (UNESCO/Council of Europe, 2001). Universities have been actively seeking opportunities to expand their educational mobility globally to other countries through international cooperation, whether this is out of commercial interests

DOI: 10.4018/978-1-6684-5226-4.ch014

or for internationalization (Hou, Montgomery, & McDowell, 2014). This international cooperation type of Transnational Higher Education (TNHE) can take the form of branch campuses, franchised degree programs, or partnerships with local universities. Especially with the aid of online learning, TNHE has become a huge global business (Hou et al., 2014).

Chinese students have accounted for a vast proportion in both international cooperation of TNHE and overseas studies. In 1978, there were just a few international exchange activities among universities in China. After the accession of the WTO in 2001, when China officially opened the TNHE market to foreign education partners, consequently, TNHE programmes had increased to 712 by the following year (Mok & Marginson, 2021). Further, TNHE in China has been greatly enhanced after the announcement of the Regulations of the People's Republic of China on Chinese-Foreign Cooperation in Running Schools in 2003, and the issuing of Measures for the Regulations of the People's Republic of China on Chinese-Foreign Cooperation in Running Schools in 2004 (Li, 2018). According to the Ministry of Education (MOE) (2022a), the number of TNHE programmes has reached more than 1230. The reasons for China to embrace "Chinese foreign cooperation in running schools" (in Chinese: Zhong Wai He Zuo Ban Xue) include learning advanced scholarships in developed countries, pushing internationalisation in China, as well as saving students' expenditure of studying abroad (Hou, et al., 2014). The UK is the largest TNHE provider, followed by the USA and Australia (Hou et al., 2014).

On the other hand, following the year after China's accession to the WTO, more than 100,000 students enrolled in universities overseas (Mok & Marginson, 2021). According to the MOE (2022b), between 2016 and 2019, over 2,510,000 Chinese involved in overseas studies. In the UK, Chinese students have formed the majority of international students, their population having increased by 50% over the five-year period 2016/17 to 2020/21 (HESA, 2022). In 2020/21, 360,000 Chinese account for one third of international students in the U.S., as the largest export country, while the UK stands second with 240,000 Chinese students (Tencent, 2022).

National, historical, socio-cultural and educational perspectives contribute to shaping learners' attributes and attitudes. Given China's unique historical and cultural background, Chinese learners' general characteristics are perceivably very different from those of their Western counterparts (Dai & Garcia, 2019). TNHE teachers must take their attributes into consideration. Only when teachers fully understand their students can they provide students with the most suitable education. However, this is particularly challenging to TNHE teachers who come from very different educational backgrounds from those of Chinese students (Wang, 2011; Zhou & Wei, 2021). With such a great deal of Chinese learners in TNHE, either in their home country or abroad, it is an important issue worthy of attention. However, very few studies have been focusing on this.

The current study set out to better understand Chinese students by studying a case in a Sino-British cooperation university in China. The TNHE teachers' and non-Chinese classmates' views on Chinese students were collected and juxtaposed with Chinese students' own accounts. It is hoped that suggestions and implications made based on this case study can be useful for TNHE policymakers and educators to offer better instruction to Chinese students, and to shed light on enhancing the quality of teaching and learning in various contexts with students from Confucian Heritage Cultures (CHC).

TNE and TNHE

Globalization has caused dramatic impacts in diverse domains, including the social, economic and political. It has also led the evolution of the knowledge-based economy towards the dissolution of territorial borders and closer interconnectedness of different countries. It has driven the mobility of higher education in unprecedently rates and directions (Mok, 2003). Foreseeing higher education's potential to be a lucrative global business, higher education institutions (HEIs) in developed countries are keen to sell their knowledge-based products, initially by attracting international students, and then taking steps further to establish branches or alternatives in the territories of 'buying countries'. Asia and Latin American countries, on the other hand, in order to meet the urgent high demand for international talents, are not only accelerating sending their students to study overseas, but also starting opening their doors welcoming knowledge providers to set up or cooperate with educational institutes in their own territories. Information technology has given rise to online or distance learning. This makes TNHE no longer confined to space and location. "Transnational Higher Education is becoming a popular format within international student mobility in the 21st century" (Hou, et al., 2014: 2).

International branch campuses and twinning programmes have been prevalent forms of TNHE. A branch campus means that a foreign sending parent HEI establishes a satellite campus in a host country. It is independent since it designs its own curriculum, delivers academic programmes, and grants qualifications without cooperation with local HEIs. A franchise programme, also called twinning programme in some countries, involves a foreign HEI setting up an independent university in the host country, and offering franchised academic programmes with no collaboration with a local HEI, either. Foreign sending HEIs provide curriculum, supervise programme delivery, and grant qualification. Both branch campuses and franchise universities are under national regulations of both host and sending countries; their faculty can be fly-in, expatriate or locally hired (Knight, 2016).

Other forms of TNHE programmes involved with collaboration with local HEIs have emerged, for instance, joint/double/multiple (JDM) degree programs. JDM means that foreign HEIs cofound or codevelop new universities with a local partner. Both HEIs are responsible for the development and delivery of the curriculum and programmes. Articulation allows further study in the foreign sending university after acquiring credits from a local host country HEI, which are recognized by the foreign sending HEI. JDM and articulation have different combinations of qualifications. For example, a joint degree programme offers one qualification with both foreign and local HEIs on certificate, while a double degree program offers two qualifications—one certificate/qualification from each partner (Knight, 2016).

In China, articulation programmes have been popular in TNHE (Dai & Garcia, 2019). Modes of articulation programmes have been developed, such as 2+2 and 3+1. In the 2+2 mode, undergraduate students usually study in China for two years, and then they can opt to move to the foreign sending university for another two years. Students can benefit from experiencing both Chinese and foreign education in one programme (Dai & Garcia, 2019) and saving expensive tuition for overseas study.

LITERATURE REVIEW

This section reviews some issues concerning Chinese students' characteristics which have been commonly drawn from the literature. We look at them from national, historical, cultural and educational influences, and discuss how these influences can manifest Chinese students' attributes and attitudes.

Collectivism

Chinese are highly collectivistic nationals (Oyserman, Coon & Kemmelmeier, 2002). Opposite to individualists, they put collective interests beyond their own benefits. Thus, Chinese students would not want to occupy the class time asking teachers questions which might only concern themselves (Xie, 2009). Collectivism values harmony; Chinese students tend to remain silent even when they do not agree with their classmates' views in order to maintain harmony. Lee (2007) conducted a questionnaire-based study on 131 East Asian students' oral participation in American university classrooms. Based on Hofstede's (1984) concepts of national cultures, she found that the participants perceived the American university classrooms as individualistic and competitive, while East Asian classrooms as collectivist and hierarchical. In Liu et al. (2019), Chinese university students' mean scores of taking classmates as ingroup members are significantly higher than those of Americans ($M = 4.12$, $SD = 0.67$ vs. $M = 3.11$, $SD = 1.07$; $t(186.2) = 8.73$). Teachers should understand students from these two cultural orientations and adopt appropriate approaches accordingly.

The Issue of 'Face'

Chinese students (also other East Asian students) are concerned about the issue of 'face' (Cortazzi & Jin, 1996). Both local and Western researchers have conducted research investigating the possible causes for Chinese learners' reluctant participation in English classrooms. A common reason is to save face for fear of making mistakes (Cortazzi & Jin, 1996; Wang, 2011). Some prefer to save face by not expressing themselves in class. However, others would take the risk for learning's sake, even when it is likely that they would make mistakes and thus lose face (Huang & van Naerssen, 1987). Tao's (2017) study indicated that even though their societies have become more westernized, over 72% of Chinese and Japanese university students still view saving face in communication very essential. When they act to save face, this could be interpreted differently by teachers. Quick judgements, such as they are simply being shy, not having an answer, or being reluctant to respond, are inappropriate. Understanding their concern for 'face' can help the teacher deal with it, for example, creating safe and encouraging atmospheres to support the students to take risks, as Chen (2016) suggests in teaching Chinese students English as a foreign language (EFL).

Confucian Influences: Modesty and Respect for Teachers

The great Chinese educator and philosopher, Confucius (551-479 BC), has a profound influence on Chinese and CHC descendants. Influenced by his teaching, Chinese people value modesty, respect, look up to teachers and regard them as authority figures (Cortazzi & Jin, 1996; Rao, 1996; Xie, 2009). These values prevent them from easily sharing ideas in class to avoid being taken as the 'show off' (Xie, 2009). Also, to show respect for their teachers, Chinese students do not interrupt teachers with questions, and avoid being perceived as challenging (Cortazzi & Jin 1996; Tan, 2008). Thus, the image of their class manners is often described as sitting quietly. However, this may not be appreciated by foreign teachers and be perceived differently, for example, as lazy or passive (Wang, 2011).

Imparting Knowledge as Teachers' Responsibility

A well-known line in a classic article of Han Yu (768-824 A.D.), a scholar in Dang Dynasty, "Shi zhe [teachers]… Chuan dao [propagate doctrine], shou ye [impart knowledge], jie huo [resolves doubts]" (Shi Shuo), pinpoints the essence of a good teacher's responsibilities. We argue that since ancient times, it has been misinterpreted by many teachers and students from CHC who take its meaning literally. Teachers have long believed that it is their responsibility to impart knowledge, including providing standard answers (Hu, 2002). Teachers' beliefs inevitably conceptualize students' expectations of teachers and shape their beliefs about learning (Brown, 2009). Such beliefs and expectations are undoubtedly different from those who are from, for example, the American educational tradition (Zhou & Wei, 2021).

It is a fallacy that this idea is from Confucius. Actually, Confucius is accredited as the 'Oriental Socrates', since both believed that knowledge is not taught, but generated through questioning and evaluating. Their teaching is inquiry-based, exploring truth through constantly asking and answering between the teacher and students. They both encourage analytical and critical thinking. However, this philosophy of teaching is not inherited by people from CHC.

Memorization and Recitation

Since the Chinese ancient time, memorizing and reciting texts has been valued as one of the best ways of learning (Huang & van Naerssen, 1987). An old Chinese saying states: "When one can understand the essence of and memorize 300 Tang poems, one is sure to be able to compose poems of one's own, even though one is not a poet" (Huang & van Naerssen, 1987: 294). This traditional way of teaching and learning is deep-rooted and still prevailing in education at all levels in China. Memorization and recitation contribute to learning only to some extent. The downside is that it may discourage the development of skills, such as reasoning, inferencing and critical thinking. Chinese students may need more instructions in such skills before being asked to perform higher cognitive levels of tasks.

THE VALUE OF EDUCATION AND CREDENTIALISM

Education has been held in very high esteem in Chinese societies. Students need to take national high school and university entrance examinations (or GaoKao), and they can give priority to the preparation of the examinations with full family support (Yi & Wu, 2004). The fact that in China, study has always bounded with examinations may date back to Keju (Imperial Examination System) era, which originated in the Sui Dynasty (581–618 A.D.) and lasted through the Qing Dynasty (1644–1911 A.D.). After standing out from the multi-tier examinations, one could be assigned to be imperial or local officials, so their fate changed, before them a bright future with fame and fortune.

Another factor contributing to the prominent status of education or study and credentialism is a well-known verse in a poem in the Song Dynasty (960–1279 A.D.). To translate it literally: Everything is inferior, but study is supreme, meaning that to be a scholar is superior to anything else. Although time changes, these influences are deep-rooted in CHC societies. The people tend to judge others by their educational levels (Liu, 2012).

These values may shape utilitarian education where the Chinese teachers and students pursue quick success and instant benefits in education, resulting in teacher-centred, test-centred and textbook-centred school education, as it in China has usually been (Li & Walsh, 2011). In order to prepare students well for these national entrance examinations, school teachers often have tight schedules to follow. Under these circumstances, giving lectures seem to be a quick way to deliver the textbook content. This intensifies long-existing teacher-centred and spoon-feeding ways of teaching. On the other hand, Chinese students are used to just listening and relying on teachers, as Cortazzi and Jin (1996) find in comparing Chinese and UK educational practices.

Difficulties for Chinese Students in TNHE Home and Abroad

The educational conceptions result in difficulties for Chinese students in TNHE, either in their home country or abroad. In Dai and Garcia (2019: 372), a Chinese student who attended a China-Australia articulation programme (2+2) found, "I did not think the Chinese experience had many positive influences on my Australian study because they were two very different contexts". Also, there were students in their study missing the traditional Chinese ways of teaching or spoon-feeding, and struggling to immerse themselves in the new environment. This reflects Gu and Maley's (2008) findings ten years earlier; Chinese International students at universities in the UK struggled to shake off the influences from years of receiving teacher-centred and spoon-fed ways of teaching.

On the other hand, the frustration is not limited to Chinese students. Wang (2011) investigated 25 foreign teachers' views on teaching Chinese students in a Southeast Ordinary university. The teachers (from six countries) were shocked, confused and uncomfortable with students' silence, and some even interpreted not answering questions as laziness. Zhou and Wei (2021) report many similar cases in the U.S.

Meanwhile, these accusations of Chinese students' features are also argued to be stereotypical (Straker, 2016). We argue that these may be a magnification of their national, historical, socio-cultural and educational influences. It is important for teachers whose own cultural and educational backgrounds are very different from Chinese to understand their learners, enabling them to offer students the most suitable education. The study aims to better understand Chinese students in TNHE by studying a case of a Sino-Anglo cooperation university in China.

The research questions are:

1. What are Chinese students' attributes in learning in TNHE from the observations of non-Chinese teachers, non-Chinese students, and Chinese students themselves?
2. How differently do Chinese students in TNHE see themselves from how their teachers and foreign classmates perceive them?
3. What factors are shaping Chinese students' attributes in TNHE?
4. What teaching suggestions can be made to best suit Chinese students in TNHE?

METHODOLOGY

This study views learners' attributes, attitudes and behaviours as socially constructed, and thus employs a qualitative case study methodology. This is in line with Merriam's (1998: 6) philosophical assumption that "reality is constructed by individuals interacting with their social worlds". She defines case study research as "an intensive, holistic description and analysis of a bounded phenomenon such as a program, an institution, a person, a process, or a social unit" (p. xiii). The purpose of a case study is to enhance the understanding of the case under study in a particular context from multiple sources (Merriam, 1998; Stake, 1995; Yin, 2002). The case in this study is Chinese students in a Sino-British university in China. The views from their expatriate teachers and non-Chinese classmates were also collected to enable a more holistic understanding of the case in this context.

Research Context

The participants are from an international joint venture university founded by a Chinese university and a British university. The city where the university locates is rich in industry, commerce and tourism. It takes less than half an hour to reach Shanghai by High-Speed Rail. It is the largest independent Sino-Foreign university approved by MOE China. The majority of students studying here are from mainland China. All programmes are taught in English.

It is ranked as a first-tier university in China, based on the students' scores on the College Entrance Examination (GaoKao). It admits students who score within the top 20% in overall subjects of the GaoKao exams, with no specific requirement of students' English level. Most students who choose undergraduate studies at this university have an intention to study for a master degree abroad.

The university offers English for Academic Purposes (EAP) courses to most year 1 and year 2 students. Students are grouped into foundation, standard and advanced level EAP, based on their placement test results. Year 2 EAP is discipline-specific; students are grouped by their programme, yet advanced modules mix programmes. With just a few students from other countries, some EAP course cohorts were entirely Chinese. Class sizes range from 20 to 27 students.

Research Participants

This study recruited thirteen participants through purposive and snowball sampling. The participants are from three groups: five expatriate teachers (hereby referred to as foreign teachers, FTs), three non-Chinese students who have the experiences of having classes with Chinese students (foreign students, FSs), and five Chinese students (CSs).

Five FTs (coded as T1, T2, and so on) were teaching EAP, four males and one female, are native English speakers from the UK, except for T3. Their experiences of teaching Chinese students in TNHE contexts range from three to fourteen years. They all taught international students in other countries before they came to China. Their details are summarised in Table 1 below.

Table 1. Summary of the teachers' teaching experiences

Place of teaching Teacher	Outside China Years/Place of teaching	In China	In this institute/ EAP
T1	14/UK with Chinese	2.5 years/ advanced EAP	
T2	1/Ireland online with Chinese	10	2/ standard
T3	8/Middle East	3/ standard	
T4	4/Australia with Chinese	5.5/ standard	
T5	13/Europe, Latin America	7	5/ advanced

Three FSs (coded as FS1, FS2, FS3) are all females. FS1, a Chinese Indonesian, was a year 2 student in Mechatronics and Robotic Systems (MRS). FS2, a Chinese Indonesian, finished her study in this university, and was carrying on studying a master degree in Biology. FS3, from Africa, was also studying MRS. They passed Level B2 of the Common European Framework of Reference (CEFR) upon entering the university, and their English is presumably further developed during the university.

Five CSs (coded as CS1, CS2, and so on), four males and one female (CS4), were all year 2 students at the School of Advanced Technology, currently taking standard EAP courses. Their English levels were estimated to be B2 (intermediate) to B2+ (upper-intermediate).

Semi-Structured Interviews

This research aims to hear the informants, gain insights and then generate theories from the data. To this end, we took an inductive approach. Therefore, semi-structured interviews were conducted to collect qualitative data. As Cohen, Manion and Morrison (2007: 351) argue, interviews allow researchers to "follow up on unexpected results, or to validate other methods, or to go deeper into the motivation of respondents and their reason for responding as they do".

Attempting to reduce our influence to a minimum, we aimed to avoid leading questions, for example: for FTs and FSs, "Describe a typical class of yours"; "What are your observations on Chinese students?"; For CSs, "What kind of learner do you think you are?"; "Describe a typical class of yours"; "How is your participation typically in class discussion?" Importantly, the CSs were asked questions based on the responses of FTs and FSs. We were cautious about ethical issues.

DATA COLLECTION AND ANALYSIS

Following approval by the university Ethics Committee, the second author approached the participants with consent forms. All participants were informed of the voluntary nature of this study and of their right to reject and withdraw. The interviews for FTs and FSs were conducted one to one, in English. CSs joined focus group interviews in Mandarin. All interviews were conducted by the second author through the Internet, and were audio-recorded with the participants' consents.

Following this, the interview data are entirely qualitative, and the transcriptions were analysed with thematic coding analysis. Similar repeated concepts emerging from the data were grouped into codes, and similar related codes were further grouped into themes (Creswell, 2007). We carried out the coding separately, and then compared it and discussed together to reach agreements. When further questions or confirmation were needed, the second author contacted the participants.

RESULTS AND DISCUSSION

The data reveal that all five CSs' previous education was very similar to the descriptions in the literature, that is, traditional Chinese styles of education. The FTs, FSs and CSs simultaneously perceived some of the educational as well as cultural influences on the Chinese students.

Influences of Traditional Chinese Styles of Education on Learning Methods

All five CSs came from a very traditional educational background. All of them used the term, 'Chuan Tong'(traditional), and three directly used 'Ying Shi' (test-oriented) education to describe the education they received in the past. They refer to "traditional" as rote learning, cramming, teachers imparting knowledge by lectures, and constantly having drills, quizzes and examinations. They explicitly expressed how their past education still has impacts on their current study in the university in the aspects of learning methods and styles.

Memorization - Four CSs have mainly used memorization and are aware that such a learning habit has been carried on since past education. They still mainly use rote learning, and comprehend learning input by finding some exercise sheets and answering questions on them. They are also aware that their critical and creative thinking skills are still underdeveloped. An exception is CS4, who is used to thinking about learning input to comprehend, and often bringing up her own thoughts.

T4's observations meet the CSs' self-reflections. "I don't think the Chinese students here understand that how they're going to be tested is much different here than in a high school context". "Why? Maybe it's because of the habits from the high school system here". "We don't have memory, rote, memorization, and stuff". T4 gave an example to show his students rejecting to try higher levels of practice. "I usually gave about 4 or 5 pieces of homework... One item will be something productive... none of them do the productive task, almost none of them!" FS1 said that she is usually the one who answers questions about critical thinking.

Waiting to be Spoon-Fed - To quote T1, "the majority of students that we teach here and I taught in the UK have mostly come from can we say like traditional Chinese learning environment?" T1 observed that Chinese students "lack engagement, sit quietly in the class expecting expert teachers to impart them with knowledge, and do not feel that it's their role or their place to challenge that knowledge, or to express their own opinion, but a feeling that they need to give the correct answer, even when there's not a correct answer, because they've come from an exam-oriented learning culture". T1's observations are echoed by the CSs. They were instructed very clearly by previous teachers.

Rarely Asking or Answering Questions - T3 commented that Chinese students do not ask questions or offer any answers unless specifically asked. In her words, "They would very, very rarely offer. I never ever got to that stage where they would just like willingly want to do that… Or what I would like to accomplish once is to have more like student led class, but [it never happened]". T5 concluded that Chinese students are "waiting for the teacher to speak, being too cautious about giving answers or waiting for more guidance...".

These were also observed by all FSs. As FS3 observed, "They are not really participating. Actually, they're just listening. Sometimes not really listening, but no one really answers questions or asks questions. It's really hard to get them to answer questions or talk during classes." All FSs also reckon that Chinese students are quieter than non-Chinese students. As FS2 shared, "In classes, they're silent for the most part. I would say when teachers ask questions, they would be a little bit more silent compared to the international students". All of the interviewed CSs agreed with such observations.

Reluctant to Speak - Comparing Chinese students with students from other countries, the FTs concluded that Chinese students are very reluctant to speak. T4 gave some examples: "if you give a class to maybe students from Columbia, we'll say, and you put them in a speaking task, they don't stop speaking. You need to stop them. But these guys, it's hard to push them." T4 recalled his experiences with Vietnamese students when he taught in Australia: "They could be a bit similar. They were reluctant, but a little bit more positive about speaking…I think the Chinese are the most reluctant". T5 pointed out that Chinese students try less to communicate, compared with Latin Americans whom he used to teach: "often the levels of English are lower…they would often be more willing to try and communicate".

The FSs also attribute Chinese students' reluctance to talk to the influences of their past education. FS1 shared that "most of the time, all the Chinese students don't really talk…they said in their high school, they were not really encouraged to talk… I heard from them it's better not to speak when teachers are teaching or even questioning anything". This phenomenon was reported by Chinese students in Wang (2011). When we asked for confirmation from the CSs, two CSs believe it is still true since teachers must keep up with the schedule, which is set based on the GaoKao. Another two experienced some teachers encouraging students to express ideas and question.

Little Idea of Group Work - FS1 reported from her friends' experiences when they have Chinese students in their groups, "there's always two scenarios": "They don't work at all, or they do all the work. It's never like we do it together". All FSs experienced that when they were grouped with Chinese students alone by themselves, Chinese students spoke in Chinese with each other, and then translated back to them. Due to Chinese students being "quite hard to talk to", "in standard class, we are forced to sit with other Chinese" (FS1). This appears not to be the solution. It becomes worse in advanced classes when students are allowed to choose their seats, so usually, international students stick with international students, and Chinese with Chinese.

Three CSs remarked that they are used to independent learning rather than cooperation and discussion. All CSs barely had group work nor discussion experiences at their formal school previously, except for CS3, who regularly had group work activities at his junior high school. CS4 took private classes with foreign teachers who used western teaching modes, such as group work. These experiences prepared her well for university. The rest of the CSs had no foreign teachers before, and thus felt a huge gap between what they had been used to and the new teaching methods of foreign teachers.

Worrying About Grammar

Chinese students worry about making grammatical mistakes; "they feel that their English needs to be perfect" (FS1). T5 made a comparison between Chinese students and Latin Americans. Latin Americans were not so worried about their grammar, but were prepared to try and use their limited English, whereas "often here, Chinese students are too aware of their limitations". FS1 feels the same: "in reality, even for us foreigners, our grammar is usually very bad. Even if our grammar is bad, we still talk". This echoes what a CS stated that it is common for Chinese students to think about grammar, and even translate mentally before speaking. This may be caused by the traditional way of English education, of which the focus has been grammar and accuracy (Chen, 2020).

Different Expectations

All groups of the stakeholders believe that previous educational experiences based on the Chinese educational system and their Chinese teachers have strong influences. Such educational influences also lead to different expectations between Chinese students and their expatriate teachers. This has been common in literature (Straker, 2016; Wang, 2011; Zhou & Wei, 2021). The FTs noticed that their expectations were very different from those of the Chinese students. The mismatches in expectations have been challenges to T1: "Traditional preparation for the GaoKao exam comprised large class sizes, not encouragement to maybe to communicate in class, not encouragement to challenge ideas, not encouragement to challenge their teachers, all of the things that we do encourage or that we say we encourage in a transnational international institution". The CSs have to say: "if you always lower your head, sit and listen to your teachers from the first day in school, then naturally in EAP classes, you are likely to wait to be spoon-fed by the teacher, as usual" (CS4).

T2 and T3 noticed that the areas where Chinese students are from affects these impacts. As T3 concluded, "they come from all over China, they come from different backgrounds. Some may come from the provinces and cities in China that have a lot of experts, and students from there can have a very good ability of English". In contrast, they may have come from places where they had very little exposure to English, as T2 encountered in his first university.

T3 continued, "And then we tried to immerse them not just into English language, but all of our cultures that we brought with us that can be overwhelming as such." In such a case, especially for the latter, the shift to the international university might be "a massive leap", and "they need some time to adjust. It might be too much of a shock pretty much" (T3). Shi's (2006) study in a Shanghai suburb middle school suggested that their classroom culture was changing towards Western classroom culture. This may only be true in the most prosperous areas, such as Shanghai. The speed of change has not reached the majority of other areas in the Chinese territory. CS4 clearly is not from Shanghai: "It is likely that, for us who grew up from our cultural background, we are too used to cramming. Therefore, at age 19, 20, it's like suddenly we are asked to open up to speak, to discuss with peers, to play games, and we feel awkward about it".

Low Levels of English - To our surprise, the Chinese students' English levels in this institute were generally considered to be low by the FTs and the FSs. T4 gave an example of his students' low levels of English abilities: "I had a student, and the lesson was on McDonald's... And I gave the students a chance to think for a minute about McDonald's. So now I asked one student, 'Do you like McDonald's?'… And she's turning to her friend and asking in Chinese, what's he talking about?" T2 and T3 understand that the students' behaviours in class have something to do with where they come from, as aforementioned. On the other hand, T5 found that when communicating with these students on a one-to-one basis, teachers can discover Chinese students' good insights and great understanding.

All FSs used the term, 'language barriers', to describe their interactions with the Chinese students, and considered them to be challenges to studying with Chinese students. FS2, an Indonesian Chinese, found that Chinese students became more willing to talk with her once they knew she could speak Chinese. FS1 noticed, from her limited encounters with Chinese students, that "they are nervous, intimidated by talking to us… I met a girl who kept apologising… A male student was difficult to be understood". Moreover, "Chinese students prefer to use formal and academic English, even for chatting" (FS1). However, as a CS shared, "we can only use some simple vocabulary and phrases to communicate". FS1 continued: "It becomes quite hard for them to interact with international students, because we tend to use informal English", and "they don't really know this". This is obvious evidence of lacking discourse competence, which should be cultivated at high school. However, T2, T5, and all FSs found that although many Chinese students' speaking is weak, their reading and writing are very good. This is a product of credentialism and utilitarianism. The GaoKao does not test speaking.

According to the CSs, the Chinese students often do not understand the very basic ideas from the beginning of the professional courses, but the teachers stick to the teaching schedule and continue. Therefore, they have to study on their own. "In more than 90% of cases, we are self-studying" (CS3). If they engaged in two-hour lectures, they needed to take extra time in finding alternative materials in

Chinese. Therefore, they came up with the idea that "don't waste time listening in class". Some even skipped classes. They went on the Internet, for example, Bilibili (YouTube equivalent), to find resources.

However, self-studying and seeking help from alternative materials in Chinese were perceived by T3 and T5 as Chinese students relying on Chinese. T5 reckoned that the Chinese students rely on translation apps in class. T3 observed that "If they can, they won't listen to an online lecture. They will find a way to subtitle it, not to listen to it or engage in English. They will use apps to translate instructions and everything." She takes this as taking shortcuts. However, these behaviours are not limited to online classes. FSs seem to have more insights into this. FS1 wanted to talk to the Chinese about Robotics, their major, but found that "they don't really know the terms. They usually know them in Chinese". A Chinese student told her that when he wants to learn about math or physics, he usually uses Chinese textbooks.

Cultural, Social and Contextual Influences on Behaviors and Attitudes

Apart from traditional educational influences, the FTs observed some features of Chinese students, which are analysed to be cultural, social and contextual influences. They may interact with each other in a complex manner.

Showing Modest - T5 also attributes Chinese students' lack of participation and reluctance to speak to their modest nature. This was not mentioned by any CSs in the initial interviews, so we asked some follow-up questions. To most of them, being modest has something to do with abilities. "If we do not know much, we know we should remain silent, not giving opinions. If we happen to know something, we should not exaggerate or boast" (CS4). There are also students whose self-esteem is too low underestimating their abilities. A CS made it clear that although they have been brought up to be modest, it is not the main reason for non-participation. For some CSs, it is their inadequate English abilities that discourage them from expressing their ideas, rather than being modest.

Not Enjoying Standing out From the Crowd - T2 met a Chinese student, who is from Shanghai, with very good English level, and is often willing to talk. T2 continued: "He saw the need for participation, and so he was participating". The CSs appreciate such a student who breaks the ice and encourages everyone else to speak. However, four of them feel awkward to play such a role: "It's like I am playing a similar role to the teacher, but I am not the teacher". They normally do not enjoy the limelight, so they opt out. CS4 tried to be the first one to participate in order to warm the atmosphere. However, when no one followed her, she felt intimidated. They all dislike students who speak up too frequently in classes only for showing off or trying to be the centre of attention. They all agreed with a CS's comment that few students are willing to volunteer to break the ice, no matter what their intentions are. Another CS stated: "In our university, students are competitive; they care more about themselves; it is not their business [to encourage the class to share ideas]".

T5 found this feature of Chinese students. He noticed that the Chinese are opposite to "Latin Americans who have to be noisy to make themselves stand out". Once a Chinese student shared with him an expression: "when the wind blows, it will hit the tall trees. If you are a tall tree, then maybe you will get hurt by the wind. So it is better not to be the tall tree". T5 thinks sometimes students just want to be collective to a certain extent. They want to be in the crowd. He feels this is a shame that they can do better, but they are reluctant to make themselves stand out. He found this especially true of female students, who often have valuable thoughts.

Worrying About Losing Face and Criticisms - The CSs in this research context were perceived to be shy and quiet. T3 supposes that it is the shyness that prevents them from speaking. T4 does not believe that shyness is an excuse. He reckons that they do not practice. T2 believed that it is Chinese culture that "Nobody really wants to lose face, so that is another reason why some students do not appear to want to take risks in class". All CSs agree with T2. They care very much what other people think of them. They feel ashamed when making mistakes, as T5 observed. They worry about criticisms from teachers, classmates, or even parents. This echoes Lee's (2007) finding that participation significantly correlated with the fear of negative evaluation. A CS continued: "I am very timid in front of strangers; I choose not to speak if I can". The main challenge for T2 is "trying to make them realize that making mistakes is a normal part of the learning process".

Worrying About Ideas Being Stolen - The reasons above are common conclusions drawn by literature (e.g. Wang, 2011). Students do not want to share ideas because they are afraid that another student will take their idea. This is considered to be a new finding. T5 attributes students' reluctance to share ideas to the competitive atmosphere in this university. He continued: "This is an odd contradiction that we often hear about the idea of collectivism." We took this question back to the CSs, and we are surprised to know that most of them confirmed this viewpoint. Two CSs eventually realized the benefits of sharing ideas in class.

Less Independent - Two FTs believe that most Chinese students' choice of universities and majors are decisions made by their parents. As T4 remarked, "We find that a lot of students do not really like their major, it's their parents' choice, not theirs." The CSs stated that they chose their majors themselves, some for the popularity and prosperous future of this industry while others for the admiration of Bill Gates and Steve Jobs. However, their parents' opinions matter, and they know that their friends may not have so much freedom in choosing their own universities and majors.

The FTs related this impression to the levels of maturity. T3 thought that being sheltered by their parents is a factor behind their quietness: "They are very shy. But then again, being here for nearly 3,4 years, I have come to understand why that is… it's not that much different to what I encountered in the Middle East. My general impression is that in both regions, China and the Middle East, that the students I taught, grew up quite sheltered. Or I suppose within the family banner." T4 considers Chinese students very immature, compared to the Irish students whom he used to teach.

Two CSs agree that many students are overprotected by parents. At home, they only need to study, and their parents take care of the rest. Therefore, they are not as mature as they should be. CS4 pointed out that there are still families with parents who are willing to cultivate their children's independence. In Gu and Maley (2008), the Chinese degree-seekers in the UK found it challenging to be on their own outside class without their parents. Liu and Vogel (2016) found a similar challenge to Chinese students in U.S. universities.

Strategies For Teachers

All three groups of stakeholders recognise that the traditional Chinese education styles and cultural background have profound influences on the students. Some of these influences strike as challenges to Chinese students, their foreign teachers, and their foreign classmates. In this section, we make suggestions, combining the CSs' true voice and the FT's suggestions.

Creating a Secure Environment

This study finds that the CSs' suggestions for increasing participation are very similar to the ones proposed by Chen (2014; 2017) in EFL teaching settings. These include selecting interesting topics, creating relaxing atmospheres as well as reducing class sizes. According to the CSs, topics are a key factor in Chinese students' participation. When they are into the topic, familiar with it, and have some knowledge or ideas about it, they would be keen to participate. Topics that are too academic or too difficult discourage them from speaking. The CSs pointed out that some activities which can improve the atmosphere can further motivate them to participate.

Atmosphere is important, as one CS claimed that even when the topic is academic, if the class atmosphere is lively, everyone is still likely to participate; otherwise, they will remain silent. T4 and T5 use banter and interesting activities to encourage more participation, similar to Oad et al.'s (2020) suggestions. T5 also reminded that in a secure learning environment where Chinese students are not being judged, they could participate well. This is in line with He's (2018) suggestions to deal with common phenomena, such as lack of confidence and fear of negative evaluation.

Chinese students consider the size of classes as an important factor in their willingness to participate. CS1 made it clear that "In big class normally there are more than a hundred students, it would be very odd to try to interact with the teacher… it's like only you and the teacher are involved in class." FS3 noticed that some Chinese students are more willing to talk in seminars when the group size is small. For large classes, breaking them into smaller groups may be a solution.

Mingling with Students - Teachers' attributes also matter. The CSs prefer to have more outgoing, friendly, and interesting teachers who understand the characteristics of Chinese learners. These attributes of teachers make interacting and mingling with students easier. The CSs enjoy classes with these teachers. One CS happened to take T4 as an example: "He is very nice, he does not force us to do childish activities to us, and he enjoys talking with us, so I feel the class atmosphere is okay". Oad et al. (2020) also concluded that interesting teachers and friendly atmospheres help reduce anxiety.

Few of these qualities are mentioned by the FTs, which does not mean that the FTs do not understand their Chinese students. On the contrary, we find that the FTs' observations are mostly precise. All FTs have witnessed their students' progress.

Nominating - T1, T2 and T3 discovered that it works well by nominating students to offer answers. As T3 claimed confidently, "Unless being nominated, there would be very little spontaneous discussion". In T1's words,

I never ask like whole open class questions like, what does anybody think about this? Does anyone have an opinion about that? Nobody will respond. So now I just ask individuals, 'What do you think, Wei?' 'What's your opinion, Sam?' And then they have to respond. Just keep track of who has contributed and who has not contributed, and then go back to students who haven't. Sometimes they need more thinking time.

Nudging, Encouraging and Watching

T3 suggests trying to nudge students and encourage them. She encourages students by saying, "Do not be afraid to try and speak a little bit". Sometimes they are just not used to it. So she goes on: "Give it a try; tell me what you think…". She praises them, saying, "you've done a good job there", "you guys have gone through all the examples you spoke for 2 minutes. Well done!" She also gives them feedback, even if it is just praising or acknowledging. When setting up a group activity or discussion activity, "you have to listen to what they're doing... even if they do not feel like doing something, they will do it because the teachers are watching".

T5 tries to be really friendly and encourage students as much as possible, and tell them: "It's okay to say, 'I don't understand that'". FS3 also suggested that teachers should encourage Chinese students to speak in English, "Also encourage them to ask questions and get them to answer, force them to answer. Sometimes that will be great. More interaction keeps them engaged in the class". For Chinese students who rely on translation apps in class, T5 considered it "a major challenge", and he advised teachers to move around the classroom during classroom activities. Chinese students are respectful to teachers, so this can work.

T2 and T5 thought Chinese students may fear giving an incorrect answer. T2 tries to make students realise that making mistakes is a normal part of the learning process. He tells students:

Yeah, where you got the feeling in primary school, middle school, high school, they have been told like you can't make mistakes or wrong mistakes about that. That is complete rubbish. If you are learning a language, you have got to make mistakes to then learn from, to reflect, to build on, because if you make the mistake, you probably will not make it again.

T2 also cautioned that in the beginning, it is quite a challenge, especially for the lower-level students because they are probably aware that their level is not so good.

Pushing - Apart from using banter, T4 tried to push students. He did not think some of his students live in reality: "they're not very realistic about what they need to do… Many of them in year two seem to think that they can pass the year, but they don't want to speak a word". The pandemic situation makes it worse. When they have online classes, "a lot of students never speak... I have several students that never ever spoke. But the good students try". Therefore, they need pushing, although sometimes they do not like that. He makes students stand up and walk around the room at the start of the lesson with a lively task. To push output, after a listening activity, he shows some false statements and asks them to discuss why they are false. The results are good, as T4 continued, "At the moment, I'm getting about half the class speaking, which I think is not bad by [this university's] standards."

Making Expectations Explicit and Having Patience

The FTs also made suggestions for foreign teachers who come from overseas and have no exposure to teaching Chinese students. The foremost advice is to be culturally aware. There are huge differences in cultural and educational conception between teachers and students. T1 and T3 both suggest making expectations explicit at the start of the course, for example, class norms and rules. For students who come from a traditional education background to shift to an international university, it can be a massive leap, and they need time to adjust. Therefore, T2 advises, "You might have to be extremely patient waiting for that breakthrough, but then maybe when the students feel relaxed, confident enough to do that, then they will do that. So you've got to be patient". FS2 also suggested that teachers need to "take the time and patience to actually understand them, because some of them do have, really, really nice thoughts and ideas, but it is difficult for them to convey those certain points and thoughts in English."

T3 feels it rewarding to witness students passing through the difficult beginning stage, gaining more confidence in speaking and teamwork, and becoming quite engaged in classes. T2 speaking from his own experience: "[Chinese students] maybe a little quiet in the beginning of Semester One. And then I think as time goes by, you built that relationship with students, as normally you would. They become more familiar with each other…then maybe in at least semester one of year one, I think students tend to build that confidence and try to participate more".

Giving More Clear Instructions and Scaffolding

T3 asserts: "There is one thing I know for sure that the Chinese students appreciate being given clear information on everything. So I think it is important to upload PowerPoints, for example, set clear deadlines for things, set reminders. So all this goes back to that they are not grownups yet. And then we need to be mindful of that". T5 noticed that Chinese students need more scaffolding. He suggests that "it can be very useful as a class to start off with some really basic things. No question. So there you go. Are all companies the same? Yes or no? Again, a whole class to say no, if they are used to the idea of a choral response, then it can make it easier for them to talk".

Some strategies should be used in combination, for example, pushing or nominating a student should be accompanied by encouragement and scaffolding in order to boost students' confidence and reduce their anxiety.

Future Directions for Teaching Methods in TNHE

We acquired precious techniques and strategies from very experienced foreign teachers, who demonstrated a good understanding of their Chinese students. These strategies inspire us with some future directions for teachers teaching Chinese students in TNHE.

1. *Forget Where You Come from And Do Not Take Everything At Face Value*

When Chinese students and foreign teachers meet, it is not only Chinese traditional education styles and cultures that make an impact. As T3 reminds, the cultures that teachers bring with them can be as much a shock. Teachers should be very culturally aware, and come with an open mind in several aspects. As T2 suggests:

The students here, the cohort, and the environment are probably completely different… Just accept how it is. Do not think about how you always used to do it and try to apply. That might not work. But I think also for teachers, especially if they haven't taught Chinese students before, is not to make a judgment just based on how much the students respond to you, because that's not everything... You might think the students are really quiet, but they're actually extremely capable. Maybe they are actually waiting for you to nominate them because that is what was common practice for them, rather than they taking the lead and actually volunteering. A lot of students may be just waiting for you to ask for them to participate.

2. *Adapt Teaching Methods to Meet the Students*

Take Chinese students' attributes into consideration when teachers plan their lessons, deliver lessons, and evaluate students' performance. This means teachers need to be more open minded, forget where they came from, and put aside what they are used to doing well in other contexts and what they are always used to. As T2 suggests:

It's the same in any context you need to get on with your students as early as you can. So what's their level? Do you really need to focus on pronunciation? They are probably quite strong at reading. So then what do you need to prioritize? Because it seems that a lot of the classes will be mixed ability, and then how do you deal with that? Yeah. Just enjoy it. You've chosen to come here, so try and enjoy it and maybe you need to adapt your teaching methods to meet the students, but I think with patience you'll find a way to get through it.

This is a realization of a more recent trend of an intercultural view, which calls for a culturally inclusive pedagogy to replace conceiving cultural imperialism or ethnocentrism, treating their own (Western) cultures as dominant and others as deficit (Straker, 2016).

3. Making Good Use of Students' Merits

The factors of Chinese students' quietness are multiple, and some are more obvious than others. The most dominant factors discussed are worrying about losing face and criticisms, not enjoying standing out from the crowd, as well as low spoken English levels. Since they are strong at reading and writing, we suggest activities to enable them to communicate in writing, for example, using the Roundtable activity. A teacher in Chen (2016) asked students to write ideas on an A3-sized whiteboard within a group, and then pass the whiteboard to the next group to further exchange ideas. The students were very engaged and excited to share. Using collaborative e-learning tools, such as Padlet, can also invite students to participate quietly and thus involve more students (Chen, 2022).

Applicability of the Study

Compared with past studies, the challenges faced by Chinese students in TNHE at home as a local student and abroad as an international student are similar in many ways, for example, feeling uncomfortable participating in classroom discussions, asking questions, having open critical arguments, and feeling unfamiliar with the teacher's expectations (Ching et al., 2017). Comparing the issues summarized by Liu and Vogel (2016), Chinese students at home and aboard share the issues of language deficiency, and academic and institutional differentiation. However, Chinese students at home avoid the problems of social exclusion, emotional issues, and financial pressures. Another difference is that Chinese students may not immerse themselves either in class or after class, as the FTs observed.

To quote T1, who has taught Chinese students in international classes both in China and in the UK for 14 years, "I think that the students that I have here are quite similar to the classes that I taught in the UK. I'm not very surprised… what I teach, the syllabus… the nature of the students, the priorities and the values of the students are very similar to in the UK". Given the similarities, the findings can also be applied to arenas beyond Chinese borders.

CONCLUSION

This study set out to understand Chinese students' attributes in TNHE and factors which contribute from three groups of stakeholders, and thus can be considered holding a more holistic view. The FTs' perceptions of Chinese students' behaviours are very similar to the aforementioned past studies, and they all reckoned that cultural factors and cultural background greatly affect students. The main challenge is students' quietness or lack of participation. Although they are common findings in a vast number of studies on CHC students' attributes, with a more open approach for this investigation, this study gains insights into these phenomena and comes up with strategies to deal with them. With the suggestions made by the very experienced foreign teachers, who demonstrated a good understanding of their Chinese students, we propose a new approach to teaching Chinese students. Teachers should forget where they come from, adapt teaching methods to meet the students, and make good use of their merits, such as respectable, obedient, and good reading and writing levels.

As shown in the previous section, the findings can also be applied to arenas beyond Chinese borders. The strategies and suggestions can be valuable to teachers who are or aim to teach students from CHC. Given the time and physical limitation, the data collected from one university cannot necessarily be generalized, but can be of useful reference to shed light on TNHE which aims to enhance the quality of teaching and learning in various contexts worldwide.

REFERENCES

Brown, A. V. (2009). Students' and teachers' perceptions of effective foreign language teaching: A comparison of ideals. *Modern Language Journal*, *93*(1), 46–60. doi:10.1111/j.1540-4781.2009.00827.x

Chen, Y. M. (2014). Observations on Teachers' Knowledge Growth in the Communicative Approach in Taiwanese EFL Classes. *Ore*.exeter.ac.uk

Chen, Y. M. (2016). *Collaborating with English teachers in developing and implementing a context sensitive communicative approach in Taiwanese EFL secondary school classes* [Doctoral dissertation, University of Exeter, England]. ORE Open Research Exeter.

Chen, Y. M. (2020). How a teacher education programme through action research can support EFL teachers in implementing communicative approaches, a case from Taiwan. *SAGE Open*, *10*(1), 215824401990016. doi:10.1177/2158244019900167

Chen, Y. M. (2022). Understanding foreign language learners' perceptions of teachers' practice with educational technology with specific reference to Kahoot! and Padlet: A case from China. *Education and Information Technologies*, *27*(2), 1439–1465. doi:10.100710639-021-10649-2

Ching, Y., Renes, S. L., McMurrow, S., Simpson, J., & Strange, A. T. (2017). Challenges facing Chinese International students studying in the United States. *Educational Research Review*, *12*(8), 473–482. doi:10.5897/ERR2016.3106

Cohen, L., Manion, L., & Morrison, K. (2007). *Research methods in education* (6th ed.). Routledge. doi:10.4324/9780203029053

Cortazzi, M., & Jin, L. (1996). Cultures of learning: language classrooms in China. In H. Coleman (Ed.), *Society and the Language Classroom* (pp. 169–206). Cambridge University Press.

Creswell, J. W. (2007). *Qualitative inquiry and research design: Choosing among five approaches* (2nd ed.). Sage.

Dai, K., & Garcia, J. (2019). Intercultural Learning in Transnational Articulation Programs: The Hidden Agenda of Chinese Students' Experiences. *Journal of International Students*, *9*(2), 362–383. doi:10.32674/jis.v9i2.677

Gu, Q., & Maley, A. (2008). Changing places: A study of Chinese students in the UK. *Language and Intercultural Communication*, *8*(4), 224–245. doi:10.1080/14708470802303025

He, D. (2018). *Foreign Language Learning Anxiety in China: Theories and Applications in English Language Teaching*. Springer. doi:10.1007/978-981-10-7662-6

HESA. (2022). *Higher Education Student Statistics: UK, 2020/21–Where students come from and go to study*. HESA. https://www.hesa.ac.uk/news/25-01-2022/sb262-higher-education-student-statistics/location

Hou, J., Montgomery, C., & McDowell, L. (2014). Exploring the diverse motivations of transnational higher education in China: Complexities and contradictions. *Journal of Education for Teaching*, *40*(3), 300–318. doi:10.1080/02607476.2014.903028

Hu, G. (2002). Potential cultural resistance to pedagogical imports: The case of communicative language teaching in China. *Language, Culture and Curriculum*, *15*(2), 93–105. doi:10.1080/07908310208666636

Huang, X. H., & van Naerssen, M. (1987). Learning strategies for oral communication. *Applied Linguistics*, *8*(3), 287–307. doi:10.1093/applin/8.3.287

Knight, J. (2016). Transnational education remodeled: Toward a common TNE framework and definitions. *Journal of Studies in International Education*, *20*(1), 34–47. doi:10.1177/1028315315602927

Lee, E. L. (2007). Linguistic and cultural factors in East Asian students' oral participation in U.S. university classrooms. *International Education*, *36*(3), 29–47.

Li, L., & Walsh, S. (2011). Technology uptake in Chinese EFL classes. *Language Teaching Research*, *15*(1), 99–125. doi:10.1177/1362168810383347

Li, S. (2018). Transnational higher education in China: Thirty years of development. *Higher Education Forum, 6*, 49–58.

Liu, D., Vogel, L., & MacLeod, J. (2016). Mitigating transitional challenges of Chinese students in U.S. higher education. *Higher Education Studies*, *6*(3), 100–113. doi:10.5539/hes.v6n3p100

Liu, J. (2012). Does cram schooling matter? Who goes to cram schools? Evidence from Taiwan. *International Journal of Educational Development*, *32*(1), 46–52. doi:10.1016/j.ijedudev.2011.01.014

Liu, S., Morris, M. W., Talhelm, T., & Yang, Q. (2019). Ingroup vigilance in collectivistic culture. *Proceedings of the National Academy of Sciences of the United States of America*, *116*(29), 14538–14546. doi:10.1073/pnas.1817588116 PMID:31249140

Merriam, S. B. (1998). *Qualitative research and case study applications in education*. Jossey-Bass.

Ministry of Education of the People's Republic of China (MOE). (2022a). *2332 programmes of Chinese foreign cooperation in running schools including 1230 in higher education*. [In Chinese]. MOE. http://www.moe.gov.cn/fbh/live/2020/52834/mtbd/202012/t20201222_506955.html

Ministry of Education of the People's Republic of China (MOE). (2022b). *Between 2016 and 2019, over 2,510,000 Chinese in overseas studies*. [In Chinese]. MOE. http://www.moe.gov.cn/fbh/live/2020/52834/mtbd/202012/t20201223_507063.html

Mok, K. (2003). Globalisation and Higher Education Restructuring in Hong Kong, Taiwan and Mainland China. *Higher Education Research & Development*, *22*(2), 117–129. doi:10.1080/07294360304111

Mok, K. H., & Marginson, S. (2021). Massification, diversification and internationalisation of higher education in China: Critical reflections of developments in the last two decades. *International Journal of Educational Development*, *84*, 1–8. doi:10.1016/j.ijedudev.2021.102405

Oad, L., Khan, N., & Khoso, F. J. (2020). Factors Affecting English Language Anxiety among Learners: A Case Study of a Public Sector University. *Pakistan Social Sciences Review*, *4*(3), 1060–1078. doi:10.35484/pssr.2020(4-III)77

Oyserman, D., Coon, H. M., & Kemmelmeier, M. (2002). Rethinking individualism and collectivism: Evaluation of theoretical assumptions and meta-analyses. *Psychological Bulletin*, *128*(1), 3–72. doi:10.1037/0033-2909.128.1.3 PMID:11843547

Rao, Z. H. (1996). Reconciling communicative approaches to the teaching of English with traditional Chinese methods. *Research in the Teaching of English*, *30*(4), 458–471.

Shi, L. (2006). The successor to Confucianism or a new generation? A questionnaire study on Chinese students'culture of learning English. *Language, Culture and Curriculum*, *19*(1), 122–147. doi:10.1080/07908310608668758

Stake, R. E. (1995). *The art of case study research*. Sage Publications.

Straker, J. (2016). International Student Participation in Higher Education: Changing the Focus From "International Students" to "Participation". *Journal of Studies in International Education*, *20*(4), 299–318. doi:10.1177/1028315316628992

Tan, Z. (2008). Questioning in Chinese university EFL classrooms: What lies behind it? *Regional Language Centre Journal*, *38*(1), 87–103.

Tao, L. (2017). Face Perception in Chinese and Japanese. *Intercultural Communication Studies*, *26*(1), 151–167.

Tencent (2022). Top 8 countries where Chinese students go for study. [In Chinese]. Tencent. https://xw.qq.com/amphtml/20210325A063VL00?ivk_sa=1024320u.

UNESCO/Council of Europe. (2001). *Code of good practice in the provision of transnational education*. UNESCO/Council of Europe.

Wang, L. (2011). Foreign English Teachers in the Chinese Classroom: Focus on Teacher-Student Interaction. *The Journal of Asia TEFL*, *8*(2), 73–93.

Xie, X. (2009). Why are students quiet? Looking at the Chinese context and beyond. *ELT Journal*, *64*(1), 1–11.

Yi, C. C., & Wu, C. I. (2004). *Teen life around the world: Introduction to teen life in Taiwan*. Sinica. https://ir.sinica.edu.tw/handle/201000000A/65566

Yin, R. K. (2002). *Case study research: Design and methods*. SAGE Publications.

Yu, X. (2021). Foreign language learning anxiety in China: Theories and applications in English language teaching. *International Journal of Bilingual Education and Bilingualism*, *24*(8), 1247–1249. doi:10.1080/13670050.2018.1545745

Zhou, Y., & Wei, M. (2021). *The Lived Experience of Chinese International Students in the US*. Springer. doi:10.1007/978-981-15-9449-6

Section 5
Enhancing Practice

Chapter 15
Scaffolding New Teacher-Trainers Through a Hybrid Co-Training Model From a Transnational Higher Education Perspective

Saif Said Rashid Al Abri
https://orcid.org/0000-0002-2360-5446
Independent Researcher, Oman

ABSTRACT

Despite the potentials of collaborative work for enhancing the knowledge, skills, and attitudes (KSA) of professionals, the educational field lacks a clear model for co-training. This article aims to develop a conceptual framework for this collaborative professional development (PD) strategy to help novice teacher trainers (TTs) grow professionally. Although a lot has been written in the educational literature about co-teaching, there are merely few self-reported reflections about the use of co-training, and it is not clear how to adopt it as a tool for TTs' PD. In an attempt to fill in this gap, a proposed co-training model is constructed based on the philosophy of co-teaching, novice TTs' needs in terms of KSA, and their role-competency in the training room. These concepts are integrated to design a co-training model that is expected to help in scaffolding novice TTs. The author argues that this model, if properly implemented, can support novice TTs.

1. INTRODUCTION

Professional development (PD) in the educational field has attracted unprecedented attention by policy-makers, researchers and individuals. This is evident from the extraordinary consideration given to the PD of teachers in both stages (pre-service and in-service), and in presenting the importance of PD in all its shapes (top-down and bottom-up, individual and collaborative, etc.). Acknowledging the importance

DOI: 10.4018/978-1-6684-5226-4.ch015

of in-service PD tools, educators should not only be encouraged to adopt these but, more importantly, should be efficiently introduced to these tools in order to garner the most out of them and to maximize their learning. PD is also seen as an integral part of transnational education, as it involves the negotiation of teaching practices and pedagogical values (Tran et al., 2021).

In transnational higher education (TNE), the PD of the host countries' institutional professionals is imperative to ensure the quality of programme delivery. Quality assurance dictates the readiness of the host country to deliver the HE programmes. "[T]he primary responsibility of the quality assurance agency is to ensure that institutions are approved to deliver HE programmes" (Knight & McNamara, 2017, p. 39). Considering the huge responsibilities of the lecturers, it is important to ensure the competency and abilities of this group in TNE. The impact these lecturers place on their students is huge, as TNE students reported to find "TNE as a way to improve their professional skills, thereby improving their career prospects." (Knight & McNamara, 2017, p. 39).

Pre-service teacher-trainers (hereafter referred to as TTs) play a significant role in the process of new teachers' preparation. This huge responsibility of TT in transnational higher education requires well-prepared TTs. The quality of training "relies on the professional skills of teacher trainers" (Courtney, 2007, p.322). Therefore, the preparation of new pre-service TTs should receive sufficient attention from those responsible for and involved in teacher preparation and training.

It is more likely that TTs have sufficient experience of teaching before they shift to teacher training. However, not all successful teachers make a successful shift to teacher-training, and this is due to the higher demands of the TTs' profession (Beaven 2004 and Wright &Bolitho, 2007). On the other hand, some academics lack the experience of teaching, and this affects their motivation to seek opportunities to improve their teaching skills. "The lack of teaching-related criteria for the appointment of academic staff or incentives for the development of pedagogical skills throughout their careers has the result of diminishing motivation to learn and innovate." (Inamorato et al. 2019, p. 15).

Joining TNE represents a necessity for expanding knowledge, enhancing skills and fostering positive attitudes towards the new profession. Thus, just like those in other professions, TTs need to work on their PD to cope with their duties, grow professionally, be competent, and show initiative. "[I]nsufficient PD … of academics creates a considerable risk to the quality of higher education and, consequently, to society as a whole." (Inamorato et al. 2019, p. 5). In addition, the study of Tran et al. (2021) shows how teaching in TNE is demanding and calls for supporting new teachers in this field to overcome the challenges "with not only the academic and cultural dimensions of offshore teaching but also the development of resilience in terms of emotional wellbeing to assist them in navigating transnational experiences" (p.1).

Hence, considering the situation in TNE, there is a need for adopting effective PD tools that involve effective preparation of new TTs, which involves the academics from the host countries and the sending countries, in order to prepare new TTs and enable them to cope with their duties. Tran et al. (2021) highlight the importance of offering more situated professional learning that equips teachers with the capabilities of … maximising the potential benefits of transnational education" (p.2). Inamorato et al. (2019) claim that for a PD design and practice to be effective in a higher education setting, it must follow certain rules, which are: offering feedback and follow up, incorporating active learning, supporting collaboration among communities of practice members, providing expert support and focusing on participants' needs. Thus, Inamorato et al. (2019) argue that there is a need for sustainability and repetitiveness of PD activities in order to provide academics with sufficient time to "learn, practice, implement, and reflect upon new teaching practices" (p.20). In transnational higher education this is crucial and can be arranged to involve locals and expats in a PD programme to maximise the benefits of the adopted PD tool.

One way to achieve this professional growth, which is based on the criteria mentioned above, is through collaborative PD, such as adopting co-training. Co-training, where two or more TTs work together planning, delivering, and evaluating training sessions, is seen as an effective tool for TTs' PD (see, e.g. Baguley, 2014 and Pohl et al., 2016).

This chapter proposes a collaborative co-training model that can help in scaffolding new TTs to their roles in TNE, raising their knowledge and skills of training and cultivating positive attitudes towards their new profession. This co-training model integrates approaches used in co-teaching with the different roles the TT plays in the training room, and therefore is called Hybrid Co-training Model.

2. TRANSNATIONAL HIGHER EDUCATION

The phenomenon termed TNE occurs due to the need to support students worldwide and disseminate knowledge beyond the borders of one state. The aim is to make learning available to students in their home by institutions different from the countries in which they operate (Wikins, 2018; Hussain 2007).

TNE has been coined to reflect the recent activities of global institutions of higher education around the world. It refers to the concept of worldwide mobility of academics in the field of training and research (Hussain, 2007). In addition to the collaboration at international level, one of the characteristics of TNE is that it aims to develop higher education in different countries through providing programmes to teach and awarding certificates.

Although the idea of TNE seems a straightforward implementation of educational programmes from the sender to the host countries, this must follow certain principles and conditions that align with the host countries' educational aims, culture and so on. Hussain (2007) stresses that transnational education must support the national educational goals that promote lifelong learning and the transmission of culture, as it is the educational embodiment of this globalization process and ways to adapt to it, and foster competition, etc. With this in mind, TNE programmes that target the preparation of new teachers at undergraduate level, for instance, require qualified TTs who are competent in the subjects they teach and aware of the situation in which they teach these programmes. Thus, there is a need to scaffold newly appointed TTs in TNE to cope with their new mission and to effectively achieve the aims of the programmes. Therefore, involving these newly appointed TTs in PD activities, to equip them with the necessary knowledge and skills to execute their everyday job, is imperative.

2.1. Professional Development in TNE

The need to provide quality TNE urge those who are responsible for delivering higher education programmes to consider their PD as an essential part of their work. Inamorato et al. (2019) argue that PD is crucial for academics "to better position themselves and attract students" and to gain the necessary knowledge and skills and to be competent in their profession (p12). In TNE educational programmes that aim to prepare new teachers, it is compulsory to ensure the capability of those assigned to run the programmes (TTs), to ensure the effectiveness of the training provided and the achievements of the aims.

Inamorato et al. (2019) state that there is often a passive participation in PD activities by academics and this is due to four main reasons: unwillingness to change their teaching style, no formal requirements for development, time constraint, and lack of organisational support. Mentioning this, for the success of programmes delivered through the unique situation of transnational education, it is important to consider the professional growth of the staff responsible for teaching these programmes. Collaborative effort is required to scaffold newly appointed TTs in TNE institutions.

2.2. The Need for Collaborative PD

The literature shows the need to move beyond the geographical boundaries of the countries that apply TNE to enhance the collaboration among academics and to have joint responsibilities for developing curriculum and enhancing joint-responsibilities among institutions (see for example Keevers et al., 2019). Collaboration of academics (in this situation TTs), that aims to promote the quality of the TNE programme, is crucial. One sort of this collaboration is the adoption of collaborative PD tools that can enhance the skills of TTs. Different collaborative PD tools can be adopted such as peer observation, mentoring, PD discussion groups and co-training (the focus of this chapter). These can be done through involving experts (either local or expat) to work with the newly appointed local TTs, set a plan, and work together to support the latter in gaining the necessary skills.

3. FROM TEACHING TO TRAINING

To be a teacher, one has to fulfil the requirements that enable him/her to be involved in the educational field and perform job tasks effectively. Examples of such requirements are: being qualified to teach and being specialized in a particular subject (De Wet, 2016). A teacher should also obtain different potentials in order to survive his/her position such as "physical and mental stamina", "good management skills", "the capacity to engage participants", "a good understanding of the content", "good classroom skills" and "the ability to get on with colleagues" Woodward (2006, p.2).

Working as a teacher before shifting to training means having a solid foundation to start successfully. Various qualities are transferred with those who move from teaching to teacher training. According to Lunenberg et al. (2014), these are teaching experience, communication skills that raise learners' involvement, awareness of group dynamics, ability to provide a stress-free learning atmosphere, ability to raise learners' motivation and ability to facilitate reflection.

While the importance of the teaching experience for this transition is acknowledged, it is seen, alone, inadequate to make a successful TT. This is because the demands of the teacher training are higher (Marshall and Edwards,1997; Lunenberg et al., 2014; Murray and Male (2005); Wright and Bolitho, 2007). TTs are obliged to "add the skill of trainer" (Marshall and Edwards,1997, p.60). The study of Murray and Male (2005) shows that the lack of prior experience in teacher education adds pressure to novice TTs during the transition time, and this is because they are novice in a situation where they are seen as experts. Inamorato et al. (2019) argues that it is imperative to raise academics' understandings of "innovative teaching in order to overcome resistance to implement innovative teaching methods" (p.14).

3.1. Requirements

Teacher training, similar to teaching, aims to foster learning. However, the learning targeted in this profession is of both teachers and students. Thus, teacher training as a profession demands broadening knowledge, skills and attitudes (KSA). These are the KSAs that evolve from their teaching experience but extend beyond their teaching background. Thus, TTs need to "amplify personal characteristics suitable for the new position they find themselves in" (O'Donoghue,1997, p.76).

Freeman (1996), cited in Wright and Bolitho (2007), demonstrates the wider circle TTs move to once they shift from teaching to training (see figure1). The increase in the responsibilities shown in this figure requires a parallel growth in KSA. This also illustrates that although the centre remains students' learning, moving to teacher training requires wider knowledge of teaching in addition to knowledge of the teaching of teaching.

Figure 1. Levels of learning, teaching, and training (Wright and Bolitho 2007, p.224)

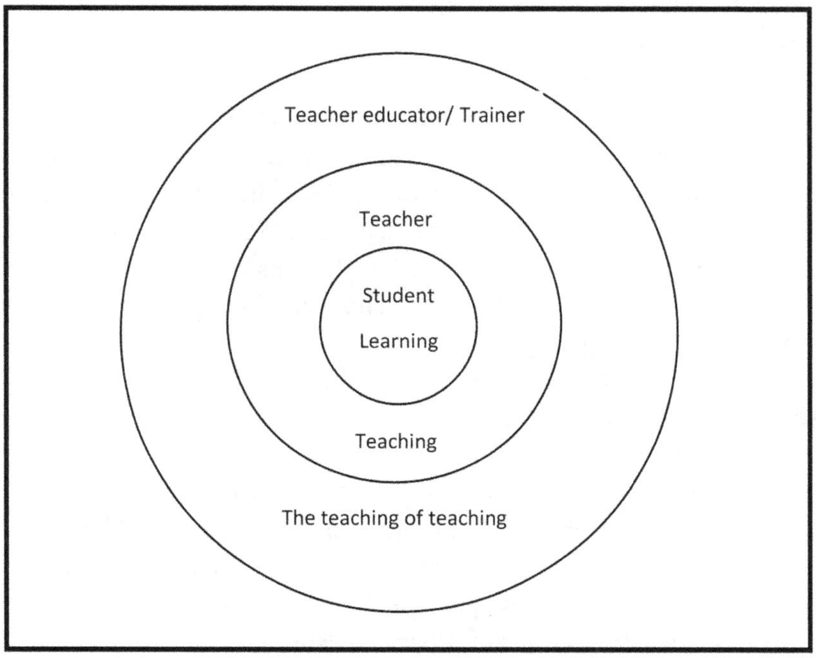

Several studies have investigated the shift to teacher training and its requirements. Some of these are related to having a wider knowledge of teaching and better skills to demonstrate it. In addition, both knowledge and skills of dealing with adult-learners, andragogy, should be acquired. Trainers also need to be able to link theories to practice and to be able to facilitate teachers' learning and development.

Although being a successful teacher does not guarantee to make a successful shift to training, knowledge and skills of teaching are compulsory in training. Knowledge of teaching is crucial when dealing with students, and it should be made explicit when dealing with teachers. This indicates the necessity to have wider knowledge and to be able to demonstrate good skills of teaching. Thus, getting meta of teaching, as stated by Woodward (2006), is necessary. This means "to have a good understanding of what you can do in a classroom, who with or to, when, how, and why" (p.2). O'Donoghue (1997) agrees with this and states, "[n]ew trainers need to be able to make explicit the beliefs they hold about teaching and to be aware of where these beliefs stem from" (p.75). Moreover, TTs need to be able to explain their practices, make explicitly adopted pedagogical approaches, in addition to being able to give a clear demonstration of best practices (O'Donoghue,1997).

Andragogy, the science of teaching adult learners, is another requirement in teacher training. It is, therefore, necessary to understand the way adults find it motivating to learn. Teachers, as trainees, have the characteristics of adult learners, some of which are "relaxed pace, longer concentration span, constructive sense of humour, ability and willingness to bring in their longer life experience, their motivation and their desire to know why you are asking them to do this or that task" (Woodward, 2006, p.2). TTs need not only to acknowledge this but more importantly, to effectively put these into practice. Therefore, KSA about this issue needs to be upgraded.

For trainees to see training beneficial to them, it is necessary to clearly see the link between the theories being articulated and their classroom practices which throws another demand for successful training and a successful teacher-trainer. Moreover, TTs need to be able to articulate experiential knowledge and link theoretical knowledge to practice (O'Donoghue,1997). By doing this, TTs work as practitioners in the field who can generate knowledge from everyday experiences and demonstrate a good understanding of the connection between the theoretical aspects of their training content and the practice of their trainees.

Furthermore, TTs need to be able to facilitate trainee-teachers' learning and development. Training is not about informing participants of what works and what does not, but it is more about helping trainee-teachers comprehend the topic being discussed and coach them to "draw their own conclusions" Woodward (2006). Trainees, as adult learners, are responsible for their learning, and this makes them also decision-makers. Their decision should be based on their understanding of their teaching and learning situation. Therefore, the role of the trainer, in such a situation, is more of a facilitator to promote teachers' reflection and decision-making skills.

3.2. Challenges

Various studies in the literature have articulated such a transition from being a teacher of students to being a teacher of teachers, which in turn enhances our understanding of the challenges these educators face (Kosnik et al., 2015). Such studies have expressed the need to expand certain qualities and obtain new ones, which is considered a necessity for playing the new role appropriately (see, e.g. Beaven, 2004a; Lunenberg et al., 2014; Murray & Male, 2005; Wright & Bolithio 2007; Williams et al. 2012). Thus, it is crucial to pay attention to this group of professionals' critical situation by the organizations and the practitioners in the field.

Formal or informal transition to teacher training requires learning about the new demands (Beaven, 2004a, p.16). The underestimation of such a shift and its requirements may result in TTs finding themselves challenged with new situations (Lunenberg et al., 2014, p.19). Davies and Northall (2018b) agrees with this and state that such challenges can make the mission of the TT "daunting" (p.48)

The confusion that the new TTs have of what is considered good practice in the profession of teacher training represents a challenge. Thus, most often, "Initial confidence in immediate success as a TT was shown to be lacking or misplaced" (Beaven, 2004a, p. 2). Bax (1995), addressing the newcomers, states that the difficulty is in identifying a "current and comprehensive set of specific indicators" for best performances which could raise their confidence and guide them in performing their everyday tasks (p.153). As a result, new TTs feel "frightened" of unexpected events during training (O'Donoghue,1997, p.74). This can, as well, lead to unfavourable training circumstances such as "resentment, embarrassment, dependency, obsequiousness, condescension, projection and irrationality" (Woodward,1997, p.7).

Novice TTs face some difficulties such as being uncertain about the requirements, feeling of anxiety, worries about lecturing skills, concerns about time-management and leading panel discussion (Murray and

Male, 2005). Hence, it is crucial to mentor novice TTs to familiarize them with their new roles (Davies and Northall, 2018a). This requires an on-going development process because depending merely on one-off induction training is not always sufficient. Velzen et al. (2010) argues that although the importance of the preparation stage has been widely articulated in literature, the induction offered to teacher-educator is often seen as insufficient. Therefore, TTs have to manage with "limited or no induction for their new role" (Beaven, 2004b, p.48).

3.3. TTs' PD

This situation of novice TTs involved in transnational higher education makes it imperative to seek ways to help themselves survive and grow professionally. Working collaboratively with other professionals in the same field is highly recommended. Kosnik et al. (2015) stress that collaborative work such as working with peers and reflecting on practice are effective ways to promote TTs' knowledge and skills. Newly appointed TTs need to be scaffolded through such collaborative CPD methods to equip them with the necessary qualities to survive.

The qualitative study conducted by Beaven (2004b) gives a clear idea of the PD paths that new TTs follow for their professional growth. The interviews with eight participants who shifted from teaching to training present the value of collaborative PD to this group of professionals. Although these show the importance of different types of PD (individual and collaborative), it can clearly be noticed that collaborative sort of PD such as interacting with colleagues and using peer-observation were helpful. Garet et al. (2001) states that "teachers who work together are more likely to have the opportunity to discuss concepts, skills, and problems that arise during their professional development experiences." (p.922)

Moreover, supporting new TTs should be done based on the job demands. Therefore, the emphasis of the CPD should focus "on what participants are expected to do and what we hope the results of their actions will be" (Guskey, 2000, p.18). Therefore, when using co-training, the suggested method of PD articulated in this paper, it is important that it focuses on enabling the participants with the job demands, such as enhancing their skills in performing the various roles they play in the training rooms.

TTs can learn from their experiences of being teachers and the way they worked to develop themselves professionally. TTs sometimes provide golden advice for their trainees for this reason, which is applicable too in the context of teacher training and can work well in improving TTs' knowledge and skills. "Teachers, when asked, often admit that they learn most from watching other people teach. Perhaps then we should set up trainer observation as the main path forward for our own training? Certainly, informal discussion and support from peers are extremely important to many trainers" (Woodward, 1997, p.6). Mentioning this, it is undoubtedly essential to consider the differences between teaching and training and to adopt these tools to suit the training context.

4. CO-TRAINING AS A SOLUTION

Co-training, where two or more TTs work cooperatively in all three stages (planning, delivery and evaluation) of training, is considered an effective tool to accelerate the learning of new TTs. Although learning through this method is not exclusive to novice TTs; as experienced ones can learn a lot from it as well, co-training can provide tremendous chances for new TTs to comprehend the vision of training clearly, cultivate appropriate attitudes towards training and build knowledge and skills required to execute training appropriately (see for example Baguley, 2014; Pohl et al., 2016). Referring to the importance of team-teaching, Carr (2019) states that "team teaching for less experienced teachers should serve as a vital part of their induction process into a new institution …" (p.55). Similarly, co-training can be of valuable benefit to the new TTs in the TNE field, especially if there is a clear model to follow.

The idea of co-training arises from the idea of the co-teaching approach. Many studies have articulated the idea of co-teaching, but, unfortunately, the idea of co-training is not much presented in the literature. Few self-reported reflections are there about TTs' practices of such a method. Therefore, considering the benefits of co-teaching, some of which are: enhancing work quality, sharing knowledge, working out of isolation, preventing burnout, building a healthy working environment etc. (Buckely, 2000), it is unwise to neglect such a tool for scaffolding new TTs, especially that it has been shown to be beneficial in enhancing TTs' KSA (e.g. Baguley, 2014; Pohl et al., 2016). However, in order to make the idea of co-training more beneficial, it is necessary to build on the idea of co-teaching and include the elements related to training in TNE, such as TTs' needs (KSA) and the way they play their roles in the training room.

5. A PROPOSED HYBRID CO-TRAINING MODEL TO SCAFFOLD NOVICE TT

This section focuses on structuring a co-training model that is extended from the co-teaching approach. Thus, the first section articulates the philosophy of co-training, which is mainly based on the literature review of the knowledge of co-teaching. This considers knowing about co-training, its conditions, procedures and the various models to adopt.

The second section focuses on novice TTs' needs. These needs are articulated based on KSA required to make an effective TT. In addition, the section also presents TTs' role-competency in the training room. This includes the various roles TTs play in the training room and what each role entails.

Focusing on these issues, the discussion is, then, presented on novice TTs' qualities that can be developed through working collaboratively with others through adopting co-training. This should lead to the structure of the proposed model for co-training.

5.1. Knowledge of Co-training

Adopting a collaborative method of PD that one has limited or no knowledge of can result in, at best, not gaining the utmost benefits of the method and, at worse, resulting in a disastrous experience that can diminish the professional relationship of those being involved in it. This was clearly demonstrated by those who reflected on their previous negative experience of conducting co-training (see, for example, Skrypnyk, 2006). For this reason, new TTs who are willing to practice training jointly with more experienced ones and those experienced trainers who work as mentors to new TTs should be aware of the co-training considerations, the appropriate procedures to follow, and the appropriate co-training approaches to adapt for a particular training setting.

Co-Training Considerations

It is imperative that TTs in transnational education who consider working with colleagues to conduct a co-training session are aware of the conditions required for a successful collaborative practice. This involves finding the right partner to work within which there is a friendly relationship between them

(Scherer & Sardone, 2013) and where both have equal chances of contributing to the work (Rao & Chen, 2019). Hence, it is important to find a willing partner who has the enthusiasm to improve and seek excellence (Blythe & Sweet, 2004). Willingness, here, does not only mean acceptance to be involved, but more importantly, it means having the desire to share insights and learn from others' experiences.

The second issue is the importance of cooperation and the use of each other's strengths which makes the collaborative work of better quality and supports professional learning of individuals. Therefore, a team's success depends to a great extent on the cooperation of the team members (Hooda & Sharma, 2017). This includes understanding each other and considering professional disagreements as a healthy phenomenon that can help individuals to accept or question ideas and insights critically. These can provide "valuable learning experiences for everyone involved" (Garran et al., 2015, p.810).

Clarity of the task and work process are also essential factors for the success of this sort of collaborative work. It is essential that all who are involved in team-teaching have a good understanding of the objectives and tasks to be accomplished (Wenger & Hornyak, 1999). Killingsworth and Xue (2015) refer to this as "mission clarity" which entails an understanding of objectives and the agreed process to perform the tasks (p.10). Furthermore, in order for members to feel secure, the roles of each member should be agreed upon. The 'turn-taking' protocol in the classroom should also go according to the planning and preparation of the lesson (Wenger & Hornyak,1999).

Co-Training Procedures

Despite the fact that many PD tools are very effective in enhancing educators' knowledge and skills and the fact that these can put a huge amount of influence over their attitudes towards their job, in case that educators do not follow the correct procedures of implementing these tools, the adoption of such will not be effective. In a situation of implementing collaborative tools such as co-training with limited or no knowledge about it, it can become worse. Thus, it is crucial to comprehend the right procedures to follow before the implementation starts.

Team-teaching practice comprises four different stages, namely: *the organizational stage, the planning stage, the performance stage, and the conclusion stage* (Tsybulsky, 2019). The knowledge of each stage and what it encounters are essential to successfully implement this PD tool. The first stage refers to the team foundation where members get to know each other, build rapport, build trust and confidence, and set rules for communications. This also includes expressing personal concerns and reasons for being involved in team-teaching (Laughlin et al., 2011). In a transnational higher education setting, this requires sufficient arrangements especially if it involves local and expat TTs as this entails meetings, co-planning, co-training and co-evolution. Therefore, in this unique situation, the arrangement should be supported by institutions from both countries.

In the planning stage, partners work together to have a mutual understanding of the materials to teach, objectives to achieve and approaches to use. They also choose the appropriate activities to use and distribute individual roles (Carr, 2019). The performance stage is the implementation stage. Participants, during this stage, put team-teaching in action and use chances to support each other, analyse performance, give feedback and work on action-points. The final stage, the conclusion stage, is the phase where partners evaluate the whole process highlighting the achievements of the team, considering the drawback of their practices, and accordingly set future plans for better implementation of team-teaching.

Applying this in a co-training setting, all four stages are essential. Similar to team-teaching, co-training requires, first, establishing mutual understanding and trust among partners, a good understanding of mission, joint preparation and agreements of role distributions and enough time to evaluate the experience once it is done. In addition, as this is considered a way to scaffold new TTs, it is important to focus on the knowledge and skills to improve and use the opportunities to learn from experienced partners.

Co-Training Approaches

The literature provides a wide range of different approaches to co-teaching. However, although these may differ in titles, they are similar in functions. Friend et al. (2010) differentiates between six approaches of co-teaching, which indicate the different roles each of the teachers plays in such a collaborative setting. These approaches are: *One teach-one assist*, *one teach-one observe*, *Station teaching*, *Parallel teaching*, *Alternative teaching,* and *Teaming*. These approaches are widely used, and they can promote "confidence and contributions of the second teacher..." (Cruz & Geist, 2019, p.2).

While *one teach-one assist* approach requires one teacher to hold the responsibility of teaching while the other teacher goes around the class and supports groups and individuals, in the one teach-one observe approach, the second teacher observes and takes notes about pre-determined focuses or general observation. *Station teaching* approach requires both teachers to be responsible for teaching different groups at the same time. The class is divided into three groups where students are expected to rotate from one group to another. While one teacher instructs one group, the other is taught by the other teacher, and the students in the third group learn independently. *Parallel teaching* approach means dividing the class into two equal groups where one teacher is responsible for each group. Same materials are used to teach both groups in *parallel teaching*. The purpose of this is to raise classroom interaction and facilitate instructional differentiation. *Alternative teaching* approach is done when one of the co-teachers works with the majority of the class and the other works with a small number of students to pre-teach, scaffold learners or for remedial work. The sixth approach is *teaming*. Here both teachers present in front of the class at the same time. This is done to present a conversation, show opposing views, and demonstrating ways to solve an issue.

To project these approaches into training settings, the table below (table 1.) shows the adaption of each approach of co-teaching into co-training. Mentioning this, co-trainers need to fully comprehend these approaches and the role of each co-trainer in each approach.

4.1. TTs' Competencies

There seems to be relatively little research on identifying the qualities of good TTs (Kandiller and Özler, 2015). However, it is undisputedly important to detect these characteristics and competencies based on which new TTs can be scaffolded to grow professionally. Few studies such as (Gauld and Miller, 2004; Johnson, 2001; Beaven, 2004a) investigated the area of TTs' profession and provided some standards for effective TTs.

Competencies of effective TTs such as the ability to blend different training techniques, use questioning to improve participation, facilitate group learning activities, evaluate the impact of training, and demonstrate effective communication skills are listed by Gauld and Miller (2004) as characteristics of effective trainers. Johnson's (2001) survey also provided a list that represented the qualities of a good TT, some of which correspond with Gauld and Miller's list. Some of the characteristics of good TT mentioned in the list are an interaction between trainers and trainees and clarity of communication. In addition, other competencies such as clear instructions, interpersonal skills, knowledge, and abilities to respond to trainees' queries and keeping training sessions lively and interesting are also seen to be important (Ghosh et al., 2012). O'Donoghue (1997) stresses the importance of TTs having "both high and low inference skills" for them to be able to evaluate and give suitable feedback to trainees (p.77).

Table 1. Co-training approaches (adapted from Friend et al., 2010, P.12)

	Co-training Approaches	Illustrations
1	***One Train, One Assist*** In this model, both co-trainers are present, but one takes a clear responsibility for training while the other is actively involved doing supplementary roles and assisting trainees when necessary. The assistant trainer does different activities such as summarizing points on the board, distributing activities to trainees, clarifying issues to certain groups, finding out individual needs etc.	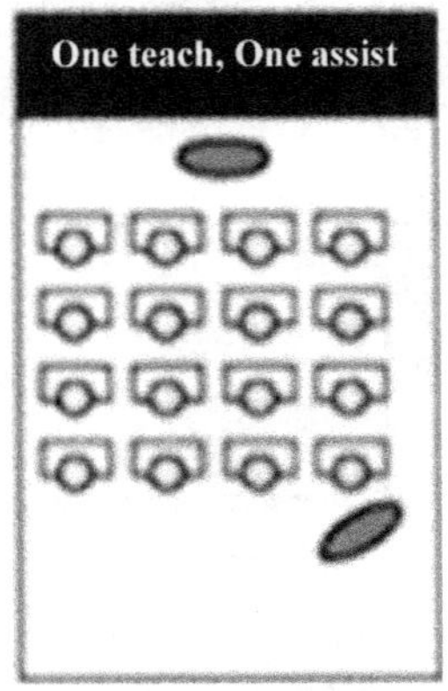
2	***One Train, One Observe*** One trainer has the full responsibility of training, and the other is observing and collecting data. The observation is planned and serves predetermined goals. This can have different focuses such as a focus on a specific group, trainer-trainee interaction, evaluating a specific training event etc.	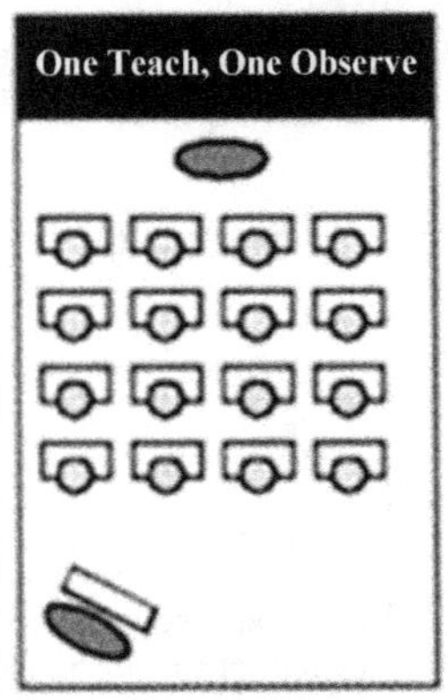
3	***Station Training*** Participants are distributed into three groups or more, which represent the stages of the topic. Each trainer is responsible for training a different aspect of the topic. The third group represents independent work. The trainees rotate from one group to another, so the trainer delivers the materials to a different group each time. This works when all the sequences are possible.	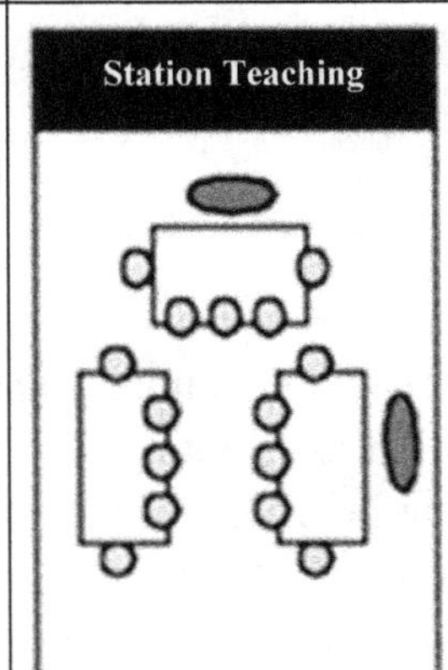

continuw on following page

Table 1. Continued

	Co-training Approaches	Illustrations
4	***Parallel Training*** Trainees are divided into two equal groups. Each trainer is responsible for delivering the same materials to one group at the same time. The purpose is to foster instructional differentiation and increase trainees' interaction and participation in the session.	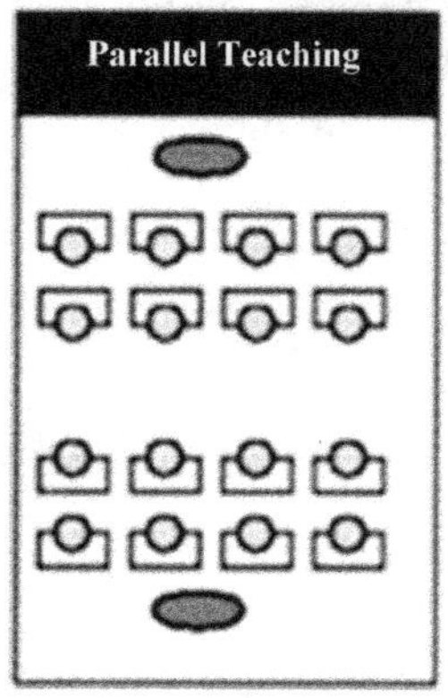
5	***Alternative Training*** In alternative training, the trainees are divided into two different groups based on the existing needs. One trainer leads the group with the majority of trainees, and the other is responsible for coaching a smaller group. The purpose can be for pre-teaching, remediation, enrichment, assessment, or other purposes.	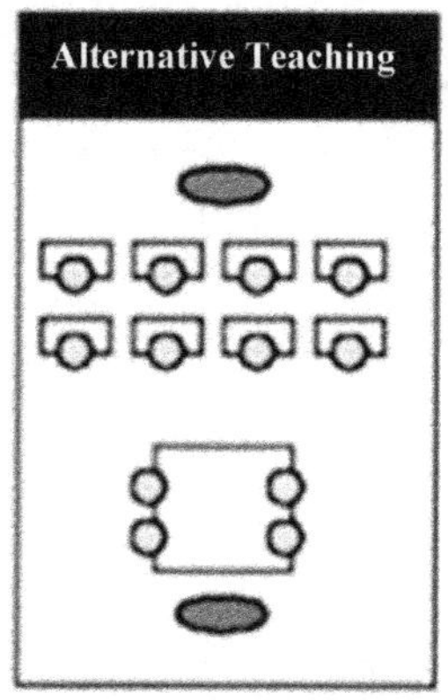
6	***Teaming*** In this model, both trainers present harmoniously at the same time for the same group of trainees. In this model, both trainers lecture, represent opposing views in a planned debate, illustrating different options of solving problems etc.	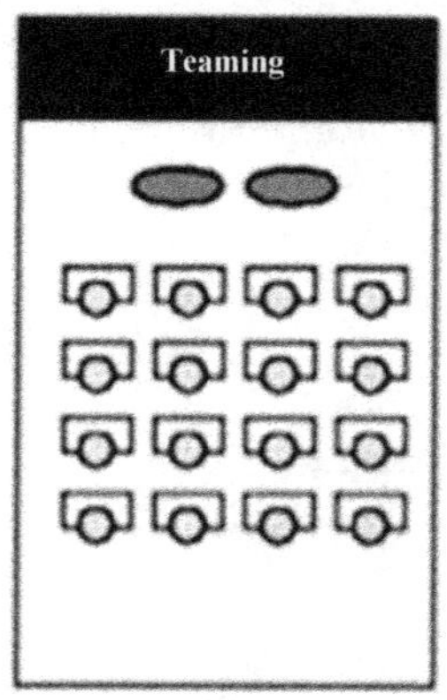

Although understanding these qualities is necessary to guide us as TTs to what makes an effective TT, it is crucial also to identify the requirements in terms of KSA once a teacher shifts to teacher training in order to understand the instant needs of new TTs and to inform the structuring of a co-training model that aims to facilitate their PD. Beaven (2004a), investigating the shift of eight TTs from teaching to training, shows the qualities that new teacher trainers ought to obtain in order to survive in this demanding profession. Based on her study, the following (figure 2.) summarises some of the important requirements of a TT in terms of knowledge, skills, attitudes and in dealing with trainees.

Figure 2. TTs' role requirements (based on Beaven,2004a).

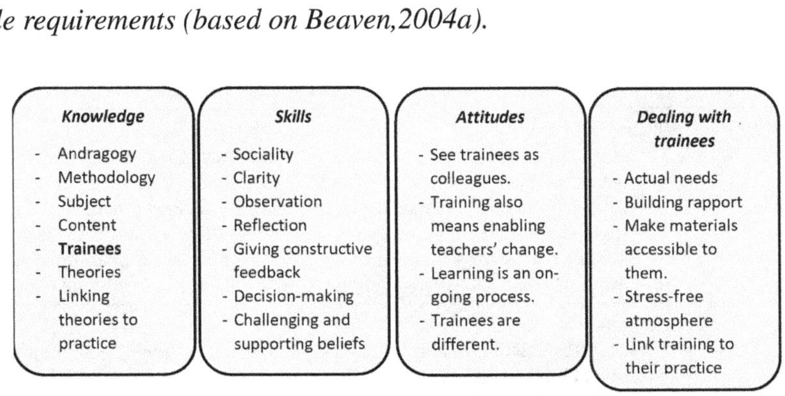

5.2. TTS' Roles In The Training Room

For the reason of supporting novice TTs, it is also necessary to present the different roles TTs play, especially during training. Different authors present different TTs' roles, and although these may differ in names, they are similar in functions. For instance, talking about the professional requirements of teacher educators, Lunenberg et al. (2014, p.21-22) explain some of these such as teacher of teachers, researcher, coach, curriculum developer, gatekeeper (admitting student teachers to the profession) and broker (a mentor in both school and institution). TTs also play the roles, as described by Gibhard (1990) cited in (O'Donoghue, 1997), directive, alternative, collaborative, non-directive, and creative. Mentioning this, moving between these professional roles necessitate an understanding of the approaches each role entails.

For the purpose of identifying the roles TTs play inside the training room so that these can be incorporated in the proposed model of co-training, I focus on the roles explored by Downey's (1996). This study identified several roles the TTs play, the behaviours of each of these required and how these roles are selected and used for facilitating trainees' professional growth. She classified the roles as follows: expert, entertainer, questioner, coach, listener, and counsellor. I find this categorization a valuable way to describe the work of a TT inside the training room.

Downey (1996) argues that the roles the TTs play are dynamic and may present a challenge for TTs to shift from one role to another. Therefore, she claims that the unsuccessful handling of these different roles presents a risk of loss to the learning of the trainees. The following (table 2.) is a summary of what each of the six roles she identified entails and which I see as crucial elements to obtain as a TT.

5.3. The Hybrid Co-training Model

The discussion above on the knowledge of co-training and its approaches, the TTs' needs, and their roles in the training room represent the main foundations of the co-training model proposed in this chapter. These elements incorporate the conditions under which the involvement of professionals in professional learning communities is appropriately executed with the various approaches to teamwork inside the training room. In addition, it presents a focus on the needs of the novice TTs and on developing the role-competency by focusing on the different roles TTs play inside the training room. The following figure presents the hybrid co-training model.

Table 2. A summary of TTs' main roles (adapted from Downey, 1996)

	The role	What it entails based on the study by (Downey 1996)
1.	***An expert***	The trainer: - is highly knowledgeable about the topic discussed (has education, training, or experience), - is skillful (able to demonstrate technical skills) - is able to link theories presented to participants' everyday practices - is able to use trainees' previous knowledge to scaffold them towards learning new issues. - Enriches discussion with ideas and thought from his/her prior knowledge and experience - Able to respond to challenging training events and ready to respond to trainees' queries.
2.	***An entertainer***	The trainer: - Energizes training sessions through stimulations and learning entertainment using stories, sense of humour, drama, or songs. - Raises participants' motivation through using purposeful activities - Chooses the right task at the right time for the right purpose of entertainment which is also linked to the expected outcomes of the training delivered. - Uses activities as exclamation points and informally sharing knowledge.
3.	***A questioner***	The Trainer: - Uses questions as an integral part of the training - uses questioning techniques as a key to the learning process - uses questioning to promote trainees' interactions, gather information, enhance understanding, and direct trainees' attention. - uses simple questions to engage, clarifies, empower, and directs participants. - Uses questions to move the learning process along. - Indicates that trainees' thoughts and contributions are sought valued. - Raises participants sense of support to guide initiatives. - Not all questions seek a direct or even an immediate answer
4.	***A coach***	The Trainer: - Discusses the desired outcomes - Is aware of individuals' actions and is able to see their needs - nurtures, reinforces or affirms the practice and behaviour of both individuals and groups in a non-threatening way. - Observes the learning process - Gives constructive feedback to the whole group in order for the trainees to develop - Makes sure that his/her interaction with the whole group focuses on public success and is less personal. - Individualizes the training process to meet the needs of individuals.
5.	***A listener***	The Trainer: - Has good listening skills, listens attentively, explores feelings and needs, builds on what he/she listens to in order to change the direction of the learning process. - Has the skill of reflective listening, can paraphrase trainees' oral contributions to check understanding? - Plays the role of a script writer to summarize participants discussions and use them to reinforce learning. - Raises trainees' motivation through adding credibility to the trainees' contributions. - Listens carefully to support their initiatives. - Listens and observes trainees closely in order to be able to understand them and support them.
6.	***A Counselor***	The Trainer: - Goes beyond addressing individual improvement in large groups (as in coaching) - Builds mutual trust with individuals - Requires the skills of attending, understanding and responding to individual needs - Gives individual and personal support - Can help individuals see their needs and privately works with them for improving their productivity. - Arrange formal conversations with individuals and work with those who need to be convinced, who are struggling and those who need attention.

Table 3. Co-training Models - The Roles that each TT plays according to the models they use

Co-training Models	The Roles that each TT plays according to the models they use	
	Co-trainer 1	Co-trainer 2
Teaming	Main (A) + (B, C, D, E)	Main (A) + (B, C, D, E)
Alternative	Main (A)	Main (D) + (B, E, F)
Station	Main (A) + (B, C, D, E)	Main (A) + (B, C, D, E)
One-train, one-observe	Main (A) + (B, C, D, E)	Main (E)
One-train, one-assist	Main (A)	Main (B) + (C, E, F)
Parallel	Main (A) + (B, C, D, E)	Main (A) + (B, C, D, E)

Figure 3. The hybrid co-training model

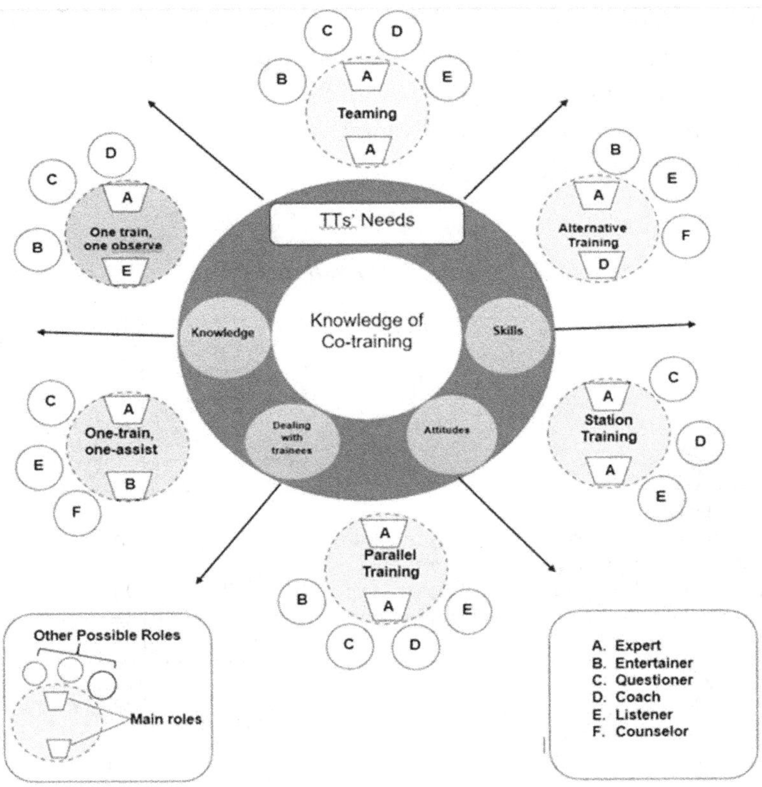

The idea of the proposed hybrid co-training model shown in Figure (3) above comprises, first of all, an understanding of the rationale of the co-training approach and the right procedures to perform it (the central circle in the model entitled Knowledge of Co-Training). After that, making decisions on the kind of knowledge, skills, and other needs to be developed is provided (the outer circle in the model) and which also includes the TTs' roles to be addressed. Next, based on the outcomes, content and procedures of the training sessions, the co-trainers decide on the approaches to follow. A training day is more likely to include more than one co-training approach. The arrows in the proposed model indicate the expansion in knowledge, skills and developing better attitudes through the adoption of this model.

Based on the proposed model, there is always a main role of each co-trainer, and there are other supplementary roles that each can perform depending on needs. Both, the main roles, and the supplementary roles should be thoroughly discussed and carefully planned during the first stage of co-training (The planning stage). As this is meant to be a tool for the PD of novice TTs, the distribution of roles should depend on co-trainers' strengths, weaknesses, preferences and professional needs.

5.4. Demonstrating the Implementation

To clarify the implementation of the model further, table (3) below is a demonstration sample of a workshop that is planned to be delivered using the co-training model. Despite the fact that this workshop includes almost all of the different approaches of co-training, normal training sessions do not necessarily involve all these approaches. The choice of approaches is determined by the aims and content of the workshop and TTs' professional needs.

This is a plan of a workshop that aims to raise participants' awareness of the significance of active learning and the possible implications in the classroom. Each phase has its distinctive features, and based on these, a proper co-training approach is planned. In Stage Two, for instance, an interactive training approach is seen as more suitable to present advantages and challenges of using active learning, and therefore the *teaming approach* is used.

Table 4. An Illustrative Example of a Co-training Workshop.

Workshop Stages	**Co-Training Approaches**	**Co-trainers' Roles**	
		Co-t. 1	**Co-t. 2**
Stage one: - Presenting theories about active learning	One-train, one-assist	**Main Expert** + Questioner	**Main Entertainer** + Questioner
Stage two (Advantages and challenges): - Observing a debate discussion (by co-trainers) on the usefulness of active learning and its expected challenges for both teachers and learners (The purpose of this stage is to highlight that even though there are some challenges, the benefits of applying such an approach are high and worth working on it.)	Teaming	**Main Expert** + **Listener** Questioner	**Main Expert** + **Listener** Questioner
Stage three (learning by doing): - Analyzing examples of active learning activities (group1) - ***Designing their own examples of active learning (group2)*** - Reflecting on their learning from the previous stages (group3)	Station Training	(group 1) **Main Expert** + Questioner	(group 3) **Main Expert** + entertainer
Stage four: (Micro-teaching) - Planning a micro-teaching lesson (each group plans using one type of active learning activities presented in the workshop) - Micro-teaching - Reflection on micro-teaching	Parallel Training	**Main Expert** + **Coach**	**Main Expert** + **Coach**
***Stage five*: (Focusing on Existing Needs)** - Based on the stage of micro-teaching, those who still need help will form a new group (2) to receive further support. The main group (1) will work on identifying the key learning elements to talk about in the final stage.	Alternative Training	(group 1) **Main Expert** + Questioner	(group 2) **Main Coach** + Questioner
Stage Six: - Reflection on learning and future practices of active learning	One train, one observes	**Main Expert** + Questioner	**Main Listener**

6. CONCLUSION

This article focuses on developing a co-training model that can provide learning opportunities for novice TTs in transnational higher education. The idea of constructing the model emerges from the need of supporting novice TTs to grow professionally through enhancing their knowledge and skills of training and developing positive attitudes towards their roles as TTs.

The Hybrid co-training model is based on the idea of co-teaching, which has been excessively presented in the literature. Thus, the foundations of the knowledge and the approaches used in the proposed model are based on the knowledge and approaches of co-teaching strategies. In addition, to make this more beneficial for TTs, elements of TTs' needs and their responsibilities are incorporated as well.

The final construction of the model considers obtaining first solid knowledge of co-training, its conditions, and procedures. It helps co-trainers determine the type of training KSA to improve and provides opportunities to improve the performance in the training room through focusing on TTs' roles in the co-training sessions.

REFERENCES

Baguley, N. (2014). Team Training. *English Teaching Professional, 91*, 58–59.

Bax, S. (1997). What are we training trainers to do? Evaluating teacher education sessions within a context-sensitive framework. In I. McGrath (Ed.), *Learning to Train: Perspectives on the Development of Language* (pp. 153–161). Prentice Hall Europe.

Beaven, B. (2004a). *How eight English language teacher trainers made the transition from teaching to training* [Ed D Thesis, Exeter University, United Kingdom].

Beaven, B. (2004b). From teacher to teacher trainer. *English Teaching Professional, 33*, 47–49.

Blythe, H., & Sweet, C. (2004). Total Team Teaching - Sharing Teaching Duties Equally. *The Teaching Professor, 18*(3), 4–5.

Buckley, F. J. (2000). *Team Teaching: What, Why, and How?* SAGE Publications. Inc. doi:10.4135/9781452220697

Carr, P. (2019). Team Teaching. *English Teaching Professional, 121*, p 53- 55.

Courtney, J. (2007). What are the effective components of in-service teacher training? A study examining teacher trainers' perceptions of the components of a training programme in mathematics education in Cambodia. *Journal of In-service Education, 33*(3), 321–339. doi:10.1080/13674580701486978

Cruz, L., & Geist, M. J. (2019). A Team-Teaching Matrix: Asking New Questions about How We Teach Together. *Transformative Dialogues: Teaching & Learning Journal, 12*(1), 1–15.

Davies, B., & Northall, N. (2018a). No One Told Me That! 1. *English Teaching Professional, 117*, 49–51.

Davies, B., & Northall, N. (2018b). No One Told Me That! 2. *English Teaching Professional, 118*, 48–51.

De Wet, C. (2016). The Status of Teaching as a Profession in South Africa. *Education Policy, Reforms & School Leadership* (143-149).

Downey, R. V. (1996). *A Study in Stand Up: Roles and Behaviors of Excellent Trainers* [PhD Thesis). Syracuse University, USA].

Friend, M., Cook, L., Hurley-Chamberlain, D., & Shamberger, C. (2010). Co-Teaching: An Illustration of the Complexity of Collaboration in Special Education. *Journal of Educational & Psychological Consultation*, *20*(1), 9–27. doi:10.1080/10474410903535380

Garet, M. S., Porter, A. C., Desimone, L., Birman, B., & Yoon, K. S. (2001). What Makes Professional Development Effective? Results from a National Sample of Teachers. *American Educational Research Journal*, *38*(4), 915–945. https://www.jstor.org/stable/3202507. doi:10.3102/00028312038004915

Garran, A. M., Aymer, S., Gelman, C. R., & Miller, J. L. (2015). Team teaching Anti-Oppression with Diverse Faculty: Challenges and Opportunities. *Social Work Education*, *34*(7), 799–814. doi:10.1080/02615479.2015.1062086

Gauld, D., & Miller, P. (2004). The qualifications and competencies held by effective workplace trainers. *Journal of European Industrial Training*, *28*(1), 8–22. doi:10.1108/03090590410513866

Ghosh, P., Satyawadi, R., Joshi, J. P., Ranjan, R., & Singh, P. (2012). Towards more Effective Training Programme: A study of trainer attributes. *Industrial and Commercial Training*, *44*(4), 194–202. doi:10.1108/00197851211231469

Guskey, T. (2000). *Evaluating professional development*. Corwin Press.

Hooda, M., & Sharma, M. (2017). The Effect of Team Teaching on Academic Achievement of 9th Grades in Science. *Scholarly Research Journal for Interdisciplinary Studies*, *3* (23), 1906-1915. https://www.academia.edu/25316443/THE_EFFECT_OF_TEAM_TEACHING_ON_ACADEMIC_ACHIEVEMENT_OF_9TH_GRADERS_IN_SCIENCE

Hussain, I. (2007). Transnational Education: Concepts and Methods. *Turkish Online Journal of Distance Education-TOJDE, 8*(1).

Inamorato dos Santos, A., Gaušas, S., Mackevičiūtė, R., Jotautytė, A., & Martinaitis, Ž. (2019). Innovating Professional Development in Higher Education: Case Studies, EUR 29669 EN, Publications Office of the European Union. doi:10.2760/712385

Johnson, J. (2001). 10 Out of 10. *English Teaching Professional*, *18*, 57.

Kandiller, S. T., & Özler, D. (2015). From teacher to trainer: What changes? Or does it? *Procedia: Social and Behavioral Sciences*, *199*, 436–452. doi:10.1016/j.sbspro.2015.07.530

Keevers, L. M., Price, O., Leask, B., Dawood Sultan, F. K., Lim, J. S., & Loh, V. (2019). Practices to improve collaboration by reconfiguring boundaries in transnational education. *Journal of University Teaching & Learning Practice*, *16*(2), 38–53. doi:10.53761/1.16.2.4

Killingsworth, B., & Xue, Y. (2015). Investigating Factors Influencing Students' Learning in a Team-Teaching Setting. *International Journal of Cognitive Research in Science. Engineering and Education*, *3*(2), 9–16.

Knight, J. and McNamara, J. (2017). *Transnational Education: A Classification Framework and Data Collection Guidelines for International Programme and Provider Mobility (IPPM)*. British Council and German Academic Exchange services.

Kosnik, C., Miyata, C., Cleovoulou, Y., Fletcher, T., & Menna, L. (2015). The Education of Teacher Educators. Falkenberg, T. (Ed.). *Handbook of Canadian research in initial teacher education*. Ottawa, ON: Canadian Association for Teacher Education. https://www.csse-scee.ca/associations/about/cate-acfe

Laughlin, K., Nelson, P., & Donaldson, S. (2011). Successfully Applying Team Teaching with Adult Learners. *Journal of Adult Education*, *40*(1), 11–18.

Lunenberg, M., Dengerink, J., & Korthagen, F. (2014). *The professional teacher educator: Roles, behaviour, and professional development of teacher educators*. Sense Publishers. doi:10.1007/978-94-6209-518-2

Marshall, N., & Edwards, C. (1997). A mentor approach to teacher trainer development. In I. McGrath (Ed.), *Learning to Train: Perspectives on the Development of Language Teacher Trainers* (pp. 60–72). Prentice Hall Europe.

Murray, J., & Male, T. (2005). Becoming a Teacher Educator: Evidence from the Field. *Teaching and Teacher Education*, *21*(2), 125–142. doi:10.1016/j.tate.2004.12.006

O'Donoghue, C. (1997). Trainer induction: reflecting on parallels between new trainers and teacher trainees. In I. McGrath (Ed.), *Learning to Train: Perspectives on the Development of Language Teacher Trainers* (pp. 73–81). Prentice Hall Europe.

Oztirk, M. (2019). An Evaluation of an Innovative In-service Teacher Training Model in Turkey. *International Journal of Higher Education*, *8*(1), 23–36. doi:10.5430/ijhe.v8n1p23

Pohl, U., Szesztay, M., & Wright, T. (2016). In Praise of Team Training. English Teaching Professional, 103, 57-61.

Rao, Z., & Chen, H. (2019). Teachers' perceptions of difficulties in team teaching between local- and native-English-speaking teachers in EFL teaching. *Journal of Multilingual and Multicultural Development*, 1–15. doi:10.1080/01434632.2019.1620753

Scherer, R. D., & Sardone, N. B. (2013). Collaboration as a Form of Professional Development: Improving Learning for Faculty and Students. *College Teaching*, *61*(1), 30–37. doi:10.1080/87567555.2012.714815

Skrypnyk, T. (2006). Moving into Teacher Training. *The Teacher Trainer Journal*, *20*(2), 2.

Tran, L. T., Thanh Le, T. T., Phan, H. L. T., & Pham, A. (2021). "Induction and off you go": Professional development for teachers in transnational education. *Oxford Review of Education*, *47*(4), 529–547. doi:10.1080/03054985.2020.1867524

Tsybulsky, D. (2019). The team-teaching experiences of pre-service science: Teachers implementing PBL in elementary school. *Journal of Education for Teaching*, *45*(3), 244–261. doi:10.1080/09589236.2019.1599505

Velzen, C. V., Klink, M. V. D., Swennen, A., & Yaffe, E. (2010). The induction and needs of beginning teacher educators. *Professional Development in Education*, *36*(1-2), 61–75. doi:10.1080/19415250903454817

Williams, J., Ritter, J., & Bullock, S. M. (2012). Understanding the Complexity of Becoming a Teacher Educator: Experience, belonging, and practice within a professional learning community, Studying Teacher Education. *Studying Teacher Education*, *8*(3), 245–260. doi:10.1080/17425964.2012.719130

Woodward, T. (1997). Trainer training: A question matrix. In I. McGrath (Ed.), *Learning to Train: Perspectives on the Development of Language Teacher Trainers* (pp. 3–10). Prentice Hall Europe.

Woodward, T. (2006). Am I Ready to be a Teacher Trainer? *The Teacher Trainer Journal*, *20*(1), 2.

Wright, T., & Bolitho, R. (2007). *Trainer Development*. Lightning Source UK Ltd.

Chapter 16
Reflection on Teaching Observation for Computer Science and Engineering to Design Effective Teaching Resources in Transnational Higher Education

Sukhpal Singh Gill
https://orcid.org/0000-0002-3913-0369
Queen Mary University of London, UK

Danielle Thibodeau
Queen Mary University of London, UK

Rupinder Kaur
Dulwich College, UK

Usman Naeem
Queen Mary University of London, UK

Tony Stockman
Queen Mary University of London, UK

ABSTRACT

Teaching observation plays an important role in the development of educators in higher education institutions, as this practice facilitates an environment where educators can share and be made aware of good pedagogic practices. This also applies to educators who teach in transnational higher education (TNE) programmes. The work in this article presents a theoretical framework for reflection on educator observations that took place on a semi-structured data and advanced data modelling module delivered to the BSc/MSc computer science programme at Queen Mary University of London. This article also provides an overview of a research methodology for designing and delivering teaching resources based on educational research and theory, as well as personal evaluations of the teaching teams' previous experience. The article illustrates how the approach adopted for the module can be transferrable to TNE programmes.

DOI: 10.4018/978-1-6684-5226-4.ch016

INTRODUCTION

Learners' expectations and pace require teaching approaches to be altered to suit their needs (Naeem et al., 2022). To ensure that educators have a better understanding of their own teaching methods, they are encouraged to adopt a practice that includes personal reflection, observations with co-workers, reflections in small groups, and university reflections (Brookfield, 1995). One of the primary purposes of teaching observation is to look for educational inequities among different groups of learners. Using this method, educators may identify and seek to eliminate biases in how different groups of learners are treated based on their gender, socioeconomic status, or other differentiating criteria. The purpose of teaching observation is to provide educators and administrators with feedback on current educational practices and to identify pedagogical problems, which could be useful to promote transnational higher education (Wilkins & Annabi, 2021).

Observing learners in the classroom allows educators to think creatively about their own practices (Gill et al., 2023a). Observational tools and interactive reflection may be used to help learners achieve learning objectives and clarify expectations while also offering targeted feedback and a chance to gather information to enhance both teaching and learning in transnational higher education (Bui, & Nguyen, (2014). Introducing evaluation tools and creative reflection into the continuous improvement cycle fosters a feeling of accountability, trust, and collaboration among employees (Gill et al., 2023b). As a result, educators are better able to implement and disseminate best practises in order to help learners achieve their educational goals while learning in transnational higher education (Gill et al., 2022a).

Motivation and Contributions

This paper presents a theoretical framework for transnational higher education through reflection on teaching observations that took place for *Semi-Structured Data and Advanced Data Modelling*, a module taught on the MSc and BSc Computer Science programmes at Queen Mary University of London. A description of a research process for developing and providing good teaching resources that are based on educational research and theory, as well as personal evaluations of prior experience, is also presented. Finally, the data and evaluation outcomes acquired after using this approach in September 2021 are presented to demonstrate its efficacy in transnational and global higher education institutions. This module was taught online to learners in the United Kingdom and other countries in late September through mid-December 2021, demonstrating that it is suited for future Transnational Higher Education (TNE).

The rest of the chapter is structured as follows: the second section presents the review of relevant literature. The third section details a theoretical framework for teaching observation in computer science education. The fourth section gives the methodology for post-observation action. The fifth section shows the preliminary results from the post-observation action. The sixth section offers recommendations for transnational higher education. Finally, the seventh section concludes the chapter.

BACKGROUND AND ANALYSIS OF LITERATURE

More and more colleges and universities are using transnational higher education (TNE) as a means of internationalising their programmes. In higher education, TNE refers to any form of programmes or educational services in which the learners are situated in a nation other than where the granting institution is located (Gill et al., 2022a). TNE is also known as cross-border, offshore, and borderless higher education in the academic literature (Knight, 2016). University programmes are increasingly being delivered across national borders as a strong indicator of higher education's internationalisation in this century. Many universities are grappling with how to ensure the quality of this innovative form of education.

It has already been shown that TNE provides learners with more flexibility to plan their futures, but it also raises the competition for jobs that need practical abilities and adaptable mindsets (Bolton, & Nie, 2010). As a result of this research, new ideas for TNE models that provide value and are long-term will be generated, as will implications for quality assurance frameworks and research into forging relationships and cultures across borders. Another study (Chapman, & Pyvis, 2012) employs an auto-ethnographic method to improve teaching and learning in transnational programmes that are given in a postcolonial environment (Hong Kong) by a university that is located in the former colonising country (UK). In order to show how TNE programmes may benefit learning and teaching in both the host and home contexts, it is necessary to acknowledge and embrace the complexity such a situation presents. Another study (Trahar, 2015) examines the factors that contribute to high-quality education in the context of Australian universities' global programmes. Using teaching observation and reflection techniques, this research provides universities with concepts for enhancing current frameworks for ensuring the quality of learning and teaching in university off-campus education programmes. Teaching observation and reflection as tools for improving quality in TNE can also provide excellent teaching and learning in university programmes offered abroad.

The above-discussed literature reported that there is a need to design effective teaching resources for providing TNE in an efficient manner (Gill et al., 2022b). It has been also identified that using different types of teaching resources (e.g. Mentimeter quizzes, case studies, animated videos, annotated exemplar and team-based activities) can be used together to design online sessions to offer transnational higher education (Gill et al., 2023a). As Queen Mary University of London (QMUL) is a very diverse university with learners from different cultures, nationalities, educational backgrounds or experiences, ages of learners, ethnicities, races and genders (Gill et al., 2023b), there is a need to utilise group-based activities (think-pair & share and case study based discussions in groups) to deal with diversity while offering TNE. Further, there is a need for different types of feedback and suggestions from tutors, senior colleagues and peers through teaching observations to implement the above-discussed plan. Therefore, there is a need to develop a new framework to design effective teaching resources in TNE, which can be improved through reflection on teaching observation. Further, Bloom's Taxonomy was used in conjunction with all resources in an efficient manner because it is a valuable tool for improving the ability to think critically and tackle real-world issues with innovation, and has been utilized successfully in many disciplines such as science & engineering (Hager et al., 1994), sustainability (Pappas et al., 2013) and music education (Hanna, 2007) to enable a sustainable learning environment. To test the practical applicability of this framework, we applied it to the teaching of *Semi-Structured Data and Advanced Data Modelling* to MSc and BSc Computer Science programmes at Queen Mary University of London. These online teaching sessions were be observed while delivering to the learners in the United Kingdom and other countries at same time due to COVID-19 pandemic, demonstrating that it is suited for future transnational higher education. Further, the evaluation data & formative assessments and the Virtual Learning Environment (VLE) analytics will be assessed to analyse its impact both in terms of learner engagement and teaching practices. Finally, various possible challenges will be identified during the implementation of this theoretical framework for TNE for future readers and researchers.

A THEORETICAL FRAMEWORK AND METHODOLOGY FOR TEACHING OBSERVATION IN COMPUTER SCIENCE EDUCATION

A methodology for reflecting on classroom observations in computer science education is discussed in this section, which may be used to create useful teaching materials for transnational higher education institutions. While pursuing a teaching qualification (PGCAP), the notion of active learning was discussed, specifically that it can be used to increase learner engagement and, as a result, teaching abilities were greatly improved (Gill et al., 2022). Additional dynamic learning methodologies were implemented, which were taught to learners throughout the module's first semester of instruction in Jan-April 2020. When it came to online instruction, a blended learning paradigm was adopted (Naeem et al., 2022). A variety of activities were used, including viewing a video clip before an online live session to develop a participant's knowledge, using a problem-solving strategy during the online educational session to encourage learners' involvement, and administering a quiz after the session to assess learners' understanding of the material. This module provides an ideal opportunity to assess new teaching strategies while also having the opportunity to gather helpful feedback from observers. Because of the COVID-19 pandemic, it is extremely difficult to teach a complete module online to more than 100 learners located in various regions (making this approach suitable for TNE) while ensuring that the maximum number of learners participate. The observation session was conducted during a *Semi-structured Data and Advanced Data Modelling* lecture at Queen Mary University of London, which is a compulsory module for learners enrolled in the MSc and BSc Computer Science programmes at the university.

Online Teaching Session

A two-part session on "XML Transformation" was held online, and 250 BSc/MSc Computer Science learners attended both sessions. CSS rules for HTML to XML transformation were the focus of the first session, which addressed "transforming XML using Cascading Style Sheets (CSS)". XSLT templates and stylesheets, as well as default templates, were covered in detail in the second session, which focused on converting XML using XSLT.

Objective

While conducting classroom observations, the major purpose of this study was to consider numerous ideas made by the tutor, a senior colleague, and other observers. In this task, it was an attempt to discover research ideas for enhancing teaching methods, whether internal or external to the organisation. Six internal areas of improvement for the teaching practise were identified, and these areas have been classified into three separate categories: academic, personal, and professional growth and development. Figure 1 shows a theoretical framework for the development of key teaching skills.

It was also determined which common aspects (lecture design and teaching method) needed to be improved in order to enhance teaching skills which could be useful for TNE. The external environments of both educators and learners can have an impact on the educational experience, which are elements which over we do not have direct control. In addition, a system for coping with these problems in order to improve teaching abilities is discussed in this work.

Figure 1. Theoretical Framework for the development of key teaching skills

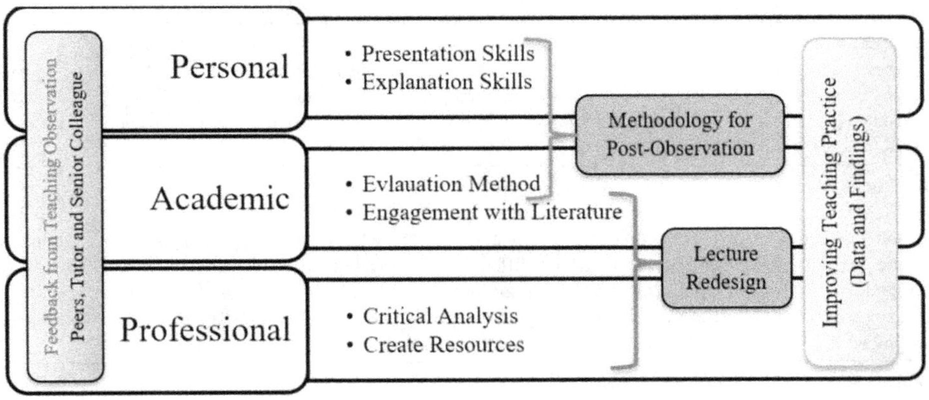

Teaching Observations

In this section, suggestions given by the tutor, senior colleague and peers during teaching observations are discussed to improve teaching based on the online teaching session delivered to the learners in the United Kingdom and other countries at same time.

Teaching Observation: By Senior Colleague

Because of the confidentiality agreement, the teaching observation undertaken by the senior colleague from QMUL and the name of the observer is not revealed. Table 1 describes the teaching session which was observed by senior colleague.

Table 1. About the teaching session observed by senior colleague

Name of Observee	**Dr Sukhpal Singh Gill**		
School/ Institute	School of Electronic Engineering and Computer Science/QMUL		
Name of Observer	Anonymous		
Topic of session	Extensible Stylesheet Language Transformations (XSLT)		
Module/Course/Unit	Semi-structured Data and Advanced Data Modelling (ECS650U/ECS789P)		
Level/Year	Level: 6/BSc 3rd Year and MSc	**No. learners**	150
Type of session (synchronous or asynchronous, lecture/seminar/practical…)	**Asynchronous**		
Date of session	7/11/2020		
Time of session	10 am (UK time)		
Length of session	15 Minutes		
Location (may be online)	Online		
How should the observer participate? (attend live webinar, watch recording, sit/stand in particular location)	Watch Recording		

continues on following page

Table 1. Continued

Name of Observee	Dr Sukhpal Singh Gill
1. What is the content and structure of the class you will be teaching? "Extensible Stylesheet Language Transformations (XSLT)" is the topic of the first 15 minutes of the two-hour class. There will be simple examples in this session to show how to use XSLT stylesheets and template defaults. There are 70 BSc Computer Science learners and 80 MSc Computer Science learners in this session, all of whom are following the QMUL teaching format. In addition, a live, one-hour Q&A session will be held to address questions from learners.	
2. Describe your learners – what is the background or composition of the group? There are 70 BSc Computer Science learners and 80 MSc Computer Science learners enrolled in this session. All of the BSc learners have completed their first and second years of computer science at Queen Mary University of London, and they are homogeneous. Although new to the programme, MSc learners come from a different educational qualifications, including bachelor's degrees in computer science, industrial engineering, information technology, and electronic engineering. All of the BSc learners are full-time students, however some of the MSc learners are enrolled in a part-time programme. Several participants are travelling from the United Kingdom to join this session, while others are staying in their native countries.	
3. What have learners been asked to do in preparation for the class? Before attending this course, learners should be familiar with the concepts of HTML, XML, and CSS and should have some prior expertise. There will be an online quiz on QMPLUS that will be based on Mentimeter to evaluate the participants' previous knowledge.	
4. What are the aims and intended learning outcomes of the session? LO1: be familiar with XSLT and its rules. LO2: be familiar with XSLT templates & stylesheets and default templates. LO3: be able to understand the transformation of XML data using XSLT. LO4: be able to transform from HTML to XML using XSLT stylesheets.	
5. How do you plan to achieve these? This lecture will be introduced with a 5-minute online quiz on QMPLUS, which will assess the learners' prior understanding of the subject.	
6. What would you like the observer to focus on during the observation? Are there particular areas you would like feedback on? The presentation of material, the teaching approach used when discussing the concepts/examples utilizing highlighter and marker, and the clarity of voice used during interaction are all significant factors.	

Table 2. Observation feedback and comments given by the senior colleague

Please comment on the following aspects of the observed session:	
1. Clarity of the aims and learning outcomes	The asynchronous video does, in fact, deliver the learning outcomes from the meeting. Maybe this information has already been supplied on the QMPlus. One option is provide an overview of this at the beginning of the video.
2. Clarity and organisation of the session including timekeeping and structure	The clarity and organisation was excellent, and the material was delivered in an understandable manner.
3. Teaching and learning methods – are they appropriate, are they innovative?	For an asynchronous session, the teaching and learning approaches are suitable; nevertheless, I suggest consider employing animation to show bullet points, since it would make it easier for learners to process the material. I really believe that Sukhpal might go into further detail on the concerns.
4. In-session assessment or review methods – are they appropriate?	This was not applicable for this session.
5. The form and extent of active learning and learner participation	I believe this was not obvious, and I urge that Sukhpal start making use of H5P to incorporate interactive questions into his lessons in way to involve his class.
6. Delivery and pace of the session	The manner in which the session was delivered and the speed at which it proceeded were suitable for this session.
7. Use of learning technologies (if applicable)	N/A
8. Specific areas identified for feedback by observee	The voice was really clear; however, I would avoid using the highlighter to underline each bullet point excessively because it might be annoying.
9. What suggestions would you make to build on strengths and/or improve teaching?	**Strengths:** The quality of the voice and the clarity of the slides were superb. Improvements: Animate bullet points (as suggested in the previous remark) and elaborate on topics more.

Table 2 shows the observation feedback and comments given by the senior colleague.

Teaching Observation: By Colleague (Peer)

Because of the confidentiality agreement, the teaching observation undertaken by the Colleague (Peer) from QMUL and the name of the observer is not revealed. Table 3 shows about the teaching session which was observed by Colleague (Peer).

Table 3. About the teaching session observed by Colleague (Peer)

<table>
<tr><th>Name of Observee</th><th colspan="3">Dr Sukhpal Singh Gill</th></tr>
<tr><td>School/ Institute</td><td colspan="3">School of Electronic Engineering and Computer Science/QMUL</td></tr>
<tr><td>Name of Observer</td><td colspan="3">Anonymous</td></tr>
<tr><td>Topic of session</td><td colspan="3">Cascading Style Sheets</td></tr>
<tr><td>Module/Course/Unit</td><td colspan="3">Semi-structured Data and Advanced Data Modelling (ECS650U/ECS789P)</td></tr>
<tr><td>Level/Year</td><td>Level: 6/BSc 3rd Year and MSc</td><td>No. learners</td><td>150</td></tr>
<tr><td>Type of session (synchronous or asynchronous, lecture/ seminar/practical…)</td><td colspan="3">Asynchronous</td></tr>
<tr><td>Date of session</td><td colspan="3">6/11/2020</td></tr>
<tr><td>Time of session</td><td colspan="3">10 am (UK time)</td></tr>
<tr><td>Length of session</td><td colspan="3">10 Minutes</td></tr>
<tr><td>Location (may be online)</td><td colspan="3">Online</td></tr>
<tr><td>How should the observer participate?
(attend live webinar, watch recording, sit/stand in particular location)</td><td colspan="3">Watch Recording</td></tr>
<tr><td colspan="4">1. What is the content and structure of the class you will be teaching?
This is the first 10 minutes of a two-hour session on "Transforming XML Using Cascading Style Sheets", which will go until the end of the day. In this session, observe explains CSS rules and their importance, as well as provide two tiny examples to illustrate main points. QMUL's teaching framework is being followed by 70 BSc Computer Science learners and 80 MSc Computer Science learners in current session, which includes both UG and PG learners. Additionally, there will be a live one-hour Q&A session to address any questions from learners.</td></tr>
<tr><td colspan="4">2. Describe your learners – what is the background or composition of the group?
The number of undergraduate computer science learners in this session is 70, whereas the number of graduate computer science learners in this session is 80. All of the BSc learners have completed their first and second years of computer science at Queen Mary University of London, and they are homogeneous. Although new to the programme, MSc learners come from a variety of educational backgrounds, including bachelor's degrees in computer science, industrial engineering, information technology, and electronics engineering. All of the BSc learners are full-time learners, however some of the MSc learners are enrolled in a part-time programme. Many participants are travelling from the United Kingdom to join this session, while the others are staying in their native countries.</td></tr>
<tr><td colspan="4">3. What have learners been asked to do in preparation for the class?
Before attending this class, learners should be familiar with the concepts of HTML and XML and should have some previous knowledge. To assess the participants' past knowledge, they will be required to complete a ten-minute online quiz on QMPLUS.</td></tr>
<tr><td colspan="4">4. What are the aims and intended learning outcomes of the session?
LO1: be familiar with CSS and its rules.
LO2: be able to understand the transformation of XML data using CSS.
LO3: be able to transform from HTML to XML using CSS stylesheets.</td></tr>
<tr><td colspan="4">5. How do you plan to achieve these?
This session will be introduced with a ten-minute online quiz on QMPLUS, which will assess the participants' prior understanding of the material covered in this session.</td></tr>
<tr><td colspan="4">6. What would you like the observer to focus on during the observation? Are there particular areas you would like feedback on?
The presentation of material, the teaching approach used when discussing the concepts/examples utilizing highlighter and marker, and the clarity of voice used during interaction are all significant factors.</td></tr>
</table>

Table 4 shows the observation feedback and comments given by the colleague (peer).

Table 4. Observation feedback and comments given by the colleague (peer)

	lease comment on the following aspects of the observed session:
1. Clarity of the aims and learning outcomes	The purpose for using CSS is well stated, and the aims and goals of the presentation are explicitly defined in the course of the session.
2. Clarity and organisation of the session including timekeeping and structure	The pace of the presentation is easy to follow even for non-experts, and the spectator is left anticipating what will happen next.
3. Teaching and learning methods – are they appropriate, are they innovative?	The techniques of teaching and learning are suitable and fascinating. We gain a true sense of why we should use CSS and how it can be altered to achieve our goal because of the usage of examples throughout the session. What I appreciate about CSS formatting is that there are two stages: the first is the most basic, and the second includes certain rules such as if/then actions and analyzing existing text to append letters.
4. In-session assessment or review methods – are they appropriate?	There is an on-line quiz well before session and it is assumed that all of the participants have finished it prior. Perhaps an introductory statement that emphasises the principles that are intended to be learned prior to the remainder of this course. In other words, "you should be acquainted with defining web pages using html or xml, and you should have finished the on-line quiz..."
5. The form and extent of active learning and learner participation	This is asynchronous so it is not applicable
6. Delivery and pace of the session	The rhythm is nice, especially because one can travel back and forth between CSS and XML and the final result to better comprehend the relationship between the two.
7. Use of learning technologies (if applicable)	It is really beneficial to give an example to show each phase of the lecture process. Additionally, the employment of a highlighter to direct the listener's attention to a particular region of interest is effective since it creates the idea that things are developing up to the final consequence.
8. Specific areas identified for feedback by observee	The presentation is well-organized, and the speed is simple to keep up with. The use of highlighters helps to draw the viewer's attention to the most important idea being covered in the presentation. The illustrations used in the lesson provide a more real sense to the presentation.
9. What suggestions would you make to build on strengths and/or improve teaching?	Just one aspect I will suggest is that you include an introduction slide or line that connects this lecture to what has gone before, such as "we've studied X, Y, and Z for establishing the web page structure, now we will show how we can enhance the display of the HTML using CSS..."

Teaching Observation: By Tutor

Because of the confidentiality agreement, the teaching observation undertaken by the Tutor from QMUL and the name of the observer is not revealed. Table 5 shows the observation feedback and comments given by Tutor.

Teaching Observation: By Attendees (Peers)

Online teaching session was also attended by two peers and their feedback is given in Table 6.

Table 5. Observation feedback and comments given by Tutor

Criteria	Description
Critical analysis	You provide some context for why motivation and teamwork are important for software engineering, but it would have been better to provide some context for that outside of your own opinion and two YouTube comments, like reference to studies about learners lacking these skills from an employer perspective, or data from learner surveys that describe their experiences as boring. It wasn't clear that organizational complexity was directly responsible for lack of motivation, or how that was addressed in your session plan.
Debating practice	You made some references to how you are using the interests of your learner to better connect their learning to real life events, like the application of real work problems to computing, which is very important. You may want to consider how you can connect that with evidence of how authentic assignments increase motivation and participation. I was also a bit confused by the challenges. If the purpose of the activities is to increase teamwork, but teamwork ends up being a challenge to the success of the activity, is the activity effective?
Engagement with scholarship and literature	You clearly link your use of certain activities to Bloom's taxonomy, which is great. You briefly reference work that supports the effectiveness of the activities you're using but it would have been more effective if you had critically engage in that research, being clearer how it supports you, how it does not, and why you consider it relevant to what you're trying to achieve.
Quality of academic writing	The presentation was clearly signposted, and you engaged with a wide range of sources though not many of them were discussed in detail during the presentation. Next time consider how to better use your time by giving less detailed descriptions of activities and more time to engage in that critical discussion about the connections your activities had to the literature, and to clarifying the challenges and how you'll overcome them.
Any other comments?	Sukhpal it's clear that you've put a lot of time and thought into the development of your lesson plan. It's still a bit unclear to me whether one of the intended learning outcomes of the session you describe are to learn teamwork skills, or if the teamwork is in service of learning other software skills. It's not necessarily the goal that every individual lesson engages every level on Bloom's taxonomy, but rather that the levels are represented thoughtfully at different points in a learner's journey through a programme of study. I would encourage you to do a bit more reading into putting Bloom's work into practice. For example, the "evaluate" level does not refer to your evaluation of the learner's learning; it refers whether the learner has developed the skills to themselves evaluate information about a topic (for example, can they evaluate which method is most appropriate for a given situation described in a case study).

Table 6. Observation feedback and comments given by Peers

Criteria	Peer 1	Peer 2
Feedback on the resource itself – does it look useful and interesting?	The resource is rich. Mentimeter and video are used. Kahoot is also used.	It's interesting to see the flow of the technique of how to encourage learners to engage with the flow of the lecture with topic to be discussed - with group activity - think pair and share. Mentimeter and kahoot tool used. Feedback survey - Google Forms.
Feedback on use of literature and scholarship	The use of literature is appropriate.	Bloom's taxonomy is applied but there's a lack of explanation on how the resources are applied in the demonstration, also, there's a lack of justification on how each level of the lecture design is related with the bloom's taxonomy.
Feedback on debating practice – links to, and learning from, other people's work	The presenter shows too much about the teaching methods, and also the teaching materials.	References are available but it would be good to show to evidence findings from other people's work on using the teaching and scholarship method.
Feedback on critical analysis – has the person justified why they've made this resource with reference to their context and the needs of key stakeholders?	Yes	The presenter has mentioned the use of bloom's taxonomy but it would be good to relate this into the work case study scenario.
Any other feedback for the presenter?	No	No

POST-OBSERVATION ACTION

Based on the constructive feedback given by the tutor, senior colleague and peers, through reflection on various internal issues for improving teaching skills for the future have been identified. Figure 2 shows the common areas (engagement with literature and content management) to improve teaching skills as suggested by a tutor, senior colleague and peers.

Figure 2. Common areas for the improvement of teaching practice

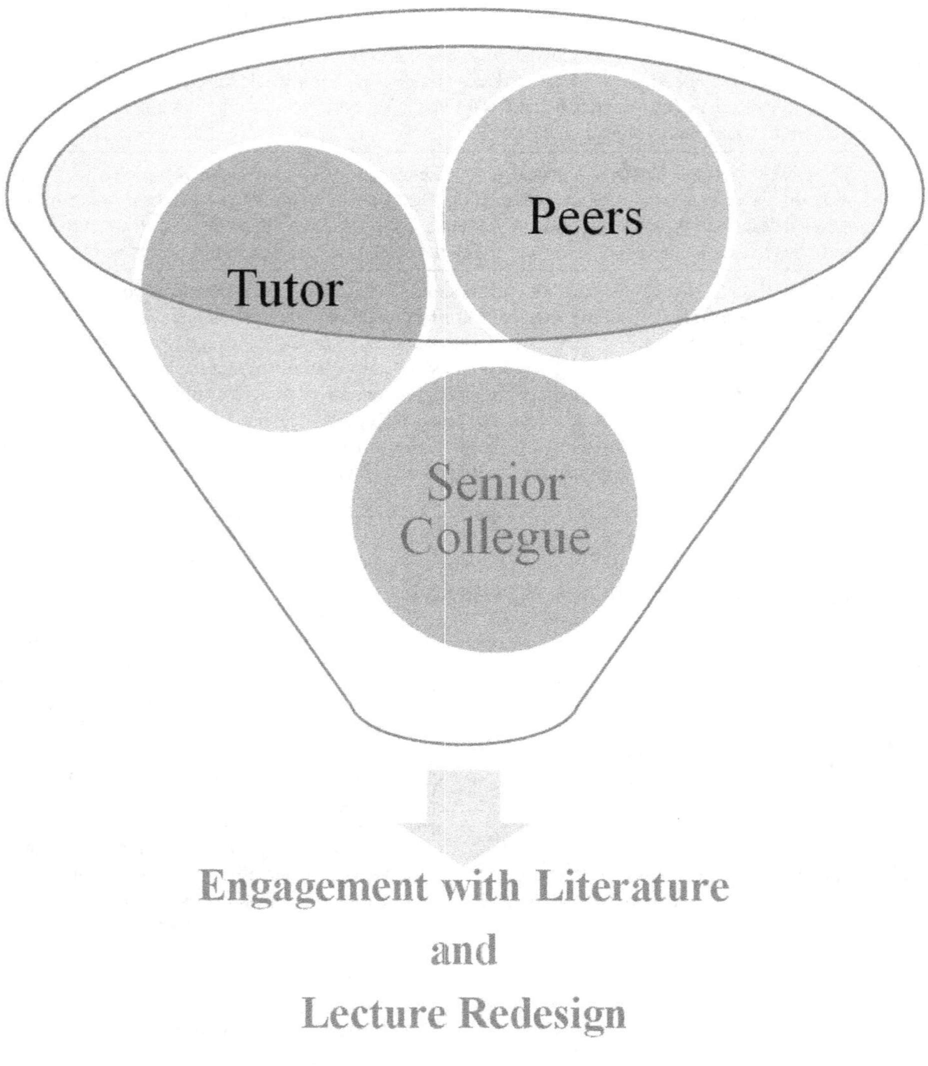

Revised Lecture

This section presents the revised lecture after learning various new teaching and learning methodologies from teaching observations. The Higher Education Academy (HEA) provides a framework for final evaluation, teaching, and learning to provide support to learners pursuing higher education in a variety of subjects at different levels (Nurunnabi, 2019). It has assisted instructors in engaging with their academic work, as demonstrated by Brooman's successful implementation and testing in the delivery of legal education (Brooman, 2011).

The "Learning and Teaching" module is an important element of PGCAP at the Queen Mary, and it assists the design of tools for practical learning, teaching, and evaluation in the workplace (Gill et al., 2022a). Educationists can benefit from the current evaluation techniques and feedback experiences in order to build successful curriculum and deliver high-quality education (Qadir et al., 2020). Innovative education boosts learners' learning performance offering a long-term favourable effect on their career to build numerous significant projects for society's advantages (Nerantzi & Hannaford, 2016). However, how can learners learn more successfully during a lecture session? The key concerns that must be addressed in order to provide better advanced learning are always evolving (Toquero, 2020).

The preparation of a session plan assists in delivering the essential information by adhering to the timetable that has been established. For the purpose of encouraging learners to participate with the lecture flow, a variety of activities have been examined (group activity, case study, quiz, and video). The lesson was opened with a quiz to get the learners to use their existing knowledge. After that, a brief video clip was played and used a case study to showcase XML-based projects to the class. In addition, annotated exemplars were used to connect the ideas of XML, XSLT, and CSS rules with real-world applications (Gill et al., 2022b). In addition, a group-based activity (i.e. think-pair-and-share) was used to assess the characteristics of XML-based projects, which motivated learners to interact in order to produce new innovative ideas. When it came to understanding XML ideas, learners drew on their existing knowledge of a variety of disciplines (including Web Technology basics and HTML). Last but not least, feedback was collected using Google forms.

It is critical to begin the session with a strong motivation for the topic, which will ensure that learners are paying attention. According to my observer, the lecture's clear and logical flow is easy to understand and maintains the viewers interest in seeing how things will unfold in the next few minutes. Furthermore, in order to present appealing material, the session's clarity and structure are essential; this was noted by my observer, who expressed appreciation for my efforts: 'The clarity of the speech was superb, and the slides were clear.' Bloom's Taxonomy (Sosniak, 1994) is an effective technique amongst various educational courses for solving real-life problems and developing key skills. It provides effective teaching approaches to solving problems with innovation in science and engineering disciplines, and it is widely used in business and industry (Pappas, 2002; Hager et al., 1994). It is interesting to see Bloom's Taxonomy being successfully used in the teaching of sustainability (Pappas et al., 2013).

As a result, although sustainability is a separate field, the same teaching method was adopted. It has been discovered that the updated Bloom's Taxonomy was applied in music education by Hanna (2010), who demonstrated that it encourages inventive thinking to enhance cognitive learning, which has a favourable influence on learning music education. As a result, a session was created in which multiple Bloom's taxonomy levels were applied to describe the utilisation of diverse resources to generate new ideas in an XML-based project, as seen in Table 7.

Table 7. Application of Bloom's levels to describe the use of various resources to create innovative ideas in XML-based project after teaching observations by tutor, senior colleague and peers

Bloom's Level	Resource	Component
Remember	Mentimeter Quiz	**Recall** the basic concepts of XML, XSLT. **Recognize** the rules of CSS.
Understand	• Case Study • Video	**Discuss** the XML based projects. **Explain** XML based projects with a case study.
Apply	Presentation on real world problems (Annotated Exemplar)	**Demonstrate** the use of XML, XSLT and CSS for the development of famous software engineering projects. **Illustrate** the application of XML, XSLT and CSS on real world problems based projects.
Analyse	Think Pair and Share (Team based activity)	**Analyze** the features of XML based Projects **Classify** the web services provided in these projects.
Evaluate	Think Pair and Share (Team based activity)	**Compare** different XML based Projects based on latest development tools & techniques, certification and quality standards. **Choose** the best XML project based on quality standard and certification.
Create	Ideation	**Generate** new ideas for future XML based Projects. **Develop** problem solving and logical thinking skills.

As a result of the COVID-19 epidemic, it has become difficult to teach a complete module online to a large number of learners (Singhal et al., 2020). Unfortunately, online education has devolved into a passive mode of information transfer, with involvement and discussion confined to a few select participants (Sonia, 2017). When there is no real teaching environment present, it is difficult to hold a learner's attention during a lesson. It is necessary to use a variety of materials to increase learner involvement, but it is difficult to manage these resources while teaching online. As a result, a lecture was created based on Bloom's Taxonomy to ensure that resources were used efficiently; the comments from my observers reflected this. The input from the observer revealed that there is a need to adequately explain how each lecture design level is connected to Bloom's taxonomy. Another observer pointed out that teaching and scholarly technique was not used to demonstrate evidence results from other people's work, which was something that needs to be done. Given the limited time available for the first presentation, several primary sources were referenced and presented a teaching style that utilised a variety of resources to help the learners understand the content. Fortunately, teaching observations provided with a wonderful opportunity to discuss the interaction with literature from other fields and to explain the thorough teaching methods using a case-study scenario, all while commenting on a number of different findings. Consequently, the necessary explanation (Table 7) for each level of Bloom's taxonomy was revised.

One observer and tutor both commented that employing all of Bloom's taxonomy levels in a single session is a difficult undertaking to accomplish. However, this method was used for teaching practise to more efficiently arrange all of the resources. Mayhew (2019) discovered that a brief quiz may be used to kick-start the session and engage learners' existing knowledge. This method has been successfully tested in the Political Science field, resulting in improved teaching and learning outcomes. As a result, the lesson was started with a Mentimeter quiz to ensure that learners can retain and recognise the XML principles (Remember). The usage of H5P in the future, according to one of the observers, should include interactive questions to increase learner involvement while teaching in an asynchronous mode. In general, the concepts were conveyed verbally and merely highlighted the most important elements on the slides. According to one of the observers, animation should be used to show bullet points in the PowerPoint presentation, which would make the presentation more dynamic and assist learners in focussing on the specific issue being discussed at any given time. To raise attention using advanced technology, the image(s) or animation will be utilized to elaborate essential topics in future sessions, as Holzl (1997) noted in his research "twelve suggestions for effective presentations" to increase attention using advanced technology.

A study conducted by Hobgood et al. (2010) discovered that educating nursing and medical learners through real-life case studies can boost learners' learning while also encouraging collaboration. In another study, researchers discovered that video-based education is a valuable teaching tool for better analysis, and they used World War II footage to teach history (Yousef et al., 2014). A short movie was played and discussed as case study to teach the XML, XSL, and CSS ideas, which was quite effective (Understand). Annotated exemplars are another active learning technique that may be used to get a true sense of what is being taught. Based on the findings, it appears to boost nursing learners' academic performance while also explaining the ideas through the use of real-life scenarios (Carter et al., 2019). As a result, two annotated exemplars (XML-based web services for software businesses) were used to demonstrate how XML is being used to solve real-world issues in practise (Apply). Using efficient teaching and evaluation methodologies, Junco (2012) discovered that naive learners might learn fundamental collaborative abilities that could be transferred to software experts working for international corporations such as Facebook or Google. Another research of healthcare workers discovered that learners lacked cooperation skills from the perspective of their employers, and it indicated that group-based learning activities such as "think-pair-share" activities might help learners enhance their teamwork abilities (Fox et al., 2018). Using creative problem solving and mathematical reasoning, Kashefi et al. (2012) discovered that cooperation is a key skill for multivariable calculus learning. To enhance active learning, the technique "Think-pair-and-share", was included which divided the large group into smaller groups for improved interaction. Then a variety of scenario-based assignments were designed and asked learners to assess the qualities of software businesses and categorise them depending on the services they provide (Analyze).

In the online session, the Bloom's Taxonomy's evaluation level was not described in detail, which was reviewed with tutor and colleague in order to fix. In order to make selections about the finest XML project, learners should consider quality standards and certifications, among other factors (Evaluate). According to (Hoegl & Parboteeah, 2007), teamwork-based learning may assist learners in instilling team spirit while also motivating them to think rationally in order to generate new ideas. Learners develop their creative abilities in order to handle software projects at this level (Create). Finally, problems were solved and teaching practises evaluated with some recommendations and feedback from learners provided using Google forms. Much of the feedback received was positive, which demonstrates that acquiring software skills through cooperation and the use of Bloom's Taxonomy is effective. When identifying the challenges, tutor pointed out one error in using the erroneous word "Teamwork Willingness", when actually the phrase "how to instil team spirit among participants" (which was mentioned as one of the external obstacles) would have been more appropriate.

PRELIMINARY RESULTS: DATA ANALYSIS AND FINDINGS

In this section, some conclusions and findings are highlighted in the form of formative assessments and feedback.

Formative Assessments

For formative assessments, a Mentimeter quizz was used during online session and every quiz contains five MCQs or T/F questions. The main aim of the quizzes was to checks learners' prior knowledge and reviews learners' understanding. There were 250 learners studying *Semi-Structured Data and Advanced Data Modelling* for the year 2021-2022 at QMUL. Figure 3 shows the Mentimeter based weekly on-line quizzes (MCQs and T/F) during online sessions (Formative assessment). Figure 3 shows that 205 learners out of 250 have participated in the Mentimeter quiz in the first week's online session, which clearly shows that using web-based tools increase learner engagement during online learning. It is noted, however, that the number of participants decreased with time for some weeks, which could be due to learners maybe being busy with assignments and coursework for other modules.

Figure 3. Mentimeter Based Weekly online quizzes (MCQs and T/F) during online session (Formative)

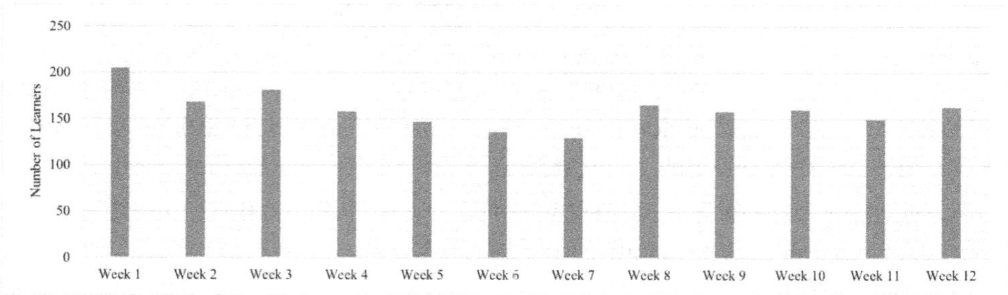

Figure 4 shows the H5P-based videos interaction before online session which learners need to watch to understand the basics of particular topic which will be covered in the online session. H5P-based videos also activates the prior knowledge about the topic which could be tested with Mentimeter based online quiz.

Figure 4. H5P-based videos interaction before online session (Formative)

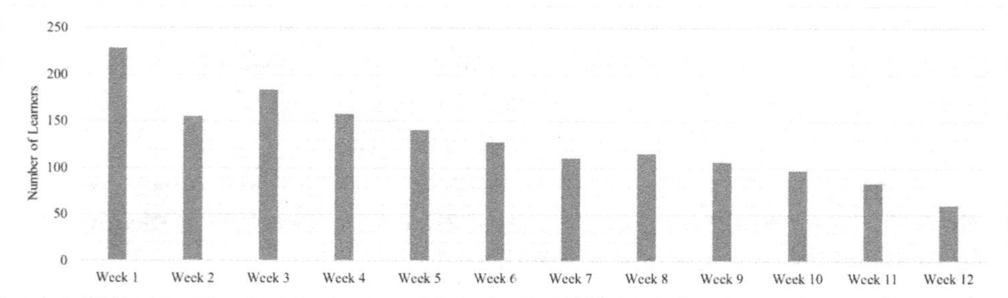

Feedback

The feedback of students was quite positive and students are happy with the teaching arrangement and organization of the module. It clearly shows that students found teaching material very useful for their career. Further, students feedback clearly shows that the teaching arrangements, delivery of module and teaching practices has been improved after reflecting on teaching observations. Furthermore, students found this module is well organized and interactive labs with different practical tasks and lecturers with Mentimeter quizzes.

The above-discussed feedback and formative assessments is clearly showing that the changes made after teaching observations were successful both in terms of student engagement and teaching practices.

RECOMMENDATIONS FOR FUTURE TRANSNATIONAL HIGHER EDUCATION

The development of this action plan occurred in response to a variety of new ideas which were learned from this module of PGCAP and a variety of sources which will assist in future academic practises (Gill et al., 2022b). The proposed teaching practice can be applied to TNE, which would be more useful for various universities around the globe. Finally, a number of external impediments have been identified when this will be implemented to TNE using online teaching (Figure 5).

Figure 5. External obstacles for delivering transnational higher education using online teaching

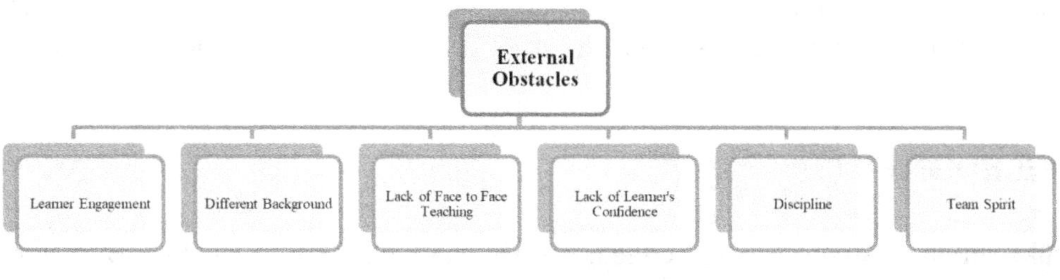

All of the observers shared a variety of beneficial ideas for keeping learners' attention while participating in online education, which could be useful for offering TNE. Furthermore, it is important to present and explain a certain topic to learners. It is critical to their interest and active involvement, especially for those who are attending these online sessions from different countries and geographical locations. As seen by the observer's response, illustrating the topic using real-life examples and relevant case studies can aid learners in comprehending the subject clearly and effectively. A small number of MSc learners come from a variety of BSc backgrounds (such as computer technology or electrical engineering), and hence require additional encouragement to work in a group to enable TNE. Demonstrations of similar historical projects can assist learners in forming a suitable team and learning the skills, technology, and tools necessary to execute the group project successfully while working from different geographical locations. Additionally, it is critical to connect with learners on a frequent basis in order to grasp their point of view when working in a group and sustaining their confidence.

Furthermore, active involvement with learners aids is key to the identification of learners who lack team spirit and who are less likely to participate in group-based activities. It is critical to monitor the progress of the learners working in a group to complete the assignment. It is also necessary to conduct constant evaluations in order to verify that all learners from different geographical locations in the group are fully engaged in the completion of their project to measure the success related of TNE.

It can be difficult to overcome external hurdles at times, but creativity and practise can assist in overcoming these difficulties for TNE. There is a need for active participation in various peer observation programmes in order to develop teaching and increase learner involvement in the classroom during online teaching to implement TNE into practice. The small focus groups from various locations/countries can be selected to receive more thorough input on these particular internal and external difficulties, which can help to evaluate the revised teaching practises for TNE in terms of learner engagement and active involvement.

CONCLUSION

This chapter has reflected on the use of teaching observation and reflection in the developing for lectures teaching Semi-Structured Data and Advanced Data Modelling to MSc and BSc Computer Science programmes at Queen Mary University of London. By implementing various pieces of feedback collected from observations from tutors, senior colleague and peers of session taught online, a framework has been developed and evaluated using student feedback and data from formative assessments and VLE analytics. This chapter has aimed to apply this framework to challenges that persist to success delivery of transitional higher education and it is our assertion that this methodology provides a roadmap to improving the experience of both students and educators in this increasingly important mode of delivery.

ACKNOWLEDGMENT

We are thankful to faculty members and colleagues who have given their valuable comments to improve the quality of this work. We declare that this work has been submitted as an ***Assignment for Learning and Teaching in the Discipline module*** in partial fulfilment of the requirements for the award of the degree of ***Postgraduate Certificate Academic Practice (PGCAP) – UK Teaching Qualification*** submitted in ***QM Academy*** of Queen Mary University of London, UK is an authentic record of research work carried out by ***Sukhpal Singh Gill (First Author)*** under the supervision of ***Danielle Thibodeau (Second Author)*** and refers other researcher's work which is duly listed in the reference section. This *Assignment* has been checked using Turnitin at Queen Mary University of London, UK and the submitted assignment has been stored in the repository for university record.

REFERENCES

Bolton, D., & Nie, R. U. I. (2010). Creating value in transnational higher education: The role of stakeholder management. *Academy of Management Learning & Education*, *9*(4), 701–714.

Brookfield, S. D. (1995). Becoming a Critically Reflective Teacher. San Francisco: Jossey-Bass.

Brooman, S. (2011). Enhancing Learner Engagement by Building upon the 'Tectonic Plates' of Legal Education. *The Liverpool Law Review*, *32*(2), 109–112. doi:10.100710991-011-9097-x

Carter, R. Halcomb, Bui, H. M., & Nguyen, N. T. (2014). Choosing a Transnational Higher Education Program: What Do Vietnamese Learners Rate as Important? Australian Association for Research in Education.

Chapman, A., & Pyvis, D. (2012). *Enhancing quality in transnational higher education: Experiences of teaching and learning in Australian offshore programs*. Lexington Books.

E., Ramjan, L. M., Wilson, N. J., Glew, P., & Salamonson, Y. (2019). Does the use of annotated exemplars by nursing learners predict academic performance? A cohort study. *Nurse education today*, *80*, 34-39.

Fox, L., Onders, R., Hermansen-Kobulnicky, C. J., Nguyen, T. N., Myran, L., Linn, B., & Hornecker, J. (2018). Teaching interprofessional teamwork skills to health professional learners: A scoping review. *Journal of Interprofessional Care*, *32*(2), 127–135. doi:10.1080/13561820.2017.1399868 PMID:29172791

Gill, S. S., Fuller, S., Cabral, A., Chen, Y., & Uhlig, S. (2023a). An Operating System Session Plan Towards Social Justice and Intercultural Development in Microteaching for Higher Education. In E. Meletiadou (Ed.), *Handbook of Research on Fostering Social Justice Through Intercultural and Multilingual Communication* (pp. 44–61). IGI Global.

Gill, S. S., Fuller, S., Cabral, A., Chen, Y., & Uhlig, S. (2023b). Curriculum Redesign for Cloud Computing to Enhance Social Justice and Intercultural Development in Higher Education. In E. Meletiadou (Ed.), *Handbook of Research on Fostering Social Justice Through Intercultural and Multilingual Communication* (pp. 62–80). IGI Global.

Gill, S. S., Naeem, U., Fuller, S. Chen, Y., & Uhlig, S. (2022a). How Covid-19 Changed Computer Science Education, *ITNOW*, *64*(2), Issue 2, 60–61.

Gill, S. S., Xu, M., Ottaviani, C., Patros, P., Bahsoon, R., Shaghaghi, A., & Uhlig, S. (2022b). AI for next generation computing: Emerging trends and future directions. *Internet of Things*, *19*, 100514. doi:10.1016/j.iot.2022.100514

Hager, P., Sleet, R., & Kaye, M. (1994). The relation between critical thinking abilities and learner study strategies. *Higher Education Research & Development*, *13*(2), 179–188. doi:10.1080/0729436940130208

Hanna, W. (2007). The new Bloom's taxonomy: Implications for music education. *Arts Education Policy Review*, *108*(4), 7–16. doi:10.3200/AEPR.108.4.7-16

Hobgood, C., & Sherwood, G., Frush, et al. (2010). Teamwork training with nursing and medical learners: Does the method matter? Results of an interinstitutional, interdisciplinary collaboration. *Quality & Safety in Health Care*, *19*(6), e25. PMID:20427311

Hoegl, M., & Parboteeah, K. P. (2007). Creativity in innovative projects: How teamwork matters. *Journal of Engineering and Technology Management*, *24*(1-2), 148–166. doi:10.1016/j.jengtecman.2007.01.008

Holzl, J. (1997). Twelve tips for effective PowerPoint presentations for the technologically challenged. *Medical Teacher*, *19*(3), 175–179. doi:10.3109/01421599709019377

Junco, R. (2012). The relationship between frequency of Facebook use, participation in Facebook activities, and learner engagement. *Computers & Education*, *58*(1), 162–171. doi:10.1016/j.compedu.2011.08.004

Kashefi, H., Ismail, Z., & Yusof, Y. M. (2012). The impact of blended learning on communication skills and teamwork of engineering learners in multivariable calculus. *Procedia: Social and Behavioral Sciences*, *56*, 341–347. doi:10.1016/j.sbspro.2012.09.662

Mayhew, E. (2019). No longer a silent partner: How Mentimeter can enhance teaching and learning within Political Science. *Journal of Political Science Education*, *15*(4), 546–551. doi:10.1080/15512169.2018.1538882

Naeem, U., Bosman, L., & Gill, S. S. (2022, March). Teaching and Facilitating an Online Learning Environment for a Web Programming Module. In *Global Engineering Education Conference (EDUCON)* (pp. 769-774). IEEE. 10.1109/EDUCON52537.2022.9766757

Nerantzi, C., & Hannaford, L. (2016). Action Learning Sets Flipping the Classroom: Advantages and Challenges. An Example from Academic Development. Teaching with Team Projects in Higher Education. Information Science Press, 119-129.

Nurunnabi, M., Abdelhadi, A., Aburas, R., & Fallatah, S. (2019). Does teaching qualification matter in higher education in the UK? An analysis of National Learner Survey data. *MethodsX*, *6*, 788–799. doi:10.1016/j.mex.2019.04.001 PMID:31032182

Pappas, E. (2002). Creative problem solving in engineering design. In *Proceedings of the American Society for Engineering Education (ASEE) Southeastern Section Meeting*. University of Florida.

Pappas, E., Pierrakos, O., & Nagel, R. (2013). Using Bloom's Taxonomy to teach sustainability in multiple contexts. *Journal of Cleaner Production*, *48*, 54–64. doi:10.1016/j.jclepro.2012.09.039

Qadir, J., Taha, A. E. M., Yau, K. L. A., Ponciano, J., Hussain, S., Al-Fuqaha, A., & Imran, M. A. (2020). *Leveraging the force of formative assessment & feedback for effective engineering education.* In *Proceedings of the ASEE Annual Conference & Exposition*, Montreal, Canada 10.18260/1-2--34923

Singhal, R., Kumar, A., Singh, H., Fuller, S., & Gill, S. S. (2020). Digital device-based active learning approach using virtual community classroom during the COVID-19 pandemic. *Computer Applications in Engineering Education*, 1–27.

Sonia, G. (2017). *Educational research and innovation pedagogical knowledge and the changing nature of the teaching profession*. OECD Publishing.

Sosniak, L. A. (1994). *Bloom's taxonomy* (L. W. Anderson, Ed.). Univ. Chicago Press.

Toquero, C. M. (2020). Challenges and Opportunities for Higher Education Amid the COVID-19 Pandemic: The Philippine Context. *Pedagogical Research*, *5*(4), 1–5. doi:10.29333/pr/7947

Trahar, S. (2015). Learning and teaching on transnational higher education programmes in Hong Kong. *Learning and Teaching*, *8*(1), 95–112. doi:10.3167/latiss.2015.080106

Wilkins, S., & Annabi, C. A. (2021). Academic Careers in Transnational Higher Education: The Rewards and Challenges of Teaching at International Branch Campuses. *Journal of Studies in International Education*, 10283153211052782. doi:10.1177/10283153211052782

Yousef, A. M. F., Chatti, M. A., & Schroeder, U. (2014), Video-Based Learning: A Critical Analysis of The Research Published in 2003–2013 and Future Visions. In *Proceeding of the Sixth International Conference on Mobile, Hybrid, and Online Learning*, Barcelona, Spain, (pp. 112–119).

ADDITIONAL READING

Eldridge, K., & Cranston, N. (2009). Managing transnational education: Does national culture really matter? *Journal of Higher Education Policy and Management*, *31*(1), 67–79. doi:10.1080/13600800802559286

Meletiadou, E. (2011). Peer assessment of writing in secondary education: Its impact on learners' performance and attitudes. [M.A. in Applied Linguistics, University of Cyprus, Nicosia].

Pyvis, D. (2011). The need for context-sensitive measures of educational quality in transnational higher education. *Teaching in Higher Education*, *16*(6), 733–744. doi:10.1080/13562517.2011.570436

Wilkins, S., & Balakrishnan, M. S. (2013). Assessing learner satisfaction in transnational higher education. *International Journal of Educational Management*, *27*(2), 143–156. doi:10.1108/09513541311297568

KEY TERMS AND DEFINITIONS

Learner: This word is used interchangeably with "learner" and "participant".

Transnational Higher Education (TNE): Teaching in a country other than the one in which the granting institution has its headquarters is known as TNE.

Think-Pair-Share: Learners work together to solve an issue or answer a question on a text they've been assigned.

Formative Assessment: Monitor learner learning to offer feedback that may be utilized by instructors to enhance their instruction as well as the learner's learning, the purpose of formative assessment.

QMPLUS: It is the online learning environment (OLE) used across the university (Queen Mary University of London) and is based on Moodle.

Educator Observation: It refers to the act of observing, learning from, and reflecting on a lesson being taught by another educator.

Chapter 17
Professional Development and Transnational Education in the Post-COVID-19 Era

Xitong Dai
Perse School Suzhou, China

ABSTRACT

This chapter will consider the impact the Covid-19 pandemic has brought on transnational education and focus on the "new normality" following the epidemic. Moreover, it will concentrate on the development of technology-enhanced education after the pandemic along with the crucial role that professional development performs in TNE. On that note, distance education and work-related challenges will be discussed, and solutions and suggestions put forward to TNE educators, with professional development providing the central focal point.

INTRODUCTION

COVID-19 pandemic has become a global health crisis in the middle of the 2019-2020 academic year, significantly impacting the education delivery mode in countless ways. Social distance as well as border closure have been emphasised as efficient measures to contain the spread of Covid-19 (TEQSA, 2021). Taking the benefits of the movement restrictions, transnational education (TNE), which differs from the traditional education delivery mode, highlights the modality of education programs that have demonstrated successful development (Wilson & Vlasceanu, 2000). Furthermore, remote learning that involves lots of technologies has been strongly encouraged by the national education sector in a number of countries for continuous student learning processing in order to replace the traditional face-to-face learning mode. The astonishing scale of education digitalising transition has become the "new normality" in higher education (Tesar, 2020). Meanwhile, the precipitate changes put a lot of strain on educators, learners, and institutions as everyone is expected to assume the new education delivery mode with technological applications (Li & Morris, 2021). Given restrictions imposed by COVID-19, educators and institutions must advance professionally so as to deliver a high standard of education. New models

DOI: 10.4018/978-1-6684-5226-4.ch017

of teacher professional development and support for teachers to acquire new skills and knowledge are indispensable (Hartshorne et al., 2020). This chapter takes into account evolving and existing TNE challenges and needs, and technology-enhanced developments draw attention to the need for professional development to help education practitioners and other providers better comprehending the challenges that would arise following the Covid pandemic.

TRANSNATIONAL EDUCATION

Transnational education (TNE) has been identified as any education delivered by an institution situated in a country other than the student's country of origin (Hussain, 2007; Kesper-Biermann, 2019; McBurnie & Ziguras, 2006). In contrast to traditional education modes in which students cross borders for their education programmes, TNE places a prime focus on the international movement of institutions and programmes (Knight, 2016). These institutions may have developed international higher education programs by franchising their degrees to the local universities, distance education provision, and/or establishing branch campuses. Franchising or partnership – the source country's institution authorises and grants permission to the partner in the host country to deliver their education programs, and the source university awards the qualification. Over 90% of programs are provided under this mode of delivery (Alam et al., 2013). Even though franchising is thought to be the most extensive mode, the quality assurance, curriculum regulation, and moderation of examinations have been queried (McBurnie & Ziguras, 2006). Distance learning is when the provider delivers the online course or digital resources through technology (computers, internet, video conferencing, etc.). The course can be accessed from any place around the world. As a result, this can aid in saving money and time on transportation. Data from UK Higher Education Statistics Agency (HESA) reveals a 16% increment of 2016/22 oversea learners in the UK TNE program with distance learning (HESA, 2022). Branch campus refers to universities that establish other campuses in order to provide education locally. The authority of education quality of provider has been placed as an obvious advantage. Take the UK as an instance, the biggest group of students (39%) in the UK TNE program were British that took programs at a branch campus (Janet et al., 2021). Moreover, Garrett et al. (2017) claimed that cooperating with the local investor as a partner to acquire financial and local resource support became increasingly popular. The contradiction between academic standards and commercial success, however, needs to be taken into consideration given the unbreakable close relationship between universities and local investors. The various modes of education delivery of TNE programs have been identified as a significant development in educational accessibility. Furthermore, in the face of the curtailed revenue by the shortage of international students in the universities in the host country, delivered TNE programmes to maintain enrolment growth have been eclipsed as a means to moderate the deficiency of finances (Alam et al., 2013; Healey, 2020).

Advantages of TNE

To set the scene, transnational education (TNE) has thrived on an unprecedented scale in the past decade. The adaptability of TNE programmes makes them well-suited to assist countries with a lack of educational resources, students who have global/bicultural learning expectations, and aspirational workers who have additional educational needs. The majority of the cross-border institutions believe TNE has become a 'mature educational market', and the developing countries with low rates (3-4%) of higher education participation have been targeted as their preferred partners (Adam, 2001). In comparison to the 72% enrolment scales in North America and Western Europe, the rate of 13% in South and West Asia exhibits a precipitous decline and extensive education demand (Chien & Kot, 2012). Taking the advantages of globalisation, the institutions with overcapacity in one country could develop and expand the market rapidly in another country with low communication as well as transportation costs by offering educational programmes. The mobility of TNE makes it easier to distribute educational resources widely while minimising the impact of borders (McBurnie & Ziguras, 2006). TNE programs also indicate a positive impact on local economies by providing work opportunities and attracting students with high-quality education to encourage local consumption (Janet et al., 2021). Moreover, Hussain (2007) mentioned that curtailing brain drain, maximising keeping the resources local, and improving the core competence in the division are some of the critical benefits of TNE. It is therefore unsurprising that more and more people are accepting TNE as a pathway for their higher education. McNamara & Knight (2014) highlighted that from the national level perspective, 'access to higher education' and 'improvement in education quality' are the top two benefits of TNE. This supplement the economic and ability benefits provided by TNE. Some developing nations heavily employ the improvement of local educational systems through the introduction of TNE initiatives, to develop human resources and increased global competitiveness (Trembath, 2016). As noted by Knight & Mcnamara (2017), in 2017 40% of local students studying at TNE providers in Mauritius, and TNE in the most populous city Dubai of UAE provided 50% of higher education. The significant proportion of TNE programs in different cities and countries shows that TNE has become an established feature and a critical component of higher education academic development in several countries. On the other hand, as globalisation continues to advance rapidly, students are under increasing pressure from the employment market once they graduate (Mok & Wu, 2016). A recent report published by the British Council in April 2021 highlights that 79% of TNE students were bilingual or multilingual speakers, which gives them a substantial advantage when applying to international companies or cross-border projects in-nation. Additionally, 89% of graduates claimed that the TNE programs helped them to get involved with good job opportunities (Janet et al., 2021). In addition, transnational education provides an extensive opportunity for full-time employees to pursue their education degrees without the risk of unemployment and migration (Alam et al., 2013). An internationally educated background can be highly competitive in the local labour market; thus, the demand for local and international higher education has grown dramatically. In order to accommodate this demand, providing and developing the TNE programs that address the future demand of the local labour market regarding identified and advanced knowledge and skills have become essential for all institutions in the 21st century (Janet et al., 2021).

Challenges of TNE

The change in the way that education is delivered received modality from the migration of learners to the mobility of education programs represents diverse education programs, greater access, and lower living expenses. The phenomenal growth of TNE demonstrates a viable solution to meet the growing needs of diversity and self-development. It might, however, endanger the existing national system (Wilson & Vlasceanu, 2000). Cultural globalisation consistently impacts the transmission and innovation of local cultural values. The influence of the TNE course on traditional thoughts, cultures, and languages, along with the permeability of regional education systems and overseas institutions arouse concern (McBurnie & Ziguras, 2006). Lack of sensitivity in the exported curriculum could harm the local culture (Adam,

2001). Alam et al. (2013)suggested enhancing deep international cooperation with local traditions and values exploration. Nevertheless, within the enhancement of the local education system in the aspects of scope and quality, the demand for TNE would constantly be declined (Healey, 2007). Regarding the concerns of enrolment standards, curriculum regulation, and education quality, the Ministry of Education of China terminated over 200 cross-border higher education programs and partnerships in 2018 (Redden, 2018).

Developments of TNE

As claimed by Wilson and Vlasceanu (2000), the provision of distance learning is an influential development in TNE, with a large number of students opting for it as their first choice. A report from the British Council titled The Scale and Scope of UK Higher Education Transnational Education (2016), analysed the 2014/15 UK TNE Survey data and results in 52% of programs delivered through virtual instruction. The UK HEI only physically provided 8 percent of the total. Regarding distance education provision, the second TNE approach being considered here, another report published by The Tertiary Education Quality and Standards Agency (TEQSA) in 2020 claimed the notable development of distance learning. Around 20% of all Australian students accepted online or blended education delivery mode already in 2018 (Martin, 2020). In addition, although the direct costs of establishing either the digital or hard copy of TNE online programs should not be understated, the expenditure on program expansion, becomes lower after the initial publication (Adam, 2001). To summarise, TNE offers a new educational internationalisation format and provides more distance education possibilities in this new era of technological advancements.

TECHNOLOGY ENHANCED TEACHING AND LEARNING

On March 11, 2020, in the middle of the 2019–2020 academic year, the World Health Organization (WHO) declared the COVID-19 outbreak a global pandemic (WHO, 2020). Social distancing had been emphasised to contain the spread of the virus; innumerable learners, educators, as well as institutions were substantially impacted by the border and school closures. The report issued by The Tertiary Education Quality and Standards Agency (TEQSA) in 2021 pointed out the tremendous impact of the border closure on international education, which was one of the key industries in Australia. The sharp decrease in revenue from international students is incapable of being superseded by other commercial activities in the short term. Reduced international student enrolment immediately threatens the existence of the institutions and the decline of the education sector financially. This situation has forced a reconsideration of the proportion of TNE programs and the development of distance education for the purpose of maintaining international and local student enrolment (TEQSA, 2021). Compared to 2020, the ICEF Monitor (2022) data has shown a 61% drop in the enrolment scale in 2021. Furthermore, Chinese students, the largest group of international students in Australia, indicated approximately a half-cut down (48%) in enrolment in 2021. Open data released by HESA in 2022 demonstrate that in both the 2019/20 and 2020/21 academic years, an intense rise of offshore enrolments in UK higher education institutions (HEIs) that around 11% increment to nearly 488,095, to compare only 9% growth in the total number of students in higher education. A restricted negative impact of pandemic activities is demonstrated by the unexpected enrolment surge of UK institutes. As one of the significant TNE program providers, the positive result of UK institutions may appreciate the extensive scope, moulded distance learning, sufficiently reputation, competitive program, and dedicated education quality of their established TNE programmes. Nevertheless, TEQSA (2021) indicated that the substantial impact of enrolment by constant border closure will start to show between 2022 and 2024.

Following the epidemic, ministries of education in a number of countries strongly recommended distance learning and facilitated implementation by enacting policies. Pandemic regulations of quarantine and lockdown have compelled all academic initiatives to rely on technology virtually overnight. For providing a similar level of educational service, a huge number of countries around the world started to move to a digital space for delivering classes through a combination of synchronous live streaming (e.g. Zoom, Teams) and asynchronous methods. UNESCO likewise provided a list of distance educational applications for educators to support student learning and offer social care during closures. Academics have had to adjust to an unprecedented age of digital development acceleration due to epidemic difficulties. This has also been documented in the literature and compared with the first *IIE Covid-19 Snapshot Survey* of online services provided by institutions in early 2020, the second survey in mid-2020 presented a significant improvement in terms of uptake, going from 37% to 93% (Martel, 2020). A recent study published by IIE (*The Institute of International Education*) examined the data from 599 institutions in the US following the Covid-19 pandemic. It has been concluded that 99.5% of colleges and universities initiated the virtual instruction program, 96% of them provided online mentoring services, while 86% of institutions digitalised the physical event with technological support (Martel, 2020). The transition of the teaching format from physical to digital is inevitable. It has become the 'new normality' in higher education (Tesar, 2020).

Emergency Remote Teaching (ERT)

Many institutions were compelled to change their original method of delivering education in favour of technology-based online or blended learning due to the spread of Covid. However, the shortage of corresponding research related to digital resources in higher education has created a dilemma for online teaching and learning (Tesar, 2020). The education delivery mode transition in the strict time limitation as an emergency solution is not the same standards as the structured online learning course. The term "emergency remote teaching (ERT)", increasingly referred to as a temporary shift of education delivery mode to face the crisis, will return to the original delivery mode once the emergency has subsided. The ERT aims not to create a high standard distance program but provide an efficient as well as a reliable solution to alternative face-to-face education. Hence, the discrepancy in objectives indicates the differentiation between online learning and ERT (Hodges et al., 2020). The exceptional digitalisation progress of all institutions must overcome issues with academic quality and technical support, nonetheless, in order to accommodate the ERT advancement. According to Hodges et al. (2020), the IT or ICT sectors on campus are available to facilitate remote learning but offering the same support for all members in the short term of preparation seems impossible. Besides, the effective online course is attributed to a careful course design, but it is unachievable with the strict time constraints of ERT. Accordingly, as a temporary replacement ERT should not be confused with concentrated online education with a well-designed curriculum and technological support.

The Covid-19 epidemic has accelerated the growth of transnational education. Since early 2020 the outbreak of covid-19 gave remote education a crucial place in higher education. In order to face the enormous challenges of emerging digital involution, experienced providers demonstrated an evident strength with well-prepared remote learning materials and efficient technical support (Croucher et al., 2020). As an outcome of the pandemic lockdown, educators and students are driven to adopt the new education delivery method quickly, which contains a massive technology involvement (Mishra et al., 2020). Moreover, online learning has been viewed as a means to address any unforeseen difficulties in the educational process (Ferri et al., 2020). ICEF Monitor reported in 2021 that the tremendous change in the international education landscape in the year 2020 provided the distance and hybrid delivery mode another golden development period. At this extraordinary time, accelerating and allowing digital delivery has emerged as a vital trend in response to social movement limitations. The global online education market was estimated at US$187.877 billion in 2019 and has been projected to a 9.23% increment per year so as to reach a total market size of about US$319.167 billion in 2025 (Research and Markets, 2020). HESA stressed that in 2022, 140,150 students took part in the UK TNE program with a distance, flexible, or distributed model. In addition, 60% of TNE learners within the European Union receiving their education online from UK institutions in 2021 exceed 31,890. Distance learning has thus replaced traditional face-to-face mode as the most popular way to deliver education in this particular era. The ubiquitous access to online learning has undoubtedly contributed to the accelerated growth of the TNE.

Challenges of Technology Enhanced

Post Covid-19 crisis, as a component of TNE, online learning has emerged as a 'new normality' education delivery method and teaching-learning pedagogical shift from physical to virtual that has allowed for more flexible course access and the potential for a wider range of review resources (KLISOWSKA et al., 2021). The advantages of distance learning, such as flexibility, time saving, and quick access to multiple learning materials, have been claimed by plenty of literature (Ferri et al., 2020; KLISOWSKA et al., 2021; Mishra et al., 2020; Montacute, 2020). Moreover, asynchronous activities are more popular in comparison to synchronous activities; students prefer pre-recorded lectures to live-streaming courses in order to understand the course content better (Chung et al., 2020). Nevertheless, the effectiveness, autonomy, motivation, and interaction of online learning have concerned a number of educators. Compared to traditional face-to-face communication, students and educators expressed negative concerns about the convincingness and interactions of online learning (Herman, 2020). In the same vein, Bista et al. (2021) argue that many experiences from cross-border learning, higher education, and national mobility cannot simply be presented via technological methods; for students receiving virtual instruction, the actual experience is unachievable. Furthermore, necessary resources for online learning, such as access to equipment, stable internet connection, and the appropriate learning space, become challenges for students living in impoverished areas (Montacute, 2020). Chung et al. (2020) likewise pointed out that even though the government published supported policies and provided economic support, poor internet connectivity remains the primary obstacle to online learning in Malaysian higher education. Again, it was a massive challenge for some subjects who rely on laboratory facilities (Gamage et al., 2020).

Developments of Technology Enhanced

Regardless of the actions taken, the TNE institutions must retain the academic standards at the professional level and a highly interactive student experience to achieve high-quality learning effects and encounter new challenges (Gamage et al., 2020). A public institution in Malaysia implemented blended learning (BL) before pure online learning in order to overcome the difficulties (Chung et al., 2020). Along with the increased technology involvement in TNE, BL is the mode that combines face-to-face and distance learning to aid students in their self-directed learning. Akma et al. (2019) also suggested the deep connection between information and communication technology (ICT) and daily education content; supporting students to acquire basic computer skills may help them feel less anxious about adopting remote learning. Some universities have formulated modes of delivering wholly online courses. For representative, institutions cooperate with Massive Open Online Courses (MOOC) platforms or dedicated online programme managers to support high-quality educational programmes (Mishra et al., 2020). Provide synchronous communication service, and find a partner in the host city to assist participants in using new technologies and media to support the online TNE program(Croucher et al., 2020). Additionally, well-designed courses that are tailored to differentiations needs can be taken into consideration. The nine dimensions of online learning design proposed by Means et al. (2014) are modality, pacing, student-instructor ratio, pedagogy, instructor role online, student role online, online communication synchrony, the role of online assessments, and source of feedback. In general, the transition of education delivery method exacerbated ICT as a compulsory part of higher education and necessary for staff professional development (KLISOWSKA et al., 2021; Mishra et al., 2020).

PROFESSIONAL DEVELOPMENT

Professional development (PD) has been widely designed to develop staff capacity with collaboration skills and individual knowledge development for the purpose of addressing challenges in the workspace. It often manifests itself in the form of workshops, formal conferences, courses, and collaborative learning among colleagues or other practitioners (Mizell, 2010). In 1985, Fenstermacher and Berliner defined professional development as the activities programs created for the knowledge and skill improvement of educators; educators perform at higher levels by engaging in high-quality PD. Professional development (PD) is an activity designed for both academic and administrative staff with the goal of enhancing student learning and provided during conventional work or even prior to new staff onboarding. To be specific, PD activities can be designed to be functional with curriculum and teaching-focused activities and to acquaint new staff with arrangements, requirements, and professional expectations in order to facilitate academic progress (Elmore, 2002). Sparks & Hirsh (1997) claimed that efficient PD programmes take into account the practical issues of student learning and enhance their learning by improving the team's professional academic skills as well as abilities and maintaining the favourable collaboration between school leaders and all staff. Research has shown that education quality and institution leadership are two essential elements that impact student learning results. Hence, enhancing educators' academic level and teaching skills to support students' better knowledge achievement is crucial (Mizell, 2010). Moreover, the prime objective of PD should be the progress of education institutions and systems rather than the limited growth of individual employees (Elmore, 2002).

After COVID-19, education digitalization has advanced at an exponential rate, posing new and different challenges for educators, students, and institutions. For adapting distance learning, to be knowledgeable about multimedia applications and new learning platforms, applications, and processes has become essential. The accessibility and reliability of distance education delivery platforms, the promptness supported and training for learners, educators, school administrators, and parents, the development of policy, and the academic quality of online programs can all have an impact on how effective distance learning is (Hodges et al., 2020). Researchers have argued that educators should be prepared for remote and blended instruction, but these states have long gone unappreciated (Kennedy & Ferdig, 2018). The majority of educators and institutions admitted the lack of preparation for digitization progression (Hodges et al., 2020). The ineffective learning of students in the in-process digital environment is caused by a lack of research and understanding of their needs for support (Borup et al., 2020). Additionally, teachers examined online teaching content and pedagogies by themselves throughout the teaching format transformation (Bergdahl & Jalal Nouri, 2020); however, many of them were newcomers to distance education and faced additional difficulties (Bond et al., 2021). Such as becoming familiar with new learning applications, creating remote teaching content, endeavouring online education pedagogy, engaging parents, and managing student mental issues (Hartshorne et al., 2020). This can present a steep learning curve for students and teachers alike. The need for PD has increased as a result of these increased difficulties(Bergdahl, 2022). A report reveals that 66% out of 256 participants suggested increasing the ERT-relevant professional development training for educators. Some of them asserted that the technology-rich academic environment prior to the pandemic helped to maintain the learning progress and reduce the pressure associated with the transition of educational format (Trust et al., 2020).

Some institutions created PD and revised the course in a limited time in order to support students and preservice teachers (Hartshorne et al., 2020). PD is also not constrained solely to academic staff. In order for administrative personnel to do their jobs effectively, they too require support. For instance, the maintenance of online data (attendance systems, teaching resources, and online platforms), and the implementation of technological solutions are often provided by the IT sector. Nevertheless, both the flexibility and accessibility of online data have been stretched during the past few years and so too the staff who are tasked with these roles (see Morris et al., 2021). Furthermore, the new digital approach to education puts a lot of pressure on educators; every teacher has to be skilled in the utilisation of technology while constantly being challenged with teaching issues as Li and Morris (2021) draw attention to.

Along with the universal access to distance learning and the growing popularity of TNE, a lack of systematic support, proper guidance of high-quality pedagogy design, and enhanced student engagement have been noted (Archambault et al., 2016a). Accordingly, a new mode of PD training especially supporting teachers with their TNE course is necessitated(Hartshorne et al., 2020). Teacher professional development (TPD) that targets online or blended learning (OBL) emphasises the teacher identity, teacher reflection and technology involvement in education(Baran et al., 2011). Tschida et al., (2016) also suggested that the role transition from professor to facilitator is the most significant difference between regular TPD and TPD for OBL. Ongoing inquiry of teacher-self encouraged teacher reflection and educator interactions. However, a stimulus such as individual further development needs or initiative from the official sector is indispensable in the PD process(Philipsen, 2019). Hence, when technology skills and new teaching pedagogy has been required under the covid-19 movement restriction, the development of TPD for OBL with teacher identity, teacher reflection and technology involvement to support educators with the TNE course implementation as a potential resolution.

Relevant PD Development

Despite the fact that the development of education digitalization may come with additional requirements for educators, students, and institutions, it could be an incentive for developing teaching practices and contribute to the growth of TNE (Bergdahl, 2022; Bond et al., 2021). In this case, traditional PD is insufficient to fulfil educators' needs; instead, the post-pandemic valuable teaching experiences should be considered, and the relevance and flexibility of PD should be increased. The following part summarised three dimensions of developing teacher PD after Covid-19, with an emphasis on online PD community, student engagement, and digital tools.

Online PD Community

In the evolution of education delivery mode evolution, PD transitions to online mode simultaneously and is anticipated to offer systematic support for interactive remote learning experiences (Archambault et al., 2016b). PD communities as collaborative support networks that establish the connection between practitioners and provide updated remote teaching resources are friendly to beginners of distance teaching (Safi et al., 2020). Elmore (2002) also suggested that educators collaborate with other practitioners who had similar problems in order to learn more effectively. Besides, the video turns to the most popular format for teachers to support their class preparation, the research depicts 60 times increment of video usage in comparison to the same period prior to Covid-19, and the search terms focused on the specific teaching practices (Cavanaugh et al., 2020). As a result, exploring the specific pedagogical practices such as group work and virtual experimentation in all subjects while including them in the teacher online PD is crucial (Evagorou & Nisiforou, 2020). In addition, creating customised online PD courses that support pedagogical practice can be considered (Affinito, 2018). Lastly, engage the assistance from other internal sectors and work corporately on the exact target of instructional improvement (Elmore, 2002).

Enhance Student Engagement

Tremendous numbers of educators posted the critical concern regarding student engagement in the online education format. As argued by students, limited online activity and learning interaction reduced social communication and motivation (Babadjanova, 2020). Additionally, it has been suggested that the increment of online interaction has a positive impact on student study motivation along with lecture engagement (Nortvig et al., 2018). Education digitalization has been reported to challenge in-person education and TPD. It could, nevertheless, be an outstanding opportunity to innovate a variety of teaching methods and instruments. Teachers are encouraged as a designer by TPD to investigate innovative approaches alongside other educators to find the solution to real classroom problems in various contexts (Getenet, 2019; Lidolf & Pasco, 2020).

Besides providing technical support and attractively designed instruction, the positive influence of student academic engagement through family emotional support also should not be underestimated, which is even more influential in contrast to that of financial support (Roksa & Kinsley, 2019). TPD that sets on the Academic Communities of Engagement (ACE) framework can promote student affective, behavioural, and cognitive engagement via the course (students, teachers, and administrators) and personal (family, friends, and others) community support in an online or blended course for the purpose of achieving academic success (Borup et al., 2020).

Digital Tools

In order to adapt to distance learning, it has also become essential to be knowledgeable about multimedia applications as well as new learning platforms, applications, and processes. Research in 2020 pointed out that 47.2% of 425 students reported that the most challenging part of online learning was the different learning methods and platforms (Chung et al., 2020). However, proficient and appropriate applicant digital tools in education may enrich the teaching process while boosting the development of an efficient class (Jesson et al., 2018).

The majority of educators delivered classes in both synchronous and asynchronous methods. Synchronist online platforms and providing a training course to support staff and students may save the time of shift between different applications and boost confidence and concentration in distance education. Moreover, the strength of synchronous activities lies in the minimal difference from physical class, the implication of breakout rooms to encourage group work and peer discussion, and the maintenance of students' interaction. Asynchronous activities have been demonstrated to support knowledge examination, aid student reflection, deliver structured feedback, interactions in different countries, and additional course options (Bergdahl, 2022).

Furthermore, The exploration of new features of digital technologies to seek innovative teaching design and digital interaction that enables personalised earning are key themes of PD as well (Bergdahl, 2022). For instance, digital poetry offers a solution to composition with engaging exploration and creation; it aids students in having a profound understanding of the composition process (Hassler et al., 2020).

CONCLUSION

Higher education throughout the world has been severely impacted by the Covid-19 outbreak (Marginson, 2020); the influence of continuous restriction control and border closure has not subsided yet in more than three years. International students, in particular, students from Mainland China and Hong Kong, place health and safety as the primary concerns while choosing universities (Mok et al., 2021), which implies that instead of the UK and USA, Asian countries or TNE courses have become their first choice. However, education quality assurance has been concerned with the unpredictable rapid progress of distance learning.

The education digitalization and technology enhancement in ongoing teaching and learning have shown more possibilities in an emergency situation. For maintaining high-level education, the innovation of TPD for OBL has been regarded as an essential avenue for accelerating TNE progression. TPD could first concentrate on building an online community that supports particular teaching practices and fosters strong collaboration with students, parents, and staff. Second, encourage teachers to discuss with educators to share experiences in a real class while creating actively online classes that promote student affective, behavioural, and cognitive engagement. Third, appropriate applicant digital tools combine both synchronous and asynchronous methods and analyse new features of digital technologies to achieve digital interaction.

Given the growing concerns about public health and safety along with the possibility of facing an emergency at any time, the potential needs of ERT, such as online teaching pedagogies and applications, must be incorporated into the teacher professional development programme. Again, the PD must constantly adapt to the demands of the new era.

REFERENCES

Adam, S. (2001). *Transnational education project. Report and recomendations*. Confederation of European Union Rectors' Conferences.

Affinito, S. (2018). *Literacy coaching : transforming teaching and learning with digital tools and technology*. Heineman, 156.

Akma, S., Seman1, A., Hashim1, M. J., Roslin3, R. M., & Ishar1, M. (2019). *Millennial Learners' Acceptance and Satisfaction of Blended Learning Environment*. Universiti Teknologi MARA.

Alam, F., Alam, Q., Chowdhury, H., & Steiner, T. (2013). Transnational Education: Benefits, Threats and Challenges. *Procedia Engineering*, *56*, 870–874. doi:10.1016/j.proeng.2013.03.209

Archambault, L., Kennedy, K., Shelton, C., Dalal, M., McAllister, L., & Huyett, S. (2016a). Incremental progress: Re-examining field experiences in K-12 online learning contexts in the United States. *Journal of Online Learning Research*, *2*(3).

Archambault, L., Kennedy, K., Shelton, C., Dalal, M., McAllister, L., & Huyett, S. (2016b). Incremental Progress:Re-examining Field Experiences in K-12 Online Learning.... *Journal of Online Learning Research*, *2*(3), 303–326.

Babadjanova, N. (2020). *Effective classroom management techniques for curriculum of 21st century*. Science and Education. https://openscience.uz/index.php/sciedu/article/view/518

Baran, E., Correia, A. P., & Thompson, A. (2011). Transforming online teaching practice: Critical analysis of the literature on the roles and competencies of online teachers. In Distance Education, 32(3). doi:10.1080/01587919.2011.610293

Bergdahl, N. (2022). Adaptive Professional Development during the Pandemic. *Designs for Learning*, *14*(1), 1–13. doi:10.16993/dfl.172

Bergdahl, N., & Jalal Nouri, D. (2020). *Covid-19 och omställning till distansundervisning i svensk skola Abstrakt*.

Bista, K., Allen, R. M., & Chan, R. Y. (2021). Impacts of COVID-19 on International Students and the Future of Student Mobility. In *Impacts of COVID-19 on International Students and the Future of Student Mobility*. Routledge., doi:10.4324/9781003138402

Bond, M., Bergdahl, N., Mendizabal-Espinosa, R., Kneale, D., Hull, P., & Ramadani, F. (2021). *Global emergency remote education in secondary schools during the COVID-19 pandemic: a systematic review*. IIEP-UNESCO Education 4 Resilience. https://education4resilience.iiep.unesco.org/index.php/resources/2021/global-emergency-remote-education-secondary-schools-during-covid-19-pandemic

Borup, J., Graham, C. R., West, R. E., Archambault, L., & Spring, K. J. (2020). Academic Communities of Engagement: An expansive lens for examining support structures in blended and online learning. *Educational Technology Research and Development*, *68*(2), 807–832. Advance online publication. doi:10.100711423-020-09744-x

Cavanaugh, C., Cavanaugh, C., & DeWeese, A. (2020). Understanding the Professional Learning and Support Needs of Educators during.... *Journal of Technology and Teacher Education*, *28*(2), 233–238.

Chien, C.-L., & Kot, F. C. (2012). New Patterns in Student Mobility in the Southern Africa Development Community. *UIS Information Bulletin*, *7*(February).

Chung, E., Subramaniam, G., & Dass, L. C. (2020). Online learning readiness among university students in Malaysia amidst Covid-19. *Asian Journal of University Education, 16*(2), 45. doi:10.24191/ajue.v16i2.10294

Croucher, G., Elliott, K., Locke, W., & Yencken, E. (2020). *Australia's higher education delivery offshore and online-trends, barriers and opportunities Melbourne Centre for the Study of Higher Education.* Melbourne Centre for the Study of Higher Education.

Elmore, R. F. (2002). Bridging the Gap between Standards and Achievement: The Imperative for Professional Development in Education. Report: ED475871. 44pp. Jul 2002.

Evagorou, M., & Nisiforou, E. (2020). Engaging Pre-service Teachers in an Online STEM Fair during COVID-19. *Journal of Technology and Teacher Education*, *28*(2), 179–186.

Fenstermacher, G. D., & Berliner, D. C. (1985). Determining the Value of Staff Development. *The Elementary School Journal*, *85*(3), 281–314. https://eric.ed.gov/?id=EJ315740. doi:10.1086/461407

Ferri, F., Grifoni, P., & Guzzo, T. (2020). Online learning and emergency remote teaching: Opportunities and challenges in emergency situations. *Societies (Basel, Switzerland)*, *10*(4), 86. doi:10.3390oc10040086

Gamage, K. A. A., Wijesuriya, D. I., Ekanayake, S. Y., Rennie, A. E. W., Lambert, C. G., & Gunawardhana, N. (2020). Online delivery of teaching and laboratory practices: Continuity of university programmes during COVID-19 pandemic. In Education Sciences, 10(10). doi:10.3390/educsci10100291

Garrett, R., Kinser, K., Lane, J. E., & Merola, R. (2017). *International branch campuses: Success factors of mature IBCs*. Observatory on Borderless Higher Education and Cross-Border Education Research Team.

Getenet, S. (2019). Using design-based research to bring partnership between researchers and practitioners. Https://Doi.Org/10.1080/00131881.2019.1677168, *61*(4), 482–494. doi:10.1080/00131881.2019.1677168

Hartshorne, R., Baumgartner, E., Kaplan-Rakowski, R., Mouza, C., & Ferdig, R. E. (2020). Special issue editorial: Preservice and inservice professional development during the COVID-19 pandemic. *Journal of Technology and Teacher Education*, *28*(2).

Hassler, D., Pytash, K. E., Ferdig, R. E., Mucha, N., & Gandolfi, E. (2020). The Use of Digital Poetry to Inform Preservice Teacher Education and In.... *Journal of Technology and Teacher Education*, *28*(2), 403–413.

Healey, N. M. (2007). Is higher education in really 'internationalising'? *Higher Education, 55*(3), 333–355. doi:10.1007/S10734-007-9058-4

Healey, N. M. (2020). The end of transnational education? The view from the UK. *Perspectives: Policy and Practice in Higher Education*, *24*(3), 102–112. doi:10.1080/13603108.2019.1631227

Herman, P. (2020). Online learning is not the future of higher education (opinion). In Inside Higher Education.

HESA. (2022). *Figure 12 - HE student enrolments based wholly overseas by location and type of provision 2016/17 to 2020/21.* HESA. https://www.hesa.ac.uk/data-and-analysis/sb262/figure-12

Hodges, C., Moore, S., Lockee, B., Trust, T., & Bond, A. (2020). *The Difference Between Emergency Remote Teaching and Online Learning*. Educause. https://er.educause.edu/articles/2020/3/the-difference-between-emergency-remote-teaching-and-

Hussain, I. (2007). Transnational education: Concept and methods. *Turkish Online Journal of Distance Education, 8*(1). doi:10.17718/tojde.99261

Janet, I., Vangelis, T., Pat, K., & Uwe, B. (2021). *Local impact of transnational education*. British Council. www.britishcouncil.org

Jesson, R., McNaughton, S., Rosedale, N., Zhu, T., & Cockle, V. (2018). A mixed-methods study to identify effective practices in the teaching of writing in a digital learning environment in low income schools. *Computers & Education, 119*, 14–30. doi:10.1016/j.compedu.2017.12.005

Kennedy, K., & Ferdig, R. E. (2018, April 12). *Handbook of Research on K-12 Online and Blended Learning (Second Edition)*. ETC Press. https://press.etc.cmu.edu/index.php/product/handbook-of-research-on-k-12-and-blending-learning-second-edition/

Kesper-Biermann, S. (2019). Transnational Education in Historical Perspective. The Deutsche Kolonialschule (1898-1944). *Diskurs Kindheits- Und Jugendforschung / Discourse Journal of Childhood and Adolescence Research, 4*(4), 417–430. doi:10.3224/DISKURS.V14I4.04

Klisowska, I., Seń, M., & Grabowska, B.KLISOWSKA. (2021). Advantages and disadvantages of distance learning. *E-Methodology, 7*(7), 27–32. doi:10.15503/emet2020.27.32

Knight, J. (2016). Transnational Education Remodeled: Toward a Common TNE Framework and Definitions. *Journal of Studies in International Education, 20*(1), 34–47. doi:10.1177/1028315315602927

Knight, J., & Mcnamara, J. (2017). *Transnational education: a classification framework and data collection guidelines for international programme and provider mobility (IPPM)*. DAAD. www.daad.de

Li, L., & Morris, G. R. (2021). *Thriving in the New Normal: In-Service Professional Development Needs and Experiences*. doi:10.4018/978-1-7998-7226-9.ch013

Lidolf, S., & Pasco, D. (2020). Educational Technology Professional Development in Higher Education: A Systematic Literature Review of Empirical Research. *Frontiers in Education, 5*, 35. doi:10.3389/feduc.2020.00035

M. (2020). COVID-19 Effects on US Higher Education Campuses. Academic Student Mobility to and from China. In *Institute of International Education*.

Marginson, S. (2020). *Global HE as we know it has forever changed | Times Higher Education (THE)*. Times Higher Education. https://www.timeshighereducation.com/blog/global-he-we-know-it-has-forever-changed# Martel,).

McBurnie, G., & Ziguras, C. (2006). Transnational education: Issues and trends in offshore higher education. *Transnational Education: Issues and Trends in Offshore Higher Education*, 1–178. doi:10.4324/9780203968352

McNamara, J., & Knight, J. (2014). *Impacts of transnational education on host countries: academic, cultural, economic and skills impacts and implications of programme and provider mobility*. British Council. www.britishcouncil.org/education/ihewww.daad.de

Means, B., Bakia, M., & Murphy, R. (2014). Learning online: What research tells us about whether, when and how. *Learning Online: What Research Tells Us About Whether, When and How*, 1–219. doi:10.4324/9780203095959

Mishra, L., Gupta, T., & Shree, A. (2020). Online teaching-learning in higher education during lock-down period of COVID-19 pandemic. *International Journal of Educational Research Open*, *1*, 100012. doi:10.1016/j.ijedro.2020.100012 PMID:35059663

Mizell, H. (2010). *Learning Forward*. Why Professional Development Matters.

Mointor, I. C. E. F. (2021, July 13). *UK: Online learning expected to drive further significant growth for TNE programmes - ICEF Monitor - Market intelligence for international student recruitment*. Monitor. https://monitor.icef.com/2021/07/uk-online-learning-expected-to-drive-further-significant-growth-for-tne-programmes/

Mok, K. H., & Wu, A. M. (2016). Higher education, changing labour market and social mobility in the era of massification in China. *Journal of Education and Work*, *29*(1), 77–97. doi:10.1080/13639080.2015.1049028

Mok, K. H., Xiong, W., Ke, G., & Cheung, J. O. W. (2021). Impact of COVID-19 pandemic on international higher education and student mobility: Student perspectives from mainland China and Hong Kong. *International Journal of Educational Research*, *105*, 101718. doi:10.1016/j.ijer.2020.101718 PMID:35719275

Monitor, I. C. E. F. (2022, April). *Australia's foreign enrolment recovering slowly in 2022 - ICEF Monitor - Market intelligence for international student recruitment*. Monitor. https://monitor.icef.com/2022/04/australias-foreign-enrolment-recovering-slowly-in-2022/

Montacute, R. (2020). *Implications of the Covid-19 crisis for educational inequality*. Sutton Trust.

Morris, G. R., Sheridan, S. M., Xu, J., Liang, W., Lv, F., Foster, R., Di, S., Zhang, C., & Perrin, S. (2021). *Educational Symbiosis: Designing English Language Learning Courses to Support Syntegrative Education*. 187–207. doi:10.4018/978-1-7998-7226-9.CH010

Nortvig, A. M., Petersen, A. K., & Balle, S. H. (2018). A literature review of the factors influencing e-learning and blended learning in relation to learning outcome, student satisfaction and engagement. *Electronic Journal of E-Learning, 16*(1).

Philipsen, B. (2019). A Professional Development Process Model for Online and Blended Learning: Introducing Digital Capital. [CITE Journal]. *Contemporary Issues in Technology & Teacher Education*, *19*(4).

Redden, E. (2018). *Closures of China-Foreign Programs*. Inside Higher Ed. https://www.insidehighered.com/news/2018/07/11/chinas-ministry-education-approves-termination-more-200-chinese-foreign-cooperative

Research and Markets. (2020). *Global Online Education Market - Forecasts From 2020 To 2025*. Research and Markets. https://www.researchandmarkets.com/reports/4986759/global-online-education-market-forecasts-from

Roksa, J., & Kinsley, P. (2019). The Role of Family Support in Facilitating Academic Success of Low-Income Students. *Research in Higher Education*, *60*(4), 415–436. doi:10.100711162-018-9517-z

Safi, F., Wenzel, T., & Spalding, L.-A. T. (2020). Remote Learning Community: Supporting Teacher Educators during Unprecedented Times. *Journal of Technology and Teacher Education*, *28*(2).

Sparks, D., & Hirsh, S. (1997). *A new vision for staff development*. Association for Supervision and Curriculum Development, 108.

TEQSA. (2021). *Forward impact of COVID-19 on Australian higher education*. TEQSA. https://www.teqsa.gov.au/sites/default/files/forward-impact-of-covid-19-on-australian-higher-education-report.pdf?v=1635905249

Tesar, M. (2020). Towards a Post-Covid-19 "New Normality?": Physical and Social Distancing, the Move to Online and Higher Education. *Policy Futures in Education*, *2020*(5), 556–559. doi:10.1177/1478210320935671

Trembath, J. L. (2016). The professional lives of expatriate academics: Construct clarity and implications for expatriate management in higher education. *Journal of Global Mobility*, *4*(2), 112–130. doi:10.1108/JGM-04-2015-0012

Trust, T., Trust, T., & Whalen, J. (2020). Should Teachers be Trained in Emergency Remote Teaching? Lessons Learned from.... *Journal of Technology and Teacher Education*, *28*(2), 189–199.

Tschida, C. M., Hodge, E. M., & Schmidt, S. W. (2016). Learning to teach online: Negotiating issues of platform, pedagogy, and professional development. In *Educational Leadership and Administration* (Vol. 4–4). Concepts, Methodologies, Tools, and Applications., doi:10.4018/978-1-5225-1624-8.ch096

UNESCO. (n.d.). *Distance learning solutions*. UNESCO. https://en.unesco.org/covid19/educationresponse/solutions

WHO. (2020, March). *WHO Director-General's opening remarks at the media briefing on COVID-19*. WHO. https://www.who.int/director-general/speeches/detail/who-director-general-s-opening-remarks-at-the-media-briefing-on-covid-19---11-march-2020

Wilson, L. A., & Vlasceanu, L. (2000). Transnational education and recognition of qualifications. In *Internationalization of higher education: an institutional perspective* (pp. 75–89). https://unesdoc.unesco.org/ark:/48223/pf0000125380

Chapter 18
Enhancing Educational Leadership in Transnational Higher Education

Gareth Richard Morris
The Perse School Suzhou, China

James Morris
IT Project Management, UK

Lei Li
Suzhou Science and Technology Town Foreign Language School, China

ABSTRACT

In every industry and field, and at every institutional level, good leadership is essential. Equally significant is the remit a leader is tasked with fulfilling, and the point in time at which this is expected and the situation one must work within, alongside the context. This all makes defining good leadership and good leaders fraught with difficulty, as what may work well in one situation, may not work so well in another. For transnational higher education, the situation is complicated further because providers can vary in terms of location, size, complexity, context, and remit. It is also challenging because of the ongoing COVID pandemic. Consequently, this chapter will briefly introduce transnational higher education, along with the idea of what successful and effective leadership constitutes. It will then go on to consider different leadership styles before examining a specific transnational higher education provider and discussing some of the leadership approaches and features that have been evidenced in a specific academic school at this institution over the past decade.

DOI: 10.4018/978-1-6684-5226-4.ch018

INTRODUCTION

Good leadership and management are essential in all industries and fields, and for all entities. This is because good leadership enhances the likelihood of success, however this may be defined. It also increases the probability that institutional effectiveness, however, it is measured, can be improved. What defines good leadership though is somewhat open to debate as it arguably encompasses many qualities, traits, behaviours, and skills,as Krakoff (2020), Watt (2009), Bryman (2008) and Eastwood (2020) highlight. Success and effectiveness may also be considered based on the remit that a leader is tasked with fulfilling, and dependent upon the point in time, context, and situation in which a leader must work. Put simply, this makes defining good leadership and leaders more challenging than it might at first appear as what may work well in one situation and with one group of people may not work so well in another. This is evidenced across professions and time periods.

For transnational higher education, the situation is complicated further because providers can vary in terms of structure, size, context, and remit among other considerations. The ongoing COVID-19 pandemic has only added to the challenges as onsite, online, and various hybrid forms of blended delivery feature, making an already complex situation even more complicated. Indeed, the working world was already increasingly challenging and unpredictable pre pandemic as the work of Orazbayeva et al. (2020) illustrated. It is also important that leadership and management are studied in a transnational higher education content for a variety of reasons. Firstly, there is very limited research regarding leadership and management in this under-researched educational area. Secondly, transnational higher education is a lucrative, important, and evolving domain, made more challenging to lead in due to macro global geopolitical developments. Thirdly, on an institutional level, good leadership can aid recruitment and retention initiatives and guard against damning reviews of employment sites like glassdoor; a significant consideration for transnational higher education providers. In addition, educators need good supportive leadership to do their job to the best of their ability. This is vital because the future of education, as Stephen Hawking (2018) states "lies in schools and inspiring teachers".

On that note, this chapter will begin by introducing background context to the case study higher education institution. Theories of educational leadership and management will then be considered. The methodologies of the various research studies which form the basis of this work will then be briefly introduced, prior to the results from these being discussed Finally, the implications will be considered with recommendations made for transnational higher education leaders, managers and administrators.

BACKGROUND

International Higher Education: On the premise that education is regarded as the engine room for future creativity, ingenuity and economic development (Watt, Richardson and Smith, 2017), it is unsurprising that in China schooling, or learning, at all levels is deemed to be essentially important. Cai and Hall (2016) highlight the important demand to internationalise higher education nationally, while Trembath (2016) notes the potential this has for future global competitiveness. The implications of all of this are that, pre COVID-19, a reasonable number of international institutions were able to start operations within the country often operating like multinational subsidiaries. Indeed, the internationalisation of higher education, in which transnational providers played an important role, has been useful in evolving educational provision (Morris, 2021a).

Transnational Higher Education: As noted, transnational higher education is a core aspect of internationalising higher education (Morris, 2021a). The notion refers to study which is undertaken by students in a different country from that of the awarding institution (Wilkins and Neri, 2019). This can therefore include joint ventures, such as Xi'an Jiao Tong-Liverpool University (XJTLU), and branch campuses like the University of Nottingham Ningbo (UNNC). Some of the challenges that providers can face include balancing local responsiveness with global integration, and international market homogeneity with market heterogeneity preferences,as Cai and Hall (2016) draw attention to. Since legislation permitted the establishment of joint ventures in 2003, nine notable Sino-Foreign universities have begun operation, with two more under construction (XJTLU, 2016). At a similar point in time, Cai and Hall (2016) highlight how Sino-Foreign ventures grew from twenty in 2013 to twenty-eight in 2015, making China the second most populous global location at one period.

Case Study Institution: The case study university under analysis in this chapter is a transnational Sino-British English Medium of Instruction (EMI) institution in eastern China. It was opened in 2006 and is the largest educational joint venture in the country (Morris et al., 2021). It is also independent of its founding parent institutions, albeit still aligned to them. Links to the overseas provider are essential for external endorsement and assurance of provisional quality, alongside dual degree awarding powers. This institution has indeed been so successful in terms of student enrolment in the past fifteen years that it has bulit and opened a state-of-the-art second campus in a satellite city of the larger metropolis in which it is based. Mirroring this macro institutional growth has been an internal division, namely its School of Languages (SoL). Starting as a Language Centre, the SoL now employs over two hundred staff as Li and Morris (2021) have noted. The SoL provides various language pathways and courses to facilitate language learning initiatives at this educational provider in order to support the academic needs of students and remit and ambitions of the provider. That said, leadership and management challenges have had to be overcome as COVID-19, growth-based restructuring and evolutionary personal and pedagogic developments have all necessitated change.

LITERATURE REVIEW

Leadership: Cambridge Assessment International Education (2017) stress that there are many definitions of leadership, albeit with most suggesting that educational leadership is the intentional influence which is exerted by an individual or group to direct group or organisational activities and relationships. Put simply, educational leadership is a social influencing process, usually associated with formal organisational positions, which varies depending on who is exerting influence and the nature of this alongside the purpose (Cambridge Assessment International Education, 2017). Given considerations such as these it is unsurprising that numerous leadership approaches exist which include but are not limited to instructional, transformational, moral, participative, managerial and contingency (Cambridge Assessment International Education, 2017).

Management: As Doyle (2019) notes, leadership and management, despite often being seen as synonymous as many leaders are managers, with the terms used interchangeably (Gavin, 2019; Toor and Ofori, 2008), are not necessarily one and the same. Sometimes they are anything but. In fact, whereas leadership may be more about motivating people, management involves a focus on executing functions (Doyle, 2019). Considered in greater detail, managers are typically concerned with day-to-day operations, evaluating performance against performance indicators (or metrics), whereas leaders are often thought to be more forward-thinking and consider organisational sustainability (Doyle, 2019). Gavin (2019) goes further,suggesting that leadership is the creation of positive non-incremental change (such as a vision), whereas management is concerned with getting staff to accomplish a common purpose on a regular recurring basis. Put simply, leadership is about vision, innovation, development and fluidity, while management concerns process implementation, administration and more static role boundaries and responsibilities (Gavin, 2019). A manager also, in contrast to a leader, tends to have to operate through hierarchical positioning with a focus more on direct measurables (Bush and Glover, 2014). A manager is also simply a title while leadership is a quality that is shaped over time,as Gavin (2019) draws attention to. Interestingly and importantly, Drucker (1954) advocated flat management structures, alongside training and testing future mangers. He also noted the importance of stimulating environments, where responsibility is devolved and work rewarding both financially and psychologically (in order to improve productivity) (Drucker, 1954). This certainly resonates with the seminal work of Maslow (1954) in many respects and some of the ideas that his hierarchy of needs draws attention to through highlighting the importance of physiological, safety, social, esteem, and self-actualisation needs.

Types of Leadership: There are various leadership models and styles that those in positions of power and influence can adopt as Bush and Glover (2014) and Gozukara (2016) draw attention to. There are additionally numerous qualities (Krakoff, 2020), traits (Watt, 2009), behaviours (Bryman, 2008) and skills (Eastwood, 2020) associated with leaders. Indeed, honesty, intelligence, decisiveness, organizational competencies, compassion, innovation and ambition are deemed essential (Pew Research Center, 2015). Leadership style is another important consideration, with democratic, autocratic, laissez-faire, strategic, transformational, transactional, coach style, and bureaucratic some forms. There are also, unsurprisingly, numerous leadership theories advocated, as the University of Cambridge Institute for Sustainability Leadership (2017b) notes, These include the great man trait theory, the behavioural or styles school of leadership, the situational or context-based theoretical school, the contingency or interactionist school, and the transactional or transformational leadership perspective (University of Cambridge Institute for Sustainability Leadership, 2017b). Which combination of features and approaches a leader actually draws upon and employs will likely be determined by personal consciousness, competencies, temporal situational considerations and contextual circumstances unless individuals are particularly wedded to a particular approach. The reason for this is that in transnational higher education staff often have to work within the confines of a given situation and context at a set point in time, which will be influenced by institutional culture. In addition to the points previously mentioned, factors associated with leadership include capacity, achievement, responsibility, participation, status and situation (University of Cambridge Institute for Sustainability Leadership, 2017b).

Transnational Higher Education Leadership and Management: At present there are relatively few studies that consider transnational higher education, and even fewer that look at the area (or areas) of leadership and management, and the practical realities of leading and managing staff. In fact, recent studies on transnational higher education do not even mention leadership and management initially, as the work of Wilkins and Annabi (2021) illustrates. Keyword searches on popular sites such as Google Scholar also highlight the dearth or work in this area. This contrasts with the vast amount of information available on education and teaching, or the topic of leadership and management more generally. For example, a quick internet search will bring up results for transnational education (for example, QAA, 2022 and/or Universities UK, 2021), and institutional level challenges (see AdvanceHE, 2020 and Wilkins, 2018), but significantly less on leading and managing staff in transnational higher education (for example, Wilkins and Neri, 2019). Given how quickly macro geopolitical changes have occurred following the COVID-19 pandemic, and how much useful material exists on leading and managing staff in general leadership and management literature, such as Owen's (2020) fifth edition handbook, this suggests that more work in this area is warranted. Indeed, the work of Morris (2021a), Li and Morris (2021) and Morris, Xu and Li (In Print) has gone some way to supporting developments in this area, but more insights are certainly needed, especially those that are drawing on practical experience and research initiatives.

METHODOLOGY

This research inspired chapter is a holistic evaluation of a collation of leadership and management research conducted,written and co-written by the author at the research site. In some respects, it is a mixed methodological review.

Research Study 1: The first piece of work is a qualitative study involving the in-depth interviews of twenty expatriate staff in terms of their employment motivation and job satisfaction (see Morris, 2021a). This exploratory study involved multiple case studies and utilised semi-structured interviews as these provide a window into an individual's world (Silverman, 2011), enabling perceptions, meaning and reality constructions to be considered (Punch, 2009). They are one of the most powerful ways to understand others (Kahn, 2011). In this instance, a semi structured interview guide was adopted, with participants selected on a purposive premise to cover a wide range of ages, gender, experiences, and employment positions. A combination of deductive and inductive coding was utilised, as Miles and Huberman (1994) and Sahakyan, Lamb and Chambers (2018) highlight can be beneficial.

Research Study 2: The second study is a quantitative one that utilised an online questionnaire which was circulated to all 215 staff within the SoL. A response rate of 41% was returned as 88 responses were received. See Li and Morris (2021). 72 of these respondents taught English for Academic Purposes (EAP). The additional 13 taught either Chinese, Spanish or Japanese. Teaching experience ranged from 6 months to 41 years. A convenience sampling strategy was employed, with the survey tool designed based upon previous research. It considered teachers' perception of and experience with teaching and learning, alongside professional development initiatives through a variety of closed question types. Those featuring a Likert scale adopted a four-point range.

Research Study 3: The third study is another qualitative study utilsiing an exploratory research methodology as defined by Cohen, Manion and Morrison (2007). In this instance a semi-structured interview approach was employed to consider pedagogic provision and staff perceptions within the SoL, notably EAP teaching and learning, before, during and post COVID-19. See Morris, Xu and Li (In Print). The interview guidelines were designed based on existing literature to best fit the purpose of the study (Li, 2014). A convenience sampling approach was adopted due to time constraints and participant access challenges during a remote learning period in the Spring 2022 due to COVID-19 protocols.

RESULTS

Research Study 1: Regarding expatriate transnational higher education staff there were three primary factors that were identified as motivating educators to seek work at this provider. See Figure 1. These were employment-based factors, personal considerations, and convenience. Employment-based factors, the most prominent, included (in rank order of preference) the new provider being regarded as a step up, a changing work situation pre-move, the remuneration package, limited alternatives, previous work experience, teaching opportunities and colleague recommendations. In terms of convenience-based features, the location was the most frequent response by far, with prior knowledge, recruitment ease and chance adverts also mentioned. Personal considerations included friends and family recommendations, family and/or partner needs, alongside lifestyle considerations and separations.

Figure 1. Expatriate employment motivation framework (Morris, 2021a)

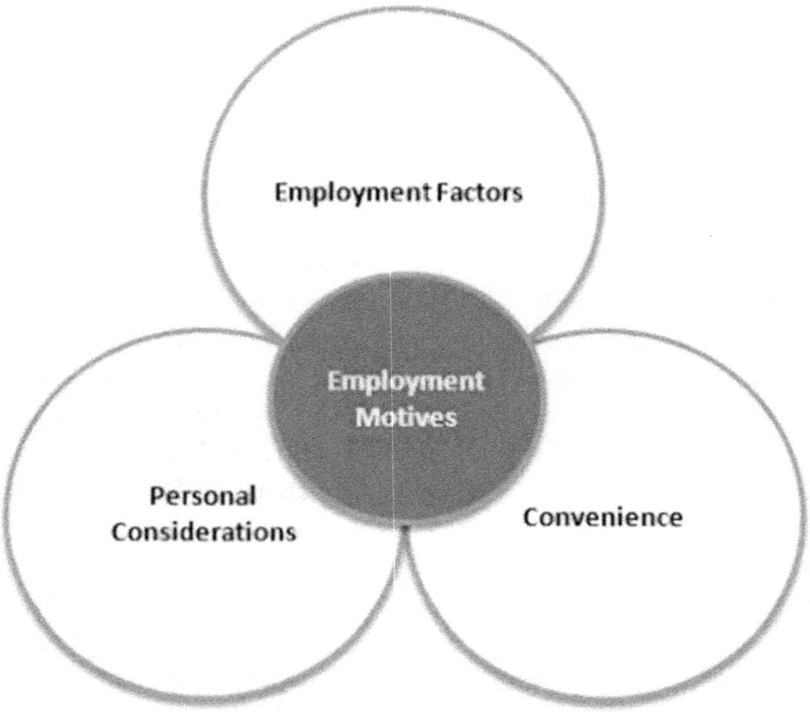

In terms of actual job satisfaction (see Figure 2), for new staff personal interactions, elements of teaching and learning, career advancement and the employment package (the most noted) all stood out. This contrasted with second and third contract staff who highlighted how personal interactions and teaching and learning features provided the greatest sources of satisfaction, along with job security and remuneration (to some extent). Similar patterns were also found with long serving staff. For the then school management some personal interaction areas and aspects of the employment package were the standout features. With regards to dissatisfaction, for new staff the area of greatest dissatisfaction was in terms of recognition and progression, and more specifically effort acknowledgment and promotion opportunities. A similar pattern was also found with second and third contract staff, with effort acknowledgement, the evaluation system and promotion opportunities especially heartfelt. For long serving staff, again, promotion opportunities stood out a source of dissatisfaction, whereas for managers the broader areas of teaching and learning and recognition and progression were areas of concern.

Figure 2. Expatriate job satisfaction framework (Morris, 2021a)

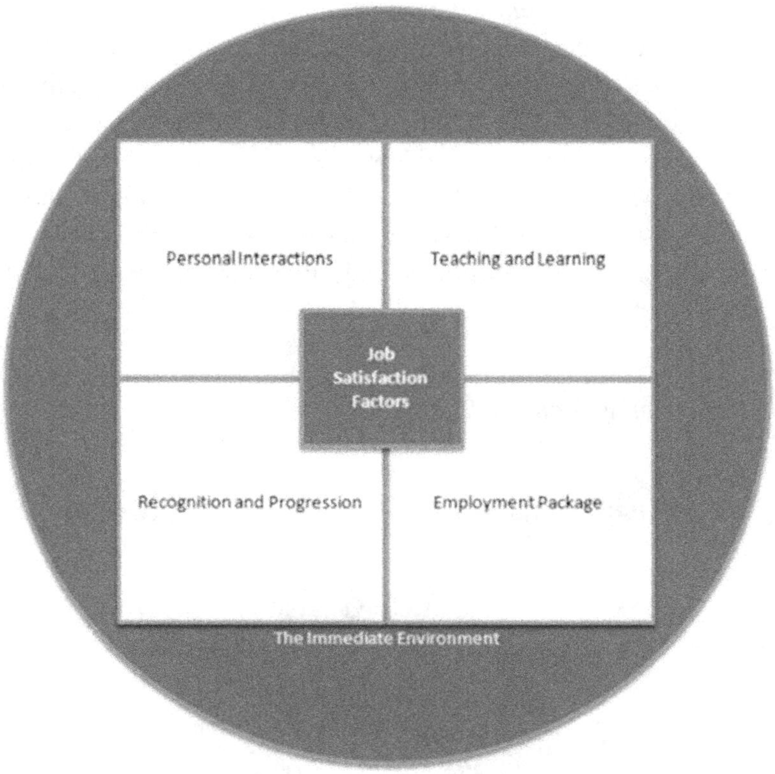

Leadership and management recommendations for the aforementioned transnational higher education SoL included stating that leadership figures ought to display good interpersonal skills (Chaaban and Du, 2017), support staff (Pourtoussi, Gharizadeh and Mousavi, 2018), promote teamwork (Middleton, 2019), encourage participation (Cansoy, 2018), ownership (Dou, Devos and Valcke, 2017), and equity (Cansoy, 2018; Norman, Ambrose and Huston, 2006). They should also communicate effectively and openly (Cansoy, 2018), manage conflict (Middleton et al., 2017), create a common vision (Cansoy, 2018), be reflective (Middleton, 2019), and not prejudiced (Robertson, 2012), clear barriers (Bowers and Seashore, 1966) and, ideally, feel a sense of pride in effective work and good relationships (Gun and Holdway, 1986). Training was also deemed important (Middleton, 2019), as too was reflective practice and the ability to change (Kaufman, 2020) and deal with uncertainty (McRaney, 2012). As Gligorovic et al. (2016) highlight, many of these aspects are important for younger staff. Recognising and rewarding staff were also essential.

Research Study 2: In this study conducted by Li and Morris (2021) which considered the impact of the COVID-19 pandemic on staff perceptions of in-service professional development needs and experiences a number of interesting findings arose, beyond the obvious fact that online learning had become increasingly prominent as Murphy (2020) and Hodges et al. (2020) had highlighted. Indeed, participant responses from the Spring of 2020 when the data was collected demonstrated that technology-enhanced language teaching and learning, associated assessments and research were all areas where additional professional development support was required. This is to some extent understandable given the macro contextual and institutional situational status quo of that point in time.

Another interesting finding from this study was the leadership and management was also identified as an area where a moderate level of need existed in 36% for the respondents and a high level of need for an additional 20% of the 88 respondents. See Figure 3. This could be attributed to internal restructuring as the Language Centre was repositioned as a School of Languages (SoL) meaning line management chains had lengthened and roles extended as Li and Morris (2021) noted. The loss of an experienced management team and the emergence of a new and relatively inexperienced new team at that time had also had a potential impact. The impact of these challenges was likely exacerbated by the speed and demands the pandemic then placed on individuals. Considerations such as these re-emphasize the importance of professional learning communities (see Richmond and Manokore, 2020) and distributed leadership as the National College for Teaching and Learning (2010) advocate.

Figure 3. Leadership and management needs (See Li and Morris, 2021)

Given how complex and demanding the educational world has become, as Orazbayeva et al. (2020) note, it is for reasons such as these that Morris (2021b) advocates the importance of considering a people-centred, or orientated approach (Mele, 2016), to leadership and management. Morris (2021b) advocates a holistic needs-based approach due to the toll the pandemic exerts of staff wellbeing in terms of feeling overwhelmed, drained and generally stressed (Civinini, 2021), and evolving COVID-19 guidelines as Roberts (2020) draws attention on add to the difficulties. This aligns with the suggestions of motivational speakers such as Simon Sinek (2017) who stress the importance of caring for the people with whom we work. In fact, Watt (2009) suggested compassion was a top five ranking leadership trait, alongside honesty, with a love of people ranked second. Of course, there is no one perfect approach as the University of Cambridge Institute for Sustainability Leadership (2017a) highlights, and Morris (2021c) has shown to be the case within this case study school, due to the role that the context, situational demands and people all play, but this institute also stressed how in China being human orientated is a core leadership feature valued by staff.

Research Study 3: Having analysed the responses from the seven participants it was apparent that there were several notable challenges that the practitioners faced. The first was technology-enhanced learning with greater training required. The second challenge was increasing student numbers, which coupled with the third challenge of staff departures was increasing the difficulties that the teachers were facing. In light of these features, Morris, Xu and Li (In Print) stressed the importance of continuing professional development and empathetic management and forward-thinking leadership. More specifically, an inclusive culture was purported, with clear open communication channels that keep employees in the loop as this can reduce anxieties and better align stakeholders (Davies et al., 2020). Also advocated were the possibilities to look at innovative pedagogic practices, such as Content Language Integrated Learning (CLIL) approaches, and initiatives that might enhance retention drives with enhanced schooling provision, and online teaching options providing greater flexi-work opportunities.

DISCUSSION

Self-Awareness: On an individual level, it is important that transnational higher education, and indeed all, leaders are self-aware. This is even more vital in transnational higher education as the complexity of working relationships is influenced by numerous differing cultural forces. This really necessitates an appreciation of conscious and subconscious thought processes and influences (See Freud, 1940), needs (See Maslow, 1954), emotions (See the US Davis Executive Leadership Program, 2014), and motives (See Dörnyei and Ushioda, 2009; Kahn, 2011; and Watt and Richardson, 2007). Leaders should also be comfortable in their own skin if they hope that others will be comfortable in their presence. This necessitates professional boundaries to be respected as the authority is partially invested in these. That said, hard and fast leadership approaches are fallible in today's working world meaning that a degree of situational flexibility is important. Indeed, this is the case across professions as Ferguson's (2013) writing suggests.

Personalised Leadership: There are numerous theories and models of leadership as Gozukara (2016) draws attention to. One such type is charismatic leadership which can be inspiring to staff, and another is situational leadership which can obviously be very pertinent and blend with other strands such as transformational demands. However, leaders ought to adopt an approach which is suited to themselves, albeit learning from others' strengths and weaknesses and reflecting on actions and reactions, the situation, content and point in time if possible. Some leaders may naturally be more charismatic, and others more managerial in orientation, but success or effectiveness will be based upon oneself and the remit alongside circumstances.

Effective Communication: Also important is communicating effectively (Krakoff, 2020). This is because good communication is more likely to ensure that educators receive clear and consistent messages which can be very reassuring and enhance rapport. Good communication also better enables leaders and organizations to adapt to situations as they arise, such as the COVID-19 pandemic. It is also very important in transnational higher education providers where staff can come from a wide variety of socio-cultural and demographic backgrounds.

Identity Creation: Ultimately, successful leadership is difficult to define as it involves many facets and it is understandably somewhat subjective. There are also degrees of success and effectiveness based on role remits. That said, one key success feature is identity creation. Having a vision is well documented in the literature (see Krakoff, 2020), and providing direction and creating identity are important for any transnational higher education entity, or entity sub-area, such as the SoL which has been discussed previously.

Building Teams: Another key feature is building good teams (University of Cambridge Institute for Sustainability Leadership, 2017). This may mean getting the best out of existing or inherited teams. It is also important to note that inherited teams may include staff who can be challenging to manage. Leaders should also not shy away from bringing in staff who have complementary, but alternative skillsets and knowledge bases, and from whom the leader can also learn. This may necessitate a degree of bravery as recruiting highly able (often junior) staff who may disagree can be daunting. However, it is also potentially advantageous if effectively managed because the insights which may be gleaned can be put to good use for the benefit of all. In addition, it is important to listen to an array of voices as this enables staff to feel appreciated and valued and allows leadership to make more informed and measured decisions that are more representative. Leaders who also demonstrate a desire for self-improvement within their teams also set strong, and potentially inspirational, examples to others. Teams also need good communication and collaboration (Baars et al., 2016). This involves guiding and empowering staff, as well as remaining actively engaged and fostering a sense of community (Hazari, 2020).

Leading Teams: Higher education transnational educational leadership is complicated by the fact that not only are leaders heading up cross-cultural teams, and potentially those who may not be entirely international in orientation, but they are also doing so in contextual conditions which may be alien to them. In addition, more senior figures may also be tasked with leading both academic or administrative or operational staff. This can present additional challenges as employment stipulations, terms of reference and employment expectations can vary, along with remuneration. To lead these differing groups successfully the Greek notions of ethos, pathos and logos are important. For academic staff, credibility, in the form of academic credentials, can be essential. In contrast, for professional service staff, who may be more goal orientated around specific tasks this may be less essential. On that note, a degree of mindset flexibility, as De Bono (2020) advocates is important. Equally important is being mindful of how non-work-related factors can affect and impact upon staff (Morris, 2021a). This can mean that as leaders rise on the career ladder all-round rather than specialist skillsets are advantageous. Cultivating a positive climate is also important (Morris, 2021a), one in which respect and trust are feature (See Sinek, 2017).

Staff Support: Successful leadership also more often than not involves supporting staff, especially junior staff, during their careers, and not simply within a specific institution. This may involve tailoring one's management style over time to get the best out of individuals as various literature demonstrates (see Ferguson, 2013). Mentoring staff is also important, and this can extend to future leaders as well due to the fact that individuals are then more ready to step up when the time arises with little or no preparation, as many do. The benefits of mentoring and support are that individuals, divisional areas, and institutions improve, and knowledge is retained. Goodwill and performance is also often enhanced. This is especially true when staff see their leaders as selfless and willing to shield as Sinek (2017) notes. It also sets a precedent for junior staff, whilst simultaneously acting as an important support mechanism if required.

Professional Development: Organisational growth relies on employee professional development (Hazari, 2020; Wertz Consulting, 2019). Leadership can be taught, as Wertz Consulting (2019) notes, but it also necessitates accepting positive and negative feedback and being open-minded. This can be difficult due to time pressures (Li and Morris, 2021). Training also needs to be tailored to specific needs and situations. This is partially why targeted training is so important as Ericsson and Pool (2016) advocate, alongside mentoring. Davies (2009) highlights the benefits of mentoring for middle managers. However, the value of mentoring is only as good as the quality of the input and interactions.

Developing Networks: The University of Cambridge Institute for Sustainability Leadership (2017a) has highlighted the importance of connections and relationships. These can be vertical and horizontal in a traditional hierarchical chain. This is because the importance of peer support cannot be underestimated as peers are an important source of time-effective information. They are also a very important support mechanism.

Leading Change: Transformational leadership can be one potential leadership approach to adopt when change is necessitated or desired. That said, it is important to note that change, or the fear of change, often leads to resistance as employees can have understandable concerns due to the likely future impact on them. Shared histories can also impact upon developments. New leaders can also be viewed with apprehension or as a potential threat, whether this is warranted or not. To lead change, it is therefore important to enhance knowledge, build support and have resources. This can be difficult to realise for new leaders in transnational higher education providers. Knowing how to work within and with policy is also essential. To act as a catalyst for change leadership figures need to be a motivational force for it as Gandhi's oft cited 'be the change you want to see' quote advocates (see UN, 2020). To this end, setting a collective vision, which others buy into, and setting up waypoints to monitor progress is essential. Staff will also need opportunities for growth and development, with staff empowered (Pieterse, 2021), and a positive (for all) collective culture fostered is likely to yield better results than an individually orientated one. This is especially important as leadership can be a draining endeavour (Macbeath, 2008), and even more so in transnational higher education.

Leadership Sustainability: Sustainability is important because constant change can lead to change fatigue. Eastwood (2020), for example, stresses the importance of building new leaders, and also providing opportunities for them is essential. This also extends to ensuring that junior leaders are ready for the step up when the opportunities arise, and this extends back to supporting staff through initiatives such as mentoring, although the mentor can come from outside of a specific institutional unit, and even the organisation itself. Transnational higher educational leaders also need to be able to manage resources as well as individuals (Baars et al., 2016), and plan for the future as the University of Cambridge Institute for Sustainability Leadership (2017) advocates.

Protecting Leaders: Drucker (1954 cited in Pierce and Newstrom, 2012) suggests that managers are an employer's scarcest and most expensive resources. They are also essential for long-term business performance (University of Cambridge Institute for Sustainability Leadership, 2017b), but are vulnerable to debilitating emotional stress (Macbeath, 2008). Certainly, leaders have to face temporal pressures and accountability concerns (Baars et al., 2016). They also need to investigate concerns and manage outcomes (Day and Sammons, 2013). In transnational higher education leaders also need to be mindful of differences between national, industrial and situational contexts where features like power distance can vary (see Ardichvili and Kuchinke, 2010). Unsurprisingly, leadership responsibility can bring unattractive tradeoffs due to the added responsibility and workload (Pont et al., 2008).

CONCLUSION

Leading others is difficult and something of an art at the best of times. Clearly good leadership is a key feature of successful organisations (Smith and Hughey, 2006), and Davies (2009) suggests that every successful school will have effective leaders, but just as management can be an element of leadership, so can effectiveness be a part of success. According to Cambridge Assessment (2019), leadership involves meeting appropriate standards in the areas of knowledge and understanding, skill and practices, values and attributes, professional relationships, teaching and learning, innovation and improvement, management systems and community engagement. This may sound reasonably straightforward, but each area is extremely broad and complex in reality. Nevertheless, like most things in life, transnational higher education leadership and management can be fine-tuned with experience, training (see Ericsson and Pool, 2016), and honest critical self-reflection.

LEADERSHIP TAKEAWAYS

What is leadership?

Leadership involves service. It involves guiding, supporting and protecting staff. It also involves a degree of selflessness. Leaders also need to promote a (common) vision as Krakoff (2020) highlights, and team ethos, but also have to find their own way when setting direction which is consistent with their values.

What qualities make a good leader?

Leaders need to have social skills and be good communicators in order to build teams (Jyoti, 2010). This is why approachability is important as Aldridge and Fraser (2016) note. They should be inclusive, recognise staff, be appreciative, as well as trustworthy (Yoshihara, 2018), and supportive (Winiger and Birkholz, 2013). They can and may need to motivate their teams, and have good organisational and time management skills. They need to support staff growth and share successes and train and mentor the next generation. Leaders also need to be able to adapt and tailor what they do and take on different roles at different times. This will all require being critically mindful and reflective in dealings with others, as well as non-judgmental.

Are there national differences in leadership?

Leadership varies between national contexts but should embrace differences. Leadership can influence and enhance institutional culture.

What should leaders remember?

Leaders cannot fix every problem and do everything. They need 360-degree support. Recruitment is therefore important. It is good to display humanistic traits, foster a positive environment (Jiang et al., 2019), build support networks, promote collaboration (Shoaib, 2004), and have the commitment to stand by their decisions. Leadership will often draw on multiple disciplines, and require support and professional development. Because time is finite leaders can learn from others. They also need to be mindful of personal beliefs, situational needs and contextual possibilities. Ultimately, leadership must be effective, successful, and sustainable. Effectiveness is linked to how well we achieve the tasks required of us. Success however is difficult to measure, multifaceted and potentially subjective and leaders must consider their own well-being.

Extended Thanks: Thanks to those transitional higher education leaders, or subject discipline experts, who have either led by example or very kindly shared some of their insights in the recent past. They include, but are certainly not limited to, Professor Stuart Perrin, Professor Joon Sik Kim, Professor Chris Harris, Professor David Goodman, Professor Youmin Xi, Dr. Bill Boland, Dr. Tao Bai, Dr. Eoin Jordan and Professor Li Li.

REFERENCES

Aldridge, J. M., & Fraser, B. J. (2016). Teachers' views of their school climate and its relationship with teacher self-efficacy and job satisfaction. *Learning Environments Research, 19*(2), 291–307. doi:10.100710984-015-9198-x

Ardichvili, A., & Kuchinke, P. K. (2010). Leadership styles and cultural values among managers and subordinates: A comparative study of four countries of the former Soviet Union, Germany, and the US. *Human Resource Development International, 5*(1), 99–117. doi:10.1080/13678860110046225

Baars, S., Parameshwaran, M., Menzies, L. & Chiong, C. (2016). *Firing on all cylinders: What makes an effective middle leader?* London: Teaching Leaders and LKMCo.

Bowers, D. G., & Seashore, S. E. (1966). Predicting organizational effectiveness with a four theory of leadership. *Administrative Science Quarterly, 2*(2), 236–263. doi:10.2307/2391247

Bryman, A. (2008). Effective leadership in higher education: A literature review. *Studies in Higher Education, 32*(6), 693–710. doi:10.1080/03075070701685114

Bush, T., & Glover, D. (2014). School leadership models: What do we know? *School Leadership & Management, 34*(5), 1–19. doi:10.1080/13632434.2014.928680

Cai, L., & Hall, C. (2016). Motivations, expectations and experiences of expatriate academic staff on an international branch campus in China. *Journal of Studies in International Education, 20*(3), 207–222. doi:10.1177/1028315315623055

Cambridge Assessment. (2019). *Cambridge school leader standards.* Cambridge. https://www.cambridgeinternational.org/teacher-and-leader-standards

Cambridge Assessment International Education. (2017). *Educational leadership.* Cambridge. https://www.cambridgeinternational.org/images/271192-educational-leadership.pdf

Cansoy, R. (2018). The relationship between school principles' leadership behaviours and teachers' job satisfaction: *A systematic review. International Education Studies, 12*(1), 37–52. doi:10.5539/ies.v12n1p37

Chaaban, T., & Du, X. (2017). Novice teachers'job satisfaction and coping strategies: Overcoming contextual challenges at Qatari government schools. *Teaching and Teacher Education, 67*, 340–350. doi:10.1016/j.tate.2017.07.002

Civinini, C. (2021). *Covid leaves teachers 'drained and frustrated.* TES. https://www.tes.com/news/covid-leaves-teachers-drained-and-frustrated

Cohen, L., Manion, L., & Morrison, K. (2007). *Research methods in education* (6th ed.). Routledge. doi:10.4324/9780203029053

Davies, B. (2009). *The essentials of school leadership: Learning-centred leadership.* Sage. doi:10.4135/9781446288290

Davies, J. A., Davies, L. J., Conlon, B., Emerson, J., Hainsworth, H., & McDonough, H. G. (2020). Responding to COVID-19 in EAP Contexts: A Comparison of Courses at Four Sino-Foreign Universities. *International Journal of TESOL Studies*, *2*(2), 32–51.

Day, C. & Sammons, P. (2013). *Successful leadership: A review of the international leadership.* Reading: CfBT Education Trust.

de Bono. (2020). *The six thinking hats.* de Bono. https://www.debono.com/six-thinking-hats-summary

Dörnyei, Z., & Ushioda, E. (2009). *Motivation, language identity and the L2 self.* Multilingual Matters. doi:10.21832/9781847691293

Dou, D., Davos, G., & Valcke, M. (2017). The relationship between school autonomy gap, principal leadership, teachers' job satisfaction and organisational commitment. *Educational Management Administration & Leadership*, *45*(6), 959–977. doi:10.1177/1741143216653975

Doyle, L. (2019*). Leadership vs. management: What's the difference?* Northeastern University. https://www.northeastern.edu/bachelors-completion/news/leadership-vs-managment/

Drucker, P. (1954). *The practice of management.* Harper & Row Publishers.

Eastwood, B. (2020). *8 essential traits for effective leadership in higher education. Northeastern University.* https://www.northeastern.edu/graduate/blog/leadership-in-higher-education/

Emery, V. & Worton, M. (2021). *Challenges for the leadership of transnational education in higher education: Balancing risk and innovation.* Advanced HE. https://www.advance-he.ac.uk/knowledge-hub/challenges-leadership-transnational-education-higher-education-balancing-risk-and-0

Ericsson, A., & Pool, R. (2016). *Peak - Secrets from the new science of expertise.* Houghton Miffin Harcourt.

Ferguson, A. (2013). *My autobiography.* Hodder & Stoughton.

Freud, S. (1940). *An outline of psychoanalysis. The standard edition of the complete psychological works of Sigmund Freud* (Vol. XXIII). W.W. Norton and Company.

Gavin, M. (2019). *Leadership vs. management: What's the difference?* Harvard Business School Online. https://online.hbs.edu/blog/post/leadership-vs-management

Gligorovic, B., Nikolic, M., Terek, E., Glusac, D., & Tasic, I. (2016). The impact of school culture on Serbian primary teacher's job satisfaction. *H.U. Journal of Education*, *31*(2), 231–248.

Gozukara, I. (2016). Leadership and managerial effectiveness in higher education. *International Journal of Academic Research in Accounting. Finance and Management Sciences*, *6*(1), 73–82.

Gun, J. A., & Holdway, E. A. (1986). Perceptions of effectiveness influences and satisfaction of senior high school principals. *Education Administration*, *22*(2), 43–62. doi:10.1177/0013161X86022002004

Hawking, S. (2018). *Brief answers to the big questions*. John Murray.

Hazari, S. (2020). *The evolution of leadership in the past decade.* Gisma. https://www.gisma.com/blog/the-evolution-of-leadership-in-the-past-decade

Hodges, C., Moore, S., Lockee, B., Trust, T., & Bond, A. (2020). The difference between emergency remote teaching and online learning. *EDUCAUSE Review, 27*(March). https://er.educause.edu/articles/2020/3/the-difference-between-emergency-remote-teaching-and-online-learning

Jiang, Y., Li, P., Wang, J., & Li, H. (2019). Relationships between kindergarten teachers' empowerment, job satisfaction and organisational climate: A Chinese model. *Journal of Research in Childhood Research, 33*(2), 257–270.

Jyoti, J. (2010). Job satisfaction of university teachers: An empirical study. *Journal of Services Research, 9*(2), 51–80.

Kahn, Z. (2011). *Factors affecting the motivation of expatriate English as a foreign language (EFL) teachers in the Sultanate of Oman.* [Unpublished EdD Thesis, University of Exeter, UK].

Kaufman, J. (2012). *Personal MBA*. Penguin.

Krakoff, S. (2020). *The top 10 qualities of a great leader.* Champlain College. https://online.champlain.edu/blog/top-qualities-of-a-great-leader

Li, L. (2014). Understanding language teachers' practice with educational technology: A case from China. *System*, *46*, 105–119. doi:10.1016/j.system.2014.07.016

Li, L., & Morris, G. (2021). Thriving in the new normal: In-service professional development needs and experience. In H. Xiang (Ed.), *Trends and developments for the future of language education in higher education* (pp. 253–272). IGI Global. doi:10.4018/978-1-7998-7226-9.ch013

Macbeath, J. (2008). Leadership for learning: Exploring similarity and living with difference. In J. Macbeath & Y. C. Cheng (Eds.), *Leadership for learning* (pp. 1–16). Sense Publishers.

Maslow, A. H. (1954). *Motivation and personality* (2nd ed.). Harper and Row.

McRaney, D. (2012). *You are not so smart*. One World.

Mele, D. (2016). Understanding humanistic management. *Humanistic Management Journal*, *1*(1), 33–55. doi:10.100741463-016-0011-5

Middleton, A. (2019). *First man in: Leading from the front*. Harper Collins.

Middleton, A., Fox, J., Ollerton, M., & Maclachlan, C. (2017). *SAS who dares wins: Leadership secrets from the special forces*. Headline Publishing Group.

Miles, M. B., & Huberman, A. M. (1994). *Qualitative data analysis*. Sage.

Morris, G. (2021a). *Investigating the employment motivation and job satisfaction of expatriate language teachers* [Unpublished EdD Thesis, University of Exeter, UK]. http://hdl.handle. net/10871/124311

Morris, G. (2021b). Leading during a pandemic: A case of prioritising Maslow ahead of Bloom. Language Teaching in China, 1(September 2021), pp. 66-71.

Morris, G. (2021c) Charting the school of languages evolutionary development: A leadership perspective. *Language Teaching in China, 1*(September 2021), pp, 78-83.

Morris, G., Perrin, S., Sheridan, S., Xu, J., Liang, W., Lv, F., Di, S., Foster, R., & Zhang, C. (2021). Educational symbiosis: Designing language learning courses to support syntegrative education. In H. Xiang (Ed.), *Trends and developments for the future of language education in higher education* (pp. 187–208). IGI Global. doi:10.4018/978-1-7998-7226-9.ch010

Morris, G., Xu, J., & Li, L. (In Print). Transitioning to the new normal: Experiences from a Sino-British institution. In Kohnke, L. (Ed.). Cases on teaching English for academic purposes (EAP) during COVID-19: Insights from around the world. IGI Global.

Murphy, M. P. A. (2020). COVID-19 and emergency eLearning: Consequences of the securitization of higher education for post-pandemic pedagogy. *Contemporary Security Policy, 41*(3), 492–505. doi:10.1080/13523260.2020.1761749

National College for Teaching and Learning. (2010). *10 strong claims about successful school leadership.* NCTL. https://www.gov.uk/government/publications/10-strong-claims-about-successful-school-leadership

Norman, M., Ambrose, S. A., & Huston, T. A. (2006). Assessing and addressing faculty morale: Cultivating consciousness, empathy and empowerment. *The Review of Higher Education, 29*(3), 347–379. doi:10.1353/rhe.2006.0013

Orazbayeva, B., Meerman, A., Galan Muros, V., Davey, T., & Plewa, C. (2020). *The future of universities thoughtbook: Universities during times of crisis*. University Industry Innovation Network.

Owen, J. (2020). *The leadership skills handbook* (5th ed.). Kogan Page Ltd.

Pew Research Center. (2015). *Women and leadership: public says women are equally qualified, but barriers persist.* Pew Research Center.

Pierce, J. L., & Newstrom, J. W. (2012). *The managers bookshelf: A mosaic of contemporary views* (10th ed.). Pearson.

Pieterse, P. (2021). *New VPAA: 'Academic leadership is about the empowerment of others.'* XJL University. https://www.xjtlu.edu.cn/en/news/2021/03/new-vpaa-academic-leadership-is-about-the-empowerment-of-others

Pont, B., Nusche, D., & Moorman, H. (2008). Policy and practice. Improving school leadership (Vol. 1). OECD.

Pourtoussi, Z., Ghanizadeh, A., & Mousavi, V. (2018). A qualitative in-depth analysis of the determinants and outcomes of EFL teachers' motivation and demotivation. *Internal Journal of Instruction, 11*(4), 175–190. doi:10.12973/iji.2018.11412a

Punch, K. F. (2009). *Introduction to research methods in education*. Sage.

QAA. (2022). *Transnational education*. QAA. https://www.qaa.ac.uk/reviewing-higher-education/types-of-review/transnational-education

Richmond, G., & Manokore, V. (2020). Identifying elements critical for functional and sustainable professional learning communities. *Science Teacher Education, 95*, 543–570.

Roberts, J. (2020). *Five ways Covid-19 has made teachers' jobs harder.* TES Magazine. https://www.tes.com/news/five-ways-covid-19-has-made-teachers-jobs-harder

Robertson, I. (2012). *The winner effect: The neuroscience of success and failure*. Bloomsbury.

Sahakyan, T., Lamb, M., & Chambers, G. (2018). Language teacher motivation: From ideal self to the feasible self. In S. Mercer & A. Kostoulas (Eds.), *Language teacher psychology* (pp. 53–70). Multilingual Matters. doi:10.21832/9781783099467-008

Shoaib, A. (2004). *The motivation of teachers of English as a second language* (PhD Thesis, University of Nottingham, UK].

Silverman, D. (2011). *Qualitative research*. Sage.

Sinek, S. (2017). *Leaders eat last: Why some teams pull together and others don't*. Penguin.

Smith, B. L., & Hughey, A. W. (2006). Leadership in higher education - Its evolution and potential: A unique role facing critical challenges. *Industry and Higher Education, 20*(3), 157–163. doi:10.5367/000000006777690972

Toor, S. U. R., & Ofori, G. (2008). Leadership versus management: How are they different and why. *Leadership and Management in Engineering, 8*(2), 61–71. doi:10.1061/(ASCE)1532-6748(2008)8:2(61)

Trembath, J. L. (2016). The professional lives of expatriate academics - Construct clarity and implications for expatriate management in higher education. *Journal of Global Mobility, 4*(2), 112–130. doi:10.1108/JGM-04-2015-0012

UK Universities. (2021). *What is UK higher education transnational education?* UK Universities. https://www.universitiesuk.ac.uk/universities-uk-international/explore-uuki/transnational-education/what-uk-higher-education-transnational

UN. (2020). Be the change you want to see. United Nations. https://www.un.org/africarenewal/webfeatures/peacekeepers/women-peacekeeping-%E2%80%98be-change-youwant-see%E2%80%99

University of Cambridge Institute for Sustainability Leadership. (2017a). *Global definitions of leadership and theories of leadership development: Literature review*. University of Cambridge.

University of Cambridge Institute for Sustainability Leadership. (2017b). *Building leaders for long-term business performance: Research findings*. University of Cambridge.

US Davis Executive Leadership Program. (2014). *Emotional intelligence: How good leaders become great.* University of Nottingham. https://moodle.nottingham.ac.uk/course/view.php?id=99200&section=4##

Watt, M. G., & Richardson, P. W. (2007). Motivational factors influencing teaching as a career choice: Development and validation of the FIT choice scale. *Journal of Experimental Education*, *75*(3), 167–202. doi:10.3200/JEXE.75.3.167-202

Watt, M. G., Richardson, P. W., & Smith, K. (2017). Why teach? How teachers' motivations matter around the world. In M. G. Watt, P. W. Richardson, & K. Smith (Eds.), *Global perspectives on teacher motivation. Current perspectives in social and behavioural sciences* (pp. 1–21). Cambridge University Press. doi:10.1017/9781316225202.001

Watt, W. (2009). Top 10 traits of an effective academic leader. *Faculty Focus.* https://www.facultyfocus.com/articles/academic-leadership/top-10-traits-of-an-effective-academic-leader/

Wertz Consulting. (2019). *How leadership has changed over the last 10 years.* Wertz Consulting. http://www.wertzconsulting.com/leadership-changed-last-10-years/

Wilkins, S. (2018). The management of transnational higher education. *International Journal of Educational Management*, *32*(2), 206–209. doi:10.1108/IJEM-10-2017-0260

Wilkins, S., & Annabi, C. A. (2021). Academic Careers in Transnational Higher Education: The Rewards and Challenges of Teaching at International Branch Campuses. *Journal of Studies in International Education*, *23*(4), 451–472. doi:10.1177/1028315318814200

Wilkins, S., & Neri, S. (2019). Managing faculty in transnational higher education: Expatriate academics at international branch campuses. *Journal of Studies in International Education*, *23*(4), 451–472. doi:10.1177/1028315318814200

Winiger, S. R., & Birkholz, P. M. (2013). Sources of instructional feedback, job satisfaction, and basic psychological needs. *Innovative Higher Education*, *38*(2), 159–170. doi:10.100710755-012-9229-9

XJTLU. (2016). *Seven Sino-foreign cooperative universities gather at XJTLU.* XJLT University. https://www.xjtlu.edu.cn/en/news/2016/07/seven-sino-foreign cooperative-universities-gather-at-xjtlu

Yoshihara, K. F. (2018). *Teachers satisfaction and staff morale in international schools* [PhD Thesis,. University of New England, USA].

Section 6
Future Trends

Chapter 19
Transnational Higher Education Trends in the Internet Era:
Case Studies in China

Wei Xu
Shanghai High School International Division, China

ABSTRACT

Under the trend of global integration, transnational higher education has become a research upsurge in recent years. In this chapter, the author focuses on the implementations and influences of the modern information technology in transnational higher education. Current research is mainly based on traditional textual research and data collection analysis. Few research mentioned the influences and changes that modern information technology could bring to the developing of transnational higher education. Furthermore, the global outbreak caused by 2019-nCOVID has also brought a full range of impacts to the whole world and profoundly affected the current situation and future process of transnational higher education. Consequently, the aim of this chapter is to provide an overview of transnational higher education trends in the internet era. The author will analyze it through several cases studies, taking China as an example, and conclude those findings to highlight efficient methods using internet technologies to contribute building a better educational world.

INTRODUCTION

Development of Transnational Higher Education

In 1985, the economist Theodore Levitt created the term 'globalization' to describe the changes in global economics (Tedlow & Abdelal, 2004). Furthermore, as Spring (2014) stated, transnational higher education has become another hot research topic apart from the corporate globalization trend in the economy. It has been around for a long time. Today, educational practices at different levels are far from satisfactory and effective at a universal level. In this respect, distance education is an important academic tool

DOI: 10.4018/978-1-6684-5226-4.ch019

that provides education options and learning environments for people with different interests, needs, skills, ages, and geographical, educational, and socioeconomic backgrounds or those with limited access to education (Durnalı et al., 2022; Orakcı, 2020; Susam et al., 2020). Thanks to distance education, without leaving their countries of residence, students have the chance to achieve a degree from a foreign post-secondary institution. As indicated by Cruz (2010) and Keller (2011), mainly in western countries, transnational higher education is considered a way of generating extra income to overcome budget cuts for some market-oriented universities. In addition, new forms of technology also facilitate the transformation of science-oriented industrial processes into international endeavors, which encourages higher education institutions with an international stance to offer a more educated workforce for global markets and ideas (Taylor, 2011).

In the past 30 years, transnational higher education has developed rapidly in China and played a significant role in developing the internationalization of higher education worldwide (Guo & Jiang, 2010). Up to 1995, the growth and development of transnational higher education in China has evolved from an informal, casual, laissez-faire activity to a more systematic and regulated program now (Huang, 2003). Under this series of the evolution of TNHE (Transnational higher education) and the trend of growing global integration, transnational higher education in running schools has become a new research upsurge. Huang (2003) took a perspective from China to analyze the primary source countries and regions that provide TNHE services in China, ranging from the USA to Australia and Hong Kong, and pointed out that Australia and Hong Kong may finally compose a significant market share in China. Yin (2014) investigated the historical development of transnational higher education in running schools from a typical period between the 19th century to now. Guo and Jiang (2010) have analyzed the status quo, problems, and countermeasures of transnational higher education based on the data published by the ministry of education. According to the official data, they found significant differences in the level of transnational higher education in different economic development regions. In economically underdeveloped regions, transnational higher education often faces problems such as the small scale of development, unbalanced structure, and lack of international courses and teachers (Gong, 2020). Adams and Song (2009) also reveal the key developments and challenges of sino-foreign cooperatively running schools in China behind the international collaboration. They pointed out that cooperative partnerships in transnational higher education need a more explicit strategy and goals by correctly assessing their contribution to the country's educational capacity building, education, and knowledge exchange.

However, in the era of rapid internet development, research on how the Internet affects transnational higher education is inadequate and limited. Current research is mainly based on traditional textual research and data collection analysis. Few studies have mentioned the influences and changes of modern information technology on the development of transnational higher education. Especially with the advent of the 5G era, the internationalization of education should usher in new challenges and opportunities. Furthermore, in 2020, the global outbreak caused by 2019-nCOVID has allowed educators to rethink education and address paradigms of education (Orakcı, & Gelişli, 2021). It has had an overall impact on China and the world, profoundly affecting the current situation and future course of transnational higher education. All of these serve as the primary motivation for this chapter.

Different Delivery Modes of Current Transnational Higher Education

Before discussing and studying the technologies used in transnational higher education, it is essential to clarify the different delivery modes in transnational higher education programs. By understanding and analyzing these different models, the impact and efficacy of applying different technologies could be better asserted. According to Francois et al. (2016), there are three main delivery models of transnational higher education: distance models, in-country delivery models, and blended models. Firstly, the distance model (DM) is a delivery model in which there is no physical contact between learner and teaching institution in the curriculum or instructional practices. It consists of online learning, instructional audio or visual, and correspondence education (Francois et al., 2016). The second delivery model is an in-country delivery model (IDM). Literally, one of the cooperated foreign institutions establishes a physical apartment in the other country directly or through a third party and then provides educational services or programs. It generally consists of overseas branch campuses (OBC) (University of Nottingham Ningbo China is one of those examples), validation, franchising, and dual/double degree (Francois et al., 2016). Unlike the previous two models without student mobility, the third type, the blended model (BM), requires students to have a short-term physical exchange from one institution to another in other countries. It includes a fly-out approach, twinning, double degree with mobility, consecutive degree, and joint degree (Francois et al., 2016).

Nowadays, different cooperative institutions adopt different delivery modes. It will affect the further implementation of different types of internet technologies. For example, the distance model (DM) requires more robust online learning technologies as there is no chance to get physical contact during the whole study period. While, for the blended model (BM), during students' exchange period, technology requirements for online learning will be reduced, and offline learning will be increased. A more detailed analysis will follow the series of discussions about this in combination with case studies in the following part of this chapter.

Aims and Methodology for This Chapter

This chapter aims to list several common internet technologies adopted widely and analyze their impact on the institutions and students to keep up with the times. Apart from that, this chapter will research three representative case studies in China and, based on analyzing different internet technologies adopted to conclude findings on how to use those technologies efficiently in China. Multidimensional analysis diagrams will be made to help analyze findings more vividly.

The Purpose of the Study

This chapter aims to offer an insight into how internet technologies are currently used in transnational higher education through the analysis of three representative universities in China.

At the same time, feasibility and practicability of these internet technologies are discussed in terms of the five evaluation criteria proposed by the author. They are the maturity of technologies, accessibility of technologies, enrichment of learning materials, student integration, and future potential. It also intends to provide reference standards for other transnational higher education institutions to discuss the use and evaluation of internet technologies they have applied. Hopefully, it will bring extraordinary vitality to the development of internet technologies in other countries and even transnational higher education in the future.

PERSPECTIVE ON TECHNOLOGIES CURRENTLY IN USE

What Specific Technologies Have Been Used in Different Countries

Over the last decade, current transnational higher education has been challenged in light of increasingly advanced technological developments and increasing requirements for educating future generations. Nowadays, to better serve transnational higher education, it is vital to find an effective way for those TNHE systems and institutions to educate and shape future global citizens through the help of pedagogical innovation and updated internet technologies. Recently, THE systems and institutions have taken various internet technologies. The following is a brief description of the internet technologies used. In Australia, 'flexible learning' is popular among students who want superb choices about when, where, and how they learn (Wade, 1994). This is based on technologically mediated learning, which is also addressed by the British Council (The British Council, 1999). The study is mainly conducted in isolation, and technologically mediated online learning takes the place of traditional face-to-face lectures. The UNESCO/Council of Europe Code of Good Practice also acknowledges the vital role of updated technologies in transnational higher education while being specific to the European higher education area (EHEA) (Bennett et al., 2010). At the same time, enhancing the use of internet technology is gaining momentum in Southeast Asia and promoting students' creativity and inventiveness. For instance, the Singaporean government applies an IT master plan in education to improve students' independent learning skills and participation in the curriculum (Ziguras, 2001). Unlike Singapore, the Malaysian higher education department is more focused on increasing the participation rate and the growth of higher education institutions (Johari, 2000). Nevertheless, their educators and private higher education institutions emphasize the central role of technology in transforming higher education (Gan, 2000).

Different countries and regions will adopt different types of technologies from the perspective of different countries and regions. Likewise, the implementation of internet technologies also varies from institution to institution. For instance, the International Medical University (IMU), which has a cooperative relationship with several foreign medical colleges, has adopted problem-based learning curriculums for students since the mid-1990s (Lim, & Mak, 2015). After students complained that they could not access detailed displays of the previous week after learning, IMU implemented an online learning system to put all the displayed content there, with announcements, research resources, assessments, and discussion forums (Ziguras, 2001). This introduction of electronic delivery of lesson materials successfully helped students adapt to PBL sessions and feel like the center of learning (Yee et al., 2006).

Similarly, Monash University Malaysia, a branch campus, adopts telecommunications like email to build connections with the Australian university. Some subjects are taught by print-based distance education, and online materials are more used as a resource other than a primary teaching method. Then under this situation, Malaysian parents and students still desire to have more face-to-face contact with teachers (Ziguras, 2001).

Apart from that, University Tun Abdul Razak (UNITAR), which first opened in 1999 as the first 'virtual' university in Malaysia, dramatically relied on mediated education and was firstly forbidden to conduct virtual teaching model (Ibrahim, & Silong, 2000). First, students must attend local study centers to study all subjects for a fixed time. Then, UNITAR established a network of local learning centers to let students carry on daily study through computers and support staff. However, since the Internet connection in Malaysia is expensive and not reliable enough, UNITAR turned to spread out teaching materials on CD-ROMs (Ziguras, 2001). Again, UNITAR requires students to be greatly independent and capable of basic computer competence. By exploring five adult students' learning experiences in taking virtual courses in UNITAR, Ibrahim and Silong (2000) also pointed out that there are institutional, dispositional, and situational barriers for students to overcome.

Another university called the Asian Institute of Technology (AIT), based in Bangkok, is an international institution to serve the engineering education demand of the Southeast Asian region. It has two branches in Vietnam. Previously, the Vietnamese campus relied extensively on fax communication with the Bangkok campus, but now email and internet are the main ways to communicate (AIT, 2022). However, as stated by teachers on the Vietnamese campus, the use of the internet did not have as much impact as contacting people worldwide in terms of teaching and research methods (Ziguras, 2001). The same, students here are also required to be greatly independent. Unlike previous institutions, the TMC Centre for Advanced Seminars in Singapore, which acts as a local partner for transnational higher education programs offered by worldwide foreign universities, provides enrollment services for transnational higher education programs other than formal teaching (Mok, 2008). Previously, due to the limit on the internet, TMC students used fax and postal to contact teachers oversea. Then, with the help of the internet, students can access internet facilities to discuss, research, and learn online. Although the internet systems established by TMC satisfy the basic requirements of communication and teaching, students still expect more face-to-face academic support (Ziguras, 2001).

All the statements above indicate that transnational institutions are seeking the help of internet technology to enhance a more flexible learning environment. They provide many materials and information online and expect students with a high independent learning spirit and basic computer competence. On the other hand, students tend to have closer contact with teachers and classmates through more face-to-face learning opportunities. This illustrates the challenge that transnational higher education now faces, how to use updated internet technologies to make students more engaged in learning and minimize the distance isolation feeling. Traditionally, when mentioning technologies currently in use for transnational higher education, it will focus on digital tools application. However, for transnational higher education, using digital tools is not the only way to improve its innovation. Developing new approaches that better meet the requirements of stakeholder organizations is also necessary (Tsiligkiris, 2021). When institutions adopt some digital tools to conduct TNHE, they should pay attention to the technology itself and how it can serve students' local context and their expectations about teaching and learning.

CASE STUDY DISCUSSION AND ANALYSIS

This part presents three brief case studies, which provide typical examples of how transnational higher education institutions operate in China in terms of using internet technology. Three representative universities are analyzed: Xi'an Jiaotong-Liverpool University (XJTLU), NYU Shanghai, and the Chinese University of Hong Kong, Shenzhen. These case studies are based on published promotional materials, website information, and interviews with school staff and students. All collection of information is focused on what and how internet technologies have been used in these universities and are concerned with difficulties and challenges that have been encountered in using these technologies to promote the quality of teaching and learning experience.

Case study 1: Xi'an Jiaotong-Liverpool University (XJTLU)

Located in Suzhou Industrial Park, Xi'an Jiaotong-Liverpool University (XJTLU) is an international joint venture university founded by Xi'an Jiaotong University in China and the University of Liverpool in the United Kingdom. By May 2020, XJTLU has more than 17,000 undergraduates and postgraduate students, including 3500 students studying at the cooperative University of Liverpool and over 920 academic staff worldwide (XJTLU, 2022). XJTLU's degree programs are taught in English, emphasizing critical thinking and independent learning to prepare students for further work and research. For the past few years, it has been a successful independent Sino-foreign cooperative university. It offers various degree programs in different fields. All those opportunities in China and the UK help XJTLU become a research-led international university in China and be recognized internationally for its unique features.

XJTLU mainly provides two forms of programs for undergraduates, and students can choose one of them freely. One is a 2+2 program in which students will spend the first two undergraduate years in Suzhou, China, and the remaining two years at the University of Liverpool, UK. The other program is called the 4+X program, in which students will spend their four undergraduate years in China, and X means unknown graduate university. All the teaching materials and assessments are shared between XJTLU and UoL, which means XJTLU has vibrant internet technologies to support students learning in China or the UK.

For students in different areas to keep the same content, XJTLU established an official study website to reach teaching materials, library facilities, discussion forums, conduct research, and submit assignments. This is quite commonly adopted in current transnational higher education institutions. However, some of them are limited to using websites to provide learning materials. Lectures are still carried out in a face-to-face way. XJTLU used to do the same thing by just taking websites as resource platforms, and there was no urgent need to change the face-to-face teaching mode. However, under the ongoing impact of COVID-19 worldwide and to prepare for future development, XJTLU started to seek changes and innovations in traditional teaching methods with the help of updated internet technologies. During the pandemic period, since students and teachers could not have face-to-face offline lectures and tutorials, XJTLU applied updated equipment, including high-definition web cameras with top-quality microphones, along with the existing BigBlueButton web conferencing software platform to enable simultaneous online teaching and keep ultimate teaching flexibility all the time. Even though students are not really in the classroom space, they still feel the teacher is interacting with them in real-time. This is due to previously mentioned updated live broadcasting technologies.

Apart from this, XJTLU also looks to the future and has established a new integrated education model called Syntegrative Education (SE), focusing on integrating specialized, industrial, and management programs in XJTLU Entrepreneur College (Taicang). It tends to educate future industry experts with the ability to lead future industry development (XJTLU, 2022). Then, under the development of AI and robotic technologies, XJTLU establishes a 'Learning Mall' center to realize the integration of learning, research, training, entrepreneurship, and business (XJTLU, 2022). The XJTLU Learning Mall is a comprehensive hub including innovative and entrepreneurial research and development, project, and partner resources. It is based on the idea of life-long learning across the university community and beyond. Hence, it is also composed of not just XJTLU schools but other partners, including Alibaba Cloud, Huawei, McGraw-Hill, and Digital China, to provide abundant resources for digital learning (XJTLU, 2022). It is like a storefront online to share partners' learning content with students and users. Based on this, it can create a wide net that gathers on-site and online programs of the university, industry, and partners' resources (XJTLU, 2022).

Furthermore, it also engages users in this system by allowing enough freedom to develop their resources and learning. The XJTLU Learning Mall facility is integrated with the university's physical environment to let people feel engaged. Partners can host their personal community space to build a symbiotic learning ecosystem from online and on-site, campus to community (XJTLU, 2022). Students also benefit from the Learning Mall as they feel fully engaged when they cannot go back to school during the quarantine period.

Generally, the following table concludes the internet technologies XJTLU has been used and its primary functions.

Table 1. The internet technologies XJTLU has been used

Technologies	Functions
Official study website	Teaching materials, library facilities, discussion forums, activity announcements, and assignment submission.
Broadcasting hardware and software like high-definition web cameras with top-quality microphones and BigBlueButton web conferencing software platform	Simultaneous teaching online and keep ultimate teaching flexibility all the time.
The Learning Mall	A comprehensive hub including innovative and entrepreneurial research and development, project, and partner resources.

Moreover, according to the different usage emphases of these internet technologies, the following multidimensional analysis diagrams are made to analyze it in five main aspects. They are the maturity of technologies, accessibility of technologies, enrichment of learning materials, student integration, and future potential. The diagram is based on current research and interviews with school staff and teachers. Three teachers from the design school and two from an international business school are invited to give their opinions about the application of internet technologies in XJTLU. Students' feedback is collected anonymously in the form of a questionnaire. Twenty students from different departments participate in the survey. Teachers and students are asked to rank five aspects on a scale of 1 to 5, with one being the least satisfied and five the most satisfied. These criteria and survey methods also apply to the two cases further studied in this chapter. The final results of the internet technologies XJTLU has been used are analyzed by taking the average value of the data and drawn into the following pentagonal analysis graph.

As shown in Figure 1, teachers and students in XJTLU recognize the convenience of the official study website by giving almost five points for this aspect. They feel that the current website is quite mature and informative. However, one student said that "the official study website is mainly used to look for teaching materials and submit homework without further expansion and extension channels." That explains satisfaction in student integration is relatively low compared with the other aspects. At the same time, students think that the website is more of a place to download teaching resources and hand in homework. However, it is a lack of interactive communication with teachers. Therefore, with the development of internet technologies in the future, this kind of online learning will be considered a traditional teaching method and have less development potential as it has been relatively mature at present.

Figure 1. The pentagonal map of the official study website technology in Table 1

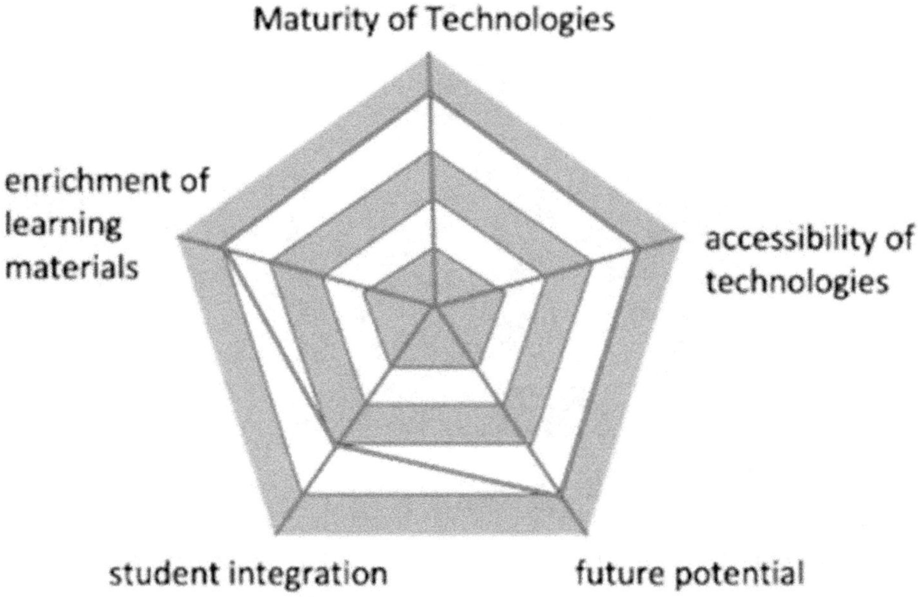

Figure 2. The pentagonal map of the broadcasting hardware and software technology in Table 1

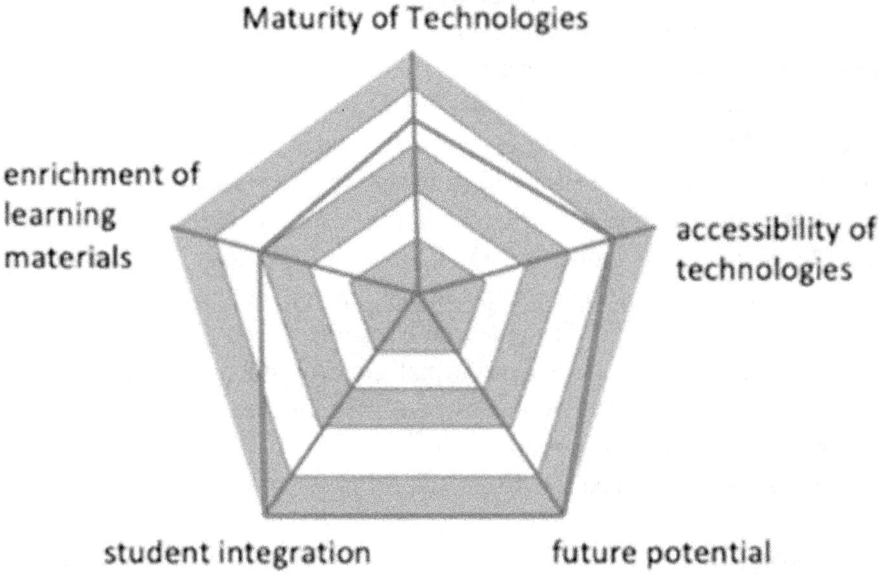

Figure 3. The pentagonal map of the Learning Mall technology in Table 1

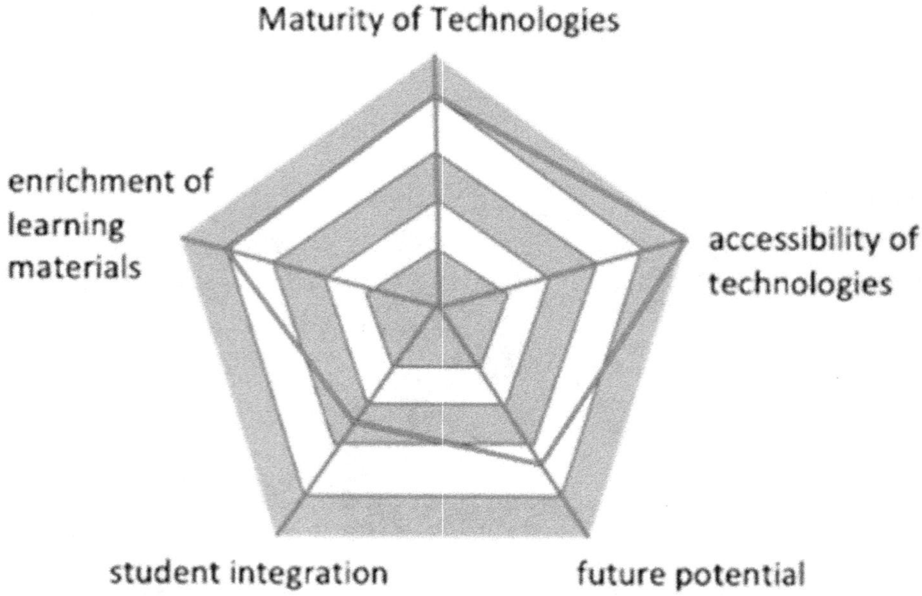

The evaluation of the broadcasting hardware and software technology is quite different. Teachers and students all think that the current live streaming software is easy to use and has many functions. So the general points for accessibility and maturity of those technologies are approximately 4 points. Meanwhile, since the software can offer teachers and students real-time communication by virtually face-to-face, students feel a strong sense of participation. Due to the unstable epidemic situation in the world, all investigators almost agree that this kind of technology will become dominant in the future and has excellent development potential. However, as the broadcasting software is mainly used for teaching at present, many learning materials still need to be obtained from official study websites. According to this reason, students and teachers do not give high points for the aspect of enrichment of learning materials.

The Learning Mall technology is one of XJTLU's recent innovative technologies. It has received widespread praise from teachers and students on campus. Investigators see this technology as a combination of an official study website and offline learning resources. It contains many learning materials, typically extra-curricular materials. As it creates the mall concept, students can choose according to their own needs, just like shopping, so there is a high level of participation. However, as the concept is new, many technical support aspects are not as mature as traditional learning websites. Students and teachers still have high expectations for this technology and expect to see its further development in the future.

Case 2: NYU Shanghai

NYU Shanghai was founded in 2012, and as indicated by the name, it is located in Shanghai. It is China's first Sino-US research university and a third degree-granting NYU Global Network campus (NYU Shanghai, 2022). It is greatly supported not only by New York University but also by East China Normal University and the district of Pudong, the city of Shanghai. Until now, NYU Shanghai has approximately

2000 undergraduate and graduate students from all over the world, typically from China and the United States. The university aims to equip students with innovative thinking and a broad knowledge base and contribute to Shanghai's public service (NYU Shanghai, 2022). The same as XJTLU, English is the language of instruction on campus. However, at NYU Shanghai, international students are required to study and achieve proficiency in Mandarin Chinese, which is not a requirement in XJTLU. There are 19 different majors for students to choose from in terms of arts, sciences, business, finance, engineering, data, and computer science (NYU Shanghai, 2022). Students here spend their first two undergraduate years working on core courses and then can deeply learn an academic specialization in the third and fourth years. Differ from XJTLU, students at NYU Shanghai spend only up to two semesters oversea to broaden their horizons.

Since students mainly study on the NYU Shanghai campus, the demand for distance learning is not strong at the beginning. In this mode, transnational higher education is more like educational activities carried out in different physical regions, emphasizing the sharing of learning materials, research resources, and assessment criteria. Then NYU Shanghai puts more effort into offline learning, applying technologies to improve teaching quality offline, such as many classrooms, lecture hall, state-of-art laboratories, and a library with extensive book and electronic collections connected to NYU's global book network (NYU Shanghai, 2022). This comprehensive wireless network coverage and powerful information technology support ensure that students and faculty are closely connected to NYU's global education network on the NYU Shanghai campus.

However, during the outbreak of 2019-nCOVID in 2020, teachers and students could not return to campus and begin regular face-to-face classes. Hence, based on the innovative advantages of internet technology in education, NYU Shanghai adopted distance learning utilizing digital technology support to ensure students finish their studies smoothly. Firstly, the previous NYU's global teaching system was fully used. Around 820 NYU Shanghai undergraduates and 130 graduate students undertake distance learning in China, the United States, Africa, and Latin America, and 620 NYU undergraduates travel to various campuses and overseas study centers in the NYU global education system (NYU Shanghai, 2022). As mentioned above, NYU Shanghai brought the educational innovation advantages of information technology into full play. Various online teaching tools are applied, such as NYU Classes, NYU Stream, NYU Zoom, and VoiceThread (NYU Shanghai, 2022). These technologies aim to help teachers interact more vividly with students and receive feedback at a time, finally creating a vibrant learning atmosphere.

Furthermore, to help teachers and students get familiar with online teaching tools and platforms, NYU Shanghai Digital Teaching Toolkit is also prepared. According to NYU Shanghai (2022), Ratan Dey, an assistant professor of computer science practice, used Gradebook, NYU Zoom, ProctorU, and other tools to carry on online teaching. He also shares her experience of using these tools with colleagues. Keith Ross, director of engineering and Computer Science, also has extensive online teaching experience and even founded a company focused on online voice message board technology for education and language learning (NYU Shanghai, 2022).

In NYU Shanghai, NYU Classes, an educational management system in NYU's global system, is frequently used and provides teachers with a platform to publish course announcements, share research resources, and assign and grade assignments (NYU Shanghai, 2022). Apart from those standard functions, there are also a lot of 'hidden features' of NYU Classes to be discovered, such as customizable course module design, interactive discussion, and a built-in media library (NYU Shanghai, 2022). This greatly enhances the interaction between teachers and students during the online learning period. NYU Zoom is also affiliated with NYU Classes for broadcasting or recording lectures. This teleconference system enables real-time class discussion or group discussion to maximize the digital interaction scene similar to an offline class, as every participant can see and hear each other in real-time and clearly.

Generally, the following table is made to conclude the internet technologies NYU Shanghai has been used and its primary functions.

Similarly, according to the different usage emphases of these internet technologies, the following multidimensional analysis diagrams are made to analyze it in five main aspects. The diagram is also based on current research and interviews with school staff and teachers. One teacher from the department of mathematics and one staff from the student support center are invited to give their opinions about the application of internet technologies at NYU Shanghai. Students' feedback is also collected anonymously in the form of a questionnaire. Fifteen students from different majors participate in the survey. Again, teachers and students are asked to rank five aspects on a scale of 1 to 5, with one being the least satisfied and five the most satisfied.

Table 2. The internet technologies NYU Shanghai has been used

Technologies	Functions
Official website	News announcements and help department
NYU Classes	Including Gradebook for recording homework scores, ProctorU for taking online exams, website platforms to share teaching and learning resources, and some 'hidden features' such as customizable course module design, interactive discussion, and a built-in media library.
NYU Zoom	A tool for broadcasting or recording lectures allows every participant to see and hear each other in real-time and clearly.

Figure 4. The pentagonal map of the official website technology in Table 2

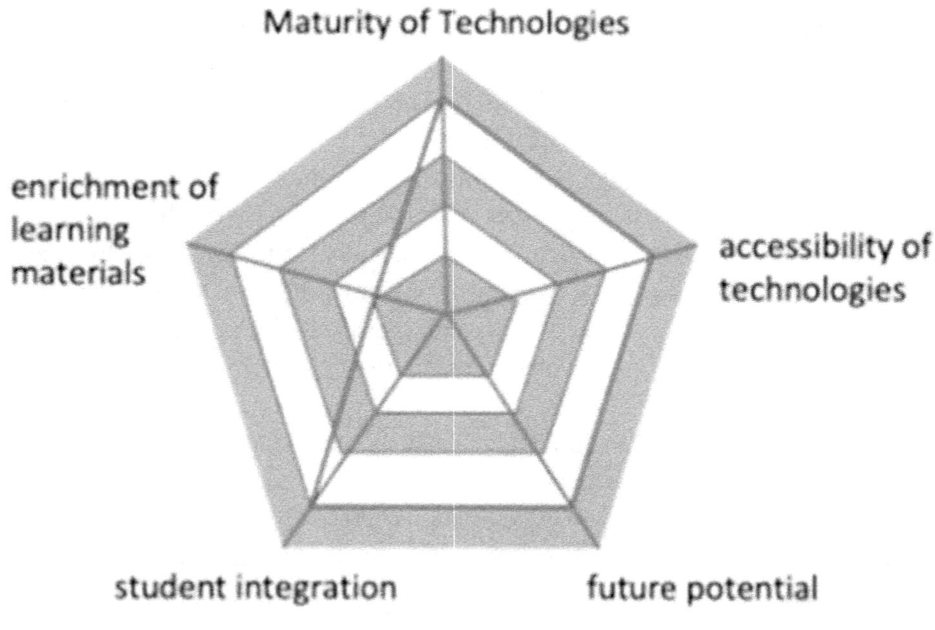

Figure 5. The pentagonal map of the NYU Classes technology in Table 2

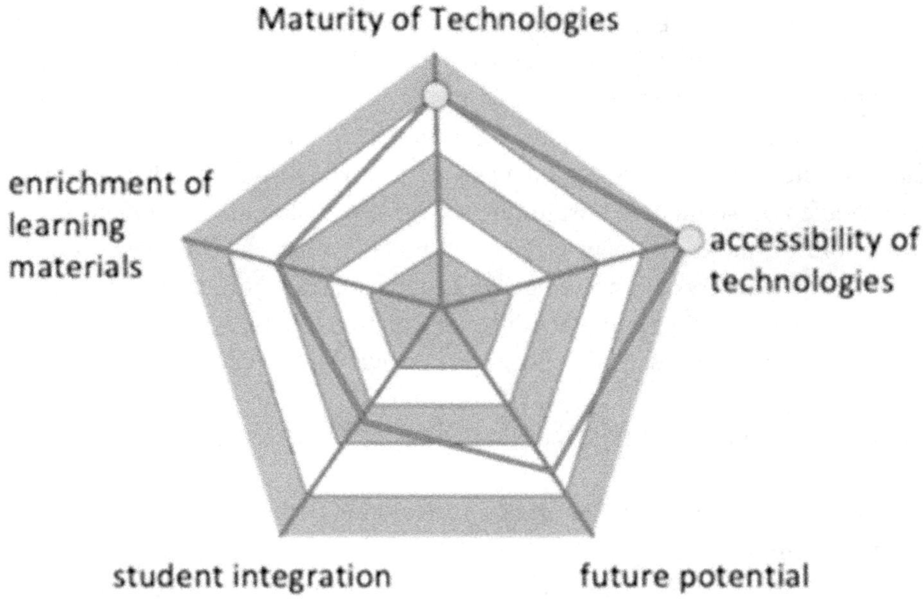

Figure 6. The pentagonal map of the NYU Zoom technology in Table 2

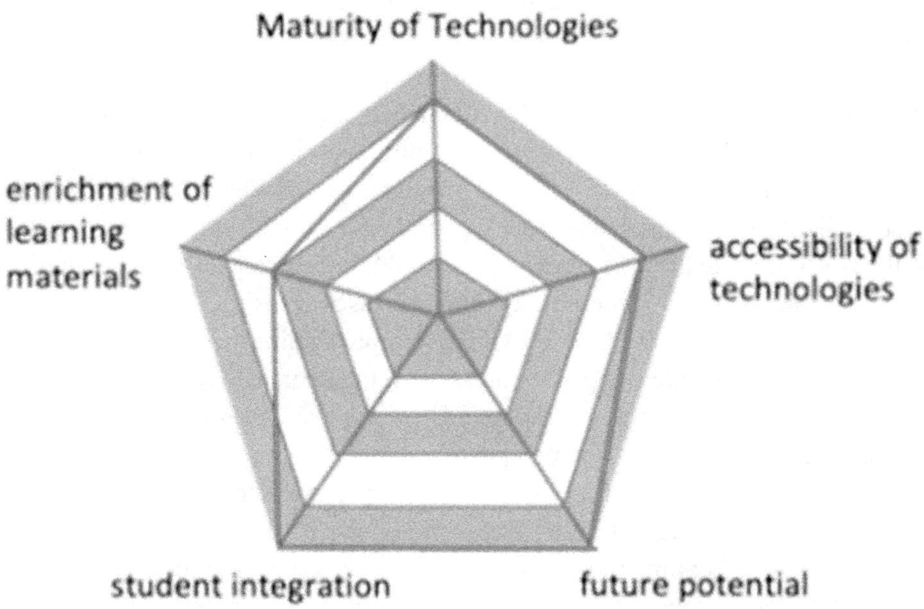

As discussed previously, the official website generally scores highly in accessibility and maturity of technologies, which is also indicated in Figure 4. However, according to students' feedback, they think that the official website is more of a platform for uploading homework and lacks some extensive materials. So they evaluate 3 points in terms of the enrichment of learning materials part. As before, students feel that the sense of participation is weak for the website technology. One student states that with the development of technology, there is not much potential for such traditional learning sites to break new ground. For NYU Classes and NYU Zoom, teachers and students generally give high points.

Regarding accessibility and maturity of technologies, they all think these two technologies are tremendous and very optimistic about their future development. Based on the survey, around 50% of students think NYU Classes include many functions such as a grade book for homework, an online exam-taking platform, customizable course module design, interactive discussion, and a built-in media library. So they give a total score for the enrichment of learning materials aspect. However, since NYU Classes does not let students and teachers communicate face-to-face, it is rated one point lower than NYU Zoom in student integration. While recognizing the high participation rate of NYU Zoom, students still hope that the live broadcasting platform can be further updated and developed with more learning resources.

Case 3: The Chinese University of Hong Kong, Shenzhen (CUHK-Shenzhen)

The Chinese University of Hong Kong (Shenzhen) is a university inheriting the school running philosophy and academic system of the Chinese University of Hong Kong since established in 2014 (CUHK-Shenzhen, 2022). It is located in Shenzhen and is committed to cultivating innovative high-level talents with global vision, Chinese tradition, and social responsibility. It has over 8,000 students, and over the past eight years, the university has established six main departments in management and economics, science and engineering, humanities and social sciences, data science, music, and medicine (CUHK-Shenzhen, 2022). Generally, there are 25 programs each for undergraduate and postgraduate study. Similarly, CUHK-Shenzhen works closely with other renowned universities worldwide, and over 60% of students here can join approximately 200 overseas academic exchange programs (CUHK-Shenzhen, 2022).

Unlike the previous two universities, CUHK-Shenzhen is under a collegiate system where every student is affiliated with one of four colleges (CUHK-Shenzhen, 2022). This system aims to communicate more closely with students with different academic and cultural backgrounds. Learning opportunities are provided within the college range by different departments in CUHK-Shenzhen. In this teaching model, the university previously focused on offline teaching on the Shenzhen campus to promote students' interpersonal skills. However, like the other universities, CUHK-Shenzhen also adopts an official website for arranging teaching and learning resources, a commonly used website called Blackboard.

At the time of the outbreak of 2019-nCOVID, CUHK adopted online learning through an online video platform called Panopto and broadcasting software Zoom, together with the original material website Blackboard. The Panopto is a platform that can manage video content, recording, and broadcasting. It can collect and manage teacher video resource updates and let students freely watch them. Blackboard, as commonly used, is a resource-sharing website. Students can check their schedules and learning materials for each class and submit assignments. Zoom, a popular broadcasting software, is also used to give live lectures and let teachers interact directly with students. Furthermore, CUHK-Shenzhen also provides online psychological support services to students and teachers to reduce the negative emotional impact during the special moment. Some students are also contacted by phone to better communicate with psychological experts.

From the perspective of students, students are satisfied with those internet technologies as it is a very efficient and effective way to deliver lectures and tutorials. Apart from that, students can save time asking questions as they do not need to wait for many students who are also eager to ask the teacher. Nevertheless, some students also mentioned that due to poor internet connection, they encountered the problem of understanding deviation. Hence, using internet technologies also needs to consider network stability.

Like the previous two case studies, the following table concludes the internet technologies CUHK-Shenzhen has been used and its primary functions.

Table 3. The internet technologies CUHK-Shenzhen has been used

Technologies	Functions
Blackboard	Arrange class schedules, activities, and learning materials and submit assignments.
Panopto	A platform that can manage video content, recording, and broadcasting. Teachers can put their teaching content in a video, and students can access it freely at any time.
Zoom	A tool for broadcasting or recording lectures and allowing every participant can see and hear each other in real-time and clearly.

Similarly, based on the different functions of these internet technologies and feedback from teachers and students, the following pentagonal map analysis is made to vividly compare those technologies in five aspects. Two teachers from the school of science and engineering are invited to give their opinions about the application of internet technologies in CUHK-Shenzhen. Students' feedback is also collected anonymously in the form of a questionnaire. Seventeen students from different colleges participate in the survey. Again, teachers and students are asked to rank five aspects on a scale of 1 to 5, with one being the least satisfied and five the most satisfied.

Figure 7. The pentagonal map of the Blackboard technology in Table 3

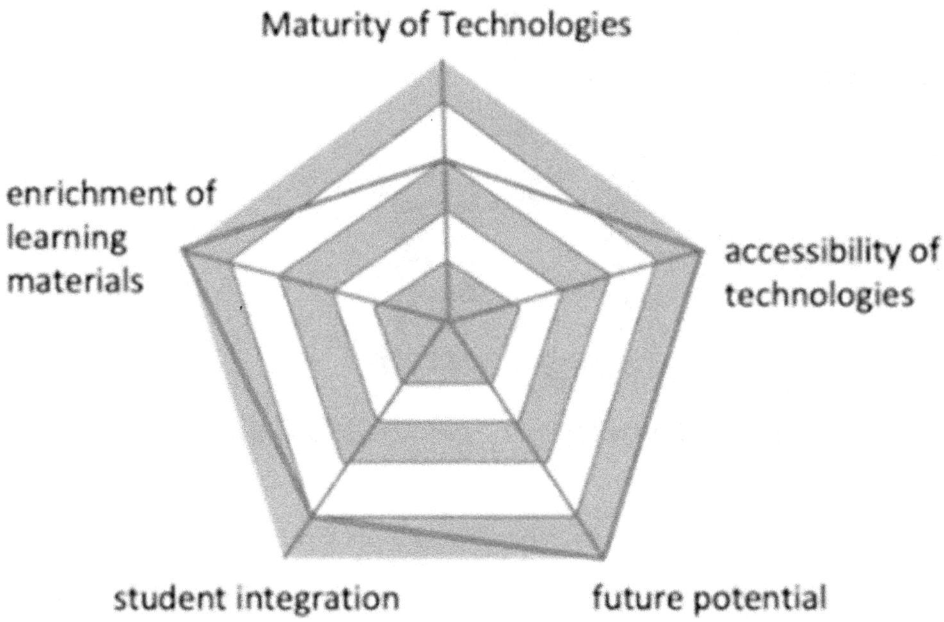

Figure 8. The pentagonal map of the Panopto technology in Table 3

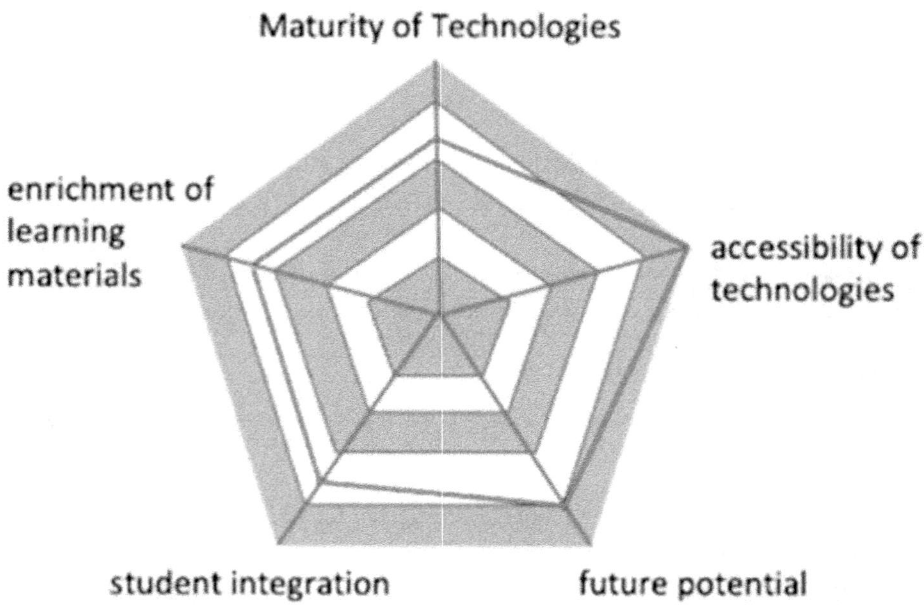

Figure 9. The pentagonal map of the Zoom technology in Table 3

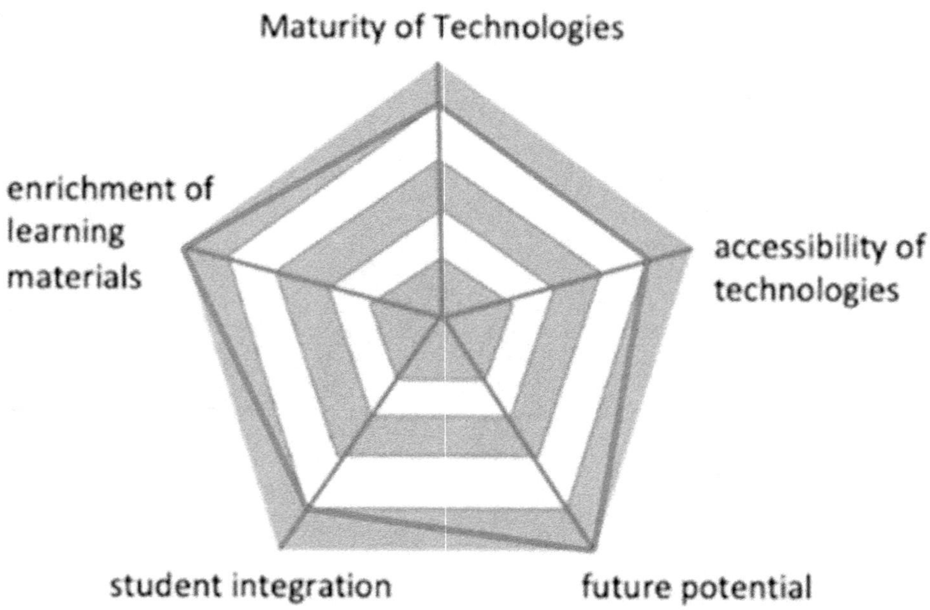

For CUHK-Shenzhen, Blackboard is a traditional learning site to spread the learning materials and submit assignments. Therefore, as investigated in XJTLU and NYU Shanghai, the maturity and accessibility of technologies are still highly evaluated. At the same time, as a notification website, students in CUHK-Shenzhen think that the content is abundant and can satisfy their needs, so they score 4 in these two aspects. Unlike the other two universities, students in CUHK-Shenzhen give 4 points for Blackboard technology in terms of future potential even though they do not feel engaged using Blackboard. For the unique Panopto technology in CUHK-Shenzhen, students think it is very convenient to operate, so they think highly of its accessibility. However, five students think it is not as abundant as the Blackboard for the enrichment of learning information, so they give points lower than 3 points, which makes the final average around 3.5 points. However, students think integrating the Panopto technology is excellent as they can watch the teacher's recorded video freely. Then, since Zoom technology can provide real-time communication between teachers and students, it scores the total points in terms of integration.

Meanwhile, the impact of individual feedback is significant because the survey sample of students in CUHK-Shenzhen is not as large as the other two universities. Apart from this, Panopto now only provides recording classes. Students in the survey expect it could involve more real-time classes in the future with the help of updated technology. They expect to combine the function of Zoom into Panopto technology instead of using two separate ones. As for the evaluation of Zoom, CUHK-Shenzhen is consistent with NYU Shanghai on the whole. Students all believe there is a very high level of integration, and they also believe that such real-time communication can be further improved with the help of future technology. However, they still expect to see more Blackboard-like displays on Zoom to improve its enrichment of learning materials.

All three universities used traditional website technology to deliver learning materials and hand in homework. Students and teachers give similar evaluations for the study website technology. They all recognize the accessibility and maturity of this technology and generally high enrichment of learning materials. However, they all pointed out that this kind of traditional study website lacks a sense of student participation, and it is easy for students to lose interest in learning if they go through a remote teaching period. Hence, they are not optimistic about its future development prospect. The three universities all have their innovative technologies. XJTLU's learning Mall is highly praised for its convenience, accessibility, rich materials, and a strong sense of student engagement. Therefore, students are looking forward to its further development. Similarly, NYU classes also highlight the possibility of its future development due to its high score in terms of enrichment of learning materials and student integration. However, as for CUHK-Shenzhen, Panopto and Zoom, which has high points of student integration, are not highly appreciated by students in terms of the enrichment of learning materials.

Concluded from the nine figures shown above, the technologies that students and teachers rated as having the tremendous potential for growth are associated with greater student engagement, convenient accessibility, and richness of learning materials. Then it can be inferred that enrichment of learning materials and student integration are the directions that updated technologies need to focus on in the future. When relevant transnational higher education institutions and universities choose to adopt new technologies, they need to think more about improving these aspects to let technologies serve the students' and teachers' demands, according to the results of previous surveys.

CONCLUSION AND FUTURE RECOMMENDATIONS

This chapter discusses three main delivery modes in transnational higher education programs: in-country delivery models, distance models, and blended models. Based on these different delivery models, the implementations and influences of modern information technology in transnational higher education under those models are also discussed. This chapter also analyzes the transnational higher education trends in the internet era through three case studies, taking China as an example. For different cases, based on the different teaching forms and program planning of universities, different internet technological means used in transnational international education are also sorted out and elaborated accordingly. Furthermore, the characteristics of different technologies in different case studies are overviewed in a table and analyzed by a pentagonal map in terms of technologies' maturity, accessibility of technologies, enrichment of learning materials, student integration, and future potential. It is indicated that technologies with more significant future development potential typically tend to have an abundant provision of learning materials and high student engagement.

Moreover, this may provide a general reference frame for future research on updating relevant internet technologies and for similar universities to adapt their technological development means during transnational higher education. Of course, this study also has its limits. More data should be collected in the future, and new influences brought by current internet technologies should be observed to improve the study and contribute to a better education world.

REFERENCES

Adams, J., & Song, H. (2009). Key developments and future challenges in Chinese-foreign cooperation in higher education. *Journal of Knowledge-based Innovation in China.*

Asian Institution of Technology. (2022). *About AIT.* Asian Institution of Technology (AIT). https://ait.ac.th/about/

Bennett, P., Bergan, S., Cassar, D., Hamilton, M., Soinila, M., Sursock, A., . . . Williams, P. (2010). *Quality Assurance in Transnational Higher Education. ENQA Workshop Report 11.* ENQA (European Association for Quality Assurance in Higher Education). Unioninkatu.

Canals, L., Burkle, M., & Nørgård, R. T. (2018). Universities of the future: Several perspectives on the future of higher education. *International Journal of Educational Technology in Higher Education, 15*(46).

Chaohong, G., & Yanqiao, J. (2010). The Status Quo, Problems and Countermeasures of Regulating Chinese-Foreign Cooperation in Running Schools in China. *Higher Education Development and Evaluation, 5.*

Cruz, T. (2010). Phillippines: Multisectoral school strike vs Aquino's budget cuts. *Asian Correspondent.* http://asiancorrespondent.com/2010/12/philippines-multisectoral-school-strike-vs- aquinos-budget-cuts/

Durnalı, M., Orakçı, Ş., & Toraman, Ç. (2022). Distance education students' acceptance of online learning systems, attitudes towards online learning and their self-directed learning skills. *Malaysian Online Journal of Educational Technology, 10*(2), 76–94. doi:10.52380/mojet.2022.10.2.236

Francois, E. J., Avoseh, M. B., & Griswold, W. (Eds.). (2016). *Perspectives in transnational higher education*. Springer. doi:10.1007/978-94-6300-420-6

Gan, S. L. (2000). Shaping education for the future: the role of IT in institutions of higher learning. *Economist Intelligence Unit.*

Gong, Y. (2020, July). The Problems and Countermeasures of Sino-Foreign Cooperation in Running Schools in Yunnan Province. In *4th International Symposium on Business Corporation and Development in South-East and South Asia under B&R Initiative (ISBCD 2019)* (pp. 138-142). Atlantis Press. 10.2991/aebmr.k.200708.027

Huang, F. (2003). Transnational higher education: A perspective from China. *Higher Education Research & Development*, *22*(2), 193–203. doi:10.1080/07294360304114

Ibrahim, D. Z., & Silong, A. D. (2000, October). Barriers to self-directed learning in a virtual environment among adult students. In *14th Annual Conference of the Asian Association of Open Universities* (pp. 25-27). Journal of Advanced Medicine Application.

Johari, B. M. (2000). Higher education planning in Malaysia. *Education Quarterly*, (July/August), 7–12.

Keller, J. (2011). Reversing course: University of California to borrow millions for online classes. *The Chronicle of Higher Education.*

Lim, P. K. C., & Mak, J. W. (Eds.). (2015). *Learning for the Future: The IMU Experiment*. International Medical University.

Liyanagunawardena, T. R., Adams, A. A., & Williams, S. A. (2013). MOOCs: A systematic study of the published literature 2008-2012. *International Review of Research in Open and Distributed Learning*, *14*(3), 202–227. doi:10.19173/irrodl.v14i3.1455

Mok, K. H. (2008). Singapore's global education hub ambitions: University governance change and transnational higher education. *International Journal of Educational Management.*

NUY Shanghai (2020, February 21). *NYU Shanghai launches innovative digital teaching on February 17.* NYU Shanghai. https://shanghai.nyu.edu/cn/news/nyu-shanghai-launch-innovative-remote-teaching-and-learning-effort-february-17

Orakcı, Ş. (2020). The future of online learning and teaching in higher education. In A. Al-Sartawi, A., Hussainey, K., Hannon, A. & Hamdan, A. (Eds.). Global Approaches to Sustainability Through Learning and Education. IGI Global. doi:10.4018/978-1-7998-0062-0.ch003

Orakcı, Ş., & Gelişli, Y. (2021). Educational policy actions in the times of Covid-19 and suggestions for future applications in Turkey. In L. Kyei-Blankson, J. Blankson, & E. Ntuli (Eds.), *Handbook of Research on Inequities in Online Education During Global Crises* (pp. 475–493). IGI Global. doi:10.4018/978-1-7998-6533-9.ch024

Spring, J. (2014). *Globalization of education: An introduction*. Routledge. doi:10.4324/9781315795843

Susam, T., Durnalı, M., & Orakcı, Ş. (2020). Administering education and training through a web-based system: E-curriculum. In M. Durnalı (Ed.), *Utilizing Technology, Knowledge, and Smart Systems in Educational Administration and Leadership*. IGI Global. doi:10.4018/978-1-7998-1408-5.ch002

Taylor, M. (2011). *Public policy in the community*. Macmillan International Higher Education. doi:10.1007/978-0-230-34409-9

Tedlow, R. S., & Abdelal, R. (2004). Theodore Levitt's "The Globalization of Markets: An Evaluation After Two Decades. *Harvard Business School, 11*.

The British Council. (1999) *Study for a UK Higher Education Qualification by Distance Learning,* The British Council, http://www.britishcouncil.org.uk/distancelearning/index.htm

The Chinese University of Hong Kong. Shenzhen. (2022). *Introducing CUHK-Shenzhen.* The Chinese University of Hong Kong, Shenzhen (CUHK-Shenzhen). https://www.cuhk.edu.cn/en/page/4987

Tsiligkiris, V. (2021). *Innovative approaches to transnational education*. THE Campus.

Wade, W. (1994). Introduction. *Flexible Learning in Higher Education*, 12-16.

Xi'an Jiaotong-Liverpool University. (2022). *XJTLU strategic growth and Integrative Education*. Xi'an Jiaotong-Liverpool University (XJTLU). https://www.xjtlu.edu.cn/en/about/overview/xjtlu-strategic-growth-and-syntegrative-education

Yee, H. Y., Radhakrishnan, A., & Ponnudurai, G. (2006). Improving PBLs in the International Medical University: Defining the 'good'PBL facilitator. *Medical Teacher*, *28*(6), 558–560. doi:10.1080/01421590600878226 PMID:17074705

Yin, L. L. (2014). *A study on the history of sino-foreign cooperation in running schools in the field of higher education*. [Thesis, The university of Xiamen, China].

Ziguras, C. (2001). Educational technology in transnational higher education in South East Asia: The cultural politics of flexible learning. *Journal of Educational Technology & Society*, *4*(4), 8–18.

Chapter 20 Transnational Education in Malaysia: Development, Challenges, and Strategic Alignment

Joseph Kee-Ming Sia
Curtin University, Malaysia

Anita Jimmie
Curtin University, Malaysia

ABSTRACT

Private higher education in Malaysia has undergone radical transformations with the aim of becoming a regional hub for higher education in Southeast Asia, and to transform the country into one that has a fully developed knowledge-based economy. To understand this transformation, the purposes of this chapter are to identify key prospects and challenges of international branch campuses (IBCs) and propose strategic alignment on the operation and administration of the IBCs in Malaysia. In order to identify and understand the challenges IBCs face when operating in Malaysia, this study adopts a review approach that is supported by findings and from academic and grey literature. The results of this review indicate that IBCs are faced with complex challenges and are on unequal footing with other local universities. This chapter uncovers various demanding issues and discusses strategic alignment of IBCs. Limitations and recommendations for future research are also incorporated in this chapter.

INTRODUCTION

Worldwide demand for quality education is growing at an exponential rate, propelled by economic growth of developing countries and the increased globalisation of countries and their economy. The demand for education has also demonstrated a sharp increase in students' participation in higher education, which puts a pressure on local domestic education systems in developing countries. Consequently, the government of these countries decided to address these demands for higher education by investing

DOI: 10.4018/978-1-6684-5226-4.ch020

in transnational education, by providing higher education study programs and services that are located in a country different from a host country (Healey, 2015). The growth and development of international branch campuses (IBC) has seen a tremendous rise in the past decade. Since 2000, the number of IBCs has seen a rapid increase, with over 250 IBCs operating around the world, and more institutions opening up in countries such as Indonesia, Morrocco and Mexico (Lane et al., 2021). There is also a marked increase in the number of IBCs penetrating the South East Asian market to date. The majority of IBCs are located in Asia, with China overtaking United Arab Emirates as the country with the highest number of IBCs (O' Malley, 2016). At the moment, China holds the record for hosting 32 IBCs, followed by UAE with 31 IBCs in the country. Singapore and Malaysia each has 12 IBCs, and Qatar, 11 IBCs. The aggregate figure makes up approximately 39% of the world's total number of IBCs (O'Malley, 2016).

Wilkins and Rumbley (2018) define IBCs as an education institution owned by an overseas organisation, and students graduate with a degree carrying the main campus' name. Hill and Thabet (2018), however, consider IBC as an international business where the university seeks to expand its enrolment through establishing a market in another country. He (2016, p.8) views IBC in a slightly different light; an IBC is seen as a *"hybrid between a branch campus and franchising"* as the partnership is between foreign and local educational enterprises. The authors concur with Lane and Kinser (2012 as cited in Hill and Thabet, 2018) in that different IBCs operate with different structures, proprietary names and governance; therefore, it would be difficult to establish a single definition to characterise the various types of IBCs and the challenges each faces when establishing these institutions in Malaysia.

The aspiration to transform Asia as an education hub has been one of the main impetuses for the growth of more IBCs in the South East Asian region. Besides improving the quality of education, this move is also seen as a strategy to develop human capital to strengthen the economy and attain economic growth (Yung et al., 2018). Knight (2011) posits that IBCs provide a linkage between research, knowledge and innovation, all essential components to national capacity building. Thus, the setting up of IBCs is seen as a way for potential economic growth by promoting a knowledge economy, particularly for developing countries such as Malaysia. At the present, the biggest education providers for IBCs in Malaysia are the UK with 5 offshore branches, followed by Australia with three offshore branches, and one IBC branch from China and Ireland respectively (Education Malaysia Global Services, n.d.).

The rapid development and establishment of IBCs in Asia signals to the increasingly important role that IBCs play in influencing international academic mobility (Alam et al., 2013). This chapter will provide a better understanding on the development of IBCs, the issues and challenges faced by IBCs in Malaysia and the implications on the stake-holders of the various IBCs in Malaysia. It is imperative to understand the socio-political factors that govern the establishment of IBCs for both the host, and the sending country. Understanding the developments and challenges faced by IBCs, in light of the current expansion and future growth of transnational education in South East Asia has enormous market potential for education. In addition, to date, there is a lack of literature related to the challenges and performances of IBCs in the South East Asian context and building strategic alignments; it is hoped that this chapter will contribute to the body of knowledge on this topic, with particular reference to the Malaysian field of private tertiary education. In the Malaysian higher education sector, there is stiff competition amongst the universities and colleges to recruit and retain both local and international students especially with the current post-pandemic climate around the globe. This chapter draws on the literature pertaining to marketing of higher education both in Malaysia and other countries. Furthermore, the chapter explores the key challenges experienced by the IBCs as they grow over the years. The strategic alignments of

IBCs are then presented, which aim at suggesting some possible improvements that could have a positive impact on sustaining student recruitment.

The first section of this chapter describes the development of IBCs in Malaysia, including the justification of establishing branch campuses in the country. Section two discusses the challenges that IBCs face when operating in Malaysia and provide insights issues such as accreditation, different standards and requirements from the feeder and host countries and the competition between various IBCs in the country which adds on to the complexities of running IBCs in Malaysia. The final section presents the strategic alignment of IBCs in Malaysia and its implications between the host university and the branch campus located in Malaysia.

DEVELOPMENT OF IBCS IN MALAYSIA

This section focuses on the development of IBCs in Malaysia, and highlights the history and establishment of IBCs, followed by the rationale for setting up the IBCs in light of the education climate in Malaysia at that time.

In the Malaysian context, the developments of IBCs were triggered by two major factors: potential contribution to economic growth and the government's decision to widen its citizens' access to quality education. In Malaysia, IBCs have emerged as significant providers of education as a result of the internationalisation, commodification of higher education, and potential economic growth of both the host country and university's home country (Escriva-Beltran, Nunoz-de-Prat & Villo, 2019). There were nine IBCs in Malaysia as of 2017 (List of IPTS, 2017) and the numbers have grown quite rapidly. As of 31 December 2021, the total number of IBCs established in Malaysia were ten, with a new IBCs set up between 2018 and 2021 (List of IPTS, 2021). This indicates the popularity of IBCs in Malaysia as branch campuses of many well-known universities from the United Kingdom such as The University of Nottingham, Herriot-Watt University, Newcastle University, the University of Southampton and the University of Reading located in Johor Bahru were established. Three Australian IBCs were also established, which are Curtin University Malaysia, Swinburne University of Technology Sarawak, and Monash University. The Royal College of Surgeons in Ireland and University College Dublin Malaysia Campus (RSCI & UCD) and Xiamen University from China were also established within a short period of time, which demonstrates the potential and attraction of establishing IBCs in Malaysia (Rashad, Majid and Subramaniam, 2020).

It is important to note that the education system in Australia and United Kingdom is quite similar. However, while the education system in United Kingdom is highly focussed on exams, Australia has a balance between coursework, assignments and exam in evaluating student performance (Mahoney, 2021). In terms of the grading system, the United Kingdom uses the honours system (First class to Third class honours) while Australia uses grading system ranging from high distinction (HD) to fail (F) (AECC Global, 2021). In comparison, the education system in China is more rigid; students are assessed based on a points system where they sit for exams and tests every semester (Smith, 2020). Conversely, the education system in Australia is based on credit system, thus, giving flexibility to students to decide what to study and total amount of time a student needs to study per semester. The differences of these IBCs education system translate into different standards, learning styles and teaching principles in Malaysia which will be further discussed in the challenges section below.

Malaysia opened up its shores to IBCs in 2007 (Rashad, Majid & Subramaniam, 2020). Initially, this initiative began in the early 1970s, to provide higher education opportunities for local students, particularly for students who could not obtain places at local public higher education institutions. This was largely due to ethnic admission policies and the lack of places in public higher education institutions to meet the needs of the growing student population at that moment (Yung et al., 2018). At the same time, reforms in higher education in Malaysia led to the idea of positioning the country as regional education hubs in South East Asia. Thus, this led to a host of opportunities to forge partnerships and collaboration between local institutions and foreign universities to offer a "localised" version of an overseas degree to Malaysian students. The government's approach to education at the time was to widen access to education for local students to ease the pressure and meet the demands of the growing education system, while promoting Malaysia as an attractive study destination in the region (Knight & Morshidi, 2011) that offers high quality, affordable education. As a result, a wide range of transnational education opportunities were offered to students, beginning with twinning programs, franchise programs, study exchange programs and credit transfer programs (Lin, Leung & Waters, 2019) which were tailored to fit the needs of the students. Eventually, the idea of establishing an offshore program locally was explored to offer opportunities for local students to pursue a foreign tertiary education at a fraction of the cost.

In addition, the establishment of IBCs also attracted a large cohort of international students who were attracted by the affordable tuition fees and lifestyle in Malaysia. This deal was seen as a good strategy to boost economic development in the nation. It is clear especially in the early stages, that the Malaysian government plays a major role in the planting of IBCs throughout the country. The National Education Policy was established in 1996 to align with the Seventh Economic Plan of developing more human capital to meet the needs of the Knowledge Economy, or K-Economy as envisioned by Tun Mahathir Mohammed, our then Prime Minister (Arachi, 2006). Due to the government changes in legislation, the government offered the IBCs attractive incentives and tax exemptions when they set up branch campuses on the Malaysian soil. In addition, the government-initiated measures to increase the number of international students in the IBCs by expediting the student visa application process. With all these favourable conditions, Malaysia, gradually but steadily, emerged as one of the prime educational hubs in Asia (Teo, 2005 as cited in Arachi, 2006).

Since it was Malaysia's intention to position itself as an international higher education hub in the region (Yung et al., 2018), the development of IBCs is viewed as an effective way to achieve economic development. The presence of these IBCs creates a robust education ecosystem and expands the market by creating an international reputation for a state, or a country. Besides attracting local and foreign students, employing international staff also helps accelerate the potential for expansion and growth in each the host states. Schulze and Kleibert (2021) assert that students and staff within the community reap benefits because of the presence of higher education institutions. The establishment of higher education institutions in surrounding area creates demands for goods and services, and increases revenue for the local communities. For example, the government came up with the initiative to create sub-national higher education hubs such as the "EduCity" project located in Iskandar Putri in Johor. This education hub was established to act as a feeder for talents to support the economic activity in Iskandar Malaysia while providing future skilled workers for the various industries in the Johor region. This in turn will drive the socio-economic development within the Johor area (Rashad, Majid & Subramaniam, 2020). It is worth noting that although other IBCs may not be situated in a centralised location such as the ones in Educity, or were strategically planned in such a manner, the IBCs are established in cities that have the potential for growth and development for the different states hosting these universities.

In recent years, the number of foreign universities interested in the local education industry has grown, and quite a few of them have set up branch campuses or offshore campuses in Malaysia to fulfil the local students' increased demand for higher education (Sato, 2005). Furthermore, parents are increasingly aware that foreign degrees command a higher "employability value"; thus, the establishments of IBCs in Malaysia are well received. The popularity of IBCs is evidenced by the number of IBCs set up in countries such as Malaysia, China, Qatar and the United Arab Emirates. Together, these countries host the largest number of IBCs in the last two decades (Pohl, & Lane, 2018).

Another reason for the establishment of IBCs in Malaysia was due to the pressure on the local education system to cope with the growing needs of students participating in higher education across the country. The development of IBCs has gained traction and become prominent in the higher education scene in Malaysia is the impact of the 1997 financial crisis on the country (Akiba, 2008). Due to the local currency depreciation and low purchasing power, many middle-class families were unable to bear the exorbitant financial costs of sending their children abroad for studies. This created a favourable situation for more IBCs to be built in the country to meet the people's demand for overseas degrees and qualifications. However, it is important to note that the 1997 financial crisis was not the sole reason for the changes in the Malaysian higher education scene. In fact, an increase in the number of higher education providers was essential to meet the manpower needs of the country (Arachi, 2006). In short, the economic forces have shaped tertiary education policies in Malaysia, from the time of the British colonial rule to the present. These policies have affected the thinking of the families and students in the way they view the value of education.

To sum up, middle-class Malaysian families place an exponentially increased value on tertiary education, making the Malaysian education system extremely competitive (Arachi, 2006). In addition, the racial quota implemented in the Malaysian national education system has created a scenario of educational and social inequalities (Schulze & Kleibert, 2021; McBurnie & Ziguras 2001). This imbalance of educational opportunity has a significant impact on the growth of the private higher education in the country, thus accelerating the development of more IBCs in Malaysia.

CHALLENGES OF IBCS IN MALAYSIA

This section examines the challenges in the development of IBCs in Malaysia, touching on several aspects. Several issues arise in relation to operational matters which are of concern to the various stakeholders. These issues stem from lack of clarity in characterising the role, purpose and objectives of IBCs between the feeder country and host country (Hill et al.,2014).

Among the issues discussed in this section include; issues related to quality assurance (accreditation and different standards set by the government), strict requirements in government policy, stiff competition from other IBCs and challenges faced by students and staff in the delivery of the curriculum.

According to Barnett (2000 as cited in Bengsten, 2017), higher education has become super complex because universities are no longer restricted to the delivery of knowledge and education, but are now involved in managing *institutional context, professional and societal arenas and also the personal life-worlds of students and teachers* (Bengsten, 2017, p.68). Hill and Thabet (2018, p. 243) supports this view as they explain, *IBCs, at face value, appear to give the home university more control over academic quality than a licensing agreement, but the financial investment may be significant and many IBCs face a similar tension between the academic goals of the university and the more overtly commercial objectives of its JV partner*. Altbach and Knight (2007) believe it will be difficult to reconcile the two objectives, as international higher education is now seen as a commodity, made available to those who can afford it, rather than as a tool for public good and access. Consequently, managing and running IBCs are getting increasingly challenging due to the numerous regulatory, cultural and normative practices of a host country (Neri & Wilkins, 2019; Shams & Huisman, 2016; Hill & Thabet, 2018).

In addition, managers and administrators are often placed in the difficult situation of having to serve *two masters* (Dobos, 2011 as cited Cai & Hall, 2016). The managers are required to maintain the quality and standard of the main campus, to safeguard the "brand" name and reputation while simultaneously needing to adapt and adhere to the conflicting local regulations. To complicate matters, they also have to adhere to instructions from the local authorities and university partners.

This section explores the complex challenges of the IBCs when operating in a fast-paced and changing environment. To remain relevant in the Malaysian education scene, the IBCs must respond very quickly to the changes in the education planning policies, research profile, student enrolment and curriculum. These issues are further examined in the following sub-sections below:

Challenges from Quality Assurance (Accreditation and Standards)

The first challenge involves ensuring that the IBCs comply with quality assurance requirements in order to operate in the country. The Malaysian government's liberalisation and internationalisation policies were instrumental in the setting up of the nine IBCs. Nevertheless, the host country puts pressure on the IBCs to change their operation and character similar to those of the local higher education providers. Compliance to strict quality assurance includes issues such as accreditation and the challenge of meeting various standards of quality assurance from the Malaysian regulatory bodies and other regulatory bodies that govern the feeder institution. To meet accreditation purposes, IBCs are often faced with the tension of reconciling between the policies set by the Malaysian government and the regulations set by the higher education accreditation body in the feeder country. This is clearly seen in the quality assurance framework imposed on the IBCs (Shams & Huisman, 2014). For instance, the IBCs have to conform to two sets of standards for both teaching and research-based activities. As far as teaching quality is concerned, the IBCs are subjected to accreditation agencies from the host country as well as the home campus. As an example, the Australian IBCs set up in Malaysia has to comply with two different accreditation bodies (Marimuthu, 2008), the Malaysian Qualification Agency (MQA) as well as the Australian Tertiary Education Quality and Standards Agency; meanwhile, the IBCs from the UK are subjected to MQA and the UK Quality Assurance Agency. These agencies are established to accredit programmes offered by the higher education institutions, and to monitor and regulate the standard of higher education institutions in their respective countries. As posited by Shams and Huisman (2014), the IBCs face "dual institutional pressure" to comply with the different requirements set by the respective individual agencies.

In addition, the IBCs based in Malaysia are subjected to the Malaysian Research Assessment (MyRA) research standard, a comprehensive system developed to assess the research capacity and performance of all Higher Education Institutions (HEIs) in Malaysia. Since 2014, all higher education institutions in Malaysia, including IBCs, are mandated to participate in annual assessment exercise by MyRA (What is MyRA?, 2015). MyRA is an instrument used to determine the university ranking based on the institution's research profile and activities. This instrument is also a measurement method used to determine if an institution should be awarded the SETARA ratings by the MoHE. For example, Australian IBCs are subjected to different rating systems; for example, the School of Business has to comply with the

Australian Business Deans Council rating system. According to Marimuthu (2008), most of the PHEIs start off as teaching universities and conduct very little research or publish academic based journals; hence, this creates a problem for institutions to move into a research-based system, while having to comply with the various research standards imposed on the IBCs.

Adding on to accreditation challenges, the IBCs face the pressure of complying with a different set of curricula; the IBCs are required to run additional units besides implementing the existing curriculum from the home campus. One example would be the implementation of general education subjects; studying of these units is compulsory for both International and Malaysian students in order for their degrees to be recognised by the Malaysian government. For instance, Malaysian students are required to enrol in subjects such as Asian and Islamic Civilisation, Ethnic Relations, National Language A (for those who did not obtain credit for Malay Language at Malaysian Certificate of Education level), Human Rights and Team Leadership and Community Service which are additions to the curriculum. Similarly, non-Malaysian students are required to enrol in Malay Language Communication, Malaysian Studies 3, Leadership and Digital Entrepreneurship, Human Rights and Team Leadership and Community Service subjects (General Education Subject, 2014). Some students of the IBCs fell it is pointless to study these units and are in a dilemma over what to do; fortunately, there is way out by transferring the credits to the main campus so that they can complete their final year there without having to complete the general education subjects. Consequently, this would result in the loss of revenues to the IBCs in Malaysia.

Challenges from Local Government

Government policies and regulations have a huge impact on the market dynamics of any industry, including higher education (Wilkins, 2016). It is not an easy job to manage IBCs due to the strict requirements to adhere to certain guidelines and the necessity to liaise with the senior government officials (Lane, 2011). As noted by Healey (2015, p.400), *these officials operate in different cultural context and have different ways of doing business.* Healey (2016) further states that IBCs can only do things with the consent of the host government, such as charging and increasing tuition fees, and setting the scopes of courses to be offered. Besides, student enrolment matters are subjected to strict government control. For instance, in Malaysia, the entry requirements and fees chargeable need to be approved by the Ministry of Higher Education (MoHE) while programme approval must be approved by the Malaysian Qualification Agency (MQA) (Dyson, 2013). Thus, two different regulatory bodies are involved in different aspects of the setting up of the university. In addition, the approval process takes a significant amount of waiting time before it is approved by either one of the ministries, further delaying the process. Healey (2017) in his study reports that the lack of autonomy and self-regulatory framework in operating the IBCs in Malaysia can be a source of frustration for the administrators. The tight control over the course fees structures by MoHE has rendered Malaysia less competitive as a regional education hub when compared with China and India. This is evidenced by the large outflow of Malaysian medical students to India (Hill & Razvi, 2015).

Furthermore, IBCs may not have full autonomy over key matters such as curriculum or staffing, and issues such as academic freedom (Wilkins, 2016). Such bureaucracy and inflexibility may not be well received by the home campus and may prevent the new IBCs from starting operations within a reasonable timescale. This is proven in a study carried out by He and Wilkins (2018), and they relate the following incident; the China-based Xiamen University recently established a branch campus in Malaysia. The university management had to adhere strictly to the regulations set by the MoHE with regard to issues such as entry requirements, and tuition fees; all the matters are subjected to the MoHE's approval. In addition, Xiamen University's courses and all the programmes offered had to be approved by the Malaysia Qualifications Agency (MQA) before they could move forward. Furthermore, the government approval process is very complex and lengthy. For instance, in the case of Newcastle University Medicine Malaysia, a branch campus of Newcastle University in the UK, the organisation had to go through a seven-month long process before they could introduce the Bachelor of Science programme. The programme had gain approval from the MQA before it could be forwarded to MoHE for another round of approval (Dyson, 2013). This caused considerable delay in establishing and offering the program. It could conceivably cause loss of opportunities in student recruitment as well, as the university would lose potential students to other universities while waiting for approval from the ministries. In the long term, as long as the government bureaucracy remains, the student enrolments of the IBCs in Malaysia will suffer (Healey, 2016).

Moreover, the viability of an IBC is affected as the government policies can change anytime (Healey, 2016). More often than not, when there is a change of Education Minister, there would be a change in education policies. For example, in 2017, the then Higher Education Minister, Datuk Seri Mohammed Khalid Nordin announced that a two-year moratorium would be placed on the setting up of new local or foreign universities, as the government felt that there were sufficient higher education institutions to meet the demands of the country. He reported that as of November 2016, there were 37 private universities, 20 university colleges, 7 foreign branch campuses and 414 private colleges in operation ("Two-year moratorium", 2017). However, after the conclusion of the 14th Malaysian General Election held in 2018, the then ruling party, Barisan National, was defeated and the then Prime Minister, Najib was ousted. Najib was replaced by Mahathir Mohamad, and the latter invited a renowned Japanese university to establish a branch campus in Malaysia ("Dr. M wants Japanese universities", 2018). The then Education Minister, Maszlee Malik, approved the setting up of the first Japanese university branch campus in early 2019, The Tsukuba University ("Japanese university branches", 2019).

The year 2020 was seen as a tumultuous and volatile time for Malaysian politics with on-going political crisis leading to further changes in the ruling government. This caused the then Prime Minister, Matahir Mohamad to resign. He was later replaced by the new Prime Minister, Muhyiddin Yassin. The political turmoil continued throughout 2020-2021, worsened by the pandemic. This crisis culminated with the resignation of Muhyiddin Yassin and was then replaced by the current Prime Minister of Malaysia in 2021. In line with the changes in the ruling government, the higher education ministers were replaced within a span of less than a year. This has implications on certain policies in higher education in the country with this change in leadership.

Challenges from Student Recruitment and Funding

To add on to the existing challenges mentioned above, there is stiff competition between members of the IBCs group in Malaysia. In addition, the former has to compete against the both private and public universities for student recruitment. IBCs mainly enrol candidates who have failed to gain admission into the public universities, and there is fierce competition amongst most of the private institutions in getting a fair share of the student enrolment. This poses a new threat to the future survival of the IBCs in Malaysia. For instance, in 1999, the Royal Melbourne Institute of Technology branch in Malaysia was closed down due to huge financial losses ("Malaysia to offer foreign universities", 2004). Adding on to the issue of competition, the condition has worsened amidst the recent pandemic, with most higher education institutions' including IBCs seeing a marked decrease in student enrolment (Sharma, 2020).

The increased competition among higher education institutions in Malaysia- Public Higher Education Institutions (PUHEs), private higher education institutions and (PHEIs) can be seen in the establishments of various IBCs, PUHEs and PHEIs, and the number of students recruited in each institution. For instance, in the year 2017, there were 10 IBCs, 20 PUHEs and 47 PHEIs in Malaysia (Ministry of Higher Education, 2017). The total students recruited numbered 29,987 in IBCs, 538,555 in PUHEs and 310,036 in PHEIs (Statistics of higher education of Malaysia, 2017). Hence, a singular IBC recruited an average of 2,999 students compared to PUHEs and PHEIs that are able to recruit 26,928 and 6,596 students respectively. Based on the ratio mentioned above, it can be deduced that each PUHE recruited about 9 times more students than an IBC. Similarly, a PHEI enrolled about 2 times more students than an IBC. Consequently, the IBCs are under tremendous pressure to find effective ways of attracting new students, within a highly competitive environment where PUHEs and PHEIs are armed with certain advantages.

Furthermore, the IBCs' existing challenges are compounded by the issues of lack of funding available. To clarify, in Malaysia, public education is highly subsidised by the government. Compared with PUHEs, IBCs received very little financial aid from the government. Based on reports, as much as 90% of the budgets for PUHEs come from the government funds, with the remainder derived from students' tuition fees, which are comparatively very small amounts (Tham & Kam, 2008). For example, according to the 2017 statistics compiled by Lim (2017), Universiti Teknologi Malaysia received a government funding of 396.54 million, Universiti Putra Malaysia 417.81 million, Universiti Sains Malaysia 524.83 million, and Universiti Kebangsaan Malaysia 472.89 million. These public universities are the premier research institutions in the country, and based on the QS global rankings, are in the top one percent globally (Lim, 2017).

In contrast, the IBCs are expected to be self-funding (Wilkins, 2020) and do not receive funding from the government for its operational costs. For example, based on a report by He and Wilkins (2018), the Xiamen University Malaysia receives its funding from various sources that include bank loans, and contributions from external parties, i.e., the overseas Chinese in South East Asia. It is pertinent to note that the IBCs in Malaysia receive very little external funding from the Malaysian government which occur in the form of scholarships and funding for potential and current students to pursue their studies at the IBCs. For example, IBCs do receive indirect support from the government, such as the National Higher Education Fund Corporation (NHEFC). However, NHEFC loans are only given to students studying in PUHEs, PHEIs and IBCs.

Due to the large amount of fundings allocated to the PUHEs, the fees payable for studying at the public universities are undeniably much lower than those of the IBCs. As such, PUHEs are a more attractive educational options for most Malaysians and even some international students. The IBCs in Malaysia have a very limited number of channels to obtain funds, and at the same time, operate in a very competitive environment.

Challenges from Students and Staff (Training, Recruitment and Retention)

One of the most challenging issues faced by IBCs operating in Malaysia is related to the teaching and learning activities experienced by students and the teaching staff working at the respective the universities. IBCs in Malaysia are a host to students and staff members from a diverse range of countries and cultural backgrounds. One of the selling points of the IBCs is the offering of the multinational and multicultural environment as part of the students' learning experience. However, this unique experience brings with it a new set of difficult situations for the IBCs; this diversity of cultures creates tension between the learners' expectations and those of the institutions. Dealing with the staff and students' expectations can be a messy job; and this topic has been discussed at length in the literature (Dobos, 2011, Shams & Huisman, 2014; Cai & Hall, 2016). Malaysia is a land of high-context cultures but the IBCs that operate in the country are of low context cultures; it can be challenging to bridge the cultural and communication gap in managing the students studying and staff working at the institutions (Healey, 2017).

It has been found that students have difficulties in adapting to the learning approaches used by the lecturers at the university. For example, in a study carried out, Pyvis and Chapman (2007) report some common issues the students face while studying in an offshore campus. These issues are related to the modes of delivery and new learning experiences students face while at university. It was found that the students experience conflicts of identities as they try to get used to a different learning environment. Based on the findings of the study, the following are the typical responses from the participants: unfamiliarity with the new environment, difficulty with transitioning from the high school learning approaches to those practised at the university, the lack of proficiency in English, which is the medium of instruction at the offshore campuses, and finally feeling burdened in coping with the learning demands and workload at the university (Pyvis & Chapman, 2007). Hence, to create a better learning experience for students, it is imperative that these issues be addressed to ensure student retention and satisfaction grows, while maintaining the university's reputation in the education market.

To complicate matters, the employees working with the IBCs face a different set of challenges. The teaching staff are also negatively affected by the students' behaviours and new experiences, as the mixed cultures of the classroom and the learning environment can come as a shock for both the students and staff members. Wilkins, Balakrishnan and Huisman (2012) report that the student-staff interactions and teaching-learning styles vary from country to country and from culture to culture. The differences in the approaches of teaching and learning inadvertently create some degree of tension in the classroom; a good case in point is that the expatriate lecturing staff feel awkward and uneasy in teaching students who have different cultural backgrounds and learning styles (Caruana and Montgomery, 2015). A campus of a diverse racial and cultural range of students and teaching staff members can be a hotbed of frustration, misunderstanding and miscommunication, especially if the expatriate staff members are not briefed about the local practices and traditions. According to Healey (2017), a principal issue with regard to teaching and learning is the students' learning styles and their lack of proficiency in the English language. This matches the experiences related by students in the paragraph above and shows that the staff, as well as students are experiencing issues with the teaching and learning, and student experience in the IBCs.

Neri and Wilkins (2019) urge the administrators to consider the issue of talent management, in terms of recruitment, training and managing academic staff in IBCs. According to the authors, an IBC has two natures-- it operates as an educational institution, and simultaneously, it is in the "business" of education; as such, the IBC is under the same pressure as other business organisations to attract, develop and retain the expatriate staff to work in the host country. Wilkins, Butt and Annabi (2017 as cited in Neri and Wilkins, 2019) claim that there are some issues concerning the staffing of IBCs and they include the following: lack of career progression, tensions between local and expatriate employees, lack of research guidance and opportunities (Cai & Hall, 2016), and these are some of the factors that exacerbate the tensions felt by the expatriate staff. Staff workload is also cited as one of the problems faced by academic staff, as lecturers of the IBCs typically have a heavier teaching workload, with little time left for research.

Salt and Wood (2014) further explain some of the more pressing issues of an IBC, and staff recruitment is one of them. They report that many UK staff members from the home campus refuse to relocate to Malaysia for a long duration. Hence, the university resorts to recruitment from the international pool of academic staff, many of whom are from other countries, and they may be unfamiliar with the culture and practices of the home campus. The university is then obligated to provide training and induction courses for these expatriate staff members. Similarly, in their study on staffing issues, Hill and Thabet (2018) report that some of the expatriate staff members, recruited from other countries but based in Malaysia, had very little knowledge of the UK or Nottingham. Without knowing the expectations of the home campus or with limited knowledge of how the Malaysian education system worked, these international staff members performed based on their perception and belief system, and created a host of problems; some of which were inappropriate teaching styles, unrealistic academic expectations, unsatisfactory work performance, and failing to understand the local customs and behaviours.

Cai and Hall (2016) contend that the staffing and recruitment of expatriate staff members for the IBCs in Malaysia are not sustainable. The authors concur with the view, and staff turnover rate is a huge concern for most of the IBCs. Hill and Thabet (2018), for example, cite that the IBCs typically attract staff members who are in the early stages of their career, and feel excited at the prospect of moving overseas for a teaching job. These young academics are often motivated and highly enthusiastic about teaching, but may lack the depth and experience in teaching, often requiring further training and academic support from the university. Once these staff members are suitably trained and fully equipped with the knowledge and expertise of teaching in an international university, many of them will end up leaving to teach at other IBCs, or return to their own country, or in some cases start employment with the rival IBCs bringing along with them valuable expertise and experiences. Salt and Wood (2014) echo similar findings in their study; they found that it was an arduous task to persuade staff members from the main campus to work in Malaysia for a long duration.

STRATEGIC ALIGNMENT OF IBCs IN MALAYSIA

The rapid expansion and growth of the IBCs in Malaysia occurs within diverse cultural, economic, political and socioeconomic settings. This complex interplay of power structure and identities (Caruana & Montgomery, 2015) has various implications on the operation and management of the IBCs.

As far as accreditation is concerned, the IBCs can reduce the pressure of bureaucracy by working towards the attainment of the self-accreditation status, which allows the university to self-monitor and evaluate their programmes and courses; the regulatory bodies will only visit the university periodically to ensure that the quality of teaching and learning and the courses are maintained (Malaysian Qualifications Agency, 2018). To date, four IBCs have been awarded self-accreditation status: Monash University, Sunway Campus; The University of Nottingham, Malaysia Campus; Swinburne University of Technology Sarawak Campus; and Curtin University Malaysia. With the self-accreditation status, the institutions concerned are able to set up an audit team to manage the accreditation process effectively. This self-accreditation status also significantly reduces the duration whilst giving respective IBCs the opportunity to ensure that the quality and standard of the programs offered still meets the requirements of the Malaysian Qualification Agency strictly. The self-accreditation is a badge of honour of which the IBCs can use it to attract more students, both locally and internationally.

As mentioned previously, a moratorium has been imposed on the foreign universities to open new branch campuses; this move has serious implications on the Malaysian education landscape. With the recent change of government and leadership after the 2018 General Election, a number of significant policy changes have taken place, one of which is the Prime Minister's effort to build partnerships with

Japan. This has resulted in a plan for a Japanese University to set up a branch campus in Malaysia. It is difficult to predict the growth and expansion of the Western-based IBCs in Malaysia in the foreseeable future. Arguably, the new move may be a positive signal for the Malaysians as presumably, it could be more affordable to study at a Japanese university, without compromising the quality of education. It may be premature to assume that the growth of the IBCs will continue as there is an adequate supply of educational providers to meet the current needs of the country. The recent Coronavirus disease (COVID-19) has also caused a decrease in student enrolment in most of the private and public universities in Malaysia, so the demand for IBCs or foreign education may experience a slower growth at least for next few years.

To encourage professional development among the employees, the staff members from the host and home countries are encouraged to collaborate in research projects, which will increase the research profile of the institution. It is a win-win situation for the IBCs to forge an international partnership with the home campus; it will benefit both institutions, especially when applying for research grants. One example is the One Curtin strategic positioning, whereby the offshore branch campuses together with mother campus in Australia, collaborate to develop international research capabilities and capacities in key research areas. This partnership builds upon, and diversifies its research income through grant schemes. Concomitantly, it impacts on student enrolment especially higher degree research students. Furthermore, working with the staff members from the home campus offers a vast number of learning opportunities, especially for offshore campus staff members who may have very little chance to participate in research. Despite the need to comply with the rules of different governing bodies on research, the collaborative efforts would be beneficial to the local staff members. As the IBCs gear towards increasing their research profile, the faculty should be encouraged to forge long-term research collaborations with the host organisations and PHEIs in Malaysia as well as to expand knowledge and widen the access to the collective pool of experts in specified fields. Although the IBCs need to comply with the different research agencies, meeting the standards set by the agency will greatly improve the quality of the university research and thereby increase the ranking; all these concerted efforts of the IBCs will help solidify the position of Malaysia as the regional hub for education. In Malaysia, informal networking forums have been established to foster better interactions between the host government, including the regulatory authorities and the IBCs of UK universities (Healey, 2015).

To build good relations between the staff and students, it is important for the management to consider some form of orientation programme for the newly hired expatriate staff and familiarise them with the local cultures and organisational practices of the institution (Tierney & Lanford, 2014). The curriculum and teaching methodology of the courses should be reviewed on a regular basis, so that adaptations and changes can be made to suit the local context and meet the students' needs. Furthermore, the IBCs can offer professional development programmes for the staff, and encourage knowledge sharing between the staff from both campuses to improve teaching quality (Clifford, 2015). Similar orientation programmes and student development schemes should be initiated to help students cope with the demands of their studies. A sustainable support programme can also be developed to guide and mentor the students to adjust themselves to the demands of learning at IBCs.

The IBCs have to be in constant communication with the teaching staff members as well as students so that teaching resources and assessments are standardised, and that the curriculum suits the needs of the students. It is imperative that the teaching staff work closely with the counterparts from the host university to maintain the uniformity of teaching and the quality of delivery. Besides that, all assessments must be moderated to ensure consistency of evaluation and fairness to the students. Crafting clear guidelines and policies for curriculum development, changes and evaluation will assist the faculty and students of the various IBCs to narrow the disparity between the Western and non-Western learning styles, while providing the necessary scaffolding for students to develop and learn more effectively.

CONCLUSION

The IBCs are unique educational institutions and offer an array of benefits to both the students and the host country. First, the students have the experience of studying in an environment quite similar to that of the home campus, with emphasis on high quality curriculum, numerous faculties offering a diverse range of courses and an international community comprising students and teaching staff members from various countries. Second, the IBCs are fully or at least partially owned by foreign entities and award credentials similar to those from the home-country universities. Third, the strong partnership between the IBCs with the local community provides rich educational opportunities to the people of the host countries. However, a home campus needs to go through a long and tedious bureaucratic process to establish a branch campus overseas. Besides this, the IBC set up has to resolve many issues and consider many aspects in order to remain sustainable and relevant, while facing the intense competition from other rival IBCs. There are some issues an IBC needs to deal with: adapting to the host country's quality assurance framework and other regulatory policies that govern the running of the IBCs; recruiting trained, qualified academic staff who can deliver the programmes with the same quality and standard similar to those of the home campus. These are the aspects which will affect the day-to-day operations of an IBC: adhering to the conflicting requirements of accreditation, curriculum development; managing talents, raising research profiles and sourcing for funding. It is imperative that the administrators examine how the decisions related to abovementioned issues and aspects will impact the various stakeholders. Meeting the expectations of the home campus and compromising on the expectations of the host country is a delicate balancing act for the administrators who operate an IBC outside of their home country. While it is inevitable to have conflicts and tensions between the students, faculties and administrators, it is also worthwhile to explore how these predicaments can be addressed and mitigated or even resolved to facilitate the smooth running of the IBCs. On the flip side of the coin, a stringent set of criteria imposed on these institutions may have a positive effect-- guaranteeing higher quality teaching and learning, which will ultimately benefit the students.

LIMITATIONS, FUTURE RESEARCH DIRECTION

As a proposal for further investigation, future researchers can explore how the IBCs have addressed or managed the issues, and difficulties of operating foreign-owned education institutions in a host country. The study results will provide a better understanding of how these institutions can continue to develop in Malaysia as there is tremendous potential for cross-border, transnational higher education to contribute to the education needs as well as economic growth of the host country. This research is not in any way exhaustive as there are limited data about how IBCs, particularly those that are Australian based, perform in Malaysia. The University of Nottingham Malaysia and Xiamen University Malaysia are the two IBCs that had carried out research on the complexity of operating IBCs in Malaysia therefore the examples and literature is based on the experiences reported in the literature. There is a lack of information from other IBCs particularly in the areas of the university's performance, student enrolment and other administrative issues. Due to the incomplete scope of this study, there are many topics related to the managing of IBCs that warrant further investigation. In addition, other areas that deserve future research are the social, cultural, and economic implications of IBCs on the host countries (Escriva-Beltran, Nunoz-de-Prat & Villo, 2019). In the same vein, future research can be conducted to investigate the extent COVID-19 pandemic impact on IBCs international student recruitment in developing countries (Sia & Abbas, 2020; Yong & Sia, 2021). Furthermore, studies can also be carried to examine the relationship between marketing mix and branding in IBCs (Lim, Jee & De Run, 2018) which may assist IBCs marketing manager in students' recruitment. It is hoped that the research findings of the abovementioned areas would help the policy makers and university marketing directors make better decisions in operating and managing the IBCs more profitably and efficiently.

REFERENCES

AECC Global. (2021). Complete Guide: University Grading System in Australia. AECC Global. https://www.aeccglobal.com.au/blog/complete-guide-university-grading-system-in-australia

Akiba, H. (2008). *The changing face of transnational education in Malaysia: a case study of international offshore university programs.* [Doctoral dissertation, the University of Minnesota, USA].

Alam, F., Alam, Q., Chowdhury, H., & Steiner, T. (2013). Transnational education: Benefits, threats and challenges. *Procedia Engineering*, *56*, 870–874. doi:10.1016/j.proeng.2013.03.209

Arachi, D. (2006). Foreign Branch Campuses in Malaysia: State Action and Consumer Choices Revisited, [Master's Thesis, Lund University, Sweden]. https://lup.lub.lu.se/luur/download?func=downloadFile&recordOId=1326386&fileOId=1326387

Bengsten, S. E. (2017). Supercomplexity and the university: Ronald Barnett and the social philosophy of Higher Education. *Higher Education Quarterly*, *72*, 65–74.

Cai, L., & Hall, C. (2016). Motivations, expectations, and experiences of expatriate academic staff on an international branch campus in China. *Journal of Studies in International Education*, *20*(3), 207–222. doi:10.1177/1028315315623055

Caruana, V., & Montgomery, C. (2015). Understanding the Transnational Higher Education landscape: Shifting personality and the complexities of partnership. *Learning and Teaching*, *8*(1), 5–29. doi:10.3167/latiss.2015.080102

Clifford, M. (2015). Assessing the Feasibility of International Branch Campuses [Doctoral Dissertation, Pardee Rand Graduate School]. https://www.rand.org/content/dam/rand/pubs/rgs_dissertations/RGSD300/RGSD354/RAN D_RGSD354.pdf

Curtin University Malaysia. (2014). *General Education Subjects*. Curtain University. https://humanities.curtin.edu.my/departments/culturelanguagestudies/mohe/

Dobos, K. (2011). "Serving two masters" – academics' perspectives on working at an offshore campus in Malaysia. *Educational Review*, *63*(1), 19–35. doi:10.1080/00131911003748035

Dyson, J. (2013, March 16). More universities attracted to Iskandar education hub. *University World News*. https://www.universityworldnews.com/article.php?story=20130315083553 21&query=iskandar+education+hub

Education Malaysia Global Services. (n.d.). *Malaysia Education in Brief.* Education Malaysia. https://educationmalaysia.gov.my/malaysia-higher-education-in-brief/#:~:text=10%20International%20Branch%20Campuses%20in,Swinburne%20University%20of%20Technology%2C%20Sarawak (Accessed 5 May 2022).

Escriva-Beltran, M., Muñoz-de-Prat, J., & Villó, C. (2019). Insights into international branch campuses: Mapping trends through a systematic review. *Journal of Business Research, 101*, 507–515. doi:10.1016/j.jbusres.2018.12.049

He, L. (2016). Transnational higher education institutions in China: A comparison of policy orientation and reality. *Journal of Studies in International Education, 20*(1), 79–95. doi:10.1177/1028315315602931

He, L., & Wilkins, S. (2018). Achieving Legitimacy in Cross-Border Higher Education: Institutional Influences on Chinese International Branch Campuses in South East Asia. *Journal of Studies in International Education, 22*(3), 179–197. doi:10.1177/1028315317738774

Healey, N. M. (2015). Managing international branch campus: What do we know? *Higher Education Quarterly, 69*(4), 386–409. doi:10.1111/hequ.12082

Healey, N. M. (2016). The challenges of leading an international branch campus: The "lived experience" of in-country senior manager. *Journal of Studies in Higher Education, 20*(1), 61–78. doi:10.1177/1028315315602928

Hill, C., Cheong, K. C., Leong, Y. C., & Fernandez-Chung, R. (2014). TNE – Trans-national education or tensions between national and external? A case study of Malaysia. *Studies in Higher Education, 39*(6), 952–966. doi:10.1080/03075079.2012.754862

Hill, C., & Razvi, S. D. A (2015). *Government and Transnational Education: challenges and opportunities in Asia*. The observatory on borderless higher education.

Hill, C., & Thabet, R. A. (2018). Managing international branch campuses: Lessons learnt from eight years on a branch campus in Malaysia. *International Journal of Educational Management, 32*(2), 310–322. doi:10.1108/IJEM-04-2017-0079

Knight, J. (2011). Education hubs: A fad, a brand, an innovation. *Journal of Studies in International Education, 15*(3), 221–240. doi:10.1177/1028315311398046

Knight, J., & Morshidi, S. (2011). The Complexities and Challenges of Regional Education Hubs: Focus on Malaysia. *Higher Education, 62*(5), 593–606. doi:10.100710734-011-9467-2

Lane, J. E. (2011). Importing Private higher education: International branch campuses. *Journal of Comparative Policy Analysis, 13*(4), 367–381. doi:10.1080/13876988.2011.583106

Lane, J. E., Brgos, J., Schueller, J., Dey, S., Kinser, K., & Zipf, S. (2021, March 13). What is the future for international branch campuses? *University World News*. https://www.universityworldnews.com/post.php?story=2021031012405285

Lim, C. B., Bentley, D., Henderson, F., Pan, S. Y., Balakrishnan, V. D., Balasingam, D. M., & Teh, Y. Y. (2016). Equivalent or not?: Beyond measuring teaching and learning standards in a transnational education environment. *Quality Assurance in Education*, *24*(4), 528–540. doi:10.1108/QAE-01-2016-0001

Lim, I. (2017, October 25). After 2017's 20 pc cut, public universities' operating budget goes up. *Malay Mail*. https://www.malaymail.com/s/1497297/after-2017s-20pc-cutpublic-universities-operating-budget-goes-up

Lim, W. M., Jee, T. W., & De Run, E. C. (2018). Strategic brand management for higher education institutions with graduate degree programs: Empirical insights from the higher education marketing mix. *Journal of Strategic Marketing*, *28*(3), 225–245. doi:10.1080/0965254X.2018.1496131

Lin Sin, I., Leung, M. W. H., & Waters, J. L. (2019). Degrees of value: Comparing the contextual complexities of UK transnational education in Malaysia and Hong Kong. *Compare: A Journal of Comparative Education*, *49*(1), 132–148. doi:10.1080/03057925.2017.1390663

MQA. (2017). List of IPTS. MQA. http://jpt.mohe.gov.my/index.php/ipt/berkaitan-ipts/ipts

MQA. (2021). List of IPTS. MQA. https://drive.google.com/drive/folders/1L_fklIz2AukzVQLV3I6_euL-BaxjZ4Lg0

MQA. (2015). Listing of Private Higher Education Institutions (IPTS). MQA. http://www.mqa.gov.my/mqr/english/eakrbyipts.cfm

Mahoney, C. (2021). Archaic examination culture of UK universities must be reformed. *Times Higher Education*. https://www.timeshighereducation.com/opinion/archaic-examination-culture-uk-universities-must-be-reformed

Malaysiakini. (2019, March 15). Japanese university branches coming to Malaysia, confirms Maszlee *Malaysiakini.* https://www.malaysiakini.com/news/468077

Malaysian Qualification Agency. (2018). *Self-Accreditation.* MQA. http://www.mqa.gov.my/portalmqav3/red/en/swaakreditasi.cfm

Marimuthu, T. (2008). The role of the Private Sector in Higher Education in Malaysia. In D. Johnson. & R. Maclean (Eds.), *Teaching: Professionalization. Development and Leadership* (271-281). https://link.springer.com/chapter/10.1007/978-1-4020-8186-6_18

McBurnie, G., & Ziguras, C. (2001). The regulation of transnational higher education in Southeast Asia: Case studies of Hong Kong, Malaysia and Australia. *Higher Education*, *42*(1), 85–105. doi:10.1023/A:1017572119543

Ministry of Higher Education. (n.d.). SETARA-2017. MOHE. http://www.mohe.gov.my/en/latest/pengumuman/790-setara-2017

Mok, K. H. (2012). The rise of transnational higher education in Asia: Student mobility and studying experiences in Singapore and Malaysia. *Higher Education Policy*, *25*(2), 225–241. doi:10.1057/hep.2012.6

Neri, S., & Wilkins, S. (2019). Talent management in transnational higher education: Strategies for managing academic staff at international branch campuses. *Journal of Higher Education Policy and Management*, *41*(1), 52–69. doi:10.1080/1360080X.2018.1522713

O'Malley, B. (2016, November 10). China overtakes UAE as top host of branch campuses. *University World News*. https://www.universityworldnews.com/post.php?story=20161110144407523

OBHE. (2014). Malaysia to offer foreign universities greater incentives to open branch campuses, but why has no new branch campus opened since 2000? *The Observatory on Borderless Higher Education.*

Pohl, H., & Lane, J. E. (2018). Research contributions of international branch campuses to the scientific wealth of academically developing countries. *Scientometrics*, *116*(3), 1719–1734. doi:10.100711192-018-2790-y

Pyvis, D., & Chapman, A. (2007). Why university students choose an international education: A case study in Malaysia. *International Journal of Educational Development*, *27*(2), 235–246. doi:10.1016/j.ijedudev.2006.07.008

Rashad, A., Majid, M., & Subramaniam, T. (2020). Capitalising on the strengths of international branch campuses in Malaysian transnational higher education landscape. *Journal of Southeast Asian Studies*, *25*(2), 201–221. doi:10.22452/jati.vol25no2.10

Sato, M. (2005). Higher education reforms in Malaysia 1957-2003. *NUCB Journal of Language Culture and Communication*, *7*(1), 73–88.

Schulze, M. P., & Kleibert, J. M. (2021). Transnational education for regional economic development? Understanding Malaysia's and Singapore's strategic coupling in global higher education. *International Journal of Training and Development*, *25*(4), 363–382. doi:10.1111/ijtd.12242

Shams, F., & Huisman, J. (2014). The role of institutional dual embeddedness in the strategic local adaptation of international branch campuses: Evidence from Malaysia and Singapore. *Studies in Higher Education*, *41*(6), 955–970. doi:10.1080/03075079.2014.966669

Sharma, Y. (2020). Private universities at risk as foreign students stay away. *University World News*. https://www.universityworldnews.com/post.php?story=20201202162834 61

Shulze, M. P. (2020). Of bumping and bending: Foreign universities' FDI strategies in Malaysia. *Journal of Economic and Human Geography*, *112*(2), 179–194. https://onlinelibrary.wiley.com/doi/full/10.1111/tesg.12472

Sia, J. K. M., & Abbas, A. A. (2020). Facing the unknown: Pandemic and higher education in Malaysia. *Asian Education and Development Studies*, *10*(2), 263–275. doi:10.1108/AEDS-05-2020-0114

Smith, A. (2020, June 9). More about Higher Education Institutions in China. *China Scholar*. https://www.china-scholar.com/higher-education-in-china/

MOE. (2017). Statistics of Private Higher Education of Malaysia. [Data set]. MOE. https://www.moe.gov.my/en/muat-turun/laporan-dan-statistik/pendidikan-tinggi/bukuperangkaan/2017-5/2394-statistik-pendidikan-tinggi-2017-bab-3-pdf/file

MOHE. (2017). Statistics of Public Higher Education of Malaysia. [Data set]. http://www.mohe.gov.my/en/download/awam/statistik/2017-3/470-statistik-pendidikan-tinggi2017-bab-2-universiti-awam/file

Study Malaysia. (2018). Foreign university branch campus. *Study Malaysia*. https://www.studymalaysia.com/education/top-stories/foreign-university-branch-campus-your-route-to-getting-a-foreign-degree-right-here-in-malaysia#:~:text=The%20very%20first%20FUBC%2C%20Monash,World%20University%20Rankings%C2%AE%202019

Tham, S. Y., & Kam, A. J. Y. (2008). Internationalising higher education: Comparing the challenges of different higher education institutions in Malaysia. *Asia Pacific Journal of Education*, *28*(4), 353–367. doi:10.1080/02188790802468880

The Star. (2018, November 5). Dr. M wants more Japanese universities to set up branch campuses in Malaysia. *The Star.* https://www.thestar.com.my/news/nation/2018/11/05/dr-m-wants-japanese-universities-toset-up-branch-campuses-in-malaysia/

Tierney, W. G., & Landford, M. (2015). An investigation of the impact of international branch campuses on organizational culture. *Higher Education*, *70*(2), 283–298. doi:10.100710734-014-9845-7

Wilkins, S. (2016). Establishing international branch campuses: A framework for assessing opportunities and risks. *Journal of Higher Education Policy and Management*, *38*(2), 167–182. doi:10.1080/1360080X.2016.1150547

Wilkins, S. (2020). Two decades of international branch campus development, 2000–2020: A review. *International Journal of Educational Management*. doi:10.1108/IJEM-08-2020-0409

Wilkins, S., Balakrishnan, M. S., & Huisman, J. (2012). Student satisfaction and student perceptions of quality at international branch campuses in the United Arab Emirates. *Journal of Higher Education Policy and Management*, *34*(5), 543–556. doi:10.1080/1360080X.2012.716003

Wilkins, S., & Rumbley, L. E. (2018). What an international branch is, and is not: a revised edition. International Higher Education, 93, 12-13. doi:10.6017/ihe.0.93.10416

Yat, W. L. W., & Chang, D. W. (2021). Revisiting the Asian regulatory regimes in transnational education: How local politics (re)oriented higher education policy in Malaysia, Singapore and Hong Kong, *Policy. The Review of Higher Education*, *5*(2), 113–130. doi:10.1080/23322969.2020.1869064

Yong, S. S., & Sia, J. K. M. (2021). COVID-19 and social wellbeing in Malaysia: A case study. *Current Psychology (New Brunswick, N.J.).* doi:10.100712144-021-02290-6 PMID:34539153

Yung, C. H. A., Hill, C., Chen, H. J. K., & Tsai, S. (2018). A comparative study of international branch campuses in Malaysia, Singapore China and South Korea: Regulation, governance and quality assurance. *Asia Pacific Education Review*, *19*(4), 543–555. doi:10.100712564-018-9550-9

Chapter 21

Envisioning and Exploring Future Transnational Higher Education and Management Models:

The Transformation of Higher Education in the UACC World

Youmin Xi
Xi'an Jiaotong-Liverpool University, China

Chengcheng Li
Xi'an Jiaotong-Liverpool University, China

ABSTRACT

This chapter aims to envision future transnational university educational and management models. In the background section, a general review of international universities in China would be outlined followed by an overview of a specific example, international Xi'an Jiaotong-Liverpool University. In the literature review section, an evaluation of relevant literature will demonstrate how the examination of key concepts like knowledge, truth, education, and enlightenment could contribute to deepened understanding of future transnational higher education. In the third section on discussion, a detailed analysis of HeXie education model, HeXie mindset model, and HeXie management model would be addressed followed by an application of these models in XJTLU's management systems. Fourthly, challenges and opportunities would be outlined in terms of student-centered and research-led education, the teaching of research, quality education, future education in the uncertain, ambiguous, complex, and changeable world, and future education, before conclusion is drawn.

DOI: 10.4018/978-1-6684-5226-4.ch021

INTRODUCTION

Covid-19 pandemic disruption prompted large scale online learning replacing the usual campus life and teaching with the digital technology, which raised questions of the value of the physical campus or university when learning could take place at home on a computer. Will the traditional university have a future? It was recently predicted that half of the United States' universities could face bankruptcy in the next decade (Horn, 2018). This could be problematic because the modern university has been an essential part of the society in its role to advance technology development, promote social transformation, shape culture and ideology, and support economic development. However, the development of society also brings new problems which entail creative and effective solutions to solve unprecedented problems like extreme weather and natural catastrophe caused by global warming, sustainable development for equality, security, and well-being of global citizens, and geopolitical conflicts and emergencies like refugee crisis due to wars such as the Ukraine war that taking place in Ukraine at present challenging humanities and civilization with possible nuclear crisis. Santos (2016, p.295) wrote in 2012 that "the university is undergoing a period of paradigmatic transition" and raised 12 questions (Figure 1) concerning whether the university has a future.

Figure 1. 12 critical questions concerning the future of universities

Is the global university a possible answer for the mission of the university in a globalized world?	*Which qualifications will be generated by which universities when job prestige goes together with job qualification and scarcity?*	*How to balance the marketable knowledge and the nonmarketable knowledge in university education?*
Can the university retain its specificity and relative autonomy while being governed by market imperatives and employment demands?	*Is it possible to standardize procedures and criteria across such different university cultures without destroying diversity and innovation?*	*Many universities play a role in disseminating certain views of the world. What is the role of knowledge of the Other in university education?*
Are we creating endless illiteracy in the same process that we create endless knowledge? Will peripheral and semi-peripheral universities be charged with solving the illiteracy problem, while the core universities will have the monopoly of highly qualified knowledge?	*Is the university prepared to recognize that the understanding of the world by far exceeds the Western understanding of the world? Is the university prepared to re-found the idea of universalism on a new, intercultural basis?*	*How does the idea of a knowledge society impact a modern university which was created on the premise that it was an island of knowledge in a society of ignorance?*
The university has historically been embedded in the three pillars of modern social regulation—the state, the market and civil society; Is the Bologna Process a creative response to neoliberal, one-dimensional demands or, on the contrary, a way of imposing them through a transnational European process that neutralizes national resistance?	*Should universities become a transnational corporation or a transnational cooperative or non-profit organization, given the modern university has been serving international flows of ideas, teachers, students and books as well as different power relations behind the distribution of the costs and benefits of globalization?*	*Modern universities have been both a product and a producer of specific models of development. The question is: In such a tumultuous time, is the university's serenity possible? And, if possible, is it desirable? Will the European university contribute to a dialogue among different models of development?*

Post Covid-19, many scholars have expressed various thoughts about future universities (Orazbayeva *et al.*, 2020) as the home base supporting lifelong learning, helping individuals' re- and up-skilling for employment, diffusing into the society with individualized and accessible education, helping various sectors in the society to provide solutions for the current crisis.

BACKGROUND

Xi'an Jiao Tong-Liverpool University: A Transnational Higher Education Pioneer

Since China joined WTO in 2001, efforts have been made to promote internationalization of universities. International universities are the most effective in enhancing cross-culture skills and students' international outlook, exchanging educational philosophy because they require internationalization of students, teachers, curriculum design and delivery, as well as independent university governance and management. In 2006, XJTLU was established with the vision and mission (See Figure 2) to become a research-led international university in China and a Chinese university recognized internationally for its unique features in learning and teaching, research, social service, and education management. XJTLU emphasizes key attributes essential for fulfilling academic performance and a full life such as critical thinking, complexity mindset, abilities to collaborate, communication skills, creativity, as well as key qualities essential for citizenship such as social responsibility, lifelong learning skills, digital literacy, senses of sustainable development, and cultural competence.

Figure 2. XJTLU Mission Statement

XJLUT Mission

- Educate technical and managerial professionals with international perspectives and competitive capabilities
- Integrate global economic and social development with expertise in business and technology
- With our unique focuses and features, conduct research in areas where humanity faces severe challenges
- Explore new models for higher education that will exert a strong influence on the development of education in China and the world.

XJTLU'S Educational Models Overview: Version 1.0/2.0/3.0

At the core of XJTLU's different education models is Research-Led education. The "research" in Research-Led education is not merely research in the narrow and literal sense of the term, but also an awareness and disposition of problem-solving and exploration. The Research-Led education model is referred to as the five-star model of student development (Xi, 2022, p. 99). Research-led education at XJTLU derailed from the traditional imposition of existing research model, process, and methodology on students. Instead, students would be provided with tools, resources, information, facilitators, and effective instructions to design their learning process as co-participant of Research-Led Education (See Figure 3).

Figure 3. XJTLU Five-star Education Model of student development of Research-Led Education

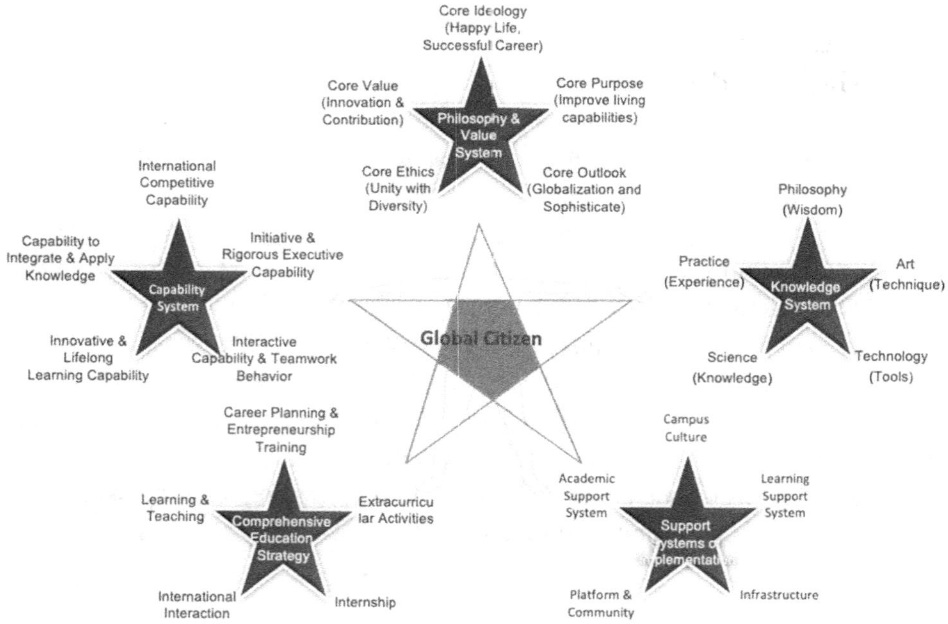

XJTLU education landscape and Five-Star strategic blueprint aim to contribute to education development and the society through three models in different phases (see Figure 4). In its first decade (XJTLU MODEL 1.0), XJTLU endeavored to establish Specialized Elite Education by integrating merits from the traditional Chinese educational system in emphasizing solid knowledge foundation, the UK system strong in quality assurance, and the US system prominent in flexibility for creativity to enhance research-led learning education emphasizing interdisciplinary or industry training. In terms of management, XJTLU adopted the principles and practices of flat and networking organizational structure and helped remove barriers within university and between university and society for collaboration.

In the second decade (XJTLU MODEL 2.0), responding to the challenges of digitalization, artificial intelligence and robotics, as well as the needs of deepened collaboration between university and the society for the transformation of future talent and social patterns, XJTLU unveiled an exploration of Syntegrative Education (SE), as XJTLU model 2.0, by establishing: 1). Industry and Enterprise Tailored Education (IETE) to enhance the development of specialized elites with higher disciplinary attainments and strengthen their industry skills; 2). Entrepreneur College (EC) to integrate comprehensively and organically general education, discipline education, industry and management training, as well as entrepreneurship education; 3). Innovation and Entrepreneur Community (IEC) to support lifelong learning, innovation, and entrepreneurship in collaboration with the society. In terms of management, XJTLU Model 2.0 strengthen the organically cooperation among its staff and units on its established networking structure with the four segments: finance and administration; academic affairs; student affairs; and information and support system to enhance productivity and efficiency and share resources.

To anticipate the future, XJTLU Model 3.0 aims to explore new, future-oriented concepts in education, universities and campuses, faculty, curriculum and pedagogy, funding, and infrastructure to form an educational ecosystem allowing efficient sharing and exchanging of resources between university

Figure 4. XJTLU education landscape and Five-Star strategic blueprint

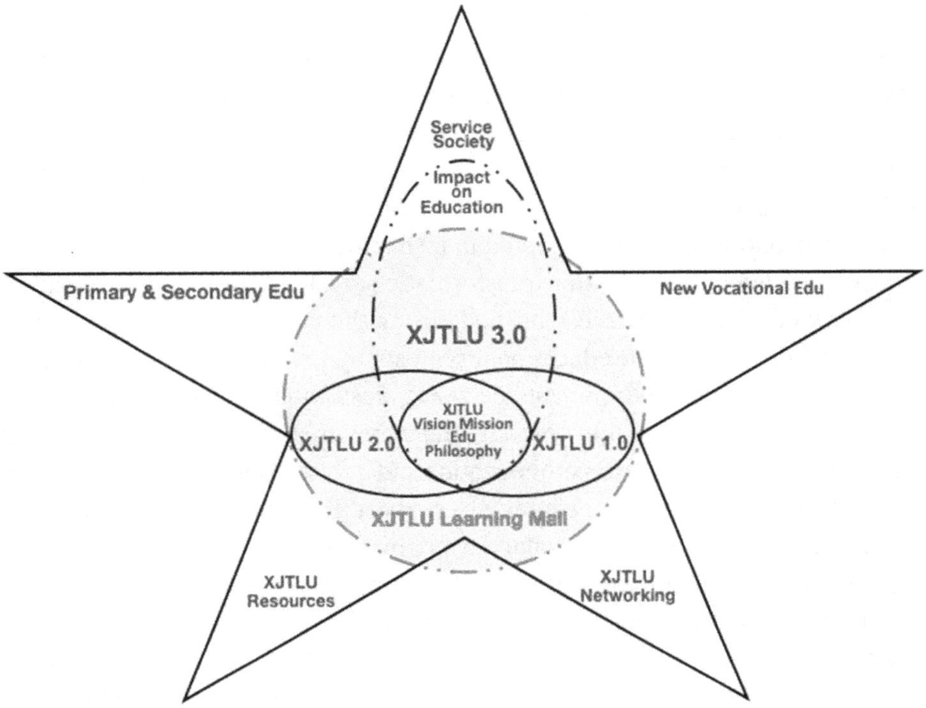

Figure 5. Five-star educational model of Version 1.0

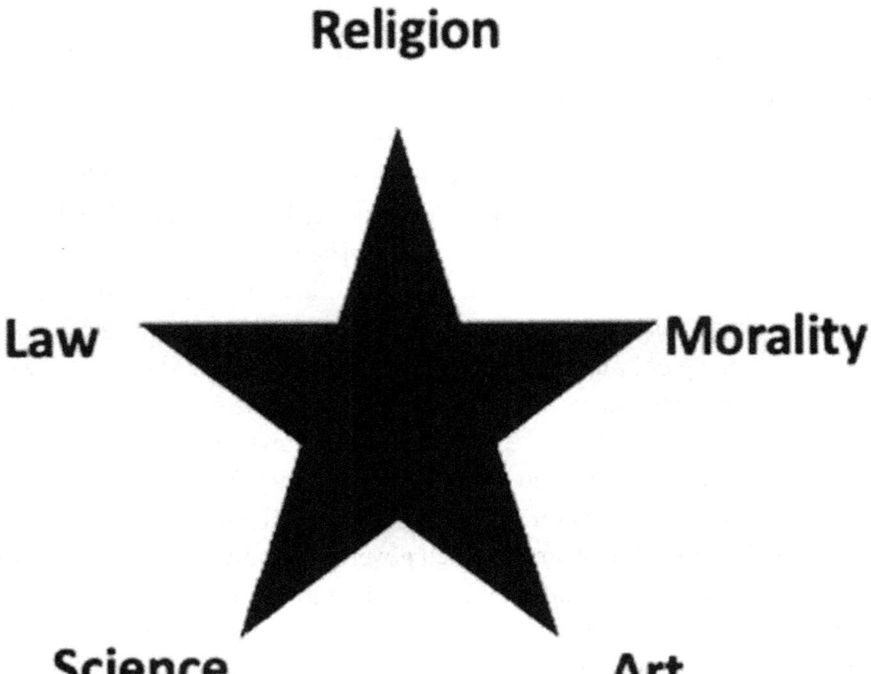

and the society to support interests-driven lifelong learning, innovation and entrepreneurship to prepare students for the fast-changing world where Artificial Intelligence will be a very important part of human productivity and citizens need continuous upskilling to survive and thrive in the digitalized new era. Education in XJTLU Model 3.0 views universities as part of a large ecosystem without clear boundaries and distinctive definition of campuses. Lifelong education could be realized through many themed Learning, Innovation and Entrepreneurship Centers (**LIECS**) all over the world by the XJTLU university systems. In terms of management models, key concepts of future management, such as HeXie Management Theory (Xi, 1987; Xi et al., 2010), Eco-management with delayering structure, diversity, syntegration, and distribution would be explored in reshaping education for the future.

As a very important element in education transformation at XJTLU through digitalization, The Learning Mall (LM), a digital platform, was established during the period of the outbreak of COVID-19 in May of 2020, informed by advanced educational philosophy and digital technology to adopt modern networks and use the academic environments of world-class campuses to put the world's best online resources and providers under one roof in order to offer experience of in-depth integration of on-campus and off-campus education, online and on-site education and industry and academic education. The Learning Mall is a core approach in XJTLU's strategy to support the running of its three models and create an ecosystem for future education and personal development to support its students and alumni as well as anyone with desires in upskilling for professional or personal development, interest-oriented lifelong learning, innovation, and entrepreneurship. Meanwhile, XJTLU developed another platforms, 1) the Institute of Leadership and Education Advanced Development (ILEAD), which formed the foundation for Academy of Future Education to enhance its influence in educational industry; 2) HeXie Management Center to support the innovative operation of university as knowledge institution; 3) XIPU-Institution, as a Think-Tank to interact with the society.

LITERATURE REVIEW

Knowledge, Truth, and Education

Understanding of the self is important because the self is where the world unfolds. Nietzsche (2008, p. 93) in *Thus Spoke Zarathustra* described how people learned to hide the true self behind so many layers of masks or wraps of colors that the true self is forgotten. The knowledge of the true self will help one live a balanced life to participate in social life and being in solitude and independent. The university has played a vital role in helping one gain knowledge of both the society and the self to develop intellect and understand the inner being or intuition that would assist the intellect. Many of the world's problems could be seen caused by the ignorance of the inner self and how the self relates to the world. The self and the world together form the totality of life in that without knowledge of the self, the world could not be understood thoroughly or genuinely, and vice versa. The fundamental reason is that the world appears as the observed world of the observer and understanding of both the observed and the observer is necessary for understanding the ultimate truth which governs the order of the world. To educate means to help draw authentic knowledge and genuine understanding from students, which could help one learn about the self. Yet, there are tremendous differences between educating and teaching. To teach means to impose something on the students. John Dewey states:

The traditional scheme ... imposes adult standards, subject-matter, and methods upon those who are only growing slowly toward maturity. The gap is so great that the required subject matter, the methods of learning and of behaving are foreign to the existing capacities of the young. They are beyond the reach of the experience the young learners already possess. Consequently, they must be imposed; even though good teachers will use devices of art to cover up the imposition so as to relieve it of obviously brutal features (Dewey, 1938, pp.18-9).

In traditional teaching, the so-called knowledge is imposed on the minds of the young who are evaluated by how well the imposition worked through memorization. However, such educational practices do not lead to genuine development of minds nor true acquisition of knowledge but mere eloquent speakers and writers who simply imitate or repeat without originality. Originality requires one to possess knowledge and understanding of both the self and the world independently. Yet, often what we know can only be considered as information rather than knowledge. The nature of knowledge entails certain beliefs as well as grounds to show the logic and validity of such beliefs, which may often come from intuition within. The more reliable and convincing the grounds, the more warranted the truthfulness of such beliefs, the more certain the knowledge. In the thought experiment, Mary's Room (Nida-Rümelin and O Conaill, 2021), the question of knowledge based on physicalism and difference and relationship between qualia and scientific theories are raised, which has profound implication for education, based on which, it is argued that knowledge should be based on experience in that language and its relationship with reality is capricious. Xi and Li (2021, p. 140) state that language does not mean truth, rather it is a tool used to refer to the truth and hence the relationship between language and meaning and truth it is intended to represent is arbitrary. Therefore, one can acquire a perfect system of language or theory with its own inherent rules and logic which may still not be able to capture the truth in that language is part of reality and not independent of and above reality. All symbols including language are socially constructed which represent the reality to some extent while they could never truly capture the reality not to mention truth. Knowledge is what one knows not what one memorizes because what one memorizes cannot become ones' knowledge when memorized information is borrowed information not warranted of its validity or truthfulness, which should be based on one's experience and genuine understanding. The only way to know is to experience the totality of life--to know the observed and the observer. Plato states that

And now, I said, let me show in a figure how far our nature is enlightened or unenlightened: — Behold! human beings living in a underground den, which has a mouth open towards the light and reaching all along the den... the truth would be literally nothing but the shadows of the images...And you may further imagine that his instructor is pointing to the objects as they pass and requiring him to name them, — will he not be perplexed? Will he not fancy that the shadows which he formerly saw are truer than the objects which are now shown to him (Jowett, 2000, pp.325-7)?

To learn or to be educated means to be able to use language to seek truth while transcend the limits of language to understand truth.

Education and Enlightenment

Practical aspects of education like obtaining qualification or degrees for exchange of social goods are necessary since citizenship is important for one's well-being in a society. Yet, it is more important for the university to help citizens in their intellectual understanding transcend the social roles and identities to discover the meaning of life by positioning the self appropriately in ultimate background of existence beyond the defined, temporal and spatial context of one's roles. The fact that humans are in a constant state of becoming means humans have the potential, possibility and power to transform and attain a much higher state of being physically, mentally, psychologically, spiritually, and consciously. In comparison, animals follow nature, spontaneity and feelings and have no sense of responsibility. The way animals respond relies on their nature programmed instinct while the way humans respond depends on education of the minds. John Dewey (1925, pp. 300-1) mentions that

To use feelings which are not the expression of a rectitude of organic action, rectitude that in civilized or artificial conditions is acquired only by taking thought, is to act like an animal without having the structural facilities of animal life. It has the fascination of all easy surrender to fatality and may be eulogized as a return to nature, spontaneity, or to the quasi-divine. It has the charm of lazy and comfortable escape from responsibility; we die, but we die, like animals, upon the field, defeated and may hap disheartened, but without knowing it.

In addition to the potentiality of transformation, humans need education also because humans have freedom to err. Humans have responsibilities because humans have the freedom to choose to err or not to err, to be or not to be. Animals and plants do not commit mistakes since their lives are perfectly aligned with their biologically and genetically programmed instinct so they follow the nature patterns very accurately and mechanically. Making mistakes is beyond the capacity of animals or plants. Animals do not have responsibility because they do not make mistakes and are protected yet limited by instinct without chance of experimenting living differently. But humans are given the greatest freedom which also means the greatest responsibility and burden as well.

Responsibility of Intellectuals and Universities

Humans need education to be enlightened and to become individuals of maturity and wisdom through understanding the self and the world. Such enlightenment is a chemical reaction between the inner self and the outer world to create a true individual with unique characters. The ultimate goal of education is to bring civilization, emancipation, liberation and compassion to humanity through enlightening the minds of individuals and helping them transform the self, dream and lead the world with creativity, compassion, and responsibility. Martin Luther King famously wrote (1947),

Intelligence plus character — that is the goal of true education...If we are not careful, our colleges will produce a group of close-minded, unscientific, illogical propagandists, consumed with immoral acts. Be careful, 'brethren!' Be careful, teachers!

Intellectuals have responsibilities to help students develop essential attributes or qualities and disposition to think independently and seek truth for both worldly goals of survival and divine goals of enlightenment and transcendence. And university should seek higher degrees of autonomy while being embedded into the regulations of the society and the market while provide quality education to help students become competent not only in the market but also in seeking truth and search for enlightenment. Chomsky (1967) stated that intellectuals with unique privileges of political liberty from access to information and freedom of expression, have much deeper responsibilities to seek truth "lying hidden behind the veil of distortion and misrepresentation, ideology and class interest". Thus, future university should continue its efforts in maintain independence given digitalization means we will be inundated with information including both true and distorted information.

Enlightenment and University

What should be the right state of human existence? And how could education help individuals achieve that ultimate state of being? Universities as a major site for knowledge creation and communication should be the focus for education transformation from the traditional models of imposing information, emphasizing practical qualifications, to new models of enlightening the minds. Universities are unique sites where the experienced meets the inquisitive, the traditional practices meet the contemporary minds, the collective society meets the individual persons, the reflection of self meets the interaction with others, the old solutions meet new problems. And in the meeting of the old and the new, universities are fated to be a place of enlightenment and innovation. While long history of a university may show excellence in accomplishments through inheritance, it may also lead to reluctance in innovation when letting go of the past is not an easy endeavor. Nevertheless, education innovation for universities must be a constant struggle because humans are in a situation where the push for changes is dire when the tradition may become more a hindrance than a safe guard for the new generation, when the old-fashioned solutions of existing problems may lead to more unpredictable problems. The new generation, who are born with and in a world of fast-developing technologies, complexity, ambiguity and uncertainty, are going to face a world which could not be fully predicted by the minds of the past. Hence education system will be challenged to meet the needs of the contemporary young individuals who will need to engage in life-long learning with flexibility and autonomy in managing learning, life, and work to create a life belongs to them instead of inheriting the no longer feasible traditional life-styles. The question is how university leaders can help envision the life of tomorrow and reform the education of today. It is of paramount importance to reflect on whether university should be part of the force of perpetuation of various existential hindrance or be part of the force of liberation, enlightenment, emancipation of humans.

The Context of Future Education Transformation

Globalization has long been a factor for shaping the transformation of education through impacting the political, economic, social, technological, demographical factors in the life of billions on the planet. It was observed that the educational practices established since the industrial revolution times have becoming inadequate in driving technological innovation, serving the need of creating a knowledge-based global economy, and supporting lifelong learning of individuals of the increasingly complex society. The standardized educational practices have become deterrence for inclusion, diversity, individual growth, and innovation when individual success may entail specific and customized instruction, interaction and communication. Universities are no longer the center for information and knowledge when technology spawned the various social media platforms and 24-hour information and news circulation. Consequently, learners are inundated with information, disinformation, false information, irrelevant and distractive information and become overloaded with information, which may create another challenge and opportunity for universities to offer students opportunities and experience in organized, instructive, safe interaction to improve information processing, organization, and management to help support lifelong learning. Moreover, the fast-changing market spurred innovation across various industries and universities are lagging behind in creating the talents desired by industries. Often the mismatch and gap between university education and skills needed in the workplace may create struggle and dissatisfaction toward university education. Hence, how to tailor university education to the real needs of young professionals and requirements of industries would be vital for future education. To this end, the traditional discrete division of disciplines would become inefficient when industries favor interdisciplinary innovation and integration. In this vein of thinking, universities should endeavor in forming symbiosis to support lifelong learning, innovation, entrepreneurship, living in open, shared, distributed centers and networks across the globe beyond geographical constraints. And this would require universities to engage in experimenting new management of knowledge organization. Globalization certainly has impacted education transformation toward the future, yet, there also exist opposing views toward the transformation, which makes education transformation remain local as small-scale skirmishes.

Globalization also contributed to the global environmental issues when companies outsourced manufacturing to less developed countries, which caused environmental and health catastrophes for the local environment as global consumption accelerated with cheap prices made available with low-cost labors. The future generation faces unprecedented sustainable development challenges as many industries' existing operational models and the consumeristic way of living may no longer be suitable for the future world. Universities should become market leaders in supporting the transformation of our current business models and economic systems, embracing culture diversity, bringing awareness and respect of nature, innovating technological advancement for green living, promoting equality to contribute to sustainable development by providing quality education for individuals to develop professional skills, grow mindset, increase awareness, become compassionate and responsible global citizens.

In addition to globalization and increasingly severe global environmental problems, the recent COVID-19 is another vital factor in accelerating the process of education transformation by forcing the adoption of digital technologies throughout the practices in higher education and even daily life. The restriction of geographical mobility has also prompted needs of flexibility in access to educational resources, curriculum, instructional design, facilities, learning platform, collaboration with industries, student enrollment, as well as staffing. Such disruption of the pandemic has indeed catalyzed the transformation and forced all stakeholders to reflect on future education especially the concept of campus, the support system and management of universities.

DISCUSSION

HeXie Educational Model for Interests-Oriented and Lifelong Learning

In Figure 6, XJTLU HeXie Education Model based on HeXie Management Theory (Xi et al., 2010): Happy Life & Successful Career demonstrates 5 different modes of learning throughout one's life, which are organically integrated to support continuous learning and growth.

Q1. Inheritance Learning: This approach refers to inheritance of existing explicit knowledge.

Q2. Reflective Cognition: This approach refers to reflection of existing knowledge or taught information for genuine understanding, emphasizing critical reflection of one's own experience and assumption as well as conceptualization of one's experience.

Figure 6. XJTLU HeXie Education Model: Happy Life & Successful Career

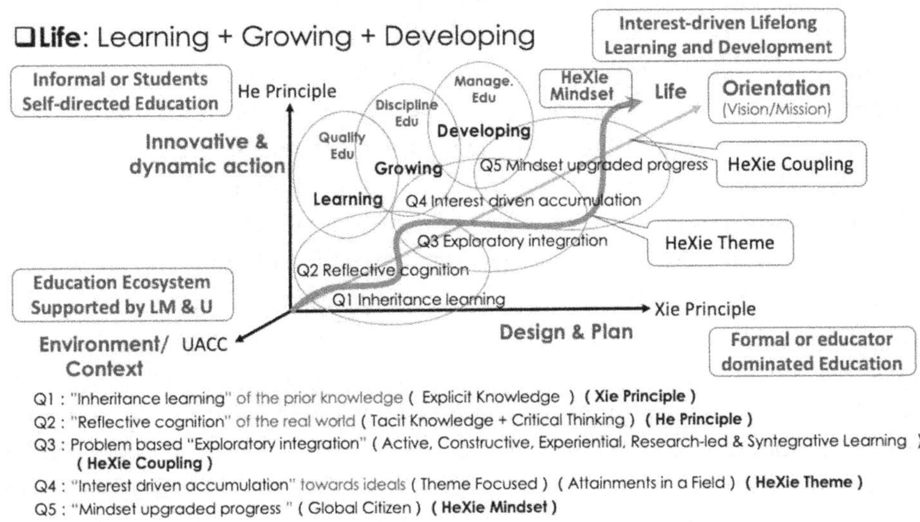

Q3. Explorative Integration: This approach aims to further develop students' creativity in exploring problems, phenomena, doubts, or confusion and integrating inherited knowledge to form a more systematic, innovative, original and genuine understanding of the world.

Q4. Interest-driven Accumulation: This approach focuses on helping learners identify the goals for the present life stage with deepened understanding of one's passion and dream to avoid unnecessary distraction and stay motivated.

Q5. Mindset Upgraded Progress: This approach emphasizes the development of mindset or intuition so that students can think deeply of the self and its relationship with the world to develop mature mindset for well-being, happiness, compassion, and harmonious relationship with existence.

HeXie Education Model helps conceptualize various types of learning for students to inherit and construct the basic knowledge system, and develop the ability of survival and lifelong learning while achieve continuous growth through forming or constantly constructing individual ideals, striving to accomplish progress according to personal interests. In the modern time, it is important to be able to fulfill a meaningful life by being able to participate successfully in the social and economic life as well as maintaining personal wellbeing. The core of learning and education should support mindset development sustainably in order to help people cope with the increasingly uncertain world full of challenges and crises that disrupt life in various ways by creating a learning ecology and necessary university support systems (Li et al., 2022). According to Bauman (2017, p.109),

the collapse of long-term thinking, planning and acting—and the disappearance or weakening of social structures in which thinking, planning, and acting could be inscribed for a long time to come—leads to the splicing of both political history and individual lives into series of short-term projects and episodes that do not combine into the logically consistent and cohesive sequences to which concepts like 'development,' 'maturation,' 'career,' or 'progress' (all suggesting a preordained order of succession) could be meaningfully applied. Such fragmentation of human lives stimulates 'lateral' rather than 'vertical' orientations.

In addition, HeXie Education Model also provides a management framework for university management from five aspects. Firstly, Vision and Mission provide the orientation for what qualities for individuals university aims to cultivate. Correspondingly, university should have clear visions and missions of what value can university deliver for helping learners develop such qualities. Secondly, HeXie Themes demonstrate themes of students' major life events such as various learning activities, assignment projects, internship experience, or entrepreneurship development. Accordingly, university should provide relevant support and resources for successful learning outcome from meaningful experience. The identification of themes helps managing the coherence of life episodes. The third element is He Principle which guides the pedagogical and management practices of university by focusing on the human factors, such as behavior, perception, mindset, creativity, motivation, multiple intelligence which are intrinsically fostered by individuals in university, an organization including students and faculty. From organization perspective, an ideal performer must be creative in mind and proactive, energetic or dynamic in action. University education needs to promote and help cultivate the inherent qualities and attributions beneficial for creativity and motivation. The management of university should address not only engagement of its staff, its students, but also, more importantly, how its staff engage with its students in effective ways. Fourthly, the Xie Principle provides frame of reference in understanding the designed activity, task, assignments individuals need to participate in to accomplish goals of activities, which are extrinsically created or co-created with other members of the organization. This principle would help measure the effectiveness of academic activities, managerial tasks, administrative work at university to ensure optimal performances. Finally, the fifth element is HeXie Coupling which refers to the evaluation, management, and intervention of the relationship between the human factors, He Principle, and the non-human factors, Xie Principle, in a system in order to ameliorate the efficiency of performance for the most desired outcome.

In other words, HeXie Education model is based on the notion that successful education should help students and teachers identify meaningful life position, periodic goals for their tasks while providing opportunities for learners' self-directed learning to enhance development of qualities beneficial for life and support for educators to transform and upgrade the educational practices for learning. Along this vein of thinking, HeXie Education model provides a solution to the question of how to balance the pursuit of knowledge with marketable value and knowledge with non-marketable value in that marketable knowledge and nonmarketable knowledge could be both inherited and promoted in formal and informal learning for students to reflect, explore, synthesize, and create based on individual interests. The total effort in one's education throughout lifetime could lead to learning, growth and being human.

HeXie Mindset Model: A Complexity Mindset Model

The society is becoming increasingly complex and uncertain which entails a much complex mindset. Bauman described the feature of our time as liquid modernity (2017) since all social forms melt before new patterns emerge. Nothing comes to stay but only to pass. Even university education become part of the passing in one's life, which turns university into a means for an end which one may never see. Bauman (2017) used the analogy of a hunter and gardener to explain how liquid modernity creates such a mentality of never-ending hunting or desiring for something new. Hunting is a means to reach an end; but in modern society, the end can never and should never be seen; otherwise, the game of hunting will not be feasible. Modern life episodes are fragmented which could lead to collapse of effective, sustainable, long-term thinking, planning, and acting (Bauman, 2017), which in turn affects what skills should be developed throughout one's life in the contemporary time. In addition, with Uncertainty, Ambiguity, Complexity, Changeability (UACC), the previously acquired skills or knowledge may no longer be feasible in the newly emerged situation, which beg four questions: First, what are essential skills that could withstand the test of time. Two, what skills are meaningful for developing new skills effectively to solve problems? Three, how to live with uncertainty? Four, what can university education do?

To answer the aforementioned questions, XJTLU proposed a Complexity Mindset Model, named HeXie Mindset Model (Xi, 2020), which is a mental model as a compass for thinking about the self and the world particularly addressing the needs of the current time.

Figure 7. Complexity Mindset Model: HeXie Mindset

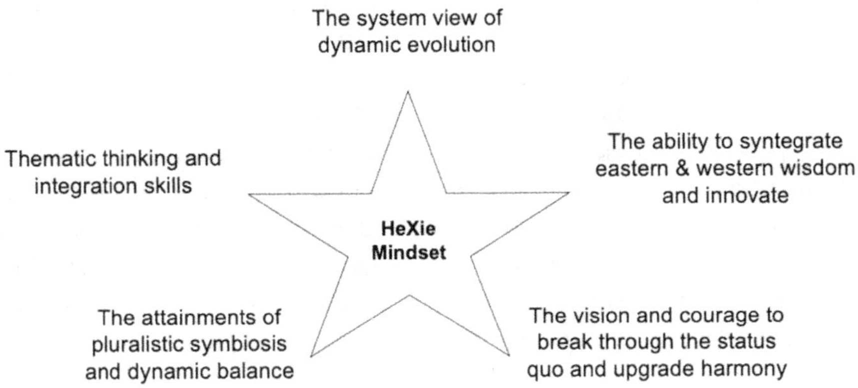

HeXie Mindset Model (Xi, 2020, p. 86) contains five elements:

1. The system view of dynamic evolution: The system view of dynamic evolution entails an ability to perceive phenomenon and situation systematically, dynamically and holistically.
2. The ability to identify themes and integrate resources: This quality helps one avoid distraction and stay focused when the UACC world creates challenges through information overload with distraction, misperception, manipulation, and fragmentation of life episodes or even daily activities.
3. The ability to syntegrate eastern and western wisdom and innovate: The synthesis and integration of both the whole and the part, both the Western and the Eastern approach, both scientific knowledge and human management, both the external environment and internal human factors is vital for understanding the reality and truth in that the syntegration could offer holistic perspectives rather than overreliance on one perspective for understanding.
4. The attainments of pluralistic symbiosis and dynamic balance: Such quality means the ability to determine the appropriate themes of the current stage of development to foster an ecosystem in which a range of diverse elements could be balanced to attain inclusion and coexistence to solve problems in harmonious ways.
5. The vision and courage to break through the status quo and upgrade harmony: The changing environment and context necessitate the evaluation of the status quo and innovation in order to achieve sustainable and evolving growth.

HeXie Mindset development could provide conditions for maturity in that these five core qualities can effectively help one cope with the Uncertainty, Ambiguity, Complexity, Changeability in modern society. Mindset development could also affect students' learning experience. Fischman and Gardener (2022) found that mindset development positively correlates to the value a student can obtain from university education. This could imply that mindset development is equally important to subject learning outcomes.

Research-Led Learning at XJTLU provides opportunities for students to engage with real world issues and develop complexity mindset, or HeXie mindset in the process of researching, solving problems, sharing and communicating the conclusion and reflection of the world. Research-Led Learning aims to enhance students' understanding of the self and world through the tool of research to develop understanding and construct knowledge (Xi and Li, 2021). From epistemology perspective, research is the way to satisfy one's inquiries of the world in that only through research one can have firsthand information or reliable data to confirm one's hypothesis and draw one's conclusion with valid evidence. From ethics perspective, research allows one to experience the complexity of reality; therefore, one could think beyond the limits of logic, the simplistic dichotomy, and could reason in critical and creative ways to obtain truth. At XJTLU, Research-Led Learning emphasizes student-centered or initiated research from observation of phenomenon, design of research questions, methodology, to analysis and conclusion instead of the traditionally teacher-assigned research of which the research for students is to simply follow instructions from teachers to complete a research task. Student-centered research could stimulate curiosity for meticulous contemplation and deep understanding. Research-Led Learning at XJTLU not only emphasize student-directed research with teachers' facilitation but also experience in socializing and relating to others as well as engage in self-transformation in the process of finding one's own truth.

HeXie Management Model

In response to the issues to improve the efficiency of Knowledge Organization raised by Peter Drucker (1985) through changing the current bureaucratic system as well as to developing a new model to adapt to the new era, XJTLU embarked on a journey of HeXie Management Experiment in HeXie Management Theory (Xi, 1987; Xi et al., 2010) application, the management of knowledge worker and organization for efficiency, and the mechanism of symbiosis and eco-management as well as the educational ecology (Li et al. 2022) and its social impact.

Theoretically, there are five pillars to HeXie Management Theory (HXMT): Orientation, HeXie Theme (HT), He Principle (HP), Xie Principle (XP), HeXie Coupling (HC) in Figure 8. Orientation refers to the long-term vision and mission and HeXie Theme refers to the short-term goal or key task or core business, both of which provide senses of direction for an organization's development. He Principle (HP) refers to principles of creating incentives to release the potentials and proactive behavior of the individuals or subunits which would drive productivity and creativity while Xie Principle refers to principles of establishing logic and process which would create orders and help maintain stability and coerce and regulate behaviors for efficiency. He Principle emphasizes Universal Rationality while Xie Principle focuses on Context Rationality. Both HP and XP form the Dual Rationality of HXMT. The strength of HXMT lies in that it provides effective rational design, incentive evolution through driving coupling of HP and XP for dynamic optimization of management practices guided by the orientation in organizations.

Figure 8. HeXie Management Theory (HXMT)

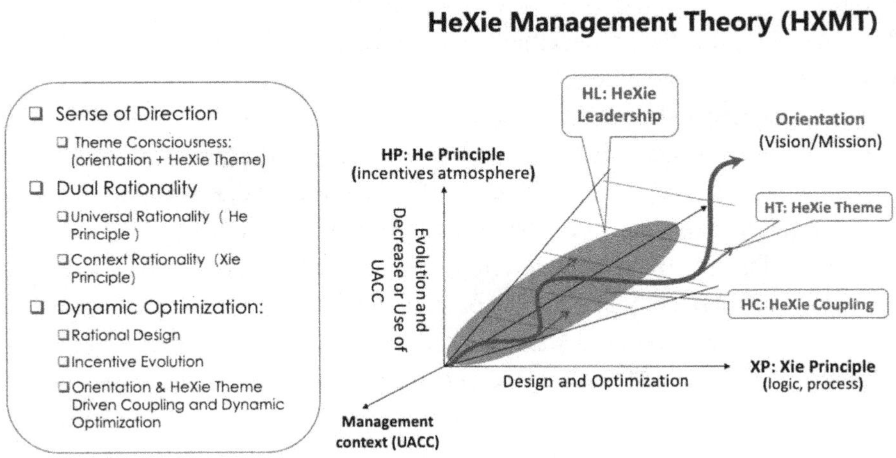

In its management practice, XJTLU management system consists of four segments: finance and administration; academic affairs; student affairs; and information and support system (see Figure 9).

Universities are typical knowledge organizations in which almost all of them are knowledge workers. In order to improve knowledge workers' efficiency, HXMT is applied to manage knowledge organization (Xi, 2022) in the following aspects: application of HXMT; HeXie Leadership experiment; ecosystem management. First, the prevalent bureaucratic organizational system was abandoned; instead, based on HXMT, a flat network organizational system was established (see Figure 9). In such a network system, the connecting agents and their roles as well as the interaction between them are supported for encouraging workers to be proactive and creative while the whole system is supported to collaborate and syntegate holistically under the shared vision and mission.

Figure 9. HXMT Experiment: XJTLU Management System

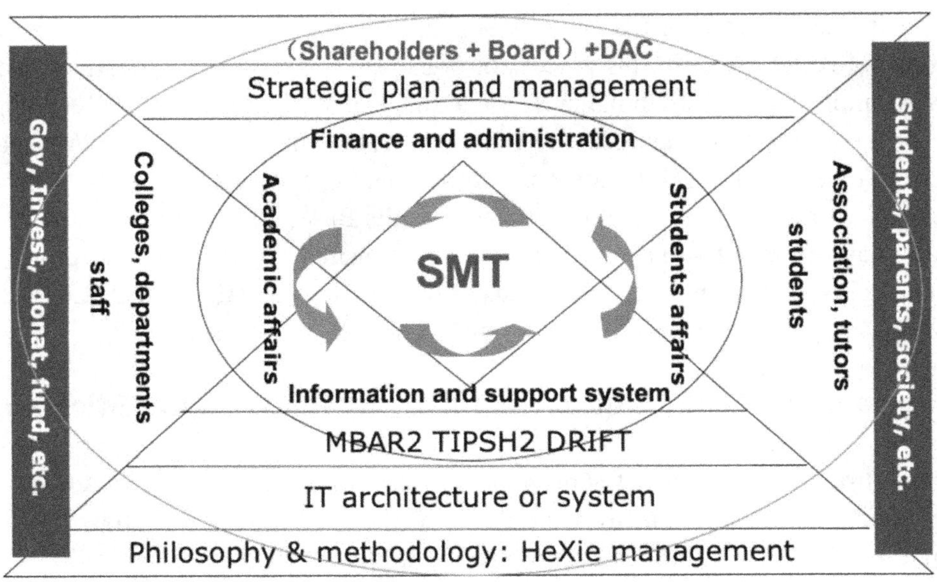

Overall, inefficiency of the bureaucracy and administration in the current universities often creates challenges for the management of universities. In terms of the university management system, Peter Drucker pointed out (1985) that the management challenge left for the 21st century is how to improve the efficiency and abilities to innovate of knowledge organizations and knowledge workers. He emphasized (1999) that knowledge workers should take responsibilities to strive to be creative and contribute to organizations in innovative ways. University is a typical knowledge organization, and its staff and students are typical knowledge workers. Drucker viewed (1999) that knowledge workers should be considered as constructive force in an organization contributing to the operation of their organization instead of a burden or costly sector. Thus, knowledge workers should be supported and to be efficient and innovative in that their efficiency and creativity positively correlate with the well-being and competitiveness of an organization. And knowledge workers' dedication to the organization they are working for is important, hence, incentives should be created to increase dedication and commitment. A management experiment with XJTLU has been conducted to explore how to improve knowledge workers' efficiency, creativity, and commitment. In this experiment, the traditional hierarchical bureaucratic system used by most universities was abandoned and instead, a flat network service platform was established to support teachers and students to carry out academic activities freely and cooperatively. This exploration may be a huge challenge for some managers who are good at the hierarchical structure of Max Weber and the professional management system and culture of Federick Taylor. First, distinctive hierarchical leadership relationships are of major concern. Second, clearly defined job responsibilities are often expected and favored. In addition, most academic managers lack or even disdain to accept necessary management learning or training. Often, work of academic leadership is subject to leaders' individual learning and teaching experience as well personal experience in management work, which is no longer suitable for a rapidly changing world and university with extremely innovative characteristics. An organization with network structure is therefore advocated to establish a hospitable and seamless support platform, emphasizing personal role, initiative and creativity, and flexible cooperation aliened to the organization's vision and mission. To this end, we should break through the traditional behavior patterns and culture, and explore an appropriate way to organically combine the efficiency of the formal organization hierarchy system with the flexibility and creativity of organizations of network structure. Therefore, employee training, organizational learning, and cultural shaping become the key. After years of experimenting efforts, XJTLU has finally preliminarily formed a flat network organization structure (see Figure 9) and an effective operation mode of cooperation. In this process of organizational structure, operation mode, behavior paradigm, and culture shaping, we took the HeXie Management Theory as XJTLU's management philosophy and methodology, and proposed XJTLU's MBAR2, five management techniques, namely MBO (management by objectives), BCO (budget constraints operation), ABC (Activity-Based Cost analysis, Activity-Based Cost role complementation), RBM (Results Based Management), RCS (Routine Case Study). We have also formed five TIPSH2 behavior modes, namely, Teamwork, Innovation, Profession, Sincerity, Hospitality, and Happiness. We have also fostered five core values of XJTLU culture- DrFIT, namely Diversity, Regulation, Freedom, Innovation and Trust.

The Management of Knowledge Worker and Organization for Efficiency

HXMT's application at XJTLU with a flat network structure has many merits. For example, it effectively addresses the productivity issues in many organizations in the information and digital era by encouraging and enabling every individual to act as a leader; hence, all members of the organization would engage

Figure 10. The organically structured knowledge organization

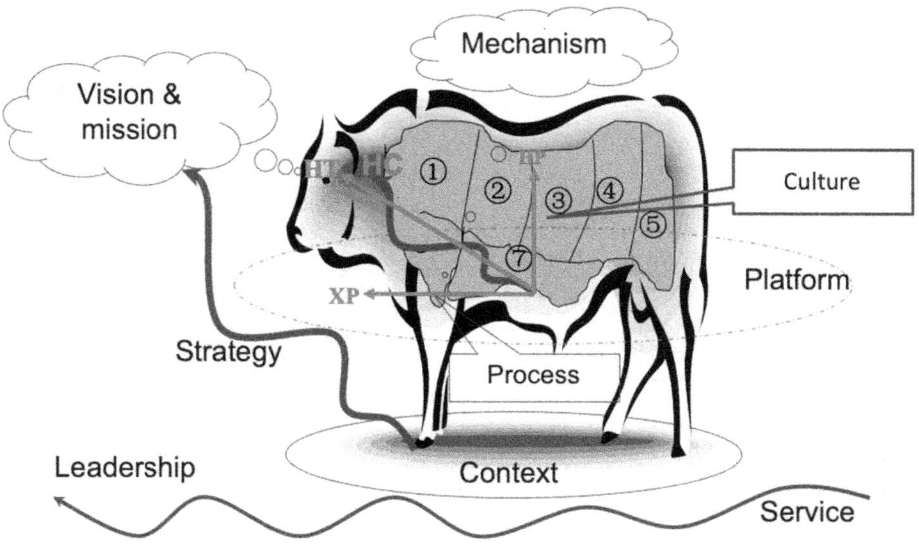

in studying and solve problems in the process of interaction and collaboration. HeXie Leadership aims to enable the agent in each connecting point of the network to manifest leadership potential as well as integrate the discrete information and localized leadership from each agent or connecting point to formulate leadership insights for the whole organization. Hence, the whole organization could work organically and harmoniously with all member's individual short-term goals and themes (HeXie Themes-HT) being aligned with the organization's long term HeXie Vision and Mission. The designed process and logic of the organization (Xie Principle-XP) could be coupled (HeXie Coupling-HC) with the motivation and incentives of its member (He Principle-HP) to form a nature knowledge organization--a three dimensioned ecosystem to manage knowledge organization organically (see Figure 10).

The Mechanism of Symbiosis and Eco-Management

HXMT not only provides effective solution for knowledge organization but also helps the collaboration between universities and the society in the era of digital technology, AI and robotics, and big data. With the development of digital technology, Internet of Things, and AI, management has become more ecologically aligned, see Figure 9. For example, XJTLU has created different themed Learning, Innovation and Entrepreneurship Centers (LIECS) in different locations by collaboration with industries and government to explore lifelong learning and innovation support system.

When management evolves from platform management with autonomy to ecosystem management with intervention and evolution, the management focus from the scientific management era on design should adapt to cater to the evolution of the ecosystem (See Figure 11). Although Big Data and AI technology could improve the predictability of complex systems and local design and optimization, the overall evolution would be more complex and uncertain. Hence, from the perspective of long-term development of the overall system, to design and control various elements in organizations would face unprecedented difficulties and challenges because of the complexity of the fast-changing world and interconnectedness.

Figure 11. The Spectrum of Management

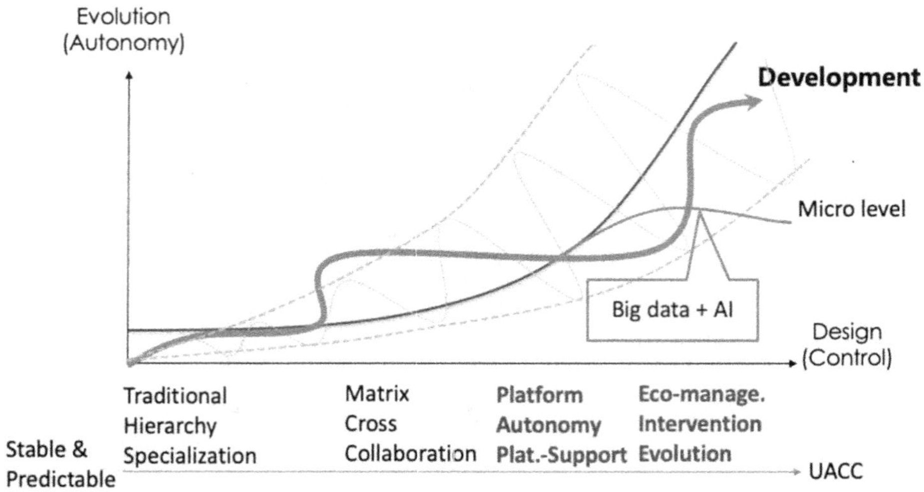

The intervention of the ecosystem relies on more evolution than design. The optimal usage of the two mechanism, evolution and design, would be critical for future management. Therefore, it is necessary to redefine management, leadership, organization, and strategies in the context of ecosystem enhanced by technology.

The Educational Ecology and Its Social Impact

HeXie Management Theory experiment has achieved positive results in creating an educational ecology, an ecosystem. For example, the XJTLU national teaching innovation competition initiated and organized by XJTLU has formed a community of millions of participants online and onsite. Also, the Higher Education Teacher Development Center at XJTLU has created a community for teacher development. Additionally, the K12 Education experiment and international collaboration has established the K12 education transformation and innovation leadership community. XJTLU Learning Mall (LM) is connecting global learners and educational resources to create a future oriented educational ecosystem and community to support personalized, interest-driven, lifelong and technology enhanced learning, innovation and entrepreneurship .

CHALLENGES AND OPPORTUNITIES

Although there are opportunities, it is still very challenging to establish and run international universities. The sudden outbreak of COVID-19 pandemic has brought new challenges to education transformation and international university operation. For example, the disruption of international traveling and domestic traveling led to the enormous challenge in carrying out normal learning and teaching activities. The pressure on moving onsite-teaching to online-teaching imposed challenges required immediate response to teaching and learning innovation by creating digital platforms and resources. The national health and safety regulations and policies halted many international travelling services which brought challenges to international personnel exchange. Additionally, the uncertainty of the global situation has negative impact on the perception and confidence of the stability of international universities. Under such conditions, even the survival of international universities is threatened, thus, the need to innovate, envision, and explore new educational model and management model of future international universities has become increasingly dire.

Student-Centered Research-Led Education: Creativity and Innovation in Knowledge Production

In the old model, students are passively engaged in pre-designed research projects in usually the narrow scope of a scientific discipline. Now, that old education praxis has to be changed for more effective knowledge production. One solution is to promote Student-Centered Research-Led Learning in two approaches: First, the students is the center of their university education, namely, they should have freedom and autonomy to design their personalized education by customizing their education experience. Secondly, students should be the center of the classroom from the pedagogical perspective where they are not taught but rather guided or facilitated. The challenges in Student-Centered Research-Led Learning lie in how ready students are in self-directed learning, how effective the support from the university is, and how feasible innovative pedagogical practices are implemented such as module design, content delivery or instruction, facilitation and feedback (see Figure 12). In addition to challenges students face to develop autonomy and independence, Student-Centered Research-Led Learning could add more challenges to teachers in that teachers would not only provide feedback and guidance in interacting with students in the classroom but also need to provide support beyond students' classroom experience. One solution is the use of digital technology such as The Learning Mall at XJTLU for teachers to continue

Figure 12. Growth Support Network

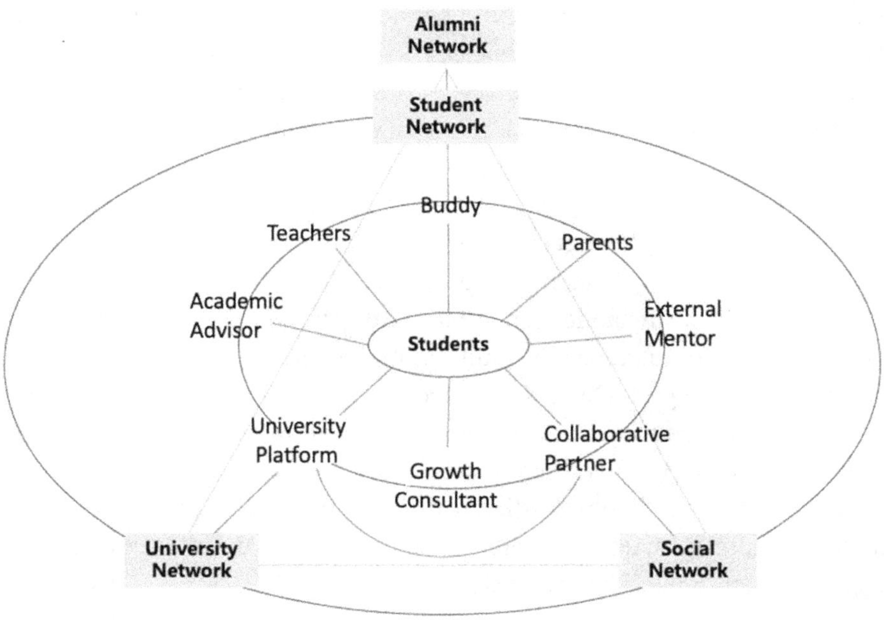

interaction with students in virtual space in both synchronous and asynchronous fashion. The use of digital platforms have such benefits as effective communication of class content in organized online space, easy exchange of files and ideas, more time for meticulous contemplation of topics for students to make meaningful and insightful contribution to discussion, recording of learning process for reviewing, multimedia content for stimulation of creativity, more opportunities and flexibility for diversity to allow students time, room, security to maneuver the content in personalized manner.

Another challenge in student-centered education is how to ensure students have meaningful experience to reflect and conceptualize their experience and creatively communicate their thoughts. The recent COVID-19 disruption has gravitated the negative impact of lack of real-world experience on the development of minds. Challenges and impacts presented by COVID-19 on education began to be manifested in students' growth and creativity. Students' lack of interaction with teachers and peers could have negative impacts in socializing skills, language skills, emotion intelligence, personality development, and creativity and intuition. The lack of human contact would hinder the whole person development of skills to relate to other people, develop compassion, enhance self-awareness, navigate ethics, form individualized mature outlook with critical and creative thinking skills. The human contact is the main approach for students to experience the society and the world directly and the lack of it could mean the intellectual aspects would be increasingly emphasized and the intuitive aspects such as compassion and the totality of human existence would be increasingly deemphasized. One response to the challenges of online teaching is to organically integrate real world experience into online education. For example, using the technology as a tool to instruct and direct students' real-world experience rather than making the learning online as the only experience. Assignments and tasks should reflect emphasis in real world experience and human interaction while the digital technology serve as a tool assisting the real-world experience.

Moreover, in order to effectively address student-centered education when digitalization has accelerated information revolution, a critical question to be asked is what is of true value for the students of the 21st century and how they could develop genuine understanding or knowledge. The traditional education model treats knowledge as static information from past experience to be imposed on students, which in one way neglects the active agency of learners in constructing knowledge and in another way perpetuates the traditional teacher-centered hierarchy in which the teacher tends to impose "adult standards, subject-matter, and methods upon those who are only growing slowly toward maturity. They are beyond the reach of the experience the young learners already possess (Dewey, 1938)." Dewey in his book Experience and Education (1938) continue to argue that this does not mean past information and knowledge does not have any value but rather the way we approach it was problematic. In our technology-infused world, the reality is dynamic and the butterfly effects are being manifested extensively to create an ever-changing world. It is not that the world has changed but rather that the human consciousness has expanding to allow deep understanding of the dynamic reality. The past scripts, narratives, perception and knowledge become inadequate as frame of reference for solutions of the contemporary problems because these are based on the experience of the past which is no longer relevant in many aspects. For example, never in the history of mankind does the planet have to feed over 7 billion people. Never before would we face environmental crisis so urgently. Never before would human beings have access to information and news 24 hours a day. The present time is drastically different in the way we live, travel, work, relate, and entertain. And the way human society is organized, structured, and develops require new type of skills in order for people to adapt to the current society.

In order to respond to such challenges in student-centered experiential experience, XJTLU strategizes its third phase of developments (XJTLU Model 3.0) in fostering student-centered campus culture to enhance a meaningful university experience consisting of cutting-edge campus infrastructure, diverse international culture, scholarly events involving students, internship, entrepreneurial development, university-industry cooperative education.

Research Transformation and the Teaching of Research

Charles M. Vest, then president of MIT, cited in (Crow and Dabars, 2020, p.54), wrote in a 1994 letter that

Our society will ask much more of these students—and they will ask more of themselves— than just to know what others have accomplished. If they are going to help us expand our knowledge and solve our problems, they are going to have to know how to research, to analyze, to synthesize, and to communicate. They must learn how to gather data, to develop hypotheses, to test and refine them, or throw them out when necessary and start over.

Crow and Dabars (2020, p.55) point out that research universities established mainly in the late 19th century in the U.S. "have prioritized the pursuit of the unknown and the isolation and analysis of increasingly specialized knowledge". In addition, the current scientific fields are developed by the experimental or observational model and theorizing model which became the successful model in competition with other different types of models or paradigms (Khun, 1970). Khun (1970) also pointed out that "Closely examined, whether historically or in the contemporary laboratory, that enterprise seems an attempt to force nature into the preformed and relatively inflexible box that the paradigm supplies (p. 24)." The way we have been practicing science is in a way like using a very small net to catch a butterfly of a much bigger size that cannot even be imagined by human beings. Hence, the current pressing issues of society and transformation of university education entail cross-disciplinary research with innovative paradigms. The teaching of research will need to evolve into guiding students in their own discovery for knowledge production while supporting and facilitating the process along the way.

Understanding of the self is crucial and challenging for research because when the observer together with the observed form the totality of the reality, observer's particular spectrum of imagination could limit perception. Thus, observer should expand the perceptual system so as not to compromise the validity of truth or knowledge. It is crucial to examine one's perceptual system consisting beliefs, prejudices, assumptions, stereotypes, bias, fallacies, error in reasoning, superstition, and unawareness. The university education should help students both in understanding the self and the world.

Institutional challenges concerning identity of research university or teaching university or research and teaching university have been under discussion of the future of universities. Universities with specialized disciplines may be more competitive compared to universities of comprehensive research, yet, simultaneously, there are increasing needs for interdisciplinary research due to the needs of the labor market. Van der Zwaan (2017) asserted that digital learning and blended learning especially for customized needs or problem-based learning from students is enhanced and promoted by technology. Hence, universities are challenged to strengthen its collaboration with the society for knowledge and resources sharing as well as collaboration with various institutions for interdisciplinary research for customized needs. The more bond universities create with other institutions, universities, and the society, the more chances for survival and prosperity. Van der Zwaan (2017, p.222) predicted for higher education in 2040 that

In the coming years research IT and big data will be ubiquitous, and this will unquestionably transform the nature of scholarship… this will reinforce the tendency towards more interdisciplinary research... if universities become more open to societal issues, then this will almost automatically mean that research will be driven more by these issues, with the consequence that in almost every case, the degree of multi-disciplinarity or interdisciplinarity will increase.

Furthermore, he also argues (Van der Zwaan, 2017) that the needs of lifelong learning also challenge universities to emphasize interdisciplinary research in collaboration with the society by serving as deep participants in societal processes to show awareness of labor market demand and balance the creation of knowledge and practical use of generated knowledge.

Quality Education

One of the key qualities for Research-Led learning in university education is critical thinking. Critical thinking is the evaluation of the minds in order to achieve clarity and accuracy in our thoughts, rationality in our beliefs, justification for our actions and genuine depth in our understanding of the self and the world to become intellectually mature and mindful beings. Professor Stephen Hawking told BBC (Cellan-Jones, 2014) "The development of full artificial intelligence could spell the end of the human race. It would take off on its own, and re-design itself at an ever-increasing rate. Humans, who are limited by slow biological evolution, couldn't compete, and would be superseded." As humans create machines to mimic human behavior and simulate humans thinking, it also alarms that that these machines could also make humans more and more like robots. Students' thinking has been strengthened in logical ways with efficiency, certainty, clarity, accuracy, which are nevertheless beneficial for practical purposes. Yet, the beauty and meaning of being has been reduced to only logic calculation. It is humiliating for humans to develop only logical thinking to be efficient because humans are reduced to robots. Jill Taylor (2021, p. 220) stated that "technology perhaps has made of an impact on our brain's development than we would have assumed." Taylor (2021, p. 31) listed 4 characters of our brain: Left Brain Thinking to be in order, follow fixed rules, think in language, focus on detail and self; Right Brain Thinking to be in flow, be open to possibilities, think in pictures, focus on bigger picture and we; Left Brain Emotional to be constricted, be fear based, be righteous, be cautious, love conditionally, be selfish; Right Brain Emotional to be expansive, be fearless, be grateful, be adventurous, love unconditionally, be sharing. Taylor (2021) concluded that now "as a society, we have reached a tipping point in the blend of humanity and technology" where computers and the Internet has created a global techno-consciousness shaping and reshaping individuals as they consume the Internet and technology in often inevitably addictive ways due to the nature of technology's impact on the brain.

Taylor's insights into human brain and mind and its relationship with technology perhaps offer a perspective to inquire how quality education should help develop whole persons and avert the effort established decades ago for a left brain dominated society in which we neglected the well-being and happiness as a human person and sacrificed honesty, compassion, kindness, gratitude, love, intuition for temporarily practical and convenient materialistic achievements. The ability to think about significant matters concerning humanities is crucial for university students.

In Figure 13, the Quality Education Diagram provides blue print for reforming educational practices at XJTLU to help develop digital literacy, personality and self-management, critical thinking, as well as complexity mindset, essential for delivering true value of university education to students who should become whole persons.

Figure 13. Quality Education

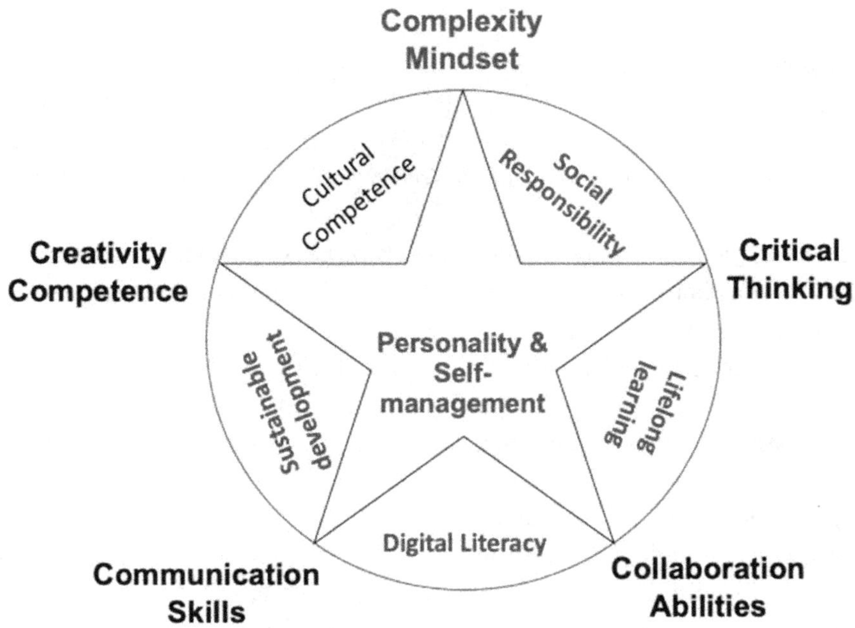

Quality education could also provide solutions to the needs to upskill professionals. The traditional model offers a separate solid 4-year education in which students engage in intensive academic studies with little real-life experience. Also, the fast development of technology also means skills learned in university may be outdated by the time students enter the force of professional career. And re-entering universities for upskilling is not easy after graduation since the traditional model requires rigid time and full. This would compel professionals to look for alternative ways for upskilling. As the societies become more based on knowledge economy, citizens inevitably will engage more in lifelong learning activities. Therefore, the current university educational model should transform the traditional standard stand-along discrete educational services into flexible units of learning activities to support lifelong learning and expand the market share of all different educational services to effectively contribute to creating a learning society for the future generation. The management, enrollment, and accreditation systems will also entail more flexibility.

Envision The Future University

There is an urgent need for pedagogical, institutional and organizational transformation. Establishing international or transnational university could be a brave move toward the endeavor to revolutionize education. In a critical moment in human history with rapid development in technology which already profoundly affected work and life of people in many ways, university should help students live in the world. University faces challenges to ameliorate the curriculum because it often reflects past more than predicts the future; hence, the imposition of the past knowledge rather than help in leading out what is inside of the learners. Universities should reshape curriculum to reflect the contemporary needs of the young in order to enhance diversity, individuality, creativity rather than to impose conformity. John Dewey (1938, p. 19) mentioned that:

The traditional scheme is, in essence, one of imposition from above and from outside. It imposes adult standards, subject-matter, and methods upon those who are only growing slowly toward maturity....But the gulf between the mature or adult products and the experience and abilities of the young is so wide that the very situation forbids much active participation by pupils in the development of what is taught.

Dewey's words imply that universities should also be a place for teachers to be more like learners in that the teachers should constantly engage in researching and finding out what are the needs of the time and how to help learners. The teachers have to transcend their past knowledge and keep tuning for the new trends of the present time and envision the future. To deal with problems from traditional university education, XJTLU focuses on innovation in university management to shape a culture in which teachers and learners are both assets of the organization contributing to the creation of knowledge society.

International university has its historical inevitability in that university since its creation has been driven by exploring knowledge and truth, an enterprise without borders and boundaries. Global communication was long achieved through various learning and teaching activities between different countries organized by medieval universities, which broke through the boundaries of nations and geography and promoted the dissemination and communication of knowledge. However, internationalization of education now is endowed with new meaning in the context of globalization. The internationalization of higher education in modern time often means personnel exchange or communication organized by the governments, relevant to diplomatic policies. Digital technology will decentralize the storage, ownership and access of information which will increase the speed and communication of information. AI and digital technology will outweigh university in the dissemination of information and creation of knowledge. Hence, such challenges should compel educators to help learners cultivate such skills as digital literacy, independent learning, questioning and being skeptical, interpersonal communication, critical and creative thinking, as well as abilities to plan and strategize for the future. Hence, universities should become more integrated into the wider society by supporting learner-centered education to transform learners, educators, universities and the society. One approach for such endeavor will be to establish learning symbiotic ecosystem of network of universities, organizations, and industries to improve productivity of knowledge workers and organizations.

Through XJTLU's education exploration in educational philosophy of student-centered research-led learning; educational model of syntegrative education; governance principle of technology enablement; organization management of coordination; relationship with external environment of symbiosis (Figure 14), some recommendations may be provided.

Firstly, universities must help individuals discover truth and construct knowledge based individualized unique experiences. Student-centered research-led learning could provide long-term sustainable strategies for enhanced learning experience and genuine understanding for shaping great minds. Secondly, university should further enhance its collaboration with partners across the society to lead knowledge creation, contribute to technology development, drive innovation in shaping knowledge society in information revolution by providing education that would go beyond the classroom to the workplace to cultivate leaders and entrepreneurs who could positively impact the world. Thirdly, future university should enhance its governance through technology enablement when digitalization will show profound impact

Figure 14. Framework of Future Exploration of XJTLU

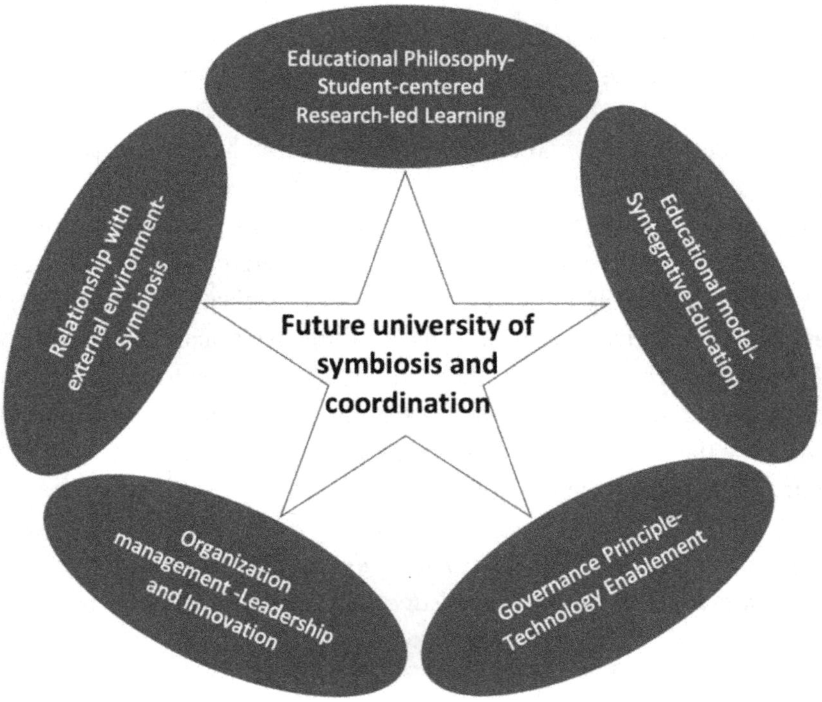

on organizations. Fourthly, leadership is key for elevating efficiency of knowledge workers, incubating innovation, and initiating constructive collaboration to create value and maintain sustainable development of future university. Future university should shift the traditional management to leadership-oriented innovative coordination for improved productivity and enhanced experience of staff and students in order to create incentives and culture for innovation and growth. Finally, future university should extend its collaboration with the society to form symbiosis for technology development, lifelong learning of future citizens, support and solution to problems and challenges facing humanities.

LEADERSHIP FOR FUTURE UNIVERSITY

At the core of the endeavor to create future universities is leadership under which leaders could formulate an effective system to effectively turn the usually disparate internal resources of talents in a university into an integrated energy for innovation while identify and prompt opportunities for collaboration across the whole spectrum of the society to stretch innovation beyond the university to spearhead changes for the society and humanities. In the UACC world, innovation has become the new norm to which universities should align its vision with the change of the society. One prominent feature of 21st century is human society has phased out the industrial revolution era and entered the information revolution era which spawned conflicts between culture residing in the old system and new emerging trends for new systems. Alvin Toffler in his book The Third Wave (1980, p. 18) writes

On one side are the partisans of the industrial past; on the other, growing millions who recognize that the most urgent problems of the world —food, energy, arms control, population, poverty, resources, ecology, climate, the problems of the aged, the breakdown of urban community, the need for productive, rewarding work— can no longer be resolved within the framework of the industrial order.

The information revolution will entail emphasis not on hierarchy and formal authority but network and collaboration to motivate innovation which is often voluntary, because network is more efficient for information sharing and communication which is a precondition for shaping a culture that is prone to incubate innovation and change. John Kotter (2021) demonstrated that 2020 has seen peak in the World Uncertainty Index and unfortunately the internal change of organizations is not keeping pace with the external change and volatility which creates challenges for organizations. He proposed leadership-centric approach to strategy in comparison to the traditionally management-centric approach to methodology to pull the lever to mitigate the gap between the slow pace of change internally to the rapid changes externally.

Universities will be at the forefront of the information revolution because the next society, or the one we are entering into, is the knowledge society. Drucker (2017, p. 208) argued that

Effective knowledge is specialized. That means knowledge workers need access to an organization—a collective that brings together an array of knowledge workers and applies their specialisms to a common end-product.

As university will play a vital role in not only providing platform and network for its knowledge workers but also helping creating knowledge workers contributing to knowledge ecosystem, leadership will become the important catalyst and the glue that connects people, resources, systems, vision, mission in coherent and logical ways to ensure continuity and inspire change. Drucker and Maciariello (2018, p.46) noted that a modern organization must innovate: "Innovation and entrepreneurship are thus needed in society as much as in the economy, in public service institutions as much as in business. The modern organization must be a destabilizer; it must be organized for innovation." Hence, key to future universities leadership is the ability to find the fulcrum to innovate.

CONCLUSION

The discussion of XJTLU's educational and management philosophy could help provide valuable insights into the exploration and transformation of future transnational university. The case analysis of its Model 1.0/2.0/3.0 may offer educators and educational leaders inspiration in their different contexts to reflect on current practices and re-conceptualize education model and management model to transform education to meet the demands of the challenges we are facing in the UACC world. Theories of HeXie Education and Management Model may shed light on exploration of principles, methodologies, practices for educators to understand key issues in transnational university transformation. Like Martin Luther King (1965) said, "The time is always right to do what is right." And the future of university is already here, it is up to us educators to do what is right.

REFERENCES

Bauman, Z. (2016). Education in Liquid Modernity. In A. Darder, P. Mayo, & J. Paraskeva (Eds.), *International critical pedagogy reader* (pp. 109–117). Routledge.

Cellan-Jones, R. (2014) Stephen Hawking warns artificial intelligence could end mankind. *BBC News*. https://www.bbc.com/news/technology-30290540.

Chomsky, N. (1967) The Responsibilities of Intellectuals. *The New York Review of Books*. https:// chomsky.info/ 19670223/ .

Crow, M. M., & Dabars, W. B. (2020). *The fifth wave: The evolution of American higher education*. Johns Hopkins University Press.

Dewey, J. (1938). *Experience and Education*. Macmillan Publishing Co. Inc.

Drucker, P. (1985). *Innovation and entrepreneurship: Practice and principles*. Butterworth Heinemann.

Drucker, P. (1999). *Management challenges in the XXI century*. Transaction Publishers.

Drucker, P. F. (2017). *A Functioning Society: Selections from Sixty-five Years of Writing on Community, Society, and Polity*. Routledge. doi:10.4324/9781315083599

Drucker, P. F., & Maciariello, J. A. (2018). *The daily Drucker: 366 days of insight and motivation for getting the right things done*. Routledge. doi:10.4324/9780080470481

Fischman, W., & Gardner, H. (2022). *The Real World of College: What Higher Education is and What it Can be*. MIT Press. doi:10.7551/mitpress/13652.001.0001

Horn, M. B. (2018) Will half colleges really closed in the next decade? Christian Institute. https://www.christenseninstitute.org/blog/will-half-of-all-colleges-really-close-in-the-next-decade/

Jowett, B. (2000). *The republic*. Dover Publication.

King, M. L. (1947) The Purpose of Education. The Maroon Tiger - Morehouse College student newspaper.

King, M. L. (1965). Remaining Awake Through a Great Revolution. Oberlin College commencement speech]. Oberlin College. https://www2.oberlin.edu/external/EOG/BlackHistoryMonth/MLK/CommAddress.html

Kotter, J. P. (2021). *Change: How Organizations Achieve Hard-to-Imagine Results Despite Uncertain and Volatile Times*. Wiley.

Kuhn, T. S. (1970). *The structure of scientific revolutions* (Vol. 111). University of Chicago Press.

Li, N., Huijser, H., Xi, Y., Limniou, M., Zhang, X., & Kek, M. Y. C. A. (2022). Disrupting the Disruption: A Digital Learning HeXie Ecology Model. *Education in Science*, *12*(2), 63. doi:10.3390/educsci12020063

Moore, J. C. (2019) *A Brief History of Universities*. Palgrave Macmillan.

Musto, R. G. (2022). *The Attack on Higher Education: The Dissolution of the American University*. Cambridge University Press.

Nida-Rümelin, M., & Conaill, O. D. (2021) Qualia: The Knowledge Argument. *The Stanford Encyclopedia of Philosophy*. https://plato.stanford.edu/archives/sum2021/entries/qualia-knowledge/

Nietzsche, F. (2008). *Thus spoke Zarathustra: A book for everyone and nobody*. Oxford University Press.

Orazbayeva, B., & ... . (2020). *The Future of Universities Thoughtbook: Universities During Times of Crisis*. University Industry Innovation Network.

Santos, B. D. S. (2016) 'The University at a Crossroads. In Darder', In A., Mayo, P. and Paraskeva, J. (ed.) International critical pedagogy reader. Routledge. pp. 295-302

Snyder, T. D. (1993). *120 years of American education: A statistical portrait*. US Department of Education, Office of Educational Research and Improvement, National Center for Education Statistics.

Taylor, J. B. (2021). *Whole brain living: The anatomy of choice and the four characters that drive our life*. Hay House, Inc.

Toffler, A. (1980). *The third wave*. William Morrow.

Van der Zwaan, B. (2017). *Higher education in 2040. A global approach*. Amsterdam University Press. doi:10.1515/9789048535163

Xi, Y. (2020). *The rarely known stories of management of XJTLU. could be and do*. Tsinghua University Press.

Xi, Y. (2022). *Be Independent: The road of HeXie Education*. Tsinghua University Press.

Xi, Y. (2022). *What Management could be and do*. Peiking University Press.

Xi, Y., & Li, C. (2021). *Research-Led Learning and Critical Thinking-EAP Practice*. Foreign Language Teaching and Research Press.

Compilation of References

Abayadeera, N., Mihret, D. G., & Dulige, J. H. (2019). Acculturation of non-native English-speaking teachers in accounting: An ethnographic study. *Accounting Research Journal*, *33*(1), 1–15. doi:10.1108/ARJ-01-2017-0005

Academic Ranking of World Universities. (2021). *2021 Academic ranking of world universities.* ARWUhttps://www.shanghairanking.com/rankings/arwu/2021

Academic Ranking of World Universities. (2022). *Academic ranking of world universities: Methodology*. ARWU. https://www.shanghairanking.com/methodology/arwu/2021

Adam, S. (2001). *Transnational education project. Report and recomendations.* Confederation of European Union Rectors' Conferences.

Adams, J., & Song, H. (2009). Key developments and future challenges in Chinese-foreign cooperation in higher education. *Journal of Knowledge-based Innovation in China.*

AECC Global. (2021). Complete Guide: University Grading System in Australia. AECC Global. https://www.aeccglobal.com.au/blog/complete-guide-university-grading-system-in-australia

Affinito, S. (2018). *Literacy coaching : transforming teaching and learning with digital tools and technology.* Heineman, 156.

Agustina, E., & Suharya, T. (2021). Zoom breakout room for students' collaborative skill enhancement in history learning during Covid-19 outbreak. *International Journal of Research in Counseling and Education*, *5*(1), 33–38. doi:10.24036/00430za0002

Ahmad, S. Z., & Buchanan, F. R. (2016). Choices of destination for transnational higher education: "pull" factors in an Asia Pacific market. *Educational Studies*, *42*(2), 163–180. doi:10.1080/03055698.2016.1152171

Ahmad, S. Z., & Buchanan, F. R. (2017). Motivation factors in students' decision to study at international branch campuses in Malaysia. *Studies in Higher Education*, *42*(4), 651–668.

Ahshan, R. (2021). A framework of implementing strategies for active student engagement in remote/online teaching and learning during the COVID-19 pandemic. *Education in Science*, *11*(9), 483. doi:10.3390/educsci11090483

Aiamy, M., & Haghani, F. (2012). The effect of Synectics & brainstorming on 3rd grade students' development of creative thinking on science. *Procedia: Social and Behavioral Sciences*, *47*, 610–613. doi:10.1016/j.sbspro.2012.06.704

AIB. (2017). *Constitution of Australian Institute of Business Pty Ltd.* AIB. https://www.aib.edu.au/wp-content/uploads/2019/03/aib-constitution.pdf

AIB. (2022). *AIB Academic Quality Assurance Framework.* AIB. https://www.aib.edu.au/wp-content/uploads/2019/05/Academic-Quality-Assurance-Framework.pdf

AIB. (n.d.). Why Study With Us. AIB. .https://www.aib.edu.au/study-with-us/why-study-with-us/

Akiba, H. (2008). *The changing face of transnational education in Malaysia: a case study of international offshore university programs.* [Doctoral dissertation, the University of Minnesota, USA].

Akma, S., Seman1, A., Hashim1, M. J., Roslin3, R. M., & Ishar1, M. (2019). *Millennial Learners' Acceptance and Satisfaction of Blended Learning Environment.* Universiti Teknologi MARA.

Alam, F., Alam, Q., Chowdhury, H., & Steiner, T. (2013). Transnational Education: Benefits, Threats and Challenges. *Procedia Engineering, 56*, 870–874. doi:10.1016/j.proeng.2013.03.209

Alamri, H., Lowell, V., Watson, W., & Watson, S. L. (2020). Using personalized learning as an instructional approach to motivate learners in online higher education: Learner self-determination and intrinsic motivation. *Journal of Research on Technology in Education, 52*(3), 322–352. doi:10.1080/15391523.2020.1728449

Al-Bayed, M. H., & Abu-Naser, S. S. (2018). Intelligent multi-language plagiarism detection system. *International Journal of Academic Information Systems Research, 2*(3), 19–34. http://dstore.alazhar.edu.ps/xmlui/handle/123456789/125

Aldridge, J. M., & Fraser, B. J. (2016). Teachers' views of their school climate and its relationship with teacher self-efficacy and job satisfaction. *Learning Environments Research, 19*(2), 291–307. doi:10.100710984-015-9198-x

Alexander, O., Argent, S., & Spencer, J. (2008). *EAP essentials: A teacher's guide to principles and practice.* Garnet Education.

Alexander, S. (2010). Flexible Learning in Higher Education. In P. Peterson, E. Baker, & B. McGaws (Eds.), *International Encyclopedia of Education* (3rd ed., pp. 441–447). Elsevier. doi:10.1016/B978-0-08-044894-7.00868-X

Alhaisoni, E., & Alhaysony, M. (2017). An investigation of Saudi EFL university students' attitudes towards the use of Google Translate. *International Journal of English Language Education, 5*(1), 72–82. doi:10.5296/ijele.v5i1.10696

Ali, M. (2020). Curriculum reconstruction for education and training of electrical engineering for construction employment in Indonesia. *Journal of Physics: Conference Series, 1625*(1), 012067. doi:10.1088/1742-6596/1625/1/012067

Allan, J., & Omarova, T. (2020). Disability and inclusion in Kazakhstan. *Disability & Society*, 1–18. https://www.tandfonline.com/doi/full/10.1080/09687599.2020.1867073?scroll=top&needAccess=true

Allen, J. (2003). Post-editing. In H. Somers (Ed.), *Computers and translation: A translator's guide* (pp. 297–318). John Benjamins Publishing. doi:10.1075/btl.35.19all

Almagro, A. E., & Vallejo, M. C. M. (2002). A case study of collaboration among the ESP practitioner, the content teacher, and the students. *Revista Alicantina de Estudios Ingleses, 15*(15), 7–21. doi:10.14198/raei.2002.15.01

Al-Quaderi, G. G., & Al Mahmud, A. (2010). English literature at English-medium schools of Bangladesh: The question of culture. *Pedagogy, Culture & Society, 18*(2), 211–226. doi:10.1080/14681366.2010.488046

Al-Samarraie, H., & Hurmuzan, S. (2018). A review of brainstorming techniques in higher education. *Thinking Skills and Creativity, 27*, 78–91. doi:10.1016/j.tsc.2017.12.002

Altbach, P. G. (2007). Globalization and the University: Realities in an unequal world. In J. J. F. Forest & P. G. Altbach (Eds.), *International handbook of higher education* (pp. 121–139). Springer.

Altbach, P. G. (2013). Is there a future for branch campuses? In *The international imperative in higher education* (pp. 101–106). SensePublishers. doi:10.1007/978-94-6209-338-6_22

Altbach, P. G., & Knight, J. (2007). The Internationalization of Higher Education: Motivations and Realities. *Journal of Studies in International Education*, *11*(3–4), 290–305. doi:10.1177/1028315307303542

Altbach, P. G., Reisberg, L., & Rumbley, L. E. (2010). Tracking a global academic revolution. *Change: The Magazine of Higher Learning*, *42*(2), 30–39. doi:10.1080/00091381003590845

Anderson, L. W., & Krathwohl, D. (2001). *A Taxonomy for Learning, Teaching and Assessing: a Revision of Bloom's Taxonomy of Educational Objectives*. Longman.

Anderson, T. (Ed.). (2008). *The theory and practice of online learning*. Athabasca University Press.

Andrade, M. S. (2009). The effects of English language proficiency on adjustment to university life. *International Multilingual Research Journal*, *3*(1), 16–34. doi:10.1080/19313150802668249

Annells, M. (2006). Triangulation of qualitative approaches: Hermeneutical phenomenology and grounded theory. *Journal of Advanced Nursing*, *56*(1), 55–61. doi:10.1111/j.1365-2648.2006.03979.x PMID:16972918

Appana, S. (2008). A Review of Benefits and Limitations of Online Learning in the Context of the Student, the Instructor and the Tenured Faculty. *International Journal on E-Learning*, *7*(1), 5–22.

Arachi, D. (2006). Foreign Branch Campuses in Malaysia: State Action and Consumer Choices Revisited, [Master's Thesis, Lund University, Sweden]. https://lup.lub.lu.se/luur/download?func=downloadFile&recordOId=1326386&fileOId=1326387

Arasaratnam-Smith, L. A. (2017). Intercultural competence: An overview. *Intercultural competence in higher education*, 7-18.

Archambault, L., Kennedy, K., Shelton, C., Dalal, M., McAllister, L., & Huyett, S. (2016a). Incremental progress: Re-examining field experiences in K-12 online learning contexts in the United States. *Journal of Online Learning Research*, *2*(3).

Archambault, L., Kennedy, K., Shelton, C., Dalal, M., McAllister, L., & Huyett, S. (2016b). Incremental Progress:Re-examining Field Experiences in K-12 Online Learning.... *Journal of Online Learning Research*, *2*(3), 303–326.

Ardichvili, A., & Kuchinke, P. K. (2010). Leadership styles and cultural values among managers and subordinates: A comparative study of four countries of the former Soviet Union, Germany, and the US. *Human Resource Development International*, *5*(1), 99–117. doi:10.1080/13678860110046225

ARG. (2002) *Assessment for Learning: 10 Principles*. ARG. www.hkeaa.edu.hk/DocLibrary/SBA/HKDSE/Eng_DVD/doc/Afl_principles.pdf

ARG. (2009). *Changing assessment practice: Process, principles and standards*. ARG. http:// www.assessment-reform-group.org/ARIA%20English.pdf

Argument-Centered Education. (n.d.). *Home*. Argument Centered Education. https://argumentcenterededucation.com

Ari, L. L., & Mula, W. (2017). "Us and them": Towards intercultural competence among Jewish and Arab graduate students at Israeli colleges of education. *Higher Education*, *74*(6), 979–996. doi:10.100710734-016-0088-7

Aristotle, Roberts, W. R., Bywater, I., & Solmsen, F. (1954). *Rhetoric*. Modern Library.

Aristovnik, A., Keržič, D., Ravšelj, D., Tomaževič, N., & Umek, L. (2020). Impacts of the Covid-19 pandemic on life of higher education students: A global perspective. *Sustainability*, *12*(20), 8438. doi:10.3390u12208438

Arnold, D. (2003). Why translation is difficult for computers. In H. Somers (Ed.), *Computers and translation: A translator's guide* (pp. 119–142). John Benjamins Publishing Company. doi:10.1075/btl.35.11arn

Arno-Macia, E., & Mancho-Bares, G. (2014). The role of content and language in content and language integrated learning (CLIL) at university: Challenges and implications for ESP. *English for Specific Purposes, 37*, 63–73. doi:10.1016/j.esp.2014.06.007

Arunasalam, N. D., & Burton, R. (2018). Investigating Malaysian Nurses' perspectives of intercultural teaching in transnational higher education learning environments. *Nurse Education Today, 69*, 165–171. doi:10.1016/j.nedt.2018.07.011 PMID:30092544

Ary, D., Jacobs, L. C., Sorensen, C. K., & Walker, D. (2013). *Introduction to research in education*. Cengage Learning.

Ashworth, F, Brennan, G, Egan, K, Hamilton, R & Sáenz, O, 2004. Learning theories and higher education. *Level 3, 2*(1), p.4.

Asian Institution of Technology. (2022). *About AIT*. Asian Institution of Technology (AIT). https://ait.ac.th/about/

Aslan, A., & Açıkgöz, Ö. (2022). Bibliometric Analysis of the Turkish Doctoral Dissertations: A Case Study of Economy, Law, Psychology, Political Science, and International Relations Disciplines. *Yükseköğretim Dergisi, 12*(2), 363–372. doi:10.2399/yod.21.820951

Aslan, A., Açıkgöz, Ö., & Günay, A. (2021). Scientific impact of the Turkish educational dissertations. *Turkish Journal of Education, 10*(3), 237–250. doi:10.19128/turje.850728

Atmaca, Ç. (2016). Contrasting perceptions of students and teachers: Written corrective feedback. *Journal of Language and Linguistic Studies, 12*(2), 166–182. https://files.eric.ed.gov/fulltext/EJ1117969.pdf

Auster, E., & Wylie, K. (2006). Creating active learning in the classroom: A systematic approach. *Journal of Management Education, USA, 30*(2), 333–353. doi:10.1177/1052562905283346

Austin, V. L. (2001). Teachers' beliefs about co-teaching. *Remedial and Special Education, 22*(4), 245–255. doi:10.1177/074193250102200408

Aziz, M. I. A., & Abdullah, D. (2014). Malaysia: Becoming an education hub to serve national development. In *International education hubs* (pp. 101–119). Springer. doi:10.1007/978-94-007-7025-6_7

Baars, S., Parameshwaran, M., Menzies, L. & Chiong, C. (2016). *Firing on all cylinders: What makes an effective middle leader?* London: Teaching Leaders and LKMCo.

Baas, M., Nevicka, B., & ten Velden, F. S. (2020). When paying attention pays off: The mindfulness skill act with awareness promotes creative idea generation in groups. *European Journal of Work and Organizational Psychology, 29*(4), 619–632. doi:10.1080/1359432X.2020.1727889

Babadjanova, N. (2020). *Effective classroom management techniques for curriculum of 21st century*. Science and Education. https://openscience.uz/index.php/sciedu/article/view/518

Bachman, L., & Palmer, A. (2010). Language Assessment in Practice. Oxford: Oxford University Press.

Bachman, L. (2004). Linking observations to interpretations and uses in TESOL research. *TESOL Quarterly, 38*(4), 723–728. doi:10.2307/3588290

Baeten, M., & Simons, M. (2014). Student teachers' team teaching: Models, effects, and conditions for implementation. *Teaching and Teacher Education, 41*, 92–110. doi:10.1016/j.tate.2014.03.010

Baguley, N. (2014). Team Training. *English Teaching Professional*, *91*, 58–59.

Bahna, M. (2018). Study choices and returns of international students: On the role of cultural and economic capital of the family. *Population Space and Place*, *24*(2), e2082. doi:10.1002/psp.2082

Bahrani, T., & Soltani, R. (2012). How to teach speaking skill. *Journal of Education and Practice*, *3*(2), 25–29.

Bailey, K. M., & Nunan, D. (2005). Practical English Language Teaching: Speaking. *Scientific Research.*

Bailey, W. (2021). Parental influence and HE decision making: The continuing power of local culture. *Journal of Further and Higher Education*, *45*(2), 149–161. doi:10.1080/0309877X.2020.1744540

Bain, K. (2004). *What the best college teachers do?* Harvard University Press.

Baker, D., & LeTendre, G. K. (2005). *National differences, global similarities: World culture and the future of schooling*. Stanford University Press. doi:10.1515/9781503624870

Baloğlu, M., & Bilgiç, Ş. (2021). *Türkiye'de akademisyenlerin WoS yayın performansları.* Nobel Yayıncılık.

Baltar, F., & Brunet, I. (2012). Social research 2.0: Virtual snowball sampling method using Facebook. *Internet Research*, *22*(1), 57–74. doi:10.1108/10662241211199960

Banks, M., Olsen, A., & Pearce, D. (2007). *Global student mobility: An Australian perspective five years on.* IDP Education Pty Ltd.

Banna, J., Lin, M. F. G., Stewart, M., & Fialkowski, M. K. (2015). Interaction matters: Strategies to promote engaged learning in an online introductory nutrition course. *Journal of online learning and teaching/MERLOT, 11*(2), 249.

Bannier, B. (2016). Global trends in transnational education. *International Journal of Information and Education Technology (IJIET)*, *6*(1), 80–84. doi:10.7763/IJIET.2016.V6.663

Baran, E., Correia, A. P., & Thompson, A. (2011). Transforming online teaching practice: Critical analysis of the literature on the roles and competencies of online teachers. In Distance Education, 32(3). doi:10.1080/01587919.2011.610293

Barnes, F., Cole, S., & Nix, I. (2018). Supporting and enabling scholarship: Developing and sharing expertise in online learning and teaching. *Journal of Perspectives in Applied Academic Practice*, *6*(1), 66–74. doi:10.14297/jpaap.v6i1.323

Barnett, R. (2000). *University Knowledge in an Age of Supercomplexity; Higher Education N. 40.* Kluwer Academic Publishers.

Barrett, M. (2018). How schools can promote the intercultural competence of young people. *European Psychologist*, *23*(1), 93–104. doi:10.1027/1016-9040/a000308

Barrett, M. D., Huber, J., & Reynolds, C. (2014). *Developing intercultural competence through education.* Council of Europe Publishing.

Barrón-Cedeño, A., Gupta, P., & Rosso, P. (2013). Methods for cross-language plagiarism detection. *Knowledge-Based Systems*, *50*, 211–217. doi:10.1016/j.knosys.2013.06.018

Baruah, J., & Paulus, P. B. (2008). Effects of training on idea generation in groups. *Small Group Research*, *39*(5), 523–541. doi:10.1177/1046496408320049

Basadur, M., & Thompson, R. (1986). Usefulness of the ideation principle of extended effort in real world professional and managerial creative problem solving. *The Journal of Creative Behavior*, *20*(1), 23–34. doi:10.1002/j.2162-6057.1986.tb00414.x

Bassot, B. (2016). *The Reflective Journal* (2nd ed.). Palgrave.

Bauman, Z. (1998b). On glocalization: Or globalization for some, localization for some others. *Thesis Eleven, 54*(1), 37–49.

Bauman, Z. (1998a). *Globalization: The human consequences*. Columbia University Press.

Bauman, Z. (1999). The self in a consumer society. *The Hedgehog Review, 1*(1), 35–40.

Bauman, Z. (2003). Educational challenges of the liquid-modern era. *Diogenes, 50*(197), 15–26. doi:10.1177/039219210305000103

Bauman, Z. (2005). Work, consumerism and the new poor. In T. May (Ed.), *Issues in society*. Open University Press.

Bauman, Z. (2009). *Does ethics have a chance in a world of consumers?* Harvard University Press.

Bauman, Z. (2013a). Liquid modernity. In *Polity*. Polity.

Bauman, Z. (2013b). *Postmodernity and its discontents*. New York University Press.

Bauman, Z. (2014). *Wasted lives: Modernity and its outcasts*. John Wiley & Sons.

Bauman, Z. (2016). Education in Liquid Modernity. In A. Darder, P. Mayo, & J. Paraskeva (Eds.), *International critical pedagogy reader* (pp. 109–117). Routledge.

Bauman, Z., & Donskis, L. (2013). Moral blindness: The loss of sensitivity in liquid modernity. *Polity.*

Bax, S. (1997). What are we training trainers to do? Evaluating teacher education sessions within a context-sensitive framework. In I. McGrath (Ed.), *Learning to Train: Perspectives on the Development of Language* (pp. 153–161). Prentice Hall Europe.

Baxter Magolda, M. (2008, July/August). Three Elements of Self-Authorship. *Journal of College Student Development, 49*(4), 269–284. doi:10.1353/csd.0.0016

Beaven, B. (2004a). *How eight English language teacher trainers made the transition from teaching to training* [Ed D Thesis, Exeter University, United Kingdom].

Beaven, B. (2004b). From teacher to teacher trainer. *English Teaching Professional, 33*, 47–49.

Becher, T., & Trowler, P. (2001). *Academic tribes and territories: Intellectual enquiry and the culture of disciplines* (2nd ed.). SHRE & Open University Press.

Bedenlier, S., Bond, M., Buntins, K., Zawacki-Richter, O., & Kerres, M. (2020). Facilitating student engagement through educational technology in higher education: A systematic review in the field of arts and humanities. *Australasian Journal of Educational Technology, 36*(4), 126–150. doi:10.14742/ajet.5477

Beerkens, E., & Derwende, M. (2007). The paradox in international cooperation: Institutionally embedded universities in a global environment. *Higher Education, 53*(1), 61–79. doi:10.100710734-007-9061-9

Bell, E., Harley, B., & Bryman, A. (2022). *Business research methods*. Oxford university press.

Bendrups, D., Candelaria, A. L. K., & Hogan, T. (2021). Collaborative transnational doctoral education: Insights from a Philippines-Australia partnership. *Innovations in Education and Teaching International, 58*(6), 682–692. doi:10.1080/14703297.2021.1991833

Bengsten, S. E. (2017). Supercomplexity and the university: Ronald Barnett and the social philosophy of Higher Education. *Higher Education Quarterly, 72*, 65–74.

Bennell, P., & Pearce, T. (2003). The internationalisation of higher education: Exporting education to developing and transitional economies. *International Journal of Educational Development*, *23*(2), 215–232. doi:10.1016/S0738-0593(02)00024-X

Bennett, P., Bergan, S., Cassar, D., Hamilton, M., Soinila, M., Sursock, A., . . . Williams, P. (2010). *Quality Assurance in Transnational Higher Education. ENQA Workshop Report 11.* ENQA (European Association for Quality Assurance in Higher Education). Unioninkatu.

Bennett, R. E. (2010). 'Cognitively based assessment of, for, and as learning: A preliminary theory of action for summative and formative assessment'. *Measurement: Interdisciplinary Research and Perspectives*, *8*(3), 70–91. doi:10.1080/15366367.2010.508686

Bennett, R. E. (2011). Formative assessment: A critical review. *Assessment in Education: Principles, Policy & Practice*, *18*(1), 5–25. doi:10.1080/0969594X.2010.513678

Benson, S., & Ward, C. (2013). Teaching with technology: Using TPACK to understand teaching expertise in online higher education. *Journal of Educational Computing Research*, *48*(2), 153–172. doi:10.2190/EC.48.2.c

Bergdahl, N., & Jalal Nouri, D. (2020). *Covid-19 och omställning till distansundervisning i svensk skola Abstrakt.*

Bergdahl, N. (2022). Adaptive Professional Development during the Pandemic. *Designs for Learning*, *14*(1), 1–13. doi:10.16993/dfl.172

Bertram Gallant, T. (2008). *Academic integrity in the Twenty-First Century: A teaching and learning imperative*. Jossey-Bass.

Bhandari, R., & Blumenthal, P. (2011). *International students and global mobility in higher education: National trends and new directions*. Palgrave Macmillan. doi:10.1057/9780230117143

Bhuian, S. N. (2016). 'Sustainability of Western branch campuses in the Gulf Region: Students' perspectives of service quality'. *International Journal of Educational Development*, *49*, 314–323. doi:10.1016/j.ijedudev.2016.05.001

Biggs, J. (1987). *Learning process questionnaire manual: student approaches to learning and studying*. Australian Council for Educational Research.

Biggs, J. (1999). *Teaching for Quality Learning at University Buckingham.* The Society for Research in Higher Education and Open University Press.

Biggs, J., & Tang, C. (2011). *Teaching for Quality Learning at University*. McGraw-Hill Education.

Bista, K., Allen, R. M., & Chan, R. Y. (2021). Impacts of COVID-19 on International Students and the Future of Student Mobility. In *Impacts of COVID-19 on International Students and the Future of Student Mobility*. Routledge., doi:10.4324/9781003138402

Black, P. (2015). Formative assessment – An optimistic but incomplete vision. *Assessment in Education: Principles, Policy & Practice*, *22*(1), 161–177. doi:10.1080/0969594X.2014.999643

Black, P., & Wiliam, D. (2005). Lessons from around the world: How policies, politics and cultures constrain and afford assessment practices. *Curriculum Journal*, *16*(2), 249–261. doi:10.1080/09585170500136218

Blondy, L. C. (2007). Evaluation and application of andragogical assumptions to the adult online learning environment. *Journal of Interactive Online Learning*, *6*(2), 116–130.

Bloom, B. (1969) 'Some theoretical issues relating to educational evaluation', In Tyler, R.W. (ed.), Educational evaluation: new roles, new means: the 63rd yearbook of the National Society for the Study of Education (part II), 69(2), pp. 26-50. doi:10.1177/016146816907001003

Bloom, B. S. (1984). The search for methods of instruction as effective as one-to-one tutoring. *Educational Leadership*, *41*(8), 4–17.

Blumenfeld, P., Kempler, T., & Krajcik, J. (2005). Motivation and Cognitive Engagement in Learning Environments. In R. Sawyer (Ed.), *The Cambridge Handbook of the Learning Sciences (Cambridge Handbooks in Psychology* (pp. 475–488). Cambridge University Press. doi:10.1017/CBO9780511816833.029

Blythe, H., & Sweet, C. (2004). Total Team Teaching - Sharing Teaching Duties Equally. *The Teaching Professor*, *18*(3), 4–5.

Bodycott, P. (2009). Choosing a higher education study abroad destination: What mainland Chinese parents and students rate as important. *Journal of Research in International Education*, *8*(3), 349–373. doi:10.1177/1475240909345818

Bodycott, P., & Walker, A. (2000). Teaching abroad: Lessons learned about inter-cultural understanding for teachers in higher education. [Code of Good Practice in the Provision of Transnational Education. UNESCO-CEPES Bucharest.]. *Teaching in Higher Education*, *5*(1), 79–94. https://www.tandfonline.com/doi/pdf/10.1080/135625100114975?needAccess=true Council of Europe/UNESCO. doi:10.1080/135625100114975

Bolton, D., & Nie, R. U. I. (2010). Creating value in transnational higher education: The role of stakeholder management. *Academy of Management Learning & Education*, *9*(4), 701–714.

Bond, M., Bergdahl, N., Mendizabal-Espinosa, R., Kneale, D., Hull, P., & Ramadani, F. (2021). *Global emergency remote education in secondary schools during the COVID-19 pandemic: a systematic review.* IIEP-UNESCO Education 4 Resilience. https://education4resilience.iiep.unesco.org/index.php/resources/2021/global-emergency-remote-education-secondary-schools-during-covid-19-pandemic

Borup, J., Graham, C. R., West, R. E., Archambault, L., & Spring, K. J. (2020). Academic Communities of Engagement: An expansive lens for examining support structures in blended and online learning. *Educational Technology Research and Development*, *68*(2), 807–832. Advance online publication. doi:10.100711423-020-09744-x

Boschman, F., Mckenney, S., & Voogt, J. (2014). Understanding decision making in teachers' curriculum design approaches. *Technology Research and Development*, *62*(4), 393–416. doi:10.100711423-014-9341-x

Bowers, D. G., & Seashore, S. E. (1966). Predicting organizational effectiveness with a four theory of leadership. *Administrative Science Quarterly*, *2*(2), 236–263. doi:10.2307/2391247

Bowker, L. (2020). Machine translation literacy instruction for international business students and business English instructors. *Journal of Business & Finance Librarianship*, *25*(1–2), 25–43. doi:10.1080/08963568.2020.1794739

Briggs, N. (2018). Neural machine translation tools in the language learning classroom: Students' use, perceptions, and analyses. *The JALT CALL Journal*, *14*(1), 2–24. doi:10.29140/jaltcall.v14n1.221

Briguglio, C. (2000) 'Language and cultural issues for English-as-a-second/foreign language students in transnational educational settings', *Higher education in Europe. Enseignement supérieur en Europe. Vysshee obrazovanie v Evrope*, *25*(3), pp. 425–434.

Brinkmann, S. (2013). *Qualitative interviewing*. Oxford University Press. doi:10.1093/acprof:osobl/9780199861392.001.0001

Britt, M., Goon, D., & Timmerman, M. (2015). How to better engage online students with online strategies. *College Student Journal*, *49*(3), 399–404.

Brookfield, S. D. (1995). Becoming a Critically Reflective Teacher. San Francisco: Jossey-Bass.

Brooks, R., & Abrahams, J. (2018). Higher education students as consumers? Evidence from England. In N. Ingram & A. Tarabini (Eds.), *Educational choices, aspirations and transitions in Europe : systemic, institutional and subjective challenges*. Routledge. doi:10.4324/9781315102368-11

Brooks, R., & Waters, J. (2010). Social networks and educational mobility: The experiences of UK students. *Globalisation, Societies and Education*, *8*(1), 143–157. doi:10.1080/14767720903574132

Brooks, R., & Waters, J. (2011). *Student mobilities, migration and the internationalization of higher education*. Palgrave Macmillan. doi:10.1057/9780230305588

Brooks, R., & Waters, J. (2015). The hidden internationalism of elite English schools. *Sociology*, *49*(2), 212–228. doi:10.1177/0038038514525517

Brooman, S. (2011). Enhancing Learner Engagement by Building upon the 'Tectonic Plates' of Legal Education. *The Liverpool Law Review*, *32*(2), 109–112. doi:10.100710991-011-9097-x

Brown, J. D. (2000). What issues affect Likert-scale questionnaire formats. *Shiken: JALT Testing & Evaluation SIG Newsletter, 4*(1).

Brown, A. V. (2009). Students' and teachers' perceptions of effective foreign language teaching: A comparison of ideals. *Modern Language Journal*, *93*(1), 46–60. doi:10.1111/j.1540-4781.2009.00827.x

Brown, H. (2017). Cooperation and collaboration in undergraduate EMI: Adapting EAP to the emergence of blended academic norms and practices in a Japanese University. In J. Valcke & R. Wilkinson (Eds.), *Integrating content and language in Higher Education: Perspectives on professional practice* (pp. 151–167). Peter Lang GmbH.

Brown, S., Rust, C., & Gibbs, G. (1994). *Strategies for diversifying assessment in higher education*. The Oxford Centre for Staff Development, Oxonion Rewley Press.

Bryant, B. (2005). Electronic discussion sections: a useful tool in teaching large university classes. Teaching of Psychology, 32(4), pp. 271-275.

Bryant, L. H., Niewolny, K., Clark, S., & Watson, C. E. (2014). Complicated spaces: Negotiating collaborative teaching and interdisciplinarity in higher education. *The Journal of Effective Teaching*, *14*(2), 83–101.

Bryman, A. (2008). Effective leadership in higher education: A literature review. *Studies in Higher Education*, *32*(6), 693–710. doi:10.1080/03075070701685114

Buckley, F. J. (2000). *Team Teaching: What, Why, and How?* SAGE Publications. Inc. doi:10.4135/9781452220697

Bullock, C., & Ory, J. (2000). Evaluating instructional technology implementation in a higher education environment. *American Journal of Evaluation, Illinois, USA*, *21*(3), 315–328. doi:10.1177/109821400002100303

Burns, A. (2019). Concepts for teaching speaking in the English language classroom. *LEARN Journal: Language Education and Acquisition Research Network*, *12*(1), 1–11.

Bush, T., & Glover, D. (2014). School leadership models: What do we know? *School Leadership & Management*, *34*(5), 1–19. doi:10.1080/13632434.2014.928680

Byrne, E. K., & Thatchenkery, T. (2019). Cultivating creative workplaces through mindfulness. *Journal of Organizational Change Management*, *32*(1), 15–31. doi:10.1108/JOCM-10-2017-0387

Cagle, L. E., & Tillery, D. (2015). Climate change research across disciplines: The value and uses of multidisciplinary research reviews for technical communication. *Technical Communication Quarterly*, *24*(2), 147–163. doi:10.1080/10572252.2015.1001296

Cai, L., & Hall, C. (2016). Motivations, expectations and experiences of expatriate academic staff on an international branch campus in China. *Journal of Studies in International Education*, *20*(3), 207–222. doi:10.1177/1028315315623055

Caillods, F., & Varghese, N. V. (2011). Preface. In J. B. G. Tilak, *Trade in higher education: The role of the General Agreement on Trade in Services (GATS)—UNESCO Digital Library* (pp. 9-10). UNESCO: International Institute for Educational Planning. https://www.iiep.unesco.org/en/trade-higher-education-role-general-agreement-trade-services-gats-9582

Cambridge Assessment International Education. (2017). *Educational leadership*. Cambridge. https://www.cambridgeinternational.org/images/271192-educational-leadership.pdf

Cambridge Assessment. (2019). *Cambridge school leader standards*. Cambridge. https://www.cambridgeinternational.org/teacher-and-leader-standards

Canals, L., Burkle, M., & Nørgård, R. T. (2018). Universities of the future: Several perspectives on the future of higher education. *International Journal of Educational Technology in Higher Education*, *15*(46).

Cansoy, R. (2018). The relationship between school principles' leadership behaviours and teachers' job satisfaction: *A systematic review. International Education Studies*, *12*(1), 37–52. doi:10.5539/ies.v12n1p37

Cao, C., & Meng, Q. (2020). Effects of online and direct contact on Chinese international students' social capital in intercultural networks: Testing moderation of direct contact and mediation of global competence. *Higher Education*, *80*(4), 1–19. doi:10.100710734-020-00501-w

Cao, C., Zhu, C., & Meng, Q. (2016). A Survey of the Influencing Factors for International Academic Mobility of Chinese University Students. *Higher Education Quarterly*, *70*(2), 200–220. doi:10.1111/hequ.12084

Carless, D. (2006). Differing perceptions in the feedback process. *Studies in Higher Education*, *31*(2), 219–233. doi:10.1080/03075070600572132

Carless, D., & Boud, D. (2018). The development of student feedback literacy: Enabling uptake of feedback. *Assessment & Evaluation in Higher Education*, *43*(8), 1315–1325. doi:10.1080/02602938.2018.1463354

Carr, P. (2019). Team Teaching. *English Teaching Professional*, *121*, p 53- 55.

Carr, R., Palmer, S., & Hagel, P. (2015). Active learning: The importance of developing a comprehensive measure. *Active Learning in Higher Education*, *6*(3), 173–186. doi:10.1177/1469787415589529

Carter, R. Halcomb, Bui, H. M., & Nguyen, N. T. (2014). Choosing a Transnational Higher Education Program: What Do Vietnamese Learners Rate as Important? Australian Association for Research in Education.

Caruana, V., & Montgomery, C. (2015). Understanding the Transnational Higher Education landscape: Shifting personality and the complexities of partnership. *Learning and Teaching*, *8*(1), 5–29. doi:10.3167/latiss.2015.080102

Case, M. (2015). Machine translation and the disruption of foreign language learning activities. *eLearning Papers*, *45*, 4–16.

Castelli, F. R., & Sarvary, M. A. (2021). Why students do not turn on their video cameras during online classes and an equitable and inclusive plan to encourage them to do so. *Ecology and Evolution*, *11*(8), 3565–3576. doi:10.1002/ece3.7123 PMID:33898009

Caswell, I., & Liang, B. (2020, June 8). Recent advances in google translate. *Google AI Blog*. https://ai.googleblog.com/2020/06/recent-advances-in-google-translate.html

Cavanaugh, C., Cavanaugh, C., & DeWeese, A. (2020). Understanding the Professional Learning and Support Needs of Educators during.... *Journal of Technology and Teacher Education*, *28*(2), 233–238.

Cellan-Jones, R. (2014) Stephen Hawking warns artificial intelligence could end mankind. *BBC News*. https://www.bbc.com/news/technology-30290540.

Centre of Research on CFCRS. (2018) Grand opening of the 9th National Conference on CFCRS in Yantai City (in Chinese). CFCRS. https://cfcrs.xmu.edu.cn/2018/0920/c4034a352953/page.htm

Chaaban, T., & Du, X. (2017). Novice teachers' job satisfaction and coping strategies: Overcoming contextual challenges at Qatari government schools. *Teaching and Teacher Education*, *67*, 340–350. doi:10.1016/j.tate.2017.07.002

Chambers, E., Parker, J., & Gregory, M. (2006). Editorial: Research-led teaching/teaching-led research? *Arts and Humanities in Higher Education*, *5*(2), 115–116. doi:10.1177/1474022206063646

Chamorro-Premuzic, T. (2015, March 25). Why group brainstorming is a waste of time. *Harvard Business Review*. https://hbr.org/2015/03/why-group-brainstorming-is-a-waste-of-time

Chandler, K. (2016). Using breakout rooms in synchronous online tutorials. *Journal of Perspectives in Applied Academic Practice*, *4*(3), 16–23. doi:10.14297/jpaap.v4i3.216

Chan, S. (1999). The Chinese learners – a question of style. *Education + Training*, *41*(6), 294–304. doi:10.1108/00400919910285345

Chaohong, G., & Yanqiao, J. (2010). The Status Quo, Problems and Countermeasures of Regulating Chinese-Foreign Cooperation in Running Schools in China. *Higher Education Development and Evaluation, 5*.

Chapman, A., & Pyvis, D. (2006). Quality, identity and practice in offshore university programmes: Issues in the internationalization of Australian higher education. *Teaching in Higher Education*, *11*(2), 233–245. doi:10.1080/13562510500527818

Chapman, A., & Pyvis, D. (2012). *Enhancing quality in transnational higher education: Experiences of teaching and learning in Australian offshore programs*. Lexington Books.

Chapman, A., & Pyvis, D. (2013). *Enhancing quality in transnational higher education*. Lexington Books.

Chen, Y. M. (2014). Observations on Teachers' Knowledge Growth in the Communicative Approach in Taiwanese EFL Classes. *Ore*.exeter.ac.uk

Chen, Y. M. (2016). *Collaborating with English teachers in developing and implementing a context sensitive communicative approach in Taiwanese EFL secondary school classes* [Doctoral dissertation, University of Exeter, England]. ORE Open Research Exeter.

Chen, C. M., & Lee, T. H. (2011). Emotion recognition and communication for reducing second-language speaking anxiety in a web-based one-to-one synchronous learning environment. *British Journal of Educational Technology*, *42*(3), 417–440. doi:10.1111/j.1467-8535.2009.01035.x

Chen, G., & Xu, D. (2020). A review of Chinese general education research [Lexical characteristics of Chinese language]. *Education Review*, *4*, 88–93.

Chen, L. (2020). 'Problematising the English-Only Policy in EAP: A Mixed-Methods Investigation of Chinese International Students' Perspectives of Academic Language Policy'. *Journal of Multilingual and Multicultural Development*, *41*(8), 718–735. doi:10.1080/01434632.2019.1643355

Chen, Q., Kettle, M., Klenowski, V., & May, L. (2013). Interpretations of formative assessment in the teaching of English at two Chinese universities: A sociocultural perspective. *Assessment & Evaluation in Higher Education*, *38*(7), 831–846. doi:10.1080/02602938.2012.726963

Chen, Q., Zhang, J., & Li, L. (2021). Problematising formative assessment in an undeveloped region of China: Voices from practitioners. *Educational Assessment, Evaluation and Accountability*, *33*(2), 649–673. doi:10.100711092-021-09369-5 PMID:34394769

Chen, Y. M. (2020). How a teacher education programme through action research can support EFL teachers in implementing communicative approaches, a case from Taiwan. *SAGE Open*, *10*(1), 215824401990016. doi:10.1177/2158244019900167

Chen, Y. M. (2022). Understanding foreign language learners' perceptions of teachers' practice with educational technology with specific reference to Kahoot! and Padlet: A case from China. *Education and Information Technologies*, *27*(2), 1439–1465. doi:10.100710639-021-10649-2

Chickering, W. & Gamson, F. (1991). Appendix A: Seven principles for good practice in undergraduate education. *New Directions for Teaching & Learning*, *1991*(47), pp. 63-69.

Chien, C.-L., & Kot, F. C. (2012). New Patterns in Student Mobility in the Southern Africa Development Community. *UIS Information Bulletin*, *7*(February).

Ching, Y., Renes, S. L., McMurrow, S., Simpson, J., & Strange, A. T. (2017). Challenges facing Chinese International students studying in the United States. *Educational Research Review*, *12*(8), 473–482. doi:10.5897/ERR2016.3106

Chiu, T. K., & Lim, C. P. (2020). Strategic use of technology for inclusive education in Hong Kong: A content-level perspective. *ECNU Review of Education*, *3*(4), 715–734. doi:10.1177/2096531120930861

Chiu, T. K., & Mok, I. A. (2017). Learner expertise and mathematics different order thinking skills in multimedia learning. *Computers & Education*, *107*, 147–164. doi:10.1016/j.compedu.2017.01.008

Choi, S. H.-J., & Nieminen, T. A. (2013). Factors influencing the higher education of international students from Confucian East Asia. *Higher Education Research & Development*, *32*(2), 161–173. doi:10.1080/07294360.2012.673165

Chompurach, W. (2021). "Please let me use Google Translate": Thai EFL students' behavior and attitudes toward Google Translate use in English writing. *English Language Teaching*, *14*(12), 23–35. doi:10.5539/elt.v14n12p23

Chomsky, N. (1967) The Responsibilities of Intellectuals. *The New York Review of Books*. https://chomsky.info/ 19670223/.

Chou, M. H. (2018). Speaking anxiety and strategy use for learning English as a foreign language in full and partial English-medium instruction contexts. *TESOL Quarterly*, *52*(3), 611–633. doi:10.1002/tesq.455

Chowdhury, M. B. (2022). Internationalisation of education and its effect on economic growth and development. *World Economy*, *45*(1), 200–219. doi:10.1111/twec.13174

Chrestensen, A. (2007). Real-world context, interest, understanding, and retention.[Thesis, Michigan Technological University, USA]. https://digitalcommons.mtu.edu/etds/536/

Christenson, S., Reschly, A. L., & Wylie, C. (2012). *Handbook of research on student engagement* (Vol. 840). Springer. doi:10.1007/978-1-4614-2018-7

Chung, E., Subramaniam, G., & Dass, L. C. (2020). Online learning readiness among university students in Malaysia amidst Covid-19. *Asian Journal of University Education*, *16*(2), 45. doi:10.24191/ajue.v16i2.10294

Chung, K.-C., Holdsworth, D. K., Li, Y., & Fam, K.-S. (2009). Chinese "Little Emperor", cultural values and preferred communication sources for university choice. *Young Consumers*, *10*(2), 120–132. doi:10.1108/17473610910964705

Civinini, C. (2021). *Covid leaves teachers 'drained and frustrated.* TES. https://www.tes.com/news/covid-leaves-teachers-drained-and-frustrated

Clarke, S. (2014). *Outstanding formative assessment: culture and practice*. Hodder Education.

Clark, S., Harbaugh, A. G., & Seider, S. (2019). Fostering adolescent curiosity through a question brainstorming intervention. *Journal of Adolescence*, *75*(1), 98–112. doi:10.1016/j.adolescence.2019.07.007 PMID:31376781

Cleaveland, N., & Packard, A. (1882). *History of Bowdoin College: with biographical sketches of its graduates from 1806 to 1879. inclusive*. J.R. Osgood & Co.

Clifford, M. (2015). Assessing the Feasibility of International Branch Campuses [Doctoral Dissertation, Pardee Rand Graduate School]. https://www.rand.org/content/dam/rand/pubs/rgs_dissertations/RGSD300/RGSD354/RAN D_RGSD354.pdf

Coates, H. (2007). A model of online and general campus-based student engagement. *Assessment & Evaluation in Higher Education*, *32*(2), 121–141. doi:10.1080/02602930600801878

CoHE. (2018). *The regulation for thesis submission to the National Thesis Center database of the CoHE.* CoHE. https://www.mevzuat.gov.tr/MevzuatMetin/1.5.2547.pdf

CoHE. (2019). *Higher education system in Turkey*. CoHE. https://www.yok.gov.tr/Documents/Yayinlar/Yayinlarimiz/2019/Higher_Education_in_Turkey_2019_en.pdf

CoHE. (2021). *University monitoring and evaluation general report 2021.* CoHE. https://www.yok.gov.tr/Documents/Yayinlar/Yayinlarimiz/2022/universite-izleme-ve-degerlendirme-genel-raporu-2021.pdf

CoHE. (2022). *Statistics for Turkish higher education.* CoHE. https://istatistik.yok.gov.tr/

Cohen, E., & Lotan, R. (1995). Producing equal-status interaction in the heterogeneous classroom. *American Educational Research Journal, Stanford University, USA*, *32*(1), 99–120. doi:10.3102/00028312032001099

Coleman, D. (2003). Quality assurance in transnational education. *Journal of Studies in International Education*, *7*(4), 354–378. doi:10.1177/1028315303255597

Commonwealth. (2016). Youth. *The Commonwealth.* https://thecommonwealth.org/youth

Connelly, F. M., & Clandinin, D. J. (1990). Stories of experience and narrative inquiry. *Educational Researcher*, *19*(5), 2–14. doi:10.3102/0013189X019005002

Conrad, R. M., & Donaldson, J. A. (2012). *Continuing to engage the online learner: More activities and resources for creative instruction.* John Wiley & Sons.

Cornell, R. M., Johnson, C. B., & Schwartz, W. C. Jr. (2013). Enhancing student experiential learning with structured interviews. *Journal of Education for Business*, *88*(3), 136–146. doi:10.1080/08832323.2012.659296

Cortazzi, M., & Jin, L. (1996). Cultures of learning: language classrooms in China. In H. Coleman (Ed.), *Society and the Language Classroom* (pp. 169–206). Cambridge University Press.

Cortazzi, M., & Jin, L. (2013). *Researching cultures of learning: International perspectives on language learning and education* [electronic version]. Palgrave Macmillan. doi:10.1057/9781137296344

Costa, P. I. D., Green-Eneix, C., & Li, W. (2021). Problematizing language policy and practice in EMI and transnational higher education: Challenges and possibilities. *Australian Review of Applied Linguistics*, *44*(2), 115–128. doi:10.1075/aral.00036.edi

Courtney, J. (2007). What are the effective components of in-service teacher training? A study examining teacher trainers' perceptions of the components of a training programme in mathematics education in Cambodia. *Journal of In-service Education*, *33*(3), 321–339. doi:10.1080/13674580701486978

Coyle, D. (2018). The place of CLIL in (bilingual) education. *Theory into Practice*, *57*(3), 166–176. doi:10.1080/00405841.2018.1459096

Craig, D. (2001). View from an electronic learning environment: Perceptions and patterns among students in an online graduate education course. *Journal of Educational Technology Systems. Middle Tennessee State University, USA*, *30*(2), 197–219.

Creswell, J. W. (2013). *Qualitative inquiry & research design: Choosing among five approaches* (3rd ed.). Sage Publications, Inc.

Creswell, J. W. (2013). *Qualitative inquiry and research design: Choosing among five approaches*. Sage Publications.

Creswell, J. W., & Creswell, J. D. (2017). *Research design: Qualitative, quantitative, and mixed methods approaches*. Sage publications.

Croker, A. (2016). Valuing ordered and organic collaboration: People, place, process and purpose. In A. Croker, J. Higgs, & F. Trede (Eds.), *Collaborating in healthcare: Reinterpreting therapeutic relationships* (pp. 55–81). Sense Publishers. doi:10.1007/978-94-6300-806-8_5

Croker, A., Higgs, J., & Trede, F. (Eds.). (2016). *Collaborating in healthcare: Reinterpreting therapeutic relationships* Sense Publishers. doi:10.1007/978-94-6300-806-8

Croker, A., Trede, F., & Higgs, J. (2014). Collaboration and collaborating. In J. Higgs, A. Croker, D. Tasker, J. Hummell, & N. Patton (Eds.), *Health practice relationships* (pp. 75–85). Sense Publishers. doi:10.1007/978-94-6209-788-9_9

Crook, A., Mauchline, A., Maw, S., Lawson, C., Drinkwater, R., Lundqvist, K., & Park, J. (2012). The use of video technology for providing feedback to students: Can it enhance the feedback experience for staff and students? *Computers & Education*, *58*(1), 386–396. doi:10.1016/j.compedu.2011.08.025

Croucher, G., Elliott, K., Locke, W., & Yencken, E. (2020). *Australia's higher education delivery offshore and online-trends, barriers and opportunities Melbourne Centre for the Study of Higher Education*. Melbourne Centre for the Study of Higher Education.

Croucher, G., Elliott, K., Locke, W., & Yencken, E. (2020). *Australia's higher education delivery offshore and online–trends, barriers and opportunities*. Melbourne Centre for the Study of Higher Education.

Crow, M. M., & Dabars, W. B. (2020). *The fifth wave: The evolution of American higher education*. Johns Hopkins University Press.

Crozet, C., Liddicoat, A. J., & Lo Bianco, J. (1999). Intercultural Competence: From language policy to language education. In J. Lo Bianco, A. J. Liddicoat, & C. Crozet (Eds.), *Striving for the Third Place: Intercultural Competence through Language Education*. Language Australia.

Cruz, T. (2010). Phillippines: Multisectoral school strike vs Aquino's budget cuts. *Asian Correspondent*. http://asiancorrespondent.com/2010/12/philippines-multisectoral-school-strike-vs- aquinos-budget-cuts/

Cruz, L., & Geist, M. J. (2019). A Team-Teaching Matrix: Asking New Questions about How We Teach Together. *Transformative Dialogues: Teaching & Learning Journal*, *12*(1), 1–15.

Cubillo, J. M., Sánchez, J., & Cerviño, J. (2006). International students' decision-making process. *International Journal of Educational Management*, *20*(2), 101–115. doi:10.1108/09513540610646091

Curhan, J. R., Labuzova, T., & Mehta, A. (2021). Cooperative criticism: When criticism enhances creativity in brainstorming and negotiation. *Organization Science*, *32*(5), 1256–1272. doi:10.1287/orsc.2020.1420

Curtin University Malaysia. (2014). *General Education Subjects*. Curtain University. https://humanities.curtin.edu.my/departments/culturelanguagestudies/mohe/

Cuzzocrea, V., & Mandich, G. (2015). Students' narratives of the future: Imagined mobilities as forms of youth agency? *Journal of Youth Studies*, *19*(4), 552–567. doi:10.1080/13676261.2015.1098773

D'Annunzio-Green, N., & Barron, P. (2019). Learning whilst working: Perceptions on barriers and enablers to transfer of learning amongst part-time students on a professional MSc programme. *Education + Training*, *61*(2), 187–200. doi:10.1108/ET-04-2018-0098

Dai, K., & Garcia, J. (2019). Intercultural Learning in Transnational Articulation Programs: The Hidden Agenda of Chinese Students' Experiences. *Journal of International Students*, *9*(2), 362–383. doi:10.32674/jis.v9i2.677

Davies, A. (1990). *Principles of language testing*. Blackwell.

Davies, B. (2009). *The essentials of school leadership: Learning-centred leadership*. Sage. doi:10.4135/9781446288290

Davies, B., & Northall, N. (2018a). No One Told Me That! 1. *English Teaching Professional*, *117*, 49–51.

Davies, B., & Northall, N. (2018b). No One Told Me That! 2. *English Teaching Professional*, *118*, 48–51.

Davies, J. A., Davies, L. J., Conlon, B., Emerson, J., Hainsworth, H., & McDonough, H. G. (2020). Responding to COVID-19 in EAP Contexts: A Comparison of Courses at Four Sino-Foreign Universities. *International Journal of TESOL Studies*, *2*(2), 32–51.

Day, C. & Sammons, P. (2013). *Successful leadership: A review of the international leadership*. Reading: CfBT Education Trust.

De Bary, W. T., & Bloom, I. (1999). *Sources of Chinese tradition from earliest times to 1600* (2nd ed., Vol. 1). Columbia University Press.

de Bono. (2020). *The six thinking hats*. de Bono. https://www.debono.com/six-thinking-hats-summary

De Hei, M. S. A., Strijbos, J. W., Sjoer, E., & Admiraal, W. (2015). Collaborative learning in higher education: Lecturers' practices and beliefs. *Research Papers in Education*, *30*(2), 232–247. doi:10.1080/02671522.2014.908407

de Hei, M., Tabacaru, C., Sjoer, E., Rippe, R., & Walenkamp, J. (2020). Developing intercultural competence through collaborative learning in international higher education. *Journal of Studies in International Education*, *24*(2), 190–211. doi:10.1177/1028315319826226

De Wet, C. (2016). The Status of Teaching as a Profession in South Africa. *Education Policy, Reforms & School Leadership* (143-149).

Deardorff, D. K. (2006). Identification and assessment of intercultural competence as a student outcome of internationalization. *Journal of Studies in International Education*, *10*(3), 241–266. doi:10.1177/1028315306287002

Debreli, E., & Demirkan, S. (2015). Sources and levels of foreign language speaking anxiety of English as a foreign language university students with regard to language proficiency and gender. *International Journal of English Language Education*, *4*(1), 49–62. doi:10.5296/ijele.v4i1.8715

Deckert, G. D. (1993). Perspectives on plagiarism from ESL students in Hong Kong. *Journal of Second Language Writing*, *2*(2), 131–148. doi:10.1016/1060-3743(93)90014-T

Department for Education and Department for International Trade. (2021). International Education Strategy: 2021 update. Supporting recovery, driving growth. DIT. https://assets.publishing.service.gov.uk/government/uploads/system/uploads/attachment_data/file/958990/International-Education-Strategy-_2021-Update.pdf. Accessed on: 16/05/2022

Department of Education. *activity 2018*. (2022). *UK revenue from education related exports and transnational education.* Department of Education. https://www.gov.uk/government/statistics/uk-revenue-from-education-related-exports-and-transnational-education-activity-2018

Dewey, J. (1938). *Experience and Education.* Macmillan Publishing Co. Inc.

Dias Lopes, A. (2020). International mobility and education inequality among Brazilian undergraduate students. *Higher Education, 80*(4), 779–796. doi:10.100710734-020-00514-5

Diehl, M., & Stroebe, W. (1991). Productivity loss in idea-generating groups: Tracking down the blocking effect. *Journal of Personality and Social Psychology, 61*(3), 392–403. doi:10.1037/0022-3514.61.3.392

Diehl, M., & Strpebe, W. (1987). Productivity loss In brainstorming groups: Toward the solution of a riddle. *Journal of Personality and Social Psychology, 53*(3), 497–509. doi:10.1037/0022-3514.53.3.497

Djahimo, S., Bili Bora, D., & Huan, E. (2018). Student anxiety and their speaking performance: Teaching EFL to Indonesian student. *International Journal of Social Science and Humanity, 2*(3), 187–195.

Dobos, K. (2011). "Serving two masters" – academics' perspectives on working at an offshore campus in Malaysia. *Educational Review, 63*(1), 19–35. doi:10.1080/00131911003748035

Doorley, S., Holcomb, S., Klebahn, P., Segovia, K., & Utley, J. (2018). *Design thinking bootleg.* Stanford University. https://dschool.stanford.edu/resources/design-thinking-bootleg

Dörnyei, Z., & Ushioda, E. (2009). *Motivation, language identity and the L2 self.* Multilingual Matters. doi:10.21832/9781847691293

Dou, D., Davos, G., & Valcke, M. (2017). The relationship between school autonomy gap, principal leadership, teachers' job satisfaction and organisational commitment. *Educational Management Administration & Leadership, 45*(6), 959–977. doi:10.1177/1741143216653975

Downey, R. V. (1996). *A Study in Stand Up: Roles and Behaviors of Excellent Trainers* [PhD Thesis). Syracuse University, USA].

Doyle, L. (2019*). Leadership vs. management: What's the difference?* Northeastern University. https://www.northeastern.edu/bachelors-completion/news/leadership-vs-managment/

Doyle, T., & Doyle, B. (2020). Learning and Teaching in harmony with the Brain. Insight from neuroscience, biology, cognitive science and psychology. In S. Hoidn & M. Klemenicic (Eds.), *The Routledge International Handbook of Student-Centered Learning and Teaching in Higher Education.* Routledge. doi:10.4324/9780429259371-6

Drucker, P. (1954). *The practice of management.* Harper & Row Publishers.

Drucker, P. (1985). *Innovation and entrepreneurship: Practice and principles.* Butterworth Heinemann.

Drucker, P. (1999). *Management challenges in the XXI century.* Transaction Publishers.

Drucker, P. F. (2017). *A Functioning Society: Selections from Sixty-five Years of Writing on Community, Society, and Polity.* Routledge. doi:10.4324/9781315083599

Drucker, P. F., & Maciariello, J. A. (2018). *The daily Drucker: 366 days of insight and motivation for getting the right things done*. Routledge. doi:10.4324/9780080470481

Ducar, C., & Schocket, D. H. (2018). Machine translation and the L2 classroom: Pedagogical solutions for making peace with Google Translate. *Foreign Language Annals*, *51*(4), 779–795. doi:10.1111/flan.12366

Dudley-Evans, T., & St. John, M. J. (1998). *Developments in ESP: A multi-disciplinary approach*. Cambridge University Press.

Dunn, L., & Wallace, M. (2006). Australian academics and transnational teaching: An exploratory study of their preparedness and experiences. *Higher Education Research & Development*, *25*(4), 357–369. doi:10.1080/07294360600947343

Durnalı, M., Orakçı, Ş., & Toraman, Ç. (2022). Distance education students' acceptance of online learning systems, attitudes towards online learning and their self-directed learning skills. *Malaysian Online Journal of Educational Technology*, *10*(2), 76–94. doi:10.52380/mojet.2022.10.2.236

Dyllick, T., & Muff, K. (2015). Clarifying the meaning of sustainable business: Introducing a typology from business-as-usual to true business sustainability. *Organization & Environment*, *29*(2), 1–19.

Dyson, J. (2013, March 16). More universities attracted to Iskandar education hub. *University World News*. https://www.universityworldnews.com/article.php?story=20130315083553321&query=iskan dar+education+hub

E., Ramjan, L. M., Wilson, N. J., Glew, P., & Salamonson, Y. (2019). Does the use of annotated exemplars by nursing learners predict academic performance? A cohort study. *Nurse education today*, *80*, 34-39.

Eastwood, B. (2020). *8 essential traits for effective leadership in higher education. Northeastern University*. https://www.northeastern.edu/graduate/blog/leadership-in-higher-education/

Eckel, P. D., & King, J. E. (2004). *An overview of higher education in the United States*. American Council on Education.

Edmondson, A. C., & Daley, G. (2020). How to foster psychological safety in virtual meetings. HBR. https://hbr.org/2020/08/how-to-foster-psychological-safety-in-virtual-meetings

Education Malaysia Global Services. (n.d.). *Malaysia Education in Brief*. Education Malaysia. https://educationmalaysia.gov.my/malaysia-higher-education-in-brief/#:~:text=10%20International%20Branch%20Campuses%20in,Swinburne%20University%20of%20Technology%2C%20Sarawak (Accessed 5 May 2022).

Edwards, A. L. (1946). A critique of 'neutral' items in attitude scales constructed by the method of equal appearing intervals. *Psychological Review*, *53*(3), 159–169. doi:10.1037/h0054184

Ehlers, U. D. (2013). *Open learning cultures: A guide to quality, evaluation and assessment for future learning*. Springer. doi:10.1007/978-3-642-38174-4

Elliott, A., & Urry, J. (2010). *Mobile lives*. Routledge. doi:10.4324/9780203887042

Elmore, R. F. (2002). Bridging the Gap between Standards and Achievement: The Imperative for Professional Development in Education. Report: ED475871. 44pp. Jul 2002.

Emery, V. & Worton, M. (2021). *Challenges for the leadership of transnational education in higher education: Balancing risk and innovation*. Advanced HE. https://www.advance-he.ac.uk/knowledge-hub/challenges-leadership-transnational-education-higher-education-balancing-risk-and-0

Ennew, C. T., & Fujia, Y. (2009). Foreign universities in China: A case study. *European Journal of Education*, *44*(1), 21–36. doi:10.1111/j.1465-3435.2008.01368.x

Erdiana, N., Daud, B., Sari, D. F., & Dwitami, S. K. (2020). A study of anxiety experienced by EFL students in speaking performance. *Studies in English Language and Education*, *7*(2), 334–346. doi:10.24815iele.v7i2.16768

Ericsson, A., & Pool, R. (2016). *Peak - Secrets from the new science of expertise*. Houghton Miffin Harcourt.

Escriva-Beltran, M., Muñoz-de-Prat, J., & Villó, C. (2019). Insights into international branch campuses: Mapping trends through a systematic review. *Journal of Business Research*, *101*, 507–515. doi:10.1016/j.jbusres.2018.12.049

European Commission. (2020). *Eurostat*. EC.https://ec.europa.eu/eurostat/web/nuts/background

European Parliamentary Research Service. (2013) 'Internationalisation of higher education', *European Parliament*. https://epthinktank.eu/2013/09/29/internationalisation-of-higher-education/

European Qualifications Framework. (2020). *European qualifications framework*. European Qualifications. https://ec.europa.eu/ploteus/content/descriptors-page

Evagorou, M., & Nisiforou, E. (2020). Engaging Pre-service Teachers in an Online STEM Fair during COVID-19. *Journal of Technology and Teacher Education*, *28*(2), 179–186.

Evans, C. (2013). Making sense of assessment feedback in higher education. Review of Educational Research, 83(1), pp. 70-120.

Evans, C. (2013). Making Sense of Assessment Feedback in Higher Education. *Review of Educational Research*, *83*(1), 70–120. doi:10.3102/0034654312474350

Evans, E., Tindale, J., Cable, D., & Hamil-Mead, S. (2009). Collaborative Teaching in a Linguistically and Culturally Diverse Higher Education Setting: A Case Study of a Postgraduate Accounting Program. *Higher Education Research & Development*, *28*(6), 597–613. doi:10.1080/07294360903226403

Evans, S., & Morrison, B. (2011). Meeting the challenges of English-medium higher education: The first-year experience in Hong Kong. *English for Specific Purposes*, *30*(3), 198–208. doi:10.1016/j.esp.2011.01.001

Exley, K., Dennick, R., & Fisher, A. (2019). *Small group teaching* (2nd ed.). Routledge. doi:10.4324/9780429490897

Fakunle, O., & Higson, H. (2021). Interrogating theoretical and empirical approaches to employability in different global regions. *Higher Education Quarterly*, *75*(4), 525–534. doi:10.1111/hequ.12345

Falchikov, N., & Boud, D. (1989). Student self-assessment in higher education: A meta-analysis. *Review of Educational Research*, *59*(4), 395–430. doi:10.3102/00346543059004395

Fang, N. (2013). Increasing high school students' interest in STEM education through collaborative brainstorming with yo-yos. *Journal of STEM Education: Innovations and Research*, *14*(4), 8–13.

Fang, Y. (2010). The cultural pedagogy of errors: Teacher Wang's homework practice in teaching geometric proofs. *Journal of Curriculum Studies*, *42*(5), 597–619. doi:10.1080/00220271003773901

Farooq, M. U. (2015). Creating a Communicative Language Teaching Environment for Improving Students' Communicative Competence at EFL/EAP University Level. *International Education Studies*, *8*(4), 179–191. doi:10.5539/ies.v8n4p179

Fenstermacher, G. D., & Berliner, D. C. (1985). Determining the Value of Staff Development. *The Elementary School Journal*, *85*(3), 281–314. https://eric.ed.gov/?id=EJ315740. doi:10.1086/461407

Ferguson, A. (2013). *My autobiography*. Hodder & Stoughton.

Ferreira, D., MacLean, G., & Center, G. E. (2018). Andragogy in the 21st century: Applying the assumptions of adult learning online. *Language Research Bulletin*, *32*(11), 10–19.

Ferri, F., Grifoni, P., & Guzzo, T. (2020). Online learning and emergency remote teaching: Opportunities and challenges in emergency situations. *Societies (Basel, Switzerland), 10*(4), 86. doi:10.3390oc10040086

Fischman, W., & Gardner, H. (2022). *The Real World of College: What Higher Education is and What it Can be*. MIT Press. doi:10.7551/mitpress/13652.001.0001

Fisher, K., Squires, K., & Woodley, I. (2016). Community collaboration beyond the red tape: Complying without being constrained. In A. Croker, J. Higgs, & F. Trede (Eds.), *Health practice relationships*. (pp. 203–211).

Fisher, R., Cavanagh, J., & Bowles, A. (2011). Assisting transition to university: Using assessment as a formative learning tool. *Assessment & Evaluation in Higher Education, 36*(2), 225–237. doi:10.1080/02602930903308241

Fletcher, J. (2015). *Teaching arguments: Rhetorical comprehension, critique, and response*. Stenhouse Publishers.

Flick, U. (2008). *Designing qualitative research*. Sage Publications.

Flowerdew, J., & Li, Y. (2007). Language re-use among Chinese apprentice scientists writing for publication. *Applied Linguistics, 28*(3), 440–465. doi:10.1093/applin/amm031

Fluckiger, J., Vigil, Y., Tixier, Y., Pasco, R., & Danielson, K. (2010). Formative feedback: Involving students as partners in assessment to enhance learning. *College Teaching, 58*(4), 136–140. doi:10.1080/87567555.2010.484031

Forman, J., & Damschroder, L. (2007). Qualitative content analysis. In L. A. S. Liva Jacoby (Ed.), *Empirical methods for bioethics: A primer* (Vol. 11, pp. 39–62). Emerald Group Publishing Limited. doi:10.1016/S1479-3709(07)11003-7

Fox, L., Onders, R., Hermansen-Kobulnicky, C. J., Nguyen, T. N., Myran, L., Linn, B., & Hornecker, J. (2018). Teaching interprofessional teamwork skills to health professional learners: A scoping review. *Journal of Interprofessional Care, 32*(2), 127–135. doi:10.1080/13561820.2017.1399868 PMID:29172791

Francois, E. J. (2016). What is transnational education? In E. J. Francois, M. B. Avoseh, & W. Griswold (Eds.), Perspectives in transnational higher education (pp. 3–23). Sense Publishers. doi:10.1007/978-94-6300-420-6_1

Francois, E. J. (2015). *Building global education with a local perspective: An introduction to glocal higher education*. Palgrave Macmillan. doi:10.1057/9781137386779

Francois, E. J., Avoseh, M. B., & Griswold, W. (Eds.). (2016). *Perspectives in transnational higher education*. Springer. doi:10.1007/978-94-6300-420-6

Frankel, M. S., Leshner, A. I., & Yang, W. (2016). Research integrity: Perspectives from China and the United States. In T. Bretag (Ed.), *Handbook of Academic Integrity* (pp. 848–864). Springer. doi:10.1007/978-981-287-098-8_65

Fredholm, K. (2019). Effects of Google Translate on lexical diversity: Vocabulary development among learners of Spanish as a foreign language. *Revista Nebrija, 13*(26), 98–117. doi:10.26378/rnlael1326300

Freud, S. (1940). *An outline of psychoanalysis. The standard edition of the complete psychological works of Sigmund Freud* (Vol. XXIII). W.W. Norton and Company.

Friend, M., & Cook, L. (2014). *Interactions: Collaboration Skills for School Professionals, Enhanced*. Pearson Education Limited.

Friend, M., Cook, L., Hurley-Chamberlain, D., & Shamberger, C. (2010). Co-Teaching: An Illustration of the Complexity of Collaboration in Special Education. *Journal of Educational & Psychological Consultation, 20*(1), 9–27. doi:10.1080/10474410903535380

Furnham, A. (2000). The brainstorming myth. *Business Strategy Review, 11*(4), 21–28. doi:10.1111/1467-8616.00154

Fussell, G., Bianco, M., & Polkina, G. (2021). Fostering Diversity, Equity, and Inclusion in Online Classes. In E. Langran, & D. Rutledge (Eds.), *Proceedings of SITE Interactive Conference* (pp. 15-19). Association for the Advancement of Computing in Education (AACE).

Galloway, N., Kriukow, J., & Numajiri, T. (2017). *Internationalisation, higher education and the growing demand for English: An investigation into the EMI movement in China and Japan* (ELT Research Papers 17.02). British Council. https://www.teachingenglish.org.uk/article/internationalisation-higher-education-and-growing-demand-english-investigation-emi-movement

Galloway, N., Numajiri, T., & Rees, N. (2020). The 'internationalisation', or 'Englishisation', of higher education in East Asia. *Higher Education*, *80*(3), 395–414. doi:10.100710734-019-00486-1

Gallupe, R. B., Bastianutti, L. M., & Cooper, W. H. (1991). Unblocking brainstorms. *The Journal of Applied Psychology*, *76*(1), 137–142. doi:10.1037/0021-9010.76.1.137 PMID:2016214

Gamage, K. A. A., Wijesuriya, D. I., Ekanayake, S. Y., Rennie, A. E. W., Lambert, C. G., & Gunawardhana, N. (2020). Online delivery of teaching and laboratory practices: Continuity of university programmes during COVID-19 pandemic. In Education Sciences, 10(10). doi:10.3390/educsci10100291

Gan, S. L. (2000). Shaping education for the future: the role of IT in institutions of higher learning. *Economist Intelligence Unit.*

Garet, M. S., Porter, A. C., Desimone, L., Birman, B., & Yoon, K. S. (2001). What Makes Professional Development Effective? Results from a National Sample of Teachers. *American Educational Research Journal*, *38*(4), 915–945. https://www.jstor.org/stable/3202507. doi:10.3102/00028312038004915

Garran, A. M., Aymer, S., Gelman, C. R., & Miller, J. L. (2015). Team teaching Anti-Oppression with Diverse Faculty: Challenges and Opportunities. *Social Work Education*, *34*(7), 799–814. doi:10.1080/02615479.2015.1062086

Garrett, R., Kinser, K., Lane, J. E., & Merola, R. (2016). *International branch campuses: Trends and developments.* The Observatory of Borderless Higher Education and C-BERT. https://www.obhe.org/resources/international-branch-campuses-trends-and-developments-2016

Garrett, R., Kinser, K., Lane, J. E., & Merola, R. (2017). *International branch campuses: Success factors of mature IBCs.* Observatory on Borderless Higher Education and Cross-Border Education Research Team.

Garrison, D. R., Anderson, T., & Archer, W. (2003). A theory of critical inquiry in online distance education. Handbook of distance education, 1(4), 113-127.

Garrison, D. R., Cleveland-Innes, M., & Fung, T. S. (2010). Exploring causal relationships among teaching, cognitive and social presence: Student perceptions of the community of inquiry framework. *The internet and higher education*, *13*(1-2), 31–36. doi:10.1016/j.iheduc.2009.10.002

Garson, B. (2005). Teaching abroad: A cross-cultural journey. *Journal of Education for Business*, *80*(6), 322–326. https://www.tandfonline.com/doi/pdf/10.3200/joeb.80.6.322-326?casa_token=7cR5erGR0nUAAAAA:LrE7Bk5dBSB_qpIpY-mVBdsWjfACX1HGHnjEtIfOqyVgS4kKqwdiOWVPg3S_XJZYtFZLHHCL4Vlz. doi:10.3200/JOEB.80.6.322-326

Garza, T. J. (2021). Raise Your Hand: Online Language and Culture Instruction, Inclusivity, and Critical Pedagogy. *Russian Language Journal*, *71*(2), 15.

Gaskell, C. (2013). 'Isolation and distress'?(Re) thinking the place of emotions in youth research. In L. van Blerk & M. Kesby (Eds.), *Doing Children's Geographies: Methodological Issues in Research with Young People* (pp. 404–439). Routledge.

Gauld, D., & Miller, P. (2004). The qualifications and competencies held by effective workplace trainers. *Journal of European Industrial Training*, *28*(1), 8–22. doi:10.1108/03090590410513866

Gavin, M. (2019). *Leadership vs. management: What's the difference?* Harvard Business School Online. https://online.hbs.edu/blog/post/leadership-vs-management

Getenet, S. (2019). Using design-based research to bring partnership between researchers and practitioners. Https://Doi.Org/10.1080/00131881.2019.1677168, *61*(4), 482–494. doi:10.1080/00131881.2019.1677168

Geuna, S., & Giacobini-Robecchi, M. G. (2002). The use of brainstorming for teaching human anatomy. *The Anatomical Record*, *269*(5), 214–216. doi:10.1002/ar.10168 PMID:12379937

Ghosh, P., Satyawadi, R., Joshi, J. P., Ranjan, R., & Singh, P. (2012). Towards more Effective Training Programme: A study of trainer attributes. *Industrial and Commercial Training*, *44*(4), 194–202. doi:10.1108/00197851211231469

Gibbons, P. (2014). *Scaffolding language, scaffolding learning: Teaching English language learners in the mainstream classroom* (2nd ed.). Heinemann.

Gibbs, G. (1988). *Learning by doing: a guide to teaching and learning methods*. Further Educational Unit, Oxford Polytechnic.

Gill, S. S., Naeem, U., Fuller, S. Chen, Y., & Uhlig, S. (2022a). How Covid-19 Changed Computer Science Education, *ITNOW*, *64*(2), Issue 2, 60–61.

Gill, S. K., & Kirkpatrick, A. (2013). English in Asian and European higher education. In C. Chapelle (Ed.), *The encyclopedia of applied linguistics*. Wiley-Blackwell., doi:10.1002/9781405198431.wbeal0383.pub2

Gill, S. S., Fuller, S., Cabral, A., Chen, Y., & Uhlig, S. (2023a). An Operating System Session Plan Towards Social Justice and Intercultural Development in Microteaching for Higher Education. In E. Meletiadou (Ed.), *Handbook of Research on Fostering Social Justice Through Intercultural and Multilingual Communication* (pp. 44–61). IGI Global.

Gill, S. S., Fuller, S., Cabral, A., Chen, Y., & Uhlig, S. (2023b). Curriculum Redesign for Cloud Computing to Enhance Social Justice and Intercultural Development in Higher Education. In E. Meletiadou (Ed.), *Handbook of Research on Fostering Social Justice Through Intercultural and Multilingual Communication* (pp. 62–80). IGI Global.

Gill, S. S., Xu, M., Ottaviani, C., Patros, P., Bahsoon, R., Shaghaghi, A., & Uhlig, S. (2022b). AI for next generation computing: Emerging trends and future directions. *Internet of Things*, *19*, 100514. doi:10.1016/j.iot.2022.100514

Giralt, R. M., & Bailey, A. J. (2010). Transnational familyhood and the liquid life paths of South Americans in the UK. *Global Networks*, *10*(3), 383–400. doi:10.1111/j.1471-0374.2010.00294.x

Gligorovic, B., Nikolic, M., Terek, E., Glusac, D., & Tasic, I. (2016). The impact of school culture on Serbian primary teacher's job satisfaction. *H.U. Journal of Education*, *31*(2), 231–248.

Gobble, M. M. (2014). The persistence of brainstorming. *Research Technology Management*, *57*(1), 64–66. doi:10.5437/08956308X5701005

Göğüş, A. (2012). Brainstorming and learning. In N. M. Seel (Ed.), *Encyclopedia of the sciences of learning* (pp. 484–488). Springer. doi:10.1007/978-1-4419-1428-6_491

Goh, C. (2016). *Teaching speaking. English Language Teaching Today, 143-159*. Springer.

Goldman, S., & Zielezinski, M. B. (2022). *Design thinking for every classroom. A practical guide for educators*. Routledge.

Gong, Y. (2020, July). The Problems and Countermeasures of Sino-Foreign Cooperation in Running Schools in Yunnan Province. In *4th International Symposium on Business Corporation and Development in South-East and South Asia under B&R Initiative (ISBCD 2019)* (pp. 138-142). Atlantis Press. 10.2991/aebmr.k.200708.027

González-Ardeo, J. M. (2012). Overlapping of ESP/EAP and Content Courses Revisited. *Revista de Lenguas para Fines Específicos*, *18*, 213–236.

González-Tennant, E. (2017). Digital Storytelling in the Classroom: New Media Techniques for an Engaged Anthropological Pedagogy. In M. Nuñez-Janes, A. Thornburg, A. Booker, I. Penier, S. Pack, & A. Leverton (Eds.), *Practicing, Teaching, and Learning Anthropology with Digital Storytelling* (pp. 152–169). De Gruyter. doi:10.1515/9783110539356-012

Gopinath, D. (2015). Discourses and practices in teaching methods and assessment: Insights from an early career academic. *SAGE Open*, *5*(1), 2158244015573371. doi:10.1177/2158244015573371

Gorgodze, S., Macharashvili, L., & Kamladze, A. (2020). Learning for Earning: Student Expectations and Perceptions of University. *International Education Studies*, *13*(1), 42–53. doi:10.5539/ies.v13n1p42

Gozukara, I. (2016). Leadership and managerial effectiveness in higher education. *International Journal of Academic Research in Accounting. Finance and Management Sciences*, *6*(1), 73–82.

Graff, G., & Birkenstein, C. (2018). *They Say, I Say*. W. W. Norton, Incorporated.

Grangeat, M., & Gray, P. (2008). Teaching as a collective work: Analysis, current research and implications for teacher education. *Journal of Education for Teaching*, *34*(3), 177–189. doi:10.1080/02607470802212306

Granovsky, Y. V., Luibimova, T. N., Murashova, T. I., & Myatlev, V. D. (1992). Information-based evaluation of the quality of doctoral theses. *Scientometrics*, *23*(3), 361–376. doi:10.1007/BF02029804

Gray, C. M. (2013, December 1). Informal peer critique and the negotiation of habitus in a design studio. *Art, Design & Communication in Higher Education*, *12*(2), 195–209. doi:10.1386/adch.12.2.195_1

Green, A. (2014). *Exploring Language Assessment and Testing*. Routledge.

Greene, H., Koh, K., Bonnici, J., & Chase, J. (2015). The value of storytelling in the marketing curriculum. *Journal of the Academy of Business Education*, *16*, 111–128.

Gribble, C. (2014). Exploring 'employability' in different cultural contexts. *Final Report: Scoping Study. Society for Research into higher Education (SRHE)*. Deakin University, Australia.

Groves, M., & Mundt, K. (2015). Friend or foe? Google Translate in language for academic purposes. *English for Specific Purposes*, *37*, 112–121. doi:10.1016/j.esp.2014.09.001

Groves, M., & Mundt, K. (2021). A ghostwriter in the machine? Attitudes of academic staff towards machine translation use in internationalised Higher Education. *Journal of English for Academic Purposes*, *50*, 100957. Advance online publication. doi:10.1016/j.jeap.2021.100957

Gu, M. (1992). *Dictionary of Education*. Shanghai Educational Publishing House.

Gunawardena, C. N., Wilson, P. L., & Nolla, A. C. (2003). Culture and online education. In M. G. Moore & W. G. Anderson (Eds.), *Handbook of distance education* (pp. 753–775). Routledge.

Gun, J. A., & Holdway, E. A. (1986). Perceptions of effectiveness influences and satisfaction of senior high school principals. *Education Administration*, *22*(2), 43–62. doi:10.1177/0013161X86022002004

Gu, Q., & Maley, A. (2008). Changing places: A study of Chinese students in the UK. *Language and Intercultural Communication*, *8*(4), 224–245. doi:10.1080/14708470802303025

Guskey, T. (2000). *Evaluating professional development*. Corwin Press.

Guskey, T. R. (2007). Closing Achievement Gaps: Revisiting Benjamin S. Bloom's "Learning for Mastery". *Journal of Advanced Academics*, *19*(1), 8–31. doi:10.4219/jaa-2007-704

Gustafsson, M., & Jacobs, C. (2013). Student Learning and ICLHE - Frameworks and Contexts. *Journal of Academic Writing*, *3*(1), ii–xii. doi:10.18552/joaw.v3i1.141

Hagen, M., Bernard, A., & Grube, E. (2016). Do it all wrong! Using reverse-brainstorming to generate ideas, improve discussions, and move students to action. *Management Teaching Review*, *1*(2), 85–90. doi:10.1177/2379298116634738

Hager, P., Sleet, R., & Kaye, M. (1994). The relation between critical thinking abilities and learner study strategies. *Higher Education Research & Development*, *13*(2), 179–188. doi:10.1080/0729436940130208

Hamdullahpur, F. (2020). Global citizens for the twenty-first century: the role of international partnerships in university education. In *Successful Global Collaborations in Higher Education Institutions* (pp. 23–30). Springer. doi:10.1007/978-3-030-25525-1_3

Hamid, P. N. (1995). Self-monitoring, locus of control, and social encounters of Chinese and New Zealand students. *Journal of Cross-Cultural Psychology*, *25*(3), 353–268. doi:10.1177/0022022194253004

Han, M., & Yang, X. (2001). Educational Assessment in China: Lessons from history and future prospects. *Assessment in Education: Principles, Policy & Practice*, *8*(1), 5–10. doi:10.1080/09695940120033216

Hannam, K., Sheller, M., & Urry, J. (2006). Mobilities, immobilities and moorings. *Mobilities*, *1*(1), 1–22. doi:10.1080/17450100500489189

Hanna, W. (2007). The new Bloom's taxonomy: Implications for music education. *Arts Education Policy Review*, *108*(4), 7–16. doi:10.3200/AEPR.108.4.7-16

Hanusch, F., Obijiofor, L., & Volcic, Z. (2009). Theoretical and practical issues in team-teaching a large undergraduate class. *International Journal on Teaching and Learning in Higher Education*, *21*(1), 66–74.

Haque, S. (2021). In-country international higher education: The right step forward. *The Daily Star*. https://www.thedailystar.net/opinion/news/country-international-higher-education-the-right-step-forward-2107257

Harbour, K. E., Evanovich, L. L., Sweigart, C. A., & Hughes, L. E. (2015). A brief review of effective teaching practices that maximize student engagement. *Preventing School Failure*, *59*(1), 5–13. doi:10.1080/1045988X.2014.919136

Harman, G. (2005). Internationalization of Australian higher education: A critical review of literature and research. In P. Ninnes & M. Hellstén (Eds.), *Internationalizing Higher Education* (Vol. 16, pp. 119–140). Springer-Verlag. doi:10.1007/1-4020-3784-8_7

Hartnett, M. K. (2015). Influences that undermine learners' perceptions of autonomy, competence and relatedness in an online context. *Australasian Journal of Educational Technology*, *31*(1). doi:10.14742/ajet.1526

Hartshorne, R., Baumgartner, E., Kaplan-Rakowski, R., Mouza, C., & Ferdig, R. E. (2020). Special issue editorial: Preservice and inservice professional development during the COVID-19 pandemic. *Journal of Technology and Teacher Education*, *28*(2).

Harvey, L. (1998). An assessment of past and current approaches to quality in higher education. *Australian Journal of Education*, *42*(3), 237–255. doi:10.1177/000494419804200303

Hasgall, A., Saenen, B., & Borrell-Damian, L. (2019). *Doctoral education in Europe today: Approaches and institutional structures*. European University Association.

Hassler, D., Pytash, K. E., Ferdig, R. E., Mucha, N., & Gandolfi, E. (2020). The Use of Digital Poetry to Inform Preservice Teacher Education and In.... *Journal of Technology and Teacher Education*, *28*(2), 403–413.

Hattie, J. (2008). *Visible learning*. Routledge. doi:10.4324/9780203887332

Hattie, J. (2012). *Visible learning for teachers: maximizing impact on learning*. Taylor and Francis. doi:10.4324/9780203181522

Hattie, J., & Timperley, H. (2007). The Power of Feedback. *Review of Educational Research*, *77*(1), 81–112. doi:10.3102/003465430298487

Hawking, S. (2018). *Brief answers to the big questions*. John Murray.

Hawkins, J. (2008). Higher education transformation: some trends in California and Asia. Policy Futures in Education, 6(5), pp. 532-544.

Hayhoe, R. (2008). Philosophy and Comparative Education: What can we learn from East Asia? In K. Mundy, K. Bickmore, R. Hayhoe, M. Madden, & K. Madjidi (Eds.), *Comparative and International Education: Issues for Teachers*. Canadian Scholars' Press Inc.

Hazari, S. (2020). *The evolution of leadership in the past decade*. Gisma. https://www.gisma.com/blog/the-evolution-of-leadership-in-the-past-decade

Healey, N. M. (2007). Is higher education in really 'internationalising'? *Higher Education, 55*(3), 333–355. doi:10.1007/S10734-007-9058-4

Healey, M., & Bordogna, C. (2014). From transnational to multinational education: Emerging trends in international higher education. In E. Beerkens, M. Magna, M. Söderqvist, & H.-G. van Liempd (Eds.), *Internationalisation of higher education*. Raabe Academic Publishers.

Healey, M., Flint, A., & Harrington, K. (2014). *Engagement through partnership: Students as partners in learning and teaching in higher education*. HE Academy.

Healey, M., Flint, A., & Harrington, K. (2016). Students as partners: Reflections on a conceptual model. *Teaching & Learning Inquiry*, *4*(2). doi:10.20343/teachlearninqu.4.2.3

Healey, N. M. (2015). Managing international branch campus: What do we know? *Higher Education Quarterly*, *69*(4), 386–409. doi:10.1111/hequ.12082

Healey, N. M. (2016). The challenges of leading an international branch campus: The "lived experience" of in-country senior manager. *Journal of Studies in Higher Education*, *20*(1), 61–78. doi:10.1177/1028315315602928

Healey, N. M. (2020). The end of transnational education? The view from the UK. *Perspectives: Policy and Practice in Higher Education*, *24*(3), 102–112. doi:10.1080/13603108.2019.1631227

Heath, H., & Cowley, S. (2004). Developing a grounded theory approach: A comparison of Glaser and Strauss. *International Journal of Nursing Studies*, *41*(2), 141–150. doi:10.1016/S0020-7489(03)00113-5 PMID:14725778

Heckler, C., Forde, R., & Bryan, C. (2013). Using writing assignment designs to mitigate plagiarism. *Teaching Sociology, USA*, *41*(1), 94–105. doi:10.1177/0092055X12461471

He, D. (2018). *Foreign Language Learning Anxiety in China: Theories and Applications in English Language Teaching*. Springer. doi:10.1007/978-981-10-7662-6

Hedin, L., & Conderman, G. (2019). Pairing Teachers for Effective Co-Teaching Teams. *Kappa Delta Pi Record*, *55*(4), 169–173. doi:10.1080/00228958.2019.1659063

Heffernan, T., Morrison, D., Magne, P., Payne, S., & Cotton, D. (2019). Internalising internationalisation: Views of internationalisation of the curriculum among non-mobile home students. *Studies in Higher Education*, *44*(12), 2359–2373. doi:10.1080/03075079.2018.1499716

Heffernan, T., Morrison, M., Basu, P., & Sweeney, A. (2010). Cultural differences, learning styles and transnational education. *Journal of Higher Education Policy and Management*, *32*(1), 27–39. doi:10.1080/13600800903440535

He, L. (2016). Transnational higher education institutions in China: A comparison of policy orientation and reality. *Journal of Studies in International Education*, *20*(1), 79–95. doi:10.1177/1028315315602931

He, L., & Wilkins, S. (2018). Achieving Legitimacy in Cross-Border Higher Education: Institutional Influences on Chinese International Branch Campuses in South East Asia. *Journal of Studies in International Education*, *22*(3), 179–197. doi:10.1177/1028315317738774

Helms, R. M. (2014). *Mapping international joint and dual degrees: US program profiles and perspectives*. American Council on Education and Center for Internationalization and Global Engagement. https://www.acenet.edu/Documents/Mapping-International-Joint-and-Dual-Degrees.pdf

Henderson, M., Barnett, R., & Barnett, H. (2017) 'New development in transnational education and the challenges for higher education professional staff.' *Perspectives: Policy and Practice in Higher Education*, *21*(1), pp. 11–19.

Henderson, M., Barnett, R., & Barrett, H. (2017). New developments in transnational education and the challenges for higher education professional staff. *Perspectives: Policy and Practice in Higher Education*, *21*(1), 11–19.

Henningsen, D. D., & Henningsen, M. L. M. (2013). Generating ideas about the uses of brainstorming: Reconsidering the losses and gains of brainstorming groups relative to nominal groups. *The Southern Communication Journal*, *78*(1), 42–55. doi:10.1080/1041794X.2012.717684

Henningsen, D. D., & Henningsen, M. L. M. (2018). Does brainstorming promote cohesiveness? How the rules of brainstorming mirror symbolic convergence. *Communication Reports*, *31*(2), 103–114. doi:10.1080/08934215.2017.1394476

Herman, P. (2020). Online learning is not the future of higher education (opinion). In Inside Higher Education.

Herrmann, K. (2013). The impact of cooperative learning on student engagement: Results from an intervention. *Active Learning in Higher Education*, *14*(3), 175–187. doi:10.1177/1469787413498035

HESA. (2022). *Figure 12 - HE student enrolments based wholly overseas by location and type of provision 2016/17 to 2020/21*. HESA. https://www.hesa.ac.uk/data-and-analysis/sb262/figure-12

HESA. (2022). *Higher Education Student Statistics: UK, 2020/21–Where students come from and go to study*. HESA. https://www.hesa.ac.uk/news/25-01-2022/sb262-higher-education-student-statistics/location

Heslin, P. A. (2009). Better than brainstorming? Potential contextual boundary conditions to brainwriting for idea generation in organizations. *Journal of Occupational and Organizational Psychology*, *82*(1), 129–145. doi:10.1348/096317908X285642

Hessler, P. (2022, May 9). A teacher in China learns the limits of free expression. *The New Yorker*.

Hewitt, E., & Stephenson, J. (2012). Foreign language anxiety and oral exam performance: A replication of Phillips's MLJ study. *Modern Language Journal*, *96*(2), 170–189. doi:10.1111/j.1540-4781.2011.01174.x

Hew, K. F., & Cheung, W. S. (2014). *Using blended learning: Evidence-based practices*. Springer Ltd. doi:10.1007/978-981-287-089-6

He, X., Shelden, D., Kraftson, A., Else, T., & Auchus, R. J. (2020). A virtual teaching clinic for virtual care during the COVID-19 pandemic. *Clinical Diabetes and Endocrinology*, *6*(1), 1–3. doi:10.118640842-020-00108-1 PMID:33251027

Higher Education Student Statistics [HESA] (2018). *Higher Education Student Statistics: UK, 2016/17 - Where students come from and go to study*. HESA. https://www.hesa.ac.uk/data-and-analysis/students/where-from

Hill, C. (2017). *Knowledge creators or knowledge hijackers? Plagiarism in international education*. The Observatory on Borderless Higher Education. https://www.obhe.org/resources/knowledge-creators-or-knowledge-hijackers-plagiarism-in-international-education

Hill, C., & Razvi, S. D. A (2015). *Government and Transnational Education: challenges and opportunities in Asia*. The observatory on borderless higher education.

Hill, C., Cheong, K. C., Leong, Y. C., & Fernandez-Chung, R. (2014). TNE – Trans-national education or tensions between national and external? A case study of Malaysia. *Studies in Higher Education*, *39*(6), 952–966. doi:10.1080/03075079.2012.754862

Hill, C., & Thabet, R. A. (2018). Managing international branch campuses: Lessons learnt from eight years on a branch campus in Malaysia. *International Journal of Educational Management*, *32*(2), 310–322. doi:10.1108/IJEM-04-2017-0079

Hillocks, G. (2011). *Teaching grades 6–12 argument writing*. Heinemann.

Hobgood, C., & Sherwood, G., Frush, et al. (2010). Teamwork training with nursing and medical learners: Does the method matter? Results of an interinstitutional, interdisciplinary collaboration. *Quality & Safety in Health Care*, *19*(6), e25. PMID:20427311

Hodges, C., Moore, S., Lockee, B., Trust, T., & Bond, A. (2020). The difference between emergency remote teaching and online learning. *EDUCAUSE Review, 27*(March). https://er.educause.edu/articles/2020/3/the-difference-between-emergency-remote-teaching-and-online-learning

Hodges, C., Moore, S., Lockee, B., Trust, T., & Bond, A. (2020). *The Difference Between Emergency Remote Teaching and Online Learning*. Educause. https://er.educause.edu/articles/2020/3/the-difference-between-emergency-remote-teaching-and-

Hoegl, M., & Parboteeah, K. P. (2007). Creativity in innovative projects: How teamwork matters. *Journal of Engineering and Technology Management*, *24*(1-2), 148–166. doi:10.1016/j.jengtecman.2007.01.008

Holloway, E. L., & Alexandre, L. (2012). Crossing boundaries in doctoral education: Relational learning, cohort communities, and dissertation committees. *New Directions for Teaching & Learning*, *2012*(131), 85-97.

Holzl, J. (1997). Twelve tips for effective PowerPoint presentations for the technologically challenged. *Medical Teacher*, *19*(3), 175–179. doi:10.3109/01421599709019377

Hong Nguyen, C. (2013). Vietnamese international student mobility: Past and current trends. *Asian Education and Development Studies*, *2*(2), 127–148. doi:10.1108/20463161311321411

Hooda, M., & Sharma, M. (2017). The Effect of Team Teaching on Academic Achievement of 9th Grades in Science. *Scholarly Research Journal for Interdisciplinary Studies*, *3* (23), 1906-1915. https://www.academia.edu/25316443/THE_EFFECT_OF_TEAM_TEACHING_ON_ACADEMIC_ACHIEVEMENT_OF_9TH_GRADERS_IN_SCIENCE

Ho, R. (2010). Assessment of Chinese students' experience with foreign faculty: A case study from a Chinese University. *Journal of Teaching in International Business*, *21*(3), 156–177. doi:10.1080/08975930.2010.504461

Horn, M. B. (2018) Will half colleges really closed in the next decade? Christian Institute. https://www.christensenin-stitute.org/blog/will-half-of-all-colleges-really-close-in-the-next-decade/

Horwitz, E. K., Horwitz, M. B., & Cope, J. (1986). Foreign language classroom anxiety. *Modern Language Journal*, *70*(2), 125–132. doi:10.1111/j.1540-4781.1986.tb05256.x

Hou, J., Montgomery, C., & McDowell, L. (2014). Exploring the diverse motivations of transnational higher education in China: Complexities and contradictions. *Journal of Education for Teaching: International research and pedagogy*, *40*(3), 300-318.

Hou, J., Montgomery, C., & McDowell, L. (2014). Exploring the diverse motivations of transnational higher education in China: Complexities and contradictions. *Journal of Education for Teaching*, *40*(3), 300–318. doi:10.1080/02607476.2014.903028

Hsu, H. C. K., Wang, C. V., & Levesque-Bristol, C. (2019). Reexamining the impact of self-determination theory on learning outcomes in the online learning environment. *Education and Information Technologies*, *24*(3), 2159–2174. doi:10.100710639-019-09863-w

Huang, C. W., & Archer, A. (2017). "Academic literacies" as moving beyond writing: Investigating multimodal approaches to academic argument. *London Review of Education*, *15*(1), 63–72. doi:10.18546/LRE.15.1.06

Huang, F. (2003). Transnational higher education: A perspective from China. *Higher Education Research & Development*, *22*(2), 193–203. doi:10.1080/07294360304114

Huang, F. (2007). Internalization of higher education in the developing and emerging countries: A focus on transnational higher education in Asia. *Journal of Studies in International Education*, *11*(3-4), 421–432. doi:10.1177/1028315307303919

Huang, F. (2014). *The internationalisation of the academic profession. The internationalization of the academy, 1-21*. Springer. doi:10.1007/978-94-007-7278-6

Huang, S. (2011). An analysis on the general education mode of universities in mainland China [Lexical characteristics of Chinese language] [Social Science Edition]. *Journal of Guangdong University of Technology*, *11*(1), 15.

Huang, X. H., & van Naerssen, M. (1987). Learning strategies for oral communication. *Applied Linguistics*, *8*(3), 287–307. doi:10.1093/applin/8.3.287

Hu, G. (2002). Potential cultural resistance to pedagogical imports: The case of communicative language teaching in China. *Language, Culture and Curriculum*, *15*(2), 93–105. doi:10.1080/07908310208666636

Hu, G. (2005, January). 'CLT is best for China'—An untenable absolutist claim. *ELT Journal*, *59*(1), 65–68. doi:10.1093/elt/cci009

Hu, K., & Cadwell, P. (2016). A comparative study of post-editing guidelines. *Baltic Journal of Modern Computing*, *4*(2), 346–353. doi:10.13140/RG.2.1.2253.1446

Hu, M., Eisenchlas, S. A., & Trevaskes, S. (2019). Factors affecting the quality of transnational higher education in China: A qualitative content analysis on Chinese host universities' self-appraisal reports. *Journal of Higher Education Policy and Management*, *41*(3), 306–321. doi:10.1080/1360080X.2019.1591679

Hussain, I. (2007). Transnational Education: Concepts and Methods. *Turkish Online Journal of Distance Education-TOJDE*, *8*(1).

Hussain, I. (2007). Transnational education: Concept and methods. *Turkish Online Journal of Distance Education, 8*(1). doi:10.17718/tojde.99261

Hussein Amoush, K. (2015). The impact of employing brainstorming strategy on improving writing performance of English major students at Balqa Applied University in Jordan. *Journal of Education and Practice, 6*(35), 88–92.

Hutchinson, T., & Waters, A. (1987). *English for Specific Purposes*. Cambridge UP. doi:10.1017/CBO9780511733031

Hutchins, W. J., & Somers, H. L. (1992). *An introduction to machine translation*. Academic Press.

Hwee Ling Koh, J., Sing Chai, C., Wong, B., & Hong, H.-Y. (2015). *Design thinking for education: Conceptions and applications in teaching and learning*. Springer.

Ibrahim, D. Z., & Silong, A. D. (2000, October). Barriers to self-directed learning in a virtual environment among adult students. In *14th Annual Conference of the Asian Association of Open Universities* (pp. 25-27). Journal of Advanced Medicine Application.

IDEO U. (2019, July 29). *IDEO brainstorming video from IDEO U*. IDEO U. https://www.youtube.com/watch?v=WIVlACbAWio

IGI Global. (2021). Call for Chapters: Developments and Future Trends. In *Transnational Higher Education*. IGI Global. https://www.igi-global.com/publish/call-for-papers/call-details/5725

Imam, S. R. (2005). English as a global language and the question of nation-building education in Bangladesh. *Comparative Education, 41*(4), 471–486. doi:10.1080/03050060500317588

Inamorato dos Santos, A., Gaušas, S., Mackevičiūtė, R., Jotautytė, A., & Martinaitis, Ž. (2019). Innovating Professional Development in Higher Education: Case Studies, EUR 29669 EN, Publications Office of the European Union. doi:10.2760/712385

InterUniversity Council. (2018). *The criteria for the promotion and appointment for the associate professorship*. UAK. https://www.uak.gov.tr/Documents/docentlik/2021-eylul-donemi/basvuru-sartlari/TA_Tablo11_2021E_15092021.pdf

Irwin, R. (2007). Culture shock: negotiating feelings in the field. *Anthropology Matters, 9*(1). https://anthropologymatters.com/index.php/anth_matters/article/view/64/124

Isaksen, S. G., & Gaulin, J. P. (2005). A reexamination of brainstorming research: Implications for research and practice. *Gifted Child Quarterly, 49*(4), 315–329. doi:10.1177/001698620504900405

Islam, R. (2018). Bangladesh ranks 143rd in corruption index. *Dhaka Tribune*. https://www.dhakatribune.com/bangladesh/2018/02/22/tib-bangladesh-progresses-two-positions-corruption-perceptions-index/

Islam, M. T. (2019). (Re)searching for the development of a conceptual model of education for citizenship in the context of young people's globalised mobility in higher education. *Globalisation, Societies and Education, 17*(2), 194–207. doi:10.1080/14767724.2019.1583093

Islam, M. T. (2021). Cultural cultivation for the mobility of Bangladeshi higher education students in Australia. *Higher Education Research & Development, 41*(5), 1572–1585. doi:10.1080/07294360.2021.1902950

Islam, M. T. (2022a). (Un)employability and (un)employment issues towards international mobility for higher education. In P. O. de Pablos, X. Zhang, & M. N. Almunawar (Eds.), *Education Institutions, Skills, and Jobs in the Digital Era: Toward a More Inclusive and Resilient Society*. IGI Global. doi:10.4018/978-1-6684-5914-0.ch008

Islam, M. T. (2022b). Bauman or Appadurai? In theorising mobilities of the Southern higher education students in the North. In K. Jermsittiparsert, P. Suanpang, A. Nuemaihom, & P. Siriattaku (Eds.), *Handbook of Research on Current Trends in Asian Education, Psychology, and Sociology*. IGI Global.

Islam, M. T. (2022c). Media mediation on academic advancement for youths' international mobility pursuing higher education. In S. Bansal, V. Ahuja, V. Chaturvedi, & V. Jain (Eds.), *Multidisciplinary Perspectives Towards Building a Digitally Competent Society*. IGI Global. doi:10.4018/978-1-6684-5274-5.ch012

Ivanov, A., & Zelchenko, P. (2020). Designing an electronic brainstorming environment for engaging East-Asian teams. *International Journal of Human-Computer Interaction, 36*(5), 414–428. doi:10.1080/10447318.2019.1649970

Jacobs, C. (2005). On being an insider on the outside: New spaces for integrating academic literacies. *Teaching in Higher Education, 10*(4), 475–487. doi:10.1080/13562510500239091

Jacobs, C. (2007). Towards a critical understanding of the teaching of discipline-specific academic literacies: Making the tacit explicit. *Journal of Education, 41*(1), 59–81.

Jaidev, R., & Blackstone, B. (2016). *Facilitating Workplace Communicative Competence. English Language Teaching Today, 293-307.* Springer.

Jameau, A., & Le Henaff, C. (2018). "Content and Language Integrated Learning" teaching in science: A didactic analysis of a case study. *Review of Science Mathematics & ICT Education, 12*(2), 21.

Janet, I., Vangelis, T., Pat, K., & Uwe, B. (2021). *Local impact of transnational education.* British Council. www.britishcouncil.org

Jesson, R., McNaughton, S., Rosedale, N., Zhu, T., & Cockle, V. (2018). A mixed-methods study to identify effective practices in the teaching of writing in a digital learning environment in low income schools. *Computers & Education, 119*, 14–30. doi:10.1016/j.compedu.2017.12.005

Jiang, L. (2010). An exploration on the development of general education in China [Lexical characteristics of Chinese language]. *China Education Innovation Heraid, 29.*

Jiang, Y., Li, P., Wang, J., & Li, H. (2019). Relationships between kindergarten teachers' empowerment, job satisfaction and organisational climate: A Chinese model. *Journal of Research in Childhood Research, 33*(2), 257–270.

Jing, X., Ghosh, R., Sun, Z., & Liu, Q. (2020). Mapping global research related to international students: A scientometric review. *Higher Education, 80*(3), 1–19. doi:10.100710734-019-00489-y

Jin, L., & Cortazzi, M. (2020). Reaching for the gold standard: Metaphors and good university teachers. [De Gruyter]. *Canadian Journal of Applied Linguistics, 43*(2), 131–149.

JISC and Internet2. (2018). *Transnational education (TNE) data report.* [Data set]. JISC and Internet2. https://wiki.geant.org/download/attachments/103713412/TNE%20data%20by%20country_v12_final.pdf?version=1&modificationDate=1525804573391&api=v2

Johari, B. M. (2000). Higher education planning in Malaysia. *Education Quarterly*, (July/August), 7–12.

Johnson, J. (2001). 10 Out of 10. *English Teaching Professional, 18*, 57.

Johnson, S. L. (2009). *Winning debates: A guide to debating in the style of the world universities debating championships*. International Debate Education Association.

Johnson, W. L. (2010). Using immersive simulations to develop intercultural competence. In *Culture and computing* (pp. 1–15). Springer. doi:10.1007/978-3-642-17184-0_1

Jones, M., & Sheridan, L. (2015). Back translation: An emerging sophisticated cyber strategy to subvert advances in 'digital age' plagiarism detection and prevention. *Assessment & Evaluation in Higher Education*, *40*(5), 712–724. doi: 10.1080/02602938.2014.950553

Jones, N., & Saville, N. (2016). *Learning Oriented Assessment: A Systemic Approach, Studies in Language Testing* (Vol. 45). Cambridge University Press.

Jordan, R. R. (1997). *English for academic purposes: A guide and resource book for teachers* (11th ed.). Cambridge University Press. doi:10.1017/CBO9780511733062

Jowett, B. (2000). *The republic*. Dover Publication.

Jullien, F. (2004). *A treatise on efficacy: Between Western and Chinese thinking*. University of Hawaii Press.

Junco, R. (2012). The relationship between frequency of Facebook use, participation in Facebook activities, and learner engagement. *Computers & Education*, *58*(1), 162–171. doi:10.1016/j.compedu.2011.08.004

Junge, M. (2008). Bauman on ambivalence: Fully acknowledging the ambiguity of ambivalence. In M. H. Jacobsen (Ed.), *The sociology of Zygmaunt Bauman: Challenges and critique* (pp. 41–56). Routledge.

Jung, J. Y. (2013). Adolescent Decision-Making Processes Regarding University Entry: A model incorporating cultural orientation, motivation and occupational variables. *Tertiary Education and Management*, *19*(2), 97–111. doi:10.1080/13583883.2012.747107

Jyoti, J. (2010). Job satisfaction of university teachers: An empirical study. *Journal of Services Research*, *9*(2), 51–80.

Kagwesage, A. M. (2012). Higher education students' reflections on learning in times of academic language shift. *International Journal for the Scholarship of Teaching and Learning*, *6*(2), 1–14. doi:10.20429/ijsotl.2012.060218

Kahn, Z. (2011). *Factors affecting the motivation of expatriate English as a foreign language (EFL) teachers in the Sultanate of Oman.* [Unpublished EdD Thesis, University of Exeter, UK].

Kandiller, S. T., & Özler, D. (2015). From teacher to trainer: What changes? Or does it? *Procedia: Social and Behavioral Sciences*, *199*, 436–452. doi:10.1016/j.sbspro.2015.07.530

Kashefi, H., Ismail, Z., & Yusof, Y. M. (2012). The impact of blended learning on communication skills and teamwork of engineering learners in multivariable calculus. *Procedia: Social and Behavioral Sciences*, *56*, 341–347. doi:10.1016/j.sbspro.2012.09.662

Katz, N. (1990). Problem solving and time: Functions of learning style and teaching methods. *OTJR (Thorofare, N.J.)*, *10*(4), 221–236.

Kaufman, J. (2012). *Personal MBA*. Penguin.

Kavadias, S., & Sommer, S. C. (2009). The effects of problem structure and team diversity on brainstorming effectiveness. *Management Science*, *55*(12), 1899–1913. doi:10.1287/mnsc.1090.1079

Kawaguchi, Y. (2005). 7010 Possibility of International Exchange Student Workshop: Case Study of Japan-Korea Architectural Design Workshop (Urban Planning). *Proceeding of the architectural research meetings: architectural planning and design, urban planning, rural planning, building economics, history and theory of architecture,* (75), 253-256.

Kaya, M., & Erbay, E. (2020). Global trends of the researches on COVID-19: A bibliometric analysis via VOSviewer. *Ankara Sağlık Bilimleri Dergisi,* 201-216. https://www.doi.org/10.46971/ausbid.817925

Keay, J., May, H., & O'Mahony, J. (2014). Improving learning and teaching in transnational education: Can communities of practice help? *Journal of Education for Teaching*, *40*(3), 251–266. https://www.tandfonline.com/doi/full/10.1080/02607476.2014.903025?scroll=top&needAccess=true. doi:10.1080/02607476.2014.903025

Keevers, L. M., Price, O., Leask, B., Dawood Sultan, F. K., Lim, J. S., & Loh, V. (2019). Practices to improve collaboration by reconfiguring boundaries in transnational education. *Journal of University Teaching & Learning Practice*, *16*(2), 38–53. doi:10.53761/1.16.2.4

Keller, J. (2011). Reversing course: University of California to borrow millions for online classes. *The Chronicle of Higher Education.*

Keller, J. M. (2010). Motivational design research and development. In *Motivational design for learning and performance* (pp. 297–323). Springer. doi:10.1007/978-1-4419-1250-3_12

Kelley, T., & Littman, J. (2001). *The art of innovation: Lessons in creativity from IDEO, America's leading design firm.* Currency/Doubleday.

Kelley, T., & Littman, J. (2005). *The ten faces of innovation: IDEO's strategies for beating the devil's advocate & driving creativity throughout your organization.* Currency/Doubleday.

Kennedy, K., & Ferdig, R. E. (2018, April 12). *Handbook of Research on K-12 Online and Blended Learning (Second Edition).* ETC Press. https://press.etc.cmu.edu/index.php/product/handbook-of-research-on-k-12-and-blending-learning-second-edition/

Kesper-Biermann, S. (2019). Transnational Education in Historical Perspective. The Deutsche Kolonialschule (1898-1944). *Diskurs Kindheits- Und Jugendforschung / Discourse Journal of Childhood and Adolescence Research, 4*(4), 417–430. doi:10.3224/DISKURS.V14I4.04

Ketelle, D. (2017). Introduction to the Special Issue: What Is Storytelling in the Higher Education Classroom? *Storytelling, Self, Society*, *13*(2), 143–150. doi:10.13110torselfsoci.13.2.0143

Key, T., & Duening, T. (2020). Strategic Entrepreneurial Storytelling: An Applied Framework for Better Pitches. *Contemporary Management Research*, *16*(4), 279–300. doi:10.7903/cmr.19684

Khanal, J., & Gaulee, U. (2019). Challenges of international students from pre-departure to post-study: A literature review. *Journal of International Students*, *9*(2), 560–581. doi:10.32674/jis.v9i2.673

Killingsworth, B., & Xue, Y. (2015). Investigating Factors Influencing Students' Learning in a Team-Teaching Setting. *International Journal of Cognitive Research in Science. Engineering and Education*, *3*(2), 9–16.

Kim, E. H., & Zhu, M. (2010). Universities as firms: The case of US overseas programs. In C. T. Clotfelter (Ed.), *American universities in a global market* (pp. 163–201). University of Chicago Press. doi:10.7208/chicago/9780226110455.003.0006

Kim, E. Y. J., & LaBianca, A. S. (2018). Ethics in academic writing help for international students in higher education: Perceptions of faculty and students. *Journal of Academic Ethics*, *16*(1), 39–59. doi:10.100710805-017-9299-5

Kim, H. R., & Bowless, M. (2019). How Deeply Do Second Language Learners Process Written Corrective Feedback? Insights Gained From Think-Alouds. *TESOL Quarterly*, *53*(4), 913–938. doi:10.1002/tesq.522

Kim, J. (2011). Aspiration for global cultural capital in the stratified realm of global higher education: Why do Korean students go to US graduate schools? *British Journal of Sociology of Education*, *32*(1), 109–126. doi:10.1080/01425692.2011.527725

Kim, T. (2009). Transnational academic mobility, internationalization and interculturality in higher education. *Intercultural Education, 20*(5), 395–405. doi:10.1080/14675980903371241

King, M. L. (1947) The Purpose of Education. The Maroon Tiger - Morehouse College student newspaper.

King, M. L. (1965). Remaining Awake Through a Great Revolution. Oberlin College commencement speech]. Oberlin College. https://www2.oberlin.edu/external/EOG/BlackHistoryMonth/MLK/CommAddress.html

Kirby, W., & van der Wende, M. (2019). New Silk Road: Implications for higher education in China and the West? *Cambridge Journal of Regions, Economy and Society, 12*(1), 127–144. doi:10.1093/cjres/rsy034

Kir, E., & Akyüz, A. (2020). An exploration of perceptions of faculty members and students: The effects of English-medium instruction on language ability. In M. L. Carrió-Pastor (Ed.), *Internationalising learning in higher education: The challenges of English as a medium of instruction* (pp. 155–177). Springer. doi:10.1007/978-3-030-21587-3_8

Kirkland, R. (2004). *Taoism: The enduring tradition.* Routledge. doi:10.4324/9780203646717

Kirkpatrick, D., & Kirkpatrick, J. (2006). *Evaluating training programs: the four levels* (3rd ed.). Berrett-Koehler Publishers.

Kit, C., & Wong, T. M. (2008). Comparative evaluation of online machine translation systems with legal texts. *Law Library Journal, 100*(2), 299–31.

Klisowska, I., Seń, M., & Grabowska, B.KLISOWSKA. (2021). Advantages and disadvantages of distance learning. *E-Methodology, 7*(7), 27–32. doi:10.15503/emet2020.27.32

Knight, J. (2018). International education hubs. *Geographies of the university*, 637-655.

Knight, J. and McNamara, J. (2017). *Transnational Education: A Classification Framework and Data Collection Guidelines for International Programme and Provider Mobility (IPPM).* British Council and German Academic Exchange services.

Knight, J., & Mcnamara, J. (2017). *Transnational education: a classification framework and data collection guidelines for international programme and provider mobility (IPPM).* DAAD. www.daad.de

Knight, J. (2011). Education hubs: A fad, a brand, an innovation? *Journal of Studies in International Education, 15*(3), 221–240. doi:10.1177/1028315311398046

Knight, J. (2015). International universities: Misunderstandings and emerging models? *Journal of Studies in International Education, 19*(2), 107–121. https://journals.sagepub.com/doi/abs/10.1177/1028315315572899. doi:10.1177/1028315315572899

Knight, J. (2016). Transnational education remodeled: Toward a common TNE framework and definitions. *Journal of Studies in International Education, 20*(1), 34–47. doi:10.1177/1028315315602927

Knight, J., & Morshidi, S. (2011). The complexities and challenges of regional education hubs: Focus on Malaysia. *Higher Education, 62*(5), 593–606. doi:10.100710734-011-9467-2

Knowles, C. L. (2022). Using an ADAPT approach to integrate Google Translate into the second language classroom. *Journal of Linguistics and Language Teaching, 14*(1), 195–236. doi:10.5070/L214151690

Knowles, M. S., Holton, E. F. III, & Swanson, R. A. (2014). *The adult learner: The definitive classic in adult education and human resource development.* Routledge. doi:10.4324/9781315816951

Kobo-Greenhut, A., Reuveni, H., Ben Shlomo, I., & Megnezi, R. (2019). Unstructured brainstorming is not enough: Structured brainstorming based on four verification and validation questions yields better hazard identification in healthcare. *International Journal for Quality in Health Care, 31*(7), G16–G21. doi:10.1093/intqhc/mzy208 PMID:30295820

Kohn, N. W., & Smith, S. M. (2011). Collaborative fixation: Effects of others' ideas on brainstorming. *Applied Cognitive Psychology, 25*(3), 359–371. doi:10.1002/acp.1699

Kolb, A. Y., & Kolb, D. A. (2009). Experiential learning theory: A dynamic, holistic approach to management learning, education and development. The SAGE handbook of management learning, education and development, 42, 68.

Kolb, D. (1984). Expenmental learning experience as a source of learning and development. Englewood Cliffs.

Kolb, D. A. (2014). *Experiential learning: Experience as the source of learning and development.* FT press.

Kolb, D., Rubin, I., & McIntyre, J. (1974). Organizational psychology: a book of readings. 2nd Edition, Englewood Cliffs.

Korde, R., & Paulus, P. B. (2017). Alternating individual and group idea generation: Finding the elusive synergy. *Journal of Experimental Social Psychology, 70*, 177–190. doi:10.1016/j.jesp.2016.11.002

Kosmützky, A., & Putty, R. (2016). Transcending borders and traversing boundaries: A systematic review of the literature on transnational, offshore, cross-border, and borderless higher education. *Journal of Studies in International Education, 20*(1), 8–33. doi:10.1177/1028315315604719

Kosnik, C., Miyata, C., Cleovoulou, Y., Fletcher, T., & Menna, L. (2015). The Education of Teacher Educators. Falkenberg, T. (Ed.). *Handbook of Canadian research in initial teacher education.* Ottawa, ON: Canadian Association for Teacher Education. https://www.csse-scee.ca/associations/about/cate-acfe

Kotter, J. P. (2021). *Change: How Organizations Achieve Hard-to-Imagine Results Despite Uncertain and Volatile Times.* Wiley.

Kozbial, S. (2022). Towards Student-Centred Learning: Using Exploratory Practice with Undergraduate Students in an International Branch Campus in China. *Inform (Silver Spring, Md.), 21*, 12–15. https://www.reading.ac.uk/web/files/inform/B28079_InForm_Issue_21_FINAL.pdf

Krakoff, S. (2020). *The top 10 qualities of a great leader.* Champlain College. https://online.champlain.edu/blog/top-qualities-of-a-great-leader

Krause, K. L., & Coates, H. (2008). Students' engagement in first-year university. *Assessment & Evaluation in Higher Education, 33*(5), 493–505. doi:10.1080/02602930701698892

Kudo, K., Volet, S., & Whitsed, C. (2020). Intercultural relationship development and higher education internationalisation: A qualitative investigation based on a three-stage ecological and person-in-context conceptual framework. *Higher Education, 80*(5), 913–932. doi:10.100710734-020-00523-4

Kuh, G. D. (2009). What student affairs professionals need to know about student engagement. *Journal of College Student Development, 50*(6), 683–706. doi:10.1353/csd.0.0099

Kuhn, T. S. (1970). *The structure of scientific revolutions* (Vol. 111). University of Chicago Press.

Kuptsch, C., & Pang, E. F. (Eds.). (2006). *Competing for global talent.* International Labour Organization.

Kuriyama, N., & Miwa, K. (2010). Report on WAT Kobe 2009, the international workshop on urban landscape and the environment in Kobe UNESCO City of Design. *Journal of the City Planning Institute of Japan, 45*(3), 295–300. doi:10.11361/journalcpij.45.3.295

Lacore-Martin, E. (2019, July 5). *The elephant in the room: Rethinking language assessment in the times of Google Translate* [Symposium]. Translation Technology in Education – Facilitator or Risk? Nottingham Trent University.

Lado, R. (1967). *Language Testing: A Teacher's Book.* Longmans.

Lambert, J. L., & Fisher, J. L. (2013). Community of inquiry framework: Establishing community in an online course. *Journal of Interactive Online Learning*, *12*(1), 1–16.

Lane, J. E., Brgos, J., Schueller, J., Dey, S., Kinser, K., & Zipf, S. (2021, March 13). What is the future for international branch campuses? *University World News*. https://www.universityworldnews.com/post.php?story=2021031012405285

Lane, J. E. (2011). Importing Private higher education: International branch campuses. *Journal of Comparative Policy Analysis*, *13*(4), 367–381. doi:10.1080/13876988.2011.583106

Larose, S., Duchesne, S., Litalien, D., Denault, A.-S., & Boivin, M. (2019). Adjustment Trajectories During the College Transition: Types, Personal and Family Antecedents, and Academic Outcomes. *Research in Higher Education*, *60*(5), 684–710. doi:10.100711162-018-9538-7

Lasagabaster, D. (2017). "I always speak English in my classes": Reflections on the use of the L1/L2 in English-medium instruction. In A. Llinares & T. Morton (Eds.), *Applied linguistics perspectives on CLIL* (pp. 251–267). John Benjamins Publishing Company. doi:10.1075/lllt.47.15las

Lasco, G. (2015). The smartphone as status symbol. *Philippine Daily Inquirer*. https://opinion.inquirer.net/89605/the-smartphone-as-status-symbol

Laughlin, K., Nelson, P., & Donaldson, S. (2011). Successfully Applying Team Teaching with Adult Learners. *Journal of Adult Education*, *40*(1), 11–18.

Le, Q. V., & Schuster, M. (2016, September 27). A neural network for machine translation, at production scale. *Google AI Blog*. https://ai.googleblog.com/2016/09/a-neural-network-for-machine.html

Leask, B. (2004). Transnational education and intercultural learning: Reconstructing the offshore teaching team to enhance internationalisation. Australia: *Australian Universities Quality Forum*.

Leask, B. (2004). Transnational education and intercultural learning: Reconstructing the offshore teaching team to enhance internationalisation. *Australian Universities Quality Forum*. https://www.researchgate.net/profile/Betty-Leask/publication/266277495_Transnational_Education_and_Intercultural_Learning_Reconstructing_the_Offshore_Teaching_Team_to_Enhance_Internationalisation/links/565dfe2608ae4988a7bd294e/Transnational-Education-and-Intercultural-Learning-Reconstructing-the-Offshore-Teaching-Team-to-Enhance-Internationalisation.pdf

Lee, R. L. M. (2005). Bauman, liquid modernity and dilemmas of development. *Thesis Eleven, 83*(1), 61–77.

Lee, E. L. (2007). Linguistic and cultural factors in East Asian students' oral participation in U.S. university classrooms. *International Education*, *36*(3), 29–47.

Lee, E., Pate, J. A., & Cozart, D. (2015). Autonomy support for online students. *TechTrends*, *59*(4), 54–61. doi:10.100711528-015-0871-9

Lee, M., & Wright, E. (2016). Moving from elite international schools to the world's elite universities: A critical perspective. *International Journal of Comparative Education and Development*, *18*(2), 120–136. doi:10.1108/IJCED-01-2016-0002

Lee, S. M. (2020). The impact of using machine translation on EFL students' writing. *Computer Assisted Language Learning*, *33*(3), 157–175. doi:10.1080/09588221.2018.1553186

Lee, S. M. (2021). The effectiveness of machine translation in foreign language education: A systematic review and meta-analysis. *Computer Assisted Language Learning*, 1–23. doi:10.1080/09588221.2021.1901746

Le-Ha, P. (2006). Plagiarism and overseas students: Stereotypes again? *ELT Journal*, *60*(1), 76–78. doi:10.1093/elt/cci085

Le-Ha, P. (2017). *Transnational education crossing 'Asia' and 'the West': Adjusted desire, transformative mediocrity and neo-colonial disguise*. Routledge.

Lehrer, J. (2012, January 30). Groupthink. The brainstorming myth. *The New Yorker*, 22–27. https://www.newyorker.com/magazine/2012/01/30/groupthink

Leijon, M., & Lundgren, B. (2019). Connecting physical and virtual spaces in a HyFlex pedagogic model with a focus on teacher interaction. *Journal of Learning Spaces*, *8*(1), 1–9. http://libjournal.uncg.edu/jls/article/view/1640

Leonardi, V. (2015). Bridging the gap between ESP and CliL in the university context. *Testi Letterature Linguaggi*, *5*, 18-26. https://www.iperstoria.it/joomla/images/PDF/Numero%205%20giusto/saggi_monografica/Leonardi_ESPCLIL.pdf

Leong, L. M., & Ahmadi, S. M. (2017). FLUENCING LEARNERS'ENGLISH SPEAKING SKILL. *International Journal of English Education.*

Levy, F., & Murnane, R. J. (2005). *The new division of labor how computers are creating the next job market*. Princeton University Press.

Li, L., & Morris, G. R. (2021). *Thriving in the New Normal: In-Service Professional Development Needs and Experiences*. doi:10.4018/978-1-7998-7226-9.ch013

Li, S. (2018). Transnational higher education in China: Thirty years of development. *Higher Education Forum, 6*, 49–58.

Liaw, M. L. (2006). E-learning and the development of intercultural competence. *Language Learning & Technology*, *10*(3), 49–64.

Lidolf, S., & Pasco, D. (2020). Educational Technology Professional Development in Higher Education: A Systematic Literature Review of Empirical Research. *Frontiers in Education*, *5*, 35. doi:10.3389/feduc.2020.00035

Liedtka, J., & Ogilvie, T. (2011). *Designing for growth.* Columbia University Press.

Lietaert, S., Roorda, D., Laevers, F., Verschueren, K., & De Fraine, B. (2015). The gender gap in student engagement: The role of teachers' autonomy support, structure, and involvement. *The British Journal of Educational Psychology*, *85*(4), 498–518. doi:10.1111/bjep.12095 PMID:26446905

Lieva, J., Tsiligkiris, V., Killingley, P., & Brandenburg, U. (2021). *Local impact of transnational education: A pilot study in selected European countries.* British Council. https://www.britishcouncil.org/education/he-science/knowledge-centre/transnational-education/local-impact-TNE-Europe

Li, L. (2014). Understanding language teachers' practice with educational technology: A case from China. *System*, *46*, 105–119. doi:10.1016/j.system.2014.07.016

Li, L., & Walsh, S. (2011). Technology uptake in Chinese EFL classes. *Language Teaching Research*, *15*(1), 99–125. doi:10.1177/1362168810383347

Li, L., & Wegerif, R. (2014). What does it mean to teach thinking in China? Challenging and developing notions of "Confucian education.". *Thinking Skills and Creativity*, *11*, 22–32. doi:10.1016/j.tsc.2013.09.003

Li, L., Xu, L. D., He, Y., He, W., Pribesh, S., Watson, S. M., & Major, D. A. (2021). Facilitating online learning via zoom breakout room technology: A case of pair programming involving students with learning disabilities. *Communications of the Association for Information Systems*, *48*(1), 12. doi:10.17705/1CAIS.04812

Lim, I. (2017, October 25). After 2017's 20 pc cut, public universities' operating budget goes up. *Malay Mail*. https://www.malaymail.com/s/1497297/after-2017s-20pc-cutpublic-universities-operating-budget-goes-up

Lim, C. B., Bentley, D., Henderson, F., Pan, S. Y., Balakrishnan, V. D., Balasingam, D. M., & Teh, Y. Y. (2016). Equivalent or not?: Beyond measuring teaching and learning standards in a transnational education environment. *Quality Assurance in Education, 24*(4), 528–540. doi:10.1108/QAE-01-2016-0001

Lim, P. K. C., & Mak, J. W. (Eds.). (2015). *Learning for the Future: The IMU Experiment*. International Medical University.

Lim, W. M., Jee, T. W., & De Run, E. C. (2018). Strategic brand management for higher education institutions with graduate degree programs: Empirical insights from the higher education marketing mix. *Journal of Strategic Marketing, 28*(3), 225–245. doi:10.1080/0965254X.2018.1496131

Lin Sin, I., Leung, M. W. H., & Waters, J. L. (2019). Degrees of value: Comparing the contextual complexities of UK transnational education in Malaysia and Hong Kong. *Compare: A Journal of Comparative Education, 49*(1), 132–148. doi:10.1080/03057925.2017.1390663

Lindgren, H. C., & Lindgren, F. (1965). Creativity, brainstorming, and orneriness: A cross-cultural study. *The Journal of Social Psychology, 67*(23), 23–30. doi:10.1080/00224545.1965.9922254 PMID:5827919

Lin, L. H., Ho, Y. L., & Lin, W. H. (2013). Confucian and Taoist Work Values: An Exploratory Study of the Chinese Transformational Leadership Behavior. *Journal of Business Ethics, 113*(1), 91–103. doi:10.100710551-012-1284-8

Litan, R. (2020). *Resolved: Debate can revolutionize education and help save our democracy*. Brookings Institution Press.

Littlefield, C. M., Taddei, L. M., & Radosh, M. E. (2015). Organic collaborative teams: The role of collaboration and peer to peer support for part-time doctoral completion. *International Journal of Doctoral Studies, 10*, 129–142. http://ijds.org/Volume10/IJDSv10p129-142Littlefield0790.pdf. doi:10.28945/2113

Liu, D. (2005). Plagiarism in ESOL students: Is cultural conditioning truly the major culprit? *ELT Journal, 59*(3), 234–241. doi:10.1093/elt/cci043

Liu, D., Vogel, L., & MacLeod, J. (2016). Mitigating transitional challenges of Chinese students in U.S. higher education. *Higher Education Studies, 6*(3), 100–113. doi:10.5539/hes.v6n3p100

Liu, J. (2012). Does cram schooling matter? Who goes to cram schools? Evidence from Taiwan. *International Journal of Educational Development, 32*(1), 46–52. doi:10.1016/j.ijedudev.2011.01.014

Liu, J., & Gao, Y. (2022). Higher education internationalisation at the crossroads: Effects of the coronavirus pandemic. *Tertiary Education and Management, 28*(1), 1–15. doi:10.100711233-021-09082-4

Liu, J., & Zheng, S. (2013). The enlightenment of Harvard University's core curriculum to China's general education [Lexical characteristics of Chinese language]. *Research and Teaching, 276*, 17.

Liu, O., Bridgeman, B., & Adler, R. (2012). Measuring learning outcomes in higher education: Motivation matters. *Educational Researcher, Princeton, NJ, USA, 41*(9), 352–362. doi:10.3102/0013189X12459679

Liu, S., Morris, M. W., Talhelm, T., & Yang, Q. (2019). Ingroup vigilance in collectivistic culture. *Proceedings of the National Academy of Sciences of the United States of America, 116*(29), 14538–14546. doi:10.1073/pnas.1817588116 PMID:31249140

Liu, W. (2016). The international mobility of chinese students: A cultural perspective. *Canadian Journal of Higher Education, 46*(4), 41–59. doi:10.47678/cjhe.v46i4.186143

Liu, Y. (2019). Choices, risks and rational conformity: Extending Boudon's positional theory to understand higher education choices in contemporary China. *Higher Education, 77*(3), 525–540. doi:10.100710734-018-0285-7

Li, Y., Cargill, M., Gao, X., Wang, X., & O'Connor, P. (2019). A scientist in interdisciplinary team-teaching in an English for Research Publication Purposes classroom: Beyond a "cameo role". *Journal of English for Academic Purposes*, *40*, 129–140. doi:10.1016/j.jeap.2019.06.005

Liyanagunawardena, T. R., Adams, A. A., & Williams, S. A. (2013). MOOCs: A systematic study of the published literature 2008-2012. *International Review of Research in Open and Distributed Learning*, *14*(3), 202–227. doi:10.19173/irrodl.v14i3.1455

Lock, J., Clancy, T., Lisella, R., Rosenau, P., Ferreira, C., & Rainsbury, J. (2016). The Lived Experiences of Instructors Co-Teaching in Higher Education. *Brock Journal of Education*, *26*(1), 22–35.

Lombardi, M. M., & Oblinger, D. G. (2007). Authentic learning for the 21st century: An overview. *Educause learning initiative, 1*(2007), 1-12.

Lörz, M., Netz, N., & Quast, H. (2016). Why do students from underprivileged families less often intend to study abroad? *Higher Education*, *72*(2), 153–174. doi:10.100710734-015-9943-1

Louis, C., Lawrence, M., & Keith, M. (2007). *Research methods in education.* Routledge.

Lowery, C. L. (2016). Critical transnational pedagogy: Toward a critical theory of transnational education and learning. In E. J. Francois, M. B. Avoseh, & W. Griswold (Eds.), Perspectives in transnational higher education (pp. 55–73). Sense Publishers.

Lozano, G. A. (2014). Ethics of using language editing services in an era of digital communication and heavily multi-authored papers. *Science and Engineering Ethics*, *20*(2), 363–377. doi:10.100711948-013-9451-6 PMID:23690133

Lu, K., Qiao, X., & Hao, N. (2019). Praising or keeping silent on partner's ideas: Leading brainstorming in particular ways. *Neuropsychologia*, *124*, 19–30. doi:10.1016/j.neuropsychologia.2019.01.004 PMID:30633875

Lunenberg, M., Dengerink, J., & Korthagen, F. (2014). *The professional teacher educator: Roles, behaviour, and professional development of teacher educators.* Sense Publishers. doi:10.1007/978-94-6209-518-2

Lunsford, A. A., & Ruszkiewicz, J. J. (2015). *Everything's an Argument* (7th ed.). Bedford/St. Martin's.

Luo, N., & Hyland, K. (2019). "I won't publish in Chinese now": Publishing, translation, and the non-English speaking academic. *Journal of English for Academic Purposes*, *39*, 37–47. doi:10.1016/j.jeap.2019.03.003

Lu, Y., & Jover, G. (2019). An anthropocosmic view: What Confucian traditions can teach us about the past and future of Chinese Higher Education. *Higher Education: The International Journal of Higher Education Research*, *77*(3), 423–436. doi:10.100710734-018-0280-z

M. (2020). COVID-19 Effects on US Higher Education Campuses. Academic Student Mobility to and from China. In *Institute of International Education.*

Maaravi, Y., Heller, B., Shoham, Y., Mohar, S., & Deutsch, B. (2021). Ideation in the digital age: Literature review and integrative model for electronic brainstorming. *Review of Managerial Science*, *15*(6), 1431–1464. doi:10.100711846-020-00400-5

Macaro, E., Curle, S., Pun, J., An, J., & Dearden, J. (2018). A systematic review of English medium instruction in higher education. *Language Teaching*, *51*(1), 36–76. doi:10.1017/S0261444817000350

Macbeath, J. (2008). Leadership for learning: Exploring similarity and living with difference. In J. Macbeath & Y. C. Cheng (Eds.), *Leadership for learning* (pp. 1–16). Sense Publishers.

MacLeod, J., Yang, H. H., & Xiang, Z. (2017). Understanding College Students' Intrinsic Motivation and Social Interdependence in Intercultural Computer-Supported Collaborative Learning between USA and China. *The Asia-Pacific Education Researcher*, *26*(3), 205–217. doi:10.100740299-017-0341-6

Ma, G. (2012). An analysis of the development situation and predicament of general education in China [Lexical characteristics of Chinese language] [Higher Education Study Edition]. *Journal of Changchun University of Technology*, *33*(2), 46.

Magne, P., Poverjuc, O., & Heffernan, T. (2017). Pedagogies across borders: Perspectives from teaching staff and students engaged with transnational programmes in Hong Kong. *Practice and Evidence of Scholarship of Teaching and Learning in Higher Education*, *12*(1), 45–62.

Mahboob, A., & Lin, A. M. (2016). *Using local languages in English language classrooms. English language teaching today, 25-40.* Springer.

Mahoney, C. (2021). Archaic examination culture of UK universities must be reformed. *Times Higher Education*. https://www.timeshighereducation.com/opinion/archaic-examination-culture-uk-universities-must-be-reformed

Malaysiakini. (2019, March 15). Japanese university branches coming to Malaysia, confirms Maszlee *Malaysiakini*. https://www.malaysiakini.com/news/468077

Malaysian Qualification Agency. (2018). *Self-Accreditation*. MQA. http://www.mqa.gov.my/portalmqav3/red/en/swaakreditasi.cfm

Malete, L. (2016). Transnational education and internationalization of education as tools for higher education: Transformation and economic development in emerging economies. In E. J. Francois, M. B. Avoseh, & W. Griswold (Eds.), Perspectives in transnational higher education (pp. 39–54). Sense Publishers.

Mareis, C. (2020). Brainstorming revisited: On instrumental creativity and human productivity in the mid-twentieth century. *Cultural Politics*, *16*(1), 50–69. doi:10.1215/17432197-8017256

Marginson, S. (2020). *Global HE as we know it has forever changed | Times Higher Education (THE)*. Times Higher Education. https://www.timeshighereducation.com/blog/global-he-we-know-it-has-forever-changed# Martel,).

Marginson, S. (2004). National and global competition in higher education. *Australian Educational Researcher*, *31*(2), 1–28. doi:10.1007/BF03249517

Marginson, S. (2006). Dynamics of national and global competition in higher education. *Higher Education*, *52*(1), 1–39. doi:10.100710734-004-7649-x

Marginson, S. (2011). The Confucian model of higher education in East Asia and Singapore. In *Higher education in the Asia-Pacific* (pp. 53–75). Springer. https://link.springer.com/chapter/10.1007/978-94-007-1500-4_3 doi:10.1007/978-94-007-1500-4_3

Marimuthu, T. (2008). The role of the Private Sector in Higher Education in Malaysia. In D. Johnson. & R. Maclean (Eds.), *Teaching: Professionalization. Development and Leadership* (271-281). https://link.springer.com/chapter/10.1007/978-1-4020-8186-6_18

Marshall, N., & Edwards, C. (1997). A mentor approach to teacher trainer development. In I. McGrath (Ed.), *Learning to Train: Perspectives on the Development of Language Teacher Trainers* (pp. 60–72). Prentice Hall Europe.

Martin, L. (2014). Assessing student learning outcomes: Research trajectories. In H. Coates (Ed.), *Higher education learning outcomes assessment: international perspectives* (pp. 49–65). Peter Lang GmbH.

Maslow, A. H. (1954). *Motivation and personality* (2nd ed.). Harper and Row.

Massey, S. (2016). Working across health and education sectors. In A. Croker, J. Higgs, & F. Trede (Eds.), *Health practice relationships*.

Matsumoto, H. (2013). Return of Scientific Knowledge to the Researched Society: Fieldwork in Other Countries. E-journal. *Geo: Geography and Environment*, *8*(1), 3–14.

Matsushita, K. (2017). 2F18 Education System of International Architectural Design Workshop, Method to Encourage Continuous Collaboration among Students. *Proceedings of Annual Conference of Japanese Society for Engineering Education*, pp. 346-347. JEE.

Matthews, K. E., Dwyer, A., Hine, L., & Turner, J. (2018). Conceptions of students as partners. *Higher Education*, *76*(6), 957–971. doi:10.100710734-018-0257-y

Matthíasdóttir, Á., Saemundsdottir, I., Audunsson, H., & Grimsdottir, H. (2016). Focusing on creativity: Faculty motivation in teaching brainstorming and creativity in an introductory course. *Proceedings of the 12th International CDIO Conference*. IEEE.

Mayhew, E. (2019). No longer a silent partner: How Mentimeter can enhance teaching and learning within Political Science. *Journal of Political Science Education*, *15*(4), 546–551. doi:10.1080/15512169.2018.1538882

McBurnie, G., & Ziguras, C. (2001). The regulation of transnational higher education in Southeast Asia: Case studies of Hong Kong, Malaysia and Australia. *Higher Education*, *42*(1), 85–105. doi:10.1023/A:1017572119543

McBurnie, G., & Ziguras, C. (2006). *Transnational education: Issues and trends in offshore higher education*. Routledge. doi:10.4324/9780203968352

McGuire, S. Y. (2006). The impact of supplemental instruction on teaching students how to learn. *New Directions for Teaching and Learning*, *2006*(106), 3–10. doi:10.1002/tl.228

Mcleod, S. (2019, March 24). The zone of proximal development and scaffolding. *Simply Psychology*. https://www.simplypsychology.org/Zone-of-Proximal-Development.html

Mcleod, S. (2020, December 29). Maslow's hierarchy of needs. *Simply Psychology*. https://www.simplypsychology.org/maslow.html

McManus, S. (2008). *Attributes of effective formative assessment*. Council for Chief State School Officers. http://www.ccsso.org/publications/details.cfm?PublicationID=362.

McNamara, J., & Knight, J. (2014). *Impacts of transnational education on host countries: academic, cultural, economic and skills impacts and implications of programme and provider mobility*. British Council. www.britishcouncil.org/education/ihewww.daad.de

McRaney, D. (2012). *You are not so smart*. One World.

Means, B., Bakia, M., & Murphy, R. (2014). Learning online: What research tells us about whether, when and how. *Learning Online: What Research Tells Us About Whether, When and How*, 1–219. doi:10.4324/9780203095959

Mehisto, P. (2012). Criteria for producing CLIL learning material. *Encuentro: Revista de investigación e innovación en la clase de idiomas*, *21*, 15-33. http://www.encuentrojournal.org/textos/3.%20Mehisto_rev.pdf

Mele, D. (2016). Understanding humanistic management. *Humanistic Management Journal*, *1*(1), 33–55. doi:10.100741463-016-0011-5

Melles, G. (Ed.). (2020). *Design thinking in higher education*. Springer. doi:10.1007/978-981-15-5780-4

Mellors-Bourne, R., Fielden, J., Kemp, N., Middlehurst, R., & Woodfield, S. (2014). *The value of transnational education to the UK*. Higher Education Academy. https://assets.publishing.service.gov.uk/government/uploads/system/uploads/attachment_data/file/387910/bis-14-1202-the-value-of-transnational-education-to-the-uk.pdf

Menestrel, S., Walahoski, J., & Mielke, M. (2014). A partnership model for evaluation: Considering an alternate approach to the internal-external evaluation debate. *American Journal of Evaluation, Washington, DC, USA*, *35*(1), 61–72. doi:10.1177/1098214013506600

Menggo, S., Suastra, I., Budiarsa, M., & Padmadewi, N. N. (2019). Needs Analysis of Academic-English Speaking Material in Promoting 21st Century Skills. *International Journal of Instruction*, *12*(2), 739–754. doi:10.29333/iji.2019.12247a

Meredith, G., & Miller, P. (2012). Transnational doctoral education and research: A case study. In P. Miller, A. Selvanathan, & G. Meredith (Eds.), *Transnational doctoral education and research: An Asian focus* (pp. 11–32). Southern Cross University Press.

Merriam, S. B. (1998). *Qualitative research and case study applications in education*. Jossey-Bass.

Merriam, S. B., Caffarella, R. S., & Baumgartner, L. (2007). Self-directed learning. In S. B. Merriam, R. S. Caffarella, & L. Baumgartner (Eds.), *Learning in adulthood: a comprehensive guide* (pp. 105–129). Jossey-Bass.

Meyer, C. (2022, June 3). *Graham's hierarchy of disagreement: How to argue like an expert*. The Mind Collection. https://themindcollection.com/revisiting-grahams-hierarchy-of-disagreement/

Meyer, K. A. (2014). Student engagement in online learning: What works and why. *ASHE Higher Education Report*, *40*(6), 1–114. doi:10.1002/aehe.20018

Miani, M. (2016). Does culture affect creativity? An integrative literature review. In P. D. Reali & C. Burnett (Eds.), *Big questions in creativity 2016* (pp. 127–141). ICSC Press.

Michinov, N. (2012). Is electronic brainstorming or brainwriting the best way to improve creative performance in groups? An overlooked comparison of two idea-generation techniques. *Journal of Applied Social Psychology*, *42*(SUPPL. 1), E222–E243. doi:10.1111/j.1559-1816.2012.01024.x

Middleton, A. (2019). *First man in: Leading from the front*. Harper Collins.

Middleton, A., Fox, J., Ollerton, M., & Maclachlan, C. (2017). *SAS who dares wins: Leadership secrets from the special forces*. Headline Publishing Group.

Miettinen, R. (2000). The concept of experiential learning and John Dewey's theory of reflective thought and action. *International Journal of Lifelong Education*, *19*(1), 54–72. doi:10.1080/026013700293458

Miles, M. B., & Huberman, A. M. (1994). *Qualitative data analysis*. Sage.

Miller, P., Selvanathan, A., & Meredith, G. (Eds.). (2012). *Transnational doctoral education and research: An Asian focus*. Southern Cross University Press.

Ministry of Education of the People's Republic of China (MOE). (2022a). *2332 programmes of Chinese foreign co-operation in running schools including 1230 in higher education*. [In Chinese]. MOE. http://www.moe.gov.cn/fbh/live/2020/52834/mtbd/202012/t20201222_506955.html

Ministry of Education of the People's Republic of China (MOE). (2022b). *Between 2016 and 2019, over 2,510,000 Chinese in overseas studies*. [In Chinese]. MOE. http://www.moe.gov.cn/fbh/live/2020/52834/mtbd/202012/t20201223_507063.html

Ministry of Higher Education. (n.d.). SETARA-2017. MOHE. http://www.mohe.gov.my/en/latest/pengumuman/790-setara-2017

Mirzoeva, L. Y. (2021). Using breakout rooms in online language teaching: Advantages and disadvantages. *International Journal of Innovative Research in Education, 8*(2), 94–101. doi:10.18844/ijire.v8i2.6807

Mishra, L., Gupta, T., & Shree, A. (2020). Online teaching-learning in higher education during lockdown period of COVID-19 pandemic. *International Journal of Educational Research Open, 1*, 100012. doi:10.1016/j.ijedro.2020.100012 PMID:35059663

Mizell, H. (2010). *Learning Forward.* Why Professional Development Matters.

Mizuno, S. (Ed.). (1979). *Management for quality improvement. The seven new QC tools.* Productivity Press.

MoE. (2010). National Education Policy-2010 (M. of Education (ed.)). Government of People's Republic of Bangladesh.

MOE. (2017). Statistics of Private Higher Education of Malaysia. [Data set]. MOE. https://www.moe.gov.my/en/muat-turun/laporan-dan-statistik/pendidikan-tinggi/bukuperangkaan/2017-5/2394-statistik-pendidikan-tinggi-2017-bab-3-pdf/file

Mohan, B., & Nair, L. R. (2018). Story tellingan effective pedagogy for multicultural education. *SCMS Journal of Indian Management, 15*(3), 81–90.

MOHE. (2017). Statistics of Public Higher Education of Malaysia. [Data set]. http://www.mohe.gov.my/en/download/awam/statistik/2017-3/470-statistik-pendidikan-tinggi2017-bab-2-universiti-awam/file

Mointor, I. C. E. F. (2021, July 13). *UK: Online learning expected to drive further significant growth for TNE programmes - ICEF Monitor - Market intelligence for international student recruitment.* Monitor. https://monitor.icef.com/2021/07/uk-online-learning-expected-to-drive-further-significant-growth-for-tne-programmes/

Mok, K. (2003). Globalisation and Higher Education Restructuring in Hong Kong, Taiwan and Mainland China. *Higher Education Research & Development, 22*(2), 117–129. doi:10.1080/07294360304111

Mok, K. H. (2008). Singapore's global education hub ambitions: University governance change and transnational higher education. *International Journal of Educational Management.*

Mok, K. H. (2012). The rise of transnational higher education in Asia: Student mobility and studying experiences in Singapore and Malaysia. *Higher Education Policy, 25*(2), 225–241. doi:10.1057/hep.2012.6

Mok, K. H., & Han, X. (2016). From 'brain drain' to 'brain bridging': Transnational higher education development and graduate employment in China. *Journal of Higher Education Policy and Management, 38*(3), 369–389. doi:10.1080/1360080X.2016.1174409

Mok, K. H., & Marginson, S. (2021). Massification, diversification and internationalisation of higher education in China: Critical reflections of developments in the last two decades. *International Journal of Educational Development, 84*, 1–8. doi:10.1016/j.ijedudev.2021.102405

Mok, K. H., & Wu, A. M. (2016). Higher education, changing labour market and social mobility in the era of massification in China. *Journal of Education and Work, 29*(1), 77–97. doi:10.1080/13639080.2015.1049028

Mok, K. H., Xiong, W., Ke, G., & Cheung, J. O. W. (2021). Impact of COVID-19 pandemic on international higher education and student mobility: Student perspectives from mainland China and Hong Kong. *International Journal of Educational Research, 105*, 101718. doi:10.1016/j.ijer.2020.101718 PMID:35719275

Molloy, E., Noble, C., & Ajjawi, R. (2019). *Attending to emotion in feedback. The impact of feedback in higher education, 83-105.* Palgrave Macmillan.

Mongeau, P. A. (1993). *The brainstorming myth.* https://files.eric.ed.gov/fulltext/ED357399.pdf

Monitor, I. C. E. F. (2022, April). *Australia's foreign enrolment recovering slowly in 2022 - ICEF Monitor - Market intelligence for international student recruitment.* Monitor. https://monitor.icef.com/2022/04/australias-foreign-enrolment-recovering-slowly-in-2022/

Monitor. (2017). Bangladesh: Middle class growth helping to drive demand for study abroad. *Monitor.* https://monitor.icef.com/2017/02/bangladesh-middle-class-growth-helping-to-drive-demand-for-study-abroad/

Montacute, R. (2020). *Implications of the Covid-19 crisis for educational inequality.* Sutton Trust.

Moore, J. C. (2019) *A Brief History of Universities.* Palgrave Macmillan.

Morris, G. (2021a). *Investigating the employment motivation and job satisfaction of expatriate language teachers* [Unpublished EdD Thesis, University of Exeter, UK]. http://hdl.handle. net/10871/124311

Morris, G. (2021b). Leading during a pandemic: A case of prioritising Maslow ahead of Bloom. Language Teaching in China, 1(September 2021), pp. 66-71.

Morris, G. (2021c) Charting the school of languages evolutionary development: A leadership perspective. *Language Teaching in China, 1*(September 2021), pp, 78-83.

Morris, G. R., Sheridan, S. M., Xu, J., Liang, W., Lv, F., Foster, R., Di, S., Zhang, C., & Perrin, S. (2021). *Educational Symbiosis: Designing English Language Learning Courses to Support Syntegrative Education.* 187–207. doi:10.4018/978-1-7998-7226-9.CH010

Morris, G., Xu, J., & Li, L. (In Print). Transitioning to the new normal: Experiences from a Sino-British institution. In Kohnke, L. (Ed.). Cases on teaching English for academic purposes (EAP) during COVID-19: Insights from around the world. IGI Global.

Morris, G., Perrin, S., Sheridan, S., Xu, J., Liang, W., Lv, F., Di, S., Foster, R., & Zhang, C. (2021). Educational symbiosis: Designing language learning courses to support syntegrative education. In H. Xiang (Ed.), *Trends and developments for the future of language education in higher education* (pp. 187–208). IGI Global. doi:10.4018/978-1-7998-7226-9.ch010

MQA. (2015). Listing of Private Higher Education Institutions (IPTS). MQA. http://www.mqa.gov.my/mqr/english/eakrbyipts.cfm

MQA. (2017). List of IPTS. MQA. http://jpt.mohe.gov.my/index.php/ipt/berkaitan-ipts/ipts

MQA. (2021). List of IPTS. MQA. https://drive.google.com/drive/folders/1L_fklIz2AukzVQLV3I6_euLBaxjZ4Lg0

Mullen, B., Johnson, C., & Salas, E. (1991). Productivity loss in brainstorming groups: A meta-analytic integration. *Basic and Applied Social Psychology, 12*(1), 3–23. doi:10.120715324834basp1201_1

Mullen, C. A. (2020). *Revealing creativity.* Springer. doi:10.1007/978-3-030-48165-0

Mun, O. (2014). Re-imagining national identity through early literacy textbooks in Kazakhstan. [Master's thesis. Lehigh University, England]. https://core.ac.uk/download/pdf/228638588.pdf

Mundt, K., & Groves, M. (2016). A double-edged sword: The merits and the policy implications of Google Translate in higher education. *European Journal of Higher Education, 6*(4), 387–401. doi:10.1080/21568235.2016.1172248

Murphy, M. P. A. (2020). COVID-19 and emergency eLearning: Consequences of the securitization of higher education for post-pandemic pedagogy. *Contemporary Security Policy, 41*(3), 492–505. doi:10. 1080/13523260.2020.1761749

Murray, J., & Male, T. (2005). Becoming a Teacher Educator: Evidence from the Field. *Teaching and Teacher Education, 21*(2), 125–142. doi:10.1016/j.tate.2004.12.006

Musthafa, M., & Sajila, K. (2014). Reconsidering the teaching–research nexus in higher education. Higher Education for the Future, 1(2), pp. 123-138.

Musto, R. G. (2022). *The Attack on Higher Education: The Dissolution of the American University*. Cambridge University Press.

Naeem, U., Bosman, L., & Gill, S. S. (2022, March). Teaching and Facilitating an Online Learning Environment for a Web Programming Module. In *Global Engineering Education Conference (EDUCON)* (pp. 769-774). IEEE. 10.1109/EDUCON52537.2022.9766757

National College for Teaching and Learning. (2010). *10 strong claims about successful school leadership*. NCTL. https://www.gov.uk/government/publications/10-strong-claims-about-successful-school-leadership

Nemeth, C. J., Personnaz, B., Personnaz, M., & Goncalo, J. A. (2004). The liberating role of conflict in group creativity: A study in two countries. *European Journal of Social Psychology*, *34*(4), 365–374. doi:10.1002/ejsp.210

Nerad, M. (2010). Globalization and the internationalization of graduate education: A macro and micro view. *Canadian Journal of Higher Education*, *40*(1), 1–12. doi:10.47678/cjhe.v40i1.1566

Nerantzi, C., & Hannaford, L. (2016). Action Learning Sets Flipping the Classroom: Advantages and Challenges. An Example from Academic Development. Teaching with Team Projects in Higher Education. Information Science Press, 119-129.

Neri, S., & Wilkins, S. (2019). Talent management in transnational higher education: Strategies for managing academic staff at international branch campuses. *Journal of Higher Education Policy and Management*, *41*(1), 52–69. doi:10.1080/1360080X.2018.1522713

Neuwirth, L. S., Jović, S., & Mukherji, B. R. (2021). Reimagining higher education during and post-COVID-19: Challenges and opportunities. *Journal of Adult and Continuing Education*, *27*(2), 141–156. doi:10.1177/1477971420947738

Neves, J., & Hewitt, R. (2021) *Students highlight the challenges of their 2021 academic experience*. Advance HE. https://www.advance-he.ac.uk/news-and-views/students-highlight-challenges-their-2021-academic-experience.

Newell, C., & Bain, A. (2018). *Team-based collaboration in higher education learning and teaching: A review of the literature*. Springer. doi:10.1007/978-981-13-1855-9

Ng, K. H., & Chiu, T. K. (2017). Emotional multimedia design for developing mathematical problem-solving skills. In *New ecology for education—Communication x learning* (pp. 131–141). Springer. doi:10.1007/978-981-10-4346-8_11

Nicol, D. J., & Macfarlane-Dick, D. (2006). Formative assessment and self-regulated learning: A model and seven principles of good feedback practice. *Studies in Higher Education*, *31*(2), 199–218. doi:10.1080/03075070600572090

Nida-Rümelin, M., & Conaill, O. D. (2021) Qualia: The Knowledge Argument. *The Stanford Encyclopedia of Philosophy*. https://plato.stanford.edu/archives/sum2021/entries/qualia-knowledge/

Nietzsche, F. (2008). *Thus spoke Zarathustra: A book for everyone and nobody*. Oxford University Press.

Nijstad, B. A., Stroebe, W., & Lodewijkx, H. F. M. (2003). Production blocking and idea generation: Does blocking interfere with cognitive processes? *Journal of Experimental Social Psychology*, *39*(6), 531–548. doi:10.1016/S0022-1031(03)00040-4

Nijstad, B. A., Stroebe, W., & Lodewijkx, H. F. M. (2006). The illusion of group productivity: A reduction of failures explanation. *European Journal of Social Psychology*, *36*(1), 31–48. doi:10.1002/ejsp.295

Niño, A. (2009). Machine translation in foreign language learning: Language learners' and tutors' perceptions of its advantages and disadvantages. *ReCALL, 21*(2), 241–258. doi:10.1017/S0958344009000172

Nisbett, R. E. (2003). *The geography of thought: How Asians and Westerners think differently and why.* Free Press.

Norman, A. (2021, May 18). The cause of America's post-truth predicament. *Scientific American.* https://www.scientificamerican.com/article/the-cause-of-americas-post-truth-predicament/

Norman, M., Ambrose, S. A., & Huston, T. A. (2006). Assessing and addressing faculty morale: Cultivating consciousness, empathy and empowerment. *The Review of Higher Education, 29*(3), 347–379. doi:10.1353/rhe.2006.0013

Normann, A. (2017). Becoming a phenomenologically skilled researcher - An account of a journey started. *Reflective Practice, 18*(5), 613–626. doi:10.1080/14623943.2017.1307720

Nortvig, A. M., Petersen, A. K., & Balle, S. H. (2018). A literature review of the factors influencing e-learning and blended learning in relation to learning outcome, student satisfaction and engagement. *Electronic Journal of E-Learning, 16*(1).

Nowlan, W. (2019, July 5). *Translation software: An insight into student use and non-EAP lecturer attitudes to translation software in university learning and assessments* [Symposium]. Translation Technology in Education – Facilitator or Risk? Nottingham Trent University.

Nunan, D. (1991). *Language teaching methodology: A textbook for teachers.* Prentice hall.

Nurunnabi, M., Abdelhadi, A., Aburas, R., & Fallatah, S. (2019). Does teaching qualification matter in higher education in the UK? An analysis of National Learner Survey data. *MethodsX, 6*, 788–799. doi:10.1016/j.mex.2019.04.001 PMID:31032182

NUY Shanghai (2020, February 21). *NYU Shanghai launches innovative digital teaching on February 17.* NYU Shanghai. https://shanghai.nyu.edu/cn/news/nyu-shanghai-launch-innovative-remote-teaching-and-learning-effort-february-17

O'Donoghue, C. (1997). Trainer induction: reflecting on parallels between new trainers and teacher trainees. In I. McGrath (Ed.), *Learning to Train: Perspectives on the Development of Language Teacher Trainers* (pp. 73–81). Prentice Hall Europe.

O'Mahony, J. (2014). *Enhancing student learning and teacher development in transnational education.* Higher Education Academy.

O'Malley, B. (2016, November 10). China overtakes UAE as top host of branch campuses. *University World News.* https://www.universityworldnews.com/post.php?story=20161110144407523

Oad, L., Khan, N., & Khoso, F. J. (2020). Factors Affecting English Language Anxiety among Learners: A Case Study of a Public Sector University. *Pakistan Social Sciences Review, 4*(3), 1060–1078. doi:10.35484/pssr.2020(4-III)77

OBHE. (2014). Malaysia to offer foreign universities greater incentives to open branch campuses, but why has no new branch campus opened since 2000? *The Observatory on Borderless Higher Education.*

OECD. (2013) Education at a Glance: 'OECD indicators', *OECD.* https://www.oecd.org/edu/eag2013%20(eng)--FINAL%2020%20June%202013.pdf

OECD. (2018). *The future of education and skills. Education 2030 the future we want.* OECD Publishing.

OECD. (2019). *OECD employment outlook 2019: The future of work.* OECD Publishing.

Offner, A. K., Kramer, T. J., & Winter, J. P. (1996). The effects of facilitation, recording, and pauses on group brainstorming. *Small Group Research, 27*(2), 283–298. doi:10.1177/1046496496272005

Ohiwa, H., Takeda, N., Kawai, K., & Shiomi, A. (1997). KJ editor: A card-handling tool for creative work support. Knowledge-Based Systems, 10, 43–50. doi:10.1016/S0950-7051(97)00015-4

Oraif, I., & Elyas, T. (2021). Applicability of collaborative work in the COVID-19 Era: Use of breakout groups in teaching L2 translation. *Electronics (Basel)*, *10*(22), 2846. doi:10.3390/electronics10222846

Orakcı, Ş. (2020). The future of online learning and teaching in higher education. In A. Al-Sartawi, A., Hussainey, K., Hannon, A. & Hamdan, A. (Eds.). Global Approaches to Sustainability Through Learning and Education. IGI Global. doi:10.4018/978-1-7998-0062-0.ch003

Orakcı, Ş. (2020). Teacher candidates' opinions on portfolio implementation. *The Journal of Turkish Educational Sciences*, *18*(1), 266–295.

Orakcı, Ş., & Gelişli, Y. (2021). Educational policy actions in the times of Covid-19 and suggestions for future applications in Turkey. In L. Kyei-Blankson, J. Blankson, & E. Ntuli (Eds.), *Handbook of Research on Inequities in Online Education During Global Crises* (pp. 475–493). IGI Global. doi:10.4018/978-1-7998-6533-9.ch024

Orazbayeva, B., & … . (2020). *The Future of Universities Thoughtbook: Universities During Times of Crisis*. University Industry Innovation Network.

Orazbayeva, B., Meerman, A., Galan Muros, V., Davey, T., & Plewa, C. (2020). *The future of universities thoughtbook: Universities during times of crisis*. University Industry Innovation Network.

Organ, A. (2019, December 10). *Blissful ignorance? Or turning a blind eye? Language departments' attitudes to student use of Google Translate* [Symposium]. Language Teaching Forum, University of York.

Orsini-Jones, M. E., Lloyd, E., Cribb, M., Lee, F., Bescond, G., Ennagadi, A., & García, B. I. (2017). The trouble with cyberpragmatics: Embedding an online intercultural learning project into the curriculum. [IJCALLT]. *International Journal of Computer-Assisted Language Learning and Teaching*, *7*(1), 50–65. doi:10.4018/IJCALLT.2017010104

Ortiga, Y. Y. (2018). Constructing a global education hub: The unlikely case of Manila. *Discourse (Abingdon)*, *39*(5), 767–781. doi:10.1080/01596306.2018.1448703

Osborn, A. (1953). *Applied imagination: Principles and procedures of creative problem solving*. Charles Scribner's Sons.

Osborn, A. F. (1948). *Your creative power. How to use imagination.* Charles Scribner's Sons.

Osigweh, C. (1986). An evaluation model of training outcomes for higher education. Educational Evaluation and Policy Analysis, 8(2), pp. 167-178.

Ottley, K. (2016). Why One-Size-Fits-All Is Not Fit for Purpose: The Problem With Mass-Produced Teaching Materials, and How One Might Creatively and Sensitively Confront this Problem. In *SLA research and materials development for language learning* (pp. 284–295). Routledge.

Owen, J. (2020). *The leadership skills handbook* (5th ed.). Kogan Page Ltd.

Oxley, N. L., Dzindolet, M. T., & Paulus, P. (1996). The effects of facilitators on the performance of brainstorming groups. *Journal of Social Behavior and Personality*, *2*(4), 633–646.

Oyserman, D., Coon, H. M., & Kemmelmeier, M. (2002). Rethinking individualism and collectivism: Evaluation of theoretical assumptions and meta-analyses. *Psychological Bulletin*, *128*(1), 3–72. doi:10.1037/0033-2909.128.1.3 PMID:11843547

Oztirk, M. (2019). An Evaluation of an Innovative In-service Teacher Training Model in Turkey. *International Journal of Higher Education*, *8*(1), 23–36. doi:10.5430/ijhe.v8n1p23

Palmer, A., Pegrum, M., & Oakley, G. (2019). A wake-up call? Issues with plagiarism in transnational higher education. *Ethics & Behavior*, *29*(1), 23–50. doi:10.1080/10508422.2018.1466301

Paniagua, J., Villó, C., & Escrivà-Beltran, M. (2022). Cross-border higher education: The expansion of international branch campuses. *Research in Higher Education*, *63*(6), 1–21. doi:10.100711162-022-09674-y PMID:35068659

Pan, M., Stiles, B. L., Tempelmeyer, T. C., & Wong, N. (2019). A cross-cultural exploration of academic dishonesty: Current challenges, preventive measures, and future directions. In D. M. Velliaris (Ed.), *Prevention and detection of academic misconduct in higher education* (pp. 63–82). IGI Global. doi:10.4018/978-1-5225-7531-3.ch003

Pappas, E. (2002). Creative problem solving in engineering design. In *Proceedings of the American Society for Engineering Education (ASEE) Southeastern Section Meeting*. University of Florida.

Pappas, E., Pierrakos, O., & Nagel, R. (2013). Using Bloom's Taxonomy to teach sustainability in multiple contexts. *Journal of Cleaner Production*, *48*, 54–64. doi:10.1016/j.jclepro.2012.09.039

Park, S.-Y., Yasue, H., & Nakao, H. (2018). The iSWOT: A web-based SWOT and TOWS analytical tool that promotes new ideas. *Agricultural Information Research (Japanese)*, *27*(1), 1–13. doi:10.3173/air.27.1

Paulus, P. B., Kohn, N. W., & Arditti, L. E. (2011). Effects of quantity and quality instructions on brainstorming. *The Journal of Creative Behavior*, *45*(1), 38–46. doi:10.1002/j.2162-6057.2011.tb01083.x

Paulus, P. B., Korde, R. M., Dickson, J. J., Carmeli, A., & Cohen-Meitar, R. (2015). Asynchronous brainstorming in an industrial setting. *Human Factors*, *57*(6), 1076–1094. doi:10.1177/0018720815570374 PMID:25850113

Paulus, P. B., & Paulus, L. E. (1997). Implications of research on group brainstorming for gifted education. *Roeper Review*, *19*(4), 225–229. doi:10.1080/02783199709553834

Paxton, M. I. J. (2009). 'It's easy to learn when you using your home language but with English you need to start learning language before you get to the concept': Bilingual concept development in an English medium university in South Africa. *Journal of Multilingual and Multicultural Development*, *30*(4), 345–359. doi:10.1080/01434630902780731

Payne, B., Cigularova, D., Costanzo, J., Das, S., Mann, M., & Perez, K. (2021). Impact of articulation agreements on student transfer between higher education institutions: A case study of a cybersecurity program. *Community College Journal of Research and Practice*, 1–16.

Peng, R. Z., & Wu, W. P. (2016). Measuring intercultural contact and its effects on intercultural competence: A structural equation modelling approach. *International Journal of Intercultural Relations*, *53*, 16–27. doi:10.1016/j.ijintrel.2016.05.003

Penington, D. (1998). Managing quality in higher education institutions of the 21st century: a framework for the future. Australian Journal of Education, 42(3), pp. 256-270.

Pennycook, A. (1994). The complex contexts of plagiarism: A reply to Deckert. *Journal of Second Language Writing*, *3*(3), 277–284. doi:10.1016/1060-3743(94)90020-5

Perez-Encinas, A., & Rodriguez-Pomeda, J. (2018). International students' perceptions of their needs when going abroad: Services on demand. *Journal of Studies in International Education*, *22*(1), 20–36. doi:10.1177/1028315317724556

Perry, B., & Stewart, T. (2005). Insights into effective partnership in interdisciplinary team teaching. *System*, *33*(4), 563–573. doi:10.1016/j.system.2005.01.006

Peters, B. D., & Anderson, M. E. (2021). Supporting nonnative English speakers at the university: A survey of faculty and staff. *Journal of International Students*, *11*(1), 103–121. doi:10.32674/jis.v11i1.1200

Pew Research Center. (2015). *Women and leadership: public says women are equally qualified, but barriers persist.* Pew Research Center.

Pham, T., & Hoang Pham, L. (2021). 'Enhancing Asian students' engagement by incorporating Asian intellectual and pedagogical resources in teaching and learning. In S. Hoidn & M. Klemenčič (Eds.), *The Routledge international handbook of student-centred learning and teaching in higher education* (pp. 171–185). Routledge.

Philipsen, B. (2019). A Professional Development Process Model for Online and Blended Learning: Introducing Digital Capital. [CITE Journal]. *Contemporary Issues in Technology & Teacher Education, 19*(4).

Pickering, J. D. (2017). Cognitive engagement: A more reliable proxy for learning? *Medical Science Educator, 27*(4), 821–823. doi:10.100740670-017-0447-8

Pieper, A., & Beall, J. (2014). *Impacts of transnational education on host countries: Academic, cultural, economic and skills impacts and implications of program and provider mobility.* British Council/ DAAD.

Pierce, J. L., & Newstrom, J. W. (2012). *The managers bookshelf: A mosaic of contemporary views* (10th ed.). Pearson.

Pieterse, P. (2021). *New VPAA: 'Academic leadership is about the empowerment of others.'* XJL University. https://www.xjtlu.edu.cn/en/news/2021/03/new-vpaa-academic-leadership-is-about-the-empowerment-of-others

Pimpa, N. (2003). The influence of family on Thai students' choices of international education. *International Journal of Educational Management, 17*(5), 211–219. doi:10.1108/09513540310484931

Pimpa, N. (2005). A family affair: The effect of family on Thai students' choices of international education. *Higher Education, 49*(4), 431–448. doi:10.100710734-004-2825-6

Pitman, J. (2021, April 28). *Google Translate: One billion installs, one billion stories.* Google. https://blog.google/products/translate/one-billion-installs/

Pittaway, S. M., & Moss, T. (2014). 'Initially, we were just names on a computer screen': Designing engagement in online teacher education. *The Australian Journal of Teacher Education, 39*(7), 140–156. doi:10.14221/ajte.2014v39n7.10

Planar, D., & Moya, S. (2016) 'The Effectiveness of Instructor Personalized and Formative Feedback Provided by Instructor in an Online Setting: Some Unresolved Issues', *The Electronic Journal of e-Learning, 14*(3), pp. 196-203. https://files.eric.ed.gov/fulltext/EJ1107130.pdf

Poggensee, A. (2016). *The effects of globalization on English language learning: Perspectives from Senegal and the United States.* WMU.

Pohl, U., Szesztay, M., & Wright, T. (2016). In Praise of Team Training. English Teaching Professional, 103, 57-61.

Pohl, H., & Lane, J. E. (2018). Research contributions of international branch campuses to the scientific wealth of academically developing countries. *Scientometrics, 116*(3), 1719–1734. doi:10.100711192-018-2790-y

Poibeau, T. (2017). *Machine translation.* MIT Press. doi:10.7551/mitpress/11043.001.0001

Pollom, E. L., Sandhu, N., Deig, C. R., Obeid, J. P., Miller, J. A., & Kahn, J. M. (2021). Networking and applying to radiation oncology during a pandemic: Cross-sectional survey of medical student concerns. *Advances in Radiation Oncology, 6*(3), 100643. doi:10.1016/j.adro.2021.100643 PMID:33748546

Pont, B., Nusche, D., & Moorman, H. (2008). Policy and practice. Improving school leadership (Vol. 1). OECD.

Poole, A. (2016) 'Complex teaching realities' and 'deep rooted cultural traditions': Barriers to the implementation and internalisation of formative assessment in China. *Cogent Education, 3*(1), pp. 1-14.

Poole, M., Harman, E., & Deden, A. (1998). Managing the quality of teaching in higher education institutions in the 21st century. Australian Journal of Education, 42(3), pp. 271-284.

Popham, W. J. (2006). Phony formative assessments: Buyer beware! *Educational Leadership*, *64*(3), 86–87.

Portnoy, L. (2020). *Designed to learn: Using design thinking to bring purpose and passion to the classroom.* ASCD.

Postholm, B. M., & Skrøvset, S. (2013). The researcher reflecting on her own role during action research. *Educational Action Research*, *21*(4), 506–518. doi:10.1080/09650792.2013.833798

Pounder, J. (2000). Evaluating the relevance of quality to institutional performance assessment in higher education. Evaluation, 6(1), pp. 66-78.

Pourtoussi, Z., Ghanizadeh, A., & Mousavi, V. (2018). A qualitative in-depth analysis of the determinants and outcomes of EFL teachers' motivation and demotivation. *Internal Journal of Instruction*, *11*(4), 175–190. doi:10.12973/iji.2018.11412a

Proctor, T. (2020). Creative problem-solving techniques, paradigm shift and team performance. *Team Performance Management*, *26*(7–8), 451–466. doi:10.1108/TPM-06-2020-0049

Puccio, G. J., Burnett, C., Acar, S., Yudess, J. A., Holinger, M., & Cabra, J. F. (2020). Creative problem solving in small groups: The effects of creativity training on idea generation, solution creativity, and leadership effectiveness. *The Journal of Creative Behavior*, *54*(2), 453–471. doi:10.1002/jocb.381

Puccio, G. J., Mance, M., & Murdock, M. (2011). *Creative leadership: Skills that drive change* (2nd ed.). Sage.

Puccio, G. J., Mance, M., Switalski, L. B., & Reali, P. (2012). *Creativity rising: Creative thinking and creative problem solving in the 21st century*. ICSC Press, International Center for Studies in Creativity.

Punch, K. F. (2009). *Introduction to research methods in education*. Sage.

Pyvis, D., & Chapman, A. (2005). Culture shock and the international student 'offshore.'. *Journal of Research in International Education*, *4*(1), 23–42. doi:10.1177/1475240905050289

Pyvis, D., & Chapman, A. (2007). Why university students choose an international education: A case study in Malaysia. *International Journal of Educational Development*, *27*(2), 235–246. doi:10.1016/j.ijedudev.2006.07.008

QAA. (2022). *Transnational education.* QAA. https://www.qaa.ac.uk/reviewing-higher-education/types-of-review/transnational-education

Qadir, J., Taha, A. E. M., Yau, K. L. A., Ponciano, J., Hussain, S., Al-Fuqaha, A., & Imran, M. A. (2020). *Leveraging the force of formative assessment & feedback for effective engineering education.* In *Proceedings of the ASEE Annual Conference & Exposition*, Montreal, Canada 10.18260/1-2--34923

Qian, F. (2020). A preliminary study on the construction of ideological and political curriculum system in Sino-foreign cooperative universities [Lexical characteristics of Chinese language]. *Chinese Character Culture, 4*, pp. 140-141.

Qiang, W. (2002). Primary school English teaching in China: New developments. *English Language Teacher Education and Development*, *7,* 99-108. http://www.elted.net/uploads/7/3/1/6/7316005/v7qiang.pdf

Quacquarelli Symonds World University Ranking. (2021). QS world university rankings 2021. *Top Universities*. https://www.topuniversities.com/university-rankings/world-university-rankings/2021

Rajitha, K., & Alamelu, C. (2020). A study of factors affecting and causing speaking anxiety. *Procedia Computer Science*, *172*, 1053–1058. doi:10.1016/j.procs.2020.05.154

Rao, Z. (2007). Training in brainstorming and developing writing skills. *ELT Journal*, *61*(2), 100–106. doi:10.1093/elt/ccm002

Rao, Z. H. (1996). Reconciling communicative approaches to the teaching of English with traditional Chinese methods. *Research in the Teaching of English*, *30*(4), 458–471.

Rao, Z., & Chen, H. (2019). Teachers' perceptions of difficulties in team teaching between local- and native-English-speaking teachers in EFL teaching. *Journal of Multilingual and Multicultural Development*, 1–15. doi:10.1080/01434632.2019.1620753

Rashad, A., Majid, M., & Subramaniam, T. (2020). Capitalising on the strengths of international branch campuses in Malaysian transnational higher education landscape. *Journal of Southeast Asian Studies*, *25*(2), 201–221. doi:10.22452/jati.vol25no2.10

Rashtchi, M., & Porkar, R. (2020). Brainstorming revisited: Does technology facilitate argumentative essay writing? *Language Teaching Research Quarterly*, *18*, 1–20. doi:10.32038/ltrq.2020.18.01

Read, D., Barnes, S. M., Hughes, O., Ivanova, I. T., Sessions, A., & Wilson, P. J. (2022). Supporting student collaboration in online breakout rooms through interactive group activities. *New Directions in the Teaching of Physical Sciences, 17*(1).

Redden, E. (2018). *Closures of China-Foreign Programs*. Inside Higher Ed. https://www.insidehighered.com/news/2018/07/11/chinas-ministry-education-approves-termination-more-200-chinese-foreign-cooperative

Reese, H. W., Treffinger, D. J., Parnes, S. J., & Kaltsounis, G. (1976). Effects of a creative studies program on structure-of-intellect factors. *Journal of Educational Psychology*, *68*(4), 401–410. doi:10.1037/0022-0663.68.4.401 PMID:1002884

Reeve, J. (2013). How students create motivationally supportive learning environments for themselves: The concept of agentic engagement. *Journal of Educational Psychology*, *105*(3), 579–595. doi:10.1037/a0032690

Reeve, J., & Tseng, C. M. (2011). Agency as a fourth aspect of students' engagement during learning activities. *Contemporary Educational Psychology*, *36*(4), 257–267. doi:10.1016/j.cedpsych.2011.05.002

Reeves, T. (2000). Alternative assessment approaches for online learning environments in higher education. *Journal of Educational Computing Research. The University of Georgia, USA*, *23*(1), 101–111.

Reidsema, C., Kavanagh, L., Hadgraft, R., & Smith, N. (Eds.). (2017). The Flipped Classroom: Practice and Practices in Higher Education. Springer Science and Business Media. doi:10.1007/978-981-10-3413-8

Reina, S. (2021). Get Creative with Your Use of Breakout Rooms. Harvard Business Publishing Education. https://hbsp.harvard.edu/inspiring-minds/get-creative-with-your-use-of-breakout-rooms?msclkid=fe01b671c50011ec9be359fd9d509506

Research and Markets. (2020). *Global Online Education Market - Forecasts From 2020 To 2025*. Research and Markets. https://www.researchandmarkets.com/reports/4986759/global-online-education-market-forecasts-from

Rice, M., & Pinnegar, S. (2010). Organic collaboration: Sustaining teachers and teacher educators in the cottage industry of curriculum making. *Teachers and Teaching*, *16*(3), 373–387. doi:10.1080/13540601003634537

Ricento, T. (2015). Political economy and English as a "global" language. In T. Ricento (Ed.), *Language policy and political economy: English in a global context* (pp. 27–47). Oxford University Press. doi:10.1093/acprof:oso/9780199363391.003.0002

Richards, C. (2019). Higher education privatisation, internationalisation and marketisation: Singaporean versus Malaysian models of Asian education hub policy. *Compare: A Journal of Comparative Education, 49*(3), 375–392. doi:10.1080/03057925.2017.1413638

Richards, J. C. (2005). *Communicative language teaching today*. SEAMEO Regional Language Centre. https://d1wqtxts1xzle7.cloudfront.net/55716819/Communicative_Language_Teaching_Today-with-cover-page-v2.pdf?Expires=1660584453&Signature=BTWrAwfHZaMKhPLa4kF~u261bnmwFYudpjiHb-14GK4xwNJkaOluuRmzqIj~7qP7zZfHJmVcF6iOPcnoqFQSPayF6WW4rM7mQ7Y07XQAw6z249O9MxcGgzun33eZzmTLa5mPV0T2hDjwMwbjl5w6yIjh-bwEtn8Fs3Jo5B36g1gjt6EcBEC-QgLt4Eao5K~yPPrvSKr9PgZXc-l7q2r~NPAPmYAL7bNwLkK-QenxqSc0TL4RRu-36RAngNzOz5QA1z51xY3Zly~3LsbCDkwDmGBqhFfJ4JYOvpYy1EkH4RgaBnXS3f~2dhfCPqFagt~kfWP7EDS1QcUN6lP-yQWX9E9g__&Key-Pair-Id=APKAJLOHF5GGSLRBV4ZA

Richmond, G., & Manokore, V. (2020). Identifying elements critical for functional and sustainable professional learning communities. *Science Teacher Education, 95*, 543–570.

Rickards, T. (1999). Brainstorming revisited: A question of context. *International Journal of Management Reviews, 1*(1), 91–110. doi:10.1111/1468-2370.00006

Risager, K. (2007). *Language and culture pedagogy: From a national to a transnational paradigm*. Multilingual Matters LTD. doi:10.21832/9781853599613

Ritchhart, R., Church, M., & Morrison, K. (2011). *Making thinking visible: how to promote engagement, understanding, and independence for all learners*. Jossey-Bass.

Ritter, S. M., & Mostert, N. M. (2018). How to facilitate a brainstorming session: The effect of idea generation techniques and of group brainstorm after individual brainstorm. *Creative Industries Journal, 11*(3), 263–277. doi:10.1080/17510694.2018.1523662

Rizi, C. E., Najafipour, M., haghani, F., & Dehghan, S. (2013). The effect of the using the brainstorming method on the academic achievement of students in grade five in Tehran elementary schools. *Procedia: Social and Behavioral Sciences, 83*, 230–233. doi:10.1016/j.sbspro.2013.06.045

Roberts, J. (2020). *Five ways Covid-19 has made teachers' jobs harder.* TES Magazine. https://www.tes.com/news/five-ways-covid-19-has-made-teachers-jobs-harder

Roberts, L. (2017). Research in the real world: Improving adult learners web search and evaluation skills through motivational design and problem-based learning. *College & Research Libraries, 78*(4), 527. doi:10.5860/crl.78.4.527

Robertson, I. (2012). *The winner effect: The neuroscience of success and failure*. Bloomsbury.

Robertson, R. (1992). *Globalization: Social theory and global culture*. Sage.

Rogers, C. (1969). Freedom to learn: a view of what education might become. Charles E. Merrill.

Roksa, J., & Kinsley, P. (2019). The Role of Family Support in Facilitating Academic Success of Low-Income Students. *Research in Higher Education, 60*(4), 415–436. doi:10.100711162-018-9517-z

Rostrong, M. (2016). A cultural other in transnational education: Impact of globalization on student and teacher identities. In L. Seawright & A. Hodges (Eds.), *Learning across borders: Perspectives on international and transnational higher education* (pp. 193–215). Cambridge Scholars Publishing.

Roy, S. (2014). Status insanity: Why the iPhone is the perfect status symbol. In *Huffington Post* https://www.huffingtonpost.com/sandip-roy/status-insanity-why-the-i_b_5801748.html

Ryabova, A. (2020). Collaborative online international learning projects in the context of contemporary pedagogical challenges. *Pedagogical Journal*, *10*(3A), 238–246.

Ryan, R. M., & Deci, E. L. (2017). *Self-determination theory: Basic psychological needs in motivation, development, and wellness*. Guilford Publications. doi:10.1521/978.14625/28806

Ryan, R. M., & Deci, E. L. (2020). Intrinsic and extrinsic motivation from a self-determination theory perspective: Definitions, theory, practices, and future directions. *Contemporary Educational Psychology*, *61*, 101860. doi:10.1016/j.cedpsych.2020.101860

Ryoo, J. H., Molfese, V. J., & Brown, E. T. (2018). Strategies to encourage mathematics learning in early childhood: Discussions and brainstorming promote stronger performance. *Early Education and Development*, *29*(4), 603–617. doi:10.1080/10409289.2018.1442095

Ryu, J., Kim, Y., Park, S., Eum, S., Chun, S., & Yang, S. (2022). Exploring foreign language students' perceptions of the Guided Use of Machine Translation (GUMT) model for Korean writing. *Journal of Linguistics and Language Teaching*, *14*(1), 136–165. doi:10.5070/L214151759

Sadler, D. (1989). Formative assessment and the design of instructional systems. *Instructional Science*, *18*(1), 119–144. doi:10.1007/BF00117714

Sadler, D. (2010). Beyond feedback: Developing student capability in complex appraisal. *Assessment & Evaluation in Higher Education*, *35*(5), 535–550. doi:10.1080/02602930903541015

Sadler, G. R., Lee, H., Lim, R. S., & Fullerton, J. (2010). Recruitment of hard-to-reach population subgroups via adaptations of the snowball sampling strategy. *Nursing & Health Sciences*, *12*(3), 369–374. doi:10.1111/j.1442-2018.2010.00541.x PMID:20727089

Safi, F., Wenzel, T., & Spalding, L.-A. T. (2020). Remote Learning Community: Supporting Teacher Educators during Unprecedented Times. *Journal of Technology and Teacher Education*, *28*(2).

Sahakyan, T., Lamb, M., & Chambers, G. (2018). Language teacher motivation: From ideal self to the feasible self. In S. Mercer & A. Kostoulas (Eds.), *Language teacher psychology* (pp. 53–70). Multilingual Matters. doi:10.21832/9781783099467-008

Sandel, M. J. (2010). Justice: What's the Right Thing to Do? (Reprint ed.). Farrar, Straus, and Giroux.

Santos, B. D. S. (2016) 'The University at a Crossroads. In Darder', In A., Mayo, P. and Paraskeva, J. (ed.) International critical pedagogy reader. Routledge. pp. 295-302

Santos, J. L. G. D., Cunha, K. S. D., Adamy, E. K., Backes, M. T. S., Leite, J. L., & Sousa, F. G. M. D. (2018). Data analysis: Comparison between the different methodological perspectives of the Grounded Theory. *Revista da Escola de Enfermagem da U S P.*, 52. PMID:29668789

Saputra, J. B. (2018). An analysis of students' speaking anxiety toward their speaking skill. *Premise: Journal of English Education*, *7*(1), 111–123. doi:10.24127/pj.v7i1.1334

Sathy, V., & Hogan, K. A. (2019). How to make your teaching more inclusive. The Chronicle of Higher Education.

Sato, M. (2005). Higher education reforms in Malaysia 1957-2003. *NUCB Journal of Language Culture and Communication*, *7*(1), 73–88.

Sawyer, K. R. (2017). Group genius. The creative power of collaboration (Revised). Basic Books.

Schädler, T. (2020, May 4). *The role of international schools amid the new anti-globalization sentiment*. Linden Education. https://www.linden-education.com/post/the-role-of-international-schools-amid-the-new-anti-globalization-sentiment

Schenker, T. (2012). Intercultural competence and cultural learning through telecollaboration. *CALICO Journal*, *29*(3), 449–470. doi:10.11139/cj.29.3.449-470

Scherer, R. D., & Sardone, N. B. (2013). Collaboration as a Form of Professional Development: Improving Learning for Faculty and Students. *College Teaching*, *61*(1), 30–37. doi:10.1080/87567555.2012.714815

Schmidt, B., Von Hippel, A., & Tippelt, R. (2010). Higher education evaluation in Germany. *Research in Comparative and International Education. Ludwig-Maximilians-University of Munich, Germany*, *5*(1), 98–111.

Schmidt, C. (2004). The analysis of semi-structured interviews. In U. Flick, E. von Kardoff, & I. Steinke (Eds.), *A companion to qualitative research* (pp. 253–258). Sage Publications.

Schmidt, H. G., Wagener, S. L., Smeets, G. A. C. M., Keemink, L. M., & van der Molen, H. T. (2015). Guus ACM Smeets, Lianne M. Keemink, and Henk T. van Der Molen. "On the use and misuse of lectures in higher education. *Health Profession Education*, *1*(1), 12–18. doi:10.1016/j.hpe.2015.11.010

Schmidt-Unterberger, B. (2018). The English-medium paradigm: A conceptualisation of English-medium teaching in higher education. *International Journal of Bilingual Education and Bilingualism*, *21*(5), 527–539. doi:10.1080/13670050.2018.1491949

Schon, D. (1983). *The Reflective Practitioner*. Temple Smith.

Schulze, M. P., & Kleibert, J. M. (2021). Transnational education for regional economic development? Understanding Malaysia's and Singapore's strategic coupling in global higher education. *International Journal of Training and Development*, *25*(4), 363–382. doi:10.1111/ijtd.12242

Schwarz, C., & Struhkamp, G. (2007). Does evaluation build or destroy trust?: Insights from case studies on evaluation in higher education reform. *Evaluation, Germany*, *13*(3), 323–339. doi:10.1177/1356389007078625

Scimago Journal Rank. (2021). *Country Rank*. Scimago. https://www.scimagojr.com/countryrank.php

Scott, P. (2011, June 7). Universities are all "internationalising" now. *The Guardian*. https://www.theguardian.com/education/2011/jun/07/universities-global-ambitions-internationalising

Scriven, M. (1967). The Methodology of Evaluation. In R. W. Tyler (Ed.), *Perspectives of Curriculum Evaluation* (pp. 39–83). Rand McNally.

Scull, J., Phillips, M., Sharma, U., & Garnier, K. (2020). Innovations in teacher education at the time of COVID19: An Australian perspective. *Journal of Education for Teaching*, *46*(4), 497–506. doi:10.1080/02607476.2020.1802701

Scupin, R. (1997). The KJ method: A technique for analyzing data derived from Japanese ethnology. *Human Organization*, *56*(2), 233–237. doi:10.17730/humo.56.2.x335923511444655

Shackelford, J. L., & Maxwell, M. (2012). Sense of community in graduate online education: Contribution of learner to learner interaction. *International Review of Research in Open and Distributed Learning*, *13*(4), 228–249. doi:10.19173/irrodl.v13i4.1339

Shams, F., & Huisman, J. (2014). The role of institutional dual embeddedness in the strategic local adaptation of international branch campuses: Evidence from Malaysia and Singapore. *Studies in Higher Education*, *41*(6), 955–970. doi:10.1080/03075079.2014.966669

Sharma, Y. (2018) Ministry ends hundreds of Sino-foreign HE partnerships. *University World News*. https://www.universityworldnews.com/post.php?story=20180706154106269#:~:text=According%20to%20official%20figures%2C%20as,Some%2070%20are%20joint%20institutes

Sharma, Y. (2020). Private universities at risk as foreign students stay away. *University World News*. https://www.universityworldnews.com/post.php?story=2020120216283461

Sheller, M. (2014). Sociology after the mobilities turn. In P. Adey, D. Bissell, K. Hannam, P. Merriman, & M. Sheller (Eds.), *The Routledge handbook of mobilities* (pp. 65–74). Routledge.

Shi, L. (2006). The Successors to Confucianism or a New Generation? A Questionnaire Study on Chinese Students' Culture of Learning English. *Language, Culture and Curriculum*, *19*(1), 122–147. doi:10.1080/07908310608668758

Shoaib, A. (2004). *The motivation of teachers of English as a second language* (PhD Thesis, University of Nottingham, UK].

Shulze, M. P. (2020). Of bumping and bending: Foreign universities' FDI strategies in Malaysia. *Journal of Economic and Human Geography*, *112*(2), 179–194. https://onlinelibrary.wiley.com/doi/full/10.1111/tesg.12472

Shweder, R. A. (1991). *Thinking through cultures: Expeditions in cultural psychology*. Harvard University Press.

Sia, J. K. M., & Abbas, A. A. (2020). Facing the unknown: Pandemic and higher education in Malaysia. *Asian Education and Development Studies*, *10*(2), 263–275. doi:10.1108/AEDS-05-2020-0114

Siddiqui, K., & Jasim, M. M. (2022). Why brain drain is set to rise. *The Business Standard*. https://www.tbsnews.net/bangladesh/migration/why-brain-drain-set-rise-403834

Sidhu, R., Ho, K. C., & Yeoh, B. (2011). Emerging education hubs: The case of Singapore. *Higher Education*, *61*(1), 23–40. doi:10.100710734-010-9323-9

Sierens, E., Vansteenkiste, M., Goossens, L., Soenens, B., & Dochy, F. (2009). The synergistic relationship of perceived autonomy support and structure in the prediction of self-regulated learning. *The British Journal of Educational Psychology*, *79*(1), 57–68. doi:10.1348/000709908X304398 PMID:18466671

Si, J. (2019). English as a lingua franca: A new approach for English language teaching in China? *Canadian Journal of Applied Linguistics*, *42*(1), 113–135. doi:10.1515/CJAL-2019-0007

Silverman, D. (2011). *Qualitative research*. Sage.

Sinek, S. (2017). *Leaders eat last: Why some teams pull together and others don't*. Penguin.

Singhal, R., Kumar, A., Singh, H., Fuller, S., & Gill, S. S. (2020). Digital device-based active learning approach using virtual community classroom during the COVID-19 pandemic. *Computer Applications in Engineering Education*, 1–27.

Singh, J. K. N., Schapper, J., & Jack, G. (2014). The importance of place for international students' choice of university: A case study at a Malaysian university. *Journal of Studies in International Education*, *18*(5), 463–474. doi:10.1177/1028315314523990

Singh, M., Rizvi, F., & Shrestha, M. (2007). Student mobility and the spatial production of cosmopolitan identities. In K. N. Gulson & C. Symes (Eds.), *Spatial theories of education: Policy and geography matters* (pp. 195–214). Routledge.

Skinner, E. A., Kindermann, T. A., & Furrer, C. J. (2009). A motivational perspective on engagement and disaffection: Conceptualization and assessment of children's behavioral and emotional participation in academic activities in the classroom. *Educational and Psychological Measurement*, *69*(3), 493–525. doi:10.1177/0013164408323233

Skipp, A., & Hopwood, V. (2017). *Alternative providers of higher education: Views of the validation and franchise process and innovation in the sector.* London Department for Education.

Skogsberg, K., & Clump, M. (2003). Do Psychology and Biology majors differ in their study processes and learning styles? *College Student Journal*, *37*(1), 27–33.

Skrypnyk, T. (2006). Moving into Teacher Training. *The Teacher Trainer Journal*, *20*(2), 2.

Sloan, D., & Porter, E. (2010). Changing international student and business staff perceptions of in-sessional EAP: Using the CEM model. *Journal of English for Academic Purposes*, *9*(3), 198–210. doi:10.1016/j.jeap.2010.03.001

Smart, K., Witt, C., & Scott, J. (2012). Toward learner-centered teaching: An inductive approach. *Business Communication Quarterly*, *75*(4), 392–403. doi:10.1177/1080569912459752

Smith, A. (2020, June 9). More about Higher Education Institutions in China. *China Scholar.* https://www.china-scholar.com/higher-education-in-china/

Smith, B. L. (1993). Interpersonal behaviors that damage the productivity of creative problem solving groups. *The Journal of Creative Behavior*, *27*(3), 171–187. doi:10.1002/j.2162-6057.1993.tb00705.x

Smith, B. L., & Hughey, A. W. (2006). Leadership in higher education - Its evolution and potential: A unique role facing critical challenges. *Industry and Higher Education*, *20*(3), 157–163. doi:10.5367/000000006777690972

Smith, E. K., & Kaya, E. (2021). Online university teaching at the time of COVID-19 (2020): An Australian perspective. *IAFOR Journal of Education*, *9*(2), 183–200. doi:10.22492/ije.9.2.11

Smith, J. A., Flowers, P., & Larkin, M. (2009). *Interpretative Phenomenological Analysis: Theory, Method and Research.* Sage Publications, Inc.

Snyder, L. G. (2009). Teaching Teams about Teamwork: Preparation, Practice, and Performance Review. *Business Communication Quarterly*, *72*(1), 74–79. doi:10.1177/1080569908330372

Snyder, T. D. (1993). *120 years of American education: A statistical portrait.* US Department of Education, Office of Educational Research and Improvement, National Center for Education Statistics.

Son, B., Liang, X., & McIntosh, A. (2021). *An exploration of attitudes towards machine translation and a consideration of good practice* [Symposium]. School of Languages Symposium, Xi'an Jiaotong-Liverpool University.

Sonia, G. (2017). *Educational research and innovation pedagogical knowledge and the changing nature of the teaching profession.* OECD Publishing.

Sosniak, L. A. (1994). *Bloom's taxonomy* (L. W. Anderson, Ed.). Univ. Chicago Press.

Sowell, T. (2014). *Basic Economics* (5th ed.). Basic Books.

Spada, N. (2007). Communicative language teaching. In *International handbook of English language teaching* (pp. 271–288). Springer. doi:10.1007/978-0-387-46301-8_20

Sparks, D., & Hirsh, S. (1997). *A new vision for staff development.* Association for Supervision and Curriculum Development, 108.

Spiel, C., Schober, B., & Reimann, R. (2006). Evaluation of curricula in higher education: challenges for evaluators. Evaluation Review, 30(4), pp. 430-450.

Spolsky, B. (1995). *Measured words: the development of objective testing.* Oxford University Press.

Spring, J. (2014). *Globalization of education: An introduction.* Routledge. doi:10.4324/9781315795843

Stafford, S., & Taylor, J. (2016). Transnational education as an internationalisation strategy: Meeting the institutional management challenges. *Journal of Higher Education Policy and Management*, *38*(6), 625–636. doi:10.1080/1360080X.2016.1202811

Stafford, S., & Taylor, J. (2016). Transnational education as an internationalization strategy: Meeting the institutional management challenges. *Journal of Higher Education Policy and Management*, *38*(6), 625–636.

Stake, R. E. (1995). *The art of case study research*. Sage Publications.

Stella, A., & Woodhouse, D. (2011). Evolving dimensions of transnational education. In A. Stella & S. Bhushan (Eds.), *Quality assurance of transnational higher education the experiences of Australia and India* (pp. 3–18). Australian Universities Quality Agency and National University of Educational Planning and Administration.

Stensaker, B., Henkel, M., Välimaa, J., & Sarrico, C. S. (2012). Introduction: How is change in Higher Education managed? In B. Stensaker, J. Välimaa, & C. S. Sarrico (Eds.), *Managing Reform in Universities: The Dynamics of Culture, Identity and Organizational Change*. Palgrave Macmillan. doi:10.1057/9781137284297_1

Stewart, E. C., & Bennet, M. (1991). *American cultural patterns. A cross-cultural perspective*. Intercultural Press.

Stewart, V. (2010). A classroom as wide as the world. In H. Hayes Jacobs (Ed.), *Curriculum 21: Essential education for a changing world* (pp. 97–114). Association for Supervision and Curriculum Development.

Stone, G., Fiedler, B. A., & Kandunias, C. (2014). Harnessing Facebook for student engagement in accounting education: Guiding principles for accounting students and educators. *Accounting Education*, *23*(4), 295–321. doi:10.1080/09639284.2014.908730

Straker, J. (2016). International Student Participation in Higher Education: Changing the Focus From "International Students" to "Participation". *Journal of Studies in International Education*, *20*(4), 299–318. doi:10.1177/1028315316628992

Strawbridge, J., Hayden, J. C., Robson, T., Flood, M., Cullinan, S., Lynch, M., Morgan, A. T., O'Brien, F., Reynolds, R., Kerrigan, S. W., Cavalleri, G., Kirby, B. P., Tighe, O., Maher, A., & Barlow, J. W. (2022). Educating pharmacy students through a pandemic: Reflecting on our COVID-19 experience. *Research in Social & Administrative Pharmacy*, *18*(7), 3204–3209. doi:10.1016/j.sapharm.2021.08.007 PMID:34483082

Study Malaysia. (2018). Foreign university branch campus. *Study Malaysia*. https://www.studymalaysia.com/education/top-stories/foreign-university-branch-campus-your-route-to-getting-a-foreign-degree-right-here-in-malaysia#:~:text=The%20very%20first%20FUBC%2C%20Monash,World%20University%20Rankings%C2%AE%202019

Study Portals. (2021). *The changing landscape of English-taught programmes*. British Council and Study Portals. https://studyportals.com/intelligence/19347-2/

Suadiyatno, T., Firman, E., Hanan, A., & Sumarsono, D. (2020). Examining the effect of contextual teaching-learning and anxiety towards students' speaking skills. *Journal of Languages and Language Teaching*, *8*(1), 100–107. doi:10.33394/jollt.v8i1.2266

Sun, K. (2014). Comprehensive education: an analysis on the path of general education in Sino-foreign cooperative universities [Lexical characteristics of Chinese language]. *Social Science Review, 4*, pp. 154-157.

Suri, H. (2011). Purposeful sampling in qualitative research synthesis. *Qualitative Research Journal*, *11*(2), 63–75. doi:10.3316/QRJ1102063

Susam, T., Durnalı, M., & Orakcı, Ş. (2020). Administering education and training through a web-based system: E-curriculum. In M. Durnalı (Ed.), *Utilizing Technology, Knowledge, and Smart Systems in Educational Administration and Leadership*. IGI Global. doi:10.4018/978-1-7998-1408-5.ch002

Sutrisno, A., & Pillay, H. (2015). Knowledge transfer through a transnational program partnership between Indonesian and Australian universities. *Asia Pacific Education Review*, *16*(3), 379–388. doi:10.100712564-015-9384-7

Sutton, R. I., & Hargadon, A. (1996). Brainstorming groups in context: Effectiveness in a product design firm. *Administrative Science Quarterly*, *41*(4), 685–718. doi:10.2307/2393872

Suzuki, N. (2017). Foreign language speaking anxiety in the English-medium instruction (EMI) program in a Japanese university. *Casele Research Bulletin*, *47*, 11–21.

Swales, J., & Feak, C. (2000). *English in today's research world: A writing guide*. University of Michigan Press. doi:10.3998/mpub.9059

Swan, K., Garrison, D. R., & Richardson, J. C. (2009). A constructivist approach to online learning: The community of inquiry framework. In *Information technology and constructivism in higher education: Progressive learning frameworks* (pp. 43–57). IGI global. doi:10.4018/978-1-60566-654-9.ch004

Tadmor, C. T., Satterstrom, P., Jang, S., & Polzer, J. T. (2012). Beyond individual creativity: The superadditive benefits of multicultural experience for collective creativity in culturally diverse teams. *Journal of Cross-Cultural Psychology*, *43*(3), 384–392. doi:10.1177/0022022111435259

Tainsh, R. (2016). Thoughtfully designed online courses as effective adult learning tools. *Journal of Adult Education*, *45*(1), 7–9.

Tan, C. (2015). 'Education Policy Borrowing and Cultural Scripts for Teaching in China'. *Comparative Education*, *51*(2), 196–211. doi:10.1080/03050068.2014.966485

Tan, Z. (2008). Questioning in Chinese university EFL classrooms: What lies behind it? *Regional Language Centre Journal*, *38*(1), 87–103.

Tao, L. (2017). Face Perception in Chinese and Japanese. *Intercultural Communication Studies*, *26*(1), 151–167.

Taras, M. (2008). Summative and formative assessment: Perceptions and realities. *Active Learning in Higher Education. University of Sunderland, UK*, *9*(2), 172–192.

Taylor, D. W., Berry, P. C., & Block, C. H. (1958). Does group participation when using brainstorming facilitate or inhibit creative thinking? *Administrative Science Quarterly*, *3*(1), 23–47. doi:10.2307/2390603

Taylor, J. B. (2021). *Whole brain living: The anatomy of choice and the four characters that drive our life*. Hay House, Inc.

Taylor, M. (2011). *Public policy in the community*. Macmillan International Higher Education. doi:10.1007/978-0-230-34409-9

Taylor, S. (2014). Student self-assessment and multisource feedback assessment: Exploring benefits, limitations, and remedies. *Journal of Management Education. University of New Mexico, USA*, *38*(3), 359–383.

Tedlow, R. S., & Abdelal, R. (2004). Theodore Levitt's "The Globalization of Markets: An Evaluation After Two Decades. *Harvard Business School, 11*.

Tencent (2022). Top 8 countries where Chinese students go for study. [In Chinese]. Tencent. https://xw.qq.com/amphtml/20210325A063VL00?ivk_sa=1024320u.

TEQSA. (2021). *Forward impact of COVID-19 on Australian higher education*. TEQSA. https://www.teqsa.gov.au/sites/default/files/forward-impact-of-covid-19-on-australian-higher-education-report.pdf?v=1635905249

Tesar, M. (2020). Towards a Post-Covid-19 "New Normality?": Physical and Social Distancing, the Move to Online and Higher Education. *Policy Futures in Education*, *2020*(5), 556–559. doi:10.1177/1478210320935671

Tham, S. Y., & Kam, A. J. Y. (2008). Internationalising higher education: Comparing the challenges of different higher education institutions in Malaysia. *Asia Pacific Journal of Education*, *28*(4), 353–367. doi:10.1080/02188790802468880

The British Council. (1999) *Study for a UK Higher Education Qualification by Distance Learning,* The British Council, http://www.britishcouncil.org.uk/distancelearning/index.htm

The Chinese University of Hong Kong. Shenzhen. (2022). *Introducing CUHK-Shenzhen.* The Chinese University of Hong Kong, Shenzhen (CUHK-Shenzhen). https://www.cuhk.edu.cn/en/page/4987

The Economist Intelligence Unit. (2014), High university enrolment, low graduate employment: Analysing the paradox in Afghanistan, Bangladesh, India, Nepal, Pakistan and Sri Lanka. *The Economist.*

The Star. (2018, November 5). Dr. M wants more Japanese universities to set up branch campuses in Malaysia. *The Star.* https://www.thestar.com.my/news/nation/2018/11/05/dr-m-wants-japanese-universities-toset-up-branch-campuses-in-malaysia/

The Times Higher Education World University Ranking. (2021). THE world university rankings 2021. *Times.* https://www.timeshighereducation.com/world-university-rankings/2021/world-ranking#!/page/0/length/25/sort_by/rank/sort_order/asc/cols/stats

The Times Higher Education World University Ranking. (2022). World university rankings 2022 methodology. *Times.* https://www.timeshighereducation.com/sites/default/files/breaking_news_files/the_2022_world_university_rankings_methodology_31082021_final.pdf

Thi Tran, L., Thi Quy Do, T., & Bui, H. (2021). 'Employability in context': The importance of considering contextual factors in reimagining employability through Australian student mobility to the Indo-Pacific region. *Higher Education Quarterly*, *75*(4), 591–607. doi:10.1111/hequ.12303

Thomas, S., Chie, Q. T., Abraham, M., Jalarajan Raj, S., & Beh, L. (2014). A qualitative review of literature on peer review of teaching in high education: An application of the SWOT framework. *Review of Educational Research*, *84*(1), 112–159. doi:10.3102/0034654313499617

Tierney, W. G., & Landford, M. (2015). An investigation of the impact of international branch campuses on organizational culture. *Higher Education*, *70*(2), 283–298. doi:10.100710734-014-9845-7

Tilak, J. B. (2002). Knowledge Society, Education and Aid. *Compare: A Journal of Comparative Education*, *3*(32), 297–310. doi:10.1080/0305792022000007463

Ting-Toomey, S., & Oetzel, J. G. (2001). Managing intercultural conflict effectively. *Sage (Atlanta, Ga.).*

Toffler, A. (1980). *The third wave.* William Morrow.

Togashi, R., Goto, H., Morita, R., Yamachika, Y., & Yamazaki, Y. (2019). Transformation of Activity and Consciousness of AA School and Residents through the Past 22 years in Koshirakura village, Niigata Prefecture. *Journal of the City Planning Institute of Japan*, *54*(3), 1460–1467. doi:10.11361/journalcpij.54.1460

Toor, S. U. R., & Ofori, G. (2008). Leadership versus management: How are they different and why. *Leadership and Management in Engineering*, *8*(2), 61–71. doi:10.1061/(ASCE)1532-6748(2008)8:2(61)

Toptal, V. M., Toptal, & Vogel, M. (2015). *Does owning an iPhone elevate a persons social standing in society?* Quora. https://www.quora.com/Does-owning-an-iPhone-elevate-a-persons-social-standing-in-society

Toquero, C. M. (2020). Challenges and Opportunities for Higher Education Amid the COVID-19 Pandemic: The Philippine Context. *Pedagogical Research*, *5*(4), 1–5. doi:10.29333/pr/7947

Toraman, C., Orakcı, S., & Aktan, O. (2020). Analysis of the relationships between mathematics achievement, reflective thinking of problem solving and metacognitive Awareness. *International Journal of Progressive Education, 16*(2), 72–90. doi:10.29329/ijpe.2020.241.6

Torres, T. (2016, February 4). *Why brainstorming doesn't work (and what to do instead).* INC. https://www.inc.com/teresa-torres/why-brainstorming-doesnt-work-and-what-to-do-instead.html

Trahar, S. (2015). Learning and teaching on transnational higher education programmes in Hong Kong. *Learning and Teaching, 8*(1), 95–112. doi:10.3167/latiss.2015.080106

Tran, L. T., Thanh Le, T. T., Phan, H. L. T., & Pham, A. (2021). "Induction and off you go": Professional development for teachers in transnational education. *Oxford Review of Education, 47*(4), 529–547. doi:10.1080/03054985.2020.1867524

Trapp, R. (2016). *Building global relations through debate.* The Foreign Language and Research Press.

Trembath, J. L. (2016). The professional lives of expatriate academics: Construct clarity and implications for expatriate management in higher education. *Journal of Global Mobility, 4*(2), 112–130. doi:10.1108/JGM-04-2015-0012

Tremblay, K. (2005). Academic mobility and immigration. *Journal of Studies in International Education, 9*(3), 196–228. doi:10.1177/1028315305277618

Trenshaw, K. F., Revelo, R. A., Earl, K. A., & Herman, G. L. (2016). Using self-determination theory principles to promote engineering students' intrinsic motivation to learn. *International Journal of Engineering Education, 32*(3), 1194–1207.

Trent, J. (2017). "Being a professor and doing EMI properly isn't easy": An identity-theoretic investigation of content teachers' attitudes towards EMI at a university in Hong Kong. In B. Fenton-Smith (Ed.), *English medium instruction in higher education in Asia-Pacific* (pp. 219–239). Springer. doi:10.1007/978-3-319-51976-0_12

Truong, Van T., Hasansen, K., & Laihonen, H. (2020). Students as knowledge mediators in transnational higher education. *Multidisciplinary Perspectives in Higher Education, 5*(2), 48–65.

Trust, T., Trust, T., & Whalen, J. (2020). Should Teachers be Trained in Emergency Remote Teaching? Lessons Learned from.... *Journal of Technology and Teacher Education, 28*(2), 189–199.

Tsai, M. N., Liao, Y. F., Chang, Y. L., & Chen, H. C. (2020). A brainstorming flipped classroom approach for improving students' learning performance, motivation, teacher-student interaction and creativity in a civics education class. *Thinking Skills and Creativity, 38*, 100747. Advance online publication. doi:10.1016/j.tsc.2020.100747

Tsai, S. C. (2020). Chinese students' perceptions of using Google Translate as a translingual CALL tool in EFL writing. *Computer Assisted Language Learning*, 1–23. doi:10.1080/09588221.2020.1799412

Tschida, C. M., Hodge, E. M., & Schmidt, S. W. (2016). Learning to teach online: Negotiating issues of platform, pedagogy, and professional development. In *Educational Leadership and Administration* (Vol. 4–4). Concepts, Methodologies, Tools, and Applications., doi:10.4018/978-1-5225-1624-8.ch096

Tsiligkiris, V. (2021). *Innovative approaches to transnational education.* THE Campus.

Tsiligkiris, V., & Ilieva, J. (2022). Global engagement in the post-pandemic world: Challenges and responses. Perspective from the UK. *Higher Education Quarterly, 76*(2), 343–366. doi:10.1111/hequ.12390

Tsuneyoshi, R. (2018). The internationalization of Japanese education: "International" without the "multicultural.". *Educational Studies in Japan, 12*(0), 49–59. doi:10.7571/esjkyoiku.12.49

Tsybulsky, D. (2019). The team-teaching experiences of pre-service science: Teachers implementing PBL in elementary school. *Journal of Education for Teaching, 45*(3), 244–261. doi:10.1080/09589236.2019.1599505

Turkish Qualifications Framework. (2015). *Turkish qualifications framework.* MYK. https://www.myk.gov.tr//TRR/File6.pdf

Turner, J. (2011). Rewriting writing in higher education: The contested spaces of proofreading. *Studies in Higher Education, 36*(4), 427–440. doi:10.1080/03075071003671786

UGC. (2020). *46th Annual Report 2019.*[Data set]. UGC.

UGC. (2022). *List of Universities.* UGC. http://www.ugc-universities.gov.bd/public-universities

UK Universities. (2021). *What is UK higher education transnational education?* UK Universities. https://www.universitiesuk.ac.uk/universities-uk-international/explore-uuki/transnational-education/what-uk-higher-education-transnational

UN. (2020). Be the change you want to see. United Nations. https://www.un.org/africarenewal/webfeatures/peacekeepers/women-peacekeeping-%E2%80%98be-change-youwant-see%E2%80%99

UNDESA. (2013). *Definition of youth* (Issue 10/08/2016). United Nations Department of Economic and Social Affairs. https://www.un.org/esa/socdev/documents/youth/fact-sheets/youth-definition.pdf

UNESCO. (n.d.). *Distance learning solutions.* UNESCO. https://en.unesco.org/covid19/educationresponse/solutions

UNESCO/Council of Europe. (2001). *Code of good practice in the provision of transnational education.* UNESCO. https://www.coe.int/en/web/higher-education-and-research/lisbon-recognition-convention

UNESCO/Council of Europe. (2001). *Code of good practice in the provision of transnational education.* UNESCO/Council of Europe.

University of Cambridge Institute for Sustainability Leadership. (2017a). *Global definitions of leadership and theories of leadership development: Literature review.* University of Cambridge.

University of Cambridge Institute for Sustainability Leadership. (2017b). *Building leaders for long-term business performance: Research findings.* University of Cambridge.

Uricchio, W. (2017). Data, culture and the ambivalence of algorithms. In K. Van Es & M. T. Schäfer (Eds.), *The datafied society: Studying culture through data* (pp. 125–137). Amsterdam University Press. doi:10.1515/9789048531011-011

Urlaub, P., & Dessein, E. (2022). From disrupted classrooms to human-machine collaboration? The pocket calculator, Google Translate, and the future of language education. *Journal of Linguistics and Language Teaching, 14*(1), 45–59. doi:10.5070/L214151790

US Davis Executive Leadership Program. (2014). *Emotional intelligence: How good leaders become great.* University of Nottingham. https://moodle.nottingham.ac.uk/course/view.php?id=99200&section=4##

Van der Zwaan, B. (2017). *Higher education in 2040. A global approach.* Amsterdam University Press. doi:10.1515/9789048535163

Vangrieken, K., Dochy, F., Raes, E., & Kyndt, E. (2015). Teacher collaboration: A systematic review. *Educational Research Review, 15*, 17–40. doi:10.1016/j.edurev.2015.04.002

Vangrieken, K., Grosemans, I., Dochy, F., & Kyndt, E. (2017). Teacher autonomy and collaboration: A paradox? Conceptualising and measuring teachers' autonomy and collaborative attitude. *Teaching and Teacher Education, 67*, 302–315. doi:10.1016/j.tate.2017.06.021

VanGundy, A. B. (1984). Brainwriting for new product ideas: An alternative to brainstorming. *Journal of Consumer Marketing, 1*(2), 67–74). doi:10.1108/eb008097

Vansteenkiste, M., Sierens, E., Soenens, B., Luyckx, K., & Lens, W. (2009). Motivational profiles from a self-determination perspective: The quality of motivation matters. *Journal of Educational Psychology*, *101*(3), 671–688. doi:10.1037/a0015083

Velliaris, D. M., & Pierce, J. M. (2019). Cheaters beware: (Re)designing assessment practices to reduce academic misconduct. In D. M. Velliaris (Ed.), *Prevention and detection of academic misconduct in higher education* (pp. 1–38). IGI Global. doi:10.4018/978-1-5225-7531-3.ch001

Velzen, C. V., Klink, M. V. D., Swennen, A., & Yaffe, E. (2010). The induction and needs of beginning teacher educators. *Professional Development in Education*, *36*(1-2), 61–75. doi:10.1080/19415250903454817

Vergolini, L., & Vlach, E. (2017). Family background and educational path of Italian graduates. *Higher Education*, *73*(2), 245–259. doi:10.100710734-016-0011-2

Vollet, J. W., Kindermann, T. A., & Skinner, E. A. (2017). In peer matters, teachers matter: Peer group influences on students' engagement depend on teacher involvement. *Journal of Educational Psychology*, *109*(5), 635–652. doi:10.1037/edu0000172

Vonderwell, S., Liang, X., & Alderman, K. (2007). Asynchronous discussions and assessment in online learning. *Journal of Research on Technology in Education*, *39*(3), 309–328. doi:10.1080/15391523.2007.10782485

Wade, W. (1994). Introduction. *Flexible Learning in Higher Education*, 12-16.

Wake, D., Ryan, G., & Ramos, E. (2020). *The scale of UK higher education transnational education 2018-19* (No. 4). Universities UK International. https://www.universitiesuk.ac.uk/universities-uk-international/insights-and-publications/uuki-publications/scale-uk-higher-education-transnational-1

Wallace, M., & Dunn, L. (2008). *Teaching in transnational higher education*. Routledge.

Wang, L. (2011). Foreign English Teachers in the Chinese Classroom: Focus on Teacher-Student Interaction. *The Journal of Asia TEFL*, *8*(2), 73–93.

Wang, W., & Curdt-Christiansen, X. L. (2016). Teaching Chinese to international students in China: Political rhetoric and ground realities. *The Asia-Pacific Education Researcher*, *25*(5-6), 723–734. doi:10.100740299-016-0316-z

Wanner, T., & Palmer, E. (2018). Formative self-and peer assessment for improved student learning: The crucial factors of design, teacher participation and feedback. *Assessment & Evaluation in Higher Education*, *43*(7), 1032–1047. doi:10.1080/02602938.2018.1427698

Waters, J. L. (2005). Transnational family strategies and education in the contemporary Chinese diaspora. *Global Networks*, *5*(4), 359–377. doi:10.1111/j.1471-0374.2005.00124.x

Waters, J. L. (2006). Geographies of cultural capital: Education, international migration and family strategies between Hong Kong and Canada. *Transactions of the Institute of British Geographers*, *31*(2), 179–192. doi:10.1111/j.1475-5661.2006.00202.x

Waters, J. L. (2012). Geographies of international education: Mobilities and the reproduction of social (dis)advantage. *Geography Compass*, *6*(3), 123–136. doi:10.1111/j.1749-8198.2011.00473.x

Waters, J., & Leung, M. (2013). Immobile transnationalisms? Young people and their *in situ* experiences of 'international' education in Hong Kong. *Urban Studies (Edinburgh, Scotland)*, *50*(3), 606–620. doi:10.1177/0042098012468902

Waters, J., & Leung, M. (2017). Trans-knowledge? Geography, mobility,and knowledge in transnational education. In H. Jöns, P. Meusburger, & M. Heffernan (Eds.), *Mobilities of knowledge. Knowledge and space* (pp. 269–285). Springer. doi:10.1007/978-3-319-44654-7_14

Waters, J., & Leung, M. W. H. (2022). Transnational higher education. In B. S. A. Yeoh & F. L. Collins (Eds.), *Handbook on transnationalism* (pp. 230–245). Edward Elgar Publishing.

Watt, W. (2009). Top 10 traits of an effective academic leader. *Faculty Focus.* https://www.facultyfocus.com/articles/academic-leadership/top-10-traits-of-an-effective-academic-leader/

Watt, M. G., & Richardson, P. W. (2007). Motivational factors influencing teaching as a career choice: Development and validation of the FIT choice scale. *Journal of Experimental Education*, *75*(3), 167–202. doi:10.3200/JEXE.75.3.167-202

Watt, M. G., Richardson, P. W., & Smith, K. (2017). Why teach? How teachers' motivations matter around the world. In M. G. Watt, P. W. Richardson, & K. Smith (Eds.), *Global perspectives on teacher motivation. Current perspectives in social and behavioural sciences* (pp. 1–21). Cambridge University Press. doi:10.1017/9781316225202.001

Weiler, A. (2004). Information-seeking behavior in generation Y students: Motivation, critical thinking, and learning theory. *Journal of Academic Librarianship*, *31*(1), 46–53. doi:10.1016/j.acalib.2004.09.009

Weiss, F., & Steininger, H.-M. (2013). Educational family background and the realisation of educational career intentions: Participation of German upper secondary graduates in higher education over time. *Higher Education*, *66*(2), 189–202. doi:10.100710734-012-9598-0

Wenger, M. S., & Hornyak, M. J. (1999). Team Teaching for Higher Level Learning: A Framework of Professional Collaboration. *Journal of Management Education*, *23*(3), 311–327. doi:10.1177/105256299902300308

Werner, M., & Zimmermann, B. (2006, February). Histoire Croisée and the Challenge of Reflexivity. *History and Theory*, *45*(1), 30–50. doi:10.1111/j.1468-2303.2006.00347.x

Wertz Consulting. (2019). *How leadership has changed over the last 10 years.* Wertz Consulting. http://www.wertzconsulting.com/leadership-changed-last-10-years/

Westerlaken, M., Christiaans-Dingelhoff, I., Filius, R. M., De Vries, B., De Bruijne, M., & Van Dam, M. (2019). Blended learning for postgraduates; an interactive experience. *BMC Medical Education*, *19*(1), 1–7. doi:10.118612909-019-1717-5 PMID:31362735

Whitsed, C., & Green, W. (2015). Internationalising the Curriculum in Education: An Overview. *Critical perspectives on internationalising the curriculum in disciplines*, 83-90.

WHO. (2020, March). *WHO Director-General's opening remarks at the media briefing on COVID-19.* WHO. https://www.who.int/director-general/speeches/detail/who-director-general-s-opening-remarks-at-the-media-briefing-on-covid-19---11-march-2020

Wholey, J. (1996). Formative and summative evaluation: related issues in performance measurement. American Journal of Evaluation, 17(2), pp. 145-149.

Widjaja, W., Yoshii, K., Haga, K., & Takahashi, M. (2013). Discusys: Multiple user real-time digital sticky-note affinity-diagram brainstorming system. *Procedia Computer Science*, *22*, 113–122. doi:10.1016/j.procs.2013.09.087

Wiliam, D., & Thompson, M. (2007). Integrating assessment with instruction: What will it take to make it work? In C. A. Dwyer (Ed.), *The future of assessment: Shaping teaching and learning* (pp. 53–82). Erlbaum.

Wilkins, S., & Rumbley, L. E. (2018). What an international branch is, and is not: a revised edition. International Higher Education, 93, 12-13. doi:10.6017/ihe.0.93.10416

Wilkinson, A., Gollan, P. J., Marchington, M., & Lewin, D. (2010). Conceptualizing employee participation in organizations. In A. Wilkinson, P. Gollan, M. Marchington, & D. Lewin (Eds.), *The Oxford handbook of participation in organizations* (pp. 1–125). Oxford University Press.

Wilkinson, R. (2018). Content and language integration at universities? Collaborative reflections. *International Journal of Bilingual Education and Bilingualism*, *21*(59), 607–615. doi:10.1080/13670050.2018.1491948

Wilkins, S. (2016). Establishing international branch campuses: A framework for assessing opportunities and risks. *Journal of Higher Education Policy and Management*, *38*(2), 167–182. doi:10.1080/1360080X.2016.1150547

Wilkins, S. (2018). Definitions of transnational higher education. *Industry and Higher Education*, *95*(95), 5–7. doi:10.6017/ihe.2018.95.10717

Wilkins, S. (2018). The management of transnational higher education. *International Journal of Educational Management*, *32*(2), 206–209. doi:10.1108/IJEM-10-2017-0260

Wilkins, S. (2020). Two decades of international branch campus development, 2000–2020: A review. *International Journal of Educational Management*, *35*(1), 311–326. doi:10.1108/IJEM-08-2020-0409

Wilkins, S., & Annabi, C. A. (2021). Academic Careers in Transnational Higher Education: The Rewards and Challenges of Teaching at International Branch Campuses. *Journal of Studies in International Education*, *23*(4), 451–472. doi:10.1177/1028315318814200

Wilkins, S., & Annabi, C. A. (2021). Academic careers in transnational higher education: The rewards and challenges of teaching at international branch campuses. *Journal of Studies in International Education*. doi:10.1177/10283153211052782

Wilkins, S., & Balakrishnan, M. S. (2013). Assessing student satisfaction in transnational higher education. *International Journal of Educational Management*, *27*(2), 143–156. doi:10.1108/09513541311297568

Wilkins, S., Balakrishnan, M. S., & Huisman, J. (2012). Student satisfaction and student perceptions of quality at international branch campuses in the United Arab Emirates. *Journal of Higher Education Policy and Management*, *34*(5), 543–556. doi:10.1080/1360080X.2012.716003

Wilkins, S., & Huisman, J. (2012). The international branch campus as transnational strategy in higher education. *Higher Education*, *64*(5), 627–645. doi:10.100710734-012-9516-5

Wilkins, S., & Juusola, K. (2018). The benefits & drawbacks of transnational higher education: Myths and realities. *Australian Universities Review*, *6*, 68–76.

Wilkins, S., & Urbanovič, J. (2014). English as the lingua franca in transnational higher education: Motives and prospects of institutions that teach in languages other than English. *Journal of Studies in International Education*, *18*(5), 405–425. doi:10.1177/1028315313517267

Williams, J., Ritter, J., & Bullock, S. M. (2012). Understanding the Complexity of Becoming a Teacher Educator: Experience, belonging, and practice within a professional learning community, Studying Teacher Education. *Studying Teacher Education*, *8*(3), 245–260. doi:10.1080/17425964.2012.719130

Wilmarth, S. (2010). Five socio-technology trends that change everything in learning and teaching. In H. Hayes Jacobs (Ed.), *In Curriculum 21: Essential education for a changing world* (pp. 80–96). Association for Supervision and Curriculum Development.

Wilson, L. A., & Vlasceanu, L. (2000). Transnational education and recognition of qualifications. In *Internationalization of higher education: an institutional perspective* (pp. 75–89). https://unesdoc.unesco.org/ark:/48223/pf0000125380

Wilson, C. E. (2007). Inverse, reverse, and unfocused methods. *Interaction, 14*(6), 54–55. doi:10.1145/1300655.1300687

Wimpenny, K., & Orsini-Jones, M. (2020). Innovation in collaborative online international learning: A holistic blend. In *Radical solutions and eLearning* (pp. 1–25). Springer. doi:10.1007/978-981-15-4952-6_1

Winiger, S. R., & Birkholz, P. M. (2013). Sources of instructional feedback, job satisfaction, and basic psychological needs. *Innovative Higher Education, 38*(2), 159–170. doi:10.100710755-012-9229-9

WMU. (n.d.). *Teaching argumentation.* The University of Michigan Writing Center. https://lsa.umich.edu/sweetland/instructors/teaching-resources/teaching-argumentation.html

Wong, C. S. (2016). *Teaching pronunciation to learners of English as a lingua franca. English language teaching today, 241-255.* Springer.

Woodward, T. (1997). Trainer training: A question matrix. In I. McGrath (Ed.), *Learning to Train: Perspectives on the Development of Language Teacher Trainers* (pp. 3–10). Prentice Hall Europe.

Woodward, T. (2006). Am I Ready to be a Teacher Trainer? *The Teacher Trainer Journal, 20*(1), 2.

Woodward, W. (1906). *Studies in education during the age of the Renaissance, 1400-1600.* Cambridge University Press.

World Economic Forum. 2020. *The future of jobs report 2020.* World Economic Forum, Geneva, Switzerland.

Wright, T., & Bolitho, R. (2007). *Trainer Development.* Lightning Source UK Ltd.

Wu, Y., Schuster, M., Chen, Z., Le, Q. V., Norouzi, M., Macherey, W., Krikun, M., Cao, Y., Gao, Q., Macherey, K., Klingner, J., Shah, A., Johnson, M., Liu, X., Kaiser, Ł., Gouws, S., Kato, Y., Kudo, T., Kazawa, H., & Dean, J. (2016). *Google's neural machine translation system: Bridging the gap between human and machine translation. ArXiv.* https://arxiv.org/abs/1609.08144

Wu, W. P., Fan, W. W., & Peng, R. Z. (2013). An analysis of the assessment tools for Chinese college students' intercultural competence. *Foreign Language Teaching and Research, 4*, 581–592.

Wylie, I. (2021) Business schools aim for an international experience at home. *Financial Times.* https://www.ft.com/content/f3e0931b-0ab3-48c1-87a5-151303327f59.

Xi'an Jiaotong-Liverpool University. (2022). *XJTLU strategic growth and Integrative Education.* Xi'an Jiaotong-Liverpool University (XJTLU). https://www.xjtlu.edu.cn/en/about/overview/xjtlu-strategic-growth-and-syntegrative-education

Xia, H., & Zhong, B. (2014). Learning outcomes assessment in China: Primitive foundations. In H. Coates (Ed.), *Higher education learning outcomes assessment: international perspectives* (pp. 113–134). Peter Lang GmbH.

Xia, W. (2021). The innovative practice of general education system under the background of new liberal arts [Lexical characteristics of Chinese language]. *Chinese Higher Education, 12*, 20–21.

Xie, K., & Ke, F. (2011). The role of students' motivation in peer-moderated asynchronous online discussions. *British Journal of Educational Technology, 42*(6), 916–930. doi:10.1111/j.1467-8535.2010.01140.x

Xie, X. (2009). Why are students quiet? Looking at the Chinese context and beyond. *ELT Journal, 64*(1), 1–11.

Xiong, J. (2011). Understanding higher vocational education in China: Vocationalism vs Confucianism. *Frontiers of Education in China, 6*(4), 495–520. doi:10.100711516-011-0143-1

Xi, Y. (2020). *The rarely known stories of management of XJTLU. could be and do.* Tsinghua University Press.

Xi, Y. (2022). *Be Independent: The road of HeXie Education.* Tsinghua University Press.

Xi, Y. (2022). *What Management could be and do*. Peiking University Press.

Xi, Y., & Li, C. (2021). *Research-Led Learning and Critical Thinking-EAP Practice*. Foreign Language Teaching and Research Press.

XJTLU. (2016). *Seven Sino-foreign cooperative universities gather at XJTLU*. XJLT University. https://www.xjtlu.edu.cn/en/news/2016/07/seven-sino-foreign cooperative-universities-gather-at-xjtlu

Xu, F., & Xu, F. (1997). Letter from China: A survey of creativity research. *Creativity and Innovation Management*, *6*(4), 249–253. doi:10.1111/1467-8691.00075

Yamamoto, R., Konno, T., Kishi, M., & Kubota, K. (2012). A Study of Learning Factors on International Fieldwork: Focus on Interaction with Partners in the Program. *Japan Journal of Educational Technology*, *36*(Suppl.), 213–216.

Yang, Y. T. C., & Wu, W. C. I. (2012). Digital storytelling for enhancing student academic achievement, critical thinking, and learning motivation: A year-long experimental study. *Computers & Education*, *59*(2), 339–352. doi:10.1016/j.compedu.2011.12.012

Yao, X. (2000). *An introduction to Confucianism*. Cambridge University Press. [electronic version] doi:10.1017/CBO9780511800887

Yarime, M., & Tanaka, Y. (2012). The issues and methodologies in sustainability assessment tools for higher education institutions: a review of recent trends and future challenges. Journal of Education for Sustainable Development, 6(1), pp. 63-77.

Yat, W. L. W., & Chang, D. W. (2021). Revisiting the Asian regulatory regimes in transnational education: How local politics (re)oriented higher education policy in Malaysia, Singapore and Hong Kong, *Policy. The Review of Higher Education*, *5*(2), 113–130. doi:10.1080/23322969.2020.1869064

Yee, H. Y., Radhakrishnan, A., & Ponnudurai, G. (2006). Improving PBLs in the International Medical University: Defining the 'good'PBL facilitator. *Medical Teacher*, *28*(6), 558–560. doi:10.1080/01421590600878226 PMID:17074705

Yi, C. C., & Wu, C. I. (2004). *Teen life around the world: Introduction to teen life in Taiwan*. Sinica. https://ir.sinica.edu.tw/handle/201000000A/65566

Yin, L. L. (2014). *A study on the history of sino-foreign cooperation in running schools in the field of higher education*. [Thesis, The university of Xiamen, China].

Yin, R. K. (2003). *Case study research: Design and methods*. Sage publications.

Yong, S. (2021). A reflective commentary about teaching international non-accounting postgraduates amid COVID-19. *Pacific Accounting Review*, *33*(5), 616–624. doi:10.1108/PAR-09-2020-0156

Yong, S. S., & Sia, J. K. M. (2021). COVID-19 and social wellbeing in Malaysia: A case study. *Current Psychology (New Brunswick, N.J.)*. doi:10.100712144-021-02290-6 PMID:34539153

York St John University. (2021). *Code of Practice for Assessment and Academic-related Matters 2021-22 (Section 23)*. York St John University. https://www.yorksj.ac.uk/media/content-assets/registry/policies/code-of-practice-for-assessment/23.Academic_Misconduct_Policy_2021-22.pdf

Yorke, M., Bridges, P., & Woolf, H. (2000). Mark distributions and marking practices in UK higher education: Some challenging issues. *Active Learning in Higher Education, UK*, *1*(1), 7–27. doi:10.1177/1469787400001001002

Yoshihara, K. F. (2018). *Teachers satisfaction and staff morale in international schools* [PhD Thesis,. University of New England, USA].

Yousef, A. M. F., Chatti, M. A., & Schroeder, U. (2014), Video-Based Learning: A Critical Analysis of The Research Published in 2003–2013 and Future Visions. In *Proceeding of the Sixth International Conference on Mobile, Hybrid, and Online Learning*, Barcelona, Spain, (pp. 112–119).

Yung, C. H. A., Hill, C., Chen, H. J. K., & Tsai, S. (2018). A comparative study of international branch campuses in Malaysia, Singapore China and South Korea: Regulation, governance and quality assurance. *Asia Pacific Education Review*, *19*(4), 543–555. doi:10.100712564-018-9550-9

Yu, X. (2021). Foreign language learning anxiety in China: Theories and applications in English language teaching. *International Journal of Bilingual Education and Bilingualism*, *24*(8), 1247–1249. doi:10.1080/13670050.2018.1545745

Yu, Y., & Moskal, M. (2019). Missing intercultural engagements in the university experiences of Chinese international students in the UK. *Compare: A Journal of Comparative Education*, *49*(4), 654–671.

Zappa-Hollman, S. (2018). Collaborations between language and content university instructors: Factors and indicators of positive partnerships. *International Journal of Bilingual Education and Bilingualism*, *21*(5), 591–606. doi:10.1080/13670050.2018.1491946

Zha, Q. (Ed.). (2013). *Education in China*. Berk Publishing Group LLC.

Zhou, R. Y., Knoke, D., & Sakamoto, I. (2005). 'Rethinking silence in the classroom: Chinese students' experiences of sharing indigenous knowledge'. *International Journal of Inclusive Education*, *9*(3), 287–311. doi:10.1080/13603110500075180

Zhou, Y., & Wei, M. (2021). *The Lived Experience of Chinese International Students in the US*. Springer. doi:10.1007/978-981-15-9449-6

Zhu, X., & Li, J. (2018). Conceptualizing the ontology of higher education with Chinese characteristics. *Educational Philosophy and Theory*, *50*(12), 1144–1156. https://www.tandfonline.com/doi/full/10.1080/00131857.2018.1504707?scroll=top&needAccess=true. doi:10.1080/00131857.2018.1504707

Ziguras, C. (2001). Educational technology in transnational higher education in South East Asia: The cultural politics of flexible learning. *Journal of Educational Technology & Society*, *4*(4), 8–18.

Ziguras, C. (2013). The Cultural Politics of Transnational Education: Ideological and Pedagogical Issues for Teaching Staff. In *Teaching in transnational higher education* (pp. 68–78). Routledge.

Zouhri, K., & Running, C. L. (2021, July). Different Zoom Breakout Room Methods and Techniques' Effects on Engineering Students' Learning Outcomes for Engineering Courses. In *2021 ASEE Virtual Annual Conference Content Access*.

Zuber-Skerritt, O., & Abraham, S. (2017). A conceptual framework for work-applied learning for developing managers as practitioner researchers. *Higher Education. Skills and Work-Based Learning*, *7*(1), 35–50. doi:10.1108/HESWBL-05-2016-0037

About the Contributors

Gareth Richard Morris currently works for the Perse School (Suzhou) leading and teaching on Business Studies, EFL, ESL and University and Careers Guidance courses. He also leads Professional Development initiatives at the institution. Gareth is a Senior Fellow of the Higher Education Academy (SFHEA), postgraduate external examiner, PDQ Mentor and previously worked in transnational higher education for fourteen years before transitioning into international schooling.

Li Li is Associate Professor in Language Education and Director of MEd in TESOL in the Graduate School of Education at the University of Exeter. Her research interests include teacher cognition, classroom discourse, developing thinking skills and integrating new technologies in language teaching. She is the author of Language Teacher Cognition and Social Interaction and Teacher Cognition. She also edited Thinking Skills and Creativity in Second Language Education.

* * *

Ömer Açıkgöz is a professor at the Social Sciences University of Ankara, Department of Economics, Ankara, Turkey. He received his Ph.D. from the Economics Program of Marmara University, Istanbul, Turkey. He served as the General Director of Vocational and Technical Education and Deputy Undersecretary at the Republic of Turkiye Ministry of National Education for three and a half years. He also served as Deputy Undersecretary of the Prime Ministry for two and a half years and was appointed as a member of the Council of Higher Education (CoHE) in 2015. He continues to serve as a member of CoHE's Executive Board. His research interests include economics and education. His articles have been published in some national and international scientific journals.

Saif Said Rashid Al Abri is an English teacher-trainer at Nizwa Educational and professional development Center - Ministry of Education, Oman.

Aydın Aslan taught English and Turkish at various K12 grades in Turkey and Belgium for 10 years. He worked as an expert in the General Directorate of European Union and Foreign Relations in the Ministry of National Education of Republic of Turkey for five years. He currently works as an assistant professor in the department of educational sciences at Selçuk University in Turkey. He holds a PhD in educational sciences from Vrije Universiteit Brussel in Belgium. His interest areas include innovation in higher education, graduates' competences and qualifications, teacher education, integration of ICT into education, curriculum evaluation, transnational education, meta-analysis and meta-thematic analysis. He has also served as an academic consultant for the Turkish Council of Higher Education in Ankara, Turkey.

Lauren Crabb is the Director of Internationalisation, Partner Colleges and Apprenticeships in the Faculty of Health, Education, Medicine and Social Care at Anglia Ruskin University. She is experienced in developing and operationalising international academic partnerships and creating Collaborative Online International Learning Projects. Lauren's research interest in critical environmental management and mega sports-events has seen her conduct research in Brazil and the Philippines and present her findings at conferences in New York, Berlin and Cambridge. She is also a Senior Fellow of the HEA.

Xitong Dai has over five years of work experience within Chinese and international schools as an EAL and CAL teacher. She has also taught both the British and IB systems. Xitong completed her master's degree in TESOL and focused on curriculum design within both bilingual and international settings. From 2019 to 2022, she has been working on professional development programs and leading staff training sessions.

Sukhpal Singh Gill is a Lecturer (Assistant Professor) in Cloud Computing at the School of Electronic Engineering and Computer Science, Queen Mary University of London, UK. Prior to his present stint, Dr. Gill has held positions as a Research Associate at the School of Computing and Communications, Lancaster University, UK and also as a Postdoctoral Research Fellow at CLOUDS Laboratory, The University of Melbourne, Australia. Dr. Gill is serving as an Associate Editor in Wiley ETT and IET Networks Journal. He has co-authored 70+ peer-reviewed papers (with H-index 30+) and has published in prominent international journals and conferences such as IEEE TCC, IEEE TSC, IEEE TII, IEEE IoT Journal, Elsevier JSS/FGCS, IEEE/ACM UCC and IEEE CCGRID. He has received several awards, including the Distinguished Reviewer Award from SPE (Wiley), 2018, Best Paper Award AusPDC at ACSW 2021 and has also served as the PC member for venues such as PerCom, UCC, CCGRID, CLOUDS, ICFEC, AusPDC. His research interests include Cloud Computing, Fog Computing, Software Engineering, Internet of Things and Energy Efficiency. For further information, please visit .

Aslı Günay is originally from Ankara, Turkey; Aslı currently works as an Assistant Professor of Economics at the Social Sciences University of Ankara, Ankara, Turkey. She received her Ph.D. from Suleyman Demirel University, Isparta, Turkey. Her research interests are public economics, applied macroeconomics, education economics, and higher education studies. She's also served as an academic consultant for the Turkish Council of Higher Education in Ankara, Turkey. Her work has been published in some national and international scientific journals including Applied Economics, Educational Technology Research and Development, Open Economies Review, and Turkish Journal of Medical Sciences.

Michael D. High, PhD, is Assistant Professor of Media Studies in the Department of Media Communication at Xi'an Jiaotong-Liverpool University. His research interests are in media piracy, Hollywood cinema, American popular culture, and digital fandom. His research papers have appeared in the International Journal of Communication and Jump Cut: A Review of Contemporary Media. He also has contributed book chapters to edited collections published Wiley-Blackwell and Routledge.

Tariqul Islam is a JSPS postdoctoral research fellow at Hiroshima University, Japan. He worked as an assistant professor at BRAC University in Bangladesh at the BRAC Institute of Educational Development (BRAC IED). Tariq earned his PhD in Education from Deakin University, Australia. He received his Bachelor's (Hons) and Master's in Education from the University of Dhaka, Bangladesh.

As a researcher, he worked with several national and international organizations, e.g., BRAC, NAEM, FREPD, UNESCO, UNICEF, ActionAid. He has written a number of peer-reviewed journal articles and book chapters that have been published in leading journals and by leading publishers. He has also given papers at national and international conferences. His research interest largely focuses on the sociology of education, with particular attention to education for sustainable development. Tariq's current research focuses on education for global citizenship, higher education, youth (un)employability, teaching-learning in higher education, teachers' professional development, ICT in education, lifelong learning, educational inclusion and exclusion, and play for learning and socio-emotional development.

Nan (Johanna) Jiang is a senior Lecturer in Entrepreneurship in the Department of Management and Human Resources at Coventry University London. Johanna has profound experience of enterprise activities across UK and China. She is specialised in developing and managing entrepreneurship and leadership training courses. She coaches young entrepreneurs in several UK and European universities. Her areas of research include entrepreneurship education, entrepreneurial learning, the transgenerational entrepreneurship in family businesses and identity construction strategies for entrepreneurial leaders. She publishes in the top academic journals and presented her research at leading academic conferences worldwide.

Anita Jimmie is a senior lecturer in the Department of Culture and Language Studies, Faculty of Humanity and Health Sciences, Curtin University Malaysia. She has 19 years of experience teaching at higher education institutes. Her research interests are on Student Engagement and Motivation, Personalised Learning and Technology and Education.

Kuldeep Kaur is a Lecturer at the Australian Institute of Business. She has a strong career history with industry and academia. Kuldeep also worked with the University of South Australia and Flinders University and has taught various subjects at undergraduate and postgraduate levels. She has over a seven-year of experience working in the industry, including companies like Nestle and Cadbury. Kuldeep holds a PhD in organisational behaviour, and the central focus of her research is on organisational climate and its impacts on attitudes and behaviour. She is a competent researcher and loves to extract new relationships in different variables with advanced knowledge of statistical techniques.

Rupinder Kaur is an employer at School of Science, Dulwich College, United Kingdom. Prior to this, Dr. Kaur has completed her Ph.D. in Chemistry from Guru Nanak Dev University, Amritsar, India. She received her M.Sc. degree in Chemistry from the Punjabi University, India and BSc Degree from Panjab University, India. Her area of research is to study the micellization behaviour of surfactants in the presence of various additives. Dr. Kaur has published her research in top ranked venues.

Keigo Kobayashi is an architect and Associate Professor at Waseda University, Tokyo. After studying at the Department of Architecture at Waseda University, Tokyo, Japan, and completing a M.Arch. at the Harvard Graduate School of Design, Cambridge, USA, in 2005, Kobayashi was involved in numerous major projects at architecture design firm called OMA in Rotterdam with Rem Koolhaas until 2012.

Chengcheng Li is currently teaching at the School of Languages of Xi'an Jiaotong-Liverpool University. From 2016 to 2019, she was the Module Convener of the first Critical Thinking course at Xi'an Jiaotong-Liverpool University. In January 2018, she won the EU Erusmus + Mobility Grant and went to the University of Liverpool to conduct international university education research. Her research interests include teaching critical thinking, Research-Led Learning, educational psychology, applied linguistics and mindset development, and cross-cultural communication, etc. She co-authored a book on critical thinking and research-led learning with EAP practices with Youmin Xi in 2021. She is currently working on research regarding higher education innovation.

Lei Li is an experienced educator and manager who has presented at a number of international conferences on a range of pedagogic topics. More recently she has completed a Cambridge Assessment PDQ in educational leadership from the University of Nottingham Ningbo and holds an MEd in TESOL from the University of Exeter, one of the Russell Group Institutions. She has been working in multicultural K12 management for over half a decade and has an extensive working knowledge of transnational higher education.

Kai Liu received his PhD from the Faculty of Law, the National University of Malaysia. Kai also received the Certificate in Professional Studies in Learning & Teaching in Higher Education from the University of Liverpool, and obtained a fellowship of Higher Education Academy in the UK. Kai is currently an Assistant Professor at Chinese Culture Teaching Center, Xi'an Jiaotong-Liverpool University.

Saadia Mahmud is an Online Facilitator at the Australian Institute of Business. Her doctoral research at the University of South Australia applied complexity theory to the handling of rapid change by SMEs. After completing her MBA as the top student, she pursued a career in banking and finance with Citibank. In higher education, she has managed large research projects to improve the quality of teaching and learning funded by the Commonwealth Government of Australia. Her work has been published in peer reviewed journals and incorporated in industry relevant outcomes.

Mattia Miani is a deputy head of the Centre for English Language Education at the University of Nottingham, Ningbo China. In this role, he supervises the content part of the preliminary year curriculum managing a team of 25 tutors delivering every year over 30 modules to 2,200 students. Prior of moving to China, he has worked in a similar transnational campus in Vietnam as a lecturer and manager of executive education programs. Before moving to Asia he spent 10 years in Italy working across academia and industry. He has published four books on professional communication subjects and he is currently interested in educational research within the context of transnational universities.

Syed Mohyuddin is a Senior Lecturer for Human Resources/Management at Australian Institute of Business. He holds a PhD in management from Curtin University, Western Australia. He has over 19 years of experience in teaching human resources and management courses in the Middle East and Australia. He worked as a full-time lecturer and a part-time tutor for various management subjects in Curtin Business School. He has also taught at La Trobe University, Mildura Campus, Victoria, Australia. His PhD research was related to the challenges faced by skilled migrants to achieve professional recognition in Australian organisations, one of his core research interests.

Gloria Molinero has worked in the field of English acquisition and EAP for many years in universities across the UK, Spain and China. She joined Queen Mary University of London after 12 years in China teaching a variety of EAP and literacy courses which preceded her work at the Universities of Birmingham, Durham and Aston. Gloria's current research interests concern the areas of Interdisciplinary Collaborations and Communications in Transnational Higher Education and Student's Independent and Autonomous Learning on Online Platforms. Published research in these areas adds to other research interests in the factors that motivate students not to plagiarise, Intercultural Communication and the field of Teacher Training.

James Morris works in a management capacity for one of the world's leading consulting companies. He has a wide range of experience working in both the private and public sectors and has also studied in transnational higher education settings in both Europe and North America. He has also recently sat on editorial boards for education publications.

Usman Naeem is a Senior Lecturer (Associate Professor) within the School of Electronic Engineering and Computer Science at Queen Mary University of London. Usman is also a Queen Mary Academy Fellow in Learner Engagement Analytics. Usman received his PhD from Queen Mary University of London in 2009. His research focus is on educational and assistive technologies, which include machine learning techniques, mobile computing, and ambient intelligent environments. Usman has taught on a variety of programmes, ranging from traditional programmes such as BSc Computer Science to degree apprenticeships programmes such as BSc Digital & Technology Solutions Professional.

Raffaele Pernice is an EU licensed architect and Senior Lecturer in Architecture and Urbanism at UNSW Sydney. He holds a PhD in Architecture from Waseda University in Tokyo, and a Laurea degree in Architecture (BArch + MArch) from the University IUAV of Venice, Italy. Dr. Pernice research interests and activities range from practice to theory and history of architecture, city planning and urban design.

Sehrish Shahid has over nine years of experience in teaching and research in the education sector. She has contributed to the global design and development of various HR systems and procedures. She is an experienced academic who previously held teaching and research positions at the school of management, RMIT University. She has worked on funded grant research projects by the City of Melbourne Council and prepared industry reports. She has played an active role in the design of culture intelligence events in the HR Course which resulted in getting an inclusion and diversity award at the College level. She has presented her research work at conferences including the prestigious Academy of Management and ANZAM. She has published her work in esteemed journals such as Personnel Review, International Journal of Organizational Analysis, and Journal of Management and Organisation. She has been an active reviewer for various journal outlets such as the International Journal of Organizational Analysis, Journal of Management and Organisation, and Leadership and Organization Development Journal.

Joseph Sia is currently a senior lecturer in the Faculty of Business at Curtin University Malaysia. His research interests include Marketing in Higher Education, Tourism, and Consumer Behavior. His publications have appeared in different academic journals namely Current Psychology, Asia Pacific Journal of Marketing and Logistics, Event Management and other journals.

Tony Stockman is a Senior Lecturer in Computer Science at Queen Mary University of London. He is an interaction designer/researcher who investigates how technology can enhance accessibility and improve human performance. He is particularly interested in technology to support spatial cognition and wayfinding, health monitoring and improve performance levels in sport and music. This includes the role of games in simulating these domains and supporting skill acquisition and enhanced performance. He is a Board member and former president of the International Community for Auditory Display. He has organised 6 international workshops on a range of HCI topics, and has been on the organising committee of 10 international HCI-related conferences. Topics on which he has recently published include participatory design and prototyping, auditory overviews for route guidance, self-monitoring of biological signals and accessible collaborative working.

Danielle Thibodeau is an Innovation & Learning Manager with the Queen Mary Academy at Queen Mary, University of London. She holds a Masters of Adult Education and Community Development from the University of Toronto, and a Masters of Public Policy, Administration and Law from York University. Danielle's work developing training and educational resources has spanned a number of disciplines, and her main areas of interest include equity and inclusion, critical citizenship, and experiential learning.

Youmin Xi is the Executive President of Xi'an Jiaotong-Liverpool University, Pro-Vice-Chancellor of the University of Liverpool, Professor of Management of Xi'an Jiaotong University, and doctoral supervisor. His main research fields include strategy, leadership, decision-making and organization research. He founded the theory of HeXie management in 1985. He has won more than 10 awards for scientific research achievements at provincial and ministerial levels, and has won honors and titles such as "Chinese Doctoral Degree Winners With Outstanding Contributions", "National Outstanding Returned Students", "National Young And Middle-Aged Experts With Outstanding Contributions", "National May 1st Labor Medal", as well as "China Youth Science and Technology Award" and "China Youth Scientists Award". He has taught in and conducted joint research with universities in Canada, America, Singapore, Japan, and other countries and regions. He has authored or co-authored 300 academic papers and 30 books.

Wei Xu received her MS in Civil Engineering from the University of Melbourne in 2019 and BS in Civil Engineering from the University of Liverpool in 2017. In 2021 she was hired as the math and physics teacher by the Shanghai High School International Division and currently still works there. She is interested in the field of education, especially the development of higher education under the internet era. She writes a chapter of Handbook of Research on Developments and Future Trends in Transnational Higher Education (2023, Morris and Li) and wants to explore more in relevant fields.

Tetsuya Yaguchi is a registered architect in Japan and California, a certified planner in the U.S, and Professor in Urban Design at Waseda University,Tokyo. He holds a PhD in Urban Design and has 20 years of professional experience as an architect/ urban designer working on a wide range of projects for private and public clients.

Hanna Yakavenka is the Associate Dean of Internationalisation and Business Development at Coventry University London, UK. She has extensive experience in setting up and growing Higher Education partnerships internationally. Hanna's previous role as a Principal Lecturer and Senior Link Tutor at the University of Greenwich in 2006 - 2017 followed the completion of her PhD in International Knowledge

Transfer at the Manchester Metropolitan University. Her research interests lie in the field of knowledge management and cross-cultural communications, where she particularly has been focusing on peer learning and professional capacity building, internationalisation of the university curricula, and programme design. She holds CMI Coaching Qualification and is a Senior Fellow of the HEA.

Jie Yang received her PhD in Linguistics from the University of Adelaide, Australia. The area of research Dr. Yang is involved in is part of a pioneering movement to reinstate language and cultural pride in Indigenous and minority communities everywhere. She is also conducting research actives in the areas of educational policy, teaching and learning practice, and higher education pedagogies.

Shuangxin Zhang is an associate English lecturer at XJTLU and her research interest is students' acquisition and development of the foreign language in class.

Index

A

B

C

D

E

S

T

U

Y

CPSIA information can be obtained
at www.ICGtesting.com
Printed in the USA
LVHW061512190123
737433LV00008B/598

9 781668 452264